SUSAN SACKETT

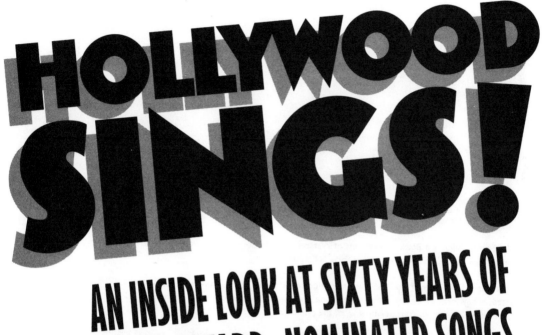

HOLLYWOOD SINGS!

AN INSIDE LOOK AT SIXTY YEARS OF ACADEMY AWARD®-NOMINATED SONGS

RESEARCHED BY MARCIA ROVINS

BILLBOARD BOOKS
an imprint of Watson-Guptill Publications/New York

First published by Billboard Books, an imprint of Watson-Guptill Publications, a division of BPI
Communications, Inc., 1515 Broadway, New York, NY 10036

Library of Congress Cataloging-in-Publication Data
Sackett, Susan.
    Hollywood Sings! : An inside look at sixty years of Academy Award-nominated songs / Susan
    Sackett ; researched by Marcia Rovins.
        p.   cm.
    ISBN 0-8230-7623-7
    1. Motion picture music--United States--Bibliography. 2. Popular music--United States--
        Bibliography. 3. Academy Awards (Motion pictures)   I. Rovins, Marcia. II. Title.
    ML128.M7S33 1995
    782.42164'1542--dc20   94-46479
                                                                         CIP

Manufactured in the United States of America

First printing, 1995

1 2 3 4 5 6 7 8 9 / 99 98 97 96 95

Edited by Paul Lukas
Cover and interior design by Jay Anning
Graphic production by Ellen Greene

To Marcia, who can zing, zing, zing practically every zong in this book, and who made it all possible,
and
To Tovar and Tasha, two loyal, loving, licking, four-footed friends — the best kind — who never left my side, especially when the earth shook and the house seemed to be broken.

CONTENTS

THE FORTIES

THE SIXTIES

THE SEVENTIES

THE EIGHTIES

THE NINETIES

PREFACE

In 1926, a group of producers, writers, and other film industry artisans, spearheaded by MGM boss Louis B. Mayer, launched a fledgling organization consisting of the movie business's most powerful movers and shakers. This exclusive clique would eventually christen itself with the grandiose designation of the Academy of Motion Picture Arts and Sciences, and while their intentions may have been as noble as their lofty name, there really was no "academy" in the traditional sense; neither were there any classes teaching arts or sciences. Instead, these professionals were bonded in a different way. Their academy was one of mind and purpose and love of their art (and science) — that of filmmaking, with the goal of maintaining excellence in their craft.

One of the first orders of business was to instigate a self-congratulatory award for the best of the members' efforts. The Academy decided on a statuette, an art deco-ish trophy of a neutered male human form, mounted on a pedestal shaped like a film reel. By 1929, the first of these trophies had been distributed. The prize, however, went nameless until 1931, when the executive director of the Academy, Margaret Herrick, upon first seeing the statuette, said it reminded her of her Uncle Oscar. (Fortunately, they decided from that time onward it would be called the Oscar, and not the Uncle.)

For the first few years, there weren't many awards given that involved sound. Films had been mostly silent, with the sound-on-film process just beginning to come into its own. But six years after the first awards, with the apparent acceptance of "talkies" as well as "movies," these Academicians decided the time had come for awards in the field of music, including Best Score and Best Song.

The first Best Song award was given in 1935, for the Best Song of 1934. There were only three nominees, but that would quickly change. Subsequent years would see six, eight, 10, and at one time as many as 14 songs per year nominated for the prestigious Best Song Oscar. In those early days, each studio was invited to submit one song it felt worthy of the award that year, and as more and more studios began to make more and more films in the heyday of the *filmusical,* the field was soon vastly overcrowded. The rules needed to be changed.

Here is how it works today: The Academy is divided into various crafts or guilds, including directors, actors, writers, editors, and songwriters. It is this latter group that secretly nominates candidates annually for the Best Song category. The rules state: "An original song consists of words and music, both of which are original. There must be a substantive rendition (not necessarily visual) of both lyric and melody (clearly audible, intelligible and recognizably performed as a song) in the film." As we shall see throughout this book, however, this rule was frequently bent in the early years.

The rulebook continues with the requirements for eligibility: "The work must be created specifically for an eligible feature-length motion picture; the measure of the work's qualification shall be its effectiveness, craftsmanship, creative substance and relevance to the dramatic whole; the work must be recorded for use in the film *prior* to any other usage, including public performance or exploitation through any of the media whatsoever." The rules continue to address voting, stating that "the five achievements in each category receiving the highest number of votes will become the nominations for final voting for the Music Awards. If there are 25 or fewer qualified works submitted . . . nominations [may] be limited to three." (This happened in 1988, the only recent year in which there were not the customary five songs nominated.) The entire Academy then votes upon the final selections, with the entry receiving the highest number of votes actually taking home the Oscar.

It sounds complicated, but the results of this competition have produced some of the most popular and memorable music of our time. If you scan the list of Best Song winners and nominees, you will no doubt be surprised that so many of these familiar tunes were first written for the screen rather than simply recorded by an artist hoping for a hit.

Now, before we ask those cheerful fellows from Price-Waterhouse for "the envelope, please," there are a few more things you ought to know as you read *Hollywood Sings!*:

First, in terms of the songs' order of presentation within the book, the entries for all of the Best Song winners are shown *first* within each given year, and are accompanied by a "winning envelope" graphic; the entries for the remaining nominees for the year are then listed *alphabetically.*

Also, as was the case in another Billboard Books publication I wrote on film — *The Hollywood Reporter Book of Box Office Hits* — all of the earnings for any given movie are reported in *North American rentals,* rather than gross receipts. This gives a consistent and more realistic picture of the take at the box office, and is also the most readily available and accurate account of of a film's profits.

Finally, a caveat: As you read the book, you may find yourself singing the familiar or long-forgotten songs in your head. Go ahead and indulge yourself, but be warned — occasionally a tune may rattle around in your brain for quite some time, refusing to leave you alone. I know; this happened to me several times. After hearing the unfamiliar title song from *The Cowboy and the Lady,* for example, I couldn't get it out of my mind for days — it followed me into the shower, to the market, walking the dogs, and so on. Even now, as I write this, it's playing on an endless loop in my head. If this happens to you, try to move on to the next tune — which will undoubtedly replace it on an endless loop of its own.

If you see some songs listed that you can't recall hearing, don't worry — many of these tunes are now obscure, but other "lost" songs may be found on videocassettes of the films in which they debuted, on late-night TV, or on classic movie cable channels.

Okay, time to dim the lights, pop some corn, pop in a cassette, settle back, and get ready to sing along with Uncle Oscar — plus Fred and Ginger, Frank, Bing, Dinah, Doris, Danny, Dean, Pat, Nat, Johnny, Barbra, Lionel, Madonna, Bruce . . . but I'm getting ahead of myself. Take your time; after all, you've got 60 years or so of listening to enjoy, as Hollywood sings just for you.

SUSAN SACKETT
Carefree, Arizona
January, 1995

ACKNOWLEDGMENTS

Chances are I'll never receive an Academy Award, so I won't be up there thanking everyone I ever knew. This, then, is my only opportunity to thank all the people who helped bring this book together.

It's been a real learning experience, and a joy, mainly because of my ever-patient, thorough, and extremely knowledgeable research associate, Marcia Rovins. Marcia has been an unrolling rock, always coming through with what I needed, and with a sunny smile too.

Fred Bronson has been not only a best friend but an invaluable resource, with an uncanny knowledge of the rock era. Perhaps that's what friends are for, but I'm still thanking my lucky stars for sending Fred into my life 24 years ago. My love and friendship is yours always.

Special thanks to the extremely talented (and modest) Richard Sherman, who in addition to sharing an afternoon of his valuable time with Marcia and me also had to put up with our caterwaulings around the piano while he played us a medley of his great songs.

Another special person is Alan Menken. If Marcia hadn't attended New Rochelle High with him, a huge section of this book would have gone without his valuable contribution. Thanks, Alan, for taking time out of your unbelievably hectic schedule to share some of your thoughts with us.

So many others made this book a pleasure instead of a chore. Wink Martindale, thanks for your generous contribution in sharing interviews with us; likewise Paul Worth, who produced many of the radio interviews that were so useful in putting this book together; Don McCulloch, too, deserves special thanks (as always) for his contribution and willingness to assist Marcia in her unenviable research efforts; also, Chuck Southcott, thanks for assistance with contacts; John Sala, your help with research material and contacts were greatly appreciated; likewise Kevin Gershan, for your help with research material; and a well-deserved thank you to John Felz at KMPC for lending your assistance to Marcia and me.

More special appreciation goes to Marvin of the Movies, a walking encyclopedia of trivia and all-round interesting guy; to Beverly Washburn, for her insights into the world of child actors; to Tata Vega, another talented person who shared valuable information with us; to Gretchen Adamson, for her help with tidbits about the music of her late husband, Harold Adamson; and Lucille Meyers, former secretary to the late Jimmy McHugh, for additional information on that songwriter.

I'd also like to thank my friend Darlene Lieblich, whose extensive knowledge of languages is probably something she never thought would help with a book about songs.

Special thanks to the gang at Eddie Brandt's Saturday Matinee, for their wonderful assistance with photo research.

Finally, I owe more than the greatest praise to my ever-patient and understanding editor, Paul Lukas. Nobody does it better.

THE THIRTIES

It helped if your name was Harry or Johnny or Sammy or Jimmy — the odds seemed to favor songwriters blessed with these first names. Of course, it helped if you had talent, too, as all of the composers of the great songs of the 1930s had in abundance.

The filmusical was alive and well then, just born in fact, in this first full decade of sound pictures. George, Cole, and Irving were also among the first names that were heard frequently during these years. Chances were that if you went to the "picture show" in the 1930s, you would hear a Gershwin tune, or perhaps a Cole Porter score would tickle your ears. And Irving Berlin's prodigious outpouring of songs might easily have filled half the pictures of the decade.

Plot was another story.

What these films may have lacked in drama (and some were accused, perhaps with some validity, of having no storyline at all), they made up for in talent. Many filmusicals were simply vaudeville presentations on celluloid, huge spectacles of songs, dances, lavish production numbers with endless white pianos topped by an endless parade of leggy, beautifully costumed showgirls hoofing their hearts out. Fred Astaire could usually be found in their midst, showing everyone how it was done. And nobody did it better.

It was during this decade that musicals on the screen began to evolve. The first Oscar for Best Song went to "The Continental" for 1934's The Gay Divorcée, a Broadway musical brought to the screen with all its inherent staginess. By 1939 and the end of the decade, a lavish film written specifically for the screen, called The Wizard of Oz, was magically transporting us "Over the Rainbow" and into a more modern world of film sophistication.

1934

THE CONTINENTAL

Music by Con Conrad; lyrics by Herb Magidson From *The Gay Divorcée*

The Chinese calendar marked 1934 as the Year of the Dog. But for millions of movie-goers, it would always be remembered as the Year of Fred and Ginger. The pair, who would later be known as the world's most famous dance team, actually made their screen bow the previous year in *Flying Down to Rio*. When the Academy of Motion Picture Arts and Sciences decided to introduce the new category of Best Song from a Motion Picture, the nominations included the hit song "The Carioca" from that film, along with two other tunes that shared the honor of being the first Oscar nominees in that category: "Love in Bloom," from *She Loves Me Not*, and another sensational Astaire/Rogers pairing in "The Continental," from *The Gay Divorcée* (which also received nominations for Best Picture,

Best Interior Decoration, Best Sound Recording, and Best Score).

While Fred Astaire and Ginger Rogers had been billed fourth and fifth, respectively, in *Flying Down to Rio* (see page 3), the release of *The Gay Divorcée* saw them receiving star billing for the first time. This lively musical was based on the popular Broadway production of the same name, with the film adding an intriguing feminist slant thanks to the second *e* in the title. The plot was a rather thin bedroom farce, an extremely popular type of comedy in the era when "gay" still meant "happy." Not unexpectedly, the story took a back seat to the film's sensational musical dance numbers. Fred and Ginger whirled their way up, over, and around various pieces of furniture throughout "The Continental" production number's 18 minutes — nearly one-fourth of the film's running time! Sung by Ginger Rogers, Lillian Miles, and Erik Rhodes, "The Continental" even propelled Fred and Ginger into multi-ethnic versions of the tune, as together they hoofed their way through a Spanish tango, Hungarian czardas, Viennese waltz, and finally a jazzy American bit.

A Leo Reisman recording of "The Continental" debuted on the *Billboard* pop charts on October 6, 1934, ultimately lasting seven weeks, including two in

Original lobby card advertising Fred Astaire and Ginger Rogers in *The Gay Divorcée*. Note billing as "The King and Queen of 'Carioca,'" a reference to their earlier picture that year, *Flying Down to Rio*.

the Number One spot. Two other recorded versions appeared simultaneously — one by Jolly Coburn and another by Lud Gluskin, spending an impressive nine and 10 weeks on the charts, and peaking at numbers two and six, respectively. Many other vocal and orchestral versions have since been recorded, including renditions by Fred Astaire, Frank Sinatra, Eddie Fisher, Ray Conniff, David Rose, Ray Anthony, Les Brown, Nat "King" Cole, and Maureen McGovern. Even the sheet music was a best-seller; the 1934 edition featured 27 action photos on the back cover so that Fred and Ginger wannabes could attempt to dance their own version of "The Continental."

The Gay Divorcée also contained Cole Porter's "Night and Day," the one holdover from the stage musical. Since its original use was not in the film but theatrical, it was ineligible for nomination. It was a small field that first year, with only three songs nominated, and given the runaway popularity of "The Continental," it came as no surprise when the song made famous by Astaire and Rogers waltzed off with the very first Oscar given for Best Song.

THE CARIOCA

Music by Vincent Youmans; lyrics by Edward Eliscu and Gus Kahn
From *Flying Down to Rio*

"Nimble-toed" is what the *New York Times* called Fred Astaire in its review of *Flying Down to Rio,* and Ginger Rogers was termed "charming." The critic's restraint was probably warranted; the duo danced on screen together for barely two minutes in the entire movie, when they butted heads — literally — to do "The Carioca."

The film stars Dolores Del Rio as a hot-blooded Latina from Rio de Janeiro (whose natives are known as "Cariocas," hence the song's title). In the rather uncomplicated plot, she's wooed by an American, played by Gene Raymond. Fred and Ginger were not the leads, and in fact were incidental to the story and received only fourth and fifth billing. Raymond plays a wealthy (was there any other kind?) American torn between his love of flying and his love of music. He books his band into the Carioca Casino down in Rio, where Astaire and Rogers are dancers.

The "Carioca" dance itself — a fast tango — included lyrics that proclaimed, "Two heads, they say,

are better than one . . . that's how the dance is begun." Taking a cue from the lyric, Dave Gould, the film's dance director, decided on a literal interpretation and had Astaire and Rogers begin their routine with an actual tête-à-tête, by touching foreheads and executing a complete turn without breaking contact.

After the head-bumping bit, the production number cuts away from the Astaire-Rogers pairing to a montage of nightclub dancers and singers. Eventually, the two return to perform a lively "Carioca" tap dance on top of seven white, revolving pianos. As elaborate as this sequence was, Astaire himself was unimpressed with their performance, later recalling the soon-to-be famous dance couple's film debut thusly: "We weren't doing anything particularly outstanding in 'The Carioca.' I had thrown in a few solos, too, in the limited time given me, but I never expected that they would register so well. However, everything clicked."

The dance clicked with the audience, too. A new "Carioca" dance craze soon developed. The answer to a studio publicist's prayers, the dance served to heighten the popularity of the film, and for a time, dance schools attempted to teach the new steps to eager clients. However, the demanding movements and complex rhythms were unsuitable for the "dance-impaired," which in this case meant just about everybody in the country except for Astaire and Rogers. The dance's popularity soon fizzled, but the song became a hit and received a nomination for a 1934 Academy Award in the newly created category.[1]

The production number lasts a full 13 minutes and is certainly outstanding. But even the antics of Fred and Ginger couldn't top the show's most spectacular sequence. For the finale, a chorus of wing-walking young ladies steal the show. In their flimsy, wind-blown gowns, they appear to defy gravity (and common sense) by fearlessly doing a precision drill, mounted atop the wings of high-flying aircraft. It was, naturally, all done on a sound stage with rear projection, but the effect was sensational. Fortunately, the talents of Astaire and Rogers weren't lost on RKO producer Pandro S. Berman. He caught their number while filming on the same lot, and gave them starring roles in his next film, *The Gay Divorcée* (see page 2).

---

1. Although the movie was released over the Christmas holiday period at the end of 1933, the Academy, as was sometimes the case in those days, allowed the picture to compete with films released in the following year.

LOVE IN BLOOM

Music by Ralph Rainger; lyrics by Leo Robin
From *She Loves Me Not*

Perhaps no song could evoke stronger feelings of warmth in American radio audiences (and, later, television viewers) than the melodic strains of "Love in Bloom." This was not, however, because people were entranced by the composers' original intent, swept away on a wave of romantic yearning. Rather, for nearly four decades' worth of Sunday nights, "Love in Bloom" announced that listeners were about to embark on a voyage of laughter. For "Love in Bloom," written as a ballad for Bing Crosby, became best known after it was appropriated by the comic Jack Benny, who used it as his theme song.

It hadn't always been that way. When Leo Robin and Ralph Rainger wrote their tune for the 1934 Paramount Pictures musical *She Loves Me Not,* the song was included among many romantic offerings warbled by the film's star, Bing Crosby. His recording of "Love in Bloom" was released by Decca Records about a month prior to the film's debut, and it quickly climbed the *Billboard* charts, peaking at Number One, holding that position for six weeks, and spending a total of 15 weeks on the charts. Three other artists — Paul Whiteman, Guy Lombardo, and Hal Kemp — all covered the tune over the next two months; Whiteman's orchestra had the greatest success, reaching number four and remaining on the charts for 10 weeks.

The song's popularity was a surprise to the brass at Paramount, who thought it "too high-class" for the general public. Nevertheless, about half a million copies of the sheet music were sold. Its huge popularity caught the attention of the Academy of Motion Picture Arts and Sciences, whose members nominated it for an Oscar in 1934, the first year of the Best Song category. And while it didn't win the big prize, Benny's use of the song ensured that it would remain more firmly entrenched in the public consciousness than hundreds of other future nominated songs that would eventually fade into obscurity.

According to his biography, *Jack Benny,* by his widow, Mary Livingstone Benny, and Hilliard Marks, Jack first played the tune at a supper club he and Mary were visiting one evening. "The band asked me to join them for their next number," said the comedian, who had once studied to be a concert violinist. "I borrowed

a fiddle and, just following the sheet music, I played 'Love in Bloom.' . . . My spontaneous performance turned up being written about in some column."

By the following week, word of Benny's antics had spread, and when he entered another club, the band immediately struck up "Love in Bloom." The tune stuck, and Benny had acquired a theme song. "I love [the song]," he later recalled, "but actually 'Love in Bloom' has nothing to do with a comedian. I mean, 'Can it be the breeze that fills the trees with rare and magic perfume . . .' sounds more like it should be the theme song of a dog — not a comic!"

Over the years, Paramount was able to get even more mileage out of its hit. The popular song popped up in two of the studio's other movies: *New York Town* (1941) and *True to the Army* (1942).

LULLABY OF BROADWAY

Music by Harry Warren; lyrics by Al Dubin
From *Gold Diggers of 1935*

"We may expect to hear that excellent song, 'Lullaby of Broadway,' on the slightest excuse for the next few months." So proclaimed the *New York Times* in its March, 1935, review of the Warner Bros.–First National musical, *Gold Diggers of 1935.* It was just a bit of an understatement; the "excellent song" became one of the most popular of the *century,* recorded over the years by scores of artists, including The Andrews Sisters, Tony Bennett, Connie Francis, and Bette Midler. Everyone, it seemed, wanted to come on along and listen to "The Lullaby of Broadway."

The Academy listened, too, and awarded it the Oscar for Best Song of 1935. In its original film, *Gold Diggers of 1935,* the song is performed in a lavish, quintessential Busby Berkeley production number (for which he received a Best Dance Direction nomination from the Academy), with Dick Powell and Winifred Shaw as the leads, and a bevy of Broadway babes dancing through the nearly 15-minute segment. (Thankfully, they were not atop those ubiquitous white pianos

Adolphe Menjou rehearses the Busby Berkeley Girls for one of the production numbers in *Gold Diggers of 1935*.

so plentiful in films of the era, although the instruments did show up elsewhere in the film.)

The song teamed Harry Warren with Al Dubin, and the two would go on to have many successful collaborations. Warren was one of the most prolific composers ever to work in Hollywood, producing a stream of hits over several decades, mostly in partnership with Dubin. Some of Warren's popular titles included "We're in the Money," "Shuffle Off to Buffalo," "I Only Have Eyes for You," "You'll Never Know" (lyrics by Mack Gordon), and the Academy Award–winning "On the Atchison, Topeka, and Santa Fe" (lyrics by Johnny Mercer; see page 88). With Harold Adamson and Leo McCarey, Warren wrote "An Affair to Remember" (see page 142), and he was also responsible for the theme to the popular television program "The Life and Legend of Wyatt Earp."

Yet for all his success in writing, Warren remained publicity-shy for most of his life. On the night of the Oscar presentation in 1935 — the first of many he would receive throughout his career — he was reluctant to attend. It took the efforts of studio boss Jack L. Warner to persuade him to show up in person, finessing the move by telling Warren the night before the ceremony that he had won the award. This may seem like a bold conjecture on Warner's part, since the envelopes were still sealed, but it actually was not such a long shot — there were only two other nominees. The ploy worked, and Warren accepted his award in person

the next evening, along with his lyricist, Al Dubin.

"Lullaby of Broadway" enjoyed continued success over the years in such films as *Lullaby of Broadway* (Warner Bros., 1951) and Woody Allen's *Radio Days* (Orion, 1987), as well as the 1980 hit Broadway show *42nd Street*. There have been numerous hit recordings of "Lullaby of Broadway," including a version by the Dorsey Brothers Orchestra, with vocal by Bob Crosby, that reached number one on the *Billboard* charts, remaining in that position for two weeks and on the charts for 11. Other renditions were recorded by Little Jack Little, Reginald Foresythe, Hal Kemp, and Chick Bullock, all charting in 1935. That "excellent song" proved to be just that.

CHEEK TO CHEEK

Music and lyrics by Irving Berlin
From *Top Hat*

Irving Berlin was already a successful songwriter when he composed the music for *Top Hat*, having achieved fame for such hits as "Alexander's Ragtime Band" as early as 1911, and "Oh, How I Hate to Get Up in the Morning" in 1918. The music for *Top Hat* was his first film score, and the prolific composer sought the input of the film's star, Fred Astaire.

Original one-sheet advertising *Top Hat*, with emphasis on "The Piccolino" rather than "Cheek to Cheek."

The dancer's initial reaction to the movie's centerpiece, "Cheek to Cheek," was not the undying enthusiasm for which Berlin had hoped. Not only would Astaire be expected to devise a dance to the tune — he would also have to sing the notes, some of which climbed to the very top of his limited vocal range. However, the two soon developed a mutual respect, and Fred agreed to do the song after spending some time together with Berlin. "You can't work with Fred without knowing you're working for him," Berlin was quoted as saying in Michael Freedland's biography, *Irving Berlin*. "He's a real inspiration for a writer. I'd never have written *Top Hat* without him. He makes you feel secure."

Essentially a redress of the first Fred-and-Ginger co-starrer, *The Gay Divorcée*, the movie *Top Hat* would forever unite these two leads in the minds of the public as the quintessential romantic dance team. Even the theretofore reluctant reviewer from the *New York Times* had to admit that "Miss Rogers, improving magnificently from picture to picture, collaborates perfectly with Mr. Astaire in 'Top Hat' and is entitled to keep the job for life." Although she fell just short of making good on this recommendation, the pairing was a happy one that endured for many years.

Ironically, the film's most famous performance of the dance team in the "Cheek to Cheek" scene nearly had to be scrubbed. The song would go on to win an Oscar nomination and future "classic" Astaire/Rogers status, but it presented director Mark Sandrich with the picture's biggest headache. The reason: feathers.

Ginger's costume called for hundreds of ostrich feathers from stem to stern. During rehearsals, she began to shed the fluffy stuff like an ostrich in molt. Fred carried on bravely, like a dancer caught in a nightmarish pillow fight, while flying feathers blinded him and tickled his nose until he had sneezing fits. Tempers flared, Fred stormed off the set, and Ginger burst into tears. The film's costume designer promised to make it right, staying up all night to sew each feather into place by hand. By the time the crew was ready to shoot the next day, Ginger's feathers were, for the most part, cooperative, and the company was able to film the dance without much problem. Later, Fred and choreographer Hermes Pan even devised a little parody of Berlin's "Heaven, I'm in heaven" lyric, serenading Ginger with "Feathers, I hate feathers, and I hate them so that I can hardly speak . . ."

In addition to the nomination for "Cheek to Cheek" as Best Song, the film also received nominations from the Academy for Best Picture, Best Interior Decoration, and Best Dance Direction, a category unique to the 1930s.

Top Hat's title song featuring Fred Astaire doing his "Top Hat, White Tie and Tails" routine would become forever associated with the debonair dancer as his signature song. It's a wonderful solo, but the film owes its success to more than just Astaire, or even Astaire and Rogers. *Top Hat* succeeds because of a dynamic *trio* — the combined talents of Berlin, Astaire, and Rogers. As classic musical films go, it just doesn't get any better than this.

LOVELY TO LOOK AT

Music by Jerome Kern; lyrics by Dorothy Fields and Jimmy McHugh
From *Roberta*

The most popular song from the Jerome Kern Broadway musical *Roberta* was ineligible for an Oscar nomination, since it was not written especially for the screen. It seems likely that if it had been allowed into contention, it would have easily won the prize, for the song, "Smoke Gets in Your Eyes," has stood the test of time much better than the film's Oscar-nominated "Lovely to Look At." "Smoke" became a pop hit in a 1958 revival by the Platters, selling an impressive two million copies and nailing down the Number One spot on the *Billboard* charts for three weeks.

When *Roberta* was translated to the screen, producer Pandro S. Berman asked composer Jerome Kern to create two new songs. One was "I Won't Dance"; the other, "Lovely to Look At." This marked the first time that two songs composed for a screen remake of a Broadway show also attained hit status.

When Kern first played his still wordless version of "Lovely to Look At" for his boss, Berman, the 29-year-old Hollywood *wunderkind* was somewhat disappointed. The song, with only 16 measures instead of the more typical 32 in most popular songs of the day, seemed to the producer to be only half-finished. Disappointed, Berman asked the composer if it the song could be made longer. "That's all I had to say," Kern shot back.

Kern's original Broadway version of *Roberta* had been written in collaboration with Otto Harbach. Berman, however, had already signed the team of Dorothy Fields and Jimmy McHugh to write the lyrics. Kern had never even met his new lyricists until the picture was being filmed. But he was pleased with their efforts, and he later became friends with Fields, who

nicknamed him "Junior" because she towered over him. Kern and Fields became collaborators on future endeavors, including the Oscar-winning "The Way You Look Tonight" (see page 7).

In the movie version of *Roberta*, Astaire and Rogers were not the leads, although Pandro Berman had persuaded RKO to purchase the rights as a starring vehicle for them. But the dancers simply were not cut out to be the leads; those roles went to Irene Dunne and Randolph Scott (the stage male lead had been Bob Hope, who later revived his role for a television version), with Astaire and Rogers relegated to the film's lighter subplot. They shared the honors of introducing Kern's new song, "Lovely to Look At," Dunne singing it and Astaire and Rogers reprising it later in the film. Incidentally, if you look closely at one of the first models to appear after Astaire's rendition, you'll spot a young, blonde Lucille Ball. Twenty years later she and husband Desi Arnaz would purchase the same studio where she had a bit part in *Roberta*, rechristening RKO as their own "Desilu."

"Lovely to Look At" was lovely to listen to as well. A recording by Eddy Duchin peaked at Number One on the *Billboard* charts in March of 1935 and held that position for four weeks, spending 14 weeks on the charts in all. Leo Reisman's version was also on the charts for four weeks, peaking at number 10, and even Dunne, the film's star, had a recording of the tune, which peaked at number 20 and then quickly disappeared.

In 1952, *Roberta* was remade as *Lovely to Look At*, starring Kathryn Grayson and Red Skelton, with dance sequences provided by Ann Miller and Marge and Gower Champion. Jerome Kern's Oscar-nominated song from 1935 had now become a film title. Lovely indeed.

1936
And the winner is....

THE WAY YOU LOOK TONIGHT

Music by Jerome Kern; lyrics by Dorothy Fields
From *Swing Time*

RKO's hot dance team of Fred Astaire and Ginger Rogers couldn't miss. To audiences, they projected style, elegance, and grace; to their studio, however, they represented only one thing: box office gold. Following the successful pairing of Jerome Kern and Dorothy Fields in the Astaire/Rogers 1935 starrer, *Roberta* (see page 7), for which they composed only two additional pieces (the rest were from the Kern-Harbach Broadway score), the studio assigned Kern and Fields the responsibility of creating an entire score for the dancing duo.

The result of their collaboration on this new musical, called *Swing Time,* was not greeted with resounding enthusiasm, at least by critics. The *New York Times* reviewer, Frank S. Nugent, said, "Maybe we have no ear for music . . .but right now we could not even whistle a bar of 'A Fine Romance,' and that's about the catchiest and brightest melody in the show. The others — 'Pick Yourself Up,' 'Bojangles in Harlem,' 'The Way You Look Tonight,' . . . — are merely adequate, or worse. Neither good Kern nor good swing."

Nor good criticism, either, if we are to believe history. "The Way You Look Tonight" took top honors at the Oscars that year, as well as providing material for a string of hit recorded versions, including one by Fred Astaire himself (Number One for six weeks; 17 weeks on the charts in 1936), another by Guy Lombardo, yet another by Teddy Wilson with Billie Holiday, and a fourth cover that year by Benny Goodman with Peggy Lee doing the vocal. In 1961, a revival by the Lettermen peaked at number 13 and spent an impressive 13 weeks on the charts — not bad for a tune that was deemed "merely adequate."

Lyricist Dorothy Fields's reaction was the complete opposite of the *Times* critic's. "The first time Jerry [Kern] played that melody for me, I went out and started to cry. The release absolutely killed me. I couldn't stop, it was so beautiful," she said in Max Wilk's *They're Playing Our Song.* Fields went on to become the first female ever to win an Academy Award for songwriting, decades before Marilyn Bergman would be the next woman to take home the Oscar for the same feat (for "The Windmills of Your Mind" — see page 193). "The Way You Look Tonight" also gave Kern the first of his two Academy Awards (the second would come in 1941, for "The Last Time I Saw Paris" — see page 41).

Though often thought of as a love ballad, "The Way You Look Tonight" was used in *Swing Time* in a comedy routine. Originally, screenwriter Howard Lindsay had written a scenario for the song that had Ginger Rogers cooking a dinner for herself and Fred in her apartment. The scene called for her hair to be in disarray, with smudges on her forehead and cheeks. Fred was to play the piano, and just as he got to the phrase

"the way you look tonight," he would glance up and see her in this disheveled state. In the end, however, the producers decided to forego an untidy Ginger, and merely had her enter the room fresh from washing her hair, the lather atop her head so perfectly sculpted it could have been a white wig.

DID I REMEMBER?

**Music by Walter Donaldson;
    lyrics by Harold Adamson**
From Suzy

Set against a background of romance, war, and espionage, *Suzy* was the first non-musical to have a song nominated for an Academy Award. It was a bittersweet story starring Jean Harlow as an American showgirl in London during World War I. She marries there, then falsely learns that her husband, played by Franchot Tone, has been killed as a spy. Fleeing to Paris, she falls for a famous French aviator, played by a young, third-billed Cary Grant. In fact, Grant's character is killed off, making this one of his few films in which he does not make it to the last reel.

The MGM film opened to mixed reviews, with many critics dissatisfied with the script and heavy dialogue. *Literary Digest* bemoaned the storyline: "Alan Campbell, Horace Jackson, Dorothy Parker and Lenore Coffee, in story conference assembled, have chosen plot No. 64 — the 'neither maid, wife nor widow' theme — in which to dip Miss Harlow's talents."

Harsh criticism, especially for Dorothy Parker, who would one day find herself in the critic's corner dishing it out for *Vanity Fair* as drama critic. This was one of her earliest screen endeavors; she would go on to pen two versions of *A Star Is Born* (1937, 1954), and was frequently brought in by studios to create additional dialogue for such films as *The Moon's Our Home* (1936) and *The Little Foxes* (1941). Further, her talent spanned several media; she was a renowned short-story writer, poet, and satirist, perhaps best remembered for noting, "Men seldom make passes at girls who wear glasses."

The song "Did I Remember?" is sung when Harlow and Grant first meet in a noisy cafe where she is torch-singing (dubbed uncannily close to Harlow's natural speaking voice by sound-alike Virginia Verrill). As she works her way through her number, Grant and his buddies become progressively louder, although he

Jean Harlow sings "Did I Remember" with wisecracking Cary Grant (center) and his buddies in *Suzy*.

makes it plain that he is aware she is singing. He simply refuses to acknowledge her, even when she sidles up to his table and sings directly to him. To get his attention, Harlow dips her finger in his drink and sprinkles his face, never missing a beat. Her facial expressions, however, come nowhere near the meaning of the happy lyrics — she sings the sweet words with looks of venom aimed directly at the unaware Grant. When she finishes, he tells her the song was great. Refusing to be patronized, Harlow says she knows he didn't hear a word. Unperturbed, Grant offers to sing it back to her, which he does, making up his own rhyming words. She's impressed, and the seeds of their relationship begin to germinate.

A popular hit in its day, "Did I Remember?" landed on the charts in August, 1936, a month after the film's debut. A recording by Shep Fields peaked at Number One, where it remained for four weeks, spending a total of 12 weeks on the charts. Tommy Dorsey's cover reached number seven and stayed on the charts for four weeks. The song was the first Academy Award nomination for lyricist Harold Adamson, who, over the next two decades, would accrue a total of five nominations, although never taking home the top honors.

I'VE GOT YOU UNDER MY SKIN

Music and lyrics by Cole Porter
From *Born to Dance*

"Bulldog, bulldog, bow-wow-wow" does not sound like the kind of lyric that might have come from the mind of a future Academy Award nominee. Nevertheless, when Cole Porter's wealthy grandfather insisted that he give up his foolish notions of becoming a composer and attend Yale instead, young Cole quickly penned the Yale "Bulldog" song, which has been the fighting chant of loyal Yalies ever since. But when, following graduation from Yale, Porter began pursuing a degree from Harvard Law School, the school's dean fortunately realized the young musician's future lay elsewhere and advised him to give up law for music. Good advice. Cole Porter wrote some of the most memorable music of his era, including "Night and Day" (from *The Gay Divorcée*), "Anything Goes," "I Get a Kick out of You," and "You're The Top," plus the musicals *Kiss Me Kate, Silk Stockings, Can Can,* and *High Society.*

In 1936, in mid-career, he wrote the music and lyrics for his first solo film, *Born to Dance.* While most of the musical's tunes failed to catch on — such ditties as "Hey Babe Hey," "Rap-Tap-Tap on Wood," "Swingin' the Jinx Away," and "Love Me, Love My Pekinese" — one song has remained a bona fide hit: the Oscar-nominated "I've Got You Under My Skin."

Easily the most memorable tune from this film, the song enjoyed success on the pop charts, recorded first by Ray Noble and His Orchestra, whose rendition peaked at number three and remained on the charts for 13 weeks. Hal Kemp's Orchestra covered with a version that peaked at number eight. In 1951, satirist Stan Freberg's rendition of the song reached number 11, while a Louis Prima and Keely Smith version in 1959 barely dented the chart at number 95. Then in 1966, the pop group the Four Seasons recorded the standard, then 30 years old, and it climbed to number nine.

Over the years, many famous artists recorded the Cole Porter tune, including Frank Sinatra, Julio Iglesias, Mel Tormé, Ella Fitzgerald, Rosemary Clooney, Dinah Washington, Shirley Bassey, and Charlie Parker. Frank Sinatra's rerecording of the tune found its way onto his 1993 *Duets* album, where he was joined, thanks to the miracle of modern mixing electronics, by U2's Bono.

Born to Dance starred Eleanor Powell, James Stewart, Virginia Bruce, and a ninth-billed Buddy Ebsen. It was a modest success for MGM (the film's only other Academy Award nomination was for Best Dance Direction), but studio chieftain Louis B. Mayer was reportedly so pleased with the picture after its first previews that he promptly signed Cole Porter to write another musical. For his efforts, Porter was paid the unheard of sum of $100,000, composing the music for the 1937 MGM musical *Rosalie.* The film was based on a Broadway musical with songs by Sigmund Romberg and George Gershwin, which Mayer tossed out in favor of the new Cole Porter score. Unfortunately, it made for a better stage production than movie. *Rosalie* proved a dismal, pretentious failure.

Meanwhile, "I've Got You Under My Skin" continued to soar. It was used in the Cole Porter screen biography *Night and Day* (Warner Bros., 1946) and again in a comedy sequence for Tony Randall and Debbie Reynolds in the non-musical movie *The Mating Game* (MGM, 1959).

A MELODY FROM THE SKY

Music by Louis Alter; lyrics by Sidney Mitchell
From *The Trail of the Lonesome Pine*

The first outdoor movie to be given the full Technicolor treatment, *The Trail of the Lonesome Pine* was a landmark film. Prior to this time, the only commercially successful movie utilizing color was the 1935 production of *Becky Sharp.* But while that pioneering film was soundstage bound, *Trail of the Lonesome Pine* used the great outdoors to fill its glorious all-color palette.

"The significance of this achievement is not to be minimized," noted the *New York Times.* "It means that we can doubt no longer the inevitability of the color film or scoff at those who believe that black-and-white photography is tottering on the brink of that limbo of forgotten things which already has swallowed the silent picture . . . It improves the case for color by lessening its importance. It accepts the spectrum as a complementary attribute of the picture, not its *raison d'être* . . . The color is not a distraction, but an attraction."

Paramount Pictures' production of *The Trail of the Lonesome Pine* was not the first time this 1908 novel had been filmed — there had been two previous movies based on the book by John Fox Jr. But since it was a natural for outdoor photography, the studio didn't hesitate to film another version. Set against the lavish backdrop of the Kentucky hills, the story centered on two feuding families — the Tollivers and the Falins. The Henry Hathaway–directed film starred Sylvia Sidney, Fred MacMurray, and Henry Fonda, and included eight-year-old Spanky MacFarland, already a veteran of dozens of "Our Gang" comedies. Unfortu-

Henry Fonda takes Spanky McFarland (of "Little Rascals" fame) for a boat ride in *Trail of the Lonesome Pine.*

nately for Spanky fans, his character, the pudgy-faced Buddy, is killed off early in the film, setting the families to more feuding.

The Oscar-nominated song "A Melody from the Sky" is used incidentally in the film, an unusual occurrence in an era when most nominated tunes were introduced in musical films. In the movie, the song is performed by Fuzzy Knight, who played the role of Tater. A musician, singer, and bandleader in nightclubs and vaudeville, this graduate of the University of West Virginia law school was best known as an awkward, stuttering sidekick in over 200 Westerns in which he provided comic relief. Fans of early-1950s Saturday-morning television may remember him as a regular on "Captain Gallant of the Foreign Legion," in which he played the comic pal of Buster Crabbe.

The Trail of the Lonesome Pine was released in February 1936, and by April "A Melody from the Sky" had provided a hit record for three artists. Jan Garber's orchestral version reached Number One on the *Billboard* charts, remaining in that position for three weeks and on the charts for 12. Eddy Duchin's cover peaked at number six and spent five weeks on the charts. Bunny Berigan's rendition reached the number 17 position and charted for only three weeks.

Composer Louis Alter had another tune in *The Trail of the Lonesome Pine*, called "Twilight on the Trail." Although not nominated, it became a favorite of President Franklin D. Roosevelt, and his original manuscript and a copy of the Bing Crosby recording can be found in the Roosevelt Memorial Library in Hyde Park, New York.

PENNIES FROM HEAVEN

**Music by Arthur Johnston;
lyrics by Johnny Burke
From *Pennies from Heaven***

Was there ever a song more representative of Depression-era motion picture optimism than "Pennies from Heaven"? The tune, introduced by Bing Crosby in the Columbia picture of the same name, did more to lift the nation's spirits than all the politicians' speeches of the decade. Sure, a bit of rain must fall in everyone's life, but hey, if you want flowers to grow, "you must have showers." By comparing raindrops to pennies, people got the message that soon everything would turn around, that things would be all right. Some of the more religious might have even interpreted the song to mean that although adversity seemed to come from "on high," God was still looking out for them; soon there would be "pennies [i.e., financial relief] from Heaven for you and me."

No wonder, then, that the song not only received an Academy Award nomination, but went on to become one of the most popular standards ever to be featured in a motion picture. During the year of its release, it spawned no less than six hit recordings. Crosby's own rendition was Number One for 10 weeks out of a 15-week chart run; Eddy Duchin's recording reached number two and spent nine weeks on the charts. Others with hit recordings of "Pennies from Heaven" that year included Teddy Wilson with Billie Holiday (peaking at number three), Hal Kemp and His Orchestra (number eight), Hildegarde (number 16), and Jimmy Dorsey (number 19). In the nearly 60 years since the song was first heard, there have been numerous other record-

ings by a variety of major artists, including Frank Sinatra, the McGuire Sisters, Dinah Washington, the Dave Brubeck Quartet, the Four Aces, Count Basie, Merle Haggard, Joe Turner, Doris Day, Woody Herman, Rosemary Clooney, and Sarah Vaughan.

The 1936 film, a light romantic musical comedy, featured several other tunes by Johnson and Burke, although none ever achieved the popularity of the title song. Their score included "Let's Call a Heart a Heart," "One, Two, Button Your Shoe," "So Do I," and "Skeleton in Your Closet," the last of which was played by Louis Armstrong and his band in one of their early film appearances.

"Pennies from Heaven" was used in several other movies as source music (music heard emanating from an external source, such as a radio or jukebox) in later years. Dick Haymes sang it in *Cruisin' Down the River* (Columbia, 1953), and it was heard in *From Here to Eternity* (Columbia, 1954) and again in another Columbia picture, *Picnic* (1956).

In 1981, a new film with the same title was made, but with a completely different storyline, based on a British television mini-series. The Steve Martin–Bernadette Peters version was ultimately much more successful — although it was rated "R" for adult situations, language, nudity, and violence (a far cry from Bing's version about an ex-con looking after a 10-year-old waif and her

Bing Crosby as a wandering minstrel serenades Edith Fellows in *Pennies from Heaven*.

elderly grandfather), the new, off-beat version received critical acclaim and a packet of nominations, including Oscar nominations for Best Costume Design, Sound, and Screenplay. Bernadette Peters picked up a Golden Globe Award as Best Actress in a Comedy or Musical, and the film also scored two other Golden Globe nominations: Best Motion Picture — Comedy or Musical; and Best Actor (Martin) — Comedy or Musical.

WHEN DID YOU LEAVE HEAVEN?

**Music by Richard A. Whiting;
lyrics by Walter Bullock
From *Sing, Baby, Sing***

In the 1930s, the era when filmusicals reigned supreme, it was generally accepted that a pair of composers would be handed the plum assignment to write the tunes for any given movie musical. *Sing, Baby, Sing* broke with this tradition in that several composers had a hand in its score. The film's tunes included "You Turned the Tables on Me," by Louis Alter and Sydney Mitchell, the title song, "Sing, Baby, Sing," by Lew Pollack and Jack Yellen, and the song that would eventually be nominated for the Oscar, the dreamy ballad entitled "When Did You Leave Heaven?" by Richard Whiting and Walter Bullock.

The movie *Sing, Baby, Sing* starred Alice Faye, the versatile actress-singer for whom composer Whiting had written several musicals. In this film, however, his song went to a newcomer, singer Tony Martin, who made his film debut in *Sing, Baby, Sing*. Martin described his nervousness at this auspicious moment in his career in his 1976 autobiography (co-written with his wife, Cyd Charisse), *The Two of Us:* "The scene called for me to sing it at an audition, and I was supposed to be dressed in absolutely dreadful clothes. I wore the worst stuff I had, but it still wasn't bad enough. They wanted something so flashy as to be laughable. They sent me down to the wardrobe department and dredged up a wild and gruesome outfit — a plaid suit with extra wide shoulders and lapels, awful shirt and tie . . . When I came back out on the stage I looked awful — which was just what they wanted. Alice [Faye] came over and said, 'Now you look better,' and winked at me."

The film proved a popular hit due to its inside story, whose relevance struck a knowing chord with the audience of the day. The storyline was a send-up of actor John Barrymore's romance with his protégée Elaine Barrie, with Adolphe Menjou hamming it up as the Barrymore-esque character.

In addition to serving as the vehicle for Martin's feature film debut, the picture also introduced the Ritz Brothers to movie audiences. The zany comic trio sang and danced their way through several of the film's production numbers, including an acrobatic-operatic aria at the film's beginning and a Jekyll-Hyde-Frankenstein number.

"When Did You Leave Heaven" became a hit recording for Guy Lombardo in the Fall of 1936. The song spent 15 weeks on the *Billboard* charts, peaking at Number One for two weeks. Ben Bernie's cover spent five weeks on the charts and peaked at the number six position, while Henry Allen's recording reached the number 16 position, spending two weeks on the charts. Ironically, Tony Martin, who had made his radio debut as a singer on "The Lucky Strike Hour," did not have a successful recording of the Oscar-nominated tune.

SWEET LEILANI

**Music and lyrics by Harry Owens
From *Waikiki Wedding***

On October 19, 1934, songwriter Harry Owens and his wife Bess welcomed their first child into the world. The little girl had her mother's laughing Irish blue eyes and black hair. The couple, who made their full-time home in Hawaii, decided to name their new daughter Leilani, which in Hawaiian means "a flower wreath from Heaven."

The name was quite a common one in the Islands; nearly every loyal Hawaiian family could boast a child named Leilani. Owens, of course, being a proper songwriter, immediately sat down and composed her a tune. He completed "Sweet Leilani" in less than an hour on October 20, when his child was one day old. "The words and music flowed like a rippling stream," he said in his 1970 autobiography, *Sweet Leilani: The Story Behind the Song.*

Shirley Ross listens as Bing Crosby croons a Hawaii tune in *Waikiki Wedding*.

Soon after that, Owens's friend Bing Crosby popped in for a visit with his old pal. By now, Owens had ordered several copies of the sheet music to his new tune, which had been distributed freely to local bands. One night, the Owenses and the Crosbys were dining and dancing at the Royal Hawaiian Hotel when the band launched into "Sweet Leilani." Bing asked Harry the name of the tune, and the crooner discovered he couldn't even pronounce it. Still, he insisted that this song was perfect for his next picture, *Waikiki Wedding*. Owens was aghast; he had written it as a lullaby for his child. "[I had] a very spiritual feeling about her song," he wrote. "To commercialize it seemed almost sacrilegious." Bing finally persuaded Owens that proceeds from the song could go to a trust fund for the child's education, and the songwriter relented.

All did not go well upon Bing's return to Hollywood. When he eagerly proffered the song to the film's producer, Arthur Hornblow, he was told that all the music had already been completed (by Leo Robin and Ralph Rainger, whose best-known tune from the pic-

ture would be "Blue Hawaii"). Moreover, Hornblow didn't even care for the song. When Bing expressed his feelings by walking off the set and onto the golf course, Hornblow reconsidered, and "Sweet Leilani" was incorporated into the picture.

Owens, however, along with most of the Hawaiians who attended the film's premiere screening in Honolulu, was appalled. At first all seemed fine — Bing began crooning to a happy, gurgling baby in a crib. Then all hell broke loose, as a squealing pig burst into his hut and was chased throughout the rest of the scene. The fact that Bing redeemed himself and the song by singing a proper version "Sweet Leilani" later in the film mattered not a whit. People fled the theater in anger; the theater manager canceled the picture's engagement and shipped his print back to Hollywood.

Owens was later consoled by the fact that Bing's recording on Decca became a smash hit and nearly single-handedly revived the Depression-era record industry, selling more than a million copies. The song soon climbed to Number One on the charts, where it remained for 10 weeks, and set a long-standing record by remaining on the charts for an unheard of 25 weeks. During his career, Crosby would achieve another record by introducing, in his various motion picures, more Academy Award–winning songs than any other performer.

On Oscar night, no one was more shocked than Harry Owens. Everyone had expected the Gershwin brothers to win for "They Can't Take That Away from Me" (see page 16). When Owens's name was called by presenter Irving Berlin, he gave full credit to Bing Crosby for having faith in the song from the start. Owens was the first Oscar winner to write both music and lyrics for a Best Song, a distinction he alone held for five years.

REMEMBER ME?

Music by Harry Warren; lyrics by Al Dubin
From *Mr. Dodd Takes the Air*

The Warner Bros. film *Mr. Dodd Takes the Air* seemed to have everything going for it: Mervyn Leroy as producer (two years later he would bring audiences *The Wizard of Oz)*, a very young and beautiful Jane Wyman as its star opposite Kenny Baker, a handsome young crooner, plus songs by Academy Award–winning composers Harry Warren and Al Dubin ("Lullaby of Broadway" — see page 4). Yet somehow, this picture became a flop. It failed to click with audiences and was soon relegated to the second half of double-feature showings. In the mid-1990s, it was rarely seen on television and had not found its way to the video rental counter.

But in spite of these problems, the film did manage to produce an Academy Award–nominated song. "Remember Me?" was introduced in the film by Kenny Baker, a former radio singer with Jack Benny's show. The song's tongue-in-cheek lyrics took a humorous look at post-wedding relationships. It was quickly reintroduced to radio audiences via a Decca recording by Bing Crosby. With "Der Bingle" crooning, there was no stopping it, and the tune landed in the Number One position for three weeks out of its six on the charts. Teddy Wilson also released a recording of the song; his orchestral version on the Brunswick label, with vocal by Boots Castle, reached number two and spent 10 weeks on the charts.

Occasionally other popular recording artists turned out their rendition of "Remember Me?" including Patti Page and Brook Benton. A slightly altered version of the song popped up in Shirley MacLaine's one-woman show, with rewritten lyrics by Fred Ebb and Bob Wells. She recorded it for a Columbia album of the show *Shirley MacLaine in Concert* at New York's Palace Theatre in 1976. The song was also performed by an unnamed soundtrack chorus for the 1946 Warner Bros. film *Never Say Goodbye,* starring Errol Flynn, Eleanor Parker, Hattie McDaniel, and Forrest Tucker.

It's difficult to say just why the picture failed to catch fire, especially in light of the song's popularity. Perhaps the problems lay in the film's premise: a young baritone with a newly signed radio contract suddenly finds (via a botched operation) that he's now a tenor. Baker in reality *was* a tenor, and the vocal confusion only served to mystify the audience, who then assumed he was singing in falsetto if, after all, he was really supposed to be a baritone. Such is not the sort of plot that could easily win over an audience in the 1930s, the heyday of the filmusical.

THAT OLD FEELING

Music by Sammy Fain; lyrics by Lew Brown
From *Vogues of 1938*

Vogues of 1938 — released in 1937 under the self-congratulatory title *Walter Wanger's Vogues of 1938* (he was the producer) — was a cinematic excuse for, as the *New York Times* termed it, "one whopper of a fashion show." The newspaper's critic had nearly as much praise for the lavish use of Technicolor ("the photogenic qualities of a Yellow cab or a Borden's milk wagon will amaze you!"), but reserved his special kudos for the Music Hall's welcome air conditioning during what had become a particularly hot and sticky New York City August. "Twenty percent cooler!" he chortled. There wasn't a whole lot else about which to remark. After admitting that the film "looks as expensive as all get-out . . . chiefly swirl, girl and frosting," plus touting the colors and the cool air, he somehow managed to overlook the film's lavish musical score, which was laden with a multitude of tunes.

As had been true of the 1936 musical *Sing, Baby, Sing,* many composers had a hand in writing musical numbers for *Vogues of 1938.* Songs were contributed to this showy Technicolor extravaganza by the teams of Frank Loesser and Manning Sherwin, Louis Alter and Paul Francis Webster, and Sammy Fain and Lew Brown. The most memorable and successful was "That Old Feeling," by Fain and Brown. In addition to being nominated for the Oscar, the song made the 1937 charts with orchestral recordings by Shep Fields (peaking at Number One during its 14 weeks on the charts) and Jan Garber (peaking at number 10 and charting for three weeks).

Vogues (the references to year and producer were later thankfully dropped) starred Warner Baxter, Joan Bennett, and Alan Mowbray. Hedda Hopper, best remembered as the dazzlingly behatted Hollywood gossip columnist of the '40s and '50s, had a brief acting role in the movie, appearing as Mrs. Van Klettering. Besides the Best Song nomination, the film also received a nod from the Academy with a nomination for Best Interior Decoration.

"That Old Feeling" was included in the 20th Century-Fox 1952 motion picture biography of Jane Froman, *With a Song in My Heart,* sung on the soundtrack by Froman herself (although she was played in the picture by Susan Hayward).

Sammy Fain, who composed the music, had a string of million-selling hits, most of which grew out of his music for the movies. He was responsible for the music of "Let a Smile Be Your Umbrella," "I'll Be Seeing You," "Secret Love" (see page 123), "Love Is a Many-Splendored Thing" (see page 132), "April Love" (see page 143), and "A Certain Smile" (see page 149). One of the last films for which he wrote tunes was the 1977 Walt Disney classic, *The Rescuers.* He died in 1989 at the age of 87.

THEY CAN'T TAKE THAT AWAY FROM ME

Music by George Gershwin; lyrics Ira Gershwin
From *Shall We Dance*

George Gershwin was at the peak of his career in 1937 when he and his brother Ira wrote "They Can't Take That Away from Me" for Pandro S. Berman's latest Fred Astaire–Ginger Rogers starrer. George had already made his mark on twentieth-century music by composing "Rhapsody in Blue" in 1925; its recognition as a classic would have sealed his future in the annals of

musical greatness. But back then, George, together with his lyricist partner and brother, had set his sights on Broadway, churning out such successes as *Funny Face* (1927), starring Fred and his sister Adele Astaire, *Girl Crazy* (1930), which introduced Ethel Merman to the musical stage, and *Of Thee I Sing* (1931), which became the first musical comedy to win a Pulitzer Prize. Many of the Gershwins' best songs would pour forth from these shows: " 'S Wonderful," "I Got Rhythm," and "Embraceable You" all became Gershwin standards. Their last musical production on Broadway was the. opera *Porgy and Bess.*

Then, in 1935, George Gershwin turned exclusively to Hollywood and the movies. The talented brothers had gotten a taste of the Big Orange in 1931, when they composed the score for *Delicious.* In 1937 they wrote the music for two films — *Damsel in Distress* and *Shall We Dance.* It was for this latter movie that the Gershwins would receive their only Academy Award nomination. Memorable tunes from these pictures included "A Foggy Day in London Town" and "Nice Work If You Can Get It" from *Damsel in Distress,* and "Let's Call the Whole Thing Off," "They All Laughed," and "They Can't Take That Away from Me," from *Shall We Dance.*

When the Academy Award nominations for 1937 were announced, nobody was surprised that "They Can't Take That Away from Me" was among those listed. Almost everyone assumed that the Gershwins were shoo-ins — until "Sweet Leilani" hulaed off with Oscar (see page 13). It would be George Gershwin's only shot at Hollywood's top prize. Sadly, he would not be among the nominees attending the ceremony the following March. On July 11, 1937, two months following the release of *Shall We Dance,* Gershwin died of an inoperable brain tumor. He was just 38 years old.

"They Can't Take That Away from Me" was one of the most popular songs ever to emerge from a film. Astaire and Rogers performed the number in two different pictures — in RKO's *Shall We Dance,* and again in the MGM movie *The Barkleys of Broadway* (1949). Yet George Gershwin was profoundly disappointed with the musical production number of the song in *Shall We Dance.* He was often quoted as saying, "The picture does not take advantage of the songs as well as it should." Be that as it may, the tunes, especially "They Can't Take . . ." were solid hits and have become undeniable standards that are still with us nearly six decades later. Fred Astaire's own recording of the tune on the Brunswick label in 1937 reached

Number One on the pop charts and remained on the charts for 11 weeks; Ozzie Nelson and His Orchestra's rendition hit number six and charted for four weeks; Tommy Dorsey's orchestration with vocal by Jack Leonard reached number 11, and Billie Holiday had a cover that made number 12. Over the years, George and Ira Gershwin's tune was recorded by such artists as Peggy Lee, Mel Tormé, Frank Sinatra, Percy Faith, Ray Conniff, Perry Como, Ella Fitzgerald and Louis Armstrong, Sarah Vaughan, Rosemary Clooney — the list is endless.

The song outlasted George Gershwin's expectations and survived his criticism. We can only speculate on all the wonderful tunes that might have been. Instead, we must be grateful for the rich legacy that he has left us. At least they can't take that away from us.

Fred Astaire and Ginger Rogers remind us "They Can't Take That Away from Me" in the Gershwin musical *Shall We Dance*.

WHISPERS IN THE DARK

**Music by Frederick Hollander;
 lyrics by Leo Robin**
From *Artists and Models*

Artists and Models was Jack Benny's first solo starrer. In this loosely plotted ensemble picture, he played a starving advertising agency head. Audiences ate it up, and Benny's film career was off and running. As Walter Winchell wrote, "Jack Benny finally gets his best break in Paramount's *Artists and Models*. The Benny magic, we mean, finally reaches out from the screen into the auditor's heart."

Starring along with Benny were Ida Lupino, Richard Arlen, Gail Patrick, Ben Blue, Judy Canova, and Hedda Hopper. Martha Raye and Louis Armstrong managed to weave their way through some musical numbers. As was becoming more and more common in 1930s musicals, a who's-who of composing talent provided the score for the various song-and-dance offerings. Ted Koehler, Harold Arlen, Victor Young, and Burton Lane all had tunes included in the movie. "Whispers in the Dark," by Frederick Hollander and Leo Robin, received an Academy Award nomination for Best Song.

The Yacht Club Boys, Judy Anne and Zeke, Russell Patterson's "Personettes," and the Water Waltzers all performed in this glorified vaudeville show on film. Songstress Connee Boswell introduced the Oscar-nominated "Whispers in the Dark," and her recording of the song spent three weeks on the *Billboard* charts, peaking at number nine. Another recorded version, by Bob Crosby (Bing's bandleader brother), became a Number One hit, holding that position for four weeks and remaining on the charts for 13. A Hal Kemp orchestral version, also recorded in 1937, peaked at number 11 and charted for three weeks.

Among the various musical production numbers strewn throughout the picture was the Oscar-nominated tune performed by Connee Boswell (who had changed the spelling of her name from the traditional Connie in mid-career). She was backed by the very reputable André Kostelanetz and His Orchestra, which no doubt gave her rendition of the song added clout. Connee and her sisters Martha and Helvetia ("Vet" for short) established their reputation in New Orleans as radio and vaudeville performers in the 1920s and '30s. Connee played cello, Martha piano, and Vet chose the

violin. But the trio soon turned to a more commercial kind of performance, adding jazz and blues numbers to their routine. In 1934 they recorded a number with Jimmie Grier, entitled "Rock and Roll," one of the earliest uses of the term. They partnered with Bing Crosby for his radio show, and also appeared in several movies, including *The Big Broadcast of 1932, Moulin Rouge,* and *Transatlantic Merry-Go-Round* (both 1934). After that, Martha and Vet retired, leaving Connee to continue as a solo act. She continued as a recording artist and in films through the late '50s, often working from a wheelchair, having contracted polio as a youngster.

THANKS FOR THE MEMORY

Music by Ralph Rainger; lyrics by Leo Robin
From *The Big Broadcast of 1938*

During the 1930s, Paramount produced a series of *Big Broadcast* films. The first, released in 1932, starred Bing Crosby, George Burns, Gracie Allen, Stuart Erwin, and the Boswell Sisters. Sequels — if they could be called that — quickly followed, each true to the same formula: Hey, radio stars, let's put on a show! Virtually every singer, musician, or comedian who ever stepped up to a mike in the heyday of radio now added his or her visage to the big screen. Burns and Allen popped up again in the 1936 and 1937 *Big Broadcast*s, along with Ethel Merman, Bing Crosby, Jack Oakie, Charlie Ruggles, Bill "Bojangles" Robinson, Jack Benny, Martha Raye, and blackfaced stars from "Amos 'n' Andy."

The last of these movies was *The Big Broadcast of 1938*. It starred W.C. Fields, the ubiquitous Raye, Dorothy Lamour, Shirley Ross, Ben Blue, and a sixth-billed fellow named Bob Hope. In fact, it served to introduce Hope to film audiences. It also introduced what would later become his theme song, a tune so closely tied to Hope that it's easy to believe he was born singing it.

"Thanks for the Memory" was originally supposed to be very humorous, since it was intended for Bob Hope, whom everyone knew was a funny guy. Ralph

Rainger and Leo Robin had earlier written "Love in Bloom," the signature song for another funny guy, Jack Benny (see page 4). So when director Mitchell Leisen told them he had a problem with the scene and needed a humorous piece about a couple who meet on an ocean liner, fall in love, but never actually say, "I love you," they promised to do their best. But a strange thing happened when the composers presented their latest creation to the production team of the 1938 *Big Broadcast:* everyone cried. Halfway through the presentation, director Leisen pulled out his hanky and began to wipe his eyes. Soon everyone from the Paramount music department was in tears. Fortunately, no one thought of pulling the song from the picture, although Rainger bet his partner Robin that the song would be a flop. He lost 10 dollars on the bet; the song went on to win the Academy Award for 1938 and became Bob Hope's signature song.

Hope liked the tune immediately. "It sounded so beautiful," he said. When Hope was asked to select a well-known theme for his new NBC radio show three months after the film's release, the sponsor suggested "Wintergreen for President," from *Of Thee I Sing,* with words modified to read, "Hope Is Here for Pepsodent."

"Nuts to that," said Hope, as he reported in his book, *The Road to Hollywood.* "I know a song that we can get much cheaper, and it'll be better." Hope was right, admitting that it was "Thanks for the Memory" that helped keep him on at Paramount, aided by famed writer Damon Runyon, who did an article saying it was the best thing he had seen in years.

When it came time to record the song on film for the movie, Leisen took an unusual step. Rather than having actors Bob Hope and Shirley Ross do the traditional lip synch to a prerecorded version of "Thanks for the Memory," he had the full Paramount orchestra assemble onstage and play the musical number live. When they finished, it was Rainger and Robin's turn to cry. "We didn't realize the song was that good," Hope remembered one of them saying. He also recalled how

W.C. Fields, Shirley Ross, and Bob Hope strut their stuff in *The Big Broadcast of 1938.*

he hated his first performance of his future theme. "Even today, when I see the 'Thanks for the Memory' number [from the film], I cringe," he wrote in *The Road to Hollywood*.

Surprisingly, it was not the Bob Hope–Shirley Ross recording of "Thanks for the Memory" that burned up the charts. Rather, the Shep Fields version spent 14 weeks on the charts, including four weeks at Number One. Perhaps Fields had an unfair edge — his recording was released three months prior to the film's opening. A 1938 version by Mildred Bailey peaked at number 11 and spent three weeks on the charts.

Paramount was so pleased with Hope's performance of the song that they decided to build an entire film around it. Later that year they featured him, again partnered with Shirley Ross, in a new picture appropriately titled *Thanks for the Memory* — one of the few times a movie song had an entire picture for an encore.

ALWAYS AND ALWAYS

Music by Edward Ward; lyrics by Chet Forrest and Bob Wright
From *Mannequin*

Until "Always and Always" was nominated for an Academy Award, Oscar-nominated songs had usually been the centerpiece of huge production numbers. Either that, or the leading man/lady had the opportunity to introduce the song while in character, ever hopeful that the tune would later soar to the top of the charts once it was released on record. Not so with "Always and Always."

The song had no dancing Astaire/Rogers teaming, no chorines blithely stepping in time to its rhythms, no moon-eyed lovers crooning to each other wistfully. Instead, "Always and Always" had the distinction of being the first tune appearing as "source music" (music heard in the background, emanating from a source such as the radio or a jukebox) to be nominated for the Academy's highest accolade.

The film *Mannequin* starred Joan Crawford, Spencer Tracy, and Alan Curtis in yet another take on that eternal theme, the love triangle. This time, Crawford plays a rags-to-riches girl from the tenements, propelled forward along with her greedy, villainous, totally loathsome husband (played by Curtis). Tracy, of course, is the wealthy good guy who wants to rescue

Joan Crawford stars as a rags-to-riches working girl in *Mannequin*.

her. It is a scene between these three characters that introduced the song "Always and Always."

Crawford is married to Curtis. The three of them are at a club where the jukebox is playing. Tracy, who has the hots for Crawford but respects her marriage, invites her to dance. (Her husband merely sees Tracy as his ticket up the ladder of ambition.) The song that is playing on the juke is "Always and Always," which has always and always been the married couple's song. Crawford politely declines Tracy's invitation, dancing instead with her husband as "Always and Always" continues on in the background. Although this is source music, eventually she does begin to sing along with the record.

Ironically, Crawford had been a dancer long before she ever uttered a line as an actress, arriving in Hollywood in 1925 at the age of 17 and hoofing her way through a series of pictures until finally making a name for herself as an actress in the film *Rain* (1932). Other dramatic roles quickly followed. Although she received favorable notices for her work in *Mannequin,* she is best remembered by movie buffs for her later films, including *Mildred Pierce* (1945), for which she won an Oscar.

"Always and Always" was recorded and played in *Mannequin* by Larry Clinton and His Orchestra. It was released in February of 1938, about a month after the film's premiere, and spent seven weeks on the charts, peaking at number nine.

CHANGE PARTNERS AND DANCE WITH ME

Music and lyrics by Irving Berlin
From *Carefree*

Irving Berlin's second foray into the Academy Award nomination ring was again with a number performed by Fred Astaire and Ginger Rogers (his first had been "Cheek to Cheek" in 1935 — see page 5). In *Carefree,* Fred for the first time plays a non-musical character, that of hypnotist Dr. Tony Flagg. Ginger plays the fiancée of another man (Ralph Bellamy), and she's forever breaking their engagement. Bellamy seeks the assistance of psychotherapist Flagg to determine the cause of this behavior, and she naturally falls for Astaire. There is a twist in all this — in previous Astaire/Rogers pictures (this was the eighth of the 10 that the couple would film together), it had always been Astaire who fell for a disinterested Rogers. Here, the tables are turned and she falls for him first.

Although playing a non-musical character, Astaire does a fair amount of dancing in the film. The couple introduce a new dance, "The Yam," the trickiest routine in the film. It was their efforts for "Change Partners," however, which garnered the attention of the Motion Picture Academy and earned an Oscar nomination.

The tune is nicely integrated into the plot, and the song was indeed a feather in Berlin's cap, since it wasn't specifically written for this picture. During the filming of *Follow the Fleet* two years earlier, Berlin began to realize that there might come a time when Astaire and Rogers might not be so dancingly joined at the hip — she was already beginning to show signs of dissatisfaction, having made a couple of successful straight comedies on her own (*Vivacious Lady* and *Having Wonderful Time,* both 1938 releases), while Astaire himself was

questioning the wisdom of continuing to work in film after film with the same partner. With a future breakup of the team apparently imminent, Berlin composed "Change Partners."

Then, in 1938, Irving Berlin received the assignment to compose the score for *Carefree,* another RKO–Pandro S. Berman production with Mark Sandrich set once again to direct the famous dance couple. The challenge this time was to devise a musical score for characters who were ostensibly non-musical. Meanwhile, Berlin and his wife had gone off to Phoenix for a seven-week holiday, which he soon turned into a working vacation. He had his specially tuned piano shipped to his retreat and managed to compose the remainder of the score to *Carefree* in a matter of days. Aside from the Oscar-nominated "Change Partners," the score featured "The Yam," "The Night Is Filled with Music," and "I Used to Be Color Blind." The latter was planned as a color sequence in Technicolor, to be inserted contrastingly into the black-and-white picture. However, RKO was riding a streak of box-office losses, and the purse strings on *Carefree* were suddenly drawn tight. At the last minute, it was decided to film "I Used to Be Color Blind" in the same black-and-white as the rest of the picture, thus completely undermining the fun in Berlin's lyrics. Despite the limitations of black and white, the film received a nomination from the Academy for Best Interior Decoration, as well as one for Best Score.

THE COWBOY AND THE LADY

Music by Lionel Newman;
** lyrics by Arthur Quenzer**
From *The Cowboy and the Lady*

Originally budgeted at $600,000, *The Cowboy and the Lady* eventually set back producer Samuel Goldwyn in excess of $1 million, a hefty amount for a simple comedy in the 1930s. The problems were blamed on that old Hollywood bugaboo, script troubles, with nearly a dozen writers hacking away at their typewriters. Several actors originally signed for the film had to be written out of it, including Thomas Mitchell and David Niven. William Wyler had been set to direct, but was replaced by lesser-known and less expensive H. C. Potter. Yet despite these behind-the-scenes difficulties, this comedy set in Montana and Palm Beach (a hopeless soundstage recreation) proved quite popular thanks to its stars, Gary Cooper and Merle Oberon.

Cooper naturally played the Cowboy of the title — not much of a stretch (coincidentally, his character's name was "Stretch") — with Oberon playing his mystery lady (he thinks she's a maid, but she's really a society Lady, as in the other half of the title). It's pure "Coop" with a sprinkling of comic sidekicks Walter Brennan and Fuzzy Knight thrown in for balance.

The title song, "The Cowboy and the Lady," is never completely sung (as was acceptable in the early days of Academy Award Best Song nominations); only a fragment of its lyrics are heard in the number when the three "maids" (Oberon, passing herself off as her own servant, along with the two real ones) and their cowboy dates return to the mansion in Palm Beach after a night at the rodeo. As they approach the grounds, they can be heard laughing and singing and "la-la-la-ing" some

of the lyrics to the tune — enough, apparently, to suit the Academy's rules about eligible songs. The melody is used quite extensively throughout the film, including over the opening and closing credits, as well as at just about every other musical opportunity — calliope music at the rodeo, a harmonica solo at the cattle round-up, a waltz, and as thematic background music. Consequently, the film received a nomination for Best Original Score, and it galloped off with a win for Best Sound Recording.

The music was composed by Lionel Newman, with lyrics by Arthur Quenzer. Lionel was the younger brother of Hollywood composer Alfred Newman, who is listed in the film's credits as musical director. This was Lionel's first film score. He joined 20th Century-Fox in the 1930s, where he began as a pianist and composer and arranger of film scores and title songs. He later became head of the music department and shared

Fuzzy Knight (seated) chows down while "cowboy" Gary Cooper seems uncertain how to proceed with "lady" Merle Oberon in *The Cowboy and the Lady*.

many assignments with his brother. Other scores included *How to Marry a Millionaire* (1953), *Love Me Tender* (1956), *The Sun Also Rises* (1957), and *North to Alaska* (1960). He also composed music for various TV shows, including "M*A*S*H" and "Planet of the Apes."

The movie is worth seeing for its intriguing look at the period of the late '30s. One of the funniest scenes (if unintentionally so) occurs immediately after the three couples half-sing "The Cowboy and the Lady" and return to the Palm Beach home's kitchen. There, the hayseeds marvel over the "latest" kitchen gadgets and appliances — an orange juice maker, a "modern" dishwasher, and so on. Intriguing, too, are the film's references to the modes of transportation of the day. When Cooper departs Florida for Galveston, he travels via cattle boat; when he goes back to his Montana ranch, he departs from a tiny one-room depot in West Palm Beach, arriving several days later, only to find that his father-in-law has beaten him there by — what a guy! — *flying* all that way.

DUST

Music and lyrics Johnny Marvin
From *Under Western Stars*

Under Western Stars introduced a new singing cowboy to the world, a handsome, shy young man named Leonard Slye, who had the good sense to change his name to Roy Rogers. In 1937, young Rogers signed a contract with Republic Pictures, which was having financial disputes with another of its cowboy stars, Gene Autry. When Autry failed to report for work on *Washington Cowboy* (the original title of *Under Western Stars)*, the role went to Rogers, who, thrilled at this "big break," reportedly accepted a salary one-fifth that of Autry.

Rogers was immediately hailed as a new cowboy hero, with, according to the *New York Times,* "a drawl like Gary Cooper, a smile like Shirley Temple and a voice like [Mexican-born singer] Tito Guizar." *Time* magazine said the 25-year-old, Wyoming-born star had a smile "like old Western star Gary Cooper, rides like a streak, and does everything Autry does." Clearly, this young cowpoke had found a new home on the silver screen.

Perhaps the most memorable moment for Rogers in any of the 102 films he would make in his career came when the producers of this first movie allowed him to select his horse. After being shown a number of poten-

tial mounts, he selected a palomino named Golden Cloud. "I got on him and rode him 100 yards and never looked at another horse," Rogers later recalled. He renamed the horse Trigger and always claimed that the animal was the best thing that ever happened to him. When Trigger died in 1965 at the age of 33, the heartbroken Rogers had him stuffed and mounted, and the horse is on display at the Roy Rogers–Dale Evans Museum in Apple Valley, California.

In the film *Under Western Stars,* Rogers played a young cowboy newly elected to Congress who hits Washington like a premature Mr. Smith (the film *Mr. Smith Goes to Washington* wouldn't be made for another year). This young maverick is a Man with a Mission — his dust bowl–shrouded home state needs Federal funds to alleviate the dryness, which is so bad that great clouds of drought-driven dust are obliterating the once-plentiful Western stars. In his lament, he sings the film's nominated song, whose beautifully poetic lyrics about even the cattle and sheep realizing their sad fate provide the film's message: "Dust, dust, must it be / Can this be Eternity?" This song by Johnny Marvin was also featured in 1948 in *Under California Skies,* a tenth anniversary Roy Rogers film.

The distributors of *Under Western Stars* were successful in their attempt to seek wider distribution than was typical for what was essentially a B-Western; Republic was able to have the film exhibited at New York City's Criterion Theatre on Broadway, the first B-Western ever to be shown there. And no doubt it was due in part to this mainstream showing that the song "Dust" received the attention of the Academy come award time, the second "cowboy" song (see "The Cowboy and the Lady," page 21) to be nominated that year.

JEEPERS CREEPERS

Music by Harry Warren;
**   lyrics by Johnny Mercer**
From *Going Places*

"Jeepers Creepers" was the first Best Song Academy Award nomination for Johnny Mercer. Eventually, he would receive a total of 18 nominations to his credit — 16 for lyrics alone, and two for music and lyrics. For the film *Going Places,* he was partnered with Harry Warren to write the lyrics for "Jeepers Creepers." Warren, already a veteran of Oscar, enjoyed his third nomination with this song. A prolific composer also, he would receive a total of 11 Oscar nominations for Best Song (music) by the end of his Hollywood career. (If you're keeping score, that brings the total combined nominations for these two to an impressive 29.)

Even today, well over half a century after it was written, nearly everyone is familiar with the simple yet catchy lyric to "Jeepers Creepers." The rhyming words to the main chorus — "creepers," "peepers," "weepers" — all were part of the then-current slang of the late '30s. In fact, all sorts of regional slang found its way into the lyrics, from country expressions like "Gosh all git up" to citified jargon like "How'd they get so lit up?" and "Got to put my cheaters [eyeglasses] on."

Mercer commented on his use of the title slang expression in the 1982 book *Our Huckleberry Friend* (written by his wife, Ginny Mercer, and Bob Bach): "I think I heard Henry Fonda say something like 'Jeepers Creepers' in a movie, and I thought it would be a cute idea for a song. I searched around quite a bit and then found that it fit so well as a title for that melody of Harry's. It was lucky casting that we got Louis Armstrong to sing it, although it wasn't written for him."

Ironically, the song as introduced in the movie *Going Places* was sung to and about a race horse. The film was based on the play *The Hottentot* and had been filmed several times before, but never as a musical. It was a farce about a horse-shy young man who poses as a famous steeplechase rider. Louis Armstrong does a couple of jam sessions, including one with the film's top two stars, Dick Powell and Anita Louise. Armstrong himself received third billing in the picture, a remarkable achievement in those days for a black man (Eddie "Rochester" Anderson, for example, received next-to-last billing for playing a groom). Also in the cast was a young Ronald Reagan as Jack Withering.

"Jeepers Creepers" appeared in many other pictures, including a 1939 Republic Western by the same title, in which Roy Rogers performed the tune; *Yankee Doodle Dandy* (Warner Bro., 1942), a brief sequence in which Joyce Reynolds and Charles Smith sang the song; *Brother Can You Spare a Dime* (1975), with Louis Armstrong recreating his original rendition, and, perhaps most outrageously, Paramount's *The Day of the Locust* (1975), where "Jeepers Creepers" is sung constantly and annoyingly by the little girl whose obnoxious, repetitive singing of this song contributes to the eventual unraveling of the film's main character.

The bouncy tune was a popular one for music buyers when first introduced in 1938. Al Donahue's release charted for 13 weeks, peaking at Number One, a position it held for five weeks; Louis Armstrong's version was released about a month after the film's premiere, peaked at number 12, and was on the charts for five weeks, while Larry Clinton's version also hit number 12 peak and was on the charts for two weeks.

MERRILY WE LIVE

Music by Phil Craig; lyrics by Arthur Quenzer
From *Merrily We Live*

Essentially derivative of the successful 1936 screwball comedy *My Man Godfrey*, *Merrily We Live* starred Brian Aherne in this variation on the all-wise tramp-cum-butler theme. He's really just a writer with a five-o'clock shadow, but once inside the household, he decides to play along.

The film was a delightful romp from producer Hal Roach, so well known for his *Laurel and Hardy* and *Little Rascals* comedies. In 1937, he produced *Topper*, one of his earliest feature-length movies. It proved a huge success, spawning two sequels (and eventually a television series and a TV movie remake). Spurred by the sequels' successes, Roach fashioned *Merrily We Live*, utilizing the same production team (including star Constance Bennett) that had made *Topper* so popular. In *Merrily We Live*, Roach incorporated his slapstick trademark in all sorts of new ways — people with pitchers of water colliding with swinging doors, Alan Mowbray as another butler getting his hand stuck in a vase, the head of the household doing a funny drunk scene on the staircase, and a scene in which the women are all fainting simultaneously.

Billie Burke, who would shortly become Glinda the Good Witch in *The Wizard of Oz* (MGM, 1939), played a scatterbrained character just one yellow brick short of a road. Her delightful performance earned her a nomination as Best Supporting Actress. Other Oscar nominations went to *Merrily We Live* for Cinematography, Interior Decoration, Sound Recording, Art Direction, and, of course, Best Song — the title song, "Merrily We Live."

In one of the most unusual presentations seen in any movie, "Merrily We Live" is sung over the opening credits in a production number featuring 10 of the top stars of the cast. Costumed as their characters, they walk up the driveway and through the wide-swinging gate of the film's mansion, arms linked, 10 abreast, laughing and stepping in time to this lively tune.

This was the second Best Song nomination for lyricist Arthur Quenzer. His previous one was another title song, "The Cowboy and the Lady," also in 1938 (see page 21). These would be the only Oscar nominations of his career. (The composer of the music for "Merrily We Live," Phil Craig, received no other nominations during his lifetime either.) Quenzer, a graduate of Columbia University with a degree in law, spent most of his early life free-lancing as a musician and lyricist. He played reeds and violin with such famous artists as David Rose, Phil Harris, Gordon Jenkins, and Victor Young. As a lyricist, he collaborated with many of the greats, including Alfred Newman, Lionel Newman, and Artie Shaw.

The music was published by Leo Feist, Inc., but was never a hit recording and is seldom remembered outside the context of this film.

A MIST IS OVER THE MOON

Music by Ben Oakland; lyrics by Oscar Hammerstein II
From *The Lady Objects*

Oscar Hammerstein II had been writing lyrics for musical stage productions since 1919, but he did not turn his attention to film until the 1930s. His most famous achievement up to that time had been the hit play *Show Boat*, in 1927, for which he teamed with Jerome Kern. Later, of course, he would be partnered with Richard Rodgers and pen some of the most memorable lyrics of the century — such Broadway hits as *Oklahoma*, *The King and I*, and *The Sound of Music* were among the dozens of products of their successful collaboration.

Billie Burke, Alan Mowbray and Brian Aherne in a scene from the Hal Roach–MGM feature *Merrily We Live*.

From left: Gloria Stuart, Lanny Ross, Bess Flowers, Pierre Watkin, and Robert Paige starred in the Columbia production *The Lady Objects*.

But for his first crack at writing a lyric for a motion picture, Hammerstein was assigned a tune written by Ben Oakland. It would be the first and only successful pairing for the team, resulting in Hammerstein's first (and Oakland's only) nomination for an Academy Award. Hammerstein would eventually receive a total of four nominations throughout his career. In 1941 he would again team with Jerome Kern for "The Last Time I Saw Paris" (see page 41), winning his first Oscar. Together with Richard Rodgers he would win the statuette again in 1945, for "It Might As Well Be Spring." And paired once again in 1946 with Kern, he would receive a nomination for "All Through the Day."

Oscar Hammerstein's first nomination came for the lyrics of "A Mist Is Over the Moon," from the 1938 film *The Lady Objects*. Lanny Ross, Gloria Stuart, and Joan Marsh starred in this drama about college sweethearts who marry and then separate when the career of "the lady" (as in the title) as a criminal lawyer takes off — a bold plot for the decade of the '30s, when women were generally frail, helpless, and usually relegated to the kitchen. (In a fascinating bit of trivia, we learn that for her efforts, she is paid $40 a week by her firm.) Later, she is called upon to defend him when he is accused of murder.

The focus of the movie seemed torn between its dramatic subject matter and its romantic comedy aspect, with lots of music tossed in. Lanny Ross's talents as a popular singer as well as actor were put to good use with his singing of the nominee-to-be "A Mist Is Over the Moon." Ross, once known as "the idol of the airwaves," first appeared on screen in 1934, in *Melody in Spring*. His other films were primarily musicals, such as *College Rhythm*, *Gulliver's Travels* (in which he was the singing voice of Gulliver — see page 30), and *Home in Oklahoma*. In 1943's *Stage Door Canteen*, he was a featured singer, performing a number that would receive another Best Song nomination (see page 66).

Ross, playing an architect, first sings "A Mist" at a cocktail party, accompanying himself on piano while singing to a potential client. He's constantly interrupted, but is later invited to perform this "song he always sings at parties" while at a nightclub. This time, the tune receives the full orchestral treatment.

Oscar Hammerstein wrote lyrics to three other songs included in *The Lady Objects:* "That Week in Paris," "Home in Your Arms," and "When You're in the Room." None made music history, and neither did any of the film's other tunes, written by Ben Oakland with another lyricist, Milston Drake.

MY OWN

**Music by Jimmy McHugh;
lyrics by Harold Adamson
From *That Certain Age***

Deanna Durbin was only 17 when she starred in Universal's *That Certain Age*. It was her first adult role — she had previously always been cast as a whistling, happy-go-lucky schoolgirl. In *That Certain Age*, she had reached that certain age when a young lady begins to think about more serious subjects — like boys, and singing beautiful operatic music. True to form, and in a voice that belied her age, Deanna's unaffected style came through.

"Sweet" and "wholesome" were terms often applied to Durbin, and *That Certain Age* further perpetuated this image. In this film, she develops a crush on her parents' house guest, an "older man" (played by Melvyn Douglas), only to eventually realize the error of her ways (after her parents' and Douglas's scheming) and return to her more appropriate teenaged boyfriend, played by Jackie Cooper. The film's highlight is when Deanna, showing off her best soprano voice, sings the future Oscar-nominated "My Own" at a party. She hopes to catch the attention of Douglas's character with her music, but it is Cooper who is really smitten with her, as he hears her performance while watching through a window.

Durbin became Universal's answer to Shirley Temple, although she was a few years older than her 20th Century-Fox counterpart. Her stardom actually survived adolescence better than Temple's did; the young Durbin pulled down as much as $300,000 a year. In 1938, Deanna received a special miniature Oscar from the Motion Picture Academy and was frequently credited with saving Universal Studios from bankruptcy. She continued making movies until 1948, wrapping up her career with *For the Love of Mary*. She retired as Hollywood's highest-paid female star at the ripe old age of 27, never to return to the public eye again, eventually emigrating to France with her third husband, Charles-Henri David (who had directed her in the 1945 film *Lady on a Train*).

"My Own" was the second Academy Award nomination for both Jimmy McHugh and Harold Adamson, but their first as a team. McHugh had received the nomination in 1935, writing the lyrics (with Dorothy Fields) for "Lovely to Look At" (see page 7). Adamson

had been the lyricist for "Did I Remember?" in 1936 (see page 8). This marked the beginning of a beautiful partnership that would eventually see the team writing songs for a total of 19 movies, including the nominated song "I Couldn't Sleep a Wink Last Night" from 1944's *Higher and Higher* (see page 68).

In addition to "My Own," other songs in the *That Certain Age* included "You're as Pretty as a Picture," "Has Anyone Ever Told You Before?" and "Be a Good Scout." The film received an additional Oscar nomination, for Best Sound Recording.

While "My Own" never became a huge hit, it did receive a substantial amount of attention during its initial release in 1938. Tommy Dorsey's version peaked at number five and spent 11 weeks on the charts, while Deanna Durbin's own recording reached the number 15 position and charted for three weeks. Another recording by Georgie Hall peaked at number 17 and was on the charts for only two weeks.

NOW IT CAN BE TOLD

**Music and lyrics by Irving Berlin
From *Alexander's Ragtime Band***

With 26 Irving Berlin songs wrapped around an all-star cast, *Alexander's Ragtime Band* was one of the happiest excuses for a movie of the '30s. Who needed plot or characterization when you had Tyrone Power, Alice Faye, Don Ameche, Ethel Merman, and Jack Haley, and that was just for starters. Commenting on the prolific music by Berlin, the *New York Times* wrote, "*Alexander's Ragtime Band* was played at the Roxy yesterday and at its finish the score stood: Irving Berlin, 26; Opposition, 0." The ecstatic reviewer went on to call it "the best musical show of the year."

The film was a veritable hit parade of classic Berlin tunes, from the title song to "Oh How I Hate to Get Up in the Morning," "When the Midnight Choo-Choo Leaves for Alabam', " "Easter Parade," "Blue Skies," "Remember," "Say It with Music," and "What'll I Do?" As if these (and more) weren't enough, Berlin created six new songs especially for the film. So great was the concentration of songs in the 105-minute film that to achieve the impressive 26-tune total (some of which were strung together in medleys), a musical number popped up on the average *every four minutes*. No wonder that the picture won the Oscar for Best Score.

(Other nominations were for Best Picture, Best Original Story, Best Interior Decoration, and Best Film Editing.)

Woven in there somewhere was a storyline about a bandleader (Power) and a singer (Faye). Although their characters interacted in a timeline running from 1911 to 1938, nary a gray hair or wrinkle dared to appear anywhere near this perfectly made-up twosome.

The new songs created especially for this picture included "My Walking Stick," "Marching Along with Time," and the film's Academy Award–nominated song, "Now It Can Be Told" (sung in the movie by Don Ameche). There was reportedly as much fun going on behind the scenes as there was in front of the cameras, with the cast involved in a number of good-natured juvenile hijinks. For instance, Power and Ameche overturned a can of garbage in Alice Faye's luxurious dressing room and later pulled away her steps so that she nearly fell out the door. Ethel Merman hid Power's temporary upper caps, which he wore in close-ups. Power retaliated by nailing her gown to a clothes tree. While he was at it, he nailed Don Ameche's shoes to the floor of his dressing room.

"Now It Can Be Told" was a big hit during the month of July for three recording artists. Tommy Dorsey's recording was on the charts for 15 weeks and peaked at number two; Bing Crosby's version peaked at number seven and remained on the charts for eight weeks, and Tony Martin's rendition charted for three weeks, peaking at number 13.

In 1994, "Now It Can Be Told," sung by Tony Bennett, was used on the soundtrack album of the movie *It Could Happen To You.*

1939
OVER THE RAINBOW

Music by Harold Arlen; lyrics by E.Y. Harburg
From *The Wizard of Oz*

"Honey, stop the car!"

Harold Arlen's wife Naya reacted immediately to her husband's words and screeched to a halt in front of the original Schwab's Drug Store in Hollywood. The movie they were headed for at Grauman's Chinese

Theatre that Sunday afternoon would have to wait. Arlen felt a song coming on. Not just any song, either. This was one that had eluded him for a week — the key ballad he and lyricist partner E. Y. Harburg needed to write for the movie *The Wizard of Oz.* It had to be a "song of yearning . . . to delineate Dorothy and to give an emotional touch to the scene where she is frustrated and in trouble," he confided in Aljean Harmetz's *The Making of the Wizard of Oz.* Quickly, he jotted down the notes as the "broad, long-lined melody" spun inside his head. Thrilled, Arlen rushed to play the newly created tune for his partner.

Harburg hated it. He thought the slow tempo was more suitable to Nelson Eddy than a little girl from Kansas. "I knew Judy [Garland] could sing 'Over the Rainbow,' but I thought it was too old for the character." Arlen refused to give up and consulted with another musical friend of his, Ira Gershwin, who suggested a quicker tempo and less harmonization. It worked, and Harburg began to create lyrics suitable to a little girl, a song full of lemon drops, stars, rainbows, and other childhood things.

At first the song was titled "Over the Rainbow Is Where I Want to Be." Harburg struggled to get the right lyric: "I'll go over the rainbow"; or maybe "Someday over the rainbow." Said Harburg, "For a while I thought I would just leave those first two notes out. It was a long time before I came to "Somewhere over the rainbow."

Judy Garland poured her 16-year-old heart into the song, yet without much discussion, MGM studio head Louis B. Mayer had the tune axed after the first sneak preview. Three times the song was deleted; three times producer Arthur Freed stormed back into Mayer's office demanding its reinstatement. Mayer finally relented, dropping instead other sequences, such as "The Jitterbugs," not restored until decades later on the laser disc version.

The film and the song were both instant hits, and it was no surprise when "Over the Rainbow" won the Academy Award for Best Song of 1939. Judy Garland, just shy of her eighteenth birthday, received a special Oscar as "the best juvenile performer of the year" and after accepting her special statuette, she was asked to sing the nominated song at the awards ceremony. Her friend and fellow "child" star Mickey Rooney presented the award to a genuinely nervous Garland, who, according to David Shipman's *Judy Garland: The Secret Life of an American Legend,* recalled, "[It was] the most

Judy Garland longs to get out of the cornfield and go "Over the Rainbow" in this classic scene from *The Wizard of Oz*.

sensational moment of my career . . . The lump in my throat was so big when I sang that I sounded more like Flip the Frog than the most excited girl in all Hollywood . . . I was so nervous I thought I'd faint. [Mickey] practically held me up through the second chorus."

The movie also won the Academy Award for Best Original Score, and received Oscar nominations for Best Picture, Best Color Cinematography, Best Interior Decoration, and Best Special Effects.

There have been numerous recordings of "Over the Rainbow" over the years, and many versions have charted. Glenn Miller had a Number One hit in 1939, which remained in that position for seven weeks; Bob Crosby's orchestral version hit number two; Larry Clinton's peaked at number 10. But no one could claim proprietorship of "Over the Rainbow" except Judy.[1] It would go on to become forever linked in the mind of the public as Judy's signature song. She sang it hundreds — maybe thousands — of times throughout the rest of her career, each time bringing the house down. It will forever remain the legacy left by Judy Garland to her adoring fans.

---

1. Ironically, Judy Garland's original soundtrack version of "Over the Rainbow" debuted three weeks after the film's release. It peaked at number five during a 12-week chart run.

FAITHFUL FOREVER

Music by Ralph Rainger; lyrics by Leo Robin
From *Gulliver's Travels*

With their highly popular cartoons of Betty Boop and Popeye in the early '30s, the production team of brothers Max and David Fleischer had been Paramount Pictures' answer to the animators at Walt Disney Studios. Then, following the 1937 release of Disney's animated hit *Snow White and the Seven Dwarfs*, the Fleischers were given a new assignment to help Paramount try to catch some animation lightning of its own.

The tunes from *Snow White* had burned up the charts, encouraging everyone to "Whistle While You Work" and sing "Heigh Ho, Heigh Ho," yet, oddly, none of the songs from that production was included in the 1937 Best Song nominations. So Paramount was espe-

cially pleased with the results of the Fleischer teaming when their animated feature *Gulliver's Travels* became the first of its genre to have a song nominated for an Academy Award. *Gulliver*, however, had one thing going for it that *Snow White* did not — a story concept built around the film's theme song.

Jonathan Swift's classic set in the year 1699 was loosely adapted into a story about two warring kings, their Romeo and Juliet–like children who fall in love, and the national song of each nation. Lilliput's anthem is called "Faithful," and the king's daughter, Princess Glory (the voice of Jessica Dragonette) plans to sing it at her wedding to Prince David of Blefuscu. But this idea doesn't sit well with the king of that country, who insists that his nation's song, "Forever," be the only tune heard at the royal wedding. What to do? What else, but merge the two tunes into one happy romantic ballad with the combined title of "Faithful Forever." Presto,

The two kings argue over which song — "Faithful" or "Forever" — should be sung at their children's wedding in *Gulliver's Travels*.

instant harmony throughout both lands, thanks to the simple suggestion of Gulliver, who has stumbled into this world in time to save the day.

At Oscar time, *Gulliver's Travels* was honored with two nominations — Best Song and Best Original Score (by Victor Young). Ralph Rainger and Leo Robin were no strangers to Oscar nominations; their "Thanks for the Memory" had taken home the statuette for 1938 (see page 18), and Paramount was hopeful to repeat that feat in '39 with "Faithful Forever." But not only were there no Oscars this time, the tune also failed to become the huge standard for weddings that its composers had hoped for. Although the song did enjoy some popularity and was a number four hit for Glenn Miller, it soon faded from memory.

In he rest of the film, Gulliver was played by the voice of Lanny Ross. His character is consistently drawn in a realistic style, well suited to his warm baritone voice, while the other characters and critters in the movie are decidedly Disneyesque. Big-eyed and silly, they could double as Dwarf stand-ins — one named Gabby is no doubt Dopey's separated-at-birth twin. This contrast in drawing styles makes it difficult to know at first if the film wants to be taken seriously. Even the kings are goofy looking, with names like Bombo and Little. Obviously, it's all meant to be good fun for the kids. And while it's nowhere near as sophisticated as today's animated gems, this is still worth a look when it shows up on local TV from time to time.

I POURED MY HEART INTO A SONG

Music and lyrics by Irving Berlin
From *Second Fiddle*

Second Fiddle is what Tyrone Power ended up playing to Olympic ice skating star–cum-actress Sonja Henie in this light-hearted spoof of David O. Selznick's search for the perfect Scarlett O'Hara for his epic film *Gone with the Wind* (1939). In *Fiddle,* produced by Darryl F. Zanuck for 20th Century-Fox, the search is on for one Violet Jansen, in an epic called *Girl of the North.* The search ends, of course, with candidate number 436 — Henie, a Norway native (and if you're looking for a girl of the north, you can't get much farther north than that!). She manages to skate several numbers throughout the picture — a real chore for the writers to work

Tyrone Power proves he has what it takes to attract the ladies in *Second Fiddle.*

into the sketchy plot, but Sonja fans expected their lady to skate, not emote. Romance helped the story along; there was a "John Alden"–type triangle between Sonja, her press agent (Power), and the film's leading man (played by Rudy Vallee).

Power had long been a favorite of Zanuck, who called him "the truest, the handsomest, the best of the lot." Power signed a deal with Zanuck's Fox studios in 1936 that would see him through 17 years of pictures. He handled nearly every aspect of his craft with considerable skill, including swashbucklers, westerns, period and contemporary dramas, and even light comedy, as called for in *Second Fiddle.*

Rudy Vallee, on the other hand, was noted mostly for his musical abilities. He popularized the song "I'm

Just a Vagabond Lover," which, in 1929, led to RKO's creation of a film for him, called, appropriately, *The Vagabond Lover.* He later crooned his way through a number of comedies and musicals.

Irving Berlin penned several new tunes for *Second Fiddle,* one of which made it into Oscar contention. "I Poured My Heart into a Song," however, is still one of Berlin's lesser-known tunes. In the movie, Vallee sings it to Henie, although her love-struck press agent (Power) is the one who actually "writes" it. Berlin poured his heart into a lot of other songs for the film, too — "I'm Sorry for Myself," "Back to Back" (Berlin's send-up of his own "Cheek to Cheek"), and a lavish production number of "An Old-Fashioned Song Is Always New." None of them became especially popular.

"I Poured My Heart" enjoyed some attention in records released in July 1939, the same time as *Second Fiddle.* Artie Shaw's version peaked at number four and was on the charts for 12 weeks; Jimmy Dorsey's rendition peaked at number 13 and charted for only two weeks.

WISHING (WILL MAKE IT SO)

Music and lyrics by Buddy DeSylva
From *Love Affair*

Love Affair owes its success to the vision of one of Hollywood's most successful "hyphenates" — writer-producer-director Leo McCarey. Using a formula of warm-hearted comedy plus sentiment, this talented man touched the hearts of movie-goers for five decades. In the early '30s he directed the likes of the Marx Brothers, Eddie Cantor, W. C. Fields, Mae West, and Harold Lloyd, and in 1937 he won his first Academy Award, for his direction of *The Awful Truth.* He would later win a pair of Oscars for directing and writing the 1944 film *Going My Way.*

McCarey wore all three of his hats in *Love Affair.* His co-written storyline for the film found Irene Dunne and Charles Boyer as unlikely lovers who meet aboard a ship and plan a rendezvous in six months atop the Empire State Building in New York, where they vow to meet to reaffirm their love. However, on her way to that appointment, Dunne is involved in a crippling accident and, not wishing to be pitied, shuns the meeting with Boyer. Eventually they do rendezvous and renew their enthusiasm for each other as she expresses her determination to walk again. (Cue the violins.)

According to *The RKO Story,* McCarey played this one close to the edge. Working without a completed script, he, along with several other writers and the cast's principal actors, "put the picture together on a day-to-day basis." The finished product was a resounding hit — so successful, in fact, that McCarey decided years later to remake his film for 20th Century-Fox; the new incarnation was called *An Affair to Remember* (see page 142). (A third version of *Love Affair,* starring the husband-and-wife acting team of Warren Beatty and Annette Bening, was released in 1994.) What is even more amazing is that both these pictures, which were decidedly non-musicals, garnered Oscar nominations for Best Song.

In the case of *Love Affair,* the tune was "Wishing (Will Make It So)." It was sung by a trio and then a full chorus of children in the film. The lyrics state the theme of the movie — that dreams do come true if people wish long and hard enough, and optimism makes all things possible.

The song quickly climbed the charts. Glenn Miller's recording went to Number One for four weeks and remained on the charts for a total of 14 weeks; Russ Morgan's version peaked at number four; Skinny Ennis' rendition hit the number nine position during its only week on the chart; and Orrin Tucker's version made number 12.

In addition to DeSylva's "Wishing," Harold Arlen and Ted Koehler were also called upon to write a song for inclusion in *Love Affair.* It was called "Sing My Heart." "Wishing" continued its popularity and was included in the motion picture musical *George White's Scandals of 1945* (RKO, 1945).

Love Affair received five additional nominations (but, unfortunately, no wins) for Academy Awards: Best Picture, Best Actress (Irene Dunne), Best Supporting Actress (Maria Ouspenskaya), Best Original Story, and Best Interior Decoration.

THE FORTIES

America's musical tastes were changing in the 1940s, and film makers hastily shifted their styles to keep up. Stage shows were still popular, both live and on screen, but more and more youngsters were boogying to a big band beat. In fact, the word "boogie" itself managed to work its way into more than a few song titles and lyrics.

As war approached, musicals and songs began to reflect the times; all-star extravaganzas cheered on our brave soldiers in uniform and brave citizens at home, as new talents emerged. Musicals still starred Astaire and Crosby, while new luminaries like Alice Faye, Eleanor Powell, Deanna Durbin, Sonja Henie, Betty Grable, Frank Sinatra, Danny Kaye, Gene Kelly, and Betty Hutton had begun emerge.

The middle of the decade — 1945 — marked the end of the war and the end of the free-for-all of the Best Song nominations, which saw a record 14 tunes up for the prize that year. After that, the rules were changed to allow a maximum of five songs per year. And while this same year did not mark the first on-air broadcast of the Academy Awards, it was the first time that the awards ceremony, celebrated in March of 1946, saw the nominated songs actually performed. With 14 tunes to sing, there wasn't much time for elaborate production numbers; Frank Sinatra, Dick Haymes, Dinah Shore, and Kathryn Grayson alternated in the performance chores in the live ceremony originating from Grauman's Chinese Theatre in Hollywood.

By the end of the decade, the need to cram multiple stars and as much singing and dancing as possible into plotless spectaculars had pretty much disappeared. Musicals were still the source of most of the nominees, but never again would there be the proliferation of filmusicals as there had been during the war years (with over 175 musical features released from 1942 to 1945). Soon there would be a new chapter in the history of cinematic song with the recognition of the importance of the title song in the next decade.

1940

And the winner is...

WHEN YOU WISH UPON A STAR

Music by Leigh Harline; lyrics by Ned Washington
From *Pinocchio*

Like a bolt out of the blue, Walt Disney and company created animagic at the movies with their 1940s offering of *Pinocchio*. Critics raved, and many awards were bestowed on this second animated feature from Disney, along with the lavish praise for what was then Walt's crowning achievement, "the best thing Mr. Disney has done and therefore the best cartoon ever made," as the *New York Times* eagerly pointed out in its 1940 review. The magic, however, did not carry over to the box office, at least not initially. *Pinocchio*'s wartime release wasn't the most financially auspicious; it wasn't until several later re-releases that the film eventually became a box office hit (it has now netted over $40 million in North American rentals) as well as critical success.

One thing, however, was successful from the start — the movie's theme song. "When You Wish Upon a Star" has, in fact, become *the* quintessential Disney theme, virtually synonymous with all things Disney —

from the opening music of the classic "Disneyland" television show of the '50s to the Disneyland theme park anthem (used in commercials until "Be Our Guest" appeared in 1991's *Beauty and the Beast)*. It is even heard in the first few intro bars used in several of the Walt Disney home videocassettes.

Not surprisingly, the song was honored with the Oscar for Best Song of 1940 (the score also received an Academy Award), the first Disney song to do so. This theme from *Pinocchio* is introduced over the opening credits by Jiminy Cricket, voiced by the soothing tenor of Cliff "Ukulele Ike" Edwards. At first we just hear the song over the film's titles, but then we see Jiminy, poised in front of the storybook of *Pinocchio*. "Pretty, huh?" he asks as the tune concludes. "I'll bet a lot of you folks don't believe that — about a wish coming true — do you? Well, I didn't either. Of course, I'm just a cricket singing my way from hearth to hearth, but let me tell you what changed my mind . . ." With that, he opens the giant book and we're off on our adventure.

The song is reprised melodically throughout the film: When woodcarver Geppetto wishes on the "first star I see tonight" that his little puppet might be a real boy, the music appears in the background; when the Blue Fairy shows up to grant Geppetto's wish, the tune is quietly present; when the story concludes and Pinocchio has become a real boy, the music swells in the picture's tag, backed by a rousing chorus.

Composer Leigh Harline himself conducted a major portion of the score, a collaboration of many

In *Pinocchio*, Jiminy Cricket promises the title puppet he can have his heart's desire in the song "When You Wish Upon a Star."

musicians. Paul Smith was involved in the composition and development of the score, and Ed Plumb, Frederick Start, and Charles Wolcott were responsible for the orchestration.

"When You Wish Upon a Star" was really a Depression-inspired homily, an attempt by Harline along with lyricist Ned Washington to give encouragement to audiences who had undergone rough times during the previous decade. It came very close in theme as well as title to a song that had been nominated for an Oscar the previous year — "Wishing (Can Make It So)" (see page 32). Ironically, the composer of the that tune, B. G. ("Buddy") DeSylva, was the presenter of the music awards at the ceremony honoring the 1940 Oscar winners.

The film's Oscar-winning score also included such Harline/Washington tunes as "Give a Little Whistle," "I've Got No Strings," and "Hi-diddle-dee-dee." It is following that last song, when Pinocchio has decided to become an actor and "fires" Jiminy Cricket as his conscience, that one of the most amusing lines in the picture is uttered, by Jiminy, who, reflecting on his situation as an outcast, sighs: "What does an actor want with a conscience anyway?" It's a throwaway line that no doubt gave the production team at Disney and other Hollywood insiders a good laugh.

"When You Wish Upon a Star" had great success as a single release in 1940. Glenn Miller's version was the Number One tune for five weeks in a row and charted for 16 weeks, while Guy Lombardo's version peaked at number five, Cliff Edwards's at number 10, and Horace Heidt's at number 12. In 1960, Dion and the Belmonts had a recording of the famous tune that peaked at number 30 and was on the charts for nine weeks.

DOWN ARGENTINE WAY

**Music by Harry Warren; lyrics by Mack Gordon
From *Down Argentine Way***

Maybe it was the sultry, tropical climate of Rio. Maybe it was something in the water everyone was warned not to drink. It certainly wasn't in the food — she didn't eat it, after all. She *wore* it, tall and swaying to the music like the trunk of some bizarre fruit-salad tree. Whatever it was, though, it was never again equaled. It — or, more properly, she — was Carmen — hot-blooded and full-bodied, like her namesake in the Bizet opera.

Carmen Miranda came to New York directly from her Brazilian homeland, taking Broadway by tropical storm in 1939. By 1940 she'd starred in her first Hollywood movie for Darryl F. Zanuck at 20th Century-Fox. Never mind that the title was *Down Argentine Way* while Miranda was Brazilian — this practically plotless picture found a way to weave in her charms by generalizing about an entire continent, reducing it in simplistic abstract to one culture, one civilization. This was epitomized in the opening song performed by Carmen, bedecked with practically every bead and shell found in South America. Along with this outfit came her trademarks — her bare midriff and tutti-frutti headdress.

The lyrics to "South American Way" (which she pronounced "*Souse* American Way") consisted mainly of a lot of "Aye, aye, aye"s, which seemed to suit Miranda and company just fine. It was, in fact, a lot easier on the ear than her rat-a-tat-tat machine-gun lyric of the title song, "Down Argentine Way," sung over the opening credits as part of an overture medley. Later, the Harry Warren–Mack Gordon tune is sung in Spanish by Don Ameche, who plays a wealthy South American horse trader in love with Betty Grable, the film's star. Betty sings an English version while performing a dance routine. Later still, the song is reprised in the Club Rendezvous number by the Nicholas Brothers, two black performers who sing it in Spanish while tap-dancing (traditionally expected of black performers in 1940). And the title song is sung yet again at the end of the picture, with story-synopsizing lyrics, and *again* over the closing cast credits.

It was no wonder, then, that this became a very popular tune of the day and received a nomination from the Motion Picture Academy. Additionally, *Down Argentine Way* received nominations for Best Color Cinematography and Best Color Interior Decoration.

At least five artists had hit recordings of "Down Argentine Way" during November and December of 1940. Bob Crosby's version peaked at number two and spent 13 weeks on the charts, and Leo Reisman, Eddy Duchin, Gene Krupa, and Shep Fields all had recordings in the top 20.

Carmen Miranda, meanwhile, proved that she had what it takes to endure. Her popularity continued through the '40s, when she appeared in a string of hit Latin-themed films, such as *Weekend in Havana* (20th Century-Fox, 1941), *That Night in Rio* (Fox, 1941), *Copacabana* (United Artists, 1947), and *Nancy Goes to Rio* (MGM, 1950). But her uninhibitedness — she reportedly wore no underwear and was once snapped by a low-angle photographer while performing a skirt-twirling dance — caused puritanical groups of the day to pressure studio boss Zanuck to drop her contract at Fox. She made several more films for various studios during the '40s and '50s before dying of a sudden heart attack in 1955 at the age of 46. She was mourned in Brazil as a national heroine.

I'D KNOW YOU ANYWHERE

Music by Jimmy McHugh;
  lyrics by Johnny Mercer
From *You'll Find Out*

Bandleader Kay Kyser managed to take the letter *k*, which also happened to be his first name, and turn it into a cottage industry when, in mid-'30s Chicago, he formed "Kay Kyser's Kollege of Musical Knowledge." Wearing a cap (kap?) and gown, Kyser and his "hep cats" (kats?) — people actually did use the term in those days — soon had their own radio show. Several other bandleaders of the time, including Benny Goodman and Harry James, had made the jump from radio to Hollywood, and it seemed only natural that a movie or two would quickly follow for Kay.

In *You'll Find Out,* Kyser and the boys show up to play at a party in a forbidding old Massachusetts house. Along for the fun are those ever-popular party animals Boris Karloff, Bela Lugosi, and Peter Lorre. They're there (uninvited, of course) to knock off the sweet debutante guest of honor and inherit all her money. So much for depth of plot.

Over the years, many popular singers became associated with Kay Kyser, including Ginny Simms, Harry Babbitt, Jane Russell, Dotty Mitchell, Georgia Carroll, and future talk-show host Mike Douglas. Simms appears with the Kollege in *You'll Find Out,* singing the song that would go on to receive a nomination for the Oscar in 1940, "I'd Know You Anywhere." In the film, she first sings it with the band as a straight number. But in one of the movie's unusual gimmicks, the next version of the song is done by the musical instruments, electronically altered to sound like they are vocalizing the words. This was a popular musical trick of the era — the technique was used frequently in children's records to teach about the various instruments of the orchestra by making them "talk." Later in the film, another Kyser singer, Harry Babbitt, performs the song.

This was one of two nominations lyricist Johnny Mercer received in 1940; the other was for "Love of My Life" from *Second Chorus* (see page 37). A prolific writer of hundreds of songs, Mercer would eventually rack up a total of 18 nominations and four Oscars — "On the Atchison, Topeka and Santa Fe" in 1946 (see page 88), "In the Cool, Cool, Cool of the Evening" in 1951 (see page 112), "Moon River" in 1961 (see page 162), and "The Days of Wine and Roses" in 1962 (see page 167).

Curiously, it was not Kay Kyser and his Kollege of Musical Knowledge whose recording of "I'd Know You Anywhere" hit the charts. While the song was featured prominently in the movie, it didn't have much appeal to the public. It was a recording by Glenn Miller's orchestra that scored, however modestly, settling into the number 24 position during its only week on the chart.

IT'S A BLUE WORLD

Music by Chet Forrest; lyrics by Bob Wright
From *Music in My Heart*

Clocking in at just 69 minutes, the barely feature-length film *Music in My Heart* had at least two good things going for it: its stars, Tony Martin and Rita Hayworth. Along with the music of the title, the rather routine plot had a love story at its heart. Martin, playing the struggling young foreign actor about to be deported, falls for Hayworth, and together they make whoopee along with all that music.

Martin was well suited to the role. In the '30s and '40s, he was touted as one of Hollywood's most promising musical stars, married to 20th Century's leading fox, Alice Faye. Just prior to the war, Martin added nightclub appearances and a hot recording career to his résumé. But his marriage to Faye lasted only three years, and in 1948 he married actress/dancer Cyd Charisse in what turned into one of Hollywood's most successful pairings. They frequently appeared together in nightclubs and published a joint memoir in 1976 called *The Two of Us.*

Co-star Rita Hayworth was born Margarita Carmen Cansino, the daughter of a Spanish dancer and his American Ziegfeld Follies partner. Young Margarita excelled in dancing, and her first films in the '30s (in which she often appeared under her real name) utilized these talents. Eventually she began to get speaking

Tony Martin sings "It's a Blue World" in *Music in My Heart.*

parts, with her first break in Howard Hawk's 1939 classic, *Only Angels Have Wings.* Later in her career, she helped swell the coffers of Columbia Pictures as a glamorous star of the '40s, kicking up her heels with the likes of Fred Astaire and Gene Kelly. She also kept Hollywood guessing about her married life, which was as dynamic as her acting career. At various times she was the wife of Victor Mature, Orson Welles, and, perhaps the most highly publicized, Aly Khan, the playboy son of the spiritual leader of millions of Moslems. They divorced two years later, leaving Hayworth enough time to squeeze in a few more husbands during her lifetime.

Martin's romantic scenes with Hayworth were some of the hottest of his career. A highlight of the film is the Academy Award–nominated song, "It's a Blue World." In the scene, Martin is crooning the tune on CBS radio to an orchestra under the musical direction of famed composer/arranger André Kostelanetz. Listening at the other end of the airwaves is Hayworth (as Patricia O'Malley), all starry-eyed over the song. Alan Mowbray, playing the part of a British publisher intent on pursuing her, is quick to observe, "You're still in love with him." She only has ears for Martin, of course.

"It's a Blue World" was a red-hot hit for Tony Martin, peaking at number two during a 13-week stay on the charts. Glenn Miller's cover peaked at number 14, and a 1952 version by the Four Freshmen hit number 30.

LOVE OF MY LIFE

Music by Artie Shaw; lyrics by Johnny Mercer From *Second Chorus*

"Love of My Life" had all the earmarks of a successful Oscar-nominated song. It had two famous musicians for its composers — Artie Shaw, whose swing band was sizzling in the early 1940s, and Johnny Mercer, who went on to become one of the leading lyricists of all time (four Oscar wins and a total of 18 nominations in his lifetime, including another one that same year for "I'd Know You Anywhere" — see page 36). Add to that a picture with the happy-toed Fred Astaire, and the formula should have effervesced at the box office like popcorn at the lobby snack bar.

It didn't. There were no second chances for *Second Chorus;* the picture was quickly forgotten, as was the tune on which Paramount had pinned its hopes of a Best Song Oscar for 1940. Maybe it was the scathing reviews. Bosley Crowther of the *New York Times* seemed to have a personal vendetta against the movie: "Seldom has a first-class talent been less effectively used than is Mr. Astaire's in his present under-burdened vehicle, and seldom has more flat, routine material been labeled top-flight musical comedy than it is in this slap-haphazard picture."

Part of the problem, Crowther surmised, was that Astaire was desperately in need of a dance partner. With Ginger Rogers having struck out on her own, Fred's attempt to recapture some of the old magic with actress Paulette Goddard, trying to follow in Ginger's dance steps, didn't fly. Goddard gave it her all, but there just wasn't any chemistry in their only on-screen routine — the "I Ain't Hep to That Step But I'll Dig It" number, written by Hal Borne and Johnny Mercer. Astaire's other two numbers were done solo — a comedy take-off of a Russian *tzazatski,* and a bit as a band leader.

There was much made of a number that, unfortunately, was cut from the final print, in which Astaire did a routine with famed Hollywood choreographer Hermes Pan, the first (and only) time Pan would appear on film with Astaire. In the routine, called "The Ghost Upstairs," Pan was covered with a veil, so he wouldn't have been recognizable in any event.

Also appearing in the cast is a young Burgess Meredith (though at 32, not as young as his character, a college student), whom the *Times* called "a juvenile Lionel Barrymore [who] will tickle a random rib." Meredith tickled a lot of ribs after that, including those of co-star Paulette Goddard, his third wife, to whom he was married from 1944–49. TV audiences will remember Meredith as the Penguin from the "Batman" series of the 1960s; filmgoers will no doubt recall his appearances in some of the first three *Rocky* pictures.

ONLY FOREVER

Music by James Monaco; lyrics by Johnny Burke
From *Rhythm on the River*

In what the *New York Times* called "one of the most likable musical pictures of the season," Bing Crosby played a musician/songwriter who meets and falls in love with an impossibly young Mary Martin. The two are unknowingly partnered as music "ghost writers" for a deceptive composer, played by Basil Rathbone. Neither knows that the other is ghosting, in a storyline some people at the time interpreted as playing a bit too close to possible reality.

There had been rumors dating back to the 1920s — later proved to be unfounded — that Irving Berlin had turned out so many hits that he must have been purchasing songs from unknowns and publishing them under his own name. What else, his jealous colleagues speculated, could explain his extraordinarily prolific production of tunes?

Berlin fought back and won several lawsuits stemming from these false accusations. All was supposedly laid to rest until *Rhythm on the River* with its very close parallel to Berlin's past troubles was produced in 1940. Rathbone's character, in fact, was described early in the film as "America's most popular songwriter." He explains his "adapting" the songs of Crosby and Martin by noting that he'd hit songwriter's block after his wife died — another remarkable similarity to Berlin's life, since his first wife had died in 1913. However, Berlin had many witnesses and friends who stood up for him, and the rumors finally subsided.

In the movie, the future Academy Award–nominated song "Only Forever" is introduced when Martin, playing a poet and lyricist, overhears Crosby working at the piano of the country inn where she's vacationing. She jots down some lyrics and shows them to him, and he croons this gentle love song. They vow to keep this as their own private love song but then discover that they are collaborative ghosts. The two agree to try their luck in the music field on their own, but they have little success until "Only Forever" pops up on the Hit Parade.

Also appearing in the cast were pianist Oscar Levant, Jean Cagney (Jimmy's sister), and a youngish William Frawley (later Fred Mertz of "I Love Lucy" fame). The film was directed by Victor Schertzinger, who also made two *Road* movies with Bob Hope and Crosby. Schertzinger himself was a concert violinist, composer, and conductor who wrote one of the film's songs — "I Don't Want to Cry Anymore."

Crosby proved the film's storyline correct when he had a Number One hit with "Only Forever." The song stayed at the top of the *Billboard* charts for nine weeks out of an impressive 20 on the charts. Tommy Dorsey had a number seven hit with his cover, while Eddy Duchin's version peaked at number 15.

Bing Crosby hits some high notes in *Rhythm on the River.*

OUR LOVE AFFAIR

Music by Roger Edens; lyrics by Georgie Stoll[1]
From *Strike Up the Band*

With the popular toothsome twosome of Mickey Rooney and Judy Garland headlining this film, moviegoers knew immediately to expect only one thing — music, music, and more music with a "Hey, kids, let's put on a show!" theme. The duo had previously been paired in producer Arthur Freed's *Babes in Arms*, in which Judy and Mickey got the gang together to put on the most professional "amateur" show this side of Kansas. With *Strike Up the Band*, as Freed's virtual sequel was called, he pulled out all the stops, hoping to top himself.

It worked: *Strike Up the Band* — which bears no resemblance to the musical originally presented on Broadway as written by the Gershwins — grossed a cool $3.5 million at the box office, a huge profit over its $838,000 cost. (Freed was so pleased with this enormous success that he turned to his favorite pair one last time in 1942, when they would be reunited for *Babes on Broadway* [see page 53]).

This variation on the amateur theatrics gimmick, directed and choreographed by Busby Berkeley, had Mickey and Judy putting together a high school

1. While this song is credited to Roger Edens and Georgie Stoll in the archives of the Academy of Motion Picture Arts and Sciences, it is credited by nearly every other major source to Edens and the film's producer, Arthur Freed.

Mickey Rooney and Judy Garland are front and center as they *Strike Up the Band.*

orchestra, with Judy as vocalist and Mickey pounding out the rhythm on a set of trap drums. Naturally, Mickey and his band end up on famed bandleader Paul Whiteman's radio show in — gasp! — Chicago, where they perform the only holdover from the Gershwin hit: the title song, "Strike Up the Band," which went on to become the UCLA fight song.

In his autobiography, *Life Is Too Short,* Rooney described the great fun of making this picture: "[Judy and I] just loved working together . . . Judy and I sang a duet, one of the most beautiful love songs ever written." The song he referred to was "Our Love Affair," which received an Academy Award nomination. In the scene — suggested by Vincente Minelli, Garland's

future husband — Mickey explains to Judy how he would orchestrate "Our Love Affair" by demonstrating on the dining room table with animated pieces of fruit representing members of an orchestra. Other songs in the film included "Do the Conga," "Nobody," "The Drummer Boy," and the Gershwins' title song.

The film received two other Academy Award nominations: Best Sound Recording, for which it won the Oscar, and Best Score.

"Our Love Affair" enjoyed three top 10 incarnations on the *Billboard* charts. Tommy Dorsey had a recording that peaked at number five, Glenn Miller's version made number eight, and Dick Jurgens's rode the tune to number 10.

WALTZING IN THE CLOUDS

Music by Robert Stolz; lyrics by Gus Kahn
From *Spring Parade*

Deanna Durbin was Universal's secret weapon in the arena of studio musicals. Her beautiful voice had already given that studio a string of six popular films since her first one in 1936 (*Three Smart Girls),* in which she starred at the age of 15. In 1940, she continued playing the ingenue in *Spring Parade,* a pseudo-Viennese operetta–costume piece set in the pre-War days.

Deanna first appears in the picture as a young peasant girl on her way to town to sell her goat. In Vienna, a fortune-teller advises her that she will marry an artist. She secures a job at a bakery and falls for a young army musician, played by Robert Cummings. The plot takes a number of absurd twists, including intervention when things get difficult by none other than the emperor, Franz Josef himself. Mainly, it was an excuse for Deanna to sing a string of songs and for lots of peasant folk in costumes to dance and waltz at the drop of a baton — with an orchestra always conveniently nearby.

The nominated song, "Waltzing in the Clouds," is performed in a beer garden. It's a fast-paced Viennese waltz sung by a dubbed Bob Cummings. Soon Deanna takes over, urging the band, "Come on, boys, let's really play it." Soon everyone is waltzing in time to the lively *um-pa-pa* beat. Cummings, dressed handsomely as a soldier, takes Deanna for a spin around the dance floor as the number concludes.

There wasn't much else to the film. Waltzes were the order of the day. There was a lilting waltz called "When April Dreams," and there was even a version of "The Blue Danube Waltz" set to words (also sung by Deanna). Bosley Crowther, the reviewer for the *New York Times,* was enthralled with Durbin, noting that "she has never been in better voice, she has never possessed more charming grace and she has never — considering her advancement now to young ladyhood — been more pleasant to behold."

All of the music, including the nominated song, "Waltzing in the Clouds," was composed by Robert Stolz, an Austrian native who escaped Hitler's takeover and fled his homeland, arriving in Hollywood just in time to write the music for *Spring Parade.* In addition to the nominated song and "When April Sings," Stolz and lyricist Gus Kahn also wrote "It's Foolish But It's Fun." Durbin recorded all three of these tunes for Decca, although none became big hits. The movie was also nominated for Best Black-and-White Cinematography, Best Sound Recording, and Best Score.

Durbin continued as a Universal star until 1947. She had reached her twenty-seventh birthday by that time, and, having starred in 21 films, decided to retire.

WHO AM I?

Music by Jule Styne; lyrics Walter Bullock
From *Hit Parade of 1941*[1]

The most intriguing thing about *Hit Parade of 1941* — released in December of 1940 and therefore optimistically dated for the upcoming year — is neither the story nor the cast nor the considerable amount of music featured in the film. While all of these are part and parcel of this rather routine movie along the lines of the *Big Broadcast* films presented during the 1930s by Paramount, there is one important statement made in this picture that went virtually ignored by the both the audience and the media: the subplot, if it could even be called that, dealt in a very matter-of-fact manner with *television.*

At a time when very few people owned television sets and there was little or no regular programming, this film's acceptance of this new upstart form of entertainment *as a given* was practically revolutionary, especially considering that TV was initially perceived as posing a huge threat to Hollywood. Unfortunately, this development is almost swept aside by the silly plot about a singer who can't sing and whose voice is dubbed on the radio.

This Republic release features Frances Langford as the woman who *can* sing, Ann Miller playing the daughter of a radio show's sponsor who doesn't have a clue about how to carry a tune (but taps up a storm), and Kenny Baker as Langford's romantic interest and musical mentor. The story involves a country antique shop owner who swaps his business for a two-watt radio station, with plans to convert it to a television station. Although there is much talk about TV in the film, we only see one actual use of the medium, then in its infancy, but it is central to the plot in a bizarre way: Phil Silvers, the host of the radio show, contrives with Frances Langford to dub Miller's screechy voice over the

---

1. Later re-released as *Romance and Rhythm.*

airwaves (unbeknownst to either her or the sponsor). All Langford has to do is watch a live TV monitor (!) and lip synch to Miller's performance — her voice will be broadcast, and no one will be the wiser. Oddly, the broadcast is still basically a *radio* show, with a surprisingly big-screen television used mostly in the secret studio where Langford's vocal switch takes place. If there were supposed to be people receiving the show on TV sets in their living rooms, no mention was made of this.

The best part of the movie is when the lip synch ploy fails (a gimmick later used successfully in the film *Singin' in the Rain*) and Miller's caterwaulings are intercut with Langford's mellifluous tones.

The song used in this scheme was "Who Am I?," which went on to receive a nomination for an Oscar. (The film received another nomination for Best Score.) "Who Am I?" was written by Jule Styne and Walter Bullock. This was the first nomination for Styne, who ultimately wrote dozens of popular songs throughout his career and received a total of 10 Academy Award nominations, winning the Oscar for "Three Coins in the Fountain" in 1954 (see page 127). He died in 1994, at the age of 88.

1941

And the winner is...

THE LAST TIME I SAW PARIS

Music by Jerome Kern; lyrics by Oscar Hammerstein II
From *Lady Be Good*

At the ceremony for the 1941 Academy Awards, composer-presenter B. G. DeSylva announced the winner of the Oscar for Best Song, but Jerome Kern, who wrote the music for "The Last Time I Saw Paris," didn't rise from the dinner table to accept his award, mainly because he wasn't present at the Awards banquet given at the Los Angeles Biltmore Hotel. Instead, Kern was listening to the proceedings at home on his radio, never dreaming that his name would be the one called.

Insiders had predicted — and Kern had wrongly believed — that the race was between "Blues in the

Ann Miller proves she can sing as well as dance in *Hit Parade of 1941*.

Ann Sothern and Robert Young play a married songwriting team in *Lady Be Good.*

Night" and "Chattanooga Choo Choo." And when Kern (and his lyricist Oscar Hammerstein II) finally did received his statuette, he accepted it only reluctantly. Kern's hesitancy was due to a bone of contention with the Academy's methodology; his protests would eventually result in a change in the rules for nominations for Best Song.

"The Last Time I Saw Paris" had a history stemming from the Nazi invasion of France. Hammerstein had fond memories of Paris from his childhood, when he had accompanied his father on a business trip; later, as a young man, he had spent five months in the City of Lights in a rented apartment. So when Hitler conquered Paris in June of 1940, Hammerstein was moved to write an unsolicited lyrical poem. "It was the only song I've ever written under any kind of compulsion," the composer revealed in a 1957 interview presented by radio host Wink Martindale on Los Angeles station "K-JOI" in a 1993 birthday tribute to Hammerstein. "The Germans had just taken Paris, and I couldn't get my mind on anything else at all. I loved the city very much, and I hated the idea of its falling. And I thought of the enemy tramping through the streets and taking all the gaiety and beauty out of the hearts of the people there

— not just the beauty of the parks or the loveliness in the museums, but everything that was Paris, good and bad, and of high quality and of cheapness — the whole thing. And this was a kind of lament."

After Hammerstein completed his lyric, he took it to Jerome Kern and asked him to set it to music. Amazingly, the notes poured out of Kern, who reportedly wrote the tune in just a single day, most of it at one sitting. They published it as an independent song, and it was then recorded in 1940 by Kate Smith. The tune peaked at number eight and remained on the charts for 11 weeks. The song was then included in the film *Lady Be Good* (sung on screen by Ann Sothern), which had been a Gershwin hit musical on Broadway in 1924. "The Last Time I Saw Paris" was the only non-Gershwin tune to be added to the film version and went on to win the Oscar, much to Kern's chagrin.

After accepting his Oscar, Kern filed a protest with the Academy, objecting to the fact that the song had been eligible in the first place, insisting it had not been written directly for the film. He was able to persuade the Academy to change the rules; subsequently they allowed nominations only for songs written expressly for the screen.

Dinah Shore sang "The Last Time I Saw Paris" in MGM's film biography of Jerome Kern, *Till the Clouds Roll By* (1946). In 1954, MGM used the tune as the title song for a non-musical movie starring Elizabeth Taylor and Van Johnson. The music was used in the background instrumentally and sung in French.

BABY MINE

**Music by Frank Churchill;
    lyrics by Ned Washington**
From *Dumbo*

With beautiful lyrics by Ned Washington and a gentle melody by Frank Churchill, "Baby Mine," a tender lullaby sung by a mother to her child, could easily have been a huge hit or even an Academy Award winner had the competition not been so fierce in 1941. But competing against songs like "Blues in the Night," "Chattanooga Choo Choo," "Boogie Woogie Bugle Boy of Company B" and the winner, "The Last Time I Saw Paris," this song never realized its full potential.

The "baby" referred to in the song's title was also the title character in Walt Disney's 1941 animated hit film, *Dumbo*. The mother, of course, was Mrs. Jumbo, a mother elephant singing her song of love to her precious baby elephant, cruelly nicknamed Dumbo by the other circus animals. A Mr. Spock precursor, Dumbo had an ear problem for which he was ostracized by his peers, but, in the movie's theme, he manages to triumph over his handicap/deformity, a neat little morality play from those magic-makers at the Mouse Factory. It was indeed a triumph: only those with the hardest of hearts couldn't find warmth and love in this charming tale about fortitude, perseverance, and love. The *New York Times* got a bit carried away, declaring *Dumbo* "the most genial, the most endearing, the most completely precious cartoon feature film ever to emerge from the magical brushes of Walt Disney's wonder-working artists!"

And why not? This was a film for everyone — parents could enjoy the music, of which there was a happy abundance, while children, who could easily sit through the film's 64-minute length, reveled in the color, the excitement of the circus, and the fantasy of a flying elephant (those big ears were just perfect for hang-gliding).

There were several outstanding musical production numbers. The Oscar-nominated song, "Baby Mine," sung to a sad-eyed little Dumbo by his incarcerated

mom, contains beautiful scenes showing mothers snuggling with their young all over the circus grounds. Another song, however, "When I See an Elephant Fly," has been criticised for its politically incorrect depiction of two crows speaking in stereotypical black dialect. In the context of the times, however, it was perfectly acceptable to have a white person imitate a black voice. Leonard Maltin, in his book *The Disney Films,* argues that "the crows are undeniably black, but they are black *characters,* not black *stereotypes.*"

Some of the other songs included "Pink Elephants on Parade," an ahead-of-its-time psychedelic sequence, and "Look Out for Mr. Stork," with the voice of Sterling Holloway as the Stork. Holloway is today best remembered for voicing Winnie the Pooh.

Although "Baby Mine" missed out on winning the Oscar, the film's score by Oliver Wallace and Frank Churchill won the Academy Award for Best Musical Score.

BE HONEST WITH ME

Music and lyrics by Gene Autry and Fred Rose
From *Ridin' on a Rainbow*

Western films had been pure oats at the box office since the days of the silents. There was something uniquely American in the genre, with a mass appeal that often masked the Western's importance as a piece of Americana. Most of the time, these "B" movies had been "they went thataway" shoot-'em-ups — good guys versus bad guys. (Unfortunately, the latter were usually generic, stereotypical Indians.) With the advent of the "talkies" in the late '20s and '30s, cowboys added one more item to their western gear of boots, saddles, and horses — the "gittar." Strumming became their thing, and singing cowboys soon found a permanent home on the range and on the screen.

Gene Autry was the number one at the western box office from 1937 to 1942 (at which point he was overtaken by Roy Rogers). Autry was also a crossover star; he ranked in the top 10 of *all* box-office stars from 1940–42, up there with the likes of Mickey Rooney, Spencer Tracy, and Clark Gable.

Unlike his western peers, Autry actually wrote much of his own music. The grandson of a Baptist minister, young Gene began singing in the church choir when he was only five. His father was an Oklahoma horse trader, so the young cowpoke was no stranger to ranches. As a young man he is said to have lost one job after another as a cowhand because his singing and self-taught guitar picking distracted the other workers. In the '20s he landed a job singing on the radio as "Oklahoma's Yodeling Cowboy." His career took off as a songwriter soon after that, and he moved to Chicago to perform regularly on national radio. Movie offers soon followed — two-reelers at first, then feature-length, less violent pictures for Republic and Columbia. In his later years, Autry became well known as a successful businessman/entrepreneur, ultimately owning radio and television stations, as well as the California Angels baseball team.

In 1941, he wrote "Be Honest with Me" (with Fred Rose), performed it in the movie, and became the first actor to be nominated for an Academy Award for a Best Song that he also performed.

Gene Autry, the original singing cowboy, also wrote much of his own music. For *Ridin' on a Rainbow,* Autry and Fred Rose co-wrote the nominated tune "Be Honest with Me."

In *Ridin' on a Rainbow,* which co-starred Smiley Burnette, Autry's early sidekick, Autry discovers that the father of a teenage showboat singer is in cahoots with bank robbers. According to Alex Gordon, Gene Autry's archivist, Autry wrote "Be Honest with Me" while sitting on a movie set. The song was recorded by three different artists in 1941, including Bing Crosby, whose version, accompanied by John Scott Trotter's Orchestra, reached the number 19 position during its sole week on the chart. Autry's own recording reached number 23, while Freddy Martin's orchestral version made number 24.

BLUES IN THE NIGHT

Music by Harold Arlen; lyrics by Johnny Mercer
From Blues in the Night

In the chicken-or-egg question of which came first when it comes to title songs from films, the answer for movies back in the '40s was almost always the song title. *Blues in the Night* was a rare exception: Harold Arlen had written the music for the song with his new partner, a Southerner named Johnny Mercer, in the late 1930s for a film to be called *Hot Nocturne*. The song turned out so well, the producers changed the movie's title to fit the song.

The original script for *Hot Nocturne* called for a jazz band to be in jail and for a black man in the adjacent cell to sing a blusey number. Composer Arlen recalled the writing process in *They're Playing Our Song*, by Max Wilk: "I said to myself, any jazz musician can put his foot on a piano and write a blues song! I've got to write one that sounds authentic, that sounds as if it were born in New Orleans or St. Louis . . . I didn't have a handle for this blues thing . . . [but] the fires went up and the whole thing poured out!" He rushed it to lyricist Mercer, who came up with the opening phrase (and alternate title): "My momma done tol' me." The lyric made it all come together.

According to Arlen, "Everything in 'Blues in the Night' was wedded well. There is no such thing as a melody doing it, or the lyric doing it alone. It's got to be a combination . . . If it weren't for that phrase *with* the melody, it wouldn't have happened." Ironically, this lyric was first stuck down at the bottom of the page until Arlen suggested to Mercer that it be moved to the top — substituting it for the original opening phrase, "Whenever the night comes, I'm heavy in my heart."

The song has managed to outlast the picture for which it was written. The Warner Bros. film about five musically talented young jazz musicians playing a string of one-night stands didn't have much of a story going for it, but the music was all that really mattered to audiences. There were several tunes besides the title song — "This Time the Dream's on Me," "Hang Onto Your Lids, Kids," and "Says Who, Says You, Says I" — although none of these stood out like "Blues in the Night" (which, strangely, is never heard in its entirety). It was heavily favored to win the Oscar, reportedly losing by a narrow margin to the Kern-Hammerstein song "The Last Time I Saw Paris" (see page 41).

"Blues in the Night" became an immediate hit. Recording artists fought over the right to record it, as reported by Margaret Whiting in *They're Playing Our Song*. Whiting first heard the music performed by the composers at their regular Saturday night get-together: "At one end of the room, Martha Raye almost passed out . . . [Mel] Tormé was so knocked out by the musicianship, he just sat there. Mickey Rooney kept saying, 'My God, this is unbelievable!' And Judy [Garland] and I raced over to the piano to see which of us could learn the song first! You knew right away the song was so *important*."

Over the next several decades many artists would get a turn at recording the song, including Frank Sinatra, Doris Day, Garland, Tormé and Buddy Rich, Raye, Doc Severinsen, the Four Freshmen, Woody Herman, Bing Crosby, and dozens more, even Johnny Mercer himself, who recorded the tune solo as well as with Jo Stafford. The most successful version belonged to Herman, who had a Number One hit in 1942; Dinah Shore's version reached number four, as did the recording by Jimmie Lunceford and His Orchestra; Cab Calloway and His Orchestra, featuring Dizzy Gillespie had a recording that went to number eight; Benny Goodman's rendition reached number 20; and in 1952, Rosemary Clooney's recording of the song made number 17.

BOOGIE WOOGIE BUGLE BOY OF COMPANY B

Music by Hugh Prince; lyrics by Don Raye
From Buck Privates

Patti, Maxine, and Laverne Andrews were just like the girls next door — if the girls next door happened to be of Norwegian-Greek parentage and could sing up a storm. Their second recording, 1937's "Bei Mir Bist Du Schön," an adaptation of a traditional Yiddish song, became an overnight sensation; by 1940, the "Queens of the Radio" were ready to move on to Hollywood and a film career that would eventually see them co-starring in 15 (most B) movies as themselves.

The tune that would become their signature song was in a comedy co-starring Bud Abbott and Lou Costello, a team who were also radio refugees. Their film was lighthearted nonsense about two street-corner con artists who accidentally enlist in the army. "If the real thing is at all like this preview of Army life — the

Messrs. A & C dropping gags once a minute and the Andrews Sisters crooning patriotic boogie-woogie airs — well, it's going to be a merry war, folks," wrote the critic for the *New York Times*. While most people would soon find the latter part of that statement debatable, there was no doubt that the picture was full of innocent musical fun. In addition to an Oscar nomination for Best Song, the movie also scored one for Best Scoring of a Musical Picture.

The sisters Andrews saw to that quite handily, although when they were first suggested for the movie, the brass at Universal weren't wild about giving them the tune "Boogie Woogie Bugle Boy of Company B" to sing in the film. According to the book *Lou's on First*, by Chris Costello, the producers lamented, "The Andrews Sisters can't sing boogie woogie . . . Boogie's too tough for them." Those executives were happily proven wrong. While the sisters sang several songs in *Buck Privates* — "You're a Lucky Fellow, Mr. Smith," "Bounce Me Brother with a Solid Four," and "I'll Be with You in Apple Blossom Time" (another Andrews

trademark) — nothing took off like "Boogie Woogie Bugle Boy." Not only was it the hit of the film, but the Andrews Sisters soon proved that they could boogie with the best of them and went on to a career that saw them sell over 30 million records, many of them boogie-woogie tunes, such as "Rhumboogie" and "The Booglie Wooglie Piggie." In 1943, the sisters revived "Boogie Woogie Bugle Boy" in another movie, *Swingtime Johnny*.

In 1973, the song became a hit all over again, with Bette Midler's recording from her very first album charting as a single all the way to number eight. In an interview with radio personality Wink Martindale on Los Angeles's "K-JOI," Midler admitted that "I had never heard that song before! Someone came up to me a long time ago and said, 'You know, you should sing "Boogie Woogie Bugle Boy of Company B," ' and I said [sarcastically], ' "Boogie Woogie Bugle Boy of Company B," oh what a great title!' . . . I searched all over until I found the song, just because the title was so outrageous."

Lou Costello (left) and Bud Abbott learn about the "Boogie Woogie Bugle Boy of Company B" from the Andrews Sisters in *Buck Privates*.

CHATTANOOGA CHOO CHOO

Music by Harry Warren; lyrics by Mack Gordon
From *Sun Valley Serenade*

In the late 1930s and early 1940s, the sounds of the big bands echoed across the United States like some primal tribal rite. Movie exhibitors soon added big band stage shows as an extra attraction, guaranteed to pull in a young audience no matter how awful the picture. Soon film producers back in Hollywood realized that if the bands were in the movies, they didn't need stories — just miles and miles of celluloid, some lights, and a camera to record the musicians, who played their hearts out in some very forgettable films that made scads of money for their backers.

By the summer of 1941, the big band craze was at its craziest. Count Basie, Xavier Cugat, Benny Goodman, Guy Lombardo, Sammy Kaye, Kay Kyser, Tommy Dorsey and his brother Jimmy, Woody Herman, Harry James — everyone, it seemed, was aboard the big bandwagon on the silver screen. So when Darryl F. Zanuck approached Glenn Miller and the boys in his band about doing a picture he had in mind for one of his contract players, former ice queen Sonja Henie, he expected Miller to add his talents to yet another silly movie. No way, said Miller. He demanded (and received) a believable script in which his band and character would be an integral part of the story, not just filler. He also reportedly received a salary of over $100,000 — nearly double that of other band leaders.

In return, Miller performed many tunes for the film in his distinct musical style, which utilized a clarinet lead over four saxes. In *Sun Valley Serenade,* the most outstanding song was "Chattanooga Choo Choo," which was performed with Miller in character as a bandleader named Phil Corey, rehearsing a song that features Paula Kelly and the Modernaires, plus a tap-dancing sequence by the Nicholas Brothers and a top-notch performance by then-teenaged Dorothy Dandridge.

Tex Beneke, Miller's lead tenor sax player, commented on a 1993 PBS special entitled "Glenn Miller, America's Musical Hero": "When we were first given our parts, the Modernaires and myself, to learn for the *Sun Valley Serenade* movie, we thought, 'Wow, what a dog this thing is. ["Chattanooga Choo Choo"'s] not gonna get off the ground.'" He was, happily, quite mistaken. *Sun Valley Serenade* was not just a hit movie, but

the film that introduced one of the biggest songs of the decade. Setting the (gold) standard for the future of the recording industry, "Chattanooga Choo Choo" became the first million-seller ever to receive a gold record; it was also the first record since Gene Austin's "My Blue Heaven" to actually sell a million copies. Miller's recording stayed in the Number One position for an enviable nine weeks and charted for a remarkable 25. The Mack Gordon–Harry Warren song proved so popular, it was used in many other motion pictures, including *Springtime in the Rockies* (1942, with Carmen Miranda singing the song in Portuguese), *Orchestra Wives* (1942 — see page 55), and *The Glenn Miller Story* (1954).

Glenn Miller gave up his public career at its peak in 1942, when he enlisted in the Army Air Corps, limiting his performances to entertaining the troops. Tragically, his plane was lost on a flight over the English Channel in 1944. Tex Beneke later assumed the baton, carrying on his legacy with a new Glenn Miller Orchestra.

DOLORES

Music by Lou Alter; lyrics by Frank Loesser
From *Las Vegas Nights*

Every studio in town was rushing a big band movie "to a theater near you," and Paramount Pictures wasted no time jitterbugging into the fray. The studio signed Tommy Dorsey and His Orchestra to a contract, tossed in a bunch of previously written stock tunes like "I'll Never Smile Again," "Song of India," and "On Miami Shores," and voilà — one big band film, *Las Vegas Nights.*

The picture, set in a primitive Las Vegas of the early '40s (no mega-hotels), certainly seems like a curiosity piece when viewed with 20/20 hindsight. But at the time of its release, it was virtually ignored. Big bands and such are okay, but as Glenn Miller proved later that year, you need more — like, say, a plot. Unfortunately, the producers of *Las Vegas Nights* forgot about the storyline.

"So woefully deficient is the story and direction of the film," moaned the *New York Times,* "that we hesitate to add to the poor actors' grief by naming them." The "poor actors" in this case needn't have worried — their careers, such as they weren't, were never in any jeopardy. Phil Regan, Bert Wheeler, Constance Moore, Lillian Cornell — not a major box office name among them. Still, most reviewers panned the film while praising the musical aspects. *Variety* suggested that audiences perk up their ears at Cornell's singing, "About the only refreshing touch in the picture . . . The girl has a delightful voice, an ingratiating personality and looks." Perhaps Cornell's feminine charms distracted the male critical establishment — the person they *should* have been watching was the male soloist with Tommy Dorsey's band, a fellow who was just beginning to emerge from the shadow of the bandstand, a young lad named Frank Sinatra.

Not many people were yet aware of the future superstar. He wasn't given any billing in the film, singing a couple of songs and then stepping aside for the more "important" cast members. And certainly no one could have suspected that the skinny little kid crooning with Dorsey's band would end up practically *owning* the town that was the movie's namesake.

Sinatra's only solo, "I'll Never Smile Again," was already a well-known song. He also sang the only original tune written for the film (not solo, but with Dorsey's singing quartet, the Pied Pipers, which also included Jo Stafford). "Dolores" became a Number One hit for Tommy Dorsey and His Orchestra. Sinatra, as part of the quartet, was not billed, although his singing helped propel the song to the top of the charts. Bing Crosby released a cover of "Dolores" on the very same day in April, 1941, and it peaked at number two.

Sinatra would have better luck in the future, of course. And while "Dolores" did not win the Oscar, he would later introduce six other nominated tunes.

OUT OF THE SILENCE

Music and lyrics by Lloyd B. Norlind
From *All-American Co-Ed*

Before there was *Some Like It Hot*, before there was television's "Bosom Buddies," before — okay, after — there was Shakespeare (men in drag played all the female parts), there was *All-American Co-Ed*, an early cross-dressing musical comedy. Clocking in at only 48 minutes, this third in a series of Hal Roach B-"features" was little more than an extended "Saturday Night Live" skit.

The late Johnny Downs, who was once one of Roach's "Our Gang"–bangers, plays a "Quinceton" man selected by his frat house to try to win a scholarship offered by the "Mar Brynn" girls' college. In drag and blonde wig, he fakes his way onto the campus, then has a number of close calls that almost expose his secret identity. (One rather racially stereotyped number has to do with a black maid in the "Steppin' Fetchit" mold freaking out when she thinks he's a ghost. The bit isn't that surprising, given that the film opens with a black tap-dancing porter on the the girls' college-bound train.)

Downs gets to get down quite a bit. He sings "I'm a Chap with a Chip on My Shoulder," "The Farmer's Daughter," and several other ditties, written by Walter G. Samuels and Charles Newman. The song that would win an Academy Award nomination, "Out of the Silence," was written by Lloyd Norlind and temporarily held the record for the Best Song nomination from the shortest-running movie (it was unseated in 1943 by at nominee from the 43-minute *Saludos Amigos* — see page 62). The film also received a nomination for Best Scoring of a Musical Picture.

In the production number for "Out of the Silence," Downs (no longer in drag) is spying on the girls who are sitting on the lawn by the bell tower, singing in beautiful Grecian-style gowns (don't these co-eds ever attend classes?). While he's peeping, he accidentally slips and grabs onto the bell rope to break his fall. Unfortunately, he must continue holding onto the rope throughout the rest of the song or he'll set off the bell. He manages to hang on until the end of the song, then loses his grip when he realizes he's in love with Virginia, played by Frances Langford.

Downs became stereotyped as Hollywood's favorite singing and dancing collegian, although he never attended college. He appeared in a string of 1930s and 1940s B-movie musicals, including *College Scandal*, *Pigskin Parade*, *College Holiday* (all 1936), and *Hold that Co-ed* (1938). As the genre wound down, Downs's movie career declined. He turned first to Broadway, then to nightclubs and live TV. By the mid-'50s, he had his own afternoon kiddie show in San Diego, a job that lasted 17 years and won him a number of awards. He later became a successful real estate salesman for a community in nearby Coronado, California. He died in 1994 at the age of 81.

It's also worth noting that *All-American Co-Ed* featured Alan Hale Jr. Hale appeared in a number of films during those same decades, but television audiences will best remember the late actor for creating the role of the Skipper on TV's "Gilligan's Island" in the 1960s, a show still wildly popular in reruns today.

SINCE I KISSED MY BABY GOODBYE

Music and lyrics by Cole Porter
From *You'll Never Get Rich*

After Rita Hayworth had kicked up her heels and shown her dancing stuff in 1940's *Music in My Heart* (see page 36), Columbia Pictures honcho Harry Cohn decided it was graduation time for the former Margarita Cansino. He planned to star her opposite Fred Astaire, as his new dance partner in *You'll Never Get Rich*. Never mind that, at 42, Astaire was 20 years her senior — love would find a way. (Less believable was the movie's storyline, which had the middle-aged but ever-dapper Astaire getting drafted for army duty.)

Although Rita was already a veteran dancer and screen presence (she would have four pictures released in 1941 in a span of only nine months!), she was nonetheless nervous at the prospect of dancing with the legendary Astaire. She worried about her height — in flat shoes, she was only three inches shorter than her partner. She bemoaned the fact that the studio boss wouldn't spring for singing lessons for her, choosing instead to dub her voice in all her musicals. But she quickly dismissed any fears she had about replacing the long-gone Ginger Rogers. "I thought about it at first," she was quoted as saying in *Rita: The Life of Rita Hayworth,* by Joe Morella and Edward Z. Epstein, "but then I put it out of my head so it wouldn't inhibit me." Fred Astaire commented in the same book at his amazement with her professionalism: "She learned steps faster than anyone I've ever known. I'd show her a routine before lunch. She'd be back right after lunch and have it down to perfection. She apparently figured it out in her mind while she was eating."

While the penny-pinching Cohn refused to pay for her singing lessons and was reportedly paying Rita a salary of only $500 a week (compared to Astaire's six-figures-per-picture fee), he did pull out all the stops when it came to the production values for *You'll Never Get Rich*, hiring top wardrobe people and hair stylists and signing Cole Porter to compose the music for the film. The well-known composer received a nomination for Best Song, for the tune "Since I Kissed My Baby Goodbye."

The plot centers on rookie life at an army basic training camp, where Astaire spends most of his time in the guardhouse. There he conveniently pulls together a black group, the Delta Rhythm Boys, to accompany him on the nominated song, "Since I Kissed My Baby Goodbye." Fred just can't sit still; first he taps out a beat on his chest, then does a seated tap number, but soon he's up on those famous feet, dancing his heart out. Rita drops by, but she doesn't perform in this number.

It's somewhat surprising that this tune was nominated, since there were more lavish song-and-dance numbers in the movie. For example, the formally attired Fred woos Rita in style in "So Near and Yet So Far." And he outdoes himself when the two of them dance in the film's finale, called "Wedding Cake Walk," with a chorus of 80 youngsters joining them for a dance number atop a huge wedding cake incongruously crowned by an army tank. Ironically, three months later, Pearl Harbor would be attacked, definitely putting a crimp in all that army life "fun."

1942

WHITE CHRISTMAS

Music and lyrics by Irving Berlin
From *Holiday Inn*

"It seemed nice enough, but no one thought it would be much else."

So said Walter Scharf (in the book *Irving Berlin,* by Michael Freedland), musical director for Irving Berlin's 1942 writing effort, a little picture over at Paramount to be titled *Holiday Inn*.[1] The gimmick Berlin had devised centered on a country inn, operated by Bing Crosby, that would open only on holidays — hence the name. Berlin had by now become synonymous with Easter, thanks to "Easter Parade," and his "God Bless America," written four years before, had caught on as

---

1. Several years later, two Memphis developers named Kemmons Wilson and Wallace Johnson decided to capitalize on this catchy name, calling their chain of motels "Holiday Inns." While they didn't have Bing Crosby greeting guests by singing "White Christmas," this first standardized roadside lodging chain caught on with American travelers. Today, Holiday Inns, Inc., is one of the largest hotel chains in the world.

an Independence Day standard. For *Holiday Inn*, he planned to write several new tunes revolving around all of the remaining major holidays (the only previously written song in the film would be "Easter Parade"). When Berlin finished, he'd penned "Let's Start the New Year Right," "Abraham" (for Lincoln's Birthday), "I Can't Tell a Lie" (for Washington's Birthday), "Be Careful, It's My Heart" (for Valentine's Day), "Let's Say It with Firecrackers" and "Song of Freedom" (two new Fourth of July songs), "Plenty to Be Thankful For" (for Thanksgiving), plus the generic "Happy Holiday" and a title song, "Holiday Inn." (One other song written for the movie, "It's a Great Country," didn't make the cut.) That left Christmas.

Working in Scharf's office with his specially tuned piano (Berlin never left home without it, composing on it using primarily the black keys), he managed to come up with the song that "seemed nice enough" amidst the surrounding chaos of people rushing in and out and telephones constantly ringing. The song was called "White Christmas," and it would forever change the way Americans sang at holiday time.

In the film, Bing Crosby sits at the piano and sings "White Christmas" to Marjorie Reynolds in front of a blazing fire. Later, on a Hollywood set designed as an exact replica of the New England lodge (in reality, one set doubled as both the lodge and "the set"), she reprises the song. Bing surprises her by joining her on the set, and the pair sing a "White Christmas" duet. Thanks to its phenomenal success, "White Christmas"

became the McDonald's of the music industry, selling millions and millions of records — at last count somewhere in the neighborhood of 125 million.

The song was popularized by Crosby, whose recording, interestingly, was released at the same time as the film — in August, 1942 — not at Christmastime. By the beginning of October, it was firmly ensconced at the top of the charts, remaining there for 11 weeks, then dropping to number six just before the actual Christmas season. The song was reissued annually for many years, several times climbing back up to its rightful place atop the charts. Eventually Crosby's version (and a re-recorded 1947 version) would sell 25 million copies for Decca. Additionally, Frank Sinatra's rendition became a Christmastime best-seller from 1944–46. Other artists who turned "White" hot during the '40s and early '50s were Charlie Spivak, Gordon Jenkins, Freddy Martin, Jo Stafford, Eddy Howard, Perry Como, and Mantovani, all with recordings in the top 25.

When the time came for the Academy Awards ceremony for the 1942 winners, Berlin found himself in the enviable position of presenting the Best Song award to himself. According to the book *Inside Oscar*, by Mason Wiley and Damien Bona, the normally shy, spotlight-shunning composer remarked, "This goes to a nice guy. I've known him all my life."

"White Christmas," now recognized as the most popular Christmas song (not to mention best-selling record) of all time, proved so successful that in 1954, Paramount decided to build a movie around it. The

Fred Astaire (right) listens to hear sleigh bells in the snow as Bing Crosby sings about a "White Christmas" in *Holiday Inn*.

title, naturally, was *White Christmas,* and the star, just as naturally, was Crosby (see page 128). Although the plot was partially recycled from the original *Holiday Inn, White Christmas* has since become even more popular than its precursor, turning up regularly on TV at holiday time.

ALWAYS IN MY HEART

Music by Ernesto Lecuona; lyrics by Kim Gannon
From *Always in My Heart*

Always in My Heart was Warner Bros.'s attempt to capitalize on Deanna Durbin's popularity by showcasing their own in-house singing talent, a 15-year-old discovery named Gloria Warren. The plot of the film was woven around her vocal abilities, and she received generally favorable recognition by reviewers for her first film. The *New York Times* said, "Miss Warren is a pleasing little lady — a bit mature for her reported fifteen years — and she has a reedy voice which she handles rather well." *Variety* noted that she "displays both screen presence and personality in her film debut [but] she's aided considerably by strong and able support from Kay Francis, Walter Huston, Una O'Connor, and Sidney Blackmer, and good direction by Jo Graham." In other words, she didn't yet have what it took to wing it on her own.

The story revolved around Walter Huston, playing a musician wrongly convicted and sentenced to life imprisonment. Kay Francis played his long-suffering ex-wife who brings up his two children, one of whom is Warren, on her own. The girl befriends her father when he's released from prison, unaware of who he is. Together, they perform the title song, "Always in My Heart," as he plays it on the piano and she sings it.

The producers decided to go for broke on this one. The song was plugged at every possible opportunity, appearing nearly a dozen times throughout the film. Gloria sings it by herself at the piano; she does the number with Walter Huston; it is even taken up by the omnipresent Borrah Minevitch and His Rascals, a popular harmonica-playing bunch well known to audiences of the day. In one of their romps, his group dances along the waterfront where they are joined by a singing and dancing throng in what seems to be a "Seventy-six Trombones" precursor. (For an interesting experience, rent *The Music Man* and *Always in My*

Heart together, watch them back to back, and compare the two production numbers for similarities.)

The push worked. "Always in My Heart" received an Academy Award nomination for Best Song. Not surprisingly, it didn't win, losing out to the hugely popular "White Christmas" (see page 50). Ironically, "Always in My Heart" lyricist James Kimble (Kim) Gannon would write the words to his most famous song the following year: "I'll Be Home for Christmas."

Mildly successful recordings of "Always in My Heart" were released by Glenn Miller's and Jimmy Dorsey's orchestras, and by the popular singer Kenny Baker, all in 1942. Miller's version did the best, peaking at number 10 and charting for five weeks. In 1964, a pair of Brazilian brothers calling themselves Los Indios Tabajaras revived the tune. Their single only managed to to make number 82.

Gloria Warren's film career soon fizzled. After *Always in My Heart,* she appeared in only four more films. Her last picture was *Bells of San Fernando* (1947). After that, she quickly disappeared from the screen into obscurity.

DEARLY BELOVED

Music by Jerome Kern; lyrics by Johnny Mercer
From *You Were Never Lovelier*

Back by popular demand, Fred Astaire and Rita Hayworth once again danced their way across Columbia Pictures' sound stages, ostensibly to a Latin beat. But the distinctly non-Latin rhythms by Jerome Kern and Johnny Mercer were contrived to have a broader appeal, and their music came off as more mainstream-romantic that could have been set anywhere.

The story focused on Adolphe Menjou as Rita Hayworth's father, who is attempting to marry her off. He'll go to any lengths, even writing anonymous love letters and sending flowers. Rita thinks they are from Astaire, which is fortunate because it gives the two several opportunities to dance together. Once again, when it came time to sing, Rita's voice had to be dubbed — this time by Nan Wynn, when Rita "sings" "I'm Old Fashioned." Other songs included "The Shorty George," "Wedding in the Spring," the title song, and the tune that would garner an Academy Award nomination — "Dearly Beloved."

When the sheet music for "Dearly Beloved" was published in 1942, it included a little note suggesting that the song was "suitable for weddings." And it actually did receive a fair amount of play at nuptials for many years following its film debut. This had been Jerome Kern's intention all along, since he fervently hoped it would replace the more popular "Oh, Promise Me." The stately music is derived from a duet in a Puccini opera; the verse is a paraphrase of another Mercer lyric in "Come Rain or Come Shine." He liked it so much he decided to recycle it "Dearly Beloved," writing, "I know that I'll be yours come shower or shine."

In the classic Hollywood tradition, everything south of Florida was treated as one big Latin-American country. Originally the film was to have been called *Carnival in Rio*, but at the last minute the setting was switched to Buenos Aires. Xavier Cugat's Cuban orchestra provided the Latin tempo necessitated by the storyline and by the varied talents of Astaire, who proved he could move his talented feet to any beat. Cugat and the band perform a number of rhythmic tunes, including one called "Chiu Chiu." But there was an even more famous-to-be Cuban in the cast: Watch for a 15-year-old Fidel Castro (minus his trademark whiskers and cigar) as an unbilled extra.

"Dearly Beloved" received considerable play on the airwaves in 1942, and three records climbed the charts. Glenn Miller's version did the best, peaking at number four and remaining on the charts for 10 weeks. Dinah Shore, whose star

was just beginning to rise at this time, had a recording that peaked at number 10, while Alvino Rey's orchestral rendition made number 21.

HOW ABOUT YOU?

Music by Burton Lane; lyrics by Ralph Freed
From *Babes on Broadway*

The frequent collaboration of producer Arthur Freed, director Busby Berekley, plus singer/actor/dancers Mickey Rooney and Judy Garland had brought lots of loot to the coffers of MGM. So it was not surprising when the team came together one last time for a film to be released at Christmas, 1941. The timing couldn't have been worse — and it couldn't have been better.

Two weeks earlier, the Japanese had attacked Pearl Harbor, an event that signaled the end of America's isolation from the war. The country's innocence now teetered on the brink from which it would never return — an innocence portrayed with carefree simplicity in the film *Babes on Broadway*. A joyful musical, it jammed

MGM studio publicity still of Judy Garland and Mickey Rooney as two literal *Babes on Broadway*.

the theaters at Christmastime with Americans eager to escape, if just for 118 minutes, the reality that awaited them once they stepped back out into the cold winter sunlight. *Babes on Broadway* became a box office smash.

Even the title suggested innocence — *babes* referred not to sexy young ladies but to all the young people in this picture, spearheaded by those two perennially young "babes" — Garland and Rooney. It was "let's put on a show" time once again, and nobody did it better. This time, the gang was part of a struggling act waiting for its big Broadway break, but in the meantime, if nobody would give them a chance, why, they'd just have to show off their stuff on their own. The vehicle in this outing was a benefit for underprivileged children.

Freed took no chances with the musical score, hiring a number of composing teams to create the many songs, including E.Y. Harburg (lyricist for Oscar-winning "Over the Rainbow"), Roger Edens, Harold Rome, and Burton Lane and Ralph Freed. Songs included the title song, "Anything Can Happen in New York" (with lyrics by Harburg), "Hoe Down" (music by Edens), "Chin Up! Cheerio! Carry On!" (Harburg again), "F.D.R. Jones" (Rome), "Mama Yo Quiero" (with Rooney doing a hilarious Carmen Miranda send-up, using her familiar Vincente Paiva–Jararaca song), "Waiting for the Robert E. Lee" (the old Lewis Muir–L. Wolfe Gilbert tune, in yet another minstrel show finale), and the Best Song nominee "How About You?"

Mickey Rooney and Judy Garland performed the nominated song, with its catchy lyrics about liking New York in June and a Gershwin tune (in an unusual instance of one songwriter paying homage to another). It became an immediate hit, but not by them. Tommy Dorsey's Orchestra had a recording that reached number eight, while Dick Jurgens's orchestral version peaked at number 21.

Babes on Broadway had mostly a second-string cast, with a few exceptions. The film marked the screen debut of a four-year-old little girl named Margaret O'Brien, who would go on to child stardom later in the decade. Also appearing in a cameo role was Joe Yule, better known as Mickey Rooney's father, a veteran burlesque, vaudeville, and stock entertainer for many years. One other young starlet, a 19-year-old still unknown to audiences, made a brief appearance in the picture. Her name was Ava Gardner. A year later, she would become known to everyone as Mrs. Mickey Rooney, and a year after that she would be the ex–Mrs. Rooney, their whirlwind romance ending in an abrupt divorce.

I'VE HEARD THAT SONG BEFORE

Music by Jule Styne; lyrics by Sammy Cahn
From *Youth on Parade*

If "Babes" could be on Broadway over at MGM, then "Youth" could be on parade at Republic. At least that was how Cy Feuer and Ernie Martin — Republic's executives in charge of musicals — saw it. Unfortunately, the studio didn't have a Mickey Rooney or Judy Garland waiting in the wings; *Youth on Parade* starred John Hubbard, Ruth Terry, and Martha O'Driscoll. Without an "A" team, the picture didn't do much (perhaps limited by its 72-minute running time), but it helped cement the pairing of one of filmdom's most renowned songwriting teams — Jule Styne and Sammy Cahn.

Cahn recalled in his 1974 autobiography, *I Should Care: The Sammy Cahn Story,* that just before he received that fateful call from Feuer, he felt he had really hit bottom. When Feuer asked if he would co-write the songs for *Youth on Parade* with Styne, Cahn recalled, "The way I felt right then, I would do a picture with Hitler." The two (Cahn and Styne, not Cahn and Hitler) clicked right away. Styne sat down at the piano and played a completed melody for Cahn. As the lyricist listened, he asked Styne to play just a bit slower. Styne obliged, Cahn listened, and said, "One more time, just a bit slower." Then Cahn blurted out, "I've heard that song before." Styne bristled, "What the hell are you, a tune detective?"

"No," said Cahn, "that wasn't a criticism, it was a title: 'I've Heard That Song Before.'" From this unusual beginning came the future Academy Award nomination from *Youth on Parade* — "I've Heard That Song Before." All together, the team wrote six songs for the picture, including "You Gotta Study, Buddy" and "You're So Good to Me."

Cahn's career as a songwriter for the movies was off and running. Over the years he would pen lyrics to 25 nominated songs, more than any other composer, winning four Oscars. He collaborated with Saul Chaplin and Jimmy Van Heusen, as well as Styne, on hundreds of popular tunes, many of which were introduced by Frank Sinatra. He was often cited for his ability to work quickly. "Other people might write better lyrics," he once joked (as reported in the book *Lullabies of Hollywood,* by Richard Fehr and Frederick G. Vogel), "but they won't do them any faster." A prolific writer, Cahn also wrote for television, winning Emmys for "Love and Marriage," from the TV version of *Our Town* and for "Call Me Irresponsible" from *Papa's Delicate Condition* (which also won an Oscar — see page 171). He died in 1993, at the age of 79.

I'VE GOT A GAL IN KALAMAZOO

Music by Harry Warren; lyrics by Mack Gordon
From *Orchestra Wives*

Back in 1941, when Glenn Miller decided to jump aboard the movie screen bandwagon, he had to play second trombone to a pair of ice skates worn by Sonja Henie. The film *Sun Valley Serenade* was a whopping success (see page 48), so Miller pressed his luck and signed up to do another picture for Darryl F. Zanuck, this time without the Olympic skating champ. To ensure he wouldn't be alone on thin ice for his first solo starrer (he received third billing, behind George Montgomery and Ann Rutherford), songwriters Harry Warren and Mack Gordon, who had composed the superhit "Chattanooga Choo Choo" for Miller's previous movie, were brought back aboard to write another round of tunes for the new film, to be called *Orchestra Wives*.

Once again, Warren and Gordon proved they had the right stuff, penning a number of new tunes for the movie, including "People Like You and Me," "At Last" (originally written for *Sun Valley Serenade* but never used in it), "Serenade in Blue," and *Orchestra Wives*'s answer to "Chattanooga Choo Choo" — another melodious city with a Native American name — "I've Got a Gal in Kalamazoo."

Future Academy Award Best Song nominee "Kalamazoo" immediately shot to the top of the charts, and it's easy to see why. Besides the sheer fun of saying the name of that town, the first line of the lyric is cleverly simple enough for a school child to learn in one try — a simple recitation of the alphabet up to the letter *I* — A,B,C,D,E,F,G,H — then into the lyric ("*I got a gal in Kalamazoo*"), with the internal rhyme of "Gal" and "Kal . . ." adding to the fun.

Before long, Miller and his band, along with vocal support from Tex Beneke, Marion Hutton, and the Modernaires, had a runaway *hit* in Kalamazoo, and just about everywhere else across the United States, as well as internationally. The recording was released simulta-

neously with the movie's premiere in August, 1942, quickly climbed the charts and stayed at Number One for eight weeks out of a 20-week *Billboard* chart run. Cover recordings, although less successful, were offered by Ted Heath, the Andrews Sisters, Jimmy Dorsey, and Benny Goodman.

For songwriters Harry Warren and Mack Gordon, "I've Got a Gal in Kalamazoo" was just one in a string of hits that would earn them the distinction as the composer and lyricist most often represented on the network radio show "Your Hit Parade" (Gordon's lyrics made the top 10 39 times; Warren's music was in the top 10 42 times).

The film itself didn't fare as well. Its plot is mediocre at best, about men who play in bands and the bitchy women who love them. The music was the only drawing card, along with some exciting dancing by the effervescent Nicholas Brothers (who do a routine to "Kalamazoo"). Watch for a young Jackie Gleason in the cast as one of the bass players. Gleason would one day have his own orchestra, but television fans best remember him for starring in "The Honeymooners" TV series.

Although this was to be Miller's last picture before his untimely death during the war, "I've Got a Gal in Kalamazoo" made at least one more appearance in a movie, in *Kiss Them for Me* (1957), starring Cary Grant and Jayne Mansfield.

LOVE IS A SONG (THAT NEVER ENDS)

Music by Frank Churchill; lyrics by Larry Morey
From *Bambi*

With the arrival of the latest animated feature from Walt Disney, children as well as adults once again had a chance to be magically transported to a fantasyland of wonder. This time, Disney selected a book by Felix Salten, which he had read in 1937. Due to the complexities of making this particular film, however, it took some time before he was able to bring the project to fruition.

For example, Disney, in his quest for realism, sent a staff member to the forests of Maine to photograph trees at various times of the year — covered in snow, during rain showers, draped in spider webs, and so on. To stimulate the creativity of his artists at the Burbank studios, he brought in two live fawns, sent by the Maine Development Commission. These were sketched time and again to capture their every movement. In addition to the attention to the minutest detail, Disney Studios was busy with other, less demanding projects, such as *Dumbo* and *Pinocchio,* as well as war training films. So although work continued on *Bambi,* it wasn't until 1942 that the story of the little orphaned deer was released.

The music was an integral part of this film, which focused more on mood than dialogue. Four new songs were written for *Bambi* by Frank Churchill and Larry Morey, who had collaborated on the tunes for *Snow White and the Seven Dwarfs* (1937). The film's basic theme is established from the opening credits, as "Love Is a Song (That Never Ends)" sets the tone for the rest of the movie. It is sung by an unnamed tenor over the opening credits, accompanied by an operatic chorus, then hummed and "ah-ah"ed by a chorale over the opening montage of the forest. A counterpoint of a bird is whistled as we find ourselves in the forest. The first five notes of "Love Is a Song . . ." are then thematically in the opening scene of an owl flying through the dim, dawn-lit woodlands.

This tune was distinctive enough to have garnered an Academy Award nomination. The pair wrote three other songs for the film: "Let's Sing a Gay Little Spring Song," "Little April Shower," and "Looking for Romance" (also known as "I Bring You a Song"). Musical themes are also used effectively in the "twitterpation" sequence and in the early scenes with Bambi's rabbit friend, Thumper. The musical score, by Frank Churchill and Edward Plumb, also received an Oscar nomination (for Best Scoring of a Dramatic or Comedy Picture). An additional nomination was for Best Sound Recording.

Bambi didn't do that well in its first outing at the box office, but the picture has since had many successful re-releases, and in the 50-plus years since its first appearance in the theaters, it has racked up enough ticket sales to become the number one film released in 1942 (as well as the top film of the entire '40s decade), earning a total of $47.2 million in North American rentals.

After making *Bambi,* Walt Disney decided to concentrate full-time on the war effort; no other full-length animated feature films would be created until the end of the war.

PENNIES FOR PEPPINO

Music by Edward Ward; lyrics by Chet Forrest and Bob Wright
From *Flying with Music*

Another one of Hal Roach's 50-minute quickie B-features, *Flying with Music* was not welcomed with open arms by either audiences or critics. The film starred Marjorie Woodworth, George Givot, William Marshall, Edward Gargan, Jerry Bergen, Norma Varden, and others equally well unknown. It was an attempt at low-budget comedy, with a practically nonexistent plot revolving around a schoolgirl with a crush on a Latin singer. Together with four young friends her age plus their chaperone, they charter a plane with a handsome pilot, and the groupies set out for Florida and the Caribbean to find the object of her fantasies. Along the way there are some forgotten misadventures and lots and lots of now-forgotten songs.

Young Bambi is greeted by Thumper, soon to become the little deer's best friend in Walt Disney's *Bambi.*

While critics panned the film ("Even 50 minutes is too long," opined one), there was praise for the music and technical aspects. As the *Hollywood Reporter* noted, "There is some good music in this triviality . . . .Photography by Robert Pittack is frequently lovely in the lush settings provided by Charles D. Hall's art direction."

Songsters Edward Ward (music) and Chet Forrest and Bob Wright (lyrics) penned five new songs for the movie: "If It's Love," "Rotana," "Caribbean Magic," "Song of the Lagoon," and the song that received an Oscar nomination (and then, like the others, was promptly forgotten), "Pennies for Peppino." The score also received a nomination from the Academy for Best Scoring of a Musical Picture.

Before turning his attention to *Flying with Music,* George "Chet" Forrest had already achieved success in films by co-writing music and/or lyrics for a number of other films, usually teaming with Robert Wright. The duo's specialty was adapting old or classical material to popular versions, as they did with Rudolf Friml's song "Chansonette," which became "The Donkey Serenade" for the movie *The Firefly.* Other Forrest/Wright tunes appeared in such films as *After the Thin Man* (1937), *Saratoga* (1937), *Three Comrades* (1938), and *Music in My Heart* (1940). In 1944, Forrest and Wright adapted Edvard Grieg's melodies for the stage show *Song of Norway.* They are perhaps best remembered for their adaptation of the Alexander Borodin melodies for *Kismet* (1953 stage show; 1955 film). These include "Stranger in Paradise" and "Baubles, Bangles and Beads."

PIG FOOT PETE

Music by Gene de Paul; lyrics by Don Raye
From *Keep 'Em Flying*

"To the United States Army Air Corps — its officers, its enlisted men — and to those unsung heroes — the ground crews who 'Keep 'Em Flying' — this picture is dedicated." With war almost a certainty, this late-1941 release had been rushed to completion at Universal, part of the studio's contribution to the war effort. But *Keep 'Em Flying*'s preamble dedication belies its genre. The team of Bud Abbott and Lou Costello were the leads, and no one was going to mistake this picture for a heavy war drama; the studio's contribution was strictly for laughs, important for the morale of the country.

In true Abbott and Costello style, there were hijinks and good humor aplenty, mixed in with a storyline involving an egotistical stunt flyer named Jinx Roberts (played by Dick Foran) who finds himself unhappily subjected to Air Corps discipline. His buddies, Bud and Lou (playing characters named Blackie and Heathcliffe), tag along for the fun. Martha Raye plays a dual role as twins Gloria and Barbara, adding to the humorous chaos.

Raye, along with the film's serious romantic leading lady, Carol Bruce, contributed most of the musical performances. Bruce sings "I'm Getting Sentimental Over You" and "Let's Keep 'Em Flying" (also sung by Foran), and she and the Raye "twins" sing "I'm Looking for the

A colorful native band performs Latin rhythms in *Flying with Music.*

Boy with the Wistful Eyes." Raye performs only one solo number, "Pig Foot Pete," which went on to receive an Academy Award nomination for 1942. (Although the film was released at the end of the previous year, the Academy was still permitting year-end releases to be included with films released and nominated for the following year.)

At first listen, "Pig Foot Pete" sounds very much like another popular tune of the day — "Boogie Woogie Bugle Boy of Company B." Not surprising, since the music was composed by the same person — Don Raye. In *Keep 'Em Flying*, Martha Raye sings and dances to the song, accompanied at first by a honky-tonk piano. Soon an unseen orchestra takes up the music, and finally a male chorus joins in. The words help clarify the strange title, about a legendary piano player who received his moniker because he "plays all night for pig's feet and beer." Simple.

From the start, it was Abbott and Costello who took creative control of the picture. Bruce recalled in *Lou's on First*, by Chris Costello, how Lou took her under his wing. It was only her second picture, and he impressed her with his sense of what worked and what didn't. "I recorded two songs for the picture: 'You Don't Know What Love Is' and 'I'll Remember April.' Lou didn't think they fit and had them cut out of the picture. I felt a lot of rejection and trauma . . . I was young and it took a long time before I realized that Lou knew what was best for the film. It was Abbott and Costello who'd get credit for the success or failure of the picture — not Carol Bruce."

Fortunately, "Pig Foot Pete" stayed. It was eventually released as a single by two recording artists — Ella Mae Morse, and Dolly Dawn. Dawn's version was on the *Billboard* charts for one week, at number 22.

WHEN THERE'S A BREEZE ON LAKE LOUISE

Music by Harry Revel; lyrics by Mort Greene
From *The Mayor of 44th Street*

Hoofer George Murphy starred in *The Mayor of 44th Street*, a lackluster musical that had fleeting success. It opened to mixed reviews and did not play long in theaters. There was a plot of sorts — an honest theatrical agent who books bands is plagued first by a group of teenaged thugs, then by a conniving paroled racketeer.

In the end, the young gangsters rush to Murphy's defense to save his business — a chain of dance halls along 44th Street.

The picture seemed to suffer from lack of direction. Was it a comedy? A musical? Perhaps a drama? At times, it seemed to be all three. There was the serious story, there were endless jitterbug numbers to bring in the teens, and there were four musical production numbers of varying lengths. Co-starring with Murphy (who only danced one routine) was Anne Shirley, who warbled many of the tunes, such as "Heavenly Isn't It?," "You're Bad For Me," "A Million Miles from Manhattan," and the song that would win an Academy Award nomination, "When There's a Breeze on Lake Louise." Music was provided by Freddy Martin's band and its so-called "sweet swing" sound.

Surprisingly, not much of the Oscar-nominated song is heard in the picture. Shirley briefly sings the chorus of "When There's a Breeze," which *Variety* described as "a sweet tune which, although not prominently displayed in the picture, looks like a candidate for popularity." The prediction was off the mark, and its popularity was short-lived, with Freddy Martin's version hitting the number 22 postion during its only week on the pop charts.

Murphy was one of a handful of Hollywood actors who parlayed his ability to speak before cameras and an audience into a political career, as did Ronald Reagan and Clint Eastwood in years to follow. (Like Reagan, Murphy served as President of the Screen Actors Guild.) After appearing in a number of '40s musicals, he retired from motion pictures in 1952. In 1953 he was chairman of the Republican National Convention. In 1964, he was elected United States Senator from California, defeating Democratic candidate Pierre Salinger.

Shirley's career began with silent films of the '20s, in which she appeared under the cutesy name of Dawn O'Day (her given name was Dawn Evelyeen Paris). Her most memorable performance was in *Stella Dallas* (1937), for which she received an Oscar nomination. She retired from films in 1945.

London-born composer Harry Revel wrote music mainly in collaboration with lyricist Mack Gordon for '30s movie musicals. Among his best-known songs are "Did You Ever See a Dream Walking?," "Goodnight, My Love," and "With My Eyes Wide Open." Other collaborators included lyricists Paul Francis Webster, Arnold Horwitt, and Mort Greene, with whom he wrote the nominated tune, "When There's a Breeze on Lake Louise."

1943

And the winner is...

YOU'LL NEVER KNOW

Music by Harry Warren; lyrics by Mack Gordon
From *Hello, Frisco, Hello*

Harry Warren and Mack Gordon were on a roll. First, they'd choo-chooed on home to Chattanooga ("Chattanooga Choo Choo," 1941 — see page 48); then they took off for Kalamazoo ("I've Got a Gal in Kalamazoo," 1942 — see page 55). In 1943, the pair again set their sights on a city, this time San Francisco, affectionately (and to the disdain of all that town's residents) known as "Frisco," as in the 20 Century-Fox release that year called *Hello, Frisco, Hello.*

Surprisingly, the songwriting team didn't write the "Hello, Frisco, Hello" title song for their latest venture into Hollywood musicals. That song harkened back — way back — to the original stage revue, Ziegfeld Follies of 1915, and was written by Gene Buck and Louis A. Hirsch. The 1943 film borrowed only the title and song, not the storyline from the original; most of the other songs were rehashed versions of older, more familiar tunes too, similar to what had been done in Irving Berlin's *Alexander's Ragtime Band* (see page 27). These included such numbers as "Strike Up the Band," "I've Got a Gal in Every Port," "They Always Pick on Me," "Tulip Time in Holland," "Sweet Cider Time," "Has Anybody Here Seen Kelly," and "By the Light of the Silvery Moon."

Obviously new songs were needed, and Gordon and Warren seemed just the ticket. What they did come up with — a sweet ballad entitled "You'll Never Know" — not only won them their third Academy Award nomination, it also won them the Oscar itself, the first for the pair as a team (Warren had won back in 1935 for "Lullaby of Broadway" — see page 4). The film also received a nomination (but no win) for Best Color Cinematography.

"You'll Never Know" was performed in *Hello, Frisco, Hello* by Alice Faye, who had absented herself from films for a year and a half. Audiences, fond of the popular star with her distinctive alto voice and straightforward way of singing, missed her greatly, and her so-

Lynn Bari, Jack Oakie, Alice Faye, and John Payne in *Hello, Frisco, Hello.*

called comeback was widely heralded. She introduces the future nominated tune by singing it into a telephone, barely moving or gesturing throughout the production number. Later the song is used in her romantic scenes and to underscore the entire picture (even more so than the title song). Faye again sang the tune in the 1944 Fox musical, *Four Jills in a Jeep.* The *Hello, Frisco, Hello* version was inserted 32 years later in the 1975 Warner Bros. movie (under the opening credits) *Alice Doesn't Live Here Anymore,* starring Ellen Burstyn.

"You'll Never Know" became a Hit Parade favorite during the war years, successfully recorded by many artists of the day. Dick Haymes had a Number One hit for Decca, charting for 18 weeks (Number One for seven) and selling well over a million records. Frank Sinatra's version went to number two and charted for nearly as long — 16 weeks — while Willie Kelly's orchestral version peaked at number six. Ten years later, in 1953, Rosemary Clooney, with Harry James's Orchestra, made a recording that made number 18, and as testimony to the Oscar-winning song's staying power, two country versions even made the country charts — Jim Reeves's recording in 1975, peaking at number 71 and, a decade later, Lew de Witt's rendition, which peaked at number 77. Others recording the tune included Willie Nelson, Johnny Mathis, Doris Day, Brook Benton, Eydie Gorme, Bobby Darin, Eddy Arnold, and Ella Fitzgerald. Surprisingly, while Alice Faye did cut a record of the tune, it never became the hit that it was for others.

CHANGE OF HEART

Music by Jule Styne; lyrics by Harold Adamson
From *Hit Parade of 1943*

In 1941, Jule Styne (along with Walter Bullock) had offered up the Academy Award–nominated song, "Who Am I?" from *Hit Parade of 1941* (see page 41). By 1943, he was ready to have another go at it. Unfortunately, *Hit Parade of 1943* didn't have much to offer in the way of story. Styne, however, did manage to snag his second Oscar nomination, while his co-writer, Harold Adamson, scored his third.

The film's plot had to do with song-snatching. John Carroll, in the lead role, steals his best "compositions" from the clever mind of a small-town gal, played by Susan Hayward. We've heard this story before, about the struggling, blocked composer who purloins tunes from others with no compunctions whatsoever about having his reputation bolstered by a "ghost." Eventually, Carroll falls for Hayward and reforms. End of picture.

When *Hit Parade of 1943* opened, *Variety* was mistakenly taken in by the first word in the film's title, proclaiming that "Republic has itself a hit picture . . . [This] filmusical will do very hefty business." Continuing, the review placed heavy emphasis on the "socko Harlem talent" (black performers) who really carried the picture. Also praised were the seven songs, "all solid," six of which were written by Styne and Adamson. These included "Do These Old Eyes Deceive Me?," "Who Took Me Home Last Night?," "Harlem Sandman," "That's How to Write a Song," and "Tahm-Boom-Bah," along with "Change of Heart," the romantic ballad Oscar nominee. The seventh song was called "Yankee Doodle Tan," written by J.C. Johnson and Andy Razaf.

Specialty acts carried most of the picture, including several black performers, such as Jack Williams (the Harlem Sandman), Dorothy Dandridge (a talented singer and actress in her own right, still struggling at the time as second-stringer, due to the color barriers of the era), Pops and Louis, the Music Maids, the Three Cheers, Chinita (billed as an Afro-Cuban dancer), the Golden Gate Quartet, and the bands of Count Basie, Ray McKinley, and Freddy Martin (whose band dominates the film and plays the best version of "Change of Heart"). Somehow, amidst all this, there was still room for the main story.

The film's star, John Carroll, had performed primarily as a stuntman in the '30s, working his way up to leading roles at RKO by 1935. His strong singing voice and black, curly hair helped secure him leading roles during the 1940s in a series of MGM pictures, and he later appeared in a number of action films for Republic and other studios. Although he never quite achieved the stardom afforded others of his generation, he invested wisely and retired to Florida a wealthy man, where he continued to produce films until his death in 1979.

Unfortunately, the blockbuster predictions of all the critics failed to materialize. The film did, however, receive a well-deserved nomination for Best Scoring of a Musical Picture along with its Best Song nomination.

HAPPINESS IS A THING CALLED JOE

Music by Harold Arlen; lyrics by E.Y. Harburg
From *Cabin in the Sky*

The first all-black musical film since 1929, *Cabin in the Sky* reunited songwriters Harold Arlen and E.Y. Harburg, who had grabbed Oscar gold in 1939 for "Over the Rainbow," from *The Wizard of Oz*. For *Cabin in the Sky*, which had its roots in a 1940 Broadway musical, the pair would be called upon to pen three new songs. Their best tune, "Happiness Is a Thing Called Joe," sung by Ethel Waters (in her only starring film role), would go on to win an Academy Award nomination, but not the top prize. Waters reprised her Broadway role, as did her co-star, Rex Ingram. Others in the outstanding cast included Lena Horne (in her feature film debut) as the seductress, Georgia Brown, and Louis Armstrong as (what else?) the Trumpeter. Even Butterfly McQueen popped up in a minor role.

Cabin in the Sky was filmed by MGM, which had also produced *The Wizard of Oz,* and bore an eerie resemblance to that film in several ways. For starters, there was the musical team of Arlen and Harburg. Then there was a tornado scene straight out of Kansas — or, more precisely, the MGM stock-footage depart-

Lobby card from *Cabin in the Sky,* one of the first hit movies with an all-black cast.

ment. Only this stock wasn't of a real tornado, but the Oz version, which the special-effects wizards had originally created by using muslin, steel gantries, lots of imagination, and lots and lots of L. B. Mayer's dollars. Some of those dollars were now amortized in an uncomfortably similar sequence in *Cabin.*

As if that weren't enough to make this seem like a black *Wizard of Oz,* there was the story itself. In *Wizard,* Dorothy finds herself in a mythical place where her friends now appear in slightly different guises as the assorted residents who people her new surroundings. In *Cabin,* Little Joe (Eddie "Rochester" Anderson) finds himself in a mythical place (Hell) from which he must try to escape. At the end, the Lord (the great and powerful Oz?) allows him to enter the Pearly Gates (implying that Kansas is heavenly!), after which he wakes up and finds out the whole thing was a dream (à la Dorothy's bump on the head). In the end, both Little Joe and Dorothy have learned similar lessons — there's no place like home to stay on the straight and narrow path.

Apart from the above "coincidences," and if one can set aside modern hindsight's perspective on this decidedly racist film, there are some delightful moments, mostly in the musical interludes. "Taking a Chance on Love" was originally introduced in the Broadway version of *Cabin,* and is one of the highlights of this film, along with "Cabin in the Sky," "Shine," and "Honey in the Honeycomb." Original songs contributed by Harlen and Harburg were "Life's Full o' Consequence," "Li'l Black Sheep," and the nominated tune, "Happiness Is a Thing Called Joe." Ironically, the song was written to soothe the ego of Ethel Waters, who was reportedly jealous over the attention being given Lena Horne's character. In the Broadway version, the character of Georgia Brown was played by Katherine Dunham and focused more on dancing. In order to enhance Horne's singing abilities, that actress's part was broadened to give her more musical numbers, including a chunk of Waters' big solo, "Taking a Chance on Love." To placate the disgruntled Waters, Arlen and Harburg created "Happiness Is a Thing Called Joe," which Ms. Waters managed to sing *twice* in the movie. Many years later, Lena Horne acknowledged a debt of gratitude to Waters (as reported in *Discovering Great Singers of Classic Pop,* by Roy Hemming and David Hajdu): realizing that she had stood on giant shoulders, she said, "Ethel Waters was the mother of us all."

The song was later sung by Susan Hayward in the biopic of Lillian Roth, *I'll Cry Tomorrow* (MGM, 1955).

61

MY SHINING HOUR

Music by Harold Arlen; lyrics by Johnny Mercer
From *The Sky's the Limit*

Another year, another Fred Astaire musical. This time, he returned to RKO for *The Sky's the Limit,* a film appropriately about the war, now an integral part of everyday life. There was no escape, even at the picture show. People trying to catch the latest diversion in movie houses were urged to "Buy War Bonds in This Theater!" at the end of every film. And most of the storylines had to do with some aspect of the war. For Fred Astaire's 1943 offering, he was cast in the role of a Flying Tiger pilot, a bit of a stretch of the imagination, considering that the always debonair Astaire, although dashing and nimble-footed as usual, was well into his 40s at the time.

Pity the poor lady who had to play opposite Astaire in two dance numbers in this movie. Cast as his dancing partner–lady love was Joan Leslie, whom the *New York Times* pegged as "a gracious and neatly attractive miss, [but who] is not a Ginger Rogers when she tries to make with her feet." What a legacy Ginger had left behind when she split with Fred!

As was to be expected, the movie introduced a number of new tunes, written by Harold Arlen, this time paired with Johnny Mercer. It was a banner year for both songsters — Arlen received three Academy Award nominations in 1943, one teamed with E. Y. Harburg ("Happiness Is a Thing Called Joe" — see page 60), and together with Mercer he received two nominations — for "That Old Black Magic" (see page 64) and "My Shining Hour," the breakaway hit song from *The Sky's the Limit.* The film also received a Best Scoring of a Musical Picture nomination from the Academy.

Among the new songs in the film, "I've Got a Lot in Common with You" and "Harvey the Victory Garden Man" have faded into obscurity. "One for My Baby (and One More for the Road)," however, has enjoyed unexpected longevity, although it was not the Oscar nominee. But no one expected much from the fourth song, "My Shining Hour." One critic judged it only "fair," and even Astaire, who sang this lofty ballad with Joan Leslie in the film, didn't have any strong feelings for it. In his autobiography, he confessed that while the picture was being produced, nobody suspected it would be a hit, but, "several months later . . . it became the number one song of the day." (Actually, it only reached the number four position.)

No doubt the song owed its immediate popularity to the hope it offered those faced with the uncertainty of war. The lyric, simple yet inspirational, speaks of a soldier heading off to war (his "shining hour"), but his lover's face will flower in his dreams through the night's (i.e., war's) darkness "till I'm with you again." The words were strongly poetic, filled with imagery about angels "watching o'er me." In the darkness of the night that was 1943, sentiments such as these were much needed, and the song touched a chord in virtually everyone.

Not surprisingly, "My Shining Hour" became a popular hit that year; the recording by Glen Gray peaked at number four and remained on the *Billboard* charts for seven weeks. Many artists have since recorded the song, including Frank Sinatra, Margaret Whiting, Mel Tormé, and Eydie Gorme.

SALUDOS AMIGOS

Music by Charles Wolcott;
lyrics by Ned Washington
From *Saludos Amigos*

With the European market all but closed to filmmakers and distributors due to the raging war, studios began searching for other sources to exhibit their product. One obvious choice was the large continent lying just to the south, in Latin America. The "Good Neighbor Policy" had been implemented by the State Department in the early 1940s, and with the blessing of Nelson Rockefeller, then Coordinator for Latin American Affairs, Walt Disney and company were invited to make a goodwill tour of several South American countries. Disney, however, wasn't interested in merely playing tourist; he convinced the State Department to back him with a grant of $200,000, in return for which he promised to produce four short films based on his experiences.

Neither the government nor the public on two continents — the real beneficiaries of this grant — were disappointed. In true Disney style, Walt found a way to combine footage he and his cohorts had shot on their Latin American junket with new animated short subjects specially created by the gang back in his California studios. The happy combination of this dovetailed footage resulted in one of the few Walt Disney commercial releases during the war — a musical "travelogue" called *Saludos Amigos.*

As promised, audiences in South America were the first to be treated to this movie, which debuted late in 1942 and was dubbed in Spanish and Portuguese (as appropriate to the country). Running only 43 minutes, *Saludos* was considered too long to be a short and too short to be a feature. Theater owners were concerned over what to use to fill the other half of what obviously had to be a double feature. But the South American public, thrilled with the whole mystique of "their" picture, would permit no other film to share billing with *Saludos Amigos*, demanding two back-to-back runnings instead of a double bill. The picture was an unqualified hit.

Fresh from its south-of-the-border triumph, the film premiered in the United States in February, 1943. It received critical praise, especially for its intermingling of live action and animation — a technique Disney had pioneered many years before and which would become a hallmark of that studio, continuing to dazzle audiences decades later with such pictures as *Mary Poppins* (1964; see page 175) and *Who Framed Roger Rabbit* (1988).

The movie opens with the title song, "Saludos Amigos," which went on to clinch an Academy Award nomination. The song plays over the credits, while we observe live humans boarding an airplane (Disney, his wife, and production people, credited only as "a group of artists, musicians and writers"), flying to Latin America "to find new personalities, music and dances for their cartoon films." Three days later (!), the group arrives in Rio. The adventure segues into four animated segments: Donald Duck as a hapless tourist at Lake Titicaca; Pedro, the Little Mail Plane That Could (could get the mail through, that is, when his Daddy plane takes "ill"); Gaucho Goofy, with the character once known as "Dippy Dog" decked out in pampas attire attempting to be a cowboy; and "Aquarela do Brasil," the most inventive of the segments. "Aquarela" introduced the new character, José ("Joe") Carioca, a colorful parrot who teaches Donald Duck the samba (and who would eventually "co-star" in a 1945 sequel, *The Three Caballeros*).

Ned Washington wrote the lyrics for "Saludos Amigos." His previous association with Disney had been a productive one, as he'd written lyrics for the Academy Award–winning "When You Wish Upon a Star," from *Pinocchio* (see page 34), as well as the other tunes from that movie and from *Dumbo* (see page 44). Musical composer Charles Wolcott, part of the Disney crew

that toured South America, based some of his melodies on actual native music heard during his visit there, especially the Donald Duck/Bolivia sequence.

Saludos Amigos also received two other Academy Award nominations: Best Sound Recording and Best Scoring of a Musical Picture.

SAY A PRAYER FOR THE BOYS OVER THERE

**Music by Jimmy McHugh;
lyrics by Herb Magidson
From *Hers to Hold***

Another topical (as well as typical) film of the day, this war-era picture managed to work its love story around scenes showing war preparation themes. The love birds this time were Deanna Durbin — in her twelfth film and first truly grown-up role — and Joseph Cotten, as her flyboy love interest, playing a Flying Tiger awaiting orders for his next crack at the enemy.

Much of the picture was shot on location at the Lockheed plant in Burbank, California, where Deanna was shown as one of hundreds of "Rosie the Riveter"–type women aircraft workers. All filming there had to be done on Sundays so as not to interfere with the actual wartime airplane production. Other filming was done at the Red Cross Blood Bank, where the scene of Durbin contributing blood was not staged — she rolled up her sleeve and gave a pint of the real stuff.

Deanna was serious about her efforts in aiding her country during wartime. The Red Cross, for example, received an even more unusual contribution from the actress. For some scenes in the picture, she rented her car to the studio, then turned the rental receipts over to the Red Cross. And her efforts as a role model paid off. Soon after the film was released, she received hundreds of letters from fans whom she had inspired to seek similar defense jobs.

In between all this war morale bolstering, there were also plenty of opportunities for songs in the movie. Deanna kept the fictional aircraft workers entertained during their efforts with songs like Cole Porter's "Begin the Beguine" and a new tune by Jimmy McHugh and Herb Magidson called "Say a Prayer for the Boys Over There," a topical number that became something of an anthem for the war effort. Although never a runaway hit, the song achieved moderate pop-

Bing Crosby and Betty Hutton in a scene from *Star Spangled Rhythm.*

ularity and scored an Academy Award nomination for its composers (the fourth for McHugh).

McHugh also showed his patriotic colors and donated his royalties to war relief agencies. He later wrote two songs that the Treasury Department used for their bond drives: "Buy, Buy, Buy a Bond" and "We've Got Another Bond to Buy." He also produced a huge bond rally in Beverly Hills that sold $28 million worth of war bonds in a single night, the largest such rally ever. For his efforts, President Truman decorated the composer with a Presidential Citation after the war ended.

His international reputation became legendary. A few years later, McHugh presented the song "Say a Prayer for the Boys Over There" in England at a command performance for the young Queen Elizabeth and her husband, Prince Philip, the Duke of Edinburgh.

THAT OLD BLACK MAGIC

Music by Harold Arlen; lyrics by Johnny Mercer
From *Star Spangled Rhythm*

Star Spangled Rhythm contributed to a banner year for the songwriting team of Harold Arlen and Johnny

Mercer. The Paramount film, with just the barest thread of a plot (something about a studio gate guard whose Navy son thinks dad's a big exec), was yet another film that essentially said, "So there's a war on, but who cares, let's just keep on singing and dancing."

Virtually every Paramount contract player had a hand, foot, and voice in this troop-entertaining stage show on film. The cast consisted of Victor Moore, Betty Hutton, Eddie Bracken, and Walter Abel, while the main thrust of the picture involved specialty acts, along with performances, songs, dances, and comedy routines by Bing Crosby, Bob Hope, Fred MacMurray, Ray Milland, Dorothy Lamour, Paulette Goddard, Mary Martin, Dick Powell, Veronica Lake, Alan Ladd, Eddie "Rochester" Anderson, William Bendix, Susan Hayward, Jerry Colonna, Macdonald Carey, Sterling Holloway, Cecil B. DeMille, and a fellow named Johnny Johnston.

It was this last person, a virtual unknown, who would make his mark in film history with this picture. In a routine that centered mostly around a dance number performed by ballerina Vera Zorina (choreographed by her then-husband, the legendary George Balanchine), Johnston introduced a new song written by Arlen and Mercer for the film, a little number called "That Old Black Magic." It was just one of the bunch written especially for this musical. Most were quickly forgettable, with titles like "Hit the Road to Dreamland," "Old Glory," "A Sweater, a Sarong and a Peek-a-Boo Bang," "Workin' on the Swing Shift," "Sharp as a Tack," and "I'm Doing It for Defense." Paramount felt strongly enough about "That Old Black Magic," to use it under the film's opening credits. Their instincts were correct — it would become one of the best-loved songs to emerge from the films of the '40s.

Johnny Mercer once described how he got the idea for the magical lyrics that seemed to fit so well to Arlen's music. He spoke of being influenced by early Cole Porter songs, especially one called "You Do Something to Me."

"It had a phrase in it — 'Do do that voo-doo that you do so well,'" Mercer recounted in the book *They're Playing Our Song*, by Max Wilk. "I've always loved Porter — those early songs of his were so clever, and later on his melodies became so rich and full. Anyway, that thing about voodoo must have stuck with me, because I paraphrased it in 'Old Black Magic.'"

Although introduced in *Star Spangled Rhythm* by Johnny Johnston, the tune was quickly appropriated as the signature song of Billy Daniels, who transformed the tune from the torch song written by Harold Arlen into something more lively and up-tempo. "Mine was a sultry, lush song," said Arlen in *They're Playing Our Song.* "Billy's version was rhythmic and terribly original."

Others latched onto the tune and added their own flair. Bing Crosby performed "That Old Black Magic" in the 1944 Paramount musical *Here Come the Waves,* delightfully spoofing the style of his rival, bobby-soxer idol Frank Sinatra. The song was later sung by Sinatra himself in the motion picture musical *Meet Danny Wilson* (Universal, 1952), and by Marilyn Monroe in the film *Bus Stop* (20th Century-Fox, 1956).

Many artists have had hit recordings of "That Old Black Magic." Glenn Miller had the only version to make Number One on the *Billboard* charts, for one week in February of 1943; his version charted for 19 weeks. Freddie Slack had a recording that peaked that year in the number 10 position, while Horace Heidt's cover stalled at number 11. In the '50s, the song enjoyed renewed popularity, with Sammy Davis Jr.'s 1955 recording reaching number 13. Louis Prima and Keely Smith's 1958 version, which made number 18, received the National Academy of Recording Arts and Sciences' Grammy award that year for the Best Vocal Group. And even 1960s teen idol-pop singer Bobby Rydell discovered there was still some magic left in the tune, when his 1961 version peaked at number 21.

THEY'RE EITHER TOO YOUNG OR TOO OLD

Music by Arthur Schwartz;
lyrics by Frank Loesser
From *Thank Your Lucky Stars*

Filmland's parade of stars continued throughout the war years. While Paramount had *Star Spangled Rhythm,* Warner Bros. offered their own galaxy of luminaries in *Thank Your Lucky Stars.* Indeed, the operative word here was "stars," as nearly the entire acting payroll of each studio showed up in these films. As an afterthought, a storyline was usually contrived, in this case a tale about three Hollywood hopefuls who appeared in an all-star benefit. So much for lofty literary content of the script.

There was no shortage of talent, however. Producer Mark Hellinger gathered some of Hollywood's biggest and best-known actors and put them in production

numbers that other producers might not have attempted. For instance, Hellinger and director David Butler cast Eddie Cantor in a dual role of an obnoxious actor named Eddie Cantor, as well as a Hollywood tour guide who bore a striking resemblance to . . . Eddie Cantor! Fortunately, the actor's ego was not as fragile as some of those in Hollywood might have been, since the Eddie Cantor he portrayed was a most unlikable boor.

In the musical numbers, the producer and director used their actors in imaginative ways. Errol Flynn poked fun at his own heroics in "That's What You Jolly Well Get"; Ann Sheridan did a number called "Love Isn't Born, It's Made"; John Garfield sang a tough guy's version of the Arlen/Mercer tune "Blues in the Night." But it was Bette Davis who stole the show with her half-sung, half-spoken rendition of "They're Either Too Young or Too Old."

The song had to do with her lamenting the fact that all the "good" men had gone away to war, with the ones left behind all being either too young or too old, a situation with which most women in the audience could easily identify. The song received a nomination for the Academy Award and had a passing popularity as a novelty tune on the *Billboard* charts, where Jimmy Dorsey's recording (with vocal by Kitty Kallen) peaked at number two and charted for 12 weeks. Years later the tune was performed by Susan Hayward in *With a Song in My Heart* (20th Century-Fox, 1952), the Jane Froman biopic, with Hayward's voice appropriately dubbed by Froman.

Other songs in the picture included "Ridin' for a Fall," "We're Staying Home Tonight," "Goin' North," "Love Isn't Born, It's Made," "Ice Cold Katie," and three tunes introduced by a newcomer — "The Dreamer," "How Sweet You Are," and the title song, "Thank Your Lucky Stars." The newcomer — a southern gal named Dinah Shore — was so nervous that she was too scared to get out of the car at a Los Angeles sneak preview of the movie. Bruce Cassiday reported in his biography, *Dinah!,* that the young singer-actress huddled alone in the parking lot during the screening, only seeing the film later at the urging of her friends, who persuaded her that she did fine. Still, she was not comfortable seeing herself on the screen for the first time, reportedly whispering to her companion through half-covered eyes, "Is that a face, or a condition?" Luckily, by the time the Oscars rolled around the following year, Shore had regained her composure enough to become the presenter for the 1943 music awards.

WE MUSTN'T SAY GOODBYE

Music by James Monaco; lyrics by Al Dubin
From *Stage Door Canteen*

In the frenzied star roundup that populated films made during World War II, United Artists put on perhaps the biggest show of all. It had its roots in reality — if a place where movie stars gathered to serve up warm meals and entertainment to the brave boys about to be shipped overseas, and possibly to their deaths, can be termed reality. On the West Coast, such a place was called the Hollywood Canteen; back East, it was known as the Stage Door Canteen. Eventually, each Canteen would become the focal point of a movie.

These films were not, as one might have imagined, documentaries. Instead, a thin wisp of a plot was devised, which created the fictional story to be sprinkled with a liberal dose of stardust — three-dimensional, living, breathing, preferably singing and dancing stardust, that is. Players from the "A" as well as "B" and even "C" lists were prevailed upon to strut and sing and otherwise perform their stuff for minimal money, with most of the film's profits going to benefit the Canteens themselves. In essence, then, these films were celluloid benefits.

The plot focused on unknown actors and their fictitious romances, a little something with which the audience could identify; but the real thrust of the picture was on the parade of talent. These stars, the biggest of their day, played themselves — whether dishing up hot soup and dispensing oranges in the Canteen kitchen while reciting lines from Shakespeare (Katharine Cornell) or washing dishes (Alfred Lunt). But the best performances were by the stars doing what they did best. Edgar Bergen did a long ventriloquist act with his well-known dummy Charlie McCarthy; Gracie Fields sang a solemn rendition of "The Lord's Prayer"; Ray Bolger did a funny dance; big bandsmen Benny Goodman, Count Basie, Xavier Cugat, Guy Lombardo, Kay Kyser, Freddy Martin, and others made their music to tunes by the likes of Rodgers and Hart. Other stars donating their talents and jockeying for a few seconds of screen time included Ethel Merman, Merle Oberon, Paul Muni, Helen Hayes, Sam Jaffe, Katharine Hepburn, Arlene Francis, Gypsy Rose Lee, Harpo Marx, George Raft, Ethel Waters, Johnny Weissmuller — all in all, perhaps the most eclectic group of entertainers ever to appear on a screen together up till that time.

The emphasis was on music, and although much of it was reprised from earlier sources, one new song was chosen to represent the picture at Academy Award time — "We Mustn't Say Goodbye," every G.I.'s lament in those difficult times. The song is performed by Lanny Ross, the voice of Gulliver in *Gulliver's Travels* (see page 30) and singer of the nominated song "A Mist Is Over the Moon" from *The Lady Objects* (see page 25). In *Stage Door Canteen*, Ross sings the nominated song in a nightclub routine as he entertains a group of troops.

In addition to an Oscar nomination for Best Song, the picture also received an Academy Award nomination for Best Scoring of a Musical Picture.

YOU'D BE SO NICE TO COME HOME TO

Music and lyrics by Cole Porter
From *Something to Shout About*

Even with names like Don Ameche, Janet Blair, and Jack Oakie, critics agreed that *Something to Shout About* really wasn't. The *New York Times,* in fact, decided that "There isn't [even] much to talk about . . . To say that the script and direction are as inept as we've seen in a month of musicals would be putting it mildly . . . 'Something to Shout About' looks as if it were still in rehearsal."

Ah, but as even the *Times* critic couldn't help noting, the film featured several new Cole Porter tunes. One, "You'd Be So Nice to Come Home To," has since become another Porter standard. It soared above this mediocre Columbia picture, receiving an Academy Award nomination and a lot of attention during those difficult war years. Designed for the first verse to be sung by a male and the second by a female (in the movie it's handled by Don Ameche and Janet Blair), "You'd Be So Nice to Come Home To" expressed the feelings of a war-weary public comprising millions of separated, lonely couples.

The song fared better than the film. Dinah Shore, just emerging from her shyness as an up-and-coming talent, had a solo hit recording of "You'd Be So Nice" that peaked at number three and remained on the *Billboard* charts for 18 weeks; Six Hits and a Miss showed they couldn't miss with this hit, reaching number 11. Over the years, the tune has been recorded by Johnny Mathis, Sarah Vaughan, Julie London, Sammy Davis Jr., Bobby Darin, George Shearing, Ray Conniff Singers, Johnnie Ray, Buddy Cole, and many others.

The film, however, has crept away not with a shout but a whimper. Although not available on video as of early 1995, it could occasionally be sighted on late-night television and is noteworthy for the Oscar-nominated tune as well as the screen debut of actress-dancer Cyd Charisse, billed here as Lily Norwood in the part of "Lily." *Something to Shout About* also received an Oscar nomination for Best Scoring of a Musical Picture.

One small historical footnote: Two years after the film's release, Porter found himself embroiled in a frivolous lawsuit brought by a man named Ira B. Arnstein, an eccentric New Yorker who had spent the past 20 years suing one after another of America's leading songwriters for plagiarism. In a federal court, he charged Porter with lifting, among other songs, "You'd Be So Nice to Come Home To," and claiming $1 million in damages. A jury deliberated for less than two hours before dismissing all charges against Porter.

1944

And the winner is...

SWINGING ON A STAR

Music by James Van Heusen; lyrics by Johnny Burke
From *Going My Way*

Going My Way introduced Bing Crosby in a new role: that of the kindly, musical priest, Father O'Malley, who, when he wasn't saving souls or helping out the neighborhood kids (all of whom seemed to belong to his warm, fuzzy parish), managed to find time to right all wrongs in this early feel-good picture. Audiences

Barry Fitzgerald is cautioned by Bing Crosby in *Going My Way*.

were soon going Bing's way too, lining up in record numbers to secure this film a place as the top box office hit of 1944, earning an impressive $6.5 million for Paramount Pictures.

Along the way, the film managed to pick up a healthy parcel of Oscars. Of the picture's 10 nominations, there were seven wins, including Best Picture, Best Actor (Crosby), Best Supporting Actor (Barry Fitzgerald), Best Director (Leo McCarey), Best Writing, Original Story (McCarey again), Best Screenplay (Frank Butler and Frank Cavett), and Best Song.

The latter, "Swinging on a Star," by James Van Heusen and Johnny Burke, had its beginnings at a dinner party in Crosby's home. Burke and Van Heusen were guests that night, when one of Bing's boys (Crosby had a houseful of them) misbehaved. Papa Bing chastised him for behaving "like a mule," sparking lyrical thoughts in the ever-alert mind of lyricist Burke. He expanded this into a song about a naughty child, stubborn as a mule, a child who would rather be a fish, or . . . someone who could swing on a star if he tried harder. The next day, Van Heusen and Burke had the beginnings of their song.

In the film, Crosby sings the tune to a group of recalcitrant youngsters — the popular Robert Mitchell Boy's Choir, dressed like neighborhood street kids. When it came time to record the song for its Decca release, a different group was used. Known as the Williams Brothers Quartet, they were a family of four kids, originally from Iowa, who'd had some success singing as a group and had soon moved to California in search of better gigs. The four brothers, including the youngest sibling, 14-year-old Howard Andrew Williams, got their first recording opportunity as back-up singers for Bing's "Swinging on a Star" recording. Later, that youngest brother shortened his name to Andy Williams, although it wasn't until 1956 that he had his first successful solo hit record.

"Swinging on a Star" proved an enormous hit for Crosby. After its simultaneous release with *Going My Way* (in May, 1944), it quickly shot to Number One on the *Billboard* charts, where it stayed, stubborn as a mule, for nine solid weeks, charting for a then-incredible total of 28 weeks and selling well over a million copies. Gray Rains covered the tune in July of that year, but his version charted for only one week, at number 28. In 1963, Big Dee Irwin and Little Eva released a version that made number 38. The delightfully amusing imagery evoked by the song has no doubt contributed to its longevity. It was recently used in a updated, soft-rock version as the theme song for the syndicated television program "Out of this World" from 1987 to 1991.

I COULDN'T SLEEP A WINK LAST NIGHT

Music by Jimmy McHugh;
**   lyrics by Harold Adamson**
From *Higher and Higher*

By 1944, Frank Sinatra was giving Bing Crosby a run for his money as the singer at the "top of the pops." Crosby had had that position all to himself for almost a decade. That year, he still controlled the charts, with "Swinging on a Star," but not for long — Sinatra's star was shooting ever higher. It was going to get very crowded up there.

Young Frankie was given his first major motion picture role in 1944, in the musical *Higher and Higher*. Originally a Broadway show with tunes by Rodgers and Hart, RKO opted to drop all but one of the original songs (retaining only "Disgustingly Rich") in favor of all-new replacements by veteran film composers Jimmy McHugh and Harold Adamson. Two hits emerged, both romantic ballads introduced in the film by Sinatra: "This Is a Lovely Way to Spend an Evening," and "I Couldn't Sleep a Wink Last Night." The latter received an Academy Award nomination and gave Sinatra a number four *Billboard* hit, which charted for an impressive 14 weeks. (The film also received a nomination for Best Scoring of a Musical Picture.)

"I Couldn't Sleep a Wink" suffered from curious birth pangs, as described by the late Jimmy McHugh's secretary, Lucille Meyers, to interviewers Marcia Rovins and Don McCulloch. Meyers tells of how Adamson and McHugh needed to come up with one more song for *Higher and Higher*, but although he tried harder and harder, the music just wouldn't come for McHugh. "He always kept a pad beside his bed, with a big red pencil," she said, "so that if something hit him, he would write it. That night he thought of something, and he couldn't sleep, and he couldn't find the pad, so he grabbed the red pencil and wrote all the music down on his sheets. He came into the studio the next morning and said to Mr. Adamson, 'I've got it! I've got the song!' He sat down at the piano — he was a very fine piano player — and he couldn't remember it. He called his housekeeper to pull the sheet off the bed, but the laundry had already been there . . . The laundry man brought the sheet out to the studio, and there was the music to 'I Couldn't Sleep a Wink' on the sheet!" Now that's *real* sheet music.

Lucille further describes her boss as a man who was constantly getting ideas for tunes. "You could go to a restaurant with him and you'd be talking and you'd think he was seriously listening to you, and he'd be thinking of a song, and he'd write on a napkin, a piece of paper, on a menu, anything!"

Other songs in the film included "You Belong in a Love Song," "The Music Stopped," and "I Saw You First," all sung by Sinatra. The movie had an exceptionally good cast, with Jack Haley, Victor Borge, and Barbara Hale, but it suffered from lack of an exciting storyline. Watch for 19-year-old Mel Tormé in his feature film debut.

I'LL WALK ALONE

Music by Jule Styne; lyrics by Sammy Cahn
From *Follow the Boys*

In what had become an instant Hollywood tradition, filmusicals were wartime *de rigeur*. Universal's take on this spreading of good cheer was to put on a typical "entertain the boys" variety show. On stage, these things worked wonders to strengthen the morale of the fighting troops; up on the screen, the jumbled acts with a thread of a plot stitching them together usually didn't fly very far. "It makes for cheap screen entertainment — and hardly a tribute to the players it presents," the *New York Times* critic Bosley Crowther groused.

Maybe so, but where else could the folks back home to be treated to the likes of Jeanette MacDonald singing "Beyond the Blue Horizon" and "I'll See You in My Dreams," Orson Welles performing a magic act with Marlene Dietrich, W.C. Fields doing his famous poolroom act, Sophie Tucker belting out two numbers, and Donald O'Connor dancing up a storm? To top it all off, there was Dinah Shore, now fully blossomed into a popular performer, singing three tunes: "I'll Get By," "Mad About Him Blues," and "I'll Walk Alone."

Shore's recording of "I'll Walk Alone," the Oscar-nominated song from *Follow the Boys*, not only put her on the map with a Number One hit that lasted for four weeks in that position while charting for 25, but it also

Michele Morgan accompanies Frank Sinatra in *Higher and Higher*, his first starring film role.

proved to be one of the most successful ballads of World War II. It reunited the songwriting team of Jule Styne and Sammy Cahn, last nominated for an Academy Award in 1942 for "I've Heard That Song Before" (see page 54). It was also the only song written by Cahn to sell over a million copies of sheet music. The song rang true once again in wartime, when no one wanted to "walk alone."

Other recording artists had success with the tune as well. Martha Tilton's cover, also released in 1944, peaked at number four and charted for 24 weeks, and Mary Martin released a recording in that same year that reached the number six spot.

The song enjoyed an unprecedented resurgence of popularity in 1952, thanks to the Jane Froman biopic, *With a Song in My Heart*. Froman dubbed the tune on-screen for Susan Hayward (who starred as the singer), and also released a recorded version, which peaked at number 14 in May, 1952. Don Cornell's recording two months earlier had done even better, peaking at number five. Both Richard Hayes's and Margaret Whiting's separate recordings also enjoyed a week each on the charts, in the number 24 and 29 positions, respectively.

I'M MAKING BELIEVE

Music by James Monaco; lyrics by Mack Gordon
From *Sweet and Lowdown*

Nobody could coax a more delicious tune from a "licorice stick" than Benny Goodman, the man who was aptly called "the King of Swing." Puckering his lips around his clarinet in *Sweet and Lowdown*, he proved the film was correctly named — his big band music was both.

The movie's *raison d'être* was still to showcase multitudinous jam sessions, even though this musical extravaganza seemed to try harder in its attempt at some semblance of a story. The film was set in Chicago, with occasional on-location appearances at the Dearborn Settlement House, where Goodman had actually been raised by his indigent immigrant parents. In the film, Goodman is performing there when an excited urchin swipes Goodman's clarinet. The kid is found in a tenement home, where his factory-worker brother is overheard improvising on the trombone. Goodman hires the talented trombonist on the spot and takes him on tour with the band.

Such plot contrivances notwithstanding, it was the music that took center stage. The tunes consisted of several standards, plus new songs written by James Monaco and Mack Gordon. Songs included "Chug, Chug, Choo-Choo, Chug" (any resemblance to "Chattanooga Choo-Choo" was strictly intentional), "Hey Bub! Let's Have a Ball," "Ten Days with Baby," and the song that would receive an Oscar nomination, "I'm Making Believe."

In the film, Lynn Bari sings "I'm Making Believe" in her inimitable deep, sultry voice in a nightclub setting in which the trombonist, played by James Cardwell, is spotlighted. While Bari worked at 20th Century-Fox (which released *Sweet and Lowdown)*, she earned the nickname "Queen of the B's," for her appearances in a string of lesser-known but lucrative movies. She had made a $1 million before she was 30, but lost most of it on bad investments. Her pictures included *Stand Up and Cheer* (1934), *Charlie Chan in City in Darkness* (1939), *Blood and Sand* (1941), *Sun Valley Serenade* (1941 — see page 48), *Orchestra Wives* (1942 — see page 55), and dozens more.

Songstress Lynn Bari sings it *Sweet and Lowdown* with Benny Goodman's Orchestra.

The hit recording of "I'm Making Believe" was not by Bari, however, whose success was tied more to the screen than to the music industry. Ella Fitzgerald and the Ink Spots had the Number One hit with the tune, on the Decca label. They held that position for two weeks and remained on the *Billboard* charts for 17 weeks. Hal McIntyre released a cover of the tune that peaked at number 14 early in 1945, but charted for only one week.

LONG AGO AND FAR AWAY

Music by Jerome Kern; lyrics by Ira Gershwin
From *Cover Girl*

When Columbia Pictures boss Harry Cohn selected Arthur Schwartz, a noted Broadway composer, to produce his next film — a starring vehicle for Rita Hayworth called *Cover Girl* — Schwartz was understandably hesitant. He had never produced a film before, but since he was anxious to get his feet wet in this medium, he immediately accepted. But when Cohn announced he would also expect Schwartz to compose the music, Schwartz put his damp foot down. Cohn, a man not used to being denied what he wanted, was stunned.

Sensing this, Schwartz let the other soggy shoe fall with a suggestion of his own — Cohn should get the best: Jerome Kern for the music, Ira Gershwin to pen the lyrics. Cohn agreed, and soon Schwartz was off to Hollywood to hear what Kern had come up with. According to biographer Gerald Bordman, in *Jerome Kern: His Life and Music,* when Jerry Kern sat down to play a new tune he'd just written, Schwartz frowned. Kern made an instant notation on the manuscript — "ADL." "What does that mean?" inquired Schwartz, to which Kern replied, "Arthur doesn't like."

By the next day, Kern had written a replacement, the melody for "Long Ago and Far Away," which Arthur *did* like. Now all that was needed were Ira Gershwin's lyrics. But Gershwin seemed blocked. He just wasn't producing the needed lyric quickly enough to suit Kern, so the frustrated composer began working on words of his own. The first line began with, "Watching little Alice pee . . ." This did the trick. Gershwin, properly shamed as well as amused, knocked out the best lyric of his career, if sales are any measure of success. The tune would eventually bring him more royalties than he'd ever earned for a lyric written with his late brother, George.

In *Cover Girl,* "Long Ago and Far Away" is sung by Gene Kelly (with Martha Mears, dubbing for Hayworth). Biographer Bordman reports that Kern's presence at the song's recording session didn't help Kelly's nerves when he entered the soundproof booth to record the tune (which would be played back when the number was filmed while Kelly lip-synched — a standard motion picture technique). Kern loved the first take, but Kelly insisted that no one ever got it right on the first take. He did several more, but Kern's instincts proved right — the first take took. After the picture was completed, Kern, at Kelly's request, sent an autographed picture, which read, simply: "To G.K. who's O.K. with J.K."

The film was a modest success, and although reviewers didn't gush over the plot ("The script is so frankly familiar that it must have come from the public domain" — the *New York Times),* it received favorable notices for the happy pairing of Kelly and Hayworth, as well as its cinematic innovation. Much was made of the "alter ego" jazz number in which Kelly dances with himself, a technique that would be successfully repeated many years later in the opening of *Singin' in the Rain* (1952).

Despite the critical hesitation, a number of Academy Award nominations went to *Cover Girl.* The movie won the Oscar for Best Scoring of a Musical Picture and was a nominee for Best Color Cinematography, Best Color Interior Decoration, and Best Sound Recording.

"Long Ago and Far Away" provided a hit for a sizable number of recording artists, among them Helen Forrest and Dick Haymes (a number two hit), Bing Crosby (number five), Jo Stafford (number six), Perry Como (number eight), Guy Lombardo (number 11), and the Three Suns (number 16).

NOW I KNOW

Music by Harold Arlen; lyrics by Ted Koehler
From *Up in Arms*

The RKO musical *Up in Arms* was primarily a showcase for the comedic talents of Danny Kaye in his first film starrer. Fresh from his triumph on the Broadway stage in something called *Let's Face It,* Kaye had been rushed by every producer in Hollywood. Samuel Goldwyn had prevailed, and Kaye debuted to raves. He played an army enlistee — no surprises here, this being the wartime theme of virtually every movie

When Dinah Shore (right) enlists as a nurse in the service, Dana Andrews and the United States Army are *Up in Arms.*

being made. The comedy antics in the film begin when he is shipped to the South Pacific and becomes involved with an Army nurse, played by Dinah Shore. Naturally, both performers get to do lots of singing. Kaye performs three songs written by his wife, Sylvia Fine (who would continue to write for all of his films), and Max Liebman.

By the time she appeared in *Up in Arms,* Dinah Shore, once a shy little southern gal, was assertive enough to receive second billing, right behind the film's star, Kaye. A protégée of Sam Goldwyn himself, Shore had no trouble adjusting to working with Kaye, even matching him in comedic style. She managed to rise above the film's featherweight storyline, with its bevy of latest "Goldwyn Girls" implausibly flitting in and out of shipboard scenes. "Miss Shore, in addition to handling an important role," wrote *Variety,* "clicks with two songs, 'Now I Know' and 'Tess' Torch Song,' both by Harold Arlen and Ted Koehler. Former is best candidate for pop attention." The *New York Times* also sensed the quality of "Now I Know," calling it "[Dinah Shore's] best — and one of the year's better — songs."

The Arlen-Koehler tune received an Oscar nomination, the sixth for Arlen and the first for Koehler. In addition to the nominated tune and the previously mentioned "Tess' Torch Song," the songwriting team's other show-stopper in the movie was a lilting march, "All Out for Freedom," delivered by a male soldier chorus. The film also received a nomination for Best Scoring of a Musical Picture.

Up in Arms was released in February of 1944, two months before *Follow the Boys,* the film that would provide Shore with her biggest hit song of the year, "I'll Walk Alone" (see page 69). By then, Shore was earning a nickname as "Queen of the Jukeboxes" (while Crosby and Sinatra battled it out in song for kingship). Between pictures, she trekked with Eddie Cantor and others in numerous war bond tours and entertained troops at bases throughout the country.

Dinah Shore spent the next five decades constantly reinventing herself. When her movie career faded, she began working in television, hosting talk shows, giving cooking demonstrations, a constant presence before the cameras. She seemed ageless. Then, in 1994, just weeks before the famous annual golf tournament that bore her name, she died suddenly. She left this world with the same grace and dignity with which she had lived — her final illness had been kept from the public, as per her wish.

REMEMBER ME TO CAROLINA

**Music by Harry Revel;
lyrics by Paul Francis Webster**
From *Minstrel Man*

For reasons now lost on contemporary (not to mention politically correct) society, folks from the first half of the twentieth century found a quaint sort of pleasure in minstrel shows. These oddities from a bygone era reached the peak of their popularity sometime in the mid-nineteenth century, but no one in their right senses waxes nostalgic about them today. In short: The men (almost never the ladies) applied shoe polish and black cork to their Caucasian faces, left a space for big, white lips, occasionally wore a hat so as not to have to bother with a kinky wig, donned white gloves, strummed banjos and/or tap-danced (preferably while eating watermelon), and pretended to be the most stereotypical African-Americans ever imagined. White audiences roared their naïve approval. While such a spectacle is unimaginable today, minstrel shows were a perfectly acceptable part of our early culture, perhaps best evoked in Al Jolson's down-on-his-knees performance in the first talkie, singing about his "Mammy."

Minstrel numbers had been quite prevalent in vaudeville, and filmusicals, especially in the '30s, frequently incorporated these numbers. This carried over even into the '40s. By 1944, movies were still being made mostly by and for whites, who apparently were not offended by the inherent racism of white men wearing blackface. *Minstel Man*, one of the more interesting pictures made that year, celebrated this form of entertainment. It starred Benny Fields, a veteran vaudevillian, who, with his wife and partner Blossom Seeley, had trod the boards of virtually every theater and vaudeville house from coast to coast. He had made his screen debut in 1937, in *The Big Broadcast of 1937*.

In *Minstrel Man*, Fields plays a minstrel who has risen from the ranks of vaudeville to star on Broadway in a show called *Minstrel Man*. The part seemed tailored especially for Fields, who got to do what he did best in vaudeville — sing. Songs by Harry Revel and Paul Francis Webster included "I Don't Care If the World Knows About It," "Cindy," and the Oscar nomi-

nee, "Remember Me to Carolina." Also tossed in is Fields's old standby, the quintessential minstrel number "Melancholy Baby."

On the minstrel show–within–a–minstrel show's opening night, Fields's character's wife dies after giving birth to their daughter — but not before he gets to belt out a blackfaced version of "Remember Me to Carolina." Then, during the encore, he gets the news that his wife has died. He walks offstage, parks the infant with friends, heads off to Europe for five years, then on to Havana for several more. While returning to the States, he is erroneously reported drowned, travels to San Francisco, is "miraculously" spotted alive by his old agent, and returns to New York just as a modern version of *Minstrel Man* is about to open, with his now-grown daughter starring as the "Minstrel Girl." He arrives backstage in time to reprise the tune "Remember Me to Carolina." Happy endings all around, fade out, the end.

Produced by Leon Fromkess and directed by Joseph H. Lewis, *Minstrel Man* was released by Producers Releasing Corporation, making it one of the earliest independent features to be nominated for an Academy Award (the film was also nominated for Best Scoring of a Musical Picture) — really a remarkable feat, since the studio system generally held sway over the entire industry at the time.

One of the big minstrel show production numbers in the film *Minstrel Man*.

RIO DE JANEIRO

Music by Ary Barroso; lyrics by Ned Washington
From *Brazil*

The "Good Neighbor Policy" found more and more studios concentrating their wartime efforts on films about our friends to the south. Walt Disney Productions had the tremendously popular *Saludos Amigos* in 1943 (see page 62). Now it was Republic's turn to shoot some footage in Brazil, and what could be more colorful than carnival time in Rio de Janeiro? What's more, the Republic film, aptly titled *Brazil*, actually had a plot to go along with the bouncy songs and dances.

The story concerns a young American author (played by Virginia Bruce) whose book, *Why Marry a Latin?* is a successful tome with an unflattering conclusion about Latin lovers. She heads off to Rio to do more research for a definitive work on that country. Her travels lead her not only to a colorful carnival, but straight into the arms of Tito Guizar, who decides to give her an object lesson and prove that Latins aren't the lousy lovers she's portrayed them to be. Of course, they are soon in love, and her theories fly out the window to a samba beat.

Apparently Brazilian singer-actors were in short supply. Guizar, starring as the leading Brazilian, was actually a popular Mexican actor. He had begun appearing in American films in 1938, with *The Big Broadcast of 1938*, and later handled Latino roles in such B-movies as *Blondie Goes Latin* (1941), *Mexicana*, *The Thrill of Brazil* (1946), *On the Old Spanish Trail* (1947), and *The Gay Ranchero* (1948). Although a native Spanish speaker, he sang *Brazil*'s tunes, by Ary Barroso and Ned Washington, in the requisite Portuguese as well as English.

In *Brazil*, Guizar introduces the song that would be nominated for an Oscar, appropriately titled "Rio de Janeiro." The melody itself, written by Barroso, is a parody of his own "Brazil," which also appears in the movie. That song, however, had already been introduced to the public in *Saludos Amigos* the previous year, and was therefore ineligible for nomination. Instead, he created a sound-alike tune in "Rio de Janeiro." However, the music to the original "Brazil" (written by S.K. Russell and Barroso) is heard continually throughout this namesake film.

The movie had a little something for everyone. There were the colorful dance numbers, the most impressive of which, depicting the harvesting of coffee, featured Aurora Miranda, Carmen's less flamboyant sister. And even Roy Rogers, on the Republic payroll as their leading cowboy star, was worked into the film. He guest-starred in the final festival sequence, singing "Hands Across the Border." Other songs composed by Barroso and Washington were "The Vaquero Song," "Tonight You're Mine," "Moonlight Fiesta," and "Upa Upa."

In 1985, Terry Gilliam directed a film by the same title. While it had an entirely different plot (it centered around an Orwellian near-future), this *Brazil* made abundant use of the original Barroso theme of the same name.

SILVER SHADOWS AND GOLDEN DREAMS

Music by Lew Pollack; lyrics by Charles Newman
From *Lady, Let's Dance*

She had one name and two legs, each of the latter terminating with an ice skate strapped underfoot. Belita, England's answer to Sonja Henie, had skated her way into the hearts of fans in her first film, entitled *Silver Skates*, only months before. Her backers thought they had struck gold and set out to tap into the mother lode.

Monogram,[1] a studio known mostly for its low-budget Westerns, serials, and other action pictures, had been home to the likes of Bill Cody, Rex Bell, Tom Keene and Tex Ritter. John Wayne made a dozen Westerns for them during the mid-'30s. "The Bowery Boys" and "Charlie Chan" series were both under the Monogram imprint. Then along came Belita; the studio immediately signed her to a seven-year contract.

She wasn't always Belita. Back in Nether Wallop, England, she was known as Belita Gladys Lyne Jepson-Turner. In 1937, at age 14, she was starring in the London spectacle "Opera on Ice." The following year she toured the United States, then headlined for two more years with "Ice Capades," when the producers from Monogram caught up with her. For her second film, *Lady, Let's Dance*, the studio put up a hefty $500,000, the largest budget in its history. They launched a huge pro-

---

1. In 1946, Monogram formed a wholly owned subsidiary, Allied Artists Productions, and in 1953, the corporate name was officially changed to Allied Artists Pictures Corporation.

motional campaign ("Belita speaks four languages, paints, sings, does needlework, plays the violin and the piano, and is proficient in boxing, wrestling, and fencing"). Alas, the film had only modest success, then faded into obscurity. Fifty years after its release, it was rarely shown on television and was not yet available on video.

A pity. Belita was indeed something to behold, not only skating through a series of delightful numbers on ice, but on the dance floor as well. With a practically nonexistent plot, there was plenty of room for orchestras (four of them), lavish production numbers, song-and-dance numbers, and so on. *Newsweek* marveled that "the only excuse for this film is the English-born, blonde, attractive, and versatile Belita, who hasn't learned how to act yet and doesn't really have to." *Variety* agreed: "Belita marks herself as a screen-comer of wide possibilities — spectacular on skates, expert at ballroom and ballet terping — and needing only more experience on the dramatic side to firmly set her box office promise." Despite these predictions of promise, Belita made only a handful of films over the next 20 years, none of her roles heavy on drama (best known: *Silk Stockings* in 1957), then drifted into retirement at age 40.

The film's nominated song, "Silver Shadows and Golden Dreams," was a gracefully poetic ice number that Belita performed with partner Eugen Mikeler, backed by Mitch Ayres's band and a male chorus. Other production numbers included the spectacular finale, billed as "Spirit of Victory," with Belita soloing in a show-stopper featuring an enormous Statue of Liberty backdrop. There was also a comedy-on-ice routine performed by a pair of Swiss comedic skaters named — honest — Frick and Frack.

SWEET DREAMS, SWEETHEART

Music by M.K. Jerome; lyrics by Ted Koehler
From *Hollywood Canteen*

In the very lucrative tradition of such "star-vaganzas" as *Thank Your Lucky Stars* and *Stage Door Canteen*, Warner Bros. pulled out all the stops for its entry into the genre with *Hollywood Canteen*. Like its New York counterpart, the Stage Door Canteen, there was a real-life Hollywood Canteen, located on the West Coast, and it too boasted celebrities serving up warm meals and entertainment to troops between their forays into combat.

Although there probably was little need for a script, the producers enlisted screenwriter Delmer Daves, who had written the 1943 *Stage Door Canteen*. This time he also signed on as director. In addition to the requisite boy-meets-girl storyline, *Hollywood Canteen* also proffered the now-familiar "every-celebrity-in-town-meets-the-cameras" storyline. And although the film was a good deal longer than the customary 90-minute running time of most musicals, clocking in at 124 minutes, most of the performances were so brief that the celebs could have phoned in their parts. The enormous collection of names sure looked good in the film's advertisements, though, if not on a movie marquee — there were none large enough to accommodate all the names.

Starring in the leads were Robert Hutton as the All-American GI Joe, while Joan Leslie played his lady love. Built around their romance were the various song-and-dance routines. There were the big band sounds of Jimmy Dorsey and His Band, as well as Carmen Cavallaro and His Orchestra, the Golden Gate Quartet, and the Sons of the Pioneers. The Andrews Sisters sang Cole Porter's "Don't Fence Me In"; Jack Benny clowned around on the violin; Eddie Cantor and Nora Martin sang "We're Having a Baby (My Baby and Me)"; actors Sydney Greenstreet and Peter Lorre did a bit, as did John Garfield (who in real life was a tireless worker at the Hollywood Canteen); ditto Bette Davis, Joan Crawford, Barbara Stanwyck, and "a cast of thousands."

Okay, *which* thousands? How about Joe E. Brown, Kitty Carlisle, Jack Carson, Faye Emerson, Alan Hale, Paul Henreid, Ida Lupino, Janis Paige, Eleanor Parker, Roy Rogers & Trigger, Robert Shayne (Inspector Henderson in the 1950s "Superman" TV series), Craig Stevens, and Jane Wyman. Before the invention of the VCR, it must have been a challenge for audiences to spot these and other famous stars of the '40s, but fortunately today's generation can simply dash down to the local video rental counter and soon have a living room filled with stars. With one finger firmly on the rewind button, each celebrity can be glimpsed again if you should blink and miss him or her.

Many of the film's songs stemmed from the popular numbers of the day, as well as new ones written especially for the movie. These included such gems as "I'm Gettin' Corns for My Country," by Jean Barry, Leah Worth, and Dick Charles, "Voodoo Moon," by Obdulio Morales, Julio Blanco, and Marion Sunshine, "You Can Always Tell a Yank," by E. Y. Harburg and Burton Lane, "What Are You Doing the Rest of Your Life?" by Ted

Koehler and Burton Lane,[1] "The General Jumped at Dawn," by Larry Neal and Jimmy Munday, and the song nominated for an Oscar, "Sweet Dreams, Sweetheart." Joan Leslie sings that song with one of the big bands the first time we hear it; actress Kitty Carlisle (playing herself), best known for appearing as a regular on the popular 1950s and '60s TV series "I've Got a Secret" and "To Tell the Truth," sings it later on.

TOO MUCH IN LOVE

Music by Walter Kent; lyrics by Kim Gannon
From *Song of the Open Road*

Yet another take on the "Hey, kids, let's put on a show" theme so familiar from the Mickey Rooney–Judy Garland–MGM days, *Song of the Open Road* was a film of both firsts and lasts. It marked the motion picture debut of Jane Powell, as well as the final film appearance of W.C. Fields. Virtually every star in the film played a character who happened to have the same name as the actor playing the role. Second-billed Edgar Bergan (right behind the film's "lead," his dummy Charley McCarthy), Jane Powell, Fields, Peggy O'Neill, Jackie Moran — all played characters of their own namesake. The film was really a showcase for the talents of all these popular performers of the day, along with the usual dancing, singing, and acrobatic acts.

Powell was only 14 at the time, and her singing presence captured the hearts of the critics. The *New York Times* described her as "a winsome youngster with a prematurely developed rich soprano voice." Wisely, United Artists made her the centerpiece of most of the musical numbers. Backed by Sammy Kaye and His Orchestra, Powell charmed audiences with several songs, including four new ones written especially for the movie by Walter Kent and Kim Gannon. The best of these was "Too Much in Love," which received an Oscar nomination. (*Song of the Open Road* was also nominated for Best Scoring of a Musical Picture.)

It was still wartime, and apparently all top writers in Hollywood had been drafted to serve their nation overseas. How else to explain the wildly improbable plot, which had Powell starring as a Hollywood child star in search of escape from all the studio and home

supervision? She disguises herself and joins a group of crop-pickers. Her new pals enlist her aid when they discover a shortage of hands to harvest Jackie Moran's brothers' oranges. It's Jane to the rescue, along with Bergan, Fields (and his nemesis, Charley McCarthy), and Kaye and the boys in the band all pitching in. Lesson learned, Jane returns to her Hollywood life.

Powell went on to a career in musical films, including *Holiday in Mexico* (1946), *A Date with Judy* (1948), *Nancy Goes to Rio* (1950), and *Royal Wedding* (1951), in which she starred opposite Fred Astaire (see page 115). Her popularity peaked with her lead in the MGM musical *Seven Brides for Seven Brothers* (1954). She was just 25 but still playing adolescents. She retired from the screen in 1958, just shy of her 30th birthday, and turned to television, summer stock, and nightclubs.

"Too Much in Love" marked the first Oscar nomination for composer Walter Kent (he would receive a second the following year (for "Endlessly" — see page 81). Surprisingly, though, he is best remembered for three other songs, none of which appeared in films: "The White Cliffs of Dover," "I'll Be Home for Christmas," and "I'm Gonna Live Till I Die."

THE TROLLEY SONG

Music by Ralph Blane; lyrics by Hugh Martin
From *Meet Me in St. Louis*

"Clang, clang, clang!"

It's virtually impossible to think of "The Trolley Song" without immediately remembering the first three words of Hugh Martin's catchy lyrics. The song first appeared in the musical *Meet Me in St. Louis,* a holiday treat in a year crowded with "musicals" consisting mainly of parades of stars. This filmusical had stars, a top director, and a wonderful score, not to mention a heartwarming story perfect for the Christmas crowd (it opened in late November). Not surprisingly, the film received nominations for Best Screenplay, Best Color Cinematography, Best Scoring of a Musical Picture, and Best Song.

Judy Garland starred as a turn-of-the-century young woman experiencing first love. Plot conflict centers around her family's impending move from their beloved St. Louis home to New York, where Leon Ames, playing the *paterfamilias*, has been transferred for business reasons. By picture's end, however, Papa realizes the error of

---

1. Not to be confused with the Legrand–Bergman song from *The Happy Ending* (see page 200).

his ways, and the family remains in St. Louis, just in time for the opening of the World's Fair. And as Judy learned so well in her last popular musical, *The Wizard of Oz* — cue the fireworks here — there's no place like home.

The film had some wonderful music, both original and old favorites. All were memorable, and the three by composers Blane and Martin were soon popular hits. "Have Yourself a Merry Little Christmas" was perfect for the season and became a best-seller; Judy had hits with "The Boy Next Door" and "The Trolley Song." She sings this Oscar-nominated tune in a lavish production number that finds her surrounded by girls in bonnets while she's hatless (and considerably blonder than in earlier pictures). The filming of this number was demanding, as related by director Vincente Minnelli in his 1974 autobiography, *I Remember It Well*. He credits director of photography, George Folsey, with making the scene — indeed, the whole picture — come off so smoothly.

"It couldn't have been done without George Folsey's fluid and mobile work," he recalled. "He proved that my thoughts on the choreography of the camera weren't half baked. He'd followed . . . Judy weaving her way from one end of the trolley to another. His work, to me, was just as lilting as 'The Trolley Song,' which accompanied the action."

Minnelli also found Judy Garland to be rather lilting. As soon as the 21-year-old singer's divorce from David Rose was final (about a year after completing *Meet Me in St. Louis),* the director married her.

Margaret O'Brien, then age seven, received second billing, and deservedly so. Her most memorable number is the cakewalk routine with Garland, called "Under the Bamboo Tree"; she simply cakewalks away with the scene.

But it was truly Judy's picture. "The Trolley Song" became the biggest hit to come out of the film. Surprisingly, a group called the Pied Pipers (who had once backed Frank Sinatra) had an even bigger hit with the tune than Judy. While her soundtrack version reached number four and lasted eight weeks on the charts, the Pipers' version climbed to number two and remained on the charts for 14 weeks. Other significant releases of "The Trolley Song" were from the King Sisters (number 13), Vaughn Monroe (number four), and Guy Lombardo (number 19).

In 1989, *Meet Me in St. Louis* was adapted as a Broadway musical, complete with the original and some new songs. After its New York run, the show began a road tour that took it all over the United States.

1945

And the winner is...

IT MIGHT AS WELL BE SPRING

Music by Richard Rodgers; lyrics by Oscar Hammerstein II
From *State Fair*

"Oscar Hammerstein II and I won an Oscar for 'It Might As Well Be Spring' in 1945. The only thing that could have made me happier than this award was the song itself," wrote Richard Rodgers (as quoted in Robert Osborne's book, *60 Years of Oscar,* 1989). And if "It Might As Well Be Spring" made the composer happy, imagine what a treat it was for war-weary audiences when they first heard it in 1945.

By then, Rodgers had been successfully paired with his musical soulmate, Hammerstein, for several years. They had scored their biggest hit to date with the Broadway sensation, *Oklahoma!* (1943). Their music had had a folksy, homespun quality in *Oklahoma!* — just what producer Darryl F. Zanuck at 20th Century-Fox was searching for when he decided to create a musical version of the 1933 bucolic film, *State Fair,* originally done as a non-musical starring Will Rogers. Zanuck commissioned Rodgers to compose the score and Hammerstein to write not only the lyrics to Rodgers's music but also the screenplay for the revised movie. Hammerstein readily agreed, but Rodgers had one demand: He refused to work in Hollywood, having previously endured some bad experiences in Tinsel Town. Zanuck knew he had no choice and agreed. *State Fair,* set in Iowa, filmed on California sound stages, had its songs written in New York, Connecticut, and Pennsylvania.

The story had always been a simplistic one, about simple folk living in a simpler time. This slice of Americana — like the mincemeat pie served up by the farmer's wife at the annual Iowa State Fair — was warm and reassuring, but it also was an endangered species. Even as the picture opened in the fall of 1945, the cheers of the crowds on August 15, V-J Day, were still ringing in the audience's ears. Unknown to the people who came to enjoy the film about the farmer's daughter, his wife, their son, their mincemeat pie, and their prize hog, this movie marking the end of those blissful times also heralded the beginning of the American coming of age.

The songwriting team outdid themselves with uplifting tunes like "Our State Fair," "That's for Me," "Isn't It Kinda Fun," and the lilting waltz, "It's a Grand Night for Singing." But the tune that waltzed away with the Oscar for Best Song was a daydreamy balled called "It Might As Well Be Spring."

At first, the team had great difficulty creating this song. Hammerstein thought that the heroine (played by Jeanne Crain, dubbed by Louanne Hogan) should be in a spring-feverish sort of mood, but state fairs are held in summer or fall, not spring. After mulling it over, he asked Rodgers's opinion, complaining to his partner, "It might as *well* be spring," since that's how she was feeling. "That's it!" shouted the composer. According to David Ewen, author of *American Popular Songs*, Hammerstein remarked, "All my doubts were gone. I had a partner behind me." After that, he completed his lyric in less than a week.

State Fair marked the only original musical that Rodgers and Hammerstein wrote together for the screen. In 1962, the picture was remade, starring Pat Boone, Bobby Darin, Ann-Margret, and Pamela Tiffin (performing "It Might As Well Be Spring," dubbed by Anita Gordon). It contained five out of the six original songs, plus five new ones with words and music by Rodgers.

"It Might As Well Be Spring" became a popular tune during late 1945. Dick Haymes (who co-starred in the film) had a recording of the tune that peaked at number five in mid-November and charted for 12 weeks. Paul Weston's version had peaked at number six three weeks earlier, in October, and stayed on the charts for 11 weeks. And Sammy Kaye's orchestral rendition made it to the number four spot in mid-December, lasting 10 weeks on the charts.

AC-CENT-TCHU-ATE THE POSITIVE

Music by Harold Arlen; lyrics by Johnny Mercer
From *Here Come the Waves*

Johnny Mercer may never have had so much fun as he did while writing the playful lyrics of "Ac-Cent-Tchu-Ate the Positive." Besides the title, whose exaggerated syllables were summed up in the way it was spelled (as opposed to "Accentuate," as some revisionists would have us believe), the song toyed with erudite words with *-ive*, *-ate*, and *-imum* suffixes, something most lyricists had never dreamed of doing. Words like positive, negative, affirmative, maximum, minimum, pandemonium (a variation on the *-imum* ending) were tossed around like alphabet soup gone haywire. Soon everyone was singing this song, especially school children, who thought it great fun to use "grown-up" words.

The song has a decidedly spiritual slant to it. There are several versions of the origins of the title. One story claims it was suggested by a newspaper clipping quoting the Harlem revivalist preacher Father Divine, to whom the phrase was attributed. According to this account, a friend sent the article to Mercer, who filed it away for future use. The lyric reportedly fell into place one day while Mercer was riding to Paramount in partner Harold Arlen's car; Harold began humming a tune he'd just written, and Mercer recalled the Divine clipping. (Another version claimed Mercer recalled the line from his southern childhood.) By the time the pair reached the studio, they had written most of the song. Arlen later commented (as reported by David Ewen in *American Popular Songs*), "It must really have pleased John. It was the first time I saw him smile."

The song was introduced by Bing Crosby, in yet another minstrel number in those politically incorrect 1940s, in a film called *Here Come the Waves*. This basic recruitment picture, couched in the guise of a musical, starred Crosby, Betty Hutton and Sunny Tufts. Crosby and Tufts perform "Ac-Cent-Tchu-Ate the Positive" in basic blackface. The Christmas release offered a number of tunes by Arlen and Mercer, including "My Mama Thinks I'm a Star," "I Promise You," "Let's Take the Long Way Home," "There's a Fellow Waiting in Poughkeepsie," and the title song. But nothing captured the imagination of the public like "Ac-Cent-Tchu-Ate the Positive."

Mercer, himself a successful performer, cut his own recording of the song. It shot to the top of the charts, lasting two weeks in the Number One position and charting for 16 weeks. Bing Crosby also cut a version of the song, assisted by the Andrews Sisters; their version peaked at number two. Other successful recordings were made by Artie Shaw, with vocal by Imogene Lynn (number five), and Kay Kyser's Kollege of Musical Knowledge, with vocal by Dolly Mitchell (number 12).

Fans of the '50s television series "Superman" will want to watch for Noel "Lois Lane" Neill as Dorothy in

Here Come the Waves. It was one of her largest movie roles before landing the part of Superman's girlfriend in the movie serials a few years prior to jumping over to the TV version.

ANYWHERE

Music by Jule Styne; lyrics by Sammy Cahn
From *Tonight and Every Night*

Tonight and Every Night was released early in 1945, when the war, although about to wind down, was still raging in Europe. It was an elaborate musical-within-a-musical about London. Although the city was being blitzed by nightly bombings, "the show must go on" — five times a day for these performers. Rita Hayworth starred as one of the members of the revue troop. Naturally, there was a subplot, in the form a romantic interest played by Lee Bowman. Also on board was Janet Blair, as the cast ingenue. Mostly, though, the movie was about the wonderful music by the popular film composing team Jule Styne and Sammy Cahn.

The audience was blitzed with plenty of song and dance. There was the title song, a patriotic march number performed by Blair; a torch song called "You Excite Me"; a ballet number, "Cry and You Cry Alone," performed, of course, by Rita Hayworth, and Hayworth's spectacular opening number, "What Does an English Girl Think of a Yank?" Hayworth also joined Blair in a comedy sketch called "The Boy I Left Behind." For her efforts, she received rave notices from the *Variety* reviewer, who gushed, "Miss Hayworth turns in a capable all-around performance, dancing magnificently, effectively putting over the song numbers and scoring solidly in the starring assignment."

Harry Cohn, studio boss of Columbia (and consequently of its contract player, Rita Hayworth) must have been greatly relieved. Especially since the mogul, not known for his genteel demeanor, flew into a rage when he learned, halfway through the filming of *Tonight and Every Night,* that his leading lady had a slight case of . . . pregnancy. She was married to Orson Welles at the time, and this would be their first child. Rita was thrilled, and so were her co-workers at the studio, who threw her a baby shower. She returned the favor by completing all her complicated dance routines before she began showing. The child, a daughter the couple named Rebecca, was born December 17, 1944, about a month before the picture opened.

None of Hayworth's songs received an Academy Award nomination. Instead, a tune called "Anywhere," performed by Blair, was entered into Oscar contention. It was the most commercial of the songs from the movie, although it never reached hit status on the charts.

Janet Blair and military chorus remind audiences what they're fighting for in a scene from *Tonight and Every Night.*

Watch for 22-year-old Shelley Winters in a bit part. The Brooklyn-born young actress had appeared mostly in a few minor plays on Broadway when she caught the eye of Cohn, who signed her to a Hollywood contract in 1943. As was customary with the old studio system, she was tossed into the background of virtually every picture Columbia produced during those years — eight of them by the time she filmed *Tonight and Every Night*. Cohn chose his talent well — Winters went on to a celebrated career as one of the busiest actresses in Hollywood, receiving a pair of Best Supporting Actress Oscars, for *The Diary of Anne Frank* in 1959 and *A Patch of Blue* in 1965, along with a third nomination for *The Poseidon Adventure* in 1972 (see page 211).

AREN'T YOU GLAD YOU'RE YOU?

**Music by James Van Heusen;
lyrics by Johnny Burke
From *The Bells of St. Mary's***

The joyous pairing of Bing Crosby and Leo McCarey had brought RKO box office gold to the tune of $6.5 million in 1944, with the smash hit *Going My Way*. Crosby played Father O'Malley, the priest who quickly became a father figure to the entire movie-going public. McCarey, who had written and directed the successful film, was asked by the studio to write, produce, and direct a sequel. This would be quite a feat under any circumstances, but was especially challenging in the mid-1940s, long before sequels were taken for granted like they are today — no one had ever pulled off such an enormous task before.

Hoping to make lightning strike twice, McCarey brought back the winning team of songwriters who had won the Oscar with "Swinging on a Star" the last time we went O'Malley's *Way*. The magic happened all over again — better, this time, if measured by success at the box office. The sequel, *The Bells of St. Mary's*, a pleasant story about nuns and their young schoolgirl charges, was an even warmer, mushier tale than the first, and it topped its predecessor with $8 million in total North American rentals. What's more, it captured eight Oscar nominations — for Best Picture, Best Actor (Crosby), Best Actress (Ingrid Bergman as the head nun), Best Director (McCarey), Best Sound Recording (the only Oscar it won), Best Scoring, Best Editing, and Best Song.

Although *The Bells of St. Mary's* didn't ring any bells with the Best Song voters of the Academy, who awarded Oscar to "It Might As Well Be Spring" that year (see page 77), the nominated song, "Aren't You Glad You're You?," was a classic Jimmy Van Heusen–Johnny Burke number, with obvious parallels to "Swinging on a Star," their winner from *Going My Way*. The earlier song asked the musical questions, "Would you rather be a mule?" and "Would you rather be a fish?" "Aren't You Glad You're You?" asked a similar question in its very title. As sung by Bing, the song featured questions like, "Every time you're near a rose, aren't you glad you've got a nose?"

Although the song's childlike lyrics might suggest limited commercial possibilities, four hit recordings of the tune were released during late 1945 and early 1946. Crosby's, naturally, had the most appeal. His Decca recording reached the number eight position and charted for nine weeks. Les Brown's orchestral version peaked at number 11, Tommy Dorsey's release made number 14, and the Pied Pipers rode the tune to number 18.

Van Heusen and Burke continued writing songs together for the next decade, most notably for the Bob Hope–Bing Crosby–Dorothy Lamour *Road* pictures.

THE CAT AND THE CANARY

**Music by Jay Livingston; lyrics by Ray Evans
From *Why Girls Leave Home***

With its spin on a tried and true formulaic plot frequently used in the earlier part of the century, Producers Releasing Corporation, one of the leading independents of the day, set out to capture some box office dollars. The story concerned an ambitious young lady who is — perish the thought — unhappy with the quiet comforts of middle-class home life and runs away to seek fame and fortune on the nightclub circuit.

Never mind that half of Hollywood's successful actresses and singers had begun in precisely this way; it was not for *our* heroine, what with her proper upbringing and obligatory kid sister and big brother. After a family squabble, she runs away and straight into the lap of trouble. Soon the plot degenerates into the cliché of the innocent girl who learns too much about the gangsters connected with the nightclub. Naturally, they plan to rub her out and make it look like a suicide; naturally, she is rescued and the plot foiled in the nick of time.

Did anyone bother to see this picture? Thanks to its scathing reviews, hardly anyone had a chance. "The picture . . . has nothing to recommend it either as entertainment or as an object lesson for disgruntled teenagers," warned the *New York Times*. There wasn't much in the way of cast to attract an audience, either. Lola Lane got top billing as the nightclub operator who takes the young girl under her wing, although it was really Pamela Blake, as the runaway, who had the meatier part. The plum role, though, went to Sheldon Leonard. He would become TV's perennial gangster in the 1950s, but he subsequently found his niche as a top producer of such shows as "Make Room for Daddy" ("The Danny Thomas Show") and "The Dick Van Dyke Show." Elisha Cook Jr. also starred as gangster Jimmie Lobo. Cook became another popular TV crime boss, primarily as Ice Pick on the 1980s series "Magnum, P.I."

In 1945, two young songwriters by the names of Jay Livingston and Ray Evans had recently arrived in Hollywood and were commissioned to write tunes for *Why Girls Leave Home*. They must have felt like packing their bags and heading back east when the picture bombed. Even the songs were panned, with *Variety* opining, "Songs are very unoriginal." The best of the bunch was "The Cat and the Canary" (not to be confused with the 1939 Bob Hope film of the same title).

As per the Academy rules at the time, the producers were invited to submit their nomination for Best Song, so "The Cat and the Canary" was proffered. (The film was also nominated for Best Scoring of a Musical Picture.) Frank Sinatra sang the tune at the Awards presentation ceremony. "We got a nomination even though we were barely getting our feet wet in Hollywood," said Evans in a 1990 interview with KMPC radio personality Don McCulloch. "It didn't mean anything," he added modestly, "because in those days there were a lot more [nominees]." In fact, 1945 was the year in which there were more nominations than any other — 14 songs were in contention for the coveted statuette.

Although their song lost, Livingston and Evans were offered a contract with Paramount Pictures that same year. They immediately grabbed this offer of full-time employment and went on to a long and happy career spanning several decades, with a half-dozen or so nominations apiece and two Oscars to their credit ("Buttons and Bows" in 1948 and "Mona Lisa" in 1950 — see pages 98 and 108, respectively).

ENDLESSLY

Music by Walter Kent; lyrics by Kim Gannon
From *Earl Carroll Vanities*

Expensive by normal Republic standards, *Earl Carroll Vanities* centered around a fictional incident in the life of an actual Broadway producer named Earl Carroll. Carroll's trademark was presenting shows loaded with bevies of beauties. In this extravaganza, Carroll, played by Otto Kruger, has discovered a visiting princess from a European postage-stamp country who is desperately in need of money to keep her country, such as it is, from being stamped out. The plot thickens — and practically turns to cement — with an all-too-familiar story of the royal who falls in love with a commoner. She decides that in spite of the opposition of her mother (the queen) and the

Dennis O'Keefe and Constance Moore star in *Earl Carroll Vanities*.

prime minister, a career in the "theatuh" is far preferable to a royal marriage and life in a stuffy old castle.

Constance Moore played the part of Princess Drina, and her performance caught the attention of many critics. "Let it be said right now," noted the *Hollywood Reporter*, "that the picture belongs to Constance Moore . . . Her voice is delightful, her dancing graceful, her acting excellent, and she looks more lovely than ever."

Her commoner romantic interest was played by Dennis O'Keefe, the author of *Vanities*, the musical in which she's supposedly starring. Producer Carroll was played by Otto Kruger, while Eve Arden (television's future "Our Miss Brooks") provided her trademark caustic comedy. Other comedy in the movie was provided by Pinky Lee in a corny routine, and a lunch counter number by popular comedian of the day with the unlikely name of Parkyakarkus ("Park your carcass" — get it?).[1] Woody Herman's orchestra also offered a few brief musical sequences.

Moore performed the Oscar-nominated song, "Endlessly," a romantic ballad and easily the best song in the film. She also sang "I've Been So Good for So Long" and "Rockabye Boogie." All three were from the songwriting team of Walter Kent and Kim Gannon, who had been nominated the previous year for "Too Much in Love" from *Song of the Open Road* (see page 76).

Woody Herman and His Orchestra did two of his compositions: "Apple Honey," an instrumental number, and "Who Dat Up Dere," with Herman doing the vocal. Pinky Lee and Eve Arden mixed it up with a song called "The Last Man in Town."

I FALL IN LOVE TOO EASILY

Music by Jule Styne; lyrics by Sammy Cahn
From *Anchors Aweigh*

What could be more topical during the war years than two sailors on leave, and where better to spend it than Hollywood? Such questions were no doubt kicked around by the producers of one of the most successful hits of 1945, a musical called *Anchors Aweigh*. Yet for director George Sidney, it wasn't as easy as it sounds, as he revealed in a 1993 radio interview.

"When we were preparing the film," explained Sidney, "they had a very good character comic actor [signed for] the part. I said, 'No, let's get Frank Sinatra.' He was doing 'The Lucky Strike Show' and a few of those things. They said, 'He's so skinny, he won't even throw a shadow,' and I said, 'He will throw the largest shadow of anybody in show business!' "

Sidney was right, of course. Even Bosley Crowther, the often-harsh critic from the *New York Times*, had some kind words for Sinatra: "Mr. Sinatra does rather nicely — and we'd be the first to say so if he did not — by such slightly sticky numbers as 'I Fall in Love Too Easily' and 'What Makes the Sunset?' " Crowther's backhanded compliment for the Jule Styne–Sammy Cahn tune, "I Fall in Love Too Easily" did manage to miss the mark. Far from being "slightly sticky," the song has become a standard today; it also brought Styne and Cahn their second Oscar nomination of the year (the other was for "Anywhere," from *Tonight and Every Night* — see page 79). Surprisingly, the hit recording of the day was made not by Sinatra, but by Mel Tormé; it peaked at number 20 and charted for only a week. In the years since the film's release, many recording artists have included the love ballad in their repertoire.

In addition to the strong presence of Sinatra (who proved in this picture that he could act as well as sing) the popularity of *Anchors Aweigh* can also be attributed to a very special production number with co-star Gene Kelly. But top-billed Kelly didn't do this number with Sinatra, or even with female lead Kathryn Grayson. Instead, he did it with Jerry, the animated mouse from the "Tom and Jerry" cartoons. In a number hailed for its innovation, little Jerry kicked up his cartoon heels for a bright dance sequence with the live actor Kelly.

It was actually the fourth or fifth time this sort of gimmick had appeared on film; Max Fleischer had done it back in the '20s in his "Out of the Inkwell" cartoons, and Walt Disney had been doing it for years. The following year Disney would again show off the technique in *Song of the South* (see page 93), and the studio would successfully reinvent itself decades later by combining animated and live action in such films as *Mary Poppins* (1964) and *Who Framed Roger Rabbit* (1988).

Anchors Aweigh was nominated for Best Actor (Gene Kelly), Best Color Cinematography, and Best Scoring of a Musical Picture, the only Oscar it won.

---

1. Parkyarkarkus's real name was Harry Einstein. His sons, Bob and Albert, both went into show business. Bob Einstein became a television writer best known for his efforts on "The Smothers Brothers Comedy Hour" and later for portraying the character Super Dave. Albert, for obvious reasons, changed his last name to Brooks and became a well known film actor, director, and writer.

I'LL BUY THAT DREAM

Music by Allie Wrubel; lyrics by Herb Magidson
From *Sing Your Way Home*

Sing Your Way Home was a cross between the "Let's put on a show" genre and an end-of-the-war celebration. The thin storyline involved the rescue of a group of French orphans, all of whom, rather conveniently, were entertainers. These talented youngsters were supposedly trapped in France for four years awaiting transportation home. Eventually the kids broadcast a show from the homeward-bound ship, hence the film's title and *raison d'être*.

Songs by Allie Wrubel and Herb Magidson predominated, and everyone — critics and record buyers alike — soon agreed that the biggest hit from the film was "I'll Buy That Dream," sung by young Marcy McGuire in the movie. Harry James and His Orchestra released a version of the song several weeks before the film's premiere. With vocal by Kitty Kallen, this rendition peaked at number two, staying on the charts for 14 weeks. Two weeks earlier, Helen Forrest and Dick Haymes had released their duet version, which also peaked at number two, while yet another recording, this one by Hal McIntyre, reached the number eight position and stayed on the charts for five weeks.

Other songs in the film included "Heaven Is a Place Called Home," "Who Did It?" and "Seven O'Clock in the Morning," all by Wrubel and Magidson. One seemingly incongruous number was a rather misplaced inclusion of Albert Hay Mallotte's musical classic, "The Lord's Prayer." Although beautifully performed by a 15-year-old named Donna Lee, the religious standard was out of its element in the film.

The musical sensation of the picture was fourth-billed actress Anne Jeffreys, then just 22 years old. She received the lioness's share of praise for her performance: "A sweet eyeful of blonde with a good voice, enough expressions for the acting job and an effective knack for selling a song," raved *Variety*, while the *Hollywood Reporter* said, "The surprise of the cast is the impression registered by Anne Jeffreys, who looks like a million and ably takes care of the songs allotted her. Possibly RKO is over-looking a real bet in Miss Jeffreys." That situation was soon remedied, and the former Powers model subsequently went on to star as the lead in scores of movies and plays. In the early '50s, she co-starred with her second husband, Robert Sterling,

in the "Topper" TV series. In the 1990s, she continued to appear as guest star on numerous television shows.

Ironically, the actor given top billing in the film, Jack Haley, received less attention than the female leads. Haley, who was best remembered as the Tin Man in 1939's *The Wizard of Oz*, shared the comedy spotlight in *Sing Your Way Home* with both Maguire and Jeffreys, but as the newspaperman charged with chaperoning the returning youngsters, he never seemed to rise about the material the way the two ladies did.

LINDA

Music and lyrics by Ann Ronell
From *The Story of GI Joe*

In the unenlightened days of the first half of the 20th century, everyone knew that music composition, especially for Broadway and the movies, was a man's realm. Female composers were a rarity, few and far between. The exception was a young composer named Ann Ronell, who broke new ground for her gender in the field of popular music. Her film work began in 1934 with the little-remembered *Down to Their Last Yacht*. That same decade, she also wrote the hits "Baby's Birthday Party," "Rain on the Roof," and the song that would become her best-known tune, "Willow, Weep for Me." It was the latter that landed her a job with Walt Disney Studios, where she wrote the popular lyrics for "Who's Afraid of the Big Bad Wolf?"

Ronell became the first woman to score a film, writing and conducting complete scores for such pictures as *Champagne Waltz* (1937), *Algiers,* (1939), and in 1945, *The Story of GI Joe*. For that film, she wrote a tune called "Linda," and she became the first woman nominated for an Oscar as a solo songwriter.

Ronell's "Linda" is often confused by various musical sources with another song of the same title (words and music by Jack Lawrence — "When I go to sleep, I never count sheep . . ."). Some sources try to partner the two composers, unaware that these are two totally different songs. Adding to the confusion is the fact that the two songs were released within two years of each other — Ronell's "Linda" in 1945, Lawrence's in 1947. In the film *The Story of GI Joe*, Ronell's "Linda" is sung by the dreaded "Axis Sally," who was a real propagandizing, sexy-voiced, unseen *femme fatale* used by the Nazis and their pals to subvert the Allied troops. In the movie, the GIs are preparing for battle the next day, when Axis Sally comes on the radio singing the plaintive, romantic ballad, "Linda," designed to make the men homesick with words like "Light for me a cigarette . . . I'll wait for you," and so on. In the scene, one of the GIs plays the melody on his guitar (without singing it), as if about to be caught in Sally's treacherous web.

The Story of GI Joe was inspired by the true stories filed by war correspondent Ernie Pyle, played by Burgess Meredith in the film. Superbly directed in pseudo-documentary style by William Wellman, the movie received several additional Oscar nominations, including Best Supporting Actor (Robert Mitchum) and Best Screenplay (Leopold Atlas, Guy Endore, and Philip Stevenson). Ronell herself received an additional nomination, for Best Score, along with co-composer Louis Applebaum.

Although she did not win any Academy Awards during her long and illustrious career, Ronell continued writing for films as well as for the Metropolitan Opera and the Los Angeles and San Francisco light opera associations, writing English librettos and adapting scores from such operettas as *The Gypsy Baron* and *The Chocolate Soldier.* She died in 1994, at the age of 85.

LOVE LETTERS

Music by Victor Young;
   lyrics by Edward Heyman
From *Love Letters*

Most literati will recognize the name of novelist Ayn Rand as the author of such classics as *The Fountainhead* (1943) and *Atlas Shrugged* (1957). Her writings stirred and inspired a generation of young conservative thinkers, creating an almost cultlike following. Yet many of Rand's fans might be surprised to learn that she also lent her talents to screenwriting. In 1945, for example, the Russian-born naturalized American author adapted Chris Massie's novel *Love Letters* for the screen.

The film starred Jennifer Jones and Joseph Cotten in a tearjerker about two British army officers on the Italian front, one of whom (Cotten) writes beautiful love letters on his friend's behalf to the friend's fiancée (Jones) back in England. The girl falls in love with the letters and their writer. She marries the man she thinks

has been her correspondent, then learns they were written by another and soon becomes disillusioned with her husband, who turns out to be a drunken lout who beats her. The girl's foster mother saves the day by stabbing the crazed, inebriated husband to death, all of which proves so traumatic that the girl is left with a case of amnesia.

But wait! There's more melodrama here, the kind Ayn Rand could really sink her teeth into. The older woman suffers a stroke and loses her ability to speak, while Jones is tried for murder and sentenced to prison because her foster mother can't speak in her defense. (Didn't anyone think to get her written statement?) Eventually, the other soldier — the letter writer — returns to England, falls in love with and marries Jones, and straightens everything out for the obligatory happy ending.

Happy, that is, for all but screenwriter Rand. Critics, although generous in their praise for the cast (especially Jones, who was trying to shake her "good girl" image from 1944's *The Song of Bernadette),* generally panned Rand, the direction, the editing — you name it. "A worse script or less expert direction has seldom been tossed at an innocent star's head," wrote Bosley Crowther in the *New York Times,* while *Variety* noted that Rand's adaptation "fails to achieve a proper distinction between theatrical artifice and reality . . . Also, the first couple of reels could have been edited better; the continuity has too static a quality in the opening minutes." The *Variety* reviewer, however, did like the production in general, with praise for the "fine directional job by William Dieterie and music score by Victor Young."

Ah yes, the music. Although this was not a musical, there was a title song, "Love Letters," composed by Young, with lyrics by Edward Heyman. It became Paramount's entry into Oscar contention for 1945 and did rather well as a hit single. Dick Haymes released a version in September, 1945, shortly after the film's premiere. It peaked at number 11 but charted only for that one week. The tune enjoyed a resurgence of popularity in the '60s, with Ketty Lester's version in February, 1962, peaking at number five and charting for 14 weeks. Four years later, Elvis Presley, released a version of "Love Letters" that peaked at number 19.

Love Letters received three additional Oscar nominations: for Best Actress (Jones), Best Black-and-White Interior Decoration, and Best Scoring of a Dramatic or Comedy Picture.

MORE AND MORE

Music by Jerome Kern; lyrics by E.Y. Harburg
From *Can't Help Singing*

Deanna Durbin had been the young darling of the 1930s, a startling talent who began starring in films at the age of 15. Although no longer an ingenue by 1944, she was still capable of pulling in a crowd to hear her lovely soprano voice. Released late that year, *Can't Help Singing* was her first Western, somewhat of a departure for her, but certainly not a stretch. She had sung in two prior films with Best Song nominations: in 1940, when she played a Tyrolean peasant girl in *Spring Parade* and sang "Waltzing in the Clouds" (see page 41), and in the 1943 film *Hers to Hold*, singing "Say a Prayer for the Boys over There" (see page 63). In *Can't Help Singing* she played a pre–Civil War debutante who goes west to California to pursue — what else? — a man. Durbin didn't realize it at the time, but *Can't Help Singing* marked the midpoint in her career; by 1948, she realized that she could indeed help singing, and took an early retirement, at age 27.

With *Can't Help Singing,* Durbin fans at last got to see the coloratura in full color, this being her Technicolor debut. They weren't disappointed. Deanna sang several Jerome Kern tunes, either solo or with her leading man, Robert Paige. Critic Bosley Crowther of the *New York Times* heralded the 1944 Christmas-released picture and claimed the "angels hit some vocal competition . . . when the caroling concession was in the hands of melodious Deanna Durbin . . . Miss Durbin's generosity with songs was none the less seasonal and triumphant than that of the seraphic choir."

The hit of the picture was "More and More," one of the best songs she ever introduced in her movies, and it appropriately received a 1945 Oscar nomination for Best Song for Kern and his latest lyricist partner, E.Y. Harburg. (Although released at the end of 1944, Academy rules at that time allowed a year-end release to be nominated the following year.) In the film, Deanna sings the love song "More and More" to Paige in a romantic moonlight setting.

"More and More" became a hit for two recording artists. Tommy Dorsey and His Orchestra had a version that peaked at number 10 and spent three weeks on the charts, while a newcomer named Perry Como made a record of the tune that peaked at number 14. The song spent 15 weeks on radio's "Your Hit Parade,"

and was the last Jerome Kern song to become a popular hit in his lifetime.

The title song, "Can't Help Singing," was perhaps the most fun, sung by Durbin in a huge wooden bathtub, shoulder-deep in suds, and joined — in song, that is — by Paige, in similar hot water on the other side of the wall. The film occasionally found itself in hot water with critics because of its not-so-subtle homage to the popular Broadway hit musical *Oklahoma*. One song, "Cal-i-for-ni-ay" cut it just a little too close in its parallel to "Oklahoma," inviting the inevitable — and not always flattering — comparisons.

SLEIGH RIDE IN JULY

Music by James Van Heusen;
lyrics by Johnny Burke
From *Belle of the Yukon*

No one would ever accuse Gypsy Rose Lee of being a serious actress. But the burlesque queen of the '30s, whose life story would one day be popularized in the biomusical *Gypsy,* did occasionally lend her talents to the screen. She appeared during the 1930s under half of her given name of Rose Louise Hovick, dropping the "Rose" when she appeared in *You Can't Have Everything* (1937) and *My Lucky Star* (1938). But acting was not in

Charles Winniger and Dinah Shore discuss a scene from *Belle of the Yukon.*

Louise Hovick's stars, so the strip-tease artist returned to the screen under the name fans knew her best — Gypsy Rose Lee — in *Stage Door Canteen* (1943).

It wasn't much of a part, this now-you-see-'em-now-you-don't parade of stars on celluloid, and in 1944 she was ready to try again for a film career under her more familiar Gypsy moniker. This time, success smiled on her as she received second billing while playing the title role in the semi-satirical *Belle of the Yukon.*

Gypsy's male co-star was Randolph Scott, in the role of Honest John Calhoun, a Klondike saloon keeper whose gal Belle attempts to set him on the straight and narrow path. Billed third was Dinah Shore, down from the second position she'd occupied the previous year in *Up in Arms,* but she apparently wasn't up in arms about it. The writers worked in a romance for her, too, as she becomes involved with a piano player, a situation that naturally gives her an opportunity to do lots of singing.

Johnny Burke and Jimmy Van Heusen were prevailed upon to create some original tunes for the film, including "Ev'ry Girl Is Diff'rent," "Like Someone in Love," and "Sleigh Ride in July," which received an Academy Award nomination. (The film was also nominated for Best Scoring of a Musical Picture.) Other tunes in the film were "I Can't Tell You Why I Love You, But I Do," by Will D. Cobb and Gus Edwards, and "Little Johnny Dugan," by Thomas Le Mack and Andrew Mack.

"Sleigh Ride in July" was a pop hit for a number of recording artists, including Shore herself. Her version peaked in the number eight position, but charted for only one week. Bing Crosby, perhaps still dreaming of white Christmases, rode a "Sleigh Ride" to the number 14 position in February of 1945, while Tommy Dorsey's version peaked at number 15 and Les Brown's Band made number 18.

Danny Kaye teams up with diva Alice Mock backstage at the Met while evading gangsters in *Wonder Man.*

SO IN LOVE

Music by David Rose; lyrics by Leo Robin
From *Wonder Man*

Wonder Man was Danny Kaye's second film, made immediately following the success of his first, *Up in Arms*. The title couldn't have been more apropos; Kaye seemed capable of doing everything. He sang, danced, and clowned; he did pantomime, impressions, and incredible glottal gymnastics that few, if any, have ever equaled.

For this new film, Kaye got to play twins in a tried-but-true plot involving the usual sort of confusion that takes place in that situation. One of the brothers dies at the hands of thugs early on, but his "spirit" continues to guide the hapless remaining brother. As *Variety* put it, "There's no mistaking that without [Kaye], this film would be decidedly commonplace."

Generally, the musical numbers in Kaye's films were written by his wife, Sylvia Fine. In *Wonder Man*, she did most of the specialty musical numbers, while the more serious songwriting was left to David Rose and Leo Robin. Their "So in Love" was performed in an elaborate nightclub production number by the ubiquitous Goldwyn Girls in diaphanous, windblown Grecian gowns. It became a complex, protracted dance number, and although the song was not very singable, there was a great tap performance by the very athletic Vera-Ellen. *Wonder Man* was her first picture, and although she wasn't Kaye's main love interest — that role would fall to blonde bombshell Virginia Mayo — Vera-Ellen received rave notices and predictions for a thriving career.

Vera-Ellen was actually born Vera-Ellen Rohe. She said her first name was given to her because "my mother saw the hyphenated name on a theater marquee in a dream several nights before I was born." In 1943, when she was only 17, Samuel Goldwyn caught her in a Broadway revival of *A Connecticut Yankee* and signed her to a Hollywood contract.

She would appear with Kaye again the following year in *The Kid from Brooklyn* (but with Virginia Mayo still playing romantic co-lead with Kaye). Later films saw her dancing with the likes of Gene Kelly, Fred Astaire, and Donald O'Connor, and she again co-starred with Kaye, along with Bing Crosby and Rosemary Clooney, in *White Christmas* (1954).

Wonder Man relied upon the magic of special effects to replicate Kaye into twin brothers, and the producers were rewarded for their outstanding work with the 1945 Oscar for Best Special Effects. In addition to the nomination for Best Song for "So in Love," the film also received nominations for Best Scoring of a Musical Picture (by Lou Forbes and Ray Heindorf) and Best Sound.

SOME SUNDAY MORNING

Music by Ray Heindorf and M.K. Jerome;
lyrics by Ted Koehler
From *San Antonio*

The story of a fighting Texas rancher who comes to town to settle a score with the boss of a gang of cattle rustlers, *San Antonio* was one of the screen's most expensive pictures to date, with Warner Bros. spending a couple of cool million on what was really a fairly routine Western. For their money, they got glorious Technicolor — Westerns up to this time had generally been made in basic black-and-white — and one big name: Errol Flynn.

Having arrived in Hollywood from his native Tasmania 10 years earlier, Flynn had mostly played heroic, swashbuckling types prior filming *San Antonio*. He'd been Captain Blood, Robin Hood, the Sea Hawk, the Earl of Essex, General Custer — and those were just for starters. Offscreen, his life was somewhat less colorful — he suffered from recurring bouts of malaria, had a heart defect and a touch of TB, and brooded over the fact that he'd been unceremoniously turned down as 4F by every branch of the service. To remedy this situation and puff up his macho image of a man who busied himself by buckling as many swashes offscreen as on, he pursued the ladies, often landing in hot water, or worse. In 1942, he was thought to have compromised the virtues of two underage teenagers aboard his yacht, and although he was acquitted of the charges, the catch phrase "in like Flynn" swept the country in direct proportion to his exploits.

San Antonio was not his first Western, and the heroic leading man was certainly a role suited to Flynn's talents, a good deal of which consisted of his dashing good looks and charisma. Nimbly assisting him was Alexis Smith, his female co-star and dance partner. Flynn proved that he was an accomplished dancer, flawlessly twirling Smith through a tricky sequence patterned after a popular Mexican dance. But most surprising of all, Flynn made his screen vocal debut by crooning a Mexican folk ballad to Smith, and even strummed the guitar for the first time on film.

Smith introduced two songs in the movie — "Somewhere in Monterey," and "Some Sunday Morning," the Heindorf-Jerome-Koehler tune that was nominated for an Oscar. Although the nominated song did have some mild popularity in its day, it really wasn't very fresh. The melody was only so-so, and, as described by Philip Furia in his book *The Poets of Tin Pan Alley,* the Koehler lyric came pretty close to the words of "For Me and My Gal," "right down to such thinly disguised borrowings as 'Bells will be chiming an old melody, 'spec'lly for someone and me.' " Not surprisingly, no bells were chiming for "Some Sunday Morning" and Oscar, either.

ON THE ATCHISON, TOPEKA AND SANTA FE

**Music by Harry Warren; lyrics by Johnny Mercer
From *The Harvey Girls***

If you had a railroad and needed a song, Harry Warren was your man. At least, that was what people were jokingly saying after Warren's tune, along with Johnny Mercer's lyrics, took top Oscar honors for 1946. His first tribute to trains had been "Chattanooga Choo Choo," which in 1941 was nominated for, but didn't receive, the Academy Award. Then, in 1945, he began working on a new railroad song, "On the Atchison, Topeka and Santa Fe." And if ever there was a railroad in need of a song, it was this one. Its very name alone sounded like the chug-chugging of an Iron Horse. By the time Engine Number 49 whistled down the line, everyone in the country was on board and humming in time to its clickity-clack beat.

The song almost didn't get written. Originally, *The Harvey Girls,* the movie in which Judy Garland introduced "On the Atchison . . ." was not even planned as a musical. According to director George Sidney, speaking

in a 1993 radio interview, "It started out as a straight picture for Clark Gable, a Western, and the studio fooled around with it, and it didn't work. Then someone got an idea — maybe we could have Clark Gable and Judy Garland together." Eventually Gable was dropped entirely, but Garland remained as the star once the story (based on the book by Samuel Hopkins Adams) was turned into a full-blown musical. Others added to the cast included John Hodiak as the gambling hall proprietor (and object of Judy's affections), Angela Lansbury as a kind of "Gunsmoke/Miss Kitty" madam — never stated as such — plus Ray Bolger, Preston Foster, Virginia O'Brien, Kenny Baker (his first film after a three-year hiatus), Marjorie Main, Chill Wills, and an eleventh-billed Cyd Charisse.

The story of a group of intrepid waitresses working for the Fred Harvey chain and coincidentally helping to tame the Wild West has become a classic (and in the 1990s was frequently seen in its newly restored Technicolor splendor on Ted Turner's TNT cable channel). As the picture opens, we are immediately immersed into the mood of the West with the spectacular production number featuring "On the Atchison . . ." All the stops are pulled out as separate women's and men's choruses sing, dance, and even mimic the movement of the train's wheels turning in big circles. The song is reiterated throughout the film and explodes into a final tap dance number by Bolger.

Mercer, along with the Pied Pipers, recorded a hit version of the tune. His rendition peaked at Number One, stayed atop the charts for eight weeks, and remained on the *Billboard* charts for 19 weeks strong. Others with hit recordings of the song included Bing Crosby (peaking at number three), Tommy Dorsey (number six), Garland (number 10), and Tommy Tucker (also number 10).

Although "On the Atchison, Topeka and Santa Fe" naturally received the most attention, there were several other noteworthy Warren/Mercer tunes in the picture. "In the Valley Where the Evening Sun Goes Down," "Wait and See," "It's a Great Big World," and the one preferred by many critics, "The Wild, Wild West." The film received a Best Scoring of a Musical Picture nomination from the Motion Picture Academy.

Part of the sequence featuring "On the Atchison . . ." was included in the 1974 MGM release *That's Entertainment!* But better still was the third installment of these films, *That's Entertainment! III,* released in early 1994. Although it had only a limited run in movie theaters, it was soon released on videocassette. It included quite a treat for Judy Garland and *Harvey Girls* fans — the restoration of a "lost" sequence called "March of the Dogies," cut from the original picture.

ALL THROUGH THE DAY

**Music by Jerome Kern;
lyrics by Oscar Hammerstein II
From *Centennial Summer***

With the commercial and critical success of MGM's 1944 hit, *Meet Me in St. Louis,* it wasn't long before the inevitable cloning process by other studios began. The concept seemed simple enough: You get two young, preferably beautiful female stars to play maturing sisters, deck them out in colorful costumes, add some comedy, a touch of an international World's Fair–type Exhibition, and toss in some memorable tunes. For its entry into the "Gee, isn't my home town wonderful and isn't it great to live in the 19th century" derby, 20th Century-Fox trotted out a filmusical called *Centennial Summer.* The title tells it all; the story took place in the summer (hard to dance and sing when encumbered in fur coats), during our nation's centennial celebration in 1876. And for a touch of authenticity and class, the story was set in Philadelphia, the city where the Declaration of Independence was signed.

It didn't work. Yes, the costumes were beautiful, the sun shone brightly on the happy stars (including Cornel Wilde, Constance Bennett, and Dorothy Gish) in their glory days of yesteryear, and the songs were singable, at least by the cast. But somehow during all this, the script got neglected. In fact, it barely existed. "This fable of a Philadelphia family is as studied and conventional an affair as its memorable predecessor was original and full of joy," groaned the *New York Times.* "It limps along heavily and slowly where the other galloped and danced, and it has no more genuine flavor than a cheap lemon lollipop."

Starring in the principal roles of the sisters were Jeanne Crain and Linda Darnell, two beauties with too little voice. Louanne Hogan sang on the soundtrack for Jeanne Crain, but she was still no Judy Garland. In fact, nearly all of the seven principals had to have their singing parts dubbed, one of the major problems with this picture. Crain's songs, written by heavy hitters Jerome Kern and Leo Robin, included the plaintive "In

Love in Vain" and the brighter "The Right Romance."

"In Love in Vain" actually landed on "Your Hit Parade" and lasted for 13 weeks. But the big hit of the movie — and the Oscar-nominated tune — was a song called "All Through the Day." For this tune, Kern partnered with Oscar Hammerstein II, and it turned out to be the best song in the film, if not at the Academy Awards ceremony, where it was sung by Dinah Shore.

Although introduced by Larry Stevens in the picture, the popular recordings were released by others. Frank Sinatra could always be counted on for a hit, and his "All Through the Day" peaked at number seven and charted for three weeks. Perry Como, whose star had begun rising unabated a few years earlier, had a number eight hit with the tune, accompanied by André Kostelanetz's Orchestra, while Margaret Whiting's version peaked at number 11. The flip side of her record was the film's other popular song, "In Love in Vain," which also proved to be a best-seller, peaking at number 12 and charting for three weeks.

Sadly, Jerome Kern never learned of his hit tunes. During November of 1945, while *Centennial Summer* was still shooting, Kern collapsed on a New York street, the victim of a cerebral hemorrhage. Two days later, he lapsed into a coma and died. He was 60 years old.

I CAN'T BEGIN TO TELL YOU

**Music by James Monaco; lyrics by Mack Gordon
From *The Dolly Sisters***

Loosely based on the vaudeville careers of two real-life Hungarian sisters who later emigrated to the United States, *The Dolly Sisters* was more fiction than true biography. Darryl F. Zanuck, chief of 20th Century-Fox, decided that platinum blondes, for example, would look better on film than brunettes, as the actual singing and dancing siblings had been. For his leading lady, Zanuck had signed the ever-popular pin-up queen Betty Grable. She had the legs, the footwork, the voice, and the star quality to make her the perfect Jenny Dolly, the older sister.

Next, Zanuck desperately tried to lure Alice Faye out of retirement to co-star with Grable as the younger of the pair, but Faye would have none of it. In stepped George Jessel, the film's producer, himself an entertainer someone once dubbed the "Toastmaster Gen-

June Haver and Betty Grable star as *The Dolly Sisters,* a biopic about two sibling vaudevillians.

eral." He suggested that Zanuck take a look at newcomer June Haver, a complete unknown to film audiences and his choice for the perfect actress to play younger sister Rosie. Zanuck agreed, but Grable wasn't so sure about working with this untried young actress. Eventually, Jessel managed to convince her that it would work, and Grable finally accepted her new co-star (they later became rivals).

Although Haver was just beginning her film career, it wouldn't be long before she would be pulling in the biggest audiences of any female star. This fact would not be lost on Zanuck, who eventually upped the budgets of her films by 33 percent in order to film only in Technicolor.

The Dolly Sisters was a musical comprised mostly of old songs; tunes from 11 solo or songwriting teams were used in the film's almost constant musical score. One new song, written especially for the picture by James Monaco and Mack Gordon, was sandwiched between the old standards: "I Can't Begin to Tell You" was a medium-paced love song, introduced in the movie by Grable and later reprised by her and male lead John Payne. Even this song wasn't entirely original, however — it was derivative of a 1906 number called "When Love Is Young in Springtime," by Rida Johnson Young and Melville Ellis. Yet it was sufficiently changed from its source to qualify as a new song in its own right, at least in the eyes of the Academy of

Motion Picture Arts and Sciences, which allowed its inclusion among the 1946 Oscar nominations (the picture was actually released late in November, 1945).

Bing Crosby released a Decca recording of the song one week after the film's debut. It shot to the Number One position and held onto that spot for six weeks, remaining on the charts for a total of 20 weeks. Grable wanted to record the song with her husband, bandleader Harry James, but her Fox contract prevented her from releasing commercial records. She did it anyway, under the pseudonym Ruth Haag. Their version peaked at number five. Others who covered "I Can't Begin to Tell You" were Andy Russell, whose rendition peaked at number seven, and Sammy Kaye's Orchestra, whose recording peaked at number nine.

OLE BUTTERMILK SKY

**Music by Hoagy Carmichael;
    lyrics by Jack Brooks**
From *Canyon Passage*

Oregon was the setting for *Canyon Passage,* a horse opera in the truest sense of the term. Everything one would expect from a Western was there — expansive outdoor Technicolor scenery, hard-drinking outlaws, high-stakes gambling, hostile Indians, action aplenty, and feminine pulchritude in the shape of Susan Hayward. She headed an all-star cast, which helped attract audiences to this Universal shoot-'em-up. Stars included Dana Andrews, Brian Donlevy, Ward Bond,

Andy Devine (and his two sons, Tad and Dennis, playing his two sons), a very young Lloyd Bridges, and even Hoagy Carmichael as a wandering minstrel.

Carmichael had been composing songs for films as well as for top artists like Bing Crosby, Louis Armstrong, Red Nichols, and many others since the 1920s. With his classic "Star Dust," written in 1929, he struck gold dust. The song has since become one of the most recorded numbers in history. Later, Carmichael partnered with such popular lyricists as Johnny Mercer and Frank Loesser. He began appearing in films featuring his songs starting with *To Have and Have Not* (1944). In 1946, he appeared in *The Best Years of Our Lives,* as well as *Canyon Passage.*

In *Canyon Passage,* Carmichael plunked out a number of tunes, the best of which, "Ole Buttermilk Sky," received an Oscar nomination, the only song from a non-musical to do so in 1946. Carmichael not only sang, but also wrote the music for the song, with Jack Brooks providing the lyrics. (True to form, Carmichael even performed his nominated tune at the Oscar ceremony that year.) It proved to be a breakaway hit whose popularity turned it into a standard, still heard with some frequency even today. Recording artists fought over the right to record it almost as much as the cowboys and Indians in the film in which it first appeared. During the fall of 1946, there were four different versions of the tune in the top 10, and six in the top 20.

First out of the chute was Kay Kyser. His recording featured a vocal by future talk-show host Mike Douglas, and it reached the Number One position, where it stayed for two weeks out of a 19-week chart run. Not to

Dana Andrews and Susan Hayward in a scene from *Canyon Passage.*

be left out, Carmichael recorded a version of his own song, which peaked at number two just two weeks later. Paul Weston's cover peaked at number six in early November, and by mid-November Helen Carroll's version had peaked in the number seven position. Danny O'Neil's recording, released in December, made number 12, and Connee Boswell had a number 14 hit with the tune. Finally, 15 years later, "Ole Buttermilk Sky" became a surprise hit when Bill Black's Combo recorded it and released their new version on June 5, 1961. The old tune reached the number 25 position and charted for an eight weeks — no small achievement for a song as long in the tooth as this one had become in 1961.

Although "Ole Buttermilk Sky" was wildly popular, it would be five more years before Hoagy Carmichael was able to take home an Oscar (for "In the Cool, Cool, Cool of the Evening" — see page 112).

YOU KEEP COMING BACK LIKE A SONG

Music and lyrics by Irving Berlin
From *Blue Skies*

There was nothing blue about the skies over Irving Berlin's talented head. He proved once again that he still had it, four years after he'd checked out of the *Holiday Inn* (see page 50). In fact, *Blue Skies,* although not technically a sequel, had enough elements in common with that original picture to qualify it at least as *Holiday Inn*–Berlin redux in terms of songs. In all, there were 22 Berlin tunes, mostly classics — the title song, "Blue Skies," and well as the ever-popular "White Christmas" (first introduced in *Holiday Inn),* "How Deep Is the Ocean?", "All By Myself," "Always," "Say It Isn't So," "Russian Lullaby," "Heat Wave," "Puttin' on

Bing Crosby and Fred Astaire, together again, in *Blue Skies.*

the Ritz," "I'll See You in C-U-B-A," "A Couple of Song and Dance Men," and the ever-popular "This Is the Army." In addition, there was a clever new tune that received an Academy Award nomination, and whose title might easily have been referring to the composer himself: "You Keep Coming Back Like a Song."

Bing Crosby kept coming back to Irving Berlin musicals, which was certainly part of Paramount Pictures's plan. So did Fred Astaire. And once again, they were indeed "a couple of song and dance men" competing (as before in *Holiday Inn)*, for the same girl. This time it was Joan Caulfield, who of course preferred Bing over the hapless Fred. Never mind. Fred knocked everyone's socks off with his fabulous "Puttin' on the Ritz" routine. If it was formulaic, it worked wonders at the box office, pulling Paramount out of a slump; along with *The Paleface, Blue Skies* became the biggest color hit of the decade. It was also the number five film in North American rentals for 1946, netting $5.7 million at the box office.

Three recording artists had hits with "You Keep Coming Back Like a Song." Dinah Shore's version reached the number five position and charted for three weeks. Jo Stafford's recording hit number 11, while Crosby's own recording peaked at a surprisingly modest number 12.

Crosby had been expected to sing "I Can't Begin to Tell You" from *The Dolly Sisters* (see page 89) at the 1946 Academy Awards ceremony the following March. But Bing startled the program's producer, Mervyn LeRoy, by bowing out, citing live performance jitters, and Dick Haymes agreed to step in. And although it was Bing who had had a hit recording of "You Keep Coming Back Like a Song," his pal Frank Sinatra was signed to sing that tune at the Oscars. But just a few days before show time, Sinatra, too, declined to appear, claiming that he was simply "following in Crosby's footsteps." Frantically LeRoy searched for a last-minute performer and came up with Andy Russell, a then-current singing sensation. (As if these troubles weren't enough, Judy Garland also got last-minute stage fright and decided she couldn't sing "On the Atchison, Topeka and Santa Fe," requiring Dinah Shore, who'd been set to sing "All Through the Day," to do double duty.) Despite all the confusion, the Awards ceremony went off rather well, although Berlin lost that year to Harry Warren and Johnny Mercer for "On the Atchison, Topeka and Santa Fe" (see page 88).

1947

And the winner is...

ZIP-A-DEE-DOO-DAH

Music by Allie Wrubel; lyrics by Ray Gilbert From *Song of the South*

The 1947 Academy Award–winning song said it best: Zip-a-dee-doo-dah! *Song of the South* was primo Walt Disney.

This purported children's film, with its obvious appeal to "children of all ages," was based on Joel Chandler Harris's tales of "Uncle Remus." It combined live action with almost other-worldly Technicolor critters and scenery in a way only Uncle Walt and his artists could. And what could be more joyful than James Baskett, portraying the dignified, kindly, fun-loving, and sensible Uncle Remus, parceling out his moralistic tales of Brers Rabbit, Fox, and Bear in a perfect marriage of live action and animation.

The Oscar-winning song comes early in the film, as Uncle Remus strolls down a country lane transfigured into an animated world of dazzling color. Disneyesque birds and animals join him as he sings "Zip-A-Dee-Doo-Dah," setting the happy mood for the remainder of the film. When he tells us "It's the truth, it's actual, everything is satisfactual," we know this is a man to be trusted and admired. The film's two small children knew it — they respected his wisdom more than their own mother's. Everyone loved Uncle Remus. Well, almost everyone.

When the picture first opened, there was a hue and cry from the NAACP, a voice to be reckoned with even back in 1946 (the picture was released in November of '46, but submitted to the Academy for consideration as a 1947 release). Walter White, the executive secretary, told the press, "Making use of the beautiful Uncle Remus folklore, *Song of the South* unfortunately gives the impression of an idyllic master–slave relationship, which is a distortion of the facts." In reality, this was not quite the truth, not quite "satisfactual." While the film did show a white-black/employer-employee relationship, the story does not depict slavery in the South, but rather takes place in the postbellum period. Walt Disney remained true to the Uncle Remus stories, and indeed, Uncle Remus himself is the only sympathetic adult character in the movie. The mother comes off as petulant and opinionated, while the closest parental figure, Uncle Remus, is the film's role model and true hero.

After the picture's initial run, the Walt Disney Studios succumbed to all the brouhaha and pulled *Song of the South* from further release. In 1986, however, they decided it might be time to reissue the picture. In taking it off the shelf once more, they discovered that the American collective consciousness had matured a bit since the late '40s. The film was well received, exceeding all expectations at the box office. The take in North American rentals, combined with the total from the previous release, made *Song of the South* the top box office hit for 1946 films.

"Zip-A-Dee-Doo-Dah" never became a Number One hit song, but its popularity proved enduring. When the film was first shown, Johnny Mercer and the Pied Pipers combined in a version of the catchy tune, which peaked in the number eight position and lasted eight weeks on the charts. (They also performed the song at the 1947 Academy Awards ceremony.) Sammy

Kaye's cover peaked at number 11, as did the one cut by the Modernaires. The song was resurrected in 1962 by Bob B. Soxx and the Blue Jeans. Session musicians for this version were Leon Russell, Glen Campbell, Nino Tempo, and Bill Strange, with lead singer Darlene Love. Their recording, produced by Phil Spector, peaked at number eight and stayed on the charts longer than any of the 1946 and '47 releases — a healthy 13 weeks — proving that, after all those years, there was still plenty of zip left in the old doo-dah.

A GAL IN CALICO

Music by Arthur Schwartz; lyrics by Leo Robin
From *The Time, The Place and The Girl*

Warner Bros. decided there was still some life in the tried-and-true "Let's put on a show" theme, so the producers there dusted off the weary idea and trotted it out one more time. *The Time, The Place and The*

From left foreground: James Baskett, Hattie McDaniel, Bobby Driscoll, Lucille Watson, and Ruth Warrick star in Walt Disney's *Song of the South.*

Girl may have had those three elements, but it was missing a crucial one — a solid story. True, the studio spent a lot of money dressing up the picture in Technicolor and giving it a swinging score by Arthur Schwartz and Leo Robin, and they even added some of the finest and liveliest talent of the day, including Dennis Morgan, Jack Carson, singer Janis Paige, and Alan Hale, plus Carmen Cavallero and His Orchestra, Chandra Kaly and His Dancers, and a specialty act called the Condos Brothers.

Critics loudly panned it. The *New York Times* reviewer, Bosley Crowther, wrote: "[It's] a hackneyed and mirthless affair in which a handful of farceurs and musicians clattered about for an hour and two-thirds . . . The combined and elaborate efforts of everybody . . . who arranged the fancy stuff, have resulted in one of those pictures that you forget even while you're watching it." Not exactly the sort of notices that the producers had hoped to receive, especially for the busy 1946 Christmas season when this picture was released (Academy rules at the time allowed a late-year release to compete for awards in the following year). Nevertheless, there was some veiled praise for the cast members, and for two of the Arthur Schwartz–Leo Robin songs — "Oh, But I Do" and "A Gal in Calico."

The latter was good enough to receive an Oscar nomination. In his in-depth technical book, *American Popular Song*, Alec Wilder writes that "A Gal in Calico" was "a great rhythm song . . . The song has a marvelous, written-at-the-same-time verse. The chorus does, with great style, precisely what it sets out to do and even goes beyond the call of duty in its last measures . . . Cheery, strong, swinging, professional. It's a good song to sing and it's a perfect big band piece."

Back in 1947, many recording artists and big bandsmen must have realized this. Johnny Mercer waxed the tune for Capitol Records; it reached number five on the *Billboard* pop charts and charted for 10 weeks. Tex Beneke, leader of the Glenn Miller Orchestra, recorded the song on the RCA label, and his version peaked at number six. Benny Goodman, the "King of Swing," made a popular recording of the tune for Columbia Records, with vocal by Eve Young; it peaked at number six as well. Finally, Bing Crosby came out with his rendition for Decca, and it reached the number eight position, staying on the charts for a total of six weeks. Subsequent recordings were made by Miles Davis, Tony Martin, Manhattan Transfer, Ahmad Jamal, and the Oscar Peterson Trio, among others.

I WISH I DIDN'T LOVE YOU SO

Music and lyrics by Frank Loesser
From *The Perils of Pauline*

Taking great liberties with the story of real-life movie serial queen Pearl White, who starred in the early days of silents in some truly harrowing cliffhangers, *The Perils of Pauline* (named for her most famous serial) was ostensibly a biomusical based on White's life. Betty Hutton starred as the "peril"-ized heroine, playing the role with all the unflinching energy and enthusiasm for which she was famous. "Give Miss Hutton an inch," wrote the *New York Times*, "which Director George Marshall did, and she takes a mile," while *Variety* proclaimed, "Betty Hutton is tiptop in the title role . . . It's a funfest for the actress and she makes the most of it."

The picture was a panoply of all that was Hollywood in those supposed glory days of silents, with several clever glimpses into the world of early movie making. One sequence depicted a multiple outdoor set where cameras were simultaneously rolling on a Western, a drama, a jungle thriller, and a slapstick comedy, complete with custard pie fight. But all this, plus the scenes recounting Pearl White's work in making those serials, didn't seem enough to producer Sol Siegel and his crew at Paramount. Not content with filming Pearl White's factual life (which, as would be expected, contained none of the excitement of her serials) they decided to pump in a hokey romantic interest — John Lund, as a hammy actor and object of White's affections — while bringing in a number of authentic old-timers to populate the film and give it just the right flavor. (Their pie-flinging worked, but the romantic angle flopped.)

Others of note in the cast included Billy De Wolfe (as a clown), Constance Collier (as a character actress), and William Demarest (later of television's "My Three Sons") as a silent director.

Frank Loesser created four songs for *The Perils of Pauline*, including "Rumble, Rumble," "Poppa, Don't Preach to Me" (not to be confused with Madonna's 1986 hit "Papa Don't Preach"), and the song that won an Academy Award nomination, "I Wish I Didn't Love You So," a plaintive ballad introduced by Betty Hutton in an audition scene.

The tune became extremely popular, with several releases jockeying for space in the top 10. Both Dinah Shore and Vaughn Monroe released separate record-

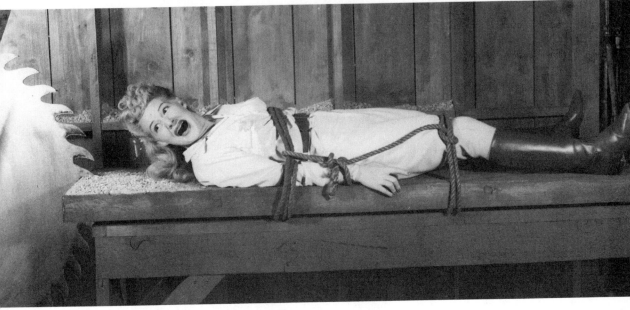

Betty Hutton plays stuntwoman Pearl White in *The Perils of Pauline.*

ings in the fall of 1947, both of which peaked at number two within a few weeks of each other. Monroe's version lasted 15 weeks on the charts, Shore's 12. Betty Hutton herself made a recording of the tune she had sung in the movie; it reached number five. Popular recording artist Dick Haymes was on the charts at the same time as these artists, with his recording peaking in the number nine spot. And yet another singer, Dick Farney, had a version that made number 13.

PASS THAT PEACE PIPE[1]

Music and lyrics by Ralph Blane, Hugh Martin, and Roger Edens
From *Good News*

Audiences today may find it strange that folks living back in what many now consider "the good old days" of the late 1940s reflected with nostalgia of their own on the previous generation. But the 1947 film *Good News* was just that for fans of the 1920s era of rah-rah college days, when students wore raccoon coats, carried

ukuleles, and sang songs constantly, if we were to believe what took place in this fond look back at that simpler time. In fact, *Good News* wasn't news at all (although it was good), having begun first as a hit Broadway musical in 1927, then as a 1930 movie.

The tried-and-true plot, all neatly tied together at the end, involved two women in love with the same man, played by heartthrob Peter Lawford. Patricia Marshall played the gold digger, who naturally lost out to sweet, honest, and true June Allyson, who was assisted in winning Lawford over by her spunky friend, played by Joan McCracken.

Most of the original songs from the stage and early film versions were included in this revival. Written by Ray Henderson, B.G. DeSylva, and Lew Brown, they included "Just Imagine," "The Varsity Drag," "The Best Things in Life Are Free," and the title song, "Good News." Mel Tormé, who was a featured player in the film, performed "Lady's Man," an extravagant music and dance number, and also lent his voice to "Lucky in Love," both from the original musical. Two new tunes were added, "The French Lesson," written by Betty Comden, Adolph Green, and Roger Edens, and "Pass That Peace Pipe," with words and music resulting from the collaborative efforts of Ralph Blane, Hugh Martin, and Roger Edens.

1. Although listed in the film's credits as "Pass *the* Peace Pipe," most sources give the title as "Pass *That* Peace Pipe," which is also a line from the lyric.

McCracken performed the song-and-dance production number created around "Pass That Peace Pipe," which went on to receive an Oscar nomination. The elaborate routine is anything but politically correct by today's standards — stereotypical pseudo–Native Americans (college kids in war paint) with tom-tom rhythms being beat out on soda fountain counter stools (and sounding a lot like the song "I'm an Indian Too," from the 1946 Irving Berlin Broadway show, *Annie Get Your Gun*, released as a movie in 1950). But the number was perfect for the times, updating the old '20s music to the "modern" swing and jazz suitable for the young audience the picture sought to capture.

Two recording artists released singles of "Pass That Peace Pipe." Margaret Whiting had a number eight hit with the song that lasted four weeks on the charts. Bing Crosby, perhaps out of his element, had a version that charted for one week, in the number 21 position.

The promising career of Joan McCracken, who played June Allyson's supportive friend in *Good News*, was cut short when the young actress died suddenly in 1961 at the age of 38, the victim of a heart condition from which she had suffered for seven years. McCracken had married and divorced twice (one husband had been Bob Fosse, then an up-and-coming dancer). Although she had performed in Broadway musicals and was once a Rockette, she appeared in only two films, *Hollywood Canteen* (see page 75) and *Good News*. After that film, she returned to New York and Broadway, where she continued to star in musical and dramatic roles until her death.

YOU DO

**Music by Josef Myrow; lyrics by Mack Gordon
From *Mother Wore Tights***

Although saddled with a rambling script, *Mother Wore Tights* proved to be a successful money maker for 20th Century-Fox. The reason can be summed up in two words: Betty Grable. The people at Fox knew a good thing when they saw it. Two good things, in fact — Grable and her world-famous legs. As the *New York Times* put it, "This new musical . . . displays the shapely gams of Betty Grable whenever it gets the chance, and it must be said that Miss Grable in Technicolor is balm for the eyes."

The story concerned a vaudeville family — husband, wife (the "Mother" of the title, played by Grable), and their two daughters, and was told in flashbacks by the younger daughter, with voice-over by Anne Baxter. Naturally, the film was packed with song-and-dance routines at every juncture.

Grable was Fox's highest paid star at the time, with a yearly salary reported at $150,000 — more than studio head Darryl F. Zanuck earned. When first cast in the starring role as Myrtle McKinley Burt, Grable expressed her desire to dance opposite Fred Astaire or Jimmy Cagney. But they were contracted to other studios, and Fox cast Dan Dailey in the role. Under contract to Fox, Dailey would eventually star in a number of musicals for the studio, mostly in roles involving show-biz personalities. (In 1948, he was nominated for a Best Actor Oscar for *When My Baby Smiles at Me*.) His career had barely begun in 1942 when he enlisted in the armed forces and served as a lieutenant during World War II, and *Mother Wore Tights* was his first film after returning home. According to the book *The Fox Girls*, by James Robert Parish, upon learning of her relatively obscure co-star, the generous Grable exclaimed, "That's swell. Dan can not only dance, he's a good actor, too!" The formula proved correct — there was definite chemistry between the two on screen.

There was also plenty of opportunity for nostalgic songs, as well as new ones penned by Josef Myrow and Mack Gordon. "You Do" became the best known. In the movie, it's performed in a production number on the vaudeville stage by Grable, Dailey, and some chorus girls. In the middle of the number, Grable's grandparents join the audience, unaware that their granddaughter, whom they believe to be away at business college, is actually performing in the act they're watching.

"You Do" became a hit song for the most popular recording artists of the day. Dinah Shore had a record of it that peaked at number four and spent 11 weeks on the charts. Vaughn Monroe, Margaret Whiting, Vic Damone, and Bing Crosby all released singles of the tune on the same date — November 1, 1947. Monroe's and Whiting's each reached the number five position, while Damone's recording peaked at number seven and Crosby (backed by Carmen Cavallaro and His Orchestra) at number eight.

While *Mother Wore Tights* did not win the Oscar for Best Song, it did win the statuette for Best Scoring for a Musical Picture, with Alfred Newman receiving the honors. In addition, there was a nomination for Best

Color Cinematography, no doubt at least in part because of Betty Grable's Technicolor legs.

1948

And the winner is...

BUTTONS AND BOWS

Music and lyrics by Jay Livingston and Ray Evans
From *The Paleface*

There is a joke told by Bob Hope in his book *The Road to Hollywood,* about his co-star in the hit movie *The Paleface.* Jane Russell was one of Howard Hughes's discoveries. "He was looking at the mountains one day," quipped Hope, "and a couple of them moved." However, the modest Mr. Hope went on to attribute the film's immense success not to his or Russell's considerable talents but to the hit song featured in the picture.

"Buttons and Bows" was already a runaway Number One song by the time the picture premiered in the winter of 1948. Dinah Shore had recorded and popularized it, eventually selling well over a million copies on the Capitol label, and it was to remain Number One on the charts for almost six months — making it the most popular song to emerge from any motion picture up till that time. Yet when people finally did get to see how the tune was used in the movie, they were disappointed to learn it was a virtual throwaway.

In the film, Hope sings the tune to Russell, accompanied only by his concertina. Audiences were bitterly disappointed with the lack of attention given the song, expecting to see a great production number. Imagine their bewilderment, then, when this tune that was on everyone's lips was tossed off comically, quickly, and never reprised. Fortunately, the picture, a spoof of shoot-'em-up Westerns, was a delight and became a box office hit independent of the use of everyone's favorite song. Hope himself later released a recording of "Buttons and Bows," which, while not as wildly popular as Shore's, was still a best-seller for Capitol.

Bob Hope braces himself as Jane Russell fends off hostile Indians in *The Paleface,* a western spoof that spawned an Academy Award–winning song "Buttons and Bows."

The hit song was written by the team of Jay Livingston and Ray Evans, who had been contracted to Paramount in 1945 (see "The Cat and the Canary," page 80). The team worked together flawlessly — Livingston composing the music and both of them working on the lyrics, then sharing equal credit. Livingston recalled in a 1990 interview with radio personality Don McCulloch, first aired on Los Angeles radio station KMPC, that the song was originally to be called "Snookum," an Indian word. "We thought it was real cute, and we played it for the director [Norman Z. McLeod], but he said, 'No way am I going to use that song . . . The Indians [in the movie] are a menace, they're dangerous. I don't want a comedy song about Indians.' So we went back to our office, disgruntled, and wrote this 'Buttons and Bows.' If he hadn't turned down 'Snookum,' we would never have written this song. Those are the kinds of breaks that come along."

However, it wasn't all buttons and bows for the composers. A $600,000 plagiarism suit was filed against them in Los Angeles Superior Court by bandleader Freddie Rich. He eventually lost his case after a jury decided his claim was unfounded.

At the 1948 Academy Awards ceremony (held in March, 1949), host Robert Montgomery introduced Jane Russell, who performed the song that had been sung in the film by her co-star, Bob Hope. "The nominated song 'Buttons and Bows' will now emanate from the lovely and talented throat of Miss Jane Russell," Montgomery announced.

"Buttons and Bows" was later interpolated as a choral episode in Paramount's non-musical picture *Sunset Boulevard* (1950). But it wasn't until 1952, with the sequel *Son of Paleface,* that the song was given proper on-screen treatment, again performed by Hope and Russell, this time joined by singing cowboy star Roy Rogers.

FOR EVERY MAN THERE'S A WOMAN

Music by Harold Arlen; lyrics by Leo Robin
From *Casbah*

Originally popularized in France as a novel called *Pepe Le Moko,* by a writer known only as Detective Ashelbe, *Casbah* had been filmed twice before this 1948 version — first in 1937, in the original French incarnation, and then in America as *Algiers* (1938), starring Charles Boyer. For this third go-round, Universal decided to turn the popular concept into a musical.

Critics were split sharply over this latest trip to the forbidden quarter of Algiers known as the Casbah. The *New York Times,* while noting that the film benefited from its predecessors, also pointed out that it "cannot sidestep comparison . . . It suffers by their shining examples." The show business bible, *Variety,* noted that "the romantic melodrama doesn't always mesh too well with the musical story [and] makes for a distraction."

Tony Martin discusses foreign intrigue with Yvonne DeCarlo in *Casbah,* a musical remake of the classic film *Algiers.*

Starring as the ill-fated Pepe was Tony Martin, upon whom most critics lavished what praise they had for the picture. "Martin is good as the dashing thief whose elusive ways are the despair of the police," said *Variety*. The *New York Daily Mirror*'s reviewer, Lee Mortimer, wrote, "Tony Martin is proving what some knew — that he is a fine and mature actor, equally at home in comedy, the boudoir or heavy villainy. Though he sings a couple of Harold Arlen's haunting melodies in virile, thrilling style, all trace of the band crooner of a decade ago is gone."

Thanks to Harold Arlen, who returned to Hollywood after a brief absence in time to pair up with lyricist Leo Robin, there were some lilting tunes in *Casbah*. "Hooray for Love" became a pop standard. "It Was Written in the Stars," a romantic number sung by Martin, accompanied by the Katherine Dunham Dancers, was also effective, as was the plaintive ballad, "What's Good About Goodbye?" "For Every Man There's a Woman" was probably the most listenable, and received an Academy Award nomination. Robin would actually receive two Oscar nominations in 1948, the second for "This Is the Moment" (see page 101). However, nothing stood a chance against shoo-in "Buttons and Bows" (see page 98).

"For Every Man . . ." wasn't as successful as some of Arlen's or Robin's other hit songs, but a couple of recordings did emerge on the pop charts. Benny Goodman and His Orchestra, with vocal by comer Peggy Lee, had a recording that peaked at number 25 and was on the charts for two weeks in February, 1948 (one month prior to the film's release). Ironically, Tony Martin himself couldn't equal Goodman's version — Martin's recording peaked at number 30. And the star of *Casbah* wasn't the one to sing this nominated tune at the Academy Awards ceremony the following Spring. Instead, that honor fell to a new star, Gordon MacRae, who, at the age of 27, had just arrived in Hollywood fresh from Broadway to film his first picture that year.

IT'S MAGIC

Music by Jule Styne; lyrics by Sammy Cahn
From *Romance on the High Seas*

When Doris Kappelhoff was in her teens, she set her sights on a career as a dancer. Then fate stepped in, in the form of an automobile accident. Doris was unable to walk for 14 months, but she put the time to good use. She studied singing, got a chance to perform on the radio, and won local fame in her hometown of Cincinnati, singing "Day by Day." Offered a job singing at a nightclub, the talented Miss Kappelhoff was told to change her name to fit the marquee, and became, appropriately, Doris Day.

She was soon singing with Bob Crosby's and Fred Waring's orchestras, and it wasn't long before she caught the attention of a Warner Bros. talent scout, who screen-tested the young singer. Director Michael Curtiz, desperate for a replacement for a very pregnant Betty Hutton in his next film, was shown Doris's test, and three days later he cast the unknown as one of the leads in *Romance on the High Seas*. Billed fourth, behind Jack Carson, Janis Paige, and Don DeFore, Doris soon caught the attention of the critics, some of whom were not too kind. Bosley Crowther, writing in the *New York Times*, noted, "Miss Day herself seems much inclined to a vicious catch-as-catch-can technique of wrestling with her material. She's the brassy type, the jive-joint cut-up . . . Maybe the Warners figured they had a new Betty Hutton in her but, even without other assets, she still lacks Miss Hutton's vital style. Also Miss Day's singing voice, while adequate . . . is nothing to herald." The American movie-going and record-buying public, as well as history, would render a very different assessment.

Doris Day launched herself on the seas of record industry history thanks to the film's hit song "It's Magic." The Styne-Cahn song became so popular internationally that in England they retitled *Romance on the High Seas*, instead naming it *It's Magic*, after the song title. Day's recording sold well over a million records, peaking at number two and staying on the charts 21 weeks. It was also magic for five other performers who covered the song during the summer months of 1948: Dick Haymes's version peaked at number nine, as did Gordon MacRae's; Tony Martin and Sarah Vaughan separately peaked at number eleven; and Vic Damone's recording made number 24. In 1962, The Platters attempted a reissue of the tune, but it only reached number 91.

Other songs sung by Day in *Romance on the High Seas* included "I'm in Love," "It's You or No One," and the bouncy tune "Put 'Em in a Box." The film was also nominated for Best Scoring of a Musical Picture.

Day reprised her performance of "It's Magic" in the 1951 film *Starlift*, appearing in a cameo in that movie.

THIS IS THE MOMENT

**Music by Frederick Hollander;
lyrics by Leo Robin**
From *That Lady in Ermine*

Born in 1892 in Berlin, Ernst Lubitsch, son of a German-Jewish tailor, grew up determined to be in show business. He quit high school at age 16, working in his father's store by day and singing and doing stand-up comedy in cabarets by night. He began directing in his 20s, and soon made his mark on the silents of the era, directing film notable Pola Negri in several films. His first trip to the United States, in 1921, was to promote one of his popular films, *Das Weib des Pharao (The Woman of Pharaoh)*. While he was on the U.S. visit, Mary Pickford, already a power to be reckoned with, tapped Lubitsch to direct her 1923 picture, *Rosita.*

Other American projects soon followed — first a string of silent hits for Warner Bros., then early sound pictures for Paramount (where today there is an Ernst Lubitsch Building on the lot, dedicated to his memory). In 1937 he was awarded a special Oscar for his "25-year contribution to motion pictures." He had yet to make his two most famous films — *Ninotchka*, starring Greta Garbo (1939) and *To Be or Not To Be* (1942), a scathing anti-Nazi comedy.

Unfortunately, Lubitsch suffered from ill health, and his brilliant career would soon be over. In 1947, he contracted with 20th Century-Fox to produce and direct Betty Grable, Douglas Fairbanks Jr., and Cesar Romero in *That Lady in Ermine*, which would become his final picture. He had suffered five heart attacks in recent years, but had always managed to bounce back. During the filming of this musical, however, he suffered a sixth — and fatal — coronary. When he died at the age of 55, before he could complete the picture, the director's reigns were taken up by Otto Preminger.

Lubitsch's last picture was a romantic Technicolor fantasy about a mythical principality, with the beautiful countess surrendering her country and heart to the conqueror. The story was difficult to follow, however, with dreams and reality confusingly overlapping. The *New York Times* reviewer Bosley Crowther, by now plainly smitten with the charms of Betty Grable, once again felt no restraint in describing her virtues: "Miss Grable, even wrapped in ermine, looks sharper than most girls in bathing suits, and the flashes she gives of territory for which she's noted are few but rewarding . . .

She sings with the gusto of a lady who understands the meaning of a song."

Even with Grable's gusto, the songs themselves weren't particularly memorable, despite lyrics by the noted Leo Robin, nominated twice that year for the Oscar (see "For Every Man There's a Woman," page 99). "Ooo, What I'll Do to That Wild Hungarian" was fun, although no one left the theater humming it. "This Is the Moment," a sweet, romantic number that Grable, dressed like a fairy tale Cinderella, croons to Fairbanks as he slips a slipper on her foot like a dashing Prince Charming, received an Academy Award nomination. It didn't become much of a hit, and neither did the picture, unfortunately — the burden of being saddled with two separate directors was evident in the film's unevenness. Despite the best promotional efforts of Fox, word of mouth quickly killed the film at the box office soon after its release.

THE WOODY WOODPECKER SONG

**Music and lyrics by Ramey Idriss
and George Tibbles**
From *Wet Blanket Policy*

With a voice provided by the legendary Mel Blanc, Woody Woodpecker burst upon the cartoon scene in 1940. His trademark cry of "Ha-ha-ha-HA-ha!", however, was provided by Grace Stafford, the actress-wife of Woody's creator, Walter Lantz. It was Gracie, in fact, who suggested that her husband create the animated character in the first place. While they were on their honeymoon at California's June Lake, the couple was constantly disturbed by a hammering woodpecker that eventually bored a hole in their cottage roof. Lantz's best-known cartoon creature at that time was Andy Panda, but his popularity was soon outstripped by that of the outrageous, hyperactive bird with the riveting laugh.

After Blanc was signed by Warner Bros. to an exclusive contract to do the voice of Bugs Bunny, Gracie asked her husband if she could assume the role of the beloved Woody Woodpecker. Lantz flatly refused, but his clever wife slipped in a tape of her voice amongst the other audition tapes. She won the part, and over the next 25 years or so, in about 200 cartoons, she was Woody's alter ego.

Walter Lantz, describing his feelings about the little red-headed character, once said, "Woody Woodpecker started out as a supporting player, but he became a star in his second picture. And he's been a nest egg to me ever since." Woody's (and Lantz's) biggest break came in 1948, when the woodpecker starred in an animated feature called *Wet Blanket Policy.* Songwriters Ramey Idriss and George Tibbles were asked to create a special song for Woody, which was called — what else? — "The Woody Woodpecker Song." The novelty tune became a runaway hit and even garnered an Oscar nomination. In reporting on the Woody phenomenon that was sweeping the country, *Time* magazine, in its June 12, 1948, issue, marveled: "Kids were driving their parents crazy with it. Waitresses in jukebox joints were going frantic. The whole U.S. seemed to be gurgling itself silly with the laughing gassiness of a goofy song called 'Woody Woodpecker.' "

The only hit song ever written about a cartoon character ("Mickey Mouse Club March" was never a top hit), "The Woody Woodpecker Song" became Kay Kyser's most popular song in five years, shooting to the top of the *Billboard* charts in the summer of 1948 and staying in the Number One position for six weeks and on the charts for 15. It became a worldwide phenomenon, number one on jukeboxes in Ethiopia, for example, while the Bedouins of the Arabian desert were reportedly playing it on camelback with portable radios.

After filing an unsuccessful lawsuit claiming royalties for his ubiquitous voice in all these airings (an out-of-court settlement was eventually reached), Blanc decided to fight back. He made his own recording of "The Woody Woodpecker Song" along with a group called the Sportsmen (the kicky flip side was called "When Veronica Plays Her Harmonica on the Pier at Santa Monica"). Not surprisingly, it too became a hit, reaching the number two position. Even the Andrews Sisters, with Danny Kaye, turned out a version of the song. It peaked at number 18.

Woodymania swept America, with theaters demanding old Woody cartoons while Universal and United Artists scrambled to their vaults to fill the exhibitors' demands.

Woody Woodpecker's voice fell sadly silent in March of 1992, with the passing of Gracie Lantz. She was 88. Walter Lantz died two years later, at the age of 92. In a tribute to the beloved animator, television's "Entertainment Tonight" played part of an early-1990s interview in which Lantz humbly thanked his, and

Woody's, many fans over the years. "It's very rewarding that people remember us," Lantz said, "and I'm so happy that we can give them joy and laughter. That's all we can do, give them joy and laughter."

1949

And the winner is...

BABY, IT'S COLD OUTSIDE

**Music and lyrics by Frank Loesser
From *Neptune's Daughter***

Three times a bridesmaid. Frank Loesser was familiar with the routine. He had been nominated three times before for an Academy Award — in 1941, as lyricist for "Dolores" (see page 48), in 1943, for his lyrics to "They're Either Too Young or Too Old" (see page 65), and again in 1947, for his composition "I Wish I Didn't Love You So" (see page 95). So with his fourth trip to the Awards ceremony, for the song "Baby, It's Cold Outside," from the film *Neptune's Daughter*, Loesser found it hard to get his hopes up. Naturally, this time he won, and no one could have been more pleased or surprised.

Not everyone was thrilled for the 1949 Oscar winner for Best Song. Several songwriters protested, perhaps jealously, that "Baby, It's Cold Outside" had been written several years before. Frank Loesser and his wife, they moaned, had been performing the song at parties for the last five years before it was sold to MGM for the filmusical. Didn't this violate Academy rules? Actually, it didn't. The Academy stuck by its decision. "Baby, It's Cold Outside" had never before been performed *professionally* or *commercially*. Those were the rules. The Award stood. Loesser was a most happy fella.

It would be the only Oscar win for the talented composer. Soon, he would leave Hollywood behind, heading to the lights of the Great White Way as he discovered his greatest fame on Broadway. *Where's Charley?* (1948), *Guys and Dolls* (1950), *The Most Happy Fella* (1956), and *How to Succeed in Business Without Really Trying* (1961) all succeeded on Broadway and, except for *Fella*, became musical motion pictures as well.

Neptune's Daughter starred Esther Williams, America's top box office swimming star (okay, so she didn't have much competition). Year after year, MGM topped itself by coming up with yet another Technicolor extravaganza for Williams, usually featuring a Latin lover. *Neptune's Daughter* was no exception: She co-starred with the dashing Ricardo Montalban. Xavier Cugat provided the Latin rhythms; Red Skelton and Betty Garrett, the comic relief. Not heavy on drama, it was the perfect summertime diversion, and audiences eagerly took the plunge, drawn as much by Loesser's score as by the swimsuit-clad bodies of Williams and Montalban.

Songs included "I Love Those Men," a tongue-in-cheek Latin number performed by Williams, "My Heart Beats Faster," with Montalban proving he'd better stick to acting, and the tune that had already been bouncing high on the charts a month before the picture's release — "Baby, It's Cold Outside." In the film, the flirtatious duet is performed by co-leads Williams and Montalban, and is reprised comically by Garrett and Skelton.

The song became a best-selling record for a number of paired artists, some likely, some not. Margaret Whiting and Johnny Mercer were the first to hit the charts. Their duet reached the number three spot and was on the charts for an impressive 19 weeks. Right behind them was Dinah Shore paired with Buddy Clark (accompanied by Ted Dale's Orchestra), whose recording peaked at number four. Ella Fitzgerald teamed up with Louis Jordan to cut a record that peaked at number nine, while Sammy Kaye's Orchestra headlined a version featuring vocals by Don Cornell and Laura Leslie, which made number 12. And country music's foremost comedy due, Homer and Jethro (real names: Henry Haynes and Kenneth Burns) released a version that also found a niche on the pop charts. It peaked at number 22.

In 1962, Ray Charles and Betty Carter dusted off the old Frank Loesser tune. It barely dented the *Billboard* Hot 100, peaking at number 91 during a two-week chart run.

IT'S A GREAT FEELING

Music by Jule Styne; lyrics by Sammy Cahn
From *It's a Great Feeling*

Billed as a hilarious behind-the-scenes romp in Hollywood, *It's a Great Feeling* was a light-hearted, although almost totally fictitious, glimpse into movie-making. The film was primarily an excuse to find a starring vehicle for Doris Day, supported by a couple of good actors and a parcel of stars in cameos. Yup, there was Gary Cooper, along with Ronald Reagan, Danny Kaye, Jane Wyman (in a fainting scene), Edward G. Robinson (doing a takeoff on his hard-boiled gangster character,

Betty Garrett and Red Skelton sing together in a scene from *Neptune's Daughter.*

Doris Day and pals discuss a musical number in *It's a Great Feeling*.

In her memoir, *Doris Day, Her Own Story*, Day confessed that she didn't really recall much of *It's a Great Feeling*. "[It] wasn't much of a picture," she wrote, "but it had a great ending, which is the one thing about it I remember very well." In the surprise ending, Doris (playing movie star wannabe Judy Adams) has returned to her hometown, Gurkey's Corners, to marry her high school sweetheart, Jeffrey Bushfinkle. As she turns to face her new husband, he lifts her veil to kiss her, and the camera moves in on his face. Surprise! It's Errol Flynn, in the film's final cameo. Smart move, Judy Adams. There's no place like Gurkey's Corners.

The film marked a turning point in Day's career. She decided that she'd found her niche in film acting rather than bandstand singing. "I felt very real in the make-believe parts I had to play," she wrote. "I felt what the script asked me to feel. I enjoyed playing and singing for the cameras and I guess that enjoyment came through on the screen, somehow communicated itself to the audience and made them feel good too . . . Acting for the camera was an immediate love affair."

played for laughs), Eleanor Parker, and Patricia Neal. Joan Crawford did a bit in a classy gown shop (no wire hangers for the gowns, you can be sure). An assortment of film directors were on hand to give folks a look at some of the seldom seen behind-the-camera names familiar to audiences of the day. Directors Michael Curtiz, King Vidor, David Butler (who actually directed *It's a Great Feeling),* and Raoul Walsh all made brief appearances.

For fans of composers Jule Styne and Sammy Cahn, the film featured a number of their pleasant, if not their most memorable, tunes. The Styne-Cahn songfest included "Blame My Absent-Minded Heart," "At the Cafe Rendezvous," "That Was a Big Fat Lie," "There's Nothing Rougher Than Love," "Give Me a Song with a Beautiful Melody," and "Fiddle-dee-dee." In addition to these, there was a cute title song, which received an Academy Award nomination. "It's a Great Feeling" was sung by Day over the opening credits, with still cartoons of her appearing as part of the titles. It neither became a big hit nor did much to advance her musical career. But the song, along with the film, proved that Day, who had begun her acting career on a rougher note, was best suited to musical comedy.

LAVENDER BLUE (DILLY, DILLY)

Music by Eliot Daniel; lyrics by Larry Morey
From *So Dear to My Heart*

"Lavender's Blue (Diddle Diddle, or, Dilly Dilly)" was a traditional English folk song dating back to around 1750. It was updated and adapted for the Walt Disney production of *So Dear to My Heart* by Eliot Daniel and Larry Morey, emerging with a slightly altered title.

A real coup in the film was the casting of Burl Ives, already famous for his down-home folk singing of such popular tunes as "Jimmy Crack Corn (The Blue Tail Fly)" and "Froggy Went A-Courtin'." *So Dear to My Heart* was only his fourth movie (three of which were made in 1948), and he took to singing "Lavender Blue" like a frog to a lily pad. Ives (born Burle Icle Ivanhoe in 1909) was a former professional football player — not surprising, given his linebacker-like build. Yet he became best known as a gentle balladeer, and was an authority on American folk music. His acting talents wouldn't truly begin to unfold until the 1950s, and he ultimately won the 1958 Academy Award as Best Supporting Actor for his role in *The Big Country*. That same year he also created what would become his most memorable role, Big Daddy, in *Cat on a Hot Tin Roof.*

In *So Dear to My Heart,* Ives, minus his trademark beard, provides light-hearted cracker-barrel wisdom to young Bobby Driscoll and Luana Patten, two of Walt Disney's original contract child actors (both were featured in the 1947 hit *Song of the South* — see page 93). Ives sings "Lavender Blue" without any fanfare, accompanying himself on his guitar while Bobby and his friend Luana do the dishes in Bobby's grandmother's simple home. Soon Beulah Bondi, playing the grandmother, and Uncle Hiram (Ives) have rolled back the rug for a kick-up-your-heels song-and-dance fest. It's pure corn pone and totally effective in this warmhearted, almost cloyingly nostalgic picture.

Other songs by various composers credited as a group (one name on the card was Mel Tormé) included "Stick-to-It-Tivity," "So Dear to My Heart" (the title song, with an "ah-ah" chorus over a beautiful scrapbook, the technique used throughout to tell the film's narrative), "Ol' Dan Patch," "It's Whatcha Do with Whatcha Got," and "County Fair." Two folk songs from the public domain were added to the score: "Billy Boy" and "Sourwood Mountain," both intoned, naturally, by the picture's resident folk singer, Ives.

"Lavender Blue" received an Oscar nomination and proved it still had what it takes two centuries later. Sammy Kaye's orchestral version was the most popular of the recordings released late in 1948 and early 1949 (the picture was a 1948 Christmas release, but was submitted for the 1949 Academy Awards). Kaye's recording peaked in the number four position and was on the charts for 16 weeks. Dinah Shore recorded the song and peaked at number nine, while Jack Smith released a version that reached number 17. Ives's own soundtrack recording wasn't as effective as it was on film; his recording, the last to be released, peaked at number 16.

Ten years later, Sammy Turner had the biggest hit of all with "Lavender Blue." His recording, debuting on June 22, 1959, peaked at number three, and was on the *Billboard* charts for 18 weeks.

MY FOOLISH HEART

Music by Victor Young;
**   lyrics by Ned Washington**
From *My Foolish Heart*

Based on a *New Yorker* story called "Uncle Wiggily in Connecticut" by J. D. Salinger (two years before he would write *The Catcher in the Rye*), *My Foolish Heart* was a melodramatic tearjerker that was generally adored by various weepy-eyed critics. *Variety* pronounced the picture "among the better romantic films. Deft and sure in wringing the utmost from a sound story by winning performances and socko[1] direction, it can't miss popular reception." Bosley Crowther of the *New York Times* even managed to shed a few tears over the picture, deeming it "Obviously designed to pull the

---

1. *Socko* and *boffo* (sometimes shortened to *sock* and *boff*) were among the more popular terms in the showbiz language invented and popularized by *Variety.* They were also the trade jounal's highest literary accolades.

Burl Ives sings "Lavender Blue (Dilly, Dilly)" to Beulah Bondi, Luana Patten and Bobby Driscoll in *So Dear to My Heart.*

plugs out of the tear glands and cause the ducts to overflow."

Variety lauded the film's star, Susan Hayward, playing an unwed mother whose lover is killed in war and marries another to give her unborn baby a name. "Her performance is a gem, displaying a positive talent for capturing reality," the paper commented. Strangely, Crowther saw it quite differently: "The casting of Susan Hayward as this lady is a bit off the beam." Hayward, however, proved she had the right stuff and pulled down the second Oscar nomination of her career. (She would receive the award on her fifth try, for *I Want to Live!* in 1958).

In *My Foolish Heart,* the title tune is sung by Martha Mears in a nightclub scene, during which Hayward bids farewell to her uniformed lover, played by Dana Andrews. Later the song is sung again over a party scene with Hayward and Kent Smith, the man she traps into what becomes an unhappy but necessary marriage. While the story seems dated today, the title song does not. The Oscar-nominated "My Foolish Heart" was heard frequently throughout in the film's score and has become a standard.

Numerous recording artists have had hits with "My Foolish Heart." Gordon Jenkins and His Orchestra, with vocal by Eileen Wilson, had a number three pop hit for Decca; Mindy Carson, on RCA, and Billy Eckstine, on the MGM label, both had pop hits that peaked at number six; Margaret Whiting's version peaked at number 17, while Richard Hayes had a number 21 hit, and Hugo Winterhalter and His Orchestra had a version that peaked at number 29. Gene Ammons did quite well with his version on the Chess label, reaching number nine on the R&B charts. Other recordings of the song through the decades have been made by Tony Bennett, Ray Conniff, Nancy Wilson, George Shearing, Vic Damone, the Shelly Manne Trio, Carmen McRae, Paul Weston and His Orchestra, Mantovani, Roger Williams, Sam Cooke, André Previn, and the Del Vikings.

THROUGH A LONG AND SLEEPLESS NIGHT

Music by Alfred Newman; lyrics by Mack Gordon
From *Come to the Stable*

Cast from the same mold as Paramount Pictures' *Going My Way* and *The Bells of St. Mary's, Come to the Stable*

was 20th Century-Fox's attempt to enter the religious-comedy genre, complete with heart-of-gold nuns stumbling through the world with blinders on, yet somehow divinely protected. Once again, the nuns in question had to procure land and money in order to establish a new children's hospital (at least it wasn't a school this time). It was a plot that could predictably find an audience willing to take on such treacle with happy abandon.

The story was written by Clare Boothe Luce, herself an intense convert to the Catholic religion, and therefore this was a work of love. She had been married to Time-Life publisher Henry Luce since 1935 and was a well-known playwright and diplomat. She served two terms (1943–47) as a United States Representative from Connecticut, and would later serve as ambassador to Italy in 1953–56.

The cast was exceptional. Loretta Young and Celeste Holm starred as the leading nuns, with Holm receiving a nomination for Best Supporting Actress. Elsa Lanchester, in a key role as an artist with whom the wanderers take refuge, also received a nomination for Best Supporting Actress. Other nominations went to Joseph LaShelle, for his cinematography, and to Luce, for Best Story. Loretta Young, of course, received a nomination for Best Actress. This was her second nomination; she had already won the Best Actress Oscar in 1947, for *The Farmer's Daughter*. Up against stiff competition — Olivia de Havilland, who took top honors for *The Heiress,* Jeanne Crain for *Pinky,* Deborah Kerr for *Edward My Son,* and Susan Hayward for *My Foolish Heart* (see page 105) — she missed out on the 1949 Oscar. Undaunted, the actress saw the light at the end of the picture tube, the one that was beginning to brighten just as the lamp from the cinema's projection booth seemed to be fading, the one called television. It called to her, and she would soon find her greatest success in that medium.

The other Academy Award nomination for *Come to the Stable* was for its one and only song, "Through a Long and Sleepless Night," an atmospheric number composed by Alfred Newman and lyricist Mack Gordon. Although they didn't win that year, both had already tasted victory on Oscar night. Gordon had won in 1947 for "You'll Never Know" (see page 59), and Newman would eventually take home nine Oscars, with a career total of 43 nominations, mostly for Best Score, having composed the scores for hundreds of films.

THE FIFTIES

The film studios were in a state of near-panic. People were deserting theaters in droves, hypnotized by the glow from the cathode-ray tube that had taken over America's living rooms like some alien invader holding the masses in thrall. Television had arrived.

To compensate, filmmakers decided that their product had to be "bigger and better than ever," as proclaimed in their slogan about the movies. The wide-screen extravaganza was invented, along with new terminology to tout it — CinemaScope (with its capital S in the middle designed to elongate the word exactly as the process did to the picture), VistaVision (ditto), Panavision, Super Technirama, Cinerama — all looming over the audiences in a way no TV set ever could. But something had to be on the screen as well, and musicals fit the bill perfectly, especially ones laden with cameos by dozens of stars whose names jockeyed for marquee space.

Although the decade started out quietly enough — just a few title songs, some source music, an animated film or two, some gentle little musicals — by the mid-1950s producers were pulling out all the stops, bringing in the big guns of composers like Irving Berlin, Jule Styne and Sammy Cahn, Dimitri Tiomkin and Ned Washington, Harry Warren and Leo Robin, Frank Loesser, Johnny Mercer, Paul Francis Webster, Jay Livingston and Ray Evans, and Cole Porter. But in 1958, the era of musicals peaked, never to rise so high again, culminating in the production of Lerner and Loewe's Technicolor wonder, Gigi. It was a true screen musical in the old style, and although the next few years would see several brave attempts to recapture this kind of excitement, Gigi had already signaled the end of the era of lavish screen musicals, at least for a while. Title songs became the order of the day by the end of the decade.

And the winner is....

MONA LISA

Music and lyrics by Jay Livingston and Ray Evans
From *Captain Carey, U.S.A.*

If all had gone as originally planned, the movie would have been called *O.S.S.*, the hit song would have been titled "After Midnight," and an unknown would have made a recording of the ditty that would quickly have disappeared. Fortunately, that's not the way it happened at all.

The picture was called *Captain Carey, U.S.A.*, a forgettable film about post-wartime cloak-and-dagger stuff, with Alan Ladd playing a former O.S.S. officer who returns to northern Italy to settle a score. The rest of the cast was fairly obscure, with the exception of two players — child actor "Rusty" Tamblyn, the future Russ Tamblyn of West Side Story fame, and Celia Lovsky, who later played T'Pau, leader of the planet Vulcan on the original "Star Trek." Oh, and there was a rather memorable song tossed off here. Something called "Mona Lisa."

"Mona Lisa" in a spy thriller? Actually, the song was the centerpiece of the picture, used as a signal of warning and played constantly throughout the film. The song is never sung in English in the movie. According to the song's co-composer, Ray Evans, speaking in a 1990 interview with KMPC radio host Don McCulloch, "The director [Mitchell Leisen] wanted to be very realistic, so he had it translated into Italian, and when you heard it in the movie, you just heard Italian lyrics." Evans went on to say that Paramount submitted the song as an Oscar contender, and MGM immediately filed a protest with the Academy, claiming the song should be sung in English. "There was no rule in the Academy that covered this," said Evans. "There was a big argument, but finally Sammy Cahn said, 'I think "Mona Lisa" should be eligible, so let's stop all this nonsense.' He lost himself an Oscar [for "Be My Love" — see page 109] by doing that."

Besides winning the Oscar, the best thing to happen to "Mona Lisa" was Nat King Cole. It was a mutually rewarding relationship between song and artist, with "Mona Lisa" becoming his biggest hit to that time, selling three million records and remaining Number One for eight weeks (and on the charts for 27). But he almost

didn't make the record. When Cole first heard the song, he reportedly said, "What kind of title is that for a song?" and gave it a pass. But Paramount insisted that he be the one to wax the official record release and prevailed upon Livingston and Evans to present their tune to him. "Through a mutual friend at Paramount," said Ray Evans, "we got to go to Nat's house in Hancock Park and do it for him, face to face. I figured we could always sell it better if we could do it for him." Jay added, "There was a little girl running around there who was giving us a lot of trouble, interrupting. That was Natalie Cole. If I had known she was going to be a big star, I would have been real nice to her!"

Nat King Cole was not pleased with his recording. In the liner notes of his album *The Nat King Cole Story*, he is quoted as saying, "When I listened to the playback after the session, I wasn't too crazy about it, so we put it on the shelf. That was in April of 1950. Later on we needed something to put out on the back of a tune I was excited about called 'The Greatest Inventor of Them All.' So 'Mona Lisa' was released [in June of 1950]."

In addition to Cole's wildly popular record (his longest-lived hit), there have been no less than eight others whose recordings of "Mona Lisa" have placed in the Top 30. Over the summer of 1950, Victor Young (number seven), Harry James (number 14), Art Lund (number 14), Ralph Flanagan (number 16), Charlie Spivak (number 16) and Dennis Day (number 29) all had success with covers of "Mona Lisa." In 1959, the song was revived, with Carl Mann's version hitting number 25, while Conway Twitty recorded the tune and hit number 29.

BE MY LOVE

Music by Nicholas Brodszky;
lyrics by Sammy Cahn
From *The Toast of New Orleans*

Alfred Arnold Cocozza was born in 1921 in South Philadelphia, the son of a disabled World War I veteran and his seamstress wife. The only moments of joy in the household came from his father's operatic record collection. Young Alfred (nicknamed Freddie) grew up idolizing Enrico Caruso, and began voice lessons as a youngster.

Music scholarships and apprenticeships saw Freddie developing his talent over the next decade and changing his name — his first to Mario, in honor of his mother Maria, his last name to Lanza, her maiden name. World War II interrupted his promising career, and he toured with the Army's Special Services. Following the war, he auditioned for Jack Warner, who failed to sign him to a screen contract because of Lanza's enormous girth. But Warner Bros.'s loss was MGM's gain, and in 1947, Louis B. Mayer caught the tenor at a Hollywood Bowl concert and signed him to a seven-year movie contract. His 1949 screen debut in *That Midnight Kiss* was but a warm-up act for 1950's *The Toast of New Orleans,* which in turn was mere preparation for his greatest role, as *The Great Caruso* (1951).

There were a number of classical operatic arias sung by Mario Lanza, solo and in duets with talented co-star Kathryn Grayson in *The Toast of New Orleans,* including "Brindisi," the drinking song from *La Traviata,* and "M'appari" from *Martha.* An excellent cast of actors and singers helped round out the Joe Pasternak production. These included David Niven, J. Carrol Naish, and a very young Rita Moreno, billed second from bottom, in the role of Tina.

But the sensation from the picture was the song "Be My Love," sung as a duet with Kathryn Grayson (while a jealous David Niven looks on). Lanza took the song and made it his own. His recording on RCA's "Red Seal" classical label sold over two millions copies, the only classical recording ever to become a Number One hit. The song stayed on the charts for an incredible 34 weeks, and Lanza became so identified with this piece that he used it as the theme for his popular CBS radio program, "The Mario Lanza Show for Coca-Cola."

Others attempted to cash in on the Oscar-nominated tune, but they were no match for Lanza. Ray Anthony's orchestral recording of "Be My Love" peaked at number 13, while baritone Billy Eckstine had a version that peaked in the number 26 position.

Lanza's career began faltering in the mid-1950s. For years he'd struggled with his weight, trying various diets and boarding that unfortunate drugs-and-alcohol roller coaster that seems to beckon to so many celebrities. By 1959, the obesity, crash diets, pills, and drinking binges had taken their toll on his heart. He died on October 7 of that year, a mere 38 years old.

Kathryn Grayson and Mario Lanza in the romantic musical *The Toast of New Orleans.*

BIBBIDI-BOBBIDI-BOO

Music and lyrics by Mack David, Al Hoffman, and Jerry Livingston
From *Cinderella*

Cinderella marked Walt Disney's long-overdue return to the magical world of animation. It was the cartoon-meister's first full-length animated feature since 1942's *Bambi*, and it was worth the wait. A team of 750 animators and writers had spent nearly six years adapting Charles Perrault's 17th-century French fable to the screen. Walt[1] personally oversaw ever aspect of the preparation, attending every story conference and giving his assembled team copious notes. He even provided his input when it came to the music for the film.

One song, "Bibbidi-Bobbidi-Boo," was a favorite of his. The title refers to the magic chant uttered by Cinderella's Fairy Godmother. Bob Thomas's biography,

---

1. A gregarious and genial studio boss, Walt Disney always insisted that everyone refer to him by his first name. Years later, Annette Funicello, his most famous discovery, admitted that she was one of the few people who just couldn't bring herself to call him that, always referring to him as "Mr. Disney."

Walt Disney, recalls Walt's comments: "We can get orchestral effects," Walt wrote in his notes. "The pumpkin can carry the beat. We might get the effect we want by having the music go up an octave . . . We can get personality into the song. It shouldn't be the Deanna Durbin type of thing. I don't see her as goofy or stupid, but rather as having a wonderful sense of humor . . . I think the Fairy Godmother should be elderly — old enough to have wisdom. She should have a certain sincerity. She should have no identity, just be a type . . ."

The songs from *Cinderella* were the first to be administered by Walt Disney's own music publishing company, giving him even further control. He raided New York's Tin Pan Alley for composers, finally choosing the pop songwriting team of Mack David, Jerry Livingston, and Al Hoffman, which had recently written a catchy novelty tune called "Chi-Baba Chi-Baba," recorded by Perry Como. Just as Walt had hoped, what emerged was an exciting soundtrack, topped off with an Academy Award nomination for the "Chi-Baba" title soundalike — "Bibbidi-Bobbidi-Boo."

Five other songs composed by the trio for the movie were "So This Is Love," "A Dream Is a Wish Your Heart Makes" (blatantly similar in lyric and meaning to "When You Wish Upon a Star," from *Pinocchio*, see page 34), the

With a "Bibbidi-Bobbidi-Boo," the Fairy Godmother transforms *Cinderella* into a princess.

title song, "Cinderella," "The Work Song," and "Sing, Sweet Nightingale." The *Cinderella* soundtrack, released along with the movie, became the third-best-selling album of the year. And the film's frequent re-releases in motion picture theaters (before its eventual move to videocassette in 1988) helped push *Cinderella* into box office history as the top film for 1950, taking in over $41 million in North American rentals. The film was also nominated for Best Scoring of a Musical Picture and Best Sound recording.

One of the stars of radio's "Your Hit Parade," Ilene Woods, provided the voice of Cinderella, and future talk show host Mike Douglas voiced her Prince Charming. "Bibbidi," is sung by Verna Felton (as the Fairy Godmother), and although she never recorded it as a single, a couple of recording artists did. Perry Como, who'd had good luck with "Chi-Baba," cut a single of "Bibbidi," and although pleasant enough, it never became a best-seller. Likewise the versions recorded by Jo Stafford and Gordon MacRae, as well as Dinah Shore. Perhaps the best pair to perform the tune were Dean Martin and Jerry Lewis, who treated audiences to their version of it at the Academy Awards ceremony in March, 1951. Dean sang the words, with Jerry chiming in on the "Boo" at the end of each chorus while clowning around in typical Jerry Lewis fashion.

MULE TRAIN

Music and lyrics by Fred Glickman, Hy Heath, and Johnny Lange
From *Singing Guns*

Republic, king of the cowboy movie studios, figured that if a singing cowboy could pack 'em in, why not a singing *outlaw?* Thus was born *Singing Guns,* from a story by noted Western writer Max Brand. The plot concerns an outlaw who, through a twist of fate, becomes the sheriff of a Western town and is assigned to hunt himself down. Republic liked their chances at the box office with this plot, especially when they signed singing bandleader Vaughn Monroe to play the lead.

Monroe had been soothing audiences with his pleasant big band sounds and mellow voice for nearly a decade when tapped to star in *Singing Guns*. While filming the picture, Monroe recorded what would become the biggest hit song to emerge from it — but ironically, not for Monroe himself.

The song was called "Mule Train." Monroe's record was released while the film was in production (enabling it to be "introduced" in the movie, rather than just as a single record, to qualify for Academy Award contention). By all accounts, Vaughn Monroe was set to have a best-seller on his hands. It was released on November 19, 1949, and immediately began to climb the charts. But Frankie Laine had released the same song just a week earlier, and he whipped this tune into shape. His recording was produced by Mitch Miller, who had the brilliant idea of adding a snapping bullwhip sound to the lyrics, emphasizing Laine's booming voice and the song's clippity-clop rhythm. It may have been gimmicky, but it worked. Soon Laine went rolling along, passing Vaughn Monroe and several others who attempted to board this gravy "Train."

Laine's version sold an estimated 1.5 million copies, one of his best-selling records of his career. The tune was nominated as Best Song for 1950 (the release year of *Singing Guns),* with Laine invited to perform it at the Oscar awards ceremony the following spring. He did, but botched the bullwhip-cracking, then covered by doing shtick with Alfred Newman, who was conducting the orchestra that night. After a bit of playful repartee between the two, the whip cracked away and he completed the song.

In a case of the tail wagging the dog, *Singing Guns* didn't fare nearly as well as the hit tune it produced. The other songs — "Singing My Way Back Home" and "Mexicali Trail" — were soon forgotten. Even the fine cast — Walter Brennan, Ward Bond, Jeff Corey, and a 14th-billed Jimmie Dodd (who became Walt Disney's head Mouseketeer in the mid-'50s) — did little to draw audiences. Critic Ann Helming, writing in the *Hollywood Citizen-News,* remarked, "Republic . . . should be given some sort of award for self-restraint in not naming the picture after the song." Perhaps the folks at Columbia Pictures saw that article, for later that year the song, sung by Gene Autry, provided the title for a B-Western called *Mule Train.*

Frankie Laine, though, had cornered the market on record sales of "Mule Train." His version held down the Number One position for six weeks and was on the *Billboard* charts for 13 weeks. Bing Crosby's recording was next in popularity, peaking at number four. Tennessee Ernie Ford found the tune a natural; his recording peaked at number nine. Monroe's own soundtrack single peaked in the number 10 position, while Gordon MacRae's release made number 14.

WILHELMINA

Music by Josef Myrow; lyrics by Mack Gordon
From *Wabash Avenue*

Although only seven years had passed since Betty Grable had made a film called *Coney Island*, her contracted studio, 20th Century-Fox, decided it was time to redo the picture. Generally, when a picture is remade, a whole new cast is sought. Not for this return to *Coney Island*, however, now retitled *Wabash Avenue* and relocated to Chicago. Fox was gambling that Grable's million-dollar legs were worth, well, millions of dollars in box office revenue. She would stay on, although her former male lead, George Montgomery, would be replaced by Victor Mature, and Phil Harris would be added to round out the love triangle.

The critics applauded the picture. In the *New York Times*, Bosley Crowther opined, "The very first time she appears as a platinum-blonde shimmy dancer in a gas-lit Chicago saloon . . . screaming an ancient lament to the effect that she wishes she could shimmy like her sister Kate, this round and voluptuous young lady proceeds to unlimber herself in a manner which we feel safe in guessing her sister could not surpass." Of course, he was referring to the old tune "I Wish I Could Shimmy Like My Sister Kate." There were other familiar songs throughout as well, some 26 oldies in total, some featuring Grable, some performed by others. These included "I've Been Floating Down the Old Green River" and "Harrigan," both performed by James Barton, playing a comic drunk. In addition, Grable offered "My Little Lovin' Honey Man," "I Remember You," and "Billy," among others.

There were plenty of new tunes, too. Josef Myrow teamed up with Mack Gordon to compose five new ones to dovetail with the older songs — "Clean Up Chicago," "Baby, Won't You Say You Love Me," "May I Tempt You with a Big Red Rosy Apple?," "Down on Wabash Avenue," and the one that went on to win an Oscar nomination, a playful tune called "Wilhelmina." Dressed in a Danish blue costume, Grable camped it up singing about her home in Copenhagen, which just happened to rhyme nicely with "toboggan." The colorful tune allowed Grable an opportunity to show off her fancy stepping — she capped off the production number with a soft shoe–style tap dance.

Grable may have had legs, but the picture didn't — it barely earned $1 million. Audiences proved just how fickle (and how glued to those newfangled television sets) they could be. The movie's sets were colorful, the period costumes lavish, the songs by Myrow and Gordon lively; all the glitter and glitz one could expect from Tinseltown was heaped upon this picture. But it wasn't enough. Even the kindest praises from critics didn't help. Grable's million-dollar legs were now devalued, marked down by an indifferent audience. She was only 34 when *Wabash Avenue* was made. In another five years, her film career would be over.

1951

IN THE COOL, COOL, COOL OF THE EVENING

Music by Hoagy Carmichael;
lyrics by Johnny Mercer
From *Here Comes the Groom*

Here Comes the Groom, a now-classic film starring Bing Crosby and directed by the renowned Frank Capra, took top honors in the Best Song category for 1951. On the warm spring night of the Oscar ceremonies, "In the Cool, Cool, Cool of the Evening" seemed just the ticket.

The award-winning song was the icing on the cake for Capra, Crosby, and the rest of the *Here Comes the Groom* team. The film, while not a runaway box office smash, did exceptionally well that year, pulling in $2.7 million in North American rentals and receiving good notices, especially for Jane Wyman, who made her singing debut in the picture. The story was, as the saying goes, pure Capra corn, a little piece of fiction about a man (Crosby) who adopts a gaggle of French orphans — Crosby films somehow always involved kids — brings them to America, then finds out he'll lose the lot unless he marries in five days. Wyman, of course, was tagged to play bride to Crosby's titular groom. The film, in an obvious attempt to compete with television's ever-growing popularity, caught and held the audience's attention with cameo appearances by Louis Armstrong, Dorothy Lamour, Phil Harris, and Cass Dailey, as well as some cute songs, like "Your Own

Little House," "Bonne Nuit," and "Misto Cristofo Columbo." For opera buffs, there was even 14-year-old Anna Maria Alberghetti, in her movie debut, singing arias from *Rigoletto*.

The best song, however (literally, according to the Academy of Motion Picture Arts and Sciences), was the very clever and upbeat, "In the Cool, Cool, Cool of the Evening." Mercer's lyrics were the perfect match for Carmichael's bouncy tune. His words were almost childlike, with things like " 'Whee!' said the bumble-bee," " 'Shore!' said the dinosaur," and " 'Where?' said the grizzly bear" in the verse leading into the chorus. Everyone was soon humming along.

In Robert Osborne's *60 Years of Oscar*, Hoagy Carmichael told of his feelings at receiving his only Academy Award: "Naturally, I was overjoyed at receiving my Oscar," he said, adding, "I'm not sure that my lyricist, Johnny Mercer, was as overjoyed as I because he already had a vulgar display of three Oscars at his home from former years."

Ironically, the song had been stashed, unused, in Paramount's files for years. It had originally been composed for a Betty Hutton film that was never made, about the life of Mabel Normand. Capra arranged for a demo record, with Mercer — a noted singer — performing the crooning chores. Both Crosby and Wyman

Bing Crosby and Jane Wyman spend the "Cool, Cool, Cool of the Evening" at home with children Jacky Gencel and Beverly Washburn in *Here Comes the Groom.*

liked the tune, and their duet was worked into a successful production number. In a departure from normal filming technique, Capra insisted on having the duo sing the number live for the cameras, rather than prerecorded. He arranged for the pair to have miniature earpieces playing the orchestral arrangement as they walked through the elaborate sets used in the number — from an office, through a corridor, into an elevator, through the lobby, and out to the street. Capra pulled it off thanks to the professionalism of his stars, whose screen chemistry he likened to that of other pairs he had directed, such as Tracy and Hepburn, and Gable and Colbert. For her part, Wyman recalled in her biography, *Jane Wyman*, "It was a holiday doing this picture with Frank and Bing."

Wyman went on to cut a record of "In the Cool . . ." with Bing Crosby. Backed by Four Hits and a Miss, their lively rendition of the song reached the number 11 position on the *Billboard* charts, charting for six weeks. Frankie Laine teamed up with Jo Stafford and released another version of the tune, which peaked at number 17.

A KISS TO BUILD A DREAM ON

Music and lyrics by Bert Kalmar, Harry Ruby, and Oscar Hammerstein II
From *The Strip*

The Sunset Strip in Hollywood has been glamorized in song and story and on screens large (as in the film *The Strip*) and small (as in the TV series "77 Sunset Strip"). Dramatizing this mile or so of once-sleazy motels, nightclubs, strip joints (sorry), and other spots that seemed to exist only for the night kept Raymond Chandler types busy churning out tales for decades. Today the Strip is as eclectic as ever, if less down and out. A few trendy restaurants, some hot night spots, a record store or two, and tremendous traffic jams now characterize these legendary few blocks of Los Angeles real estate.

It was portrayed at its tackiest in a low-budget MGM musical called, simply and appropriately, *The Strip*. There were some big names attached to the project — Joe Pasternak as producer, Mickey Rooney as the lead, supported by the likes of Louis Armstrong, William Demarest, and a guest appearance by Vic Damone. But it lacked a good story, believable characters, and, most importantly, an audience to play to. It

was Rooney's first picture in three years; he was desperately in need of work, as he admitted in his 1991 autobiography, *Life Is Too Short:* "It was work, and I needed work. The Strip made only a little more than it cost ($885,000), and I brought in just enough to pay a few outstanding bills."

Part of the problem was the senseless story. Rooney played a drummer in a band who was falsely accused of murdering a racketeer. The trouble was that the picture didn't seem to have any balance. One minute it was a whodunit, then a melodrama, then a jazzy musical. All of the budget, it seems, went for the musical talent, not the screenwriters.

The best of the songs was the Academy Award nominee, "A Kiss to Build a Dream On," reprised a number of times throughout the film. According to *American Popular Songs,* by David Ewen, the number originated as a song called "Moonlight on the Meadows," by Kalmar and Ruby. When it didn't work, Oscar Hammerstein II was called in to punch it up and provide a new title. In the film it is sung by Demarest and Rooney as a harmonized duet, then later by Kay Brown, and finally by Armstrong.

The movie quickly faded, but fortunately the song did not. Hugo Winterhalter had a recording of it that peaked at number 10 and charted for nine weeks. But it was Armstrong — whose own version fell short of Winterhalter's mark, peaking at number 16 — who would take the song and make it his own. His recording of "A Kiss to Build a Dream On" has been reprised frequently in recent years. It was interpolated in the Broadway play *Tru,* with Robert Morse, who played the classic Armstrong recording in one of the scenes. And in the 1993 hit movie *Sleepless in Seattle* (see page 308), the same recording is used as background music and was included as part of the original motion picture soundtrack.

NEVER

Music by Lionel Newman; lyrics by Eliot Daniel
From *Golden Girl*

The colorful careers of bloomer-clad showgirls have often been fodder for the film industry, affording the opportunity to "put on a show," complete with costumes, lavish dance numbers, and new (and old) music in huge production numbers. Occasionally there's even a script.

So it was only a matter of time before Hollywood decided to film the life story of Lotta Crabtree, the so-called Golden Girl who charmed Californians during its gold-rush days following the Civil War. The picture was called, naturally, *Golden Girl,* and producer George Jessel (the sometimes stand-up comic and "toastmaster") brought all the ingredients together like a recipe for a scrumptious cake: a talented cast, including Mitzi Gaynor, Dale Roberton, Dennis Day, James Barton, and Una Merkel; pretty color photography by Charles G. Clarke to show off the colorful costumes and location settings; and some bouncy tunes, penned by Jessel himself, plus others by top songwriters of the day. Stir well, add an audience, and voilà — instant box office hit.

Well, not exactly. This "pseudobiography," as *Time* magazine dubbed it, seemed to have cornered the market on corn. The time-honored plot has Mitzi falling for the rotten, no-good Dale Robertson, a gambler and Confederate spy stealing Yankee gold shipments. After a lot of song-and-dance numbers, he vanishes from Mitzi's life, reportedly taken prisoner and killed by damn Yankees. At picture's (and Civil War's) end, she's onstage, singing "Dixie" for the umpteenth time, when Robertson miraculously appears by her side, seemingly back from the dead, for the big, happy Hollywood ending. ("Dixie" was played so much, in fact, that, as Mitzi Gaynor wrote in the *Saturday Evening Post,* "An English fan said he thought I should play Scarlett O'Hara in a musical version of *Gone with the Wind.")*

Mitzi didn't have an easy time of it. During the production, she broke her toe, sprained her back, and caught the flu and laryngitis. Still, trooper that she was, she managed to complete her work in the film successfully and received general praise from critics. "Her dancing talent and pert personality are attributes that help carry a stock characterization," proclaimed *Variety,* and the *New York Times* called her "youthful and fresh as the noted music hall artists."

Between endless rounds of "Dixie," "Oh, Dem Golden Slippers," and "When Johnny Comes Marching Home Again," there were several new tunes. George Jessel and Sam Lerner did lyrics and Joe Cooper the music for "California Moon," Eliot Daniel and Ken Darby wrote "Sunday Morning," and Lionel Newman (Alfred's younger brother) teamed with Eliot Daniel to contribute "Never." The song was introduced by Dennis Day in the film, his tenor voice highly familiar to audiences from his appearances on radio's "The Jack Benny Show." While no hit record was produced, "Never" was among the five nominees for a Best Song Academy Award that year.

TOO LATE NOW

Music by Burton Lane; lyrics by Alan Jay Lerner
From *Royal Wedding*

Jane Powell was only 21 when she made *Royal Wedding,* a fictitious film centered around a real event — the marriage of Princess Elizabeth of England (before she became queen) to Prince Philip, a wedding that had actually taken place years before. Audiences couldn't get enough about the fairy-tale princess and her young, handsome husband, and a film set during this "Wedding of the Century" afforded an opportunity to bring together great stars, like Fred Astaire and Peter Lawford.

Jane Powell recalled how she got the role in her 1988 autobiography, *The Girl Next Door . . . and How She Grew:* "It was the first film in which I played an adult. I got the role quite by accident — I replaced *both* June Allyson and Judy Garland! June was taken pregnant and Judy was taken ill." During the picture's filming, Powell herself became pregnant with her first child, born four months after the film premiered in 1951.

As one might expect from a Fred Astaire picture, the film had some great music and dance numbers. One of the most charming was a routine involving Astaire and Powell, which may have had the world's longest title: "How Could You Believe Me When I Said I Loved You When You Know I've Been a Liar All My Life." Another was a big production number called "I Left My Hat in Haiti." Powell danced and sang two numbers, "The Happiest Day of My Life," and the song that would be nominated for the Oscar, "Too Late Now," a love song she croons to Lawford.

"Too Late Now" was written by Burton Lane, with lyrics by Alan Jay Lerner, who had paired with Frederick Loewe in 1947 for *Brigadoon* and again in 1951 for *Paint Your Wagon.* Lerner and Loewe would ultimately write some of the finest musicals of the era, including *My Fair Lady, Camelot,* and *Gigi,* for which the composers would earn the Oscar (see page 147).

Royal Wedding, which is frequently seen on television, has become a classic not for its story content or its wonderful singing and dance performances, but rather as an early example of a special effects technique — the one in which Astaire dances up the walls and

Don't try this at home: Fred Astaire makes like Spiderman in this classic scene from *Royal Wedding*.

onto the ceiling of his hotel room. The effect was created by utilizing a camera synched to revolve in time with a turning room in which everything was nailed down tightly, with Astaire himself simply maintaining his position. The cameraman, however — attached to a similarly revolving wall — did indeed rotate, at one point filming from an upside-down position! It was a method that would find its most renowned success in the 1968 MGM film *2001: a space odyssey*, in which a Pan Am flight attendant, ostensibly using Velcro shoes, does a 180-degree twirl around the spacecraft galley, and later still in the Gary Lockwood–centrifuge sequence. Although the effect was by then a bit more refined, it was essentially the same one pioneered in *Royal Wedding*.

WONDER WHY

**Music by Nicholas Brodszky;
 lyrics by Sammy Cahn**
From *Rich, Young and Pretty*

While working on *Rich, Young and Pretty*, Jane Powell frequently found herself having to suppress the urge to throw up. It had nothing to do with the movie or her part in it; she had nearly completed her work on *Royal Wedding* (see page 115) when she learned she was pregnant with her and husband Geary Steffen's first child.

As soon as that film wrapped, she quickly moved over to the set of her next project, *Rich, Young and Pretty* (and also pregnant, they might have added). Morning sickness was upon the 21-year-old actress, who vividly tells of the experience in her autobiography, *The Girl Next Door . . . and How She Grew:* "I was a lovely shade of green most of the time. The studio sent a car for me every day because I couldn't drive; I could barely stand up . . . I sang one dumb song called 'How Do You Like Your Eggs in the Morning.' That *really* turned my stomach, for more reasons than one."

Once again, the songs in this MGM musical were a mixture of old and new. "Deep in the Heart of Texas," "There's Danger in Your Eyes, Cherie," and "Old Piano Roll Blues" were a few of the recycled tunes dredged up one more time. There were some new ones as well, written by the recently teamed Nicholas Brodszky and Sammy Cahn. They had already received their first Academy Award nomination for "Be My Love" in 1950 (see page 109), and would be in Oscar contention for several years to come, both together and paired with others. In *Rich, Young and Pretty,* their tunes included the aforementioned stomach-turner about eggs (a surprise modest hit recording by the Four Freshmen, who also appeared in the film), "I Can See You" (also popularized by the Four Freshmen), and "Wonder Why," the Oscar-nominated song that was introduced in the movie by Powell.

Rich, Young and Pretty never became the box office sensation MGM had hoped for. It may have been the fault of the film's fairly weak story, in which a young Texas lass (the 21-year-old Powell was still playing adolescents, much to her dismay) visits Paris with her rancher dad, falls for a young fella, and meets her mother for the first time. Aware of this uninspired plotting, MGM made it clear that the purpose of the picture was to showcase the exciting song-and-dance numbers.

Co-screenplay credit for *Rich, Young and Pretty* was shared by Sidney Sheldon (teamed with Dorothy Cooper). Sheldon had won an Academy Award for best screenplay in 1947 for *The Bachelor and the Bobby Soxer.* Among his best known screenplays were *Easter Parade* (1948) and *Annie Get Your Gun* (1950). He became famous mainly as a blockbuster novelist beginning in the mid-1970s, penning such popular page-turners as *The Other Side of Midnight, Memories of Midnight, Bloodline, Rage of Angels, Master of the Game,* and *If Tomorrow Comes.* Most have been adapted as screenplays, usually with Sheldon's name above the title (*Sidney Sheldon's Bloodline,* for example). He was also

Jane Powell and Vic Damone are joined by Fernando Lamas (seated at piano) in this scene from *Rich, Young and Pretty.* The film marked the American debut for Argentine native Lamas as well as the film debut of Damone.

creator of such long-running television shows as "Hart to Hart" and "I Dream of Jeannie," which he produced and directed as well.

1952

HIGH NOON (DO NOT FORSAKE ME)

**Music by Dimitri Tiomkin;
lyrics by Ned Washington
From *High Noon***

Every so often, a rare event occurs in the cinematic world: They get everything right. Producer, director, screenwriter, casting, music — somehow, magically, everything clicks. The film is a hit. Eventually it becomes a classic.

High Noon was such a picture. Produced by Stanley Kramer, directed by Fred Zinnemann, written by Carl Foreman, starring Gary Cooper, Grace Kelly, Thomas Mitchell, and Lloyd Bridges, this picture was more than an amalgam of some of the standard, more-or-less clichéd elements of Western drama that the public had known for years. In a way, it was more than the sum of its parts. Simple in plot — the sheriff, who is getting married in 90 minutes, learns that a killer he once put away is arriving on the noon train, gunning for him — yet equally complex in characters and moral issues, *High Noon* found itself in the enviable position of being compared not only to such fine Western dramas as *Stagecoach* and *The Virginian* but even to works by classic playwright Henrik Ibsen. Yet curiously, when the film was first previewed, it was deemed a total failure. It was saved, oddly enough, by the composer of the film's musical score.

After *High Noon*'s first run-through for the producer and director, the mood was dismal. Tiomkin suggested that a strong theme song might set the mood before the story even got underway. In his autobiography *Please Don't Hate Me*, he wrote: "The rule book says that in movies you can't have singing while there's dialogue; but I convinced Stanley Kramer that it might be a good idea to have the song sung, whistled and played by the orchestra."

Dimitri Tiomkin's career would see him win four Oscars and provide the score for almost 150 films, including *Lost Horizon* (1937), *Red River* (1948), *The High and the Mighty* (1954, Academy Award winner), and *Giant* (1956). The song Tiomkin composed for *High Noon*, with words by multiple Academy Award nominee Ned Washington — "High Noon (Do Not Forsake Me)" — was sung by Tex Ritter over the opening credits and scenes of cowboys riding, as the story begins to unfold. Ritter recorded the song for the movie's soundtrack, but at first he refused to cut the record for popular release. While the film was still in production, Tiomkin persuaded Frankie Laine to cut the tune for Columbia. His version, which peaked at number five and charted for 19 weeks, became a hit and helped to pre-sell audiences on the film. Ritter's release was a hit three months later (but didn't do nearly as well as Laine's), peaking at number 12 and charting for eight weeks.

High Noon received a fistful of Academy Award nominations, along with four Oscars. Nominations were for Best Picture, Best Actor (Gary Cooper, winner), Best Director (Fred Zinnemann), Best Screenplay (Carl Foreman), Best Song (winner), Best Scoring of a Dramatic Picture (Tiomkin, winner), and Best Film Editing (Elmo Williams and Harry Gerstad, winners). Ironically, although Carl Foreman was lauded by the Academy for his excellence in writing, he was soon blacklisted as a communist, due in part to his writing of *High Noon*, which some saw, in those days of the McCarthy witch hunts, as an allegory for a rejection of American values and ethics. When Gary Cooper dropped his badge in the dust and turned his back on this metaphor for small-town America, some twisted minds construed this as sympathy for communism. It would be a while before light would appear at the end of this tunnel.

AM I IN LOVE?

**Music and lyrics by Jack Brooks
From *Son of Paleface***

It took four years, but Paramount finally released a sequel to its huge 1948 comedy box office hit *The Paleface*. Even its title was intended as somewhat of a joke, a salute to all those "Son of" sequels so popular in the '30s and '40s, like *Son of Frankenstein, Son of Lassie,*

Son of Fury, Son of Kong, and so on. *Paleface*'s offspring was a chip off the old blockhead, with Bob Hope at his campiest. In many ways, this film was even more humorous than its progenitor.

Hope was reunited with his previous co-star, Jane Russell, for this sequel. Playing a Harvard grad, the son of the previous *Paleface* film's dentist–Indian fighter, he heads west to claim his inheritance of gold and finds all sorts of trouble along the trail. Mixing it up with them was Roy Rogers as a sheriff, and his horse Trigger as Trigger, who had perhaps the funniest bit in the picture, a classic comedy scene in which the horse and Hope share sleeping quarters.

All sorts of outrageous sight gags abound: Hope shoots a stuffed moose which pays off like a Las Vegas slot machine; he throws banana peels to trip up the Indians in pursuit; when a photographer arrives to film him in the bathtub, he grabs a towel with a big *H* monogram and says, "Hurry up. Who do you think you are — Cecil B. DeMille?" (Of course, that's just who it is!) Hope's famous running gag about Bing Crosby was also worked into the film. Referring to the multi-millionaire singer, he quips: "He's just an old, broken-down character actor on the Paramount lot; we try to keep him working." At the end, Hope gets the girl (Russell), while Rogers naturally gets Trigger.

Songs by various composers were plentiful. Jay Livingston and Ray Evans's Academy Award winner, "Buttons and Bows" (see page 98) was reprised. Other songs by the pair included "California Rose," "Wing-Ding Tonight," and "What a Dirty Shame." "There's a Cloud in My Valley of Sunshine" was written by Jack Hope and Lyle Moraine, and Jack Brooks served up "Four-Legged Friend" and "Am I in Love?," the latter of which received an Academy Award nomination. In the film, Hope and Russell sing the song while she shaves him.

Hope was available on Oscar night but Russell wasn't, so he performed the song with Marilyn Maxwell. Walt Disney, who was the presenter of the music awards that night, managed to mangle the pronunciation of most of the composers' names. It wasn't entirely his fault — nominees for Best Score had names like Miklos Rosza (which became "Miklos Rosca") and Dimitri Tiomkin, which Walt valiantly attempted and trampled. Other composers with complex names like Gian-Carlo Menotti didn't help. Flustered, he misread the nominated song from *Son of Paleface,* proclaiming, "I Am in Love!" Although Mrs. Disney was no doubt pleased, no one knows for sure just how composer Jack Brooks felt, since he lost to the highly unpronounceable Dimitri Tiomkin (and Ned Washington) for "High Noon" (see page 118).

BECAUSE YOU'RE MINE

**Music by Nicholas Brodszky;
lyrics by Sammy Cahn**
From *Because You're Mine*

Producer Joe Pasternak had his hands full. Mario Lanza, the self-proclaimed successor to Enrico Caruso, suffered nervous disorders brought about by excessive boozing and eating, along with various attempts at crash dieting. He had mood swings, he had bouts of drunkenness, he was often violent — in short, he was a very sick man.

In his Lanza biography, *The Mario Lanza Story,* the singer's conductor, Constantine Callinicos, describes the "nightmare world" in which those surrounding this great, self-destructive talent dwelled. He tells a story of the confrontation between Lanza and Pasternak, who had worked with Lanza before and was now meeting with him to discuss their next picture, *Because You're Mine.* "I think it would be a natural for your talents," Pasternak said of the film. "Your fans would love you in it, as a plain GI. It's only a few years since the war, and the GI role would be a very sympathetic one for you."

Lanza's ego shrugged off the stroking. "Are you serious?" he snapped. "How can you put Caruso in the Army? I don't think Mario Lanza will ever do it." Pasternak launched his final salvo: "Do you want to play God? I'll get you the rights!"

The film was made, however, between Lanza's bouts of eating and drinking, alternating with starvation. Chemically imbalanced, he continued to battle with his producer. "Once he rammed his Cadillac into the mailbox in front of Pasternak's home," Callinicos reports. "Another time, when he had been drinking heavily, he paid a nocturnal call on the Pasternak home and stood out front bellowing threats to assault Joe and his wife." An intervention was attempted by Callinicos and some close friends, who chartered a private plane to bring the opera singer to a New York psychiatric clinic specializing in nervous disorders. Unfortunately, the doctors there could do nothing for him without his cooperation, which was not forthcoming.

Amidst this turmoil, Lanza's talent managed to emerge. According to Callinicos, "With the help of constant strategy meetings, conferences, prolonged persuasion, intermittent severity and coddling, *Because You're Mine* was finally completed." Not only that, but critics heralded Lanza's performance, unaware of his inner turmoil. While *Variety* inadvertently fanned the singer's flames, proclaiming "Lanza slimmer than in *Caruso*. Sometimes seems heavier. Reminder of long delay in making film while Lanza made weight," it also acknowledged the "terrific Lanza singing," which should have been the only concern in the first place. Otis L. Guernsey Jr. of the *New York Herald Tribune* echoed that sentiment: "Mario sings with all the vigor and expression that have made him one of the most popular phenomena of the modern musical screen."

The plot of the picture — Lanza as a young soldier in love with the top sergeant's sister — was secondary to the real purpose of the film, that of showing off Lanza's tenor vocal chords at approximately five-minute intervals. Nicholas Brodszky and Sammy Cahn, perennial also-rans in the Academy Award derby at this point in their careers, again received a nomination for one of their tunes, in this case the title song, "Because You're Mine." As it turned out, this would be the last pairing for the two, who had also composed "Be My Love" for Lanza in 1950's *The Toast of New Orleans* (see page 109). They would garner future Oscar nominations with new partners after going their separate ways.

Lanza recorded the song, and it became a popular request on the radio, if not a top hit. Additionally, Lanza sang "Granada," "O Paradis," from the opera *L'Africaine*, "The Songs Angels Sing," "Lee-Ah-Loo," "Miserere" from *Il Trovatore*, "The Lord's Prayer," "Mama Mia, Che Vo Sape?" and several other selections, some in duets with female co-star Doretta Morrow, others with James Whitmore (who played the sergeant).

The film was a moderate success, and Lanza eventually apologized to Pasternak for all the trouble he had caused. Sadly, he never regained his health; he died after years of alcohol and drug abuse in 1959 at the age of 38.

Mario Lanza sings the nominated title song from *Because You're Mine*.

THUMBELINA

Music and lyrics by Frank Loesser
From *Hans Christian Andersen*

A fairy tale to warm the hearts of children everywhere, *Hans Christian Andersen* was a Christmas treat when it opened in theaters across America. Everyone adored Danny Kaye as the handsome storyteller who spun his tales for children, arrived in "wonderful, wonderful Copenhagen," and fell in love with a Danish ballerina. Everyone, that is except the Danes themselves.

While the $4 million production of the life of Andersen was making box-office history in the United States (final take: $6 million in rentals, making it the fifth-ranked hit for 1952), the Danish government, without actually having seen the film, refused to allow the picture to be exhibited. They condemned it because the film was as fictitious as any of Andersen's yarns.

Aside from the fact that Andersen did write children's stories, very little else in *Hans Christian Andersen* actually happened in his life. To resolve the situation, a disclaimer was added to introduce the movie, explaining that it was "a fairy tale about a great spinner of fairy tales." Finally, after eight months, the film had its Danish premiere, to critical acclaim. When Queen Ingrid herself attended the opening-night benefit performance, all doubt was shunted aside. *Hans Christian Andersen* was at last welcomed home.

The film had all the bells and whistles — production by Samuel Goldwyn, script by Moss Hart (reportedly there were 20 predecessors), direction by Charles Vidor, and a lavish musical score by Frank Loesser. Billed as a children's picture, although obviously popular with adults, kids figured prominently in all the musical production numbers, and at least half of the songs were based on Andersen's fairy tales — "Inch Worm," "The King's New Clothes," "The Ugly Duckling," and the nominated tune, "Thumbelina."

In "Thumbelina," one of the most charming songs, Danny Kaye, as the jailed Hans C. Andersen, improvises a story for child actress Beverly Washburn (who stops below his window to ask if he's scared) by turning his thumb into a storybook character. Washburn, who was nine at the time, remembers having to learn to use the Danish toy with which she plays in the scene: "They trained me for two or three days and made a big deal about it," she recalls. She must have gotten it right, since the scene plays flawlessly. In addition to the tune's Oscar nomination, Kaye's recording of "Thumbelina," a true children's song, made number 28 on the pop charts in October of 1952, prior to the film's release.

Those deciding which one of the film's songs to submit for nomination must have had a difficult time. Besides the fairy tale–based ditties mentioned above, the picture featured several other strong tunes: "Wonderful Copenhagen" is practically the anthem of that city now; "No Two People," "Anywhere I Wander," and the opening song, "I'm Hans Christian Andersen" were equally memorable.

The Motion Picture Academy honored the film with six nominations in all. In addition to Best Song, there were nominations (but no wins) for Best Color Cinematography, Best Color Art Direction/Set Decoration, Best Sound Recording, Best Scoring of a Musical Picture, and Best Color Costume Design.

The character of "Thumbelina" has proved to be one of the most popular ever created by Andersen. In 1994, animator Don Bluth (director of *An American Tail,* 1986) released a new animated movie called *Thumbelina;* although the cartoon had musical numbers, it was not based on the song nor the character from *Hans Christian Andersen,* nor did it contain any of the Frank Loesser songs.

ZING A LITTLE ZONG

Music by Harry Warren; lyrics by Leo Robin
From *Just for You*

Jane Wyman had proved she could hold her own against Bing Crosby when the two had first been paired to sing the Academy Award–winning "In the Cool, Cool, Cool of the Evening" in 1950 (see page 112). It was a cute novelty song — just the sort of tune that was needed for their second teaming two years later, when Paramount brought them together in *Just for You.* To create a vehicle for displaying the obvious musical chemistry between Wyman and Crosby, the producers brought in two top songwriters — composer Harry Warren and lyricist Leo Robin. They hadn't produced any Academy Award nominations as a team before, but both could boast several nominations over the preceding three decades while partnered with others, beginning with the very first year of the Best Song Oscar's presentation.

They managed to come up with a song very similar to "Cool, Cool, Cool" in feeling and rhythm. In fact, "Zing a Little Zong" began almost exactly like its predecessor. Where "Cool, Cool, Cool" has begun with "In the cool, cool of the evening," Warren and Robin's new song led off with, "Zing, zing, zing a little zong." It was fun, singable for audiences, and playable for disc jockeys, if not a chart-burner. The pair cut a record, released a couple of months before the film came out — just early enough to stir up interest. It peaked at number 18 and charted for six weeks.

There was another noteworthy novelty tune in the film, performed by Crosby, and perhaps another inten-

Bing Crosby gives Jane Wyman a lesson in how to "Zing a Little Zong" in *Just for You*.

tional stab at the elusive statuette. It was called "On the 10:10 from Ten-Ten-Tennessee." Could that be anywhere near Chattanooga? "The songs and song numbers," wrote Bosley Crowther in the *New York Times,* "while pleasant, are nothing to set the screen on fire."

Bolstered by her success as a recording artist and Academy Award–winning actress, Jane Wyman continued doing records for Decca, both solo and partnered in duets with artists like Danny Kaye. For one single, she teamed up with Kaye, Jimmy Durante, and Groucho Marx. "Black Strap Molasses" was on the A-side, with "How Di Ye Do and Shake Hands" on the flip side. "Records are a whole new field," Wyman was quoted as saying in the biography *Jane Wyman,* by Joe Morella and Edward Z. Epstein. "I'm just coasting. I think I can

make a few more sides before they get wise to me . . . Records are great fun, but I'm not that serious about it."

The storyline of *Just for You* in many ways paralleled that of Wyman's own life. The film's basic conflict involved a single parent (Crosby) who is a famous producer, struggling to balance a show-biz career and parenthood. Wyman, who had been divorced from Ronald Reagan since 1948, was in a similar situation, a divorced mom trying to make time for her two children, Michael and Maureen, while living the full-time life of a glamorous Hollywood star.

This second film with Crosby, while diversionary fun for Wyman, would be their last teaming. "I think we've about had it," she said. "We should just let it lie there."

SECRET LOVE

Music by Sammy Fain;
lyrics by Paul Francis Webster
From *Calamity Jane*

When Doris Day, America's freckle-faced sweetheart, debuted as the raucous girlfriend of Wild Bill Hickok in *Calamity Jane,* a wave of controversy seemed to follow her. Critics panned her for attempting to become another Betty Hutton, who had played a similarly tomboyish Annie Oakley three years earlier in *Annie Get Your Gun* (which, not so coincidentally, had had the same co-star, Howard Keel). "Doris Day works very, very hard at being Calamity and is hardly realistic at all," proclaimed *Variety.* "Strain shows through in her essaying of the hard and dynamic Calamity character." Writing in the *New York Times,* Bowley Crowther opined, "Miss Day could afford to be less violent, occasionally a little more relaxed."

They thought they were speaking of the character Doris Day played in the film. They didn't realize that they could have been speaking of her personal life.

In her autobiography, *Doris Day: Her Own Story,* Day tells of the problems that began almost as soon as the picture wrapped. At about that time, she found a small lump in her breast, and she also began having shortness of breath and heart palpitations. At first she was afraid to tell anyone and tried to get through it on her own. When things seemed to get worse, she turned to her religion, Christian Science, convinced she could overcome whatever ailments her body threw at her by using the healing powers of her mind. After she fainted one night, her husband rushed her to a doctor, who confirmed that there was nothing physically wrong with her (the lump proved benign), but that she had been hyperventilating. Too much oxygen and not enough carbon dioxide had caused the physical manifestations. She was caught in a vicious circle, suffering from nervous exhaustion. Through proper treatment, including medication and therapy, she made a complete recovery, but not before the episode took its toll on her reputation.

She was careful not to publicize her struggle. The press never learned about her illness. "Since I had

always been very cooperative in the past," Day wrote, "the media people interpreted these turndowns [for interviews] as an indication that I had become snooty, a movie queen aloof on her thrown . . . That upset me very much." When she failed to appear at the Academy Awards to sing "Secret Love,"[1] the song nominated from *Calamity Jane,* columnists began criticizing her, even giving her the "Sour Apple Award" as the most uncooperative actress in films.

"Secret Love" went on to win the Oscar. (Other nominations for *Calamity Jane* were for Best Sound Recording and Best Scoring of a Musical Picture.) Motion picture veterans Sammy Fain, who had been doing movie tunes since 1929, and Paul Francis Webster, whose film career began in 1935, wrote this beautiful love ballad for Day to sing in the film. Its mood contrasted greatly with her pistol-packin', two-fisted, rowdy character. This was the Doris Day the world knew and loved — so much so, in fact, that her single of "Secret Love" (backed with "The Deadwood Stage," also from the movie) became a Number One hit for four weeks and charted for 18 more.

A surprising array of singers from various genres had hits with "Secret Love." Slim Whitman, for instance, had a number two hit on the country charts in 1954, and Freddy Fender had a crossover hit with the tune — number 20 on the pop charts and Number One on the country charts in 1975. Ahmad Jamal took the song to number 18 hit on R&B charts, while Billy Stewart's version made number 11 R&B and number 29 pop in 1966. Numerous other artists have recorded the song over the years, and several have made the top 40.

THE MOON IS BLUE

Music by Herschel Burke Gilbert; lyrics by
Sylvia Fine
From *The Moon Is Blue*

Before there was a sexual revolution, or even a call to arms, Hollywood had a strict code about what it deemed proper subject matter for films. And as is usually true in

---

1. Ann Blyth substituted for her. During reheasals, someone voiced concern about whether Blyth, who was in the early stages of pregnancy and just beginning to show, should be singing lyrics like "my secret love's no secret anymore." Since the actress was married, those in charge decided that it was acceptable.

such cases, it violated that code as frequently as possible. One instance of this hypocrisy was *The Moon Is Blue,* a serious drama about a woman and her virginity (discretely referred to by some reviewers, who still refused to discuss such things in writing, as "maidenly virtue"). The so-called adult comedy seems tame by contemporary standards, but in a cinematic era when bedroom doors were never closed, one foot was always kept on the floor, and married couples routinely slept in twin beds, some of the language was considered scandalous. Shocking terms like "virgin," "seduce," and "pregnant" were bandied about with impunity. •

Based on the successful Broadway play by F. Hugh Herbert, who also wrote the screenplay, *The Moon Is Blue* was really an innocuous, remarkably moral play with heavy emphasis on the lesson to be learned when a "good girl" retains her virtue and gets the man. Unfortunately, it wasn't the story that ultimately caused this United Artists production to fail; rather, it was the film's stage-bound nature, with its three main characters and constant dialogue. William Holden did a convincing job as the seducer, as did Maggie McNamara, as the seducee, with David Niven adding spice as the upstairs neighbor.

Maggie McNamara was poised to launch what seemed to be a promising career when this picture appeared. She had starred in the stage version of *The Moon Is Blue* and easily segued to the part on film. "Newcomer Maggie McNamara [presents] an interesting talent as the femme lead," proclaimed *Variety.* But not all the critics were kind. Bosley Crowther of the *New York Times* was particularly hard on the young lady, writing, "Maggie McNamara . . . tends to be slightly annoying with her endless chatter and her sing-song speaking voice in which she was probably directed but which certainly lacks quality and charm. She is also a bit oddly shapen — long of neck and short of leg — which leaves one, at least, wondering mildly wherein lies her vaunted allure."

Nevertheless, the Academy managed to see past these remarks and nominated McNamara for the Best Actress Oscar that year (won by Audrey Hepburn in *Roman Holiday*). Unfortunately, her career would have few subsequent highlights. She was signed by Fox, but starred in only two more roles in the '50s — *Three Coins in the Fountain* (1954) and *Prince of Players* (1955). She then vanished from the public eye, later resurfacing in *The Cardinal* in 1963. She also appeared on Broadway in 1962's *Step on a Crack*. Her career again foundered, she sought work as a typist, and her marriage ended in divorce. In 1978 she committed suicide by overdosing on sleeping pills. She had just turned 50.

The title song from the film, "The Moon Is Blue," also received an Oscar nomination. The song, written by Herschel Burke Gilbert, with lyrics by Sylvia Fine (Mrs. Danny Kaye), is played and sung over the film's opening credits by the Sauter-Finegan Orchestra and an unnamed vocalist. The orchestra had only been organized for about a year. Both Eddie Sauter and Bill Finegan had worked with many of the big band biggies, including Benny Goodman, Artie Shaw, Tommy Dorsey, Woody Herman, and Glenn Miller. By the time the two teamed up, big bands were on their way out, and observers predicted doom for Sauter-Finegan. Yet they survived for five years, due in part to their own innovations to the big band sound. The two leaders, a novelty in itself, featured such infrequently highlighted instruments as the flute, piccolo, oboe, English horn, bass clarinet, and harp, and provided unusual percussion effects emphasizing the timpani.

The opening music to *The Moon Is Blue* was released as a single by the Sauter-Finegan Orchestra. It was a surprising hit, if not a monstrous one, peaking at number 20 on the *Billboard* charts.

MY FLAMING HEART

**Music by Nicholas Brodszky;
lyrics by Leo Robin**
From *Small Town Girl*

Small-town girl meets big-town boy — that was the theme of the Joe Pasternak–MGM musical *Small Town Girl*. The story was not particularly original: a wealthy New Yorker (Farley Granger) gets a speeding ticket while zipping through Duck Creek, USA — population 4,516. The judge, who naturally has a lovely daughter (Jane Powell), sentences him to 30 days in the local hoosegow. It turns into a life sentence, however, when said lovely young daughter and rich but foolish big city boy fall in love, tossing aside his show-girl fiancée (Ann Miller). This plot, a sure winner, has been frequently recycled, more recently (with contemporary changes) in 1991's *Doc Hollywood*, starring Michael J. Fox (premise: promising, future rich plastic surgeon lands in the small town from Hell and discovers happiness and love).

It all made for light-hearted fun in the traditional Pasternak style. The plot does a nice job of staying out of the way of the film's *raisons d'être* — the eight songs by veteran film music writers Nicholas Brodszky and Leo Robin, and the snazzy Busby Berkeley dance routines.

Pasternak, a native Hungarian who began his career directing European films, was noted for pictures that brought classical music to the attention of unsuspecting audiences who might otherwise not have attended such "highbrow" fare. He is credited with saving the career of Marlene Dietrich when it was faltering in the late '30s, and saved Universal from financial ruin with a string of highly successful Deanna Durbin musicals in the '40s. Moving to MGM in the late '40s, he produced all of Mario Lanza's films despite a love-hate relationship with the temperamental star (see page 109).

Small Town Girl featured a lavish Brodszky/Robin score. Songs included a waltz, "The Fellow I'd Follow"; a hymnal chant, "Lullaby of the Lord" (sung by Powell); "Small Towns Are Smile Towns"; and "Fine, Fine, Fine" (also by Powell), plus two hot production numbers showing off Miller's fast and flashy tapping — "I've Gotta Hear That Beat" and "My Gaucho," a south-of-the-border rhythm. Hoofer Bobby Van, a featured performer who the *New York Times* compared to a "young Ray Bolger," steps lively in the show-stopping "Take Me to Broadway."

But the best song in the film, nominated for the Best Song Oscar, was performed by Nat "King" Cole. Singing and playing a slow, jazzy number called "My Flaming Heart," Cole appears in a nightclub sequence in the picture, where people out for a night on the town stop in to see him at the "Club Del Rio." It was one of many film appearances by the late entertainer. Over the years he had brief roles in films like *Here Comes Elmer* (1943), *Swing in the Saddle* (1944), *See My Lawyer* (1945), *Kiss Me Deadly* (1955), and *The Night of the Quarter Moon* (1959). His last picture was the highly popular *Cat Ballou* (1965 — see page 181).

The unforgettable Nat "King" Cole sang "My Flaming Heart," the Oscar-nominated tune from *Small Town Girl*.

SADIE THOMPSON'S SONG (BLUE PACIFIC BLUES)

Music by Lester Lee; lyrics by Ned Washington
From *Miss Sadie Thompson*

Television was winning. Motion picture studios were frantic to find ways to recapture the distracted attention of fickle audiences. Big name stars, lavish Technicolor productions, musicals, dancing girls, you name it — nothing seemed to be working. Then someone remembered stereoscopy, a process actually conceived in the 19th century. Three-dimensional motion picture processes were first patented around 1900, but they were never technically feasible. Experiments continued through the silent era, and by the time of the New York World's Fair of 1939, a fairly good process had been developed. But like so many other things that teased audiences with a look into the future, it was never really put to the commercial test.

Then, in the 1950s, with the advent of the living room TV set, desperate film producers again turned to gimmickry to attract wayward audiences. Soon people began drifting back into the theaters and donning special glasses to see a whole array of stereoscopic films, now renamed "3-D." Some of these were nothing more than novelty movies — people tossing balls at the camera or poking broom handles out into the audience. But in some 3-D films, the process actually took a back seat to storytelling.

Such was the case in the remake of the W. Somerset Maugham story *Rain*, redone and updated for the '50s as *Miss Sadie Thompson*. The new Columbia release starred Rita Hayworth in the role of the sex symbol of the South Pacific, and Columbia's advertising department made full use of her assets in their promotional campaign. A full-figure photo showed Rita, provocatively twirling her purse, cigarette dangling from her pouty lips; she wore a low-cut blouse and slit-up-the-thigh skirt, while the posters proclaimed, "Rita Turns It On In 3-D!"

Maybe so, but she still didn't do much to turn audiences on. The picture was, by all accounts, a loser. It wasn't the acting — Rita, José Ferrer, Aldo Rey, and the rest of the cast all received critical praise; so did the cinematography, done on location against Hawaii's lush, photogenic island scenery. But the updated screenplay seemed to suffer in its transition from the original version. The material was dated; somehow the story about sex, sin, and salvation in the tropics wasn't as salacious as it had seemed when Gloria Swanson first strutted her stuff back in 1928 or Joan Crawford succumbed to the fire-and-brimstone preacher in the 1932 version of *Rain*. In fact, in *Miss Sadie Thompson*, the preacher was no longer a missionary, just a bigoted fanatic who is ineffectual at best. Unfortunately, none of this worked as a drawing card for audiences.

What did the most to draw patrons to the theaters was the music. There was a much-publicized 3-D dance in a smoke-filled barroom in a production number called "The Heat Is On," along with other musical numbers by Lester Lee and veteran film lyricist Ned Washington. "Hear No Evil, See No Evil," which Rita sings to a group of children, had also been heavily plugged. But the outstanding song in the film — and the one that received an Oscar nomination — was one called "Blue Pacific Blues" or, alternately, "Sadie Thompson's Song." It's a sexy number performed by a reclining Rita, surrounded by Marines. "Blue Pacific Blues" was released as a single and enjoyed five weeks on the *Billboard* charts with a recording by Richard Hayman, which peaked at number 20.

THAT'S AMORE

**Music by Harry Warren; lyrics by Jack Brooks
From *The Caddy***

Dean Martin and Jerry Lewis were an unlikely pair, the oddest of all possible odd couples: a handsome Italian singer teamed with a rubber-legged scrawny young Jewish man who whined in a little-boy voice. Yet what should have been a booking agent's nightmare instead became a fountain of gold. They complemented each other perfectly with their equally matched talents, becoming overnight sensations onstage, in nightclubs, and eventually in movies. Martin and Lewis were like ham and . . . ham. Perfect comedic timing and a mutual respect — while it lasted — made them the darlings of the American public as well as box office champions.

In 1953, they brought their latest antics to the screen in *The Caddy*, their tenth picture together (they would make 16 before splitting up in 1956). It was pure M & L, with Jerry clowning it up by roller skating through a china shop, impersonating a Continental sophisticate, and fleeing from a pack of watchdogs. For his part, Dino, the act's straight man, had little more to do than look handsome, romance Donna Reed, and sing some pretty songs. He made it look easy, the way George Burns used to do with Gracie Allen, but anyone who has worked in show business knows that if the comedic partner comes off looking great while the other half looks laid back, then the straight man's doing his job. When the *New York Times*, in its review of *The Caddy*, noted, "Mr. Lewis is slowly taking over. Just give him a couple of more years," this was in fact an unwitting acknowledgment that Dino was an expert straight man — although he certainly was not given as much to do as he would have liked.

Martin was also a fine singer. Fortunately for him, composer Harry Warren knew this. When called upon to write a song for the film, Warren dug back to his (and Martin's) Italian roots to write "That's Amore," which compares love to having the moon hit your eye "like a big pizza pie." Dean Martin would eventually take the song with its quirky lyrics (by Jack Brooks) and make it his own. But not before he panned the tune altogether.

As was so often the case with some of the great songs to emerge from the cinema, Martin hated "That's Amore" when he first heard it. He wanted to do an old Italian standard, "Oh, Marie" — a sure thing — rather than some unknown tune. Under pressure from Paramount, which had paid Warren (a four time Oscar-winner) a good deal of money to compose the song, Dino reluctantly agreed to sing "That's Amore" in the film. But that was all. He flatly refused to cut a record for Capitol, stating it wasn't worthy of his talents. Paramount couldn't get him to budge, so they did the next best thing — they gave Capitol Records the rights to the sound track version. Two months after the picture's release, "That's Amore" made its debut in record stores and on the radio. It climbed the charts rapidly, peaking at number two and remaining there for five weeks (and on the charts for 22), reportedly selling more than two million copies. It was Martin's first hit in seven years — the sort of dry spell that makes his stubbornness about the song all the more remarkable — and also won an Oscar nomination (Dino broke down and sang it at the Oscar ceremonies the following Spring). While it lost to "Secret Love," the song set Dean Martin firmly on the road to stardom as a solo performer.

THREE COINS IN THE FOUNTAIN

Music by Jule Styne; lyrics by Sammy Cahn
From *Three Coins in the Fountain*

"Three Coins in the Fountain" added up to jingling coins in many pockets. For 20th Century-Fox, the film studio that produced the picture *Three Coins in the Fountain*, it represented $4.8 million in rental take at the box office, a tidy sum for the film, which ranked in the year's top 15. For Jule Styne and Sammy Cahn, there were lots of royalties (they owned a combined 50 percent of the profits) and an Oscar for writing the film's title song, the icing on a cake they almost didn't get to eat.

Fox producer Sol Siegel thought he had a dog of a

picture on his hands, something called *We Believe in Love*. He brought in the team of Styne and Cahn, hoping that a nifty song might somehow elevate the film. It was a lavish new CinemaScope production (Fox's wide-screen attempt to lure TV viewers back into theaters), set against the background of the glory that was Rome, not to mention Dorothy McGuire, Jean Peters, and Maggie McNamara. After Siegel described the picture's opening sequence of these three ladies tossing coins into Rome's Trevi Fountain, Styne asked, "Why don't you call it *Three Coins in the Fountain*?"

Siegel questioned whether the songsters could write a song by that title, to which lyricist Cahn replied, "It's a helluva lot easier than 'We Believe in Love.' " According to Cahn, he finished his lyric in 20 minutes and handed it to Styne, who spent another 20 minutes creating a melody. With time of the essence (as it always seems to be in Hollywood), the front office boss in New York, Spyro Skouras, was notified of the song and film title change. He balked: Why lose a good word like *Love* in the title? Eventually, Styne volunteered "to get Frank" (as in Sinatra) to do it; he was recording the song the following Monday just as the New York brass walked onto the sound stage. Timing being everything, the song with Sinatra behind it struck just the right chord with Skouras. And with the American public. And with the Academy of Motion Picture Arts and Sciences.

Sinatra's recording, which was sung under the film's opening title sequence, became a number four hit, on the charts for four weeks. But surprisingly, it was a recording by a new group, the Four Aces, that captured the hearts of the record-buying public, who pushed the Aces' version of the song to the top of the charts for one week. It remained on the charts for a total of 18 weeks. An additional version was recorded by Julius La Rosa; it peaked at number 21.

When Oscar time rolled around, Sammy Cahn was less than confident. He'd made the trip to the altar 13 times before but was always a best man, never a groom. The fourteenth time is always the charm. (Over the years, Cahn would win three more times; this would be the only win for the oft-nominated Styne.) Director of photography Milton Krasner also won an Oscar that night for Best Color Cinematography.

The film told the story of three young American women — "predatory dames," as the *New York Times* called them in the vernacular of the day — searching for husbands in the Eternal City of Rome. The title and lyrics of the song refer to the legend that throwing a

Bing Crosby, Rosemary Clooney, Vera-Ellen, and Danny Kaye sing about White Christmas in the 1954 film named after the 1942 Academy Award–winning song. The new movie spawned another Irving Berlin Oscar-nominated song, "Count Your Blessings Instead of Sheep."

coin in Rome's Trevi Fountain will make one's wish come true. The song was largely responsible for making this fountain a major tourist attraction, crowded mostly with Americans, backs to the fountain, tossing *lire* over their shoulders and wishing for happiness. (Actually, the legend only promises a return to Rome, not a happily-ever-after marriage, as in the film.) While there are no statistics on the success of the wishers, the whole scene certainly was the answer to Rome's public-relations prayers — even to this day, crowds of people can be seen at Trevi on any given day, pitching coins into the fountain.

COUNT YOUR BLESSINGS (INSTEAD OF SHEEP)

Music and lyrics by Irving Berlin
From *White Christmas*

Irving Berlin was famous for making films based on his song titles. "Blue Skies," "Alexander's Ragtime Band," "Easter Parade" — all became hit films. It seemed only natural, then, following the success of the 1942 picture *Holiday Inn*, which produced the biggest-selling song of the century — "White Christmas," with sales that have now reached 30 million and counting — that there should be a film based on that title. It took 12 years, but in 1954 Paramount finally corralled Bing Crosby to star in a sequel and Irving Berlin to write new tunes for it.

Originally, it was to be a Crosby–Fred Astaire starrer, but Astaire was ill and unable to appear in the picture. Donald O'Connor was then signed, and when he became ill as well, Danny Kaye was brought in as a last-minute replacement. Since he wasn't the top-billed star, there was less for him to do than in his own vehicles. Although he clowned and cut up a few times, it was one of his tamest comedy performances and certainly not his most memorable role.

There were nine new songs by Berlin, along with seven recycled ones. Naturally, "White Christmas" opened and closed the show, with all the drama and nostalgia Crosby and company could muster. It made the classic even more classical, as audiences wiped at a tear or two at picture's finale (even though it was only October when the film was released). Among the songs included were "The Old Man," a sentimental military march about an army general; "Sisters," a cute number with Crosby and Kaye in drag and the voices of co-stars Vera-Ellen and Rosemary Clooney dubbed in; "The Best Things Happen While You're Dancing"; "Snow"; "Mandy," a minstrel number; "Love, You Didn't Do Right by Me"; and "Count Your Blessings (Instead of Sheep)."

"Count Your Blessings," a sweet lullaby performed by Clooney and Crosby, received an Oscar nomination for Berlin — his seventh and last. Both Crosby and Clooney made recordings of the tune; each one peaked at number seventeen on the charts. They might have done better had a popular new singer not gotten the drop on them by six weeks or so: Eddie Fisher's version debuted at the end of October, as compared to Crosby's the first week in December and Clooney's a week later. It became one of Fisher's biggest-selling records, appearing on "Your Hit Parade" 13 times. His record peaked in the number five position, and was on the *Billboard* charts for 15 weeks.

Still, it was "White Christmas" (which won Berlin the Academy Award in 1942 — see page 50) that everyone remembered from *White Christmas*. A holiday perennial, the filmusical can be found popping up all over the dial at Christmastime, proving that for Paramount, Berlin, and Crosby, there's no business like snow business.

THE HIGH AND THE MIGHTY

**Music by Dimitri Tiomkin;
lyrics by Ned Washington
From *The High and the Mighty***

The High and the Mighty was the original *Airport,* a sky-high disaster film set aboard an aircraft bound from Honolulu to San Francisco, beset by every flyer's worst nightmare — something gone wrong in midair. Don't look for this one as an in-flight movie.

The "high" and the "mighty" of the title refer to the brave pilots fighting to bring their craft home safely, in this case John Wayne as the veteran pilot, second in command yet more in control of things than Robert Stack, as the captain. It was a people story, too, with all the drama this genre usually brings with it.

The lofty film called for a lofty score, and Dimitri Tiomkin was pressed into service. The theme he created, appropriately called "The High and the Mighty," was prevalent throughout the picture. It is frequently whistled and is secondarily named "The Whistling Song." But when it came time for Oscar nominations, Tiomkin was informed that it would not be eligible for an Academy Award nomination, since there were no lyrics heard in the film.

There are two versions of what happened next. In one, Tiomkin, irate because the lyrics had originally appeared in the film but had been later removed, immediately had Warner Bros. issue one print with reinstated lyrics. The print was exhibited in Los Angeles, and Tiomkin took to the air in a skywriting plane to announce the fact. This makes for a dramatic tale, but a second version of the same story is probably more accurate: Tiomkin, upon learning that the song was ineligible because the "lyrics" were only whistled, enlisted the aid of lyricist Ned Washington, a multiple Oscar-nominee, to create words for Tiomkin's music. The studio then quickly inserted these, sung under the closing title. One would be hard-pressed to find someone today who can sing a few bars, but most people will readily recognize the melody (and accompanying whistling) upon hearing it.

Tiomkin had better luck with his complete musical score for *The High and the Mighty*. He received his third Oscar, having previously won two for *High Noon* (see page 118). His acceptance speech was memorable. In a town where movie composers had frequently been accused of plagiarism, the Russian-born composer stated (with tongue firmly planted in cheek): "I'd like to thank Johannes Brahms, Johann Strauss, Richard Strauss, Richard Wagner, Beethoven, Rimsky-Korsakov . . ." As the audience laughed, Bob Hope's voice could be heard rising above the din: "You'll never get on *this* show again!" Hope was wrong, of course — Tiomkin would receive a fourth Oscar, for *The Old Man and the Sea* in 1958.

"The High and the Mighty" achieved success as a popular recording, generally without lyrics. Les Baxter's orchestral version peaked at number four and was on the charts for 13 weeks. Victor Young's orchestral recording peaked in the number six position, while Johnny Desmond (who sang the song at the Awards ceremony, along with Muzzy Marcellino) released a vocal recording, which reached the number 17 position. Tiomkin himself conducted his orchestra and reached the number 29 position. Over the years, the haunting, ethereal song has been recorded by many others, including Billy Eckstine, Perez Prado, the Shadows, Lionel Hampton, Los Indios Tabajaras, Harry James, Roger Williams, and Arthur Lyman.

HOLD MY HAND

**Music by Jack Lawrence;
   lyrics by Richard Myers**
From *Susan Slept Here*

It's hard to say whether or not it was just wishful thinking on the part of Harriet Parsons — that rarity among rarities in the '50s, a female producer — or simply an inside joke. But the occasional narration in *Susan Slept Here* is done by an Academy Award statuette. It was one of the many inside jokes in this comedy, described by *Variety* with that all-encompassing and vastly overused term, "wacky."

The story centers around a Hollywood writer, played by Dick Powell, whose subject matter is juvenile delinquency (the narrating Oscar is his). Enter Debbie Reynolds, who becomes his guinea pig after being deposited at his doorstep one Christmas Eve by two detectives. Soon there's romance in the air as the May–December affair takes hold.

Much of the cast would soon find their way into motion pictures' arch-rival medium, television. One

Anne Francis, Dick Powell and Debbie Reynolds in a scene from *Susan Slept Here*.

inside joke in the film had Dick Powell catching one of his old movies on TV. By 1961, Powell would be hosting his own TV anthology series, "The Dick Powell Show." Co-star Debbie Reynolds would have a show with her name on it in 1969, a comedy about the unpredictable wife of a sports columnist. Anne Francis, who played Reynolds's rival love interest in *Susan Slept Here,* starred in several movies, including the sci-fi cult film *Forbidden Planet* (1956), before being featured in her own TV series, the popular detective show "Honey West."

Alvy Moore, listed fourth in the credits, played Powell's ex–Navy buddy and handyman. He, too, would go on to co-star in a television series, playing Hank Kimball, the talkative agricultural representative in "Green Acres."

Ellen Corby probably did better than any of the lesser players in *Susan Slept Here.* Billed close to the bottom simply as "Waitress," she went on to co-star as Grandma Walton in the highly acclaimed television series *The Waltons.* Better still, she won three Emmys for Outstanding Continuing Performance by a Supporting Actress in a Drama Series (1973, 1975, 1976).

Despite the cute hint, there were no Oscars for *Susan Slept Here,* although there was one nomination: "Hold My Hand," for Best Song. Written by Jack Lawrence and Richard Myers, it is heard as source music in the movie as Debbie Reynolds fixes breakfast while listening to the radio. The recording was made by Don Cornell, who released the actual hit record. It peaked at number two during an 18-week run on the charts. Today the song is frequently heard on over 200 radio stations across the United States, as part of Unistar's nostalgia format.

THE MAN THAT GOT AWAY

Music by Harold Arlen; lyrics by Ira Gershwin
From *A Star Is Born*

Every now and then Hollywood submits to a degree of soul-searching, turning the cameras on itself and laying bare the inner workings that make up the body and soul of this passionate, if cruel, city. Against this setting for high drama, a story was born.

Adela Rogers St. Johns wrote the original version, based on an actual incident she witnessed in the 1920s, wherein an alcoholic male star, John Bowers, swam to his death in the Pacific Ocean. Her story, *What Price Hollywood?,* was filmed in 1932 by George Cukor, and

starred Constance Bennett and Lowell Sherman. In 1937, David O. Selznick, who had produced it, decided to do a remake. Under its new title — *A Star Is Born* — and directed by William Wellman, the film starred Janet Gaynor as the new kid in town destined for glory; Frederic March played her star-crossed mentor/husband whose destiny lay in the ocean depths. Then, in 1954, producer Sid Luft optioned the property. He took it to George Cukor, his choice for director. The film would be a starring vehicle for Luft's wife. Her name was Judy Garland.

Warner Bros. wasted no time in pulling out all the stops. DeLuxe color, which was used in the tests, wasn't as brilliant as Technicolor, so the latter was selected, along with the new CinemaScope process. Approximately $300,000 worth of footage had already been shot in standard format; it was summarily scrapped in favor of the wide-screen process. A top actor was sought for the male lead. Names like Humphrey Bogart and Frank Sinatra were tossed around; the studio pushed for Cary Grant, but at the last minute negotiations fell through. Finally, they decided upon James Mason. Many would later call this was his finest role.

Surely, there were many who felt that the part of Vicki Lester was Judy Garland's quintessential screen performance as well. And there was no doubt that the torch song she performs at the beginning of the picture, "The Man That Got Away," was her best on-screen musical number since "Over the Rainbow," if not her finest ever. Not surprisingly, the music was written by Harold Arlen, who had composed "Over the Rainbow." With lyrics by Ira Gershwin, it became legendary.

"The Man That Got Away" immediately clicked with lyricist Gershwin. Upon hearing Arlen play it for him the first time, he promptly suggested the title, to which the composer replied, simply, "I like." Judy Garland liked, too. The tune became her theme song. As *Time* magazine said, "Her big dark voice sobs, sighs, sulks, and socks it out like a cross between Tara's harp and the late Bessie Smith." Ironically, her record, timed to coincide with the release of the film, only reached number 22 on the pop charts. Frank Sinatra also made a recording, gender-bendered as "The Gal That Got Away," which charted to the number 21 position. Dozens of others have recorded it over the years, including Tony Bennett, Ella Fitzgerald, Pia Zadora, Rosemary Clooney, Dinah Washington, Pearl Bailey, Julie London, Vikki Carr, Sarah Vaughan, and Shirley Bassey. None has captured the essence as well as Garland.

Judy Garland mourns "The Man That Got Away" in *A Star Is Born*.

On Oscar night, Judy was scheduled to sing the nominated song. She was also up for an Oscar as Best Actress. (Other nominations: James Mason for Best Actor; Best Color Art Direction; Best Scoring — Ray Heindorf; and Best Color Costume Design. There were no wins.) But Judy was to have another event overshadow her appearance at the Oscars — two days before the ceremony, she had her own blessed event, the birth of son Joey Luft. Rosemary Clooney belted out Judy's song on Oscar night.

A Star Is Born would have another birth, too. It was remade in 1976, starring Barbra Streisand, who not only gave the time-honored story a new spin, but took home an Oscar for Best Song that year (see page 228).

1955

And the winner is...

LOVE IS A MANY-SPLENDORED THING

**Music by Sammy Fain;
lyrics by Paul Francis Webster**
From *Love Is a Many-Splendored Thing*

"Love Is a Many-Splendored Thing" proved to be just that for all concerned. The theme song had been widely popularized even before the film had been released, doing much to establish interest in this opera-ish love story, set in Hong Kong, about an American war correspondent (William Holden) and his Eurasian lover

(Jennifer Jones, with a stretch of the imagination — she's supposed to be a physician of mixed Chinese and English parentage).

Although the title is derived from Francis Thompson's poem "The Kingdom of God," the original name for the movie (based on the best-selling book by Han Suyin) was to have been simply "A Many-Splendored Thing." Sammy Fain and Paul Francis Webster, who had won the Academy Award for "Secret Love" in 1953 (see page 123) and had numerous nominations between them, were selected by the film's producer, Buddy Adler, to create a title song, which they obligingly did. The producer loved the song and thought it would be a big hit. Then, shortly before the film's release date, Adler hit Fain with the bad news: The film's title had been changed to include the words "Love Is." Apparently someone in the front office thought this would look bigger and better on a marquee and attract a wider audience.

Fain scrapped his original tune and wrote a new one, which he then took to his partner. Webster re-did his lyrics for the new version, the tune received the go-ahead from the studio, and Fain set about finding just the right recording artist. Tony Martin turned it down, claiming the song was "too heavy." Doris Day, Nat "King" Cole, Eddie Fisher — none of them would

touch it. One group finally agreed to do it — the Four Aces, the same artists who'd had a hit with "Three Coins in the Fountain." Fain's timing couldn't have been better. With the rock 'n' roll era breathing down their necks, the Four Aces had decided to fold; they were on the verge of breaking up when they agreed to do this one final tune.

Their version reached the top of the *Billboard* charts, where it held on for two weeks, and charted for a total of 21 weeks. Following the Aces' success with the song, some of the other artists who had originally turned it down released recordings of it. Other hit versions were posted by Don Cornell, whose recording peaked at number 26, David Rose, whose orchestral version peaked in the number 54 position, and Don, Dick 'n' Jimmy, who barely cracked the chart at number 96.

The film was not an immediate hit with critics and had only mild success at the box office ($4.2 million in North American rentals). Nevertheless, it was the darling of the Motion Picture Academy. Fain and Webster took home the Oscar for Best Song. (Ironically it was Eddie Fisher, one of the artists who had first turned down a chance to record it, who performed the number at the Awards ceremony.) In addition, the film bagged Oscars for Best Color Costume Design and Best

Jennifer Jones and William Holden play romantic leads in *Love Is a Many-Splendored Thing.*

Scoring of a Dramatic Picture, as well as nominations for Jennifer Jones as Best Actress and for the film for Best Picture, Best Cinematography, Best Sound, and Best Color Art Direction.

I'LL NEVER STOP LOVING YOU

Music by Nicholas Brodszky; lyrics by Sammy Cahn
From *Love Me or Leave Me*

Filmusical maven Joe Pasternak, who had produced a string of big-budget song-and-dance films for MGM, decided he wanted Doris Day to star in his next movie, a biopic about the life of Ruth Etting. Etting was a torch singer of the '20s whose life hadn't been the most exemplary, but it made for a colorful film biography. She was married to a former Chicago mobster named Martin Snyder, nicknamed "The Gimp," and James Cagney was set for the role of the small-time hoodlum who devoted his life to furthering his wife's career. But Day wasn't so sure she could carry off the part. She felt she was constantly being cast against type, and worried that the audience wouldn't believe her in the role.

"I had several discussions with Joe Pasternak about that," she wrote in her autobiography, *Doris Day: Her Own Story.* "The part would require me to drink, to wear scant, sexy costumes, to string along a man I didn't love in order to further my career. There was a vulgarity about Ruth Etting that I didn't want to play." Eventually, she gave in, partly because of the opportunity to play opposite Cagney, partly because of the great musical score.

She prepared for this demanding role by listening to all of Ruth Etting's records. "She had a quiet way of speaking and singing," wrote Day. "It was not my intention to mimic her, but to suggest her style with little inflections and shadings that I picked up from the recordings."

She did a convincing job, receiving lavish praise from the critics, but she was right about one thing — her fans were in an uproar. "I was deluged with mail attacking me for drinking, for playing a lewd woman, for the scant costumes I wore in the nightclub scenes . . . What's involved in this kind of protest is the movie realism that made me hesitate to play the role in the first place . . . To the audience I am Doris Day and I shouldn't be doing those dreadful things on the screen." She politely answered all her letters, and eventually returned to playing virgins.

The score of *Love Me or Leave Me* included many of the old standards, like "Ten Cents a Dance," "Everybody Loves My Baby," and "You Made Me Love You," plus some new ones composed especially for the film. One of these, "I'll Never Stop Loving You" garnered an Academy Award nomination for Nicholas Brodszky and Sammy Cahn, already multiple nominees. Although they would not take home the Oscar that night, the film's writer, Daniel Fuchs, received the statuette for Best Writing of a Motion Picture Story.

Doris Day's recording of "I'll Never Stop Loving You" (backed with the title song, "Love Me or Leave Me") became a modest hit, peaking at number 13 during a nine-week run on the charts.

SOMETHING'S GOTTA GIVE

Music and lyrics by Johnny Mercer
From *Daddy Long Legs*

The story for Fred Astaire's latest film, *Daddy Long Legs,* had been kicking around for quite a long time. It first appeared as a novel by Jean Webster in 1912, and three versions of it had been produced: in 1919 (with Mary Pickford and Mahlon Hamilton), in 1931 (with Janet Gaynor and Warner Baxter), and as *Curly Top* (with Shirley Temple) in 1935. So it had been a while since audiences had been treated to the story of the orphan who falls in love with a millionaire playboy/benefactor she has never met. Leslie Caron starred as the orphan — French for this incarnation — while Astaire played her sponsor. In the end, despite their age differences (he was mid-50s, she twentysomething), they end up dancing cheek to cheek.

But not before they dance on screen for well over two hours. Some critics thought this a bit much, but for others it was a rare treat to see these two dancing sensations together in the same picture. There was a dream-sequence ballet, created by Roland Petit (with music by Alex North), with lots of pastel colors shown off in the wide-screen CinemaScope format. There also was an acrobatic dance number called "Sluefoot," in which Caron proved her versatility; Astaire's skills proved equally wide-ranging, particularly in a sequence in which he played drums.

Johnny Mercer, who usually stuck to lyrics, created both words and music for this film. (He would receive one other nomination for both lyrics and music, for 1960's "The Facts of Life" — see page 159.) His songs for this film included "Dream," "History of the Beat," "Sluefoot," and "Something's Gotta Give." This last tune, sung by Astaire, received an Academy Award nomination.

The song is sung to Caron by Astaire before they dance together on a hotel balcony. The lyrics are witty and apt: Astaire, the immovable object, meets Caron, an irresistible force, and the implied laws of physics state that "something's gotta give" — in this case, love.

Hit recordings of the song were released by the McGuire Sisters, whose recording on the Coral label reached the number five position on the pop charts, and by Sammy Davis Jr., whose Decca version peaked at number nine. As was so often the case when the film-recorded version was beaten to the marketplace by other versions, Astaire's recording of the tune didn't

even make the charts. Other artists who have recorded the tune over the years include Rosemary Clooney, Les Brown and His Band of Renown, Dinah Washington, Frank Sinatra, Peter Duchin and His Orchestra, Jack Jones, and Johnny Mercer himself, who frequently recorded his own songs.

In addition to the two leads in the cast, there was an unusual pairing of two actors who later played the same role in a television series. Both Larry Keating and Fred Clark appeared in *Daddy Long Legs,* and both men, at varying times, would later play the role of George and Gracie's next-door neighbor, Harry Morton, on "The George Burns and Gracie Allen Show" in the '50s. *Daddy Long Legs* marked the only time these two Harrys appeared together in the same production.

(LOVE IS) THE TENDER TRAP

**Music by James Van Heusen;
lyrics by Sammy Cahn
From *The Tender Trap***

As was becoming more and more common in the decade of the 1950s, films were including "title songs," tunes that worked the name of the picture into the song. Paul Francis Webster had handled this aptly with "Love Is a Many-Splendored Thing," which, with its full-sentence title and uplifting words and music, would manage to take home the Oscar for 1955 (see page 132).

In the same year, MGM released a film starring Frank Sinatra. Naturally, it called for a title song, preferably sung by Old Blue Eyes himself. Sammy Cahn recalled in his autobiography, *I Should Care,* that the title came first, so in this case the lyrics came before the music. The picture was to be called *The Tender Trap.* "Now when I heard the word 'trap,' " wrote Cahn, "I also heard the word 'snap.' Think about it — 'trap' and 'snap' and you're almost home." Well, maybe if you're a talented songwriter like Cahn. Other rhyming pairs soon followed — "whap" and "map," and soon he was home free. He presented these lyrics to his new partner, Jimmy Van Heusen, who instantly whipped up a tune he was certain fit the words perfectly.

"I thought [it] was one of the worst melodies I'd ever heard," Cahn recalled. But he was cautious and refrained from telling his new collaborator. "We weren't really adjusted to the effect our styles had on

Fred Astaire and Leslie Caron show off their lengthy appendages in *Daddy Long Legs*.

Debbie Reynolds prepares to spring *The Tender Trap* on an unsuspecting Frank Sinatra.

each other; we were just feeling each other out on our first song." Cahn went home to brood over the music. When they got together the next day, Van Heusen greeted him with the news. "That tune last night wasn't very good, was it?" Van Heusen proceeded to play a new melody, much to Cahn's delight. "[It] sounded as though it had always been there," he wrote.

Their song went on to receive an Academy Award nomination, the second recognition for Cahn that year. After this first effort, the team continued working together for many productive years, receiving several nominations and winning Oscars in 1957 for "All the Way" (see page 142), in 1959 for "High Hopes" (see page 151), and in 1963 for "Call Me Irresponsible" (see page 171).

In *The Tender Trap*, Frank Sinatra played prey to trapper Debbie Reynolds. He was a bachelor who found himself the object of "ladies of desperate disposition who have their traps out for any fair game," as the *New York Times* so sexistly put it. But such was the case, more or less, in the '50s, when any woman over the age of 25 fell into a panic if she hadn't "trapped" herself a man.

The film was a comedy, not a musical, with Sinatra, who had won the Oscar for Best Supporting Actor in 1953's *From Here to Eternity*, receiving considerable critical acclaim for his comedic abilities. His recording of "The Tender Trap," released about a month after the film's debut, climbed the charts to number seven, and spent 15 weeks charting.

UNCHAINED MELODY

Music by Alex North; lyrics by Hy Zaret
From *Unchained*

One of the most romantic and durable modern songs to emerge from the world of film, "Unchained Melody" had its roots in an obscure movie called *Unchained*. The picture was the brainchild of one man, Hall Bartlett, who wrote, produced, and directed this movie about life in the California Institute for Men, an "honor farm" state prison at Chino. Hardly the stuff of romance.

The film was based on the career of Kenyon J. Scudder, former supervisor at Chino, as detailed in Scudder's book, *Prisoners Are People*. Most of the scenes were actually filmed on location at the prison. Former football player Elroy "Crazylegs" Hirsch played the lead character, while other inmates, each with a story to tell, were played by Chester Morris and Jerry Paris, among others. Television buffs will recognize Paris as a top TV director who got his start playing Dick Van Dyke's buddy on "The Dick Van Dyke Show" of the early '60s. Others in the cast included Peggy Knudsen and Barbara Hale, who appeared as women visiting the prisoners. Hale went on to star as Della Street in the long-running "Perry Mason" television series.

The song "Unchained Melody" has fared considerably better than the film, which quickly sank into obscurity. The movie was released in January, 1955, and, as was required in order for songs to be eligible for Academy Award nomination, the words and music were sung on the soundtrack, in this case by Al Hibbler, a blind black singer. His version of the song and an instrumental recording by Les Baxter were released simultaneously on April 9, 1955. Baxter's orchestral version on the Capitol label actually went higher on the charts, reaching the Number One position and holding it for two weeks in the course of a 21-week chart run. Although it seems hard to believe, it was the only version of the song ever to make it to the Number One position. Hibbler's version peaked at number three, while two other artists who released records of "Unchained Melody" that year, Roy Hamilton and June Valli, had more moderate success, charting at number six and 29, respectively.

The song was revived briefly in 1963, when Vito and the Salutations recorded a version of it that climbed the charts to number 66. But its most popular revival would come two years later, in 1965, with a brand-new hit recording by the Righteous Brothers, whose special sound helped "Unchained Melody" find a new audience and reach the number four position. Three years later, the Sweet Inspirations recorded the perennial favorite; it rose only to number 73. And once again, in 1981, Heart took a turn with "Unchained Melody," but by now it was a case of diminishing returns — their version made it only to number 83.

"Unchained Melody," the love song that began as a prison movie theme, was most recently used in the 1990 hit movie *Ghost*, starring Patrick Swayze and Demi Moore. The Righteous Brothers' version is prominently used in the sexy pottery-throwing love scene between the film's two leads.

1956

And the winner is....

WHATEVER WILL BE, WILL BE (QUE SERA, SERA)

Music and lyrics by Jay Livingston and Ray Evans

From *The Man Who Knew Too Much*

Alfred Hitchcock was adamant. He didn't want a song in his new picture. Never had one before, didn't need or want one now. But Paramount Pictures insisted that this was a Doris Day film, and people would expect Doris Day to sing. And that was that.

Hitch called in Jay Livingston and Ray Evans, who had won Oscars back in 1948 for "Buttons and Bows" (see page 98). His first words to the team were, "I don't want a song," a rather unusual greeting. But he told the pair about the film, a true Hitchcock gem about a man (Jimmy Stewart) in the diplomatic service, working in Europe, traveling with wife Doris and their little boy. Then the director informed them that he needed a song for her to sing to the child, although he had no idea what kind of song he wanted. They promised Hitch they'd get right on it.

"Now, we had written 'Que Sera, Sera' two weeks before," Ray Livingston told Don McCulloch in a 1990 radio interview. "It was just sitting in our office. We waited for two weeks so that Hitchcock would think we were working hard." Two weeks later, sweat all but pouring from their brows, the two played their "new" song for Hitchcock. "Gentlemen," he announced, "I told you I didn't know what kind of a song I wanted. *That's* the kind of song I wanted." And with that, he walked out of the room in a typical Hitchcockian dramatic exit.

The song had originally been called "Che Sera," the Italian spelling, but the songwriters changed it to "Que," reasoning that there were more Spanish-speaking people in the world who would relate to it. However, neither title flew with the studio's legal department, which wouldn't let them use that title, since songs submitted for Academy Award nominations had to have English titles. "So we had to call it 'Whatever Will Be, Will Be,' with 'Que Sera, Sera' in parentheses."

Doris Day and James Stewart star as the frightened parents of a kidnapped boy in Alfred Hitchcock's *The Man Who Knew Too Much.*

Doris Day was the next one to balk. She didn't want to record it, but the studio pressured her into it. "It's a kiddie song," she complained to her husband and manager, Marty Melcher. "I was hoping it would be more than that. You know — 'whatever will be, will be' — that's not really my kind of lyric." Her husband disagreed, telling her he thought it would be a big hit.

About a month after the film was released, Doris Day's recording hit the airwaves. It climbed the pop charts, peaking at number two, where it remained for three weeks (and on the charts for 27). Her husband was correct — it was a hit, and the actress-singer managed to work it into two of her other films — *Please Don't Eat the Daisies* (1960) and *The Glass Bottom Boat* (1966). She also used it as the theme for her CBS television series, "The Doris Day Show," which ran from

1968 to 1973. The song she had started out disliking had ended up becoming her signature song once she realized it was a true reflection of her philosophy of life: "I strongly believe in the inevitability of everyone's life pattern. Our destinies are born with us," she wrote. In other words, que sera, sera. What will be, will be.

What would be for the Livingston/Evans song was a statuette named Oscar. It caught the songsters completely by surprise. Everyone's money that year had been on Cole Porter to at long last win his well-deserved Best Song Oscar, which he was expected to take home for "True Love" (see page 140). Said Jay: "The show was partly in New York in those days, and when Carroll Baker announced the winning song and said, 'Back to Hollywood,' I was just slumped in my seat. It took me a little while to get up. It was a big surprise."

He should have realized it was inevitable. After all, who better to have known that que sera, sera?

FRIENDLY PERSUASION (THEE I LOVE)

Music by Dimitri Tiomkin; lyrics by Paul Francis Webster
From *Friendly Persuasion*

It was a shameful time in United States history. In the late 1940s through the mid-1950s, a country panicked by the awesome specter of potential atomic warfare felt the need to give a name to its fear: communism. These insidious communists were supposedly lurking everywhere, bogeymen of a society's collective nightmare. The United States Senate, under the misguidance of Senator Joseph McCarthy, held hearings to beat the bushes for these would-be destroyers of our freedoms here at home. The cancer had to be excised before it spread. One supposed source of this disease was Hollywood, our very own dream-spinners, purveyors of mythology, tellers of tales. Danger lurked everywhere.

Many of Hollywood's finest actors, producers, directors, and screenwriters were the first to feel the sting of these self-appointed witch-hunters. Talented and creative people were criticized, ostracized, and, ultimately, totally expunged from memory. Most were completely innocent of any wrongdoing. Many lost their jobs; others, working anonymously at their typewriters, were able to create alternate personae for themselves. They had dealt in fiction all their lives — now they too became fictitious, as they put pseudonyms to their work. Others simply left their names off their work and were quietly paid off by brave producers who realized the folly of it all.

Such was the situation with the film *Friendly Persuasion*. It was adapted from the stories by Jessamyn West, who was fully credited for these original tales. But no screenwriter's name appeared on the screen. Had the movie created itself? Did the actors, producer, director, camera crew, and others just make it up as they went along? Of course not. Yet no name was ever mentioned until many years later, when people came to their senses.

Today we know that Michael Wilson wrote this motion picture full of drama, suspense, comedy, quaintness, and charm about the lives of a group of Quakers — the Society of Friends (hence the title pun, *Friendly Persuasion*). The film, which starred Gary Cooper, Dorothy McGuire, Marjorie Main, and a very young, pre-*Psycho* Anthony Perkins, was widely praised by critics and received six Academy Award nominations: Best Picture, Director, Supporting Actor (Perkins), Sound, Song, and Adapted Screenplay. Oddly, no one was named for the latter, and had the award for writing gone to this film, it would have been interesting to see who accepted, since writer Wilson, under the Academy bylaws at the time, was deemed "ineligible for nomination" (read: blacklisted).

On a brighter note, a Best Song nomination went to the theme "Friendly Persuasion" (also called "Thee I Love" — the second-person singular with its quaint "thee"s and "thy"s and "thou"s being perpetuated by this sect during the time of the film's setting, just after the Civil War). A young singer who was just beginning to make a name for himself recorded the title song. In the early part of the decade, Pat Boone had been known to only a few followers of TV's "Arthur Godfrey and His Friends"; he was one of the regular "Friends," having graduated after his discovery on "Arthur Godfrey's Talent Scouts." Dot Records had caught his act and signed him to an exclusive contract, and by 1956 he'd already had eight hit records. Dimitri Tiomkin, who wrote and conducted the score for *Friendly Persuasion* as well as the title tune (with veteran lyricist Paul Francis Webster), became a fan of the young, clean-cut Columbia University student in white bucks, and felt that he was the perfect voice for "Friendly Persuasion."

The song is heard over the opening credits, is used thematically throughout (music only), and is again heard at the end of the film. Boone only earned $3,000 for cutting the record on his assignment for the movie, but his payoff would come later. Dot Records, mindful of a good thing when they saw it, released Boone's recording of the title song. It climbed the charts to the number four position and remained on the charts for 24 weeks.

The Four Aces also recorded this tune, but their version, released in September of 1956, a week after Boone's, only reached the number 45 position.

JULIE

Music by Leigh Stevens; lyrics by Tom Adair
From *Julie*

Before Doris Day became everyone's favorite girl next door, her husband, Marty Melcher, had been guiding her career in a different direction. This time, he practically piloted her onto the rocks.

She had done straight dramatic parts before, but at least she'd managed to incorporate musical numbers. In *Love Me or Leave Me* (see page 134), she had played torch singer Ruth Etting; in *The Man Who Knew Too Much*, she had managed to work in a song that would become the Oscar winner — "Whatever Will Be Will Be (Que Sera, Sera)" (see page 137). Now, Melcher wanted her to appear in a totally non-musical picture, *Julie*, which he planned to produce. Doris Day balked.

It wasn't the script itself (which would eventually receive an Oscar nomination for Best Original Screenplay) that caused her distress, but rather the direction the storyline took. She would play the part of a wife who learns that her jealous husband has murdered her first husband. Would he try to kill her too? It was not a part she longed to play.

The whole picture proved to be an ordeal. The climax of the film had to do with Day assuming the controls of an airplane after her husband and two co-pilots are shot. She prepared for the part by taking flying lessons so she could realistically handle the controls. On the day she was scheduled for her first lesson, her new Cadillac was demolished when she, her husband, and son were broadsided by a hot-rodder as she drove to the airfield. The others were fine, but Day had to be rushed to the hospital for X-rays, which, fortunately, showed that nothing was broken.

Almost the entire picture was shot on location on California's Monterey coast, in the resort town of Carmel-by-the-Sea. Between takes, Doris and her co-star, Louis Jourdan, often took long walks on the beach, the Frenchman and his leading lady chatting about acting, their problems, their children, and so on. Nothing other than a proper friendship ever occurred, but Melcher began showing a jealousy that made her uneasy, given the plot of the film.

On the plus side, Day fell in love with Carmel, and eventually made it her home. Another plus was the title song of the film, "Julie." Doris sang the song under the credits, not onscreen as in the past, making this her first completely non-musical starring role (as Melcher had promised). And when the song "Julie," by first-timers Leigh Stevens and Tom Adair, received a nomination for an Academy Award (it would prove to be their only nomination), it was Doris's second singing effort to be nominated that year. Only one could win, of course — "Que Sera, Sera."

"Julie" was released as a single but didn't do much for Day's musical career. The song spent 10 weeks on the charts, topping out at number 64.

TRUE LOVE

Music and lyrics by Cole Porter
From *High Society*

Based on the Broadway play of the same name, the 1941 film *The Philadelphia Story* had been a box office hit, the number four picture for that year, raking in $1.5 million — big bucks in those days. Katharine Hepburn had starred onstage and in the movie as socialite Tracy Lord in the highly acclaimed comedy. Then, in 1956, Cole Porter was enlisted by MGM to crank out some tunes for a musical version of the play, to be titled *High Society*.

Now, 15 years later, a younger actress was sought to play the blue-blooded heiress, and Grace Kelly was selected for the part. She herself was a true Philly blue blood, so it wasn't much of a stretch. Nor was the singing, which she carried off quite successfully opposite Bing Crosby and Frank Sinatra, cast as her suitors. *High Society* marked the first joint motion picture appearance of these two world-class singers (they would go on to make *The Road to Hong Kong* in 1962 and *Robin and the 7 Hoods* in 1964 — see page 179).

Bing Crosby and Grace Kelly sing "True Love" in *High Society*, Kelly's last film before she left Hollywood to marry Prince Rainier of Monaco.

Porter, himself an aristocrat among composers, was certainly up to the task of creating some memorable tunes. There was a wonderful number with Louis Armstrong and Bing Crosby called "Now You Has Jazz" — the setting for this version of the story conveniently being transferred to the site of the Newport Jazz Festival. Crosby sang "I Love You, Samantha," and Sinatra performed "Mind If I Make Love to You," "You're Sensational," and "Who Wants to Be a Millionaire?" (the latter along with Celeste Holm, playing a fellow reporter). One of the best numbers in the picture was the duet between Crosby and Sinatra called "Well, Did You Evah! (What a Swell Party This Is)," which was originally written for Broadway's *DuBarry Was a Lady*. Other tunes included the title song, "High Society Calypso," "Little One," and the song that was nominated for an Academy Award, "True Love."

"True Love" was the name of a boat, and the song, performed by Crosby (Kelly joins in later, harmonizing) begins with a close-up of a toy boat. Then the scene flashes back to an earlier, happier time when their characters had been married. The scene dissolves into one of the real, full-sized sailboat as Bing "plays" a concertina and Grace joins him in song. It was fairytale romance all the way, and proved one of the highlights of the film.

Their soundtrack song was released as a single by Capitol and climbed the pop charts to number three, remaining on the charts a healthy 31 weeks. Others soon booked passage aboard the "True Love," including Jane Powell, whose version of the song reached number 15. In 1963, Richard Chamberlain, TV's "Dr. Kildare," recorded a version that made an anemic showing at number 98. Meanwhile, two hit versions of the song appeared on the country charts: In 1973, Red Steagall's version reached number 51, and in 1978, the LeGardes released a rendition that hit number 88. Over the years, the song has also been recorded by major artists of the rock era, including the Everly Brothers, Pat Boone, Bobby Vinton, Elvis Presley, and Elton John and Kiki Dee.

Despite the fact that everyone thought Porter a shoo-in, he did not go home with the Oscar, which instead went to Jay Livingston and Ray Evans, for "Whatever Will Be, Will Be (Que Sera, Sera)" (see page 137). Grace Kelly, however, captured a prize when she went home with a prince — Prince Rainier of Monaco, that is. *High Society* was her last picture before her own fairy-tale romance came true — true love, indeed.

WRITTEN ON THE WIND

Music by Victor Young; lyrics by Sammy Cahn
From *Written on the Wind*

Texas figured heavily in films in 1956. First there was *Giant,* which was certainly that in every respect — a monumental picture starring Rock Hudson, James Dean, Elizabeth Taylor, and a stellar supporting cast. Later in the year, Hudson appeared in another film featuring the Lone Star state, this one called *Written on the Wind.* Again, Hudson was cast as a Texan, but this was more coincidence than typecasting, with the two characters bearing no resemblance to each other whatsoever.

Written on the Wind was a melodramatic portrayal of wealthy, upper-crust Texas oil millionaires — their morals (or lack thereof), their foibles, loves, and disasters. Hudson played the stalwart, well-adjusted friend of a psychotic, character-flawed loser, played by Robert Stack. Normalcy doesn't usually attract too much critical or peer attention, while performances of psychos always do; at Oscar time, Hudson was bypassed for a nomination in favor of Stack, who received a Best Supporting Actor nod from his peers. The normal, nice-girl female lead, played by Lauren Bacall, was similarly overlooked, while Dorothy Malone, as the totally immoral sister, struck a chord with the Academy. She won the year's Best Supporting Actress Oscar for her juicy role as Stack's nymphomaniacal sister.

The title song, "Written on the Wind," written on paper by veterans Victor Young and Sammy Cahn, was also nominated for an Oscar. There was nothing immoral about this song, however. The full-bodied tune is sung under opening credits, with scenes of windblown trees and leaves, by the Four Aces, a barbershop-style group who had by now become the title songsters of choice for filmmakers. With "Three Coins in the Fountain" (see page 127) and "Love Is a Many-Splendored Thing" (see page 132), the foursome had already been behind two Oscar-winners, to say nothing of million-sellers. But by the time they recorded "Written on the Wind" — which managed to make only number 61 on the charts, despite charting for 15 weeks — their heyday had passed.

The Four Aces, four clean-cut young men from Chester, Pennsylvania, rose to prominence in Philadelphia in the late 1940s. Their first success came with a self-financed recording on the local Victoria label. It was called "Sin," and in 1951 it reportedly sold a million copies. After that, Decca signed the foursome — lead baritone and sometime-composer Al Alberts, plus Dave Mahoney, Sol Voccaro, and Lou Silvestri. Shortly after their success with "Written on the Wind," Alberts left the group in search of a solo career, without much success. Bereft of their leader, the group began to disintegrate; by the early '60s, they were making way for other "Four" groups — the Four Freshmen, the Four Lads, the Four Preps, the Four Seasons, and the Four Coins, to say nothing of the Fab Four — the Beatles.

ALL THE WAY

**Music by James Van Heusen;
lyrics by Sammy Cahn**
From *The Joker Is Wild*

Sammy Cahn, lyricist, just couldn't stop writing. What's more, he couldn't seem to stop writing Oscar-nominated tunes, no matter who he worked with. Over the years, after his first nomination in 1945, there had been Jule Styne and Sammy Cahn, Nicholas Brodszky and Sammy Cahn, Victor Young and Sammy Cahn, and now James Van Heusen and Sammy Cahn. It was this last pairing that would bring yet another statuette to the prolific writer, as well as seeing him through several more successful years of songwriting for motion pictures, with nomination after nomination — not to mention win after win — for the Academy Award.

A lot of it had to do not only with the talented team, but also with the person doing the performing. Once Frank Sinatra got hold of a Van Heusen–Cahn tune, the song became a triple threat. As Cahn wrote in his autobiography, *I Should Care*, "Frank Sinatra never turned down a song of mine." He goes on to tell of the first time he played "All the Way" for Sinatra. Cahn and his partner went to Las Vegas to sing their latest tune for Sinatra, who, as is customary for nighttime performers, was just arising when they arrived at 4:00 P.M. "Van Heusen gave me an intro," wrote Cahn, "and we went into 'All the Way.' When I'd sung the last immortal word

and note, Frank said, 'Let's eat.' " After they had left, Cahn's agent, Lillian Small, who had come along for the ride, turned to him in tears. "How could he not like that song?" she asked him. "Oh, he loved it," Cahn replied. "How do you know?" she said. Cahn responded with infinite confidence, "Because he loves them all."

If Frank Sinatra suppressed his initial enthusiasm, it was never apparent to the public. Besides being the show-stopping number in *The Joker Is Wild*, the musical biopic of the life of comedian Joe E. Lewis, Sinatra took the tune and made it his signature song for many years. The song, which was performed in Sinatra's absence at the Oscar ceremony by pal Dean Martin, went on to win the Academy Award for 1957.

Ironically, "All the Way" never made it all the way to the top of the *Billboard* charts. Released on the Capitol label shortly after the premiere of the picture, the song quickly climbed the charts, but peaked at number two. However, it remained on the charts a very long time — 30 weeks — which was enough to generate sales of over a million copies.

Despite the fine acting performances by Sinatra and the supporting cast of Eddie Albert, Mitzi Gaynor, and Jeanne Crain, the film was not a huge money-maker for Paramount. Its total take in North American rentals at the box office was $3.1 million — even after being reissued under the more promising name of *All the Way*. Sinatra's other picture that year, *Pal Joey*, fared much better, clocking as the seventh-ranked film of the year at $4.6 million.

AN AFFAIR TO REMEMBER

**Music by Harry Warren; lyrics by Harold
Adamson and Leo McCarey**
From *An Affair to Remember*

Leo McCarey, the multi-talented writer-producer-director, decided to recycle one of his favorite pictures, the 1939 romantic weeper *Love Affair*, starring Charles Boyer and Irene Dunne. A new cast, a few more songs, and soon women all across America were dragging their dates to movie houses to see this new, updated version of the fated lovers.

Cary Grant was now the suave male lead who falls in love with co-star Deborah Kerr on a transatlantic sea voyage. Their plight is foreshadowed by such trite, yet somehow classic, dialogue as, "We're heading into a rough sea, Nicky," to which Grant replies, "I know. We changed our course today." Heavy. Ominous. Perfect.

To set the mood, director Leo McCarey and his producer, Jerry Wald, decided to hire Harry Warren to compose the musical theme that would be used throughout. Warren preferred to write his music first, then turn it over to his lyricist — in this case Harold Adamson (with McCarey also contributing to the lyric). "When I did 'An Affair to Remember,' " Warren told biographer Max Wilk in *They're Playing Our Song,* "I knew I had to get some sort of a melody that would sound good with the old lady [Cathleen Nesbitt in the role of 'Grandmère'] playing it on the piano, one that would sound almost classical. Well, I must've written about twenty-five tunes before I finally hit that one."

The theme was perfectly mated to the film. It was sung by Vic Damone under the credits (his recording would later reach number 16 and chart for 16 weeks), hummed and sung during the scene with the old French grandmother at the piano, and sung in a nightclub by Deborah Kerr's character, dubbed by Marni Nixon.[1] Kerr did sing one number herself — a cute scene in which she leads a children's chorus — reminiscent of her singing with the children in *The King and I.* It seemed out of place, however, and for a while the picture, like the ship, changed course.

The song went on to win an Academy Award nomination — the final one of Harry Warren's long career. The original film version had also spawned an Oscar contender — "Wishing (Will Make It So)" (see page 32), making *An Affair to Remember* the first of only two pairs of films based on the same story to contain a Best Song nominee. (The other pair was the two versions of *A Star Is Born,* made in 1954 and remade in 1976 — see pages 131 and 228 respectively.)

The film was all but forgotten until the summer of 1993. One woman who never forgot her experience of seeing *An Affair to Remember* for the first time was Nora Ephron. The picture, which she first viewed as a teen, left a lasting impression on her. Many years later, Ephron became a successful screenwriter and director. In one of 1993's biggest box office hits, *Sleepless in Seattle,* she was able to incorporate frequent allusions to *An Affair to Remember,* making the original a picture to remember (and demand) at the video rental

counter. Cassettes seemingly flew off the shelves and into the VCRs of a whole new generation.

In 1994, Warren Beatty and his wife, actress Annette Bening, starred in a third version of this story, with the same title as the original film, *Love Affair.* It did only so-so business at the box office.

APRIL LOVE

Music by Sammy Fain;
  lyrics by Paul Francis Webster
From *April Love*

With no plot but lots of charm, the film *April Love* served to introduce Pat Boone to movie audiences for the second time in 1957. Earlier that year, he had appeared in a songfest called *Bernadine,* marking his screen debut. Today it might pass as one long music video, since the movie was actually a showcase for Boone's ever-growing popularity as a singer. With that in mind, 20th Century-

---

1. Marni Nixon had also dubbed Kerr's voice in *The King and I.* She would become the dubber of choice for many years to come in musical films, ghost-singing for such actresses as Natalie Wood and Audrey Hepburn.

Fox rushed to complete *April Love*, which teamed Boone with pony-tailed co-star Shirley Jones.

Sammy Fain composed the music, while Paul Francis Webster, who had written the words to Boone's previous Oscar-nominated song, "Friendly Persuasion" (see page 138), again performed the lyricist's chores. The *New York Times*, while panning the film for having "nifty Kentucky scenery in good color and absolutely no plot," had nothing but praise for Boone and the songs in general: "The tunes, which he and Miss Jones share . . . are sweet, lilting and practically sketch the plot . . . the dramatic highlight [of which] is a sick horse."

The "sweet and lilting" tunes, now mostly forgotten, included "Do It Yourself," "The Bentonville Fair," "Clover in the Meadow," "Give Me a Gentle Girl," and the title song, "April Love." It was apparent to all involved that "April Love" would emerge from the pack as the odds-on favorite to push for the Oscar derby, as well as the one to boost Boone's rapidly rising career. Apparent to all, that is, except Boone himself.

According to an interview in *The Billboard Book of Number One Hits*, by Fred Bronson, Boone didn't find the original arrangement of "April Love" upbeat enough to become a hit. "It didn't sound commercial. In the heyday of rock and roll, what chance did a sweet, simple little song have?" Boone said. So he effected a change during the recording session that would contribute greatly to the song's marketability. He told Billy Vaughn, the arranger, that "we need something to goose this song up a little bit." Boone, working in a corner of the recording studio, penciled in 12 rapid-fire notes as an intro to the melody, something he thought would help set up the song.

No one will ever know whether or not this did the trick; it couldn't have hurt. Boone's recording of "April Love" was released on October 28, 1957, and steadily climbed the charts. By December 23, Pat had a Christmas present for his wife Shirley and their four children — his song had reached the Number One position, where it remained for two weeks; it also charted for 26 weeks.

Happily for Boone (a great-great-great-great-grandson of frontiersman Daniel Boone), people liked his "sweet, simple little song." In a field crowded with the likes of Elvis, the Everly Brothers, and Buddy Holly and the Crickets, the self-effacing young Columbia University student who had once wanted to be a schoolteacher found himself with his second Number One song of the year (the first had been "Love Letters

in the Sand" six months earlier, which would prove to be his most successful single of his career.)

The promoters were happy too, especially at Oscar time. Although "April Love" didn't win, the producers of the Academy Awards ceremony at the Pantages Theater in Hollywood gave the song the most elaborate of production numbers, with Shirley Jones, Ann Blyth, Anna Maria Alberghetti, Jimmie Rodgers, Tommy Sands, and Tab Hunter — all the cool, young stars, it would seem, except Pat Boone himself, who was not present to recreate his hit.

TAMMY

Music and lyrics by Jay Livingston and Ray Evans
From *Tammy and the Bachelor*

Tammy and the Bachelor was, by all accounts, a flop. People seemed to be avoiding this melodramatic film about an innocent girl from the bayou who nurses a downed airplane pilot (Leslie Nielsen) back to health, then naturally falls for him. It was a flop, that is, until the movie's title song, "Tammy," sung midway through the film, was released as a single by the picture's star, Debbie Reynolds.

It hadn't been planned that way. Academy Award–winning composers Jay Livingston and Ray Evans ("Buttons and Bows," see page 98, and "Whatever Will Be, Will Be [Que Sera, Sera]," see page 137) were brought on board at Universal to create a song called "Tammy," the original title of the picture. According to Livingston (as related in a 1990 interview), the script called for Reynolds to sing a song in her attic room while gazing out the window, dreaming of romance. Asked, "What is that?" she replies that it's a song she learned from her great-grandmother. "So it had to have that folk-song feeling," Jay recalled. "We gave that song to Debbie Reynolds, and she sang it exactly as she did on the record. She's the best sight reader I ever saw — read it right off the music."

Debbie recorded it with only a piano player to guide her. When they shot the scene, she lip-synched to her pre-recorded track. Later, more instruments were added to the track, along with a Henry Mancini arrangement. Ray Evans recalled that no one wanted to re-record Debbie. "They figured instead of spending all the money on a big recording session, they liked the soundtrack," said Evans. "They said, 'Let's put this out,' because it wasn't really that important of a picture. So, to everybody's surprise, including ours, it just took off."

Indeed, no one thought it would sell, especially since the recording timed out at three and a half minutes, nearly double the preferred length of a single in those days. Reynolds's recording of "Tammy" was released on July 22, 1957, three weeks after the version by the Ames Brothers (who sang the tune under the opening credits), and both records soon became hits on the *Billboard* charts. The Ames Brothers version peaked in the number five position and charted for 24 weeks, while Debbie's wistful recording reached Number One the week of August 26 and stayed atop the charts for three weeks, charting for 31 weeks in all.

Meanwhile, Universal had pulled *Tammy and the Bachelor* from theaters. Reynolds, who had gone to London with her then-husband, Eddie Fisher, for his Palladium appearance, recalled what happened in her autobiography, *Debbie: My Life:* "A few days after we arrived in England, I got a wire from the United States informing me that 'Tammy' was one of the Top Ten on the *Billboard* charts. Everyone was amazed because it was a sweet, simple little ballad in contrast to the hits by Elvis Presley, Jerry Lee Lewis, Paul Anka and Buddy Holly . . . The record had such impact that when Universal re-released *Tammy and the Bachelor,* it grossed millions." Well, $3.2 million, actually, far from placing in 1957's top films.

Nevertheless, the movie launched Reynolds's career as a full-fledged star, although for years, producers continued to insist that she play ingenue roles. She managed to transcend the typecasting, and went on to make many feature films, two TV series, and became popular as a Las Vegas nightclub performer. In fact, she became owner of the Debbie Reynolds Hotel, Casino and Hollywood Movie Museum in that town. In the mid-1990s, she could frequently be found performing in the hotel's Celebrity Cafe, where the most requested songs were "Singin' in the Rain" and "Tammy." The Oscar-nominated song was still going strong after all those years, with one concession to modern times — occasionally, as a salute to her younger fans, she performed a rap version of "Tammy."

A goat steals the scene from Tammy (Debbie Reynolds) and her boyfriend (Leslie Nielsen) in *Tammy and the Bachelor.*

WILD IS THE WIND

**Music by Dimitri Tiomkin;
   lyrics by Ned Washington**
From *Wild Is the Wind*

It was another instance of the song wagging the film. Just as "Tammy" had spearheaded a return to the box office for people familiar with that tune now eager to see *Tammy and the Bachelor* (see page 144), the Johnny Mathis hit song "Wild Is the Wind" began stirring up interest in the otherwise floundering film that served as its namesake.

Mathis's career, like those of so many newcomers in the early stages of the rock era, was just beginning to rise. His style, though, was what made him different. Never a rocker, Mathis appealed to young lovers (or those just dreaming of love), especially women. In 1957, his recording of "Chances Are" and "The Twelfth of Never" became a double-sided hit. But while his singles and albums sold in the millions, he never had a Number One hit until 1978 (with Deniece Williams,

Anna Magnani and Anthony Franciosa discuss the "joys" of birthing lambs in a spring snow storm as Anthony Quinn helps a ewe with her delivery in *Wild Is the Wind*.

"Too Much, Too Little, Too Late"). His recording of "Wild Is the Wind," sung under the opening credits in the movie of the same name, peaked in the number 22 position and remained on the charts for 18 weeks.

Even with the push from Mathis, the film never became a box office hit, earning less than $1 million in North American rentals. It suffered from a weak script that just didn't seem able to find its center. It started off as a comedy, starring Anthony Quinn as a wealthy Italian-born sheep rancher from Nevada who goes back to the old country to wed the sister of his long-dead wife. Anna Magnani played the new wife, and the film quickly turns soapy when she returns with Quinn to Nevada, but without the love she expects. She falls for much younger Anthony Franciosa, and the suds start flying. The film had its moments, though. *Variety* noted that "George Cukor directs with taste and imagination and his skillful handling is evident in many scenes, particularly the sequence showing a film audience how a lamb is dropped, or one in which Franciosa trains sheep dogs, and in his handling of the affair between Magnani and Franciosa."

However, Lambing 101 and sheep dog obedience lessons did little to herd audiences into theaters. The lambing lessons reportedly didn't sit too well with the film's leading lady, either. It was a particularly cold spring, and even though the calendar said May, snowflakes were falling. Magnani wondered aloud to director Hal Wallis if the scene could be postponed. No, he gently replied to the hot-tempered, expletive-hurling Italian actress. "You have to understand," he explained (as reported in his autobiography, *Starmaker*), "the lambs are dropped only on a certain date. The sheep aren't going to change their habits just because you aren't satisfied with the script!" She continued to "sulk like a spoiled child" throughout the whole ordeal of getting *Wild Is the Wind* on film.

Whatever problems they might have had were set aside at Oscar time. When the nominations were announced, Quinn received one for Best Actor and Magnani was nominated for Best Actress. Neither won, however, and neither did "Wild Is the Wind," which received a Best Song nomination, one of many for Dimitri Tiomkin and Ned Washington.

1958

And the winner is...

GIGI

**Music by Frederick Loewe;
   lyrics by Alan Jay Lerner**
From *Gigi*

Cute, spoiled, tomboyish, and worth every ounce of her adolescent weight in francs, Gigi burst upon the scene in the spring of 1958 with all the charm and spontaneity of the film that bore her name.

It had begun simply enough with the 1944 novella by 70-year-old French writer Colette. Her little piece went unperformed until a small French film was made in 1950. It was followed shortly by a non-musical Broadway play, starring Audrey Hepburn. Then, in 1957, Arthur Freed and Vincente Minnelli, MGM's top musical producer and director, respectively, decided to produce *Gigi* as a wide-screen musical. To that end, they sought out the two hottest composers on Broadway, Frederick Loewe and Alan Jay Lerner, to write the music and lyrics. Lerner and Loewe had done *My Fair Lady,* an

unprecedented Broadway phenomenon that had been playing to capacity crowds for the past three years.

The team's efforts became one of the screen's all-time greatest musical hits. Some critics disdained *My Fair Gigi,* as several saw it. Indeed, comparisons could be made between the two. The musical numbers, for instance: "The Rain in Spain" had similarities to "The Night They Invented Champagne," and the title song, "Gigi," sung-spoken by Louis Jourdan, was frequently compared to "I've Grown Accustomed to Her Face," as sung-spoken by Rex Harrison in *My Fair Lady.* There were similar story lines, to a degree — the older, wiser gentleman who bears witness to the transformation of a gangling duckling into a regal swan. As if to hammer this point home, during Jourdan's singing of "Gigi," numerous swans, personally selected by Vincente Minnelli after four days of swan auditions, swim in the fountain just behind Jourdan.

Yet the presentation of the title song is one of the most effective in any film's climactic moment. Minnelli had a thorough knowledge of music, lyrics, comedy, and drama and utilized these with unmatched skill and imagination. As Alan Lerner wrote in his autobiography, *The Street Where I Live,* "The night scene with Louis Jourdan pacing up and down in silhouette [singing "Gigi"] in front of a shimmering fountain and

Louis Jourdan, Leslie Caron, and Maurice Chevalier in a scene from the Academy Award–winning film *Gigi*.

being shaken into a decision when a horse and carriage, also in silhouette, pull up short to avoid hitting him, is among the most memorable effects ever filmed and uniquely Minnelli."

Minnelli brushed aside any implications that there were intentional similarities between *My Fair Lady* and *Gigi*, writing in his own autobiography, *I Remember It Well*, "They were completely different stories, as I saw them, the one we were involved in showing the manners and morals of the French aristocracy at the time [of the turn of the century]." He also was quick to point out, that "since *Gigi* was essentially a dramatic story, there was no reason to mount production numbers in the film. Dance sequences, like the songs in the picture, had to look as if they were spontaneous."

And what songs they were! The Lerner and Loewe score included "Thank Heaven for Little Girls," "The Parisians," "It's a Bore," "Gossip," "She Is Not Thinking of Me," "The Night They Invented Champagne," "I Remember It Well," "I'm Glad I'm Not Young Anymore," "Say a Prayer for Me Tonight," and the Oscar-winning title song, "Gigi." While the Vic Damone–released single of "Gigi" only reached number 88 on the charts for one week, the soundtrack album of the film rose to Number One.

On Oscar night, *Gigi*, already jailer of America's (and most of the world's) hearts, captured nine Oscars, winning every one for which the film was nominated and setting a new record in Academy Award history. There were Oscars for Best Picture, Director, Adapted Screenplay, Color Cinematography, Art Direction/Set Decoration, Score, Film Editing, Costume Design, and, of course, Song. Although no one from the wonderful cast (which included Leslie Caron, Maurice Chevalier, Louis Jourdan, Hermione Gingold, and Eva Gabor) was nominated, Chevalier received an honorary statuette for "his contributions to the world of entertainment for more than half a century."

Gigi was a milestone in one other respect: It signaled the end of the era of lavish MGM musicals, a genre that had risen to such great heights during the preceding three decades. Those glory days would never again be equaled.

ALMOST IN YOUR ARMS

Music and lyrics by Jay Livingston and Ray Evans
From *Houseboat*

Sophia had arrived. After a tremendous buildup campaign, designed to entice the American public into believing that God himself had perhaps reinvented Woman with Sophia Loren as the prototype, the widely heralded Ms. Loren landed on American shores.

She was not a newcomer to the picture business. The former beauty contest winner had been appearing in

Cary Grant and Sophia Loren seem to enjoy playing *Houseboat.*

films in her native Italy since 1949, when she and her mother both worked as extras in *Quo Vadis?*(released in 1951). Following that, she appeared in numerous Italian films seen mainly on that side of the Atlantic. In 1957, she co-starred in two American movies produced overseas — *Boy on a Dolphin* and *The Pride and the Passion,* plus a forgettable U.S./Italian effort called *Timbuktu, Legend of the Lost.* Her American debut would come in 1958, when she appeared in two films, *Desire Under the Elms* and the far more lucrative *Houseboat,* which was the fourteenth-ranked film for the year, earning $3.6 million in domestic rentals.

Critics either loved or loathed her in the comedy, which starred Cary Grant as the single parent of three rowdy youngsters in need of taming by Loren. The actress played a combination nanny/housekeeper who comes aboard the title vessel where the family has taken up residence. Could love soon be in the air? Bet on it. "It misses on two scores," wrote Bosley Crowther of the *New York Times.* "First, it is in bad taste. The trumped-up pathos of motherless children and the aura of Miss Loren do not mix . . . a tasteless mishmash of essentially clean sentiment and leering sex. With Miss Loren slinking about the houseboat in various revealing states of décolletage, designed to catch the audience's attention, as well as Mr. Grant's, it is offensive to pretend to be interested in the emotional disturbances of kids."

Well, designed to catch the reviewer's attention, anyway. When he managed to tear his eyes away from Loren's plunging neckline, Crowther's second complaint was the story, the jokes, the casting — just about everything. Meanwhile, the reviewer at *Variety* was kinder, especially to Loren: "Miss Loren continues to act better in irate Italian than in emotional English, but despite a physical appearance that overcomes any inner talents, she is believable and sometimes downright warm as the lover of Grant and his children."

Two Livingston-Evans songs were introduced in the film — a catchy tune called "Bing, Bang, Bong" (which Loren sings at every opportunity) and one that would receive the Academy Award nomination, "Almost in Your Arms" (also called "Love Song From Houseboat" in the credits). When we first hear it, Loren sings it in her native Italian, while Paul Peterson, playing the eldest of Grant's children, translates it into English. But Academy rules at the time stated that the song title and lyrics must include the English version, so later in the film, the song is heard at a country club dance, sung by an unseen Sam Cooke, while Loren and Grant do a turn around the floor and gaze into each other's eyes.

Cooke had hit the top of the *Billboard* charts for the first time the previous year with "You Send Me," but the only version of "Almost in Your Arms" to make the Hot 100 was Johnny Nash's rendition, which peaked at number 78 and was on the charts for four weeks.

A CERTAIN SMILE

**Music by Sammy Fain;
lyrics by Paul Francis Webster**
From *A Certain Smile*

Rock 'n' roll may have been king, but a certain singer who specialized in romantic ballads held his ground and built a career around softer sounds. Johnny Mathis, once dubbed "the king of necking music," with his tender, sensuous voice, was in the middle of a series of hit love songs when he was tapped to sing the title theme for *A Certain Smile.*

The film, based on the novel by Françoise Sagan, involved a "shocking" story of a young girl having a week-long affair with an older, married man. Despite objections from the industry's self-imposed watchdogs, whose job it was to assure that films abided by the Production Code, cinema was beginning to grow up. The movie starred Christine Carére as the girlish lead, Italian heartthrob Rosanno Brazzi (best known for singing "Some Enchanted Evening" in the year's top box office hit, *South Pacific),* Bradford Dillman (in his film debut) as her younger boyfriend and Sorbonne classmate, and Joan Fontaine as Brazzi's long-suffering wife.

Carére was given a tremendous buildup by 20th Century-Fox for this, her American film debut. The Dijon, France, native was 28 years old at the time, and had been appearing in films in her native country since 1950. Her reception by American critics was mostly warm. The *New York Times* noted, "[Carére] does project a bit of the feeling needed in a girl about to step from youthful innocence to a wiser and sadder maturity," while *Variety* said, "Carére is charming and petite, turning in a capable performance that's just a shade too much on the wholesome side." Why, then, didn't her career blossom? It's difficult to say; she appeared in only three other American films — *Mardi Gras* (1958), *A Private's Affair* (1959), and *I Deal in Danger* (1966) — before returning permanently to France, where she married French actor Philippe Nicaud.

A Certain Smile received a lot of attention for its use of the French Riviera scenery, which was seemingly photographed from every possible angle. Part of the reasoning was that despite the restrained use of the main theme of the original Sagan novel, the storyline still had to be toned down quite a bit, and something was needed to lure in theater patrons. Thanks to these vistas of the Riviera, the picture was among those nominated for Best Art Direction at Oscar time. Other nominations were for Best Costume Design, and yet another nomination for Sammy Fain and Paul Francis Webster for Best Song — the title song of this non-musical, "A Certain Smile."

Mathis's single release of "A Certain Smile" was a moderately successful hit. It peaked in the number 14 position and charted for 14 weeks. It had greater success as part of his *Greatest Hits* album, also released that year. This compilation of tunes like "Chances Are," "Twelfth of Never," "Wonderful, Wonderful," and "It's Not for Me to Say" was issued because the singer's busy schedule prevented him from recording a new album. It proved to be one of the most successful albums released, remaining on the *Billboard* charts for almost 10 years.

TO LOVE AND BE LOVED

**Music by James Van Heusen;
  lyrics by Sammy Cahn**
From *Some Came Running*

By 1958, Frank Sinatra, the blue-eyed heartthrob of millions of bobby-soxers of the '40s, had proven himself a skilled actor, even winning an Academy Award in 1954 for *From Here to Eternity*. Meanwhile, his buddy Dean Martin had given up comedy with partner Jerry Lewis. Martin had always voiced the desire to be a singer. Now he had moved into the realm of dramatic acting.

The picture was called *Some Came Running*, and besides Sinatra and Martin, it co-starred yet another member of the evolving Rat Pack — Shirley MacLaine. Oozing with gamblers, thugs, drunks, prostitutes, and honky-tonks, *Some Came Running* was based on James Jones's best-selling, 1,200-page novel that described the lives, loves, and struggles in small-town America, a veritable soap opera splashed across the wide screen.

"I decided to use the inside of a jukebox as my inspiration for the settings — garishly lit in primary colors," director Vincente Minnelli related in his autobiography, *I Remember It Well*. Minnelli, so famous for his MGM grand musicals, was delighted to be drafted as director for this decidedly non-musical feature. It was his first post-*Gigi* effort, and it gave him the opportunity to show his ability to handle just about any genre that the studio tossed his way.

All did not go smoothly with *Some Came Running*'s location filming in Madison, Indiana. "Frank and Dean were pretty much prisoners during our three weeks in Madison," wrote Minnelli. "Every time they ventured out, some incident seemed to occur. The townspeople were offended when Frank was quoted as saying — I don't know how accurately — that Madison was worse than the skid row in Los Angeles. Another, time, it was said he'd torn a phone from the wall because an operator was listening in on his conversation. Yet another incident had Sinatra's and Dean's manager involved in a shoving match with an elderly hotel clerk, all over an order of hamburgers." Regardless of his antics, Sinatra was a skilled professional. When the crew returned to Los Angeles to complete shooting, it was he who suggested to Minnelli that they work from noon to eight, rather than the usual nine-to-five routine, theorizing that performers work better in the afternoon and the ladies looked better then. Minnelli, deciding he was on to something, indulged the actor. The performances went flawlessly.

At Oscar time, it was a banner year for Vincente Minnelli. *Gigi*, his hit musical film, received nine nominations (see page 147), while *Some Came Running* received five — Shirley MacLaine for Best Actress (her first nomination), Arthur Kennedy for Best Supporting Actor, Martha Hyer for Best Supporting Actress, plus Best Costume Design, and Best Song.

The nominated song was written by Academy Award winners James Van Heusen and Sammy Cahn, who had authored Sinatra's Oscar-winning theme song, "All the Way" the previous year. But their song from *Some Came Running* — "To Love and Be Loved" — would not be performed by Sinatra. The tune, sung by a male vocal group, is played in the background over a scene between Sinatra, MacLaine, and a third actress, Betty Lou Kelm (playing Sinatra's niece). The unnamed chorus also sing a couple of standards in the film, such as "Don't Blame Me" and "After You've Gone" (with MacLaine trying to sing along).

The nominated song was one of Van Heusen's and Cahn's less successful efforts. It was not released as a single, included instead as part of the original film soundtrack album.

A VERY PRECIOUS LOVE

Music by Sammy Fain;
lyrics by Paul Francis Webster
From *Marjorie Morningstar*

Herman Wouk's best-selling novel *Marjorie Morningstar* was an in-depth examination of upper-middle-class Jewish families of Manhattan, with particular emphasis on the teenaged daughter, a student at Hunter College who spends a summer at a Borsht Belt retreat for adults and falls in love with its social director. Much of the book focused on religious experiences of the principals, Wouk writing from his own Orthodox Jewish background. However, as might be expected, the film shifted to the more dramatic aspects to be found in the love situation, with a post-adolescent actress in the title role.

Barely 20 years old, Natalie Wood had been making movies for most of her life. In the 1940s, the popular child actress co-starred in the original *Miracle on 34th Street* (1947), now viewed as a Yuletide classic. By the 1950s, she was appearing in less noteworthy pictures, the exception being *Rebel Without a Cause* (1955), a landmark film in which she starred opposite James Dean and received an Academy Award nomination. *Marjorie Morningstar* was her first successful venture as a top-billed actress; Wood was on her way to stardom.

The critics thought so too. "Natalie Wood gives a glowing and touching performance as the title heroine," wrote *Variety*, while the *New York Times* was even less restrained, amazed that "Natalie Wood, who only yesterday was playing with dolls in films, has blossomed into a vivacious, pretty brunette who very likely is as close to a personification of Marjorie as one could wish."

Cast opposite Wood was Gene Kelly as Noel Airman, her summer romance interest, assigned to "put on a show" at the South Wind resort. Although twice her age at 46, his youthful energy enabled him to play the role a bit younger, but still as the older and more experienced man to her ingenue character. She fawns after him like a puppy throughout the film, but comes to her senses just in time to realize that this relationship has no future.

The pair have their own theme song, seemingly the only music heard at the resort. When Marjorie first meets Noel, a so-so writer from Broadway, he's at the piano, surrounded by adoring fans as he plays the song

that would win an Oscar nomination — "A Very Precious Love." Later, at the film's end, after Marjorie has made her decision, she sees Noel from a distance as we hear the song again.

Sammy Fain and Paul Francis Webster, two-time Academy Award winners (for 1953's "Secret Love" and 1955's "Love Is a Many-Splendored Thing" — see pages 123 and 132, respectively) composed this non-winning but very likable tune. Several artists made recordings of it, with the Ames Brothers' version having the most success on the *Billboard* charts, peaking at number 23. Others recording the tune included Doris Day, Mantovani and His Orchestra, Carmen Cavallaro, Slim Whitman, and the Mystic Moods Orchestra.

And the winner is...

HIGH HOPES

Music by James Van Heusen;
lyrics by Sammy Cahn
From *A Hole in the Head*

The only Oscar-winning song to become the theme for a presidential campaign, "High Hopes" began simply as a title buzzing around in Sammy Cahn's head. When the Academy Award–winning team of James Van Heusen and Sammy Cahn were asked to write a song for Frank Sinatra's latest picture, *A Hole in the Head*, they knew it would be sung by Sinatra and child actor Eddie Hodges, who played Sinatra's son, in a light scene designed to alleviate tension between the two characters.

Van Heusen's first tune, stemming from the "High Hopes" title, didn't sit well with Cahn. "He comes back with one of those two-four tunes," he told biographer Max Wilk in *They're Playing Our Song*, "very martial: 'When you're down and out, lift up your head and shout, you're gonna have some high hopes!' I didn't like it . . . He came back the next day, and he had a spiritual: 'Sing Hallelujah, Hallelujah, and you're bound to have some high hopes!' " Wrong. Finally, Cahn remembered Van Heusen's Oscar-winner, "Swinging on a Star" (see page 67), which contained references to mules and fish and such, and suggested they write their song from an animal's point of view. "I'm looking on the bungalow floor at Fox, where we're working . . . ants running around. '*Insects!*' I said . . . you just take an ant. An ant has a sense of fulfillment when it moves from one place to another." From there, it wasn't long before, oops, there goes another Academy Award for the team.

Sinatra's recording of the novelty song reached number 30 on the *Billboard* charts, and charted for 17 weeks. Meanwhile, the popular singer had been hanging with the Kennedy clan; he arranged for the songwriting team to meet the future President at a party at Peter Lawford's house. Those gathered at the event asked if Van Heusen and Cahn would be willing to write a campaign song for JFK. The songwriters suggested "High Hopes."

"They loved the title, and Van Heusen and I went to work on a Kennedy version," Cahn wrote in his autobiography, *I Should Care*. "We were in trouble; the name Kennedy just wouldn't fit anywhere . . .'What the hell, why don't we spell it?' I suggested . . .'K-E-double-N-E-D-Y,/Jack's the nation's favorite guy./Everyone wants to back Jack,/Jack is on the right track/And he's got high hopes . . .' " The song was a brilliant choice, with its familiarity from both the film and the Sinatra record, and Sinatra even recorded the campaign version. Soon "everyone" did back Jack, and the Oscar winners were off to the inauguration.

The song became a bigger hit than the movie. *A Hole in the Head* was the first effort from Frank Capra since his 1951 film *Here Comes the Groom* (see page 112). The producer/director had been behind such classic films as *It Happened One Night* (1934), *Mr. Deeds Goes to Town* (1936), *Mr. Smith Goes to Washington* (1939), and *It's a Wonderful Life* (1946). With a self-imposed legacy such as this, nothing short of perfection was expected from the filmmaker. *A Hole in the Head* was warmly received by some critics, but audiences didn't fully embrace it. It earned a respectable $5 million, ranking number 14 for the year.

THE BEST OF EVERYTHING

**Music by Alfred Newman;
 lyrics by Sammy Cahn**
From *The Best of Everything*

The best thing about *The Best of Everything* was "The Best of Everything," the Best Song nominee. The worst thing seemed to be the movie's title, lambasted with

glee by multiple critics, proclaiming such things as, "Everything considered, *The Best of Everything* should have been better" (The *New York Times*) and "*The Best of Everything* might be considered a little over-optimistic in its title" (*Variety*).

The film had all the ingredients that should have added up to a box office hit: a good cast, including Joan Crawford, Hope Lange, Stephen Boyd, Suzy Parker, Diane Baker, Martha Hyer, and Brian Aherne; a good, sudsy script, in the same vein as *Peyton Place* and *The Long Hot Summer,* popular genres of the day; good Technicolor; CinemaScope; and a musical score by Alfred Newman. The picture was also blessed with a top director, Jean Negulesco, the Romanian whiz responsible for *Johnny Belinda* (1948), *How to Marry a Millionaire* (1953), *Three Coins in the Fountain* (1954), *Daddy Long Legs* (1955), and *A Certain Smile* (1958). At 59, the onetime painter and Parisian stage decorator was at the peak of his career. But following the failure of *The Best of Everything,* demand for his directorial services waned; he would make only four more pictures during the next decade, none of them noteworthy.

If these elements didn't succeed in helping the picture find its audience, then perhaps it was the failure of the story to rise above its basic premise of a bed-hopping, extra-marital affair. All of the movie's female characters, it seemed, were involved in affairs with married men. With the production code relaxing more each year, sex was now a movie preoccupation, along with "shockingly" more frequent usage of such words as "damn" and "hell" — still harsh-sounding to many old-school critics as the 1950s drew to a close.

Some interesting names were connected with this picture. The novel on which the Edith Sommer–Mann Rubin screenplay was based had been an early bestseller by Rona Jaffe; the author quckly became a popular writer of "trashy" novels, such as *The Fame Game, The Other Woman,* and *Mazes and Monsters.* And one of the minor roles, that of a slick playboy, went to Robert Evans, a former child actor who eventually migrated into production and wound up as studio head at Paramount. He produced some of the studio's most successful films of the '70s, including *Chinatown* (1974), *Marathon Man* (1976), and *Black Sunday* (1977).

The Best of Everything received two Oscar nominations: Best Color Costume Design and Best Song. The lyrics to "The Best of Everything" were written by Sammy Cahn, who received his second nomination of the year.

Director Negulesco had selected Johnny Mathis to record "A Certain Smile" for his film by the same name the previous year. For "The Best of Everything," he turned once more to Mathis. The title song is sung under the opening credits as scenes of New York City, the film's setting, progress from the peaceful aspects of the city to the more bustling, familiar metropolis.

Mathis released a single of "The Best of Everything," but it was not one of his major hits; the song peaked in the number 62 position and charted for only five weeks.

THE FIVE PENNIES

Music and lyrics by Sylvia Fine
From *The Five Pennies*

In 1959, Danny Kaye, noted for his bouncing-off-the-walls-and-ceiling humor, turned his talents toward a biographical film. *The Five Pennies* was based on the life of trumpet and coronet player–bandleader Red Nichols, whose band, in reality comprising anywhere from six to 10 men, served as the home to many jazz greats during the '20s and '30s. Nichols, the son of a Utah college music professor, had been playing in public since he was five, and by the mid-1920s had started his own group, the Five Pennies. At various times, his band provided the training ground for some of the great bandleaders, including Miff Mole, Jimmy Dorsey, Glenn Miller, Joe Venuti, and Benny Goodman.

The movie told the story of Nichols, but also attempted to depict his family life. Barbara Bel Geddes played his wife and vocalist with the band (her songs were dubbed by Eileen Wilson). The film's score featured many of the tunes Nichols made famous, such as "Runnin' Wild," "Out of Nowhere," "Indiana," and the trademark Five Pennies theme song, "Wail of the Winds," composed by Harry Warren. Some of the best moments in the film occur when Kaye, whose coronet playing was dubbed by the real Red Nichols, teams up with Louis Armstrong for "When the Saints Go Marchin' In" and a jazzy version of "The Battle Hymn of the Republic." Armstrong also is heard in his rendi-

Louis Armstrong and Danny Kaye star in *The Five Pennies*, a biopic about bandleader Red Nichols.

tion of "Bill Bailey, Won't You Please Come Home."

Kaye's wife, Sylvia Fine, had been writing songs for his films for years. One of the few females to achieve success in this male-dominated field, she'd had a previous Academy Award nomination in 1953 for "The Moon Is Blue" (see page 123). For *The Five Pennies*, she composed three new numbers — "Lullabye in Ragtime," "Good Night, Sleep Tight," and the title song, "The Five Pennies," which Danny, as Nichols, sings to his daughter (played by Susan Gordon). At the end, the number is reprised by Barbara Bel Geddes (voiced by Eileen Wilson). It would bring Fine — Mrs. Kaye — her second Academy Award nomination. (Kaye's daughter Dena also got in on the act, making her screen debut as one of the young polio patients.)

While cute as used in the film's context, the song "The Five Pennies" didn't have much chance as a single release. It was recorded by Dodie Stevens and was on the *Billboard* charts for one week, reaching the number 89 position.

The screenplay for *The Five Pennies* was co-written by Jack Rose and Mel Shavelson, the latter of whom also directed. The onetime contract writer for most of the Goldwyn comedies of the 1940s (who would write and direct Kaye's 1961 comedy hit, *On the Double*) found a sympathetic ear at Paramount Studios when he brought his screenplay to the executive producer, Don Hartman. The story, while mainly centered on the history of the band, also focused on Nichols's daughter, who was stricken with polio. Executive producer Don Hartman's daughter also had polio, which brought this story close to home and gave Shavelson an added edge with the studio.

The film also received Academy Award nominations for Best Color Cinematography, Best Scoring of a Musical Picture, and Best Color Costume Design.

THE HANGING TREE

Music by Jerry Livingston; lyrics by Mack David
From *The Hanging Tree*

Panning for gold, drinking whiskey, playing poker, and making love to the womenfolk — these were the primary occupations of the men of Skull Creek, Montana, circa 1870. Stagecoach hold-ups, killings, unrestrained lust, street brawling, and yes, hangings from the title tree were also tossed in for good measure in *The Hang-*

ing Tree, Warner Bros.'s attempt to draw people out of their living rooms, where TV cowboys were kings, and back to the the movie theaters where they belonged.

This literate, "adult" Western, based on the book by Dorothy Johnson, boasted a talented cast, including Gary Cooper, nearing the end of his fourth decade in film (he would die two years after this picture was made), Viennese-born actress Maria Schell (older sister of actor Maximilian Schell) as the strange, blind foreigner and female lead, Karl Malden as an evil gold prospector, and in his motion picture debut, George C. Scott. Several in the cast received high marks from Bosley Crowther in the *New York Times:* "Mr. Cooper, Mr. Malden, Miss Schell and Ben Piazza . . . perform expertly, as if they were acting *High Noon*."

Composer Jerry Livingston and lyricist Mack David wrote an appropriate theme for *The Hanging Tree*. The tune, sung under the opening credits by Marty Robbins, landed the songwriting team their second Academy Award nomination; the first had been in 1950, for "Bibbidi-Bobbidi-Boo" (see page 110). They would be nominated again in 1965, for "The Ballad of Cat Ballou" (see page 181), and David, writing with others, would eventually amass eight Oscar nominations in the course of his career. The team of Livingston and David also wrote the popular theme song for the television show "77 Sunset Strip," as well as for several others in the Warner Bros. stable.

Robbins recorded "The Hanging Tree" with Ray Conniff and His Orchestra. It was released as a single on the Columbia label, and peaked at number 38, remaining on the charts for 13 weeks.

Robbins, a native of the Phoenix suburb of Glendale, had begun his career mainly as a country and Western singer, with early emphasis decidedly on country, but his later songs, many of which he wrote, leaned more towards a Western flavor. His first major hit was in 1954, with a country version of Elvis Presley's "That's All Right," which gained him a country top 10 hit. Other successes were "A White Sport Coat (and a Pink Carnation)" (1957), "The Story of My Life" (1957), and "She Was Only Seventeen (He Was One Year More)" (1958). Following the success of "The Hanging Tree," Robbins had his first international hit with "El Paso," another original composition and his biggest hit. It topped the charts for two weeks in January of 1960. Clocking in at an unprecedented five minutes and telling a complete short story, the song also became the first country song to win a Grammy award.

Gary Cooper in a scene from *The Hanging Tree*.

STRANGE ARE THE WAYS OF LOVE

Music by Dimitri Tiomkin;
   lyrics by Ned Washington
From *The Young Land*

Before there was a Hollywood, before Disneyland or orange trees or tract houses or beaches or freeways or smog — there was another California. Some of it had been portrayed in films about the gold rush days, but none was done with any degree of accuracy. *The Young Land* attempted to right that wrong. It was set in the Golden State in the year 1848, just after the territory had been acquired by the United States. The film's theme, about a young American gunman who has ruthlessly murdered a Mexican and now must stand trial, invokes timeless lessons about prejudice and justice. Indeed, it is American justice itself that is on trial in this frontier film, which concerned itself more with the law, courtroom, jury selection, and trial than the usual shoot-'em-ups of the era.

Unfortunately, the film failed to live up to its potential. "One aspect of this failure," wrote *Variety*, "[is that] even with the paucity of action, real or implied, and wasteful dialog, pointless of any implication or interesting in itself, some greater interest might have been aroused through more skillful use of photography . . . The cast is beset with stock characterizations."

The movie had a youthful cast of virtual unknowns, many of whom would later become more recognizable names as their careers took off. Pat Wayne, as the young sheriff, received top billing. Then 20 years old, the son of John Wayne had cut his teeth playing juvenile parts in John Ford movies, then graduated to supporting roles in his father's productions.

Third-billed Dennis Hopper played the American killer. It would be 10 more years before he'd be heading out on the highway in his biggest picture, *Easy Rider*, which he would co-write and direct.

Dan O'Herlihy played the Federal judge. The Irish-born actor had made a name for himself in a number of adventure films and swashbucklers, including the title role in *The Adventures of Robinson Crusoe* (1952), *At Sword's Point* (1952, as musketeer Aramis), *The Black Shield of Falworth* (1954, as Prince Hal), *The Purple Mask* (1955), and *The Virgin Queen* (1955).

Yvonne Craig played the leading lady and romantic interest, Elena de la Madrid. She would later find her niche and most famous role as Batgirl on television's "Batman."

Ken Curtis was cast as one of the young locals. He would also find steady work in television, appearing as Festus Haggen on "Gunsmoke" from 1964 to 1975.

Variety managed to give composer Dimitri Tiomkin a left-handed compliment, stating, "Tiomkin's score is good, but it rather shows up the thinness of the film itself." Tiomkin, along with lyricist Ned Washington, wrote a theme song for the film, "Strange Are the Ways of Love." The tune was sung by Randy Sparks, who also released a single of the tune. Although it received an Academy Award nomination for the oft-nominated songwriting team, it didn't have much success as a record. In 1962, Sparks founded his own group, the New Christy Minstrels, who performed ersatz folk songs. They had a number of hits, including "This Land Is Your Land," "Green, Green" (their biggest hit — it climbed to number 14), "Saturday Night," and even a version of "Chim, Chim, Cheree" from *Mary Poppins* (1964 — see page 175)

THE SIXTIES

Rock 'n' roll had things all shook up by the 1950s, but its influence was not yet strongly felt in the hallowed halls of the Motion Picture Academy. Nominated songs in the late '50s and early '60s were still mostly traditional, and most stayed close to the middle of the road. Lyrical, musically rich tunes were often used as the film's opening credits rolled, with more and more title songs becoming nominees and Best Song winners. Nominees that were not title songs were usually featured as the film's main theme, used under opening or closing credits.

Until the 1960s, most film composers were brought in from the outside to create melodies especially for the picture. Some were partnered with a favorite lyricist; others composed both music and words. At the turn of the decade, however, more and more themes and title songs were being composed by the person assigned by the producers to write the picture's full score. People like Dimitri Tiomkin, Henry Mancini, Michel Legrand, John Barry, and Elmer Bernstein, composers best known for their fine, feature-length scores, suddenly became songwriters, with lyrics being provided by the likes of Paul Francis Webster, Jay Livingston and Ray Evans, Johnny Mercer, and Mack David.

By the late 1960s, the horrors of war were once again tormenting the nation, with the conflict in Vietnam being played out nightly on television news shows. Escapism at the movies was the order of the day, and studios began reviving the filmusical concept — musicals written especially for the screen, a genre that had largely been mothballed after its heyday in the '30s and '40s. Movies like Doctor Dolittle, Thoroughly Modern Millie, Chitty Chitty Bang Bang, *and* Star! *attempted to recapture some of those glory days, bringing audiences a sort of neo-filmusical. It helped for a while, but the interest soon subsided once again, with title songs and "themes from" still the order of the day by decade's end.*

1960

And the winner is...

NEVER ON SUNDAY

Music and Greek lyrics by Manos Hadjidakis; English lyrics by Billy Towne
From *Never on Sunday*

When asked what they recall most about the Greek-produced film *Never on Sunday,* the majority of people would undoubtedly answer, "The title song." A similar number of people might recall the film's stunning Greek female star, Melina Mercouri. But most assuredly, almost no one would remember the person most responsible for the picture — its American writer-director–male lead, Jules Dassin.

Yet *Never on Sunday* really was his brainchild. He wrote the screenplay, then went about filming the picture on location in the Greek seaport of Piraeus. It was to be his vehicle, with he himself serving as the driver, until his female lead bounced him right out of the driver's seat.

Mercouri, a tall, blonde, classically trained actress, came from a politically oriented Athens family. Her grandfather, Spyros Mercouris, was a conservative mayor of Athens for more than a quarter-century, and her father, Stamatis, served as a member of Parliament. But the young Melina knew what she wanted and broke family tradition by studying drama in the country that had invented and perfected this art form so many centuries before. After completing her studies at Greece's National Theater school of drama, she had a series of minor starring roles on the Greek stage and in films in that country, before landing the plum role of the big-hearted prostitute in Jules Dassin's *Never on Sunday.*

The title does not refer, as some would believe, to her taking a day off from providing her services for the sailors at the port of Piraeus. (The English lyrics, speaking euphemistically of "kissing," suggest that she is never, ever to be kissed on a Sunday because "that's my day of rest.") Instead, Mercouri's character, Ilya, spends her Sundays studying the ancient Greek tragedies. As her patron, Dassin, spends time trying to reform her, as he observes her reaction to the plays she studies. Soon he begins to realize that although she is a classic "working girl," she is truly virginal at heart. She

refuses, for example, to believe that Oedipus was anything other than a good son who loved his mother, or that the infanticidal Medea could have killed her children — after all, aren't they all there at the end of the play, to take their bows?

The film was an overwhelming success with American audiences, proving that an inexpensively produced European "art" film could win over patrons who were used to slick Hollywood productions. Dassin was nominated for Oscars for Best Director and Best Screenplay, and Mercouri received a nomination for Best Actress, and while neither won the statuette, Melina won the heart of her director and co-star. Following the finalization of her divorce from a man she had hastily married as a teen, she and Dassin were married in 1966. She continued to star in films like *Topkapi* (1964) and *Jacqueline Susann's Once Is Not Enough* (1975). But politics was literally in her blood, and she chose to devote most of her life to this calling. She was stripped of her citizenship from 1967 to 1974 for speaking out against the military dictatorship that then ruled Greece, but she returned to her beloved homeland from her exile in Paris after the election of the New Democracy Party. She served as a Member of Parliament from Piraeus from 1977 to 1989 and as Culture Minister from 1981 to 1989. A chain smoker, she was diagnosed with lung cancer in 1989, but continued to smoke until her death from the disease in March of 1994.

"Never on Sunday," became an enormous hit and won the Academy Award for its composer, Manos Hadjidakis. The self-taught musician drew heavily on Greek folk music for his score. In the film, Melina Mercouri introduced the song in Greek under its original title, "Ta Pedia Tou Pirea" ("The Children of Piraeus"). English words were written by Billy Towne, and there were two popular records of the tune released in the United States. Don Costa and His Orchestra recorded an instrumental version in August of 1960, which peaked in the number 19 position and was on the charts for 26 weeks. The following June, the Chordettes recorded the hit vocal version, in English, of course; their recording peaked at number 13. In April of 1961, Lale Anderson recorded a German-language version called "Ein Schiff Wird Kommen" ("A Ship Will Come"). It had modest success on the *Billboard* charts, peaking at number 88.

Composer Manos Hadjidakis also scored the film *America, America,* by Elia Kazan (1963), and another Dassin film (starring Mercouri), *Topkapi* (1964). He died in 1994, of a heart attack.

THE FACTS OF LIFE

Music and lyrics by Johnny Mercer
From *The Facts of Life*

Bob Hope and Lucille Ball, together again!

That's what producer Norman Panama and director Melvin Frank had in mind when they packaged their script for a bedroom farce called *The Facts of Life*. The story concerned two married people who fall for each other. Thrown together against their will by a series of comedic events, they find their initial loathing for each other soon turning to love. Will they consummate their relationship? Get serious. This was 1960, and these were America's most popular comedians.

Still, it was a risqué premise. Twenty years earlier, it would have been unheard of; 20 years later, it would have been considered naïve. In 1960, however, American mores and their reflection in the cinema stood poised in the middle ground between innocence and worldliness. Who better to bridge this vast ocean between the two worlds than Hope and Ball, heroes from the past, now heroes from the most popular medium of the day — television.

Hope and Ball had made two previous films together —*Sorrowful Jones* (1949) and *Fancy Pants* (1950). Would audiences pay to see the Clown Prince and Princess of the airwaves when they could see them for free in their living rooms? United Artists was betting on it. The film was made at Ball's and recent ex-husband Desi's Desilu Studios in Hollywood. Her biggest concern while making the film was that she might inadvertently be playing her television character instead of the one in the script for *The Facts of Life*. As Bob Hope recalled in his book, *The Road to Hollywood*, "Both Lucy and I were determined to submerge our own personalities in the roles we were playing. After a scene, Lucille would ask Mel Frank: 'Was I "Lucy"? Was I "Lucy"?'" The talented actress proved she wasn't, as noted by *Variety*, which wrote, "Somewhat more subdued than her well-known 'Lucy' image, Miss Ball thoroughly brightens up the comedy, be it farce, slapstick, sophisticated or satire, all of which are incorporated into the picture."

The production was not without its problems, mostly in the form of a series of accidents that put filming behind schedule and the principals in considerable discomfort. For instance, while rehearsing a scene in which she was supposed to step into a rowboat, Ball missed her footing and fell more than eight feet, hitting her head on the boat. She was knocked unconscious and had black eyes, a bruised face, and a gashed leg. Production had to shut down for a month while she recuperated. Hope, meanwhile, had caught his finger in a door, and the director sprained his ankle on the golf course. "When we went back to work," wrote Hope, "Lucy needed heavy makeup to hide her injuries, I had my hand in a bandage, and Mel was on crutches. We looked like the original cast of *War and Peace*."

The title song, "The Facts of Life," was sung by popular recording artists Steve Lawrence and Eydie Gorme during the opening credits. The Johnny Mercer tune received a nomination for Best Song, one of several in the long career of the prolific composer. At the time of the picture's release, Steve and Eydie had been charting with other records, both singly and as a couple; "The Facts of Life," however, was not released as a single.

THE FARAWAY PART OF TOWN

Music by André Previn; lyrics by Dory Langdon
From *Pepe*

Actor Mario Moreno Reyes was born in Mexico City in 1911. By the time of his death over 80 years later, he had become a national treasure. The Mexican people knew him by a softer, more familiar name — they called him Cantinflas.

The picture in which Cantinflas found himself at the turn of the decade, amidst a parade of Hollywood actors and cameo stars, was called *Pepe*. Following semi-closely on the heels of his other American success, as David Niven's valet Passepartout in 1956's *Around the World in 80 Days*, *Pepe* was designed to capitalize on Catinflas's newfound celebrity.

The simple storyline had the droopy-trousered comedian playing the groom for a Mexican stallion brought to the United States after it is purchased by a Hollywood director. In the course of his meanderings, which take him from Hollywood to Vegas to Acapulco and other spots in Mexico, he crosses paths with all the stars Columbia could squeeze onto the screen and into the picture's budget — a total of 28, enough to fill the three-hour-plus film with a steady parade of glitz.

The main cast surrounding Cantinflas included Dan Dailey, Shirley Jones, Carlos Montalban, Edward G. Robinson, and Ernie Kovacs. Among the 28 shoot-

Shirley Jones whoops it up with Cantinflas in *Pepe*.

ing stars were Joey Bishop, Maurice Chevalier, Bing Crosby, Bobby Darin, Sammy Davis Jr., Jimmy Durante, Zsa Zsa Gabor, Greer Garson, Peter Lawford, Janet Leigh, Jack Lemmon, Jay North (TV's "Dennis the Menace"), Kim Novak, Donna Reed, Debbie Reynolds, Cesar Romero, and Frank Sinatra. Unfortunately, all this was merely window dressing. There was very little for these stars to do, other than wander onto the set, mutter a few words or do a routine before the bemused Cantinflas, and collect their paychecks.

Some chroniclers would have you believe that the film was a certified flop. In fact, the picture earned a respectable $4.6 million in North American rentals, ranking 16th for all films released that year. And it served to catapult its young Mexican star, Cantinflas, to a place of prominence in his homeland. The actor continued making films in Mexico, but became even more renowned for his philanthropy. He personally constructed more than 60 apartment houses and sold them to poor families for a fraction of their worth. He also gave away much of his personal wealth in the form of cash donations to those who needed a handout, reportedly close to $175,000 a year to people who had only to knock on his door. No wonder the whole country declared a national day of mourning when he died on April 20, 1993, at the age of 81.

Pepe included a scene in which Shirley Jones dances with Dan Dailey while Pepe watches. The tune is source music, on the radio — a song called "The Faraway Part of Town." It was sung by Judy Garland, and although it received an Academy Award nomination, it was not one of her more successful recordings. The song was composed by André Previn, with lyrics by Dory Langdon (the pair were later married). Previn, who had previously received the Best Score Oscar for *Gigi* (1958 — with Ken Darby) and for *Porgy and Bess* (1959), can also be seen briefly in the movie as one of the 28 guest stars.

Pepe proved a hit with the Academy if not with the critics. At Oscar time, the film was nominated for seven Academy Awards. In addition to Best Song, nominations were for Best Color Cinematography, Best Color Art Direction-Set Direction, Best Sound, Best Scoring of a Musical Picture, Best Film Editing, and Best Color Costume Design.

THE GREEN LEAVES OF SUMMER

**Music by Dimitri Tiomkin;
lyrics by Paul Francis Webster**
From *The Alamo*

With 1,500 horses, a $1.5 million replica of the real Alamo, and John Wayne himself as Davy Crockett (spouting lines like: "I want ya to listen tight"), the film portrayal of *The Alamo* may not have been too historically accurate, but it took box offices with all the fury of Santa Anna and his men attacking that famous fort. After the dust had cleared, the United Artists release had grabbed nearly $8 million in domestic rentals, making it the number five film of 1960.

While history has shown the real Davy Crockett to have been somewhat less than heroic — he tried to convince Santa Anna that he was merely a tourist who had taken refuge in the Alamo — John Wayne portrayed him as being larger than life itself. He was supported in this 200-minute epic by an all-star cast that included Richard Widmark, Laurence Harvey, Wayne's son Patrick Wayne, Richard Boone, and even Frankie Avalon, far from his surfboard and Annette.

The film was was anything but critically acclaimed. Bosley Crowther of the *New York Times* proclaimed it a "horrendous representation of the last battle for the Alamo." The Academy, however, disagreed — the film, which Wayne also produced and directed, received seven Oscar nominations, for Best Picture, Best Supporting Actor (Chill Wills), Best Color Cinematography, Best Film Editing, Best Scoring (Dimitri Tiomkin), Best Sound (the only win), and Best Song.

Blessed with lyrics that did nothing to bind it to the film, "The Green Leaves of Summer," by Dimitri Tiomkin and Paul Francis Webster, took on a life of its own. It was sung by a chorus on the soundtrack, and had moderate success as a single. The Brothers Four, another ersatz folk singing group in the popular revivalist style of the day, released a version just after the film's premiere in October. Their recording peaked at number 65 and charted for seven weeks. Kenny Ball recorded the tune two years later; his version reached number 87.

Although never a megahit, the movie's main theme has since become a nostalgic favorite, due in part to the outstanding Webster lyrics coupled with Tiomkin's minor-keyed, plaintive melody. *Variety* commented at length about the Tiomkin score, calling it "distinguished . . . incorporating and intertwining melodies of Latin and country-style-U.S.A. flavors . . . An important contribution to the product. There are compelling choral passages and even a few pleasant little ditties."

At the Academy Awards ceremony, the Brothers Four sang the nominated song; this was a rarity, since nearly all the song nominees at this time were being performed by celebrities rather than the artists of record. A few weeks prior to the event, the outspoken

Tiomkin expressed his hopes to an interviewer: "What is the duty of the Academy? I will tell you. I am interested in the Awards as a businessman. They increase my royalties. [Winning the Oscar for] *High Noon* did more for me than all of my symphonic work combined. It doubled my royalties . . . I suffer for recognition here, and the Academy Awards show to me is recognition . . . Four weeks was all I was allowed to write *The Alamo* . . . It is ruining my health and my heart." Perhaps, but although "The Green Leaves of Summer" would not win the Oscar, there were still two other nominations (and, presumably, a healthy share of dollars) in Tiomkin's future (see "Town Without Pity," page 166, and "So Little Time," page 174).

THE SECOND TIME AROUND

Music by James Van Heusen; lyrics by Sammy Cahn
From *High Time*

College comedies were all the rage in the 1940s. So what was Bing Crosby doing in a campus film at the beginning of the 1960s? Had he flipped his wig? Well, no, not exactly. In fact, he donned one — along with a dress, earrings, and makeup. Crosby in drag? What was going on?

Over at Twentieth, someone thought it might be fun to return to the days of yesteryear when Dick Powell and Betty Grable wandered ivy-covered halls, cheered at football games, and tore down goal posts. So writers Tom and Frank Waldman devised a screenplay that had the Old Groaner returning to campus as a middle-aged student. Sure enough, kids were up to the same old antics this "second time around," playing fraternity pranks, shooting the breeze and hoops, building bonfires, and creating mischief. Occasionally they even studied French or chemistry. The script called for Crosby to pledge a fraternity, the fictitious Chi Delta Pi, and then attend a party disguised as a southern belle — cue the drag number.

The producers sought a youthful audience, so they corralled the acting talents of rock star Fabian, along with Tuesday Weld, Richard Beymer, Yvonne Craig, Jimmy Boyd, and future "Love Boat" captain Gavin MacLeod. Rock 'n' roll had replaced the big band swing music, but nothing could save the sagging script. "The screenplay by Tom and Frank Waldman, based on a story by Garson Kanin, is awfully sad, awfully burdened with hackneyed situations. And Mr. Crosby, alas, is no kid," lamented the *New York Times.* "He tries to be casual and boyish, to prove modestly that he's in the groove...[but] there is a terrible gauntness and look of exhaustion about Mr. Crosby when the camera gets close and peers at his face."

James Van Heusen and Sammy Cahn wrote a memorable song for *High Time,* "The Second Time Around" (whose lyrics refer to love, not college, being easier the second time around). It is sung by Crosby in the picture, and received yet another nomination for the Van Heusen–Cahn team. Frank Sinatra cut the song as a single in March, 1961, on Capitol. It coincided with a new film called *The Second Time Around,* which starred Debbie Reynolds and Andy Griffith and used "The Second Time Around" as its theme. Sinatra's record peaked in the number 50 position and charted for seven weeks; today it is regarded as a standard.

The score for *High Time,* an early Blake Edwards–directed film, was by Henry Mancini. It marked the beginning of a legendary cinematic partnership between these two talents (they had already worked together in television, most notably on the "Peter Gunn" series), a collaboration that would reach its most memorable heights with the *Pink Panther* films.

1961

MOON RIVER

**Music by Henry Mancini;
lyrics by Johnny Mercer
From *Breakfast at Tiffany's***

"Moon River." Most film critics and music buffs agree that a song like this comes along maybe once in a decade. Yet, it was nearly tossed out of *Breakfast at Tiffany's,* the movie in which it first appeared.

Composer Henry Mancini, who had been creating music for Blake Edwards since he had first produced

Bing Crosby tries to get in step with Tuesday Weld in *High Time.*

the soundtrack for the acclaimed "Peter Gunn" television series, was invited by Edwards to create not only a score for *Tiffany's*, but also a song for the leading actress, Audrey Hepburn, to sing in a gentle balcony scene.

"That song was the toughest I have ever had to write," said Mancini in his autobiography, *Did They Mention the Music?*. "It took me a month to think it through. What kind of song would this girl sing? What kind of melody was required? Should it be a jazz-flavored ballad? Would it be a blues? One night at home, I was relaxing after dinner. I went out to my studio off the garage, sat down at the piano (still rented), and all of a sudden I played the first three notes of a tune. It sounded attractive. I built the melody in [Hepburn's] range of an octave and one. It was simple and completely diatonic: in the key of C, you can play it entirely on the white keys. It came quickly. It had taken me one month and half an hour to write that melody."

Edwards loved it and asked who Mancini would like as lyricist. "I went for the best," wrote Mancini. "Johnny Mercer." Mercer, however, was more reserved. "Hank," he asked, "who's going to record a waltz? We'll do it for the movie, but after that it hasn't any future commercially." Mercer wanted to call his song "Blue River," but several of his friends already had songs by that title, and while a song title cannot be legally copyrighted, he wanted his to be different. He suggested one from the bottom of the pile: "Moon River." Mancini wasn't so sure — he remembered a talk show on Cincinnati radio that had gone by that title. But since that wasn't actually a song, they agreed to use it.

Then came the first preview screening of *Breakfast at Tiffany's*, whose screenplay was based on Truman Capote's tale of a young, eccentric southern girl on the make for a rich husband in New York.

When the picture ran overly long at the preview, Marty Rackin, one of the producers, had a quick suggestion: "The fucking song has to go." Blake Edwards and Audrey Hepburn shot a daggered look at Rackin, murder clearly on their minds. The song stayed.

When it came time to find a recording artist to release a single, the pair approached Andy Williams, whom they accosted one night in a Beverly Hills restaurant. "I took it back to [orchestra leader] Archie Bleyer," said Williams in a 1993 interview with Wink Martindale, written and produced by Paul Worth and first aired on the Los Angeles radio station "K-JOI." "He said, 'I don't think the kids will buy a record that has the phrase in it, "my huckleberry friend," ' so we passed on it. Henry [Mancini] had a million-selling single on it as an instrumental, Jerry Butler recorded it and had a million seller, and I never recorded [at that time]."

In fact, the "huckleberry friend" lyric threw a lot of people. "I don't know *why* I thought of it," Mercer said in an interview in the book, *They're Playing Our Song*, by Max Wilk. "Probably stems from the days of my childhood, when we'd go out in the fields and pick wild berries; they were everywhere. I was free-associating about the South for that song. The heroine [in *Breakfast at Tiffany's*], Holly Golightly, was from down there." Mancini recalled in *Did They Mention the Music?* just how moving he found the line. "Every once in a while you hear something so right that it gives you chills, and when [Mercer] sang that 'huckleberry friend' line, I got them. I don't know whether he knew what effect those words had or if it was just something that came to him, but it was thrilling. It made you think of Mark Twain and Huckleberry Finn's trip

Audrey Hepburn strikes a classic pose as Holly Golightly in *Breakfast at Tiffany's*.

down the Mississippi. It had such echoes of America. It was one of those remarkable lines that gives you a rush. It was the clincher."

In the end, Andy Williams agreed. After the number received the Best Song nomination, Columbia, his recording company, decided to put out an album called *Moon River and Other Movie Themes*. The day after the Academy Awards, Columbia rushed a fresh shipment to the stores. After all, 80 million people had just witnessed Williams singing what would become his signature song. It introduced his television series for 10 years, and in the mid-1990s he even used the song's title for his musical theater, where the popular singer welcomed thousands of visitors annually to his "Andy Williams–Moon River Theater" in Branson, Missouri.

Mancini's career, meanwhile, was also kicked off in earnest with "Moon River." By the time of his death in 1994, he had picked up four Oscars (three for Best Song, one for Best Score — for *Breakfast at Tiffany's),* having been nominated 18 times; he'd also won 20 Grammys (with 72 nominations), with five alone for *Breakfast at Tiffany's,* including record, soundtrack and song of the year. He was working on music for a Broadway version of Blake Edwards's 1983 movie *Victor/Victoria* when he died from pancreatic cancer.

BACHELOR IN PARADISE

Music by Henry Mancini; lyrics by Mack David
From *Bachelor in Paradise*

If Crosby could cause the brass at 20th Century-Fox to allow him to have a fling "the second time around" in *High Time* (see page 161), it seemed only fitting that Hope could hope for some of the same. That was the sentiment over at MGM, where Bob Hope was signed to do a film called *Bachelor in Paradise.* From Hope's point of view, it must have seemed a dream come true. The actor was cast as a writer in a mythical San Fernando Valley development called Paradise Valley, where he was working on a book about life in suburbia — and the sexual habits of the female residents in particular — to pay off a tax debt. In this subdivision laden with young, pretty wives — all secretly panting after our hero, the script would have us believe — Hope was the only bachelor in "Paradise" — get it?

The problem was the premise — it simply wasn't believable. Here was Hope, at age 59, attempting to portray a playboy role suited to someone 20 or 30 years his junior. To top it off, he falls for the only available woman on the screen, the development's manager,

Surrounded by feminine pulchritude, Bob Hope has become a *Bachelor in Paradise.*

played by Lana Turner, who herself had recently turned 41. Would happiness find these two young lovebirds? Who cared? "Their first fine rapture actually suggests a desperate last fling, their romantic moments sometimes seem mildly necromantic," opined *Time* magazine.

Further, the dialogue did nothing to aid the cause of these two miscast actors. When Turner tells Hope that the builder had to stop work on another tract nearby, he quips: "I knew this was a man with an arrested development." When Janis Paige coos at Hope, "Tom and I are separated. Does that put your mind at ease?," he shoots back, "Just my conscience. My mind is having a ball." Paige, brandishing a morning martini, doesn't give up easily: "Aren't you having a drink?" Hope: "It's a little early for me." Paige: "Early? It's April!"

Perhaps the best thing about the film was the title song, "Bachelor in Paradise," sung under the cute, animated opening credits by an unnamed chorus. The song was the second Henry Mancini tune to be nominated for Best Song that year, giving him his third Oscar nomination for 1961 (the others were Best Song for "Moon River" and Best Score for *Breakfast at Tiffany's*, both of which he won — see page 162). "Bachelor in Paradise" had lyrics by Mack David, who was now on everyone's "A" list as the lyricist of choice for title songs; over the next decade he would pen several more.

At the Academy Awards ceremony the following spring, "Bachelor in Paradise" was performed by newcomer Ann-Margret. A virtual unknown who was working with a little group at a club down in Newport Beach at the time, her appearance on the television broadcast that night helped launch her career. Clad in a tight gown and topped with her trademark red hair, the singer received a standing ovation.

LOVE THEME FROM *EL CID* (THE FALCON AND THE DOVE)

Music by Miklos Rozsa;
lyrics by Paul Francis Webster
From *El Cid*

Miklos Rozsa was a man to be envied. In a fickle town such as Hollywood, the Hungarian-born composer had done something few had been able to do successfully — he had worked steadily. Year after year, he cranked out his lavish musical scores for films, some epic, some modest, some well-known, some relatively obscure. Rozsa, too, was relatively obscure. Unless you were a soundtrack aficionado, you most likely wouldn't have recognized his name.

Yet Rozsa was a three-time Academy Award winner. His scores for *Spellbound* (1945), *A Double Life* (1947), and his most prestigious win, *Ben-Hur* (1959), all took home Oscars. Throughout his career, he continued churning out music for psychological dramas and later for sweeping historical epics. In the 1940s, he composed the music for such disparate pictures as *So Proudly We Hail* (1943), *Blood on the Sun* (1945), and *Adam's Rib* (1949). In the 1950s he turned his attention to epics like *Ivanhoe* (1952), *Knights of the Round Table* (1954), *Lust for Life* (1956), and *Something of Value* (1957). Rozsa's epic period culminated in 1961, when he was called upon to compose the score for *El Cid*. This time there was a bonus.

His main theme for the three-hour picture was titled "Love Theme from *El Cid*"; when lyrics by Paul Francis Webster were added to it and sung on the soundtrack, it became known as "The Falcon and the Dove." Although the song had no life of its own outside the film, it was well received by the Academy. Rozsa had crossed the bridge from composer to songwriter — something not every composer can do (even Henry Mancini once feared he might not be able to make the journey). For his efforts, he received his first — and last — Academy Award nomination for Best Song. For Webster, it was something like his jillionth nomination — the lyricist had received his first nomination in 1944 for "Remember Me to Carolina" (see page 72); he would receive his final one in 1976, for "A World That Never Was" (see page 231).

El Cid was a surefire box office hit, ranking number four for 1961, with a North American rental take of $12 million. Of course, producer Samuel Bronston had spent $8 million for the finest special effects, cast (Charlton Heston, Sophia Loren), extras by the score, plus 70-millimeter Super Technirama, with Rozsa's score thundering behind lavish scenery, battles, and no end of big-screen hoopla. Unfortunately, there was very little interaction between the characters. "The spectacle is terrific," wrote Bosley Crowther, then in his fourth decade as critic for the *New York Times*. "Only the human drama is stiff and dull." He did, however, reserve his praise for the music while summing up the plot's shortcomings: "A musical score by Miklos Rozsa is rhythmic and rousing to the extent that it is likely to have one's ears ringing long after one leaves this massive film, which is actually no more than a big drama of a king-serving Robin Hood."

While the producers no doubt cringed over this assessment, this last reference was perfect from Rozsa's point of view — another epic notched on his baton. He received an Oscar nomination for Best Scoring of a Dramatic or Comedy Picture, and the film received a nomination for Best Color Art Direction–Set Direction.

POCKETFUL OF MIRACLES

**Music by James Van Heusen;
    lyrics by Sammy Cahn**
From *Pocketful of Miracles*

Characters with names like Dave the Dude, Apple Annie, Queenie Martin, Flyaway, Cheesecake, Big Mike, and Shimkey populated the fictional world of Damon Runyon, a place peopled with kind-hearted guys and dolls, gangsters and molls, dressed in the snappiest of duds and whose speech patterns religiously avoided contractions ("I do not"; never "I don't"). Runyon's short stories about these heart-of-gold thugs were a major contribution to the legacy of contemporary literature, and many of them made their way to stage and screen, including one called "Madam La Gimp."

In 1933, director Frank Capra brought "Madam La Gimp" to the screen under the title *Lady for a Day*; a sequel, *Lady by Choice*, followed a year later. In 1961, he decided to do a remake of the first *Lady*, called *Pocketful of Miracles*. Like its predecessors, the story concerns a Depression-era apple seller, appropriately named Apple Annie, who is transformed, in Cinderella-like fashion, into Mrs. E. Worthington Manville, an ersatz socialite, in order to impress her daughter, who has been educated in Spain and hasn't seen her in years. All the kindly hoods in the 'hood get in on the act — a parade of some of the finest talent in Hollywood portraying this really swell bunch of thugs, racketeers, murderers, and other assorted Runyon types. (Nary a drop of blood is ever spilt, of course — this is family entertainment.)

The cast made it all worthwhile. Glenn Ford starred as Dave the Dude, while a deliciously witchy Bette Davis played the haggish Apple Annie. "All Miss Davis seems to need is a broom to qualify as the leading lady

in a Charles Addams cartoon," wrote A. H. Weiler of the *New York Times*. "This portion of the role is a tribute to her artistry and make-up." Others in the superb cast included Hope Lange, Peter Falk (typecast as a thug long before donning his "Columbo" trenchcoat to become a crimefighter), Sheldon Leonard (the epitome of thuggery), character actors Benny Rubin and Jack Elam, and, in her screen debut, Ann-Margret.

A title song was needed, preferably one sung by Frank Sinatra. Enter Jimmy Van Heusen and Sammy Cahn. The pair had won an Oscar for another Frank Capra/Sinatra film, *A Hole in the Head* (see page 151), with their song "High Hopes." This time, their catchy tune and quirky lyrics were good enough for an Academy Award nomination, although they actually had no hopes against *Moon River*. Cahn recalled in his autobiography, *I Should Care*, that his partner Van Heusen had once written a song with Johnny Burke called "Pocketful of Dreams." Songwriters were always mindful of offending their colleagues. How could they do a another song by that name, Cahn wondered. "If I wrote that song with Burke," Van Heusen said, "I can also give you permission to write another with me."

The song was noted for its stretching out of the first letter of some of the words. "Practicality doesn't interest me" became "Pee-racticality dee-uzn't int'rest me"; "Troubles, more or less, bother me, I guess" became "Tee-roubles, more or less, bee-ahther me, I guess." The rhythm worked well with the music, giving it an added push. And while Frank Sinatra's single wasn't a chartburner, it managed to reach the number 34 position and remain on the charts for eight weeks.

Pocketful of Miracles received two additional Academy Award nominations — for Best Color Art Direction–Set Direction and Best Scoring of a Dramatic or Comedy Picture.

TOWN WITHOUT PITY

**Music by Dimitri Tiomkin;
    lyrics by Ned Washington**
From *Town Without Pity*

Filmed on location in Germany, the riveting drama of *Town Without Pity* centered around a trial involving rape, always a daring topic, although it was becoming less so as the '60s began to unfold. The film was based on the novel *The Verdict*, by Manfred Gregor, and was a combined effort of the Mirisch Company and United Artists in the United States, and Gloria Film of Munich, Germany.

The story centered around a 16-year-old German girl who is assaulted by four drunken, off-duty American soldiers. The drama comes from the trial, as justice is sought by the girl's family and the local townsfolk. Kirk Douglas played the army officer assigned as the defense attorney, and additional drama stems from his inner conflict between his own revulsion at the crime his clients have committed and his duty to defend them in the courtroom. E. G. Marshall played the prosecuting attorney, while a cast of fine German actors played the townspeople — you know, the ones without pity.

One of the soldiers was played by Robert Blake. A former child actor, "Bobby" Blake, as he was then known, had been a member of "Our Gang" in the old Hal Roach comedies. He went on to star in a number of films, generally playing thugs and petty crooks, like a convict in *Revolt in the Big House* (1958) and one of the murderers in *In Cold Blood* (1968). His most popular starring role was as TV's "Baretta" in the 1970s. Frank Sutton played another one of the soldiers on trial. He later found fame as Gomer Pyle's Sergeant Carter on the 1960s television series "Gomer Pyle, U.S.M.C."

Nearly every film in the 1960s seemed to have a title song performed under the opening credits, and *Town Without Pity* was no exception. Dimitri Tiomkin, who composed the score, proved he was up for the job of songwriter as well, and selected longtime partner Ned Washington to do the lyricist's honors. The song was not only nominated for an Academy Award (it lost to "Moon River"), but also received the Hollywood Foreign Press Association's prestigious Golden Globe Award for Best Original Song.

"Town Without Pity" also became a best-selling single, recorded by Gene Pitney, who had one of his biggest hits with the song. His recording debuted on October 30, 1961, about two weeks after the film opened, and climbed the charts to the number 13 position. It charted for 19 weeks.

Pitney was born in Hartford, Connecticut, in 1941, and became proficient on piano, guitar, and drums during his youth. He began writing songs and soon was selling to popular artists of the day, including Rick Nelson, for whom he wrote the hit song "Hello Mary Lou" in 1961. For the Crystals he wrote "He's a Rebel" in 1962, and he co-wrote (under the pseudonym Orlowski) Bobby Vee's 1960 hit "Rubber Ball." His own first successful recording was "Town Without Pity," followed by a trio of million-selling songs written by Burt Bacharach and Hal David — "The Man Who Shot Liberty Valance" (from the film of the same name), "Only Love Can Break a Heart," and "Twenty Four Hours from Tulsa."

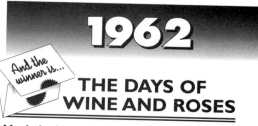

1962
And the winner is...
THE DAYS OF WINE AND ROSES

Music by Henry Mancini; lyrics by Johnny Mercer
From *The Days of Wine and Roses*

The preview was a disaster. *The Days of Wine and Roses*, a new Warner Bros. film, had just been shown to a "test" audience. What happened during that screening nearly sent the studio executives into collective shock. There were talks of retakes, revisions.

The film's producer, Blake Edwards (best known for his private-eye series and romantic comedies), and star, Jack Lemmon (also primarily associated with comedy at the time), were mystified. They were sure their work was Academy Award material, yet 40 couples had walked out on film during the first 45 minutes. Later it became clear what had happened, as recalled by Lemmon in his Don Widener–penned biography, *Lemmon*: "Some ding-dong had run newspaper advertisements without mentioning that the picture was a drama. All the ads said was: Jack Lemmon's Newest Movie. Families came, some with children, expecting to see a comedy, and within the first twenty minutes this raving drunk shows up on the screen. That's when they started to bail out."

Although off to a rocky start, the film, originally broadcast as a "Playhouse 90" television drama by J. P. Miller, received the highest critical acclaim. It also received Academy Award nominations in five categories: Best Actor (Lemmon), Best Actress (Lee Remick), Best Black-and-White Art Direction, Best Black-and-White Costumes, and Best Song. The film's only Oscar went to Henry Mancini and Johnny Mercer for their song, "The Days of Wine and Roses."

It was their second Oscar in as many years, an Academy first. What's more, the song had proven one of the easiest for them to write. "The title determined the melody," Mancini wrote in his autobiography, *Did They Mention the Music?*. "I went to the piano and started on middle C and went up to A, 'The days . . .' The first phrase fell right into place. That theme was written in about half an hour. It just came, it rolled out." Mercer, too, had little trouble with the lyric, reportedly jotted down in five minutes. When it came time to play their song for producer Edwards, they commandeered an empty sound stage on the Warners lot. It had a sole upright piano in the center of this hangar-sized empty building, with a single light shining down. As Mancini sat down to play, Mercer took a crumpled piece of paper out of his pocket — the lyrics — and began to sing. Lemmon later recalled, "Blake, Lee, and I just stand there. I swear to God, I'm beginning to cry. He started to sing this song, and I have never been through anything like it in my life. I knew. The strange thing is that I think that even for people who are musical, or who are in the business to some extent, when you first hear a piece of music, you do not necessarily make a very keen judgment of it, but when I heard this, I was wiped out — I was gone. It was one of the most thrilling moments that I've ever had in 35 years of being in this business."

Johnny Mercer's hauntingly poetic lyrics and Mancini's easy-flowing melody not only won the Oscar for Best Song, but also took home two Grammy Awards, for Song of the Year and Record of the Year.

Andy Williams's recording, released the following spring, peaked at number 26 and charted for 12 weeks; Mancini's own orchestral version made number 33.

LOVE SONG FROM MUTINY ON THE BOUNTY (FOLLOW ME)

**Music by Bronislau Kaper;
  lyrics by Paul Francis Webster**
From Mutiny on the Bounty

Clocking in at nearly three hours, MGM's remake of their original 1935 Best Picture Oscar-winner, *Mutiny on the Bounty* (which then starred Clark Gable and Charles Laughton), spared no expense. The 1962 version, complete with Technicolor and Ultra Panavision 70, reportedly cost $8 million (it barely broke even). For its money, the studio got authentic Tahitian locations, a nearly full-sized replica of the ship *H.M.S. Bounty*, special effects of tempest-tossed seas, handsomely (although barely) clad natives frolicking and dancing with the seamen, and a whole boatload of new Oscar nominations.

Marlon Brando starred as Fletcher Christian, the leading mutineer, while Trevor Howard played the *Bounty*'s misguided captain. Most kudos went to Brando, who, according to *Variety*, "gives the finest performance of his career" (this was years before *The Godfather*, of course). Richard Harris, as the sailor accused of stealing a head of cheese, was also notable in the cast.

The film's plot was based on an actual historical incident. In 1787, the *Bounty* sailed from England under the by-the-book captaincy of William Bligh. After completing her business in Tahiti, the *Bounty* set sail for the long voyage home, but her crew, on the verge of starvation, had had enough of the captain's seemingly whimsical tormentings. With Fletcher Christian as their leader, they seized the ship and set Bligh and 18 loyalists adrift in a dinghy. Somehow Bligh made it to the Dutch East Indies — one for the record books. Christian, meanwhile, landed at Pitcairn Island, where he and some of the others took native wives. As of 1994, 41 out of the 46 islanders living on Pitcairn were descendants of the mutineers, many with the surname of "Christian."

The location filming in the Society Islands (the South Pacific chain that includes Tahiti) took almost two years. During that time, Brando married a native woman, and the two later had a child. Succumbing to what anthropologists call the Tahiti syndrome, he fell under the spell of those lush, romantic islands and eventually purchased one of his own.

Bronislau Kaper's musical score effectively enhanced the various dramatic moods of the film. For one number, "Love Song from *Mutiny on the Bounty*," he received an Academy Award nomination for Best Song. The song, also known as "Follow Me" (with words by veteran lyricist Paul Francis Webster), is sung by an unnamed chorus early in the film. After Captain Bligh is told that it would be insulting for his men not to have sex with the Tahitian women, his crew dutifully returns to shore, and the tune is heard during the ensuing intimate scenes. The song, along with the sweeping

Sailors mingle with Polynesian natives in this celebration scene from *Mutiny on the Bounty.*

soundtrack album, was never as popular with the public as the critics predicted it might be.

In addition to the nomination for Best Song, Bronislau Kaper also received an Oscar nomination for Best Score. Other nominations for this epic film were for Best Picture, Color Cinematography, Color Art Direction, Editing, and Special Effects. Despite this impressive total of seven nominations, there were no wins.

SECOND CHANCE

Music by André Previn; lyrics by Dory Langdon
From *Two for the Seesaw*

Fresh from its Broadway success, *Two for the Seesaw* was given the full treatment for its big-screen debut: a big-name director in Robert Wise, a big-name male lead in Robert Mitchum, and hotter-than-hot female talent in the form of Shirley MacLaine as the leading lady. MacLaine had been wowing them at the Motion Picture Academy the last few years, having been nomi-

nated as Best Actress for *Some Came Running* in 1959 and for *The Apartment* in 1960. (She was subsequently nominated several additional times, winning the Oscar for *Terms of Endearment* in 1983).

With all this going for it, the film should have been a smash. For some reason, however, it was a disappointment at the box office, earning only $1.8 million in North American rentals. Perhaps the problem was the inherent staginess. The story of a love affair between Jerry Ryan (Mitchum), a Nebraska lawyer, and Gittel Mosca (MacLaine), a nice Jewish girl from the Bronx, was a talkative play that just didn't seem that suited to a screen translation. Critics had a field day slashing and dissecting the picture's main problems. "There is a fundamental torpor about *Seesaw* that is less troublesome on stage than it is on screen, a medium of motion that exaggerates its absence, that emphasizes the slightest hint of listlessness," wrote *Variety*. Bosley Crowther of the *New York Times* agreed, finding additional fault in the film's casting: "Where the fellow in [playwright] Mr. Gibson's gimmicked and talkative little play was (and must be) an obviously withdrawing, self-pitying, apologetic type, on the order of Henry Fonda, who, miraculously, originated the role, Mr. Mitchum is plainly a two-fisted, self-assertive and generally supercilious brute whose feeble attempts to act downtrodden are on the painful side of absurd. And where the girl in the play was a fireball of emotional vibrancy and energy, Miss MacLaine simply isn't a fireball. She tries to portray one without sufficient fuel."

There were, however, two Oscar nominations for this film. One was for Best Black-and-White Cinematography, and the other was for Best Song. The song, entitled "Second Chance," was sung in the background of a scene where Jerry Ryan goes to a party to look for Gittel. It was written by André Previn (who also wrote the film's score) and his wife, Dory Langdon. Although neither the unspectacular song nor the score would win any awards, the following year was a much better one for Previn — he won an Oscar for Best Score for *Irma La Douce*, a film that, ironically, also starred MacLaine (she received an Oscar nomination for her role in that film).

In 1973, *Two for the Seesaw* returned to Broadway, this time as a musical called *Seesaw*, starring Ken Howard as Jerry Ryan and Michele Lee as Gittel Mosca. Written by Cy Coleman and Dorothy Fields, it ran for less than a year.

TENDER IS THE NIGHT

**Music by Sammy Fain;
lyrics by Paul Francis Webster**
From *Tender Is the Night*

Set against the background of the French Riviera and Paris, *Tender Is the Night* was based on F. Scott Fitzgerald's story of a former American psychiatrist and his rich wife during pre-Depression days. The screenplay was written by Ivan Moffat, who was obligated to ignore much of Fitzgerald's unfilmable prose, which, of course, was the essence of the book's literary value. Like most novels translated to the screen, the writer distilled it as best he could, and it was evident that those involved with the filming had painstakingly attempted to stay as close to the book's plot as possible.

Despite all their efforts, this CinemaScope film from 20th Century-Fox seemed to plod along. There were endless talky, two-person scenes in this character-driven picture about Dick Diver, a psychiatrist (Jason Robards Jr.), and his former-patient-turned wife, Nicole Diver (Jennifer Jones). Part of the problem may have been that the source material was just too good to live up to — few films are as good as their literary inspirations, and classics are especially hard to re-create. Moffat found his screenplay under a microscope, where it couldn't help but suffer by comparison to Fitzgerald's original novel. "Mr. Moffat has written very long scenes, but he has not written sharply and clearly," said the *New York Times*. "He has not clinched dramatic points. He has let the development get fuzzy."

On the plus side, there was a very moving, very lyrical theme song created for the film. Written by two veteran film composers — Sammy Fain and Paul Francis Webster — "Tender Is the Night" was sung on the soundtrack by a chorus under the main and end titles. Introduced during the film by Earl Grant, the song was an integral part of the drama. The romantic, melancholy composition received an Academy Award nomination, the only one bestowed upon the picture.

Grant, who did not release the song as a single, was best known for his instrumental version of "Ebb Tide," which sold in the millions. During his career as an organist, he recorded nearly 50 albums. Besides appearing on screen in *Tender Is the Night,* he was seen in *Imitation of Life* (1959) and appeared in numerous television shows. He died in an automobile accident in the New Mexico desert in 1970, at the age of only 39.

"Tender Is the Night" was recorded by Tony Bennett, and was also popularized by Johnny Mathis, who used it as the title track for a 1964 LP that made number 16 on the album charts.

WALK ON THE WILD SIDE

Music by Elmer Bernstein; lyrics by Mack David
From *Walk on the Wild Side*

Prostitution. Lesbianism. The underworld of pimps and whores. Themes of lost innocence and redemption. Not the sort of film topics that usually garnered a positive response from Hollywood's Production Code board. But by 1962, it was clear these self-appointed watchdogs would soon be on the unemployment line. *Walk on the Wild Side* was just one of the reasons.

Producer Charles Feldman had brought *A Streetcar Named Desire* to the screen a decade before *Walk on the*

Wild Side. At the time, that picture was considered a breakthrough film, mirroring an unseemly side of contemporary society that few wished to acknowledge. With *Wild Side,* Feldman again attempted to break new ground.

The film, based loosely on a 1956 novel by Nelson Algren (with a screenplay by John Fante and Edmund Morris) was set in 1930s New Orleans. It was peopled with an excellent cast: Laurence Harvey as Dove Linkhorn, the Texas vagabond who heads to the Big Easy to find Hallie, his lost love (played by the mono-named Capucine), who he finds working in a brothel; Jane Fonda as the sluttish Kitty Twist; Barbara Stanwyck as the madam with designs on Capucine; and Anne Baxter as the Mexican cafe owner Teresina Vidaverri.

Walk on the Wild Side was directed by Edward Dmytryk, who first made his mark helming such intriguing, stylish productions as *Hitler's Children* (1943) and Till the End of Time (1946). In the '50s, he turned his attention to large-budgeted adaptations of best-selling novels, like *Raintree County* (1957) and *The Young Lions* (1958).

But apart from the outstanding performances and controversial script (which reportedly included drafts by veteran writers Ben Hecht and Clifford Odets), *Walk on the Wild Side* is often remembered for its opening credits. The Saul Bass title sequence is a masterpiece of variable-speed photography and optical work, featuring a sleek alley cat (Bass's own feline) wending its way through a concrete maze of pipes and iron fences, all underscored by composer Elmer Bernstein's main title music.

Bernstein's creation of the bluesy theme, "Walk on the Wild Side," with lyrics by Mack David, earned the pair an Academy Award nomination. Bernstein, who composed over 90 film scores during his long career, became known for his skill at composing jazz scores, beginning in 1955 with his melding of symphonic and jazz elements in *The Man with the Golden Arm.* He was also adept at producing full-bodied scores for epic pictures and swashbucklers, such as *The Ten Commandments* (1955), *The Buccaneer* (1959), and *The Magnificent Seven* (1960). He won an Oscar in 1967 for his vibrant score for *Thoroughly Modern Millie.*

"Walk on the Wild Side" was sung by Brook Benton. His single release, however, peaked at only number 43 position and charted for seven weeks, while a version by Jimmy Smith peaked at number 21 and was on the *Billboard* charts for 13 weeks.

And the winner is...

CALL ME IRRESPONSIBLE

**Music by James Van Heusen;
lyrics by Sammy Cahn
From *Papa's Delicate Condition***

In 1956, Henry and Phoebe Ephron completed a script for a film that would star Fred Astaire. The story concerned the father of silent film star Corinne Griffith, who followed her screen career with an even more successful stint as a writer. One of her dozen or so books, an autobiography, was called *Papa's Delicate Condition,* and the rights were bought by Paramount. The Ephrons' script was fairly true to the book: Papa Griffith, a railroad superintendent and heavy boozer (his "delicate" condition), loved his daughter so much that when she wanted a pony, for example, he bought her an entire circus.

Fred Astaire was signed to play Papa, while Academy Award–winning composers James Van Heusen and Sammy Cahn were brought on board to create five songs for the film. Cahn was thrilled — for years it had been his dream to write for Fred Astaire. One of the songs they created was called "Walking Happy," a tune about how a drunk walks; the other key song found Papa explaining some of his more questionable acts (like buying that circus) to his wife, inviting her to "Call me irresponsible . . . ."

As it turned out, Astaire was unable to get out of his MGM commitments, and the picture was shelved before Cahn and Van Heusen could realize their dream of seeing Astaire perform one of their songs in a film. The team figured that was the end of it. "Walking Happy" and "Call Me Irresponsible" also ended up on the shelf.

Seven years later, Martin Rackin, a production executive at Paramount, revived the project and signed Jackie Gleason to play "Papa" Jack Griffith. After reading about this sudden turn of events in the *Hollywood Reporter,* Sammy Cahn rushed to the telephone to remind Rackin that he had written five songs for that picture. "There aren't going to be songs in this picture," Rackin informed the lyricist. Undaunted, Cahn and

Van Heusen insisted on auditioning their tunes for Rackin and Jack Rose, the new writer-producer. They loved "Walking Happy" but nixed "Call Me Irresponsible." According to Cahn, writing in his autobiography *I Should Care*, Rose said, "I can't see the character singing such a self-pitying song." Cahn was insistent: "This song has been on the shelf for seven years. Damn near every singer from Frank Sinatra to Tony Bennett to Billy Eckstine to Peggy Lee has been waiting to sing it. It could win an Oscar." Reluctantly, Rackin allowed the two songs to stay.

At the preview tryout, it was deemed that "Walking Happy" slowed the film's action, so it was cut out (it was later used as the title song in a Sammy Cahn–James Van Heusen Broadway production in 1966). "Call Me Irresponsible," however, remained prominently in the film. It is first established as a melody on the music box in Papa's daughter's room. When Jackie Gleason finally sings it, he's alone, drunk and singing to himself. It was popularized by numerous recording artists long before the Academy Awards that year. No one had a huge hit with the tune (Jack Jones's version reached number 75 and charted for four weeks, while Frank Sinatra's made number 78), but it proved to be a steady seller and eventually became something of a standard.

The competition for the Oscars was strong that year, with both "Charade" and "More" given even odds along with "Call Me Irresponsible." As luck would have it, Cahn's divorce became final on the day of the Oscars, so he decided to skip the awards ceremony, where he might face further trauma; but as luck would also have it, "Call Me Irresponsible" brought home the Oscar that year. Van Heusen and Cahn's daughter, Laura Cahn, accepted the award.

CHARADE

Music by Henry Mancini; lyrics by Johnny Mercer
From *Charade*

A combination suspense thriller, black comedy, adventure, and romance, *Charade* had several things going for it. First, it had an outstanding cast: Cary Grant and Audrey Hepburn as the leads, Walter Matthau as an American Embassy contact, and James Coburn, George Kennedy, and Ned Glass as a trio of bad guys. Grant and Hepburn were masters at tongue-in-cheek comedy, and although there was no mistaking this picture for anything other than the sometimes violent whodunit that it was, the lighter moments just added to the deliciousness. When Grant, for example, asks Hepburn if she'd like to see where he was tattooed, and she eagerly replies in the affirmative, he quips, "All right. We'll drive 'round that way." In another scene, pretending to be shy, he refuses to undress in front of Hepburn and steps, fully clothed, into the shower, calmly lathering up while explaining with his famous grin, "Drip dry." All of the levity helped to soften the constant thumping of bodies in what *Newsweek* labeled "an absolute delight" and *Variety* termed a "superb comedy . . . [set] against a colorful background of witty dialogue, humorous situations, and scenic beauty."

Jackie Gleason and Glynis Johns star in *Papa's Delicate Condition*, which introduced the Academy Award–winning song "Call Me Irresponsible."

That scenic beauty was another of the film's major strengths. From the breathtaking views of the French Alps in the movie's opening to the location filming in Paris, the incredible Technicolor photography made *Charade* a visual treat.

But what attracted almost as much attention as the picture itself was the Henry Mancini score — "as tunefully brittle as the dialog," said *Variety*. This was Mancini's second time scoring an Audrey Hepburn film (the first was *Breakfast at Tiffany's*, for which he received two Oscars — see page 162). Mancini reteamed with Johnny Mercer, his Oscar-winning lyricist for "Moon River" and "The Days of Wine and Roses" (see page 167) to create the title song for *Charade*. In addition to the song's one vocal turn in the film, it is also heard thematically throughout the picture.

To create and score the picture, Mancini was called to London, where producer-director Stanley Donen was headquartered. "I was concerned about the quality of the British musicians," Mancini wrote in *Did They Mention the Music?* But he soon learned that there was nothing to fear from the professionals there. After spending two months holed up in the penthouse suite of the Mayfair Hotel, he turned his main theme over to Mercer, who penned some of his most poetic (if somewhat abstract) lyrics. The score was then recorded at the Cine Tele Sound Studios in London on the same stage that would later serve to record most of John Barry's James Bond film scores. "Charade" was nominated for an Academy Award, but this time the team of Mancini and Mercer lost out to Van Heusen and Cahn for "Call Me Irresponsible" (see page 171).

There were three hit single releases of "Charade." Sammy Kaye's orchestral arrangement peaked in the number 36 position, as did Mancini's own soundtrack single release. Andy Williams's vocal recording just barely made the Hot 100 chart, sneaking in at number 100.

IT'S A MAD, MAD, MAD, MAD WORLD

Music by Ernest Gold; lyrics by Mack David
From *It's a Mad, Mad, Mad, Mad World*

Filmed in something United Artists touted as "70-millimeter Ultra Panavision," *It's a Mad, Mad, Mad, Mad World* was boastfully excessive. It had an excessively large, large, large, large budget — $9.4 million; it had

an excessively star-heavy cast, including Spencer Tracy, Milton Berle, Sid Caesar, Buddy Hackett, Ethel Merman, Mickey Rooney, Dick Shawn, Phil Silvers, and Jonathan Winters. In addition, it had dozens of cameo appearances from nearly every ambulatory Hollywood actor or comedian crammed into its excessive, 192-minute running time, barely enough to contain them all. Among the stars taking bows were Jim Backus, Eddie "Rochester" Anderson, Ben Blue, Buster Keaton, Paul Ford, Peter Falk, Don Knotts, Carl Reiner, the Three Stooges, Joe E. Brown, Andy Devine, Sterling Holloway, Jack Benny, Jerry Lewis, and a modestly last-billed Jimmy Durante.

Producer-director Stanley Kramer's homage to Hollywood, past and present, was, as he put it, "a comedy to end all comedies," but also "a comedy about greed." Although this last description probably referred to the treasure hunt that formed the basis of the film's plot, the talented filmmaker might just as easily have been speaking of the picture itself. United Artists executives greedily watched it earn over $20 million in domestic rentals for 1963, making it the second-ranked picture of the year.

The film's Saul Bass–designed animated opening credits set the tone for the entire picture, which is essentially a giant, live-acted cartoon full of car chases, slapstick, wild stunts, and banana-peel slippage. At the same time, Ernest Gold's theme music set the mood, careening to jaunty lyrics by Mack David, a multiple Academy Award nominee for movie theme lyrics.

"It's a Mad, Mad, Mad, Mad World" was nominated for Best Song, making this Gold's first (and only) Best Song nomination and David's fifth. Gold was not, however, a stranger to Oscar, having won the Academy Award for his stirring score for *Exodus* in 1960, the culmination of a career that began in the late 1940s and included scores for such pictures as *Witness for the Prosecution* (1957), *On the Beach* (1959), *Judgment at Nuremberg* (1961), *Ship of Fools* (1965), and *The Runner Stumbles* (1979).

"It's a Mad, Mad, Mad, Mad World" had only a modicum of success as a single record. The Shirelles' recording of the song peaked in the number 92 position, and stayed on the *Billboard* charts for just two weeks.

The film received several Academy Award nominations, including Best Sound Effects, for which it won the Oscar. Other nominations were for Best Color Cinematography, Best Sound, Best Original Score, and Best Film Editing.

MORE

**Music by Riz Ortolani and Nino Oliviero;
lyrics by Norman Newell**
From *Mondo Cane*

One of the most shocking, bizarre, and depressing films ever to be exhibited in mainstream theaters was an Italian import posing as a documentary. It was called *Mondo Cane* (pronounced *CAHN-ay*) — translated as *A Dog's World* — and ultimately inspired a slew of "shockumentaries," as they were called. Ironically, this unlikely picture featured one of the loveliest songs ever to emerge from a motion picture. A beautiful melody with a romantic lyric, it was called, simply, "More."

In the case of the film, less would certainly have been more. The camera first leers at jiggling, bare-breasted Trobriand Island women as they engage in their man-trapping rituals. Cut to: U.S. sailors aboard a ship in the Mediterranean, ogling topless native French Riviera females as they buzz the ship in their motor boat. Cut to: New Guinea cannibals slaughtering pigs (in gory, living color) for a special feast. Cut to: A Los Angeles pet cemetery. We see the graves of pets who once belonged to the Jerry Lewis family, to the Jack Warners, to the Grables, to Julie London. Cut to: Taipei, Taiwan, where we are told that dogs are bred for food, with the choicest puppies costing the most. A series of repulsive food-related scenes follows. And so on.

Finally, after this barrage of disturbing imagery, we get to hear the first strains of the movie's highlight — the musical theme, "More." It is first heard as a march, as the "Lifesavers Girls' Association of Australia" stages a rescue simulation on Manly Beach near Sydney (lots of mouth-to-mouth resuscitation here). Next, the theme is played as the camera visits Bikini Island, former site of postwar atomic bomb testing, where the local wildlife is depicted in assorted states of radiation-induced dementia and disarray. The theme music rises symphonically as birds fly off into the glowing sunset, leaving behind thousands of sterile eggs.

Soon, there's more "More." Now it's a waltz in a German beer garden, now a careening background accompaniment to drunks, staggering through the streets of Hamburg. Finally, we hear the song's magnificent lyrics — hastily written in English in order to qualify for the Academy Award nomination — in a slow, sultry song, complete with symphonic violins, to whose strains Czech painter Yves Kline covers models in brilliant blue paint, to become his human brushes. He presses their flesh to canvas as "More" is sung in the background.

Today *Mondo Cane* has been relegated to the "Cult" section of most video stores, while the beautiful theme song has emerged from the tawdriness of the film that spawned it. There have been several hundred recordings of "More," beginning with Kai Winding's orchestral version in 1963 on the Verve label, which peaked in the number eight position and spent 15 weeks on the charts. Vic Dana also had some success with the tune, peaking at number 42.

Composer Riz Ortolani also wrote the music for another Oscar-nominated song, "Till Love Touches Your Life," which appeared in the 1970 film *Madron* (see page 205).

SO LITTLE TIME

**Music by Dimitri Tiomkin;
lyrics by Paul Francis Webster**
From *55 Days at Peking*

Although billed as an historical epic, *55 Days at Peking* was mostly the kind of history Hollywood was best noted for — fictitious. Certainly there was a modicum of truth to this story of the final gasps of the Manchu Dynasty in and around the Forbidden City of Peking circa 1900. But history usually isn't dramatic enough for filmmakers; accordingly, the story of the Boxer Rebellion was given the full cinematic treatment.

The Samuel Bronston–Allied Artists spectacular was filmed on location, of course — in Madrid, Spain — where a complete "city" was constructed. Characterizations? Who needed 'em, when they had Charlton Heston starring as a tough United States Marines major and David Niven as the British envoy who stubbornly refuses to surrender, risking the safety of all about him, including his immediate family? For the love interest, Ava Gardner was tossed in, playing a Russian baroness whose husband has killed himself after learning she has been unfaithful to him with a Chinese official.

But enough about people. The real point of this film was cowboys and Indians. Well, all right, Chinese Boxers and imperialist Americans, Brits, French, Russians, and so on. Guess who the good guys are? Guess who wins? The cavalry even arrives in the nick of time. Thousands of Spanish extras, lavishly costumed and made up to resemble the rebellious Chinese, added to the film's epic scope. So did the musical score, another majestic effort from the era's maestro of cinemusic, Dimitri Tiomkin.

Tiomkin received two nods from the Academy for his work on *55 Days at Peking*. His sweeping score received one Oscar nomination, while the song "So Little Time," co-written with his frequent lyrical partner Paul Francis Webster, received another. The song was peculiarly placed at the end of the film, sung by Andy Williams *after* the completion of the end titles and appearance of the words "The End," apparently intended for use as exit music while people filed out of the theater. Odder still, Williams did not reprise this song at the Oscar Award ceremony, although he sang two of the other nominated tunes — "Call Me Irresponsible" and "Charade" — leaving "So Little Time" to be sung by Harve Presnell.

1964

CHIM CHIM CHEREE

Music and lyrics by Richard M. Sherman and Robert B. Sherman
From *Mary Poppins*

"Part of the magic of creating words is to make them sound very real, like they've always been around."

Richard Sherman and his older brother, Robert, had been working with Walt Disney ever since they wrote "Tall Paul" and other songs for a teenager and former Mouseketeer named Annette. While working on tunes

Ava Gardner and Charlton Heston star as ill-fated lovers in *55 Days at Peking*.

for Disney films like *The Parent Trap* (1961) and *Summer Magic* (1963), Walt asked the brothers to assist Don DaGradi in developing story ideas for a new project, based on the *Mary Poppins* books by P. L. Travers. "My brother Bob, Don, and I sat in a room for weeks and months developing concepts and ideas for how to make the *Mary Poppins* books come to life," says Richard. Eventually, they came up with a storyline and 14 songs.

One of the those, "Chim Chim Cheree" had luck written all over it. "In the third book," Richard continues, "there was a passing character of a chimney sweep, and Mary Poppins remarks, 'It's luck when you shake with a sweep.' So Don's imagination flowered, and he drew a picture of a sweep with his arms swung over his broom handles and his bristles sticking out in the back, all covered with soot, whistling with his cheeks puffed out, and under it he wrote, 'It's luck when you shake with a sweep.' " As soon as Bob and Richard walked into the office, they spotted the picture. "My God, wow, what a song idea!" exclaimed Richard. "There's music in that picture!" Thus was born the concept for "Chim Chim Cheree."

Creating the music and lyrics was a joint effort, as were all the brothers' musical endeavors. Grandsons of a famous European conductor and son of Al Sherman,

who composed such American classic pop tunes as "You've Got to Be a Football Hero" and "Potatoes Are Cheaper, Tomatoes Are Cheaper," the brothers Sherman had been discouraged as youngsters from entering the musical profession, but there was no stopping them — music flowed in their veins from generation to generation.

Initially frustrated in their efforts to write a tune about a chimney sweep, Richard recalls that they locked onto the song after a long period of "twiddling around with our minds. One day Bob said, 'One Chiminey, two chiminey, three chiminey, sweep.' I said, 'What is that supposed to be? It feels nice.' [Actually] I thought it was a lousy idea, and I walked down the hall to the men's room thinking, 'This guy's lost his mind.' And all of a sudden, this melody starts coming into my head." He rushed back to the room, hit a few notes on the piano, and remarked, "Hey, that sounds like it's always been there." He knew then they were three-quarters of the way home. With input from Walt ("He was the most brilliant and inspiring man that I have ever known in my life," Richard enthuses), the character of Bert

Dick Van Dyke and Julie Andrews in a combined live action–animation scene from Walt Disney's *Mary Poppins.*

the Chimney Sweep was fleshed out, the words were changed to something the brothers Sherman liked much better than "One chiminey, two chiminey" — instead it became, simply, "Chim chiminey, chim chiminey, chim chim cheree." The following year, the tune waltzed off with the Oscar, and the Shermans took home two apiece that night — one each for Best Song and another for Best Score.

Mary Poppins became one of Disney's greatest hit films, earning $45 million in domestic rentals, making it the top movie for 1964. There was also another sweep in store for *Mary Poppins;* the picture, "practically perfect in every way" (as Mary herself might have said), received 13 Academy Award nominations, with five actual wins — Julie Andrews for Best Actress, Best Song, Best Original Music Score, Best Film Editing, and Best Visual Effects. And that, as the Brothers Sherman wrote in another of the film's songs, was pretty "supercalifragilisticexpialidocious."

DEAR HEART

Music by Henry Mancini;
lyrics by Jay Livingston and Ray Evans
From *Dear Heart*

Jay Livingston and Ray Evans had been co-writing movie songs and lyrics since the 1940s, and had received their first Oscar in 1948, for "Buttons and Bows" (see page 98). In those days, as Jay later recalled in a 1990 radio interview, "the songwriters wrote the songs and the scorers wrote the background scores, the dramatic music. Somewhere around this time [1964], the scorers said, 'If there is any music in this picture, we want to write it.' And they took over the songwriting duties. But they needed lyric writers. So, we thought in order to keep working in pictures, we would start writing lyrics, which we wrote together anyway, for other composers. I must say that scorers are very talented people, and it's very difficult to do. But they write with their heads, and we write with our stomachs. You know, when it feels good down there, you know it's good."

Livingston was quite obviously distressed at the shift in the business, but he had only the highest praise for Henry Mancini. Not surprisingly, Mancini had similar feelings towards Livingston and Evans as lyricists. Mancini recalled in his memoirs that when Johnny Mercer — his lyricist on "Moon River," "Days of Wine

and Roses," "Charade," and so on — wasn't available to write the lyrics for an opening song for a Warner Bros. film called *The Out-of-Towners,* he didn't hesitate to call upon Jay and Ray, "fine lyricists who are always happy to tell people that they got their break in motion pictures when Mercer got too busy for a job and recommended them for it," as Mancini jokingly wrote.

The song by Livingston and Evans was called "Dear Heart." The picture was originally called *The Out-of-Towners,* but according to Jay, "When [the producers] heard the song, they decided to call the picture *Dear Heart.*" The film starred Geraldine Page as an Ohio postmistress attending a convention in New York City. She's an old maid type who falls for Glenn Ford, also an out-of-towner, in the Big Apple for a sales convention. Love soon follows.[1]

"Dear Heart" was sung in the picture under the opening titles by an unnamed chorus. Andy Williams recorded it for Columbia and made number 24, charting for 11 weeks. Jack Jones's version did well, too, peaking at number 30. Mancini's orchestral version was also on the charts, peaking at number 77.

HUSH . . . HUSH, SWEET CHARLOTTE

Music by Frank De Vol; lyrics by Mack David
From *Hush . . . Hush, Sweet Charlotte*

There was a time when Oscar-nominated songs came from lilting musicals, or at least uplifting pictures. Think Crosby. Think Astaire. Think Garland. Think . . . slashers?

Well, 1964's slashers may not exactly have ranked up there with today's Cuisinart hack-'em-ups in the gore department; call them *choppers,* maybe. Any way you slice it, though, it seems Bette Davis had a way of leaving it to cleavers in *Hush . . . Hush, Sweet Charlotte.* Heads and other body parts rolled with regularity in this gruesome picture, a follow-up to Davis's mid-life crisis picture, *Whatever Happened to Baby Jane?* (1962). *Charlotte* came from the same blood-dipped pen as *Baby Jane,* that of Henry Farrell (working this time

---

1. Six years later, Neil Simon wrote a movie called *The Out-of-Towners* for Paramount. While this film, starring Jack Lemmon and Sandy Dennis, had the original title and involved rubes in New York, the plots were totally different.

with co-writer by Lukas Heller), and was produced and directed by Robert Aldrich, who had also helmed *Baby Jane.* Joan Crawford had starred opposite Davis in that one; she had been set again to co-star in this film, but was replaced due to a last-minute illness by Olivia de Havilland. Let the games begin.

Aided by haggard makeup, outlandish wardrobe, and an effective Southern accent, Davis and her fellow loonies continued to shock with schlock as the picture took bizarre twists and turns. Most reviewers hated the film. Bosley Crowther of the *New York Times* (well into his fourth decade of critiquing and seeming to loathe nearly everything he saw) was particularly venomous: "Miss Davis, made up to look like Hydra, with heavy eyebrows and lines in her face, is plainly directed to accomplish a straight melodramatic tour de force. And Agnes Moorehead as her weird and crone-like servant is allowed to get away with some of the broadest mugging and snarling ever done by a respectable actress on the screen. If she gets an Academy Award for this performance — which is possible, because she's been nominated for it — the Academy should close up shop!" (She didn't; neither did they.)

The film actually received seven Academy Award nominations: Best Supporting Actress (Moorehead), Best Black-and-White Cinematography, Best Black-and-White Costume Design, Best Art Direction, Best Editing, Best Original Music Score, and Best Song. The score, written by Frank De Vol, was "a valuable assist in building atmospheric mood," said *Variety,* which also noted that the "title song cleffed by Mack David and De Vol and sung by Al Martino carries a certain haunting quality."

"Hush . . . Hush, Sweet Charlotte" is first heard as "Chop, Chop Sweet Charlotte" about 13 minutes into the film, which is when opening credits finally begin to roll. There is a tinkling music box accompaniment as children, making fun of Davis's "Charlotte" character, sing about her supposed past. The song then swings into a musical theme heavy on the violins. Martino sings the actual "Hush . . . Hush" version over the end titles, to a harmonica accompaniment.

Patti Page, however, had the only successful single release, on the Columbia label. The lullaby-ish, uncomplicated lyrics to the verse made for a natural sing-along, and helped Page's recording climb to the number eight position on the *Billboard* pop charts, where the song charted for 14 weeks.

Bette Davis in a scene from
Hush...Hush, Sweet Charlotte.

MY KIND OF TOWN

**Music by James Van Heusen;
lyrics by Sammy Cahn**
From *Robin and the 7 Hoods*

Sometime in the late '50s or early '60s, a group of actors began hanging together. Although the names changed from time to time, there was never any doubt about who was the leader: the self-proclaimed Chairman of the Board, Frank Sinatra. Others in this clique included Dean Martin, Sammy Davis Jr., Joey Bishop, Peter Lawford, and Shirley MacLaine. With its racial and religious diversity, this "Rat Pack," as it came to be known, constituted a cross between a miniature United Nations and a latter-day, grown-ups' "Little Rascals."

In 1960, a number of the guys, along with Angie Dickinson, starred in the comedy film *Ocean's Eleven,* with Sinatra starring as Danny Ocean, a two-bit hood intent on robbing Las Vegas casinos. By 1964, the Pack had been reshuffled; Sinatra, Martin, Davis, Bing Crosby, and Peter Falk and several others were tossed together in a film called *Robin and the 7 Hoods.* This comedy, set in 1928, featured Sinatra as leader of a pack of really nice mobsters — so nice that they robbed from crooks and gave the loot to charity. The film made no pretensions of being anything other than an updated version of the "Robin Hood" legend, right

down to the characters' names: Sinatra played Robbo (the head hood), Dino was John (as in Little John), Sammy Davis Jr. was Will Scarlet, Crosby was Alan A. Dale, Peter Falk played heavy Guy Gisborne, and Barbara Rush was Marian (no "Maid" designation for her). There were a few twists, of course — literally. For example, Gisborne ends up in the foundation of a new pretzel factory and Marian organizes a women's reform movement. And everyone sings — eight songs in all, by Jimmy Van Heusen and Sammy Cahn.

Most of the song-and-dance numbers were playfully tongue-in-cheek; Falk sings the comedic "All for One," Rush does "Any Man Who Loves His Mother," Crosby and company do "Mr. Booze," Sammy Davis has his moment in a big production number called "Bang, Bang," Sinatra, Martin, and Crosby don straw hats for "Style," and Crosby has fun with "Don't Be a Do-Badder," crooning with kids in an orphanage (his on-camera specialty, as constantly demonstrated in films like *Going My Way* and *The Bells of St. Mary's).* But the show-stopper was "My Kind of Town," which became one of Sinatra's signature songs for many years before he defected to "New York, New York." In the movie, the Chicago-touting song is sung after Robbo (Sinatra) has been acquitted of the sheriff's murder. It begins on the courthouse steps, accompanied by a Dixieland jazz band, and soon turns into an full-blown finale production number.

Frank Sinatra sings the praises of Chicago in the song "My Kind of Town," from *Robin and the 7 Hoods.*

Sinatra's recording of "My Kind of Town" had some success. And although the song didn't win the Oscar, in 1965 the All-American Press Association, comprised of 31 domestic and foreign periodicals, chose "My Kind of Town" as the best motion-picture song of the year. The film also received a nomination from the Motion Picture Academy for Best Adapted Score.

WHERE LOVE HAS GONE

**Music by James Van Heusen;
   lyrics by Sammy Cahn
From *Where Love Has Gone***

In 1958, glamorous movie star Lana Turner became the center of newspaper headlines when her teenaged daughter, Cheryl Crane, stabbed to death Turner's underworld boyfriend, Johnny Stompanato. The killing was later termed justifiable homicide, based on evidence that Crane actually saved her mother's life. In addition to creating a media frenzy — small potatoes by today's standards, but frenetic nonetheless — the incident spawned a salacious novel by one of the popular muses of the day, Harold Robbins. Of course, Robbins used fictitious characters, but the Turner episode was clearly the inspiration for the book, which became a best-seller.

Where Love Has Gone, the book, begat *Where Love Has Gone,* the movie. In the film, the place where love had gone was to San Francisco (as opposed to Hollywood), where the teen's mother was now a society woman with a knack for sculpture. Still, what would the plot be without the daughter (played by a young Joey Heatherton) plunging a chisel into the gut of the deranged lover? Some things never change.

Excellent casting helped give this film merit. Susan Hayward played the mother, while Bette Davis played Hayward's mother (to the hilt, complete with overdone Bette Davis eyes, lips, and white wig). Also in the cast were two future television stars: Michael Conners (who would later shorten his name to Mike and play the lead in "Mannix," which ran from 1967 to 1975) played Hayward's husband, the father of the girl, who returns to support his daughter's cause; and DeForest Kelley (later known as Dr. McCoy on the original "Star Trek") was seen here as an unscrupulous art critic promoting Hayward's sculpting career.

The title song, "Where Love Has Gone," was composed by those busy songsters James Van Heusen and Sammy Cahn. For their efforts, they received their second Oscar nomination of 1964 (the first was for "My Kind of Town" — see page 179). The tune was sung under the titles by Jack Jones, who recorded it on the Kapp label. His single, released in August, nearly two months in advance of the film's debut, hit number 62 and was on the charts for six weeks.

Jones, born in 1938, was the son of Allan Jones, a popular singer of the 1930s and 1940s. Jack made his debut in 1957 at the age of 19, singing together with his father on the Las Vegas nightclub circuit. Eventually he broke free of his father's shadow and became a name in his own right. Twenty-twenty hindsight later led many to criticize his early songs as sexist ("Lollipops and Roses" depicted women as children to be kept complacent with gifts, and "Wives and Lovers" urged a "little girl" to comb her hair, touch up her makeup, and always be at her husband's beck and call), but in later years Jones was able to break free of these dated songs. The singer was voted 1962's "Most Promising Male Vocalist" in a *Cashbox* poll of deejays but had few genuine hits. He did have success with the familiar theme for "The Love Boat," and continued to perform before delighted audiences in the 1990s.

THE SHADOW OF YOUR SMILE

**Music by Johnny Mandel;
   lyrics by Paul Francis Webster
From *The Sandpiper***

"Liz and Dick's beach blanket party" is how Bob Hope referred to *The Sandpiper* when he introduced the Oscar-nominated song "The Shadow of Your Smile" at the 1965 Academy Awards ceremony. Most of the audience, of course, knew that Liz and Dick were Elizabeth Taylor and Richard Burton, the on-again/off-again/on-again married couple who had first fallen in love two years before, while making *Cleopatra.*

The Sandpiper, a beautifully photographed film directed by Vincente Minnelli, also starred Eva Marie Saint and Charles Bronson. The elegant score was by

Johnny Mandel, while Paul Francis Webster was in his element with the poetic lyrics to "The Shadow of Your Smile." It was multiple Oscar winner Johnny Mercer, however, who had been the producers' initial lyricist of choice.

As Mercer recalled in the Max Wilk book *They're Playing Our Song*, "A couple of years ago they asked me to do the song for a picture called *The Sandpiper*. I worked up a lyric and brought it in, and the producer turned it down. He went and got another one — 'The Shadow of Your Smile.' Huge hit. That can be pretty depressing . . . It sort of sounded to me as if it were about a lady with a slight mustache." He also recalled, in an interview, that when he was told that his lyrics were unsuitable, "I said, 'Well, get Paul Francis Webster' and they did and had a great big hit."

Mandel composed the entire score for *The Sandpiper*. "I decided to attempt something different in soundtrack music," he wrote in the liner notes for the album. "Usually, a cinema composer tries to dazzle the listener with the wildest possible variety of sounds and tempos. For *The Sandpiper*, I have, instead, tried to sustain a constant mood throughout. It's a haunting mood matching the poignancy of the story, underscored by the beauty and loneliness of the magnificent Big Sur [California] location. I have attempted, with this music, to capture the sounds of the surf, the grandeur of the mountains, the beauty of the land."

"The Shadow of Your Smile" is sung by an unnamed chorus under closing credits of the film. In addition to winning the Academy Award, it also scored a Grammy for Song of the Year. Tony Bennett's recording became the best-known version, although it only reached the number 95 position on the pop charts. Boots Randolph recorded the tune a year later, with similar results, peaking at number 93.

THE BALLAD OF CAT BALLOU

Music by Jerry Livingston; lyrics by Mack David
From *Cat Ballou*

A rollicking send-up of the Old West, *Cat Ballou* was played broadly, entirely for laughs, with an outstanding cast headed by Jane Fonda and Lee Marvin. Fonda plays the local schoolmarm, a pretty young thing dead set on avenging her father's murder. Along the way,

Nat "King" Cole and Stubby Kaye appear as balladeers in *Cat Ballou.*

this gun-toting "innocent" robs a train and falls in with the Hole in the Wall Gang, assisted by Michael Callan, Dwayne Hickman (TV's "Dobie Gillis"), and Tom Nardini, a Three Stooges–like bunch that keep things moving. Lee Marvin, in one of the most memorable roles of his career, played a has-been gunslinger and amusing drunk. He also played a second role within the same film, that of the killer Silvernose. Marvin was rewarded with the Best Actor Oscar for his outstanding characterizations.

Critically, the picture was a hit. Even the curmudgeonly Bosley Crowther of the *New York Times* had a few kind words: "It is a carefree and clever throwing together of three or four solid Western stereotypes in a farcical frolic that follows — and travesties — the ballad form of Western story telling made popular in *High Noon*."

Crowther was referring to the picture's gimmick involving the "Balladeers" — Nat 'King" Cole and Stubby Kaye, wandering minstrels of the early West, whose job it is to tell the story as it unfolds and keep it flowing smoothly and humorously.

The song with which they relate the tale is called "The Ballad of Cat Ballou." At the beginning of the movie, before the credits role, we see the trademark Columbia Pictures "Lady," who, through animation, turns into a cowgirl, setting up the fun to follow. This is immediately followed by Kaye and Cole's introduction, getting us into the story. They continue their narration throughout the film via the title ballad, a-pickin' and a-strummin' these musical interludes.

The song was nominated for an Oscar, one of many in the careers of both nominees, Jerry Livingston and Mack David. Other nominations for *Cat Ballou* included Best Adapted Screenplay, Best Editing, and Best Adapted Score.

Nat "King" Cole was playing gigs at Lake Tahoe during the filming of *Cat Ballou* in late 1964. He would perform at Harrah's Club until two in the morning, then catch a flight to Los Angeles to film sequences for the picture, then hop a plane back to Tahoe for his nightclub act. Friends and family began to notice that the talented singer was losing weight. When confronted with this, he simply ignored it, but it was clear he was not well. Cole was a heavy smoker, and his loved ones soon learned he had lung cancer. He passed away at the age of only 45 the following February. *Cat Ballou* was his last film.

I WILL WAIT FOR YOU

**Music by Michel Legrand;
lyrics by Jacques Demy**
From *The Umbrellas of Cherbourg*

It was known as *Les Parapluies de Cherbourg* in France, where it was born; once arriving on American shores, this film, originally shown mostly in art houses, received its literal English title, *The Umbrellas of Cherbourg*. The title was deceptive in both languages — the film had little to do with umbrellas or Cherbourg. Instead it focused on what all French folk focus on: *l'amour*.

The story of universal love had more than just a French accent going for it. Winner of the grand prize at the Cannes Film Festival in the spring of 1964, the film had no spoken dialogue. Instead, all of the words were

sung, as an opera or operetta might be. But *Umbrellas* wasn't opera. Today, this sort of thing is much more commonplace in modern stage musicals like *Les Misérables* and *Miss Saigon*, which are almost entirely sung. But nothing like this had ever been done directly for the screen, and in France it was virtually unheard of.

The film introduced future French superstar and sex symbol Catherine Deneuve in the role of a 16-year-old in love with a local boy (Nino Castelnuovo). She's pregnant; he's army-bound. Each marries another, and eventually they get on with their lives. (The title stems from an umbrella store owned by the girl's mother.) Critical acclaim accompanied the film's American debut.

The score, by Michel Legrand, brought the composer his first international recognition. His music had to carry the entire picture, sung as it was. *Variety* noted that "Michel Legrand has supplied a richly tuneful score that still is not ostentatious and also serves as a sharp counterpart to help story points and enhance the moods." The Oscar-nominated song, "I Will Wait for You," had French lyrics by Jacques Demy, who also directed. The picture was sung entirely in French (with English subtitles). Norman Gimble, the lyricist who would receive

Nino Castelnuovo and Catherine Deneuve, stars of the French film *The Umbrellas of Cherbourg*.

future Oscar nominations for "Richard's Window" (see page 226) and "Ready to Take a Chance Again" (see page 239), and who won for "It Goes Like It Goes" (see page 241), wrote the now-familiar English lyric called "I Will Wait for You." It is used in the dubbed (American) version of the film, which was not a direct translation from the French, as clearly revealed by the subtitles that appear as Catherine Deneuve and her young lover, Nino Castelnuovo sing. In English, the lyrics tell us that she'll wait for him even if it takes forever, while the French singing is all about how he is going off to Algeria for two years, and she begs him not to leave her.

Legrand, born in 1932 in Paris, was the son of Raymond Legrand, who wrote numerous scores for 1930s and 1940s French films. His success with *The Umbrellas of Cherbourg* guaranteed his acceptance in the Hollywood community. In addition to the Academy Award nomination for "I Will Wait for You," Legrand and Demy received a nomination for Music Score — Substantially Original, and Legrand himself (whose name means "The Great") also received a nomination for Scoring of Music — Adaptation or Treatment.

After arriving in the States, Legrand soon teamed up with Alan and Marilyn Bergman, and the trio received their first Oscar in 1968, for "The Windmills of Your Mind" (see page 193). He won an Oscar for scoring *The Summer of '42* (1971) and had several additional Best Song nominations.

THE SWEETHEART TREE

**Music by Henry Mancini;
lyrics by Johnny Mercer
From *The Great Race***

Henry Mancini's long-term working relationship with Blake Edwards saw him pressed into service again in 1965. Edwards had just finished *A Shot in the Dark*, the second film in the *Pink Panther* series, and Mancini had composed the score. Next, the writer-producer-director wanted to turn his attention to a big-budget period comedy about an automobile race from New York to Paris. *The Great Race* needed a great score, and Mancini was selected to provide it.

In addition to the score, Mancini wrote two songs for the film with his lyricist partner Johnny Mercer. One was for a production number featuring actress Dorothy Provine, called "He Shouldn't-a, Hadn't-a,

Oughtn't-a Swang on Me." (The catchy title alone was practically the entire Mercer lyric.) The second song comes closer to the end of the film, just after a huge pie fight (for which Mancini wrote a tune called "The Pie in the Face Polka"). Stars Tony Curtis and Natalie Wood are racing each other to reach the Eiffel Tower. Edwards wanted a song here, but Natalie Wood didn't sing (her voice in the musical *West Side Story* had been dubbed by Marni Nixon). Eventually, Wood would be dubbed by Jackie Ward.

Mercer showed his stuff by presenting Mancini with two lyrics. According to Mancini's autobiography, *Did They Mention the Music?*, the first lyric began, "There are ninety-nine cars on the freight train." "It was a weird lyric," wrote Mancini. "He sang the whole thing for me, and I said, 'Whoa, John. What else do you have?' He then sang me the second version, that touching lyric that begins, 'They say there's a tree in the forest . . .'" It wasn't a tough decision. The "tree in the forest" fell where everyone could hear the sound — up on the screen, with a bouncing ball for all to follow and sing along with Wood/Ward. Johnny Mathis later popularized the song in a Mercury recording.

The film was a hit, but cost a reported $12 million to make. It barely broke even, netting $11.4 million in North American rentals, plus a bit more in the international market.

The Great Race was plagued with problems, most of them having to do with Natalie Wood's dissatisfaction with her role in the film. According to the book *Natalie & R.J.: Hollywood's Star-Crossed Lovers,* by Warren G. Harris, the actress was distressed at the prospect of being stuck on location in Europe for two months, endured chauvinistic harassment from co-stars Jack Lemmon and Tony Curtis, as well as from Edwards, and hated her tightly corseted wardrobe. Plus, she was having to turn down roles she really longed to do. Unable to break her contract, she resorted to other means. "Natalie suddenly became very temperamental, arriving late on the set or calling in sick, claiming she was having her period," said William Orr, the Warner Bros. production executive. "Then she started running up huge bills at the Paris dressmakers and charging them to Warner Bros. The accounting department went bananas, so she was packed off to L.A. the next day. Her remaining scenes were either cut from the script or shot with a double."

Somehow, though, it all came together in one of the funniest pictures of the decade. At Oscar time, the film took home the honors for Best Sound Effects;

other nominations included Best Color Cinematography, Editing, Sound, and Best Song for "The Sweetheart Tree."

WHAT'S NEW, PUSSYCAT?

Music by Burt Bacharach; lyrics by Hal David
From *What's New, Pussycat?*

Off-beat and irreverent, like the film for which it was created, "What's New, Pussycat?" was the first Oscar-nominated song by the team of Burt Bacharach and Hal David. It would not be the last. Over the next several years, they would continue writing tunes together, eventually winning the Oscar for "Raindrops Keep Fallin' on My Head" (see page 197).

Burt Bacharach met Hal David (younger brother of Mack David, another frequent Academy Award–nominated composer) in 1957; they pooled their talents for a couple of songs, then parted for a few years. In 1962, the songwriters joined forces again when they signed with Scepter Records to write tunes for Dionne Warwick. Hit followed hit as the pair became known for their low-key, gentle, quasi-rock songs, such as "Don't Make Me Over," "Anyone Who Had a Heart," "I'll Never Fall in Love Again" (from their Broadway show *Promises, Promises),* "What the World Needs Now," and "Do You Know the Way to San Jose?"

While "What's New, Pussycat?" sounds like it should have been an easy write, since the title was already in place, David indicated otherwise in a 1993 radio interview: "I used to complain constantly that they would come to me with the titles that nobody else could do, like 'The Man Who Shot Liberty Valance' and 'Wives and Lovers.' Why don't they give me a good title once in a while? So they gave me 'What's New, Pussycat?,' which is one of the great titles. It turned out to be a very difficult song to write. I wrote lyrics and Burt wrote a tune, and it was bad, and then he wrote a tune and I wrote a lyric, and it was bad; and we kept trying." Eventually, working on Easter Sunday from their base in London (the picture was actually filmed in Paris and the French countryside), David finally was inspired. "I was stretched out on the couch and I started writing, and I got, 'Pussycat, Pussycat, I've got flowers and lots of hours to spend with you,' and all of a sudden, we had a song . . . we finished it later that day. That was like getting a monkey off my back."

There were a lot of "firsts" with *What's New, Pussycat?:* It featured the first Bacharach/David song to be nominated for an Oscar; it was Woody Allen's first feature-film writing and acting effort, and it was the first (and last) picture in which audiences would get to see a cast containing Peter Sellers, Peter O'Toole, Romy Schneider, Capucine, Paula Prentiss, Ursula Andress, and Richard Burton.

It was also the first soundtrack song for Tom Jones, whose popularity was just beginning. The title song is sung in the opening sequence as the credits appear as a Tiffany-type colored-glass slide show. The tune was a big hit for Jones, landing in the number three position in June of 1965 and charting for 12 weeks.

1966

BORN FREE

Music by John Barry; lyrics by Don Black
From *Born Free*

Based on the best-selling book by Joy Adamson, *Born Free* was the true story of Elsa, the lion cub that Joy and her game warden husband George raised to young adulthood after finding her orphaned in the Kenya bush. The film was shot on location in Africa, with the real Adamsons acting as technical advisors. Husband-and-wife actors Bill Travers and Virginia McKenna played the Adamsons, adding to the believability of the film.

The plot centers on the need for Joy Adamson to teach Elsa to fend for herself in the wild, where this lioness, born free but raised almost as a pet, must now return to live the life nature intended or face the alternative of being sent to a zoo. At a time when ecological consciousness was just beginning in our society, the film was poignant without being maudlin and earned the praise of critics and the appreciation of audiences both young and old.

John Barry's moving theme music and score earned him two Oscars that year — for Best Score and Best Song. The opening notes of "Born Free" are instantly recognizable and strangely reminiscent of two other memorable motion picture themes. The same two ini-

Husband-and-wife actors Virginia McKenna and Bill Travers relax with one of several lionesses used to play Elsa in *Born Free.*

tial notes, of approximately the same duration and in rather similar melodies, can be heard in Maurice Jarre's score for *Lawrence of Arabia* (1962), which also won for Best Score, and again in John Williams's work for *Star Wars,* again winning Best Score (1977).

In an interview for the cable network Bravo, John Barry described working with the music for *Born Free* as "one of the most unhappy movies I ever worked on . . . I'd never read the original book, so I didn't know what this was about. Then I read the script, and I thought, 'This isn't really my thing.' " He met with director James Hill and strongly disagreed with his point of view. Eventually, Barry told the producer, Carl Foreman, that "the only way I can bring myself around and find a style is if I say to myself, 'This is Disney — this is lions — this is youthful — it's lovely, but the style has to be a pastiche on a Disney-esque attitude towards filmmaking.' " The change in attitude worked. With lyrics by Don Black, the "Born Free" theme won the Oscar for Best Song.

Barry was already well-known for his James Bond scores, beginning in 1963 with *From Russia with Love,* and continuing with *Goldfinger* (1964) and *Thunderball* (1965). He won a third Oscar in 1968 for the score to *The Lion in Winter,* a fourth in 1985 for *Out of Africa,* and a fifth for 1990's *Dances with Wolves.* Over the years he has also received several additional Academy Award nominations for Best Score.

"Born Free" was sung on the original soundtrack by Matt Monro, but the most popular single recording was the instrumental by Roger Williams, which peaked in the number seven position and charted for 16 weeks. In 1968 it was covered by the Hesitations in a soul version, which peaked at number 38.

Born Free spawned a 1972 sequel, *Living Free.* There was also a short-lived TV series that ran in the fall of 1974 and starred Gary Collins and Diana Muldaur as the Adamsons.

Travers and McKenna were so moved by their participation in the original film that when they returned to live in their native England, they established the Born Free Foundation to support animal rights and conservation. Travers died in 1994, but their son, William, continued the important work of the foundation, located in Coldharbour, 25 miles south of London.

Sadly, the Adamsons did not fare as well as their beloved lion cub. George Adamson was killed in 1989 by armed bandits at his home on a remote game reserve in Kenya. His wife had been killed nine years earlier in a wage dispute with a servant.

ALFIE

Music by Burt Bacharach; lyrics by Hal David
From *Alfie*

In the mid-1960s, England was clearly the cultural focus of the world. The fashion industry was influenced by London's "Carnaby Street" look, while music was taking its downbeat from those mop-top Lads from Liverpool, the Beatles. All things British were practically guaranteed success, including films. Such a picture was *Alfie,* based on Bill Naughton's popular London and Broadway play. Naughton adapted his story for the screen version, which starred Michael Caine, in probably the best-known performance of his career, as the title character. Co-starring were Shelley Winters, Millicent Martin, Vivien Merchant, and Jane Asher (Beatle Paul McCartney's one-time steady).

Alfie was the story of a male chauvinist who exists primarily to chase "birds," as the Cockney expression goes. The film ends much as it began, with Alfie not really having learned too much, generally a writing defect in proper literature, but effective in this instance, due largely to the outstanding performance of Caine. For his efforts, he received an Oscar nomination for Best Actor; the film was also nominated for Best Picture, Best Supporting Actress (Vivien Merchant), Best Screenplay (Bill Naughton), and Best Song, the latter a title tune penned by Burt Bacharach and Hal David, marking their second nomination as a team (the first was for "What's New, Pussycat?" — see page 184).

In a 1993 radio interview, David described "Alfie" as one of his two favorite songs (the other was "What the World Needs Now Is Love"). But it posed some problems. "Picture being asked to write a song called 'Alfie' that's not supposed to be a comedic song," he said. "You don't mind writing a song called 'Sally' or 'Irene' or 'Mary' — but 'Alfie?' I kind of said, 'I think it's impossible.' I wrote 'The Man Who Shot Liberty Valance' and I thought, 'It's getting worse and worse!' I didn't know how to approach it . . . Somewhere along the line, I thought of 'What's it all about, Alfie?' and all of a sudden, it had a significance to me."

The song makes sense in light of the amoral character who really doesn't have a clue as to what "it" — life — is all about. At the end of the picture, Alfie reminisces: "When I look back on my little life and the 'birds' I've known and think of all the things they've done for me and the little I've done for them, you'd think I had the best of it all along the line. But what have I got out of it? I got a bob or two, some decent clothes, a car. I got me 'ealth back and I ain't attached. But I ain't got me peace of mind, and if you ain't got that, you ain't got nothing. I don't know. It seems to me if they ain't got you one way, they got you another. So what's the answer? That's what I keep asking meself — what's it all about? Know what I mean?" After this final speech in the film, he walks off along the Thames as end credits begin to roll, and the title song begins playing.

Although Cher sang on the soundtrack, her release was not the most successful. Her single peaked in the number 32 position and spent six weeks on the charts. Dionne Warwick, who recorded everything Bacharach and David wrote in those days, had a number 15 hit with the tune (she also performed it at the Oscar awards ceremony). Cilla Black covered the song in Great Britain, but only made number 95 with the tune in the States. Stevie Wonder recorded the song under the name Eivets Rednow ("Stevie Wonder" backwards), riding "Alfie" to number 66.

GEORGY GIRL

Music by Tom Springfield; lyrics by Jim Dale
From *Georgy Girl*

Yet another British import in a year when the cry "The British are coming!" would have been heralded as good news, *Georgy Girl* introduced Lynn Redgrave to the American public in the role of a shlumpy, dumpy caterpillar about to become a butterfly, if not in beauty, then in spirit. James Mason played her wealthy employer/paramour/eventual husband in this comedy based on the novel by Margaret Forster, who also co-wrote the screenplay.

Redgrave received high marks from American reviewers. Michael Stern of the *New York Times* noted that "the daughter of Sir Michael Redgrave and Rachel Kempson (who has a minor role in the picture) — and younger sister of the Vanessa you met in *Morgan!* — cannot be quite as homely as she makes herself in this film. Slimmed down, cosseted in a couture salon and given more of the brittle, sophisticated lines she tosses off with such abandon here, she could become a comedienne every bit as good as the late Kay Kendall." The Redgraves, of course, are today a well-known dynasty of actors. Vanessa became the controversial one; Lynn did slim down — way down, in fact, becoming spokesperson for Weight Watchers International. And she not only fulfilled the predictions of becoming a comedy performer, she proved her worth in all forms of acting, including drama (she received an Oscar nomination for her work in *Georgy Girl*), although most critics would agree her best work has been in comedy.

Georgy's character is established in a scene played over the title song and preceding the opening credits. The theme was performed by the Seekers, whose record made it to the number two position and spent six weeks on the charts, selling over a million copies. The Seekers were a commercial folk group whose peak popularity was in the '60s and '70s. The members were mainly Australians, with one of the group a native of Sri Lanka. In 1965 they had a top 10 hit in America (and Number One in Britain) with "I'll Never Find Another You." One of their most famous songs was the Coca-Cola jingle, "I'd Like to Buy the World a Coke."

"Georgy Girl" was also recorded as an instrumental by the Baja Marimba Band. Their rendition barely made the Hot 100 chart, appearing for one week at number 98.

The music for "Georgy Girl" was written by Tom Springfield, brother of popular singer Dusty Springfield. The lyrics were by singer/actor Jim Dale, who had appeared in the British *Carry On* films. He indulged in what he termed his "hobby" of lyric writing when he wrote the words to "Georgy Girl." He also went on to contribute music to the films *Shalako* (Cinerama Releasing, 1968) and *Lola* (American-International, 1979).

MY WISHING DOLL

Music by Elmer Bernstein; lyrics by Mack David
From *Hawaii*

"Can't you just see it? 'Mary Poppins married Jesus.' "

Julie Andrews, as quoted in the biography, *Julie Andrews*, by Robert Windeler, was referring to her upcoming role, cast alongside co-star Max Von Sydow as an 1840s missionary and his wife who leave their New England home for Polynesia in the film *Hawaii*. Andrews had previously played the title character in Walt Disney's *Mary Poppins*; Von Sydow had been Jesus in *The Greatest Story Ever Told*. *Hawaii*, based on the best-selling novel by James Michener, would find them on location in the Hawaiian Islands, as well as in New England, at sea off Norway, in Tahiti, and on Hollywood soundstages.

"She must have flown up to him and said, 'Listen, with my magic and your talent, we'd make a great team,' " Andrews continued, still joking about Mary Poppins and Jesus. " 'I can fly. You can walk on water. What more do we need?' Actually, come to think of it, who else could she have married? It's the classic mother and father image for all children." She felt she could afford to make such slightly irreverent jokes about her surprise at finding herself cast in such a role; her "star" status now granted her a reported salary of $400,000.

The film turned out to be the top-grossing movie of 1966, with a North American rental take in excess of $15.5 million. The cast was expanded to include people

Max von Sydow preaches to the Hawaiian queen (Jocelyne LaGarde) as Julie Andrews looks on in a scene from *Hawaii*.

of all nationalities, ranging from those with star power, like Englishman Richard Harris, to American actors Gene Hackman and Carroll O'Conner (the future Archie Bunker of TV's "All in the Family"), a young Bette Midler as a passenger on board the Hawaii-bound ship, and a six-foot, 418-pound, French-speaking Tahitian of royal blood, Jocelyne La Garde, who played the Hawaiian queen.

Since Andrews was a renowned singer, it seemed logical to work in at least one song for her fans. Composer Elmer Bernstein (who also did the score), wrote "My Wishing Doll," with lyrics by film veteran Mack David. Bernstein's score received an Academy Award nomination, as did his and David's song. The film was also nominated for Best Supporting Actress (La Garde, in her debut performance), Best Color Cinematography, Best Color Costume Design, Best Sound, and Best Special Visual Effects, making seven Oscar nominations (but no wins) in all.

"My Wishing Doll" is sung early in the film. Prior to Andrews's departure from her New England home, she is seen playing with some children, and she begins singing the song to them. But before she can finish, she is interrupted by Von Sydow, in the role of her future husband. Alas, she never finishes the song, which she had barely begun. However, even this slight effort was enough for the Academy to allow the tune to qualify for a Best Song nomination.

A TIME FOR LOVE

Music by Johnny Mandel;
lyrics by Paul Francis Webster
From *An American Dream*

Based on the Norman Mailer novel, *An American Dream* was the rather depressing story of a psychotic, rich, alcoholic shrew (played by Eleanor Parker) who is murdered early in the film by her husband, a TV talk-show host. In a frenzied fight, he pushes her out of their penthouse to her death 30 floors below. The film then goes melodramatic, dealing with gangsters, gumshoes, hoods, and the underworld.

Parker got rave reviews for her brief role, but most critics agreed that the film was a poor one. "With four months still to go, the year's worst movie may well turn out to be *An American Dream*," predicted the *New York Times*. "Like a tired, jaded, mire-splattered old turkey,

the Warner version of Norman Mailer's novel roosted yesterday at the Forum . . . Stuart Whitman, Janet Leigh, Eleanor Parker and Barry Sullivan are the hapless — and we do mean hapless — prisoners of this Technicolored claptrap."

In fact, there were were plenty of big names attached to the picture. William Conrad — later to star on TV in "Cannon" and "Jake and the Fatman," was the film's executive producer. The excellent supporting cast included Lloyd Nolan, J. D. Cannon, Murray Hamilton, and George Takei (the future Mr. Sulu on TV's "Star Trek"). The highlight of the film, however, was the widely acclaimed musical score by Johnny Mandel, which received what little praise the critics doled out. "Johnny Mandel's score is good," noted *Variety*, "particularly in representation of traffic noise" — not an insignificant point, because Parker's 30-floor plunge creates, not surprisingly, a major traffic jam.

Despite working within the parameters of a dreadful picture, Mandel even managed to wangle a Best Song nomination for his efforts. Co-written with his frequent lyricist Paul Francis Webster, "A Time for Love" was not one of the pair's better-known songs. Although John Davidson, then an up-and-coming popular recording artist, sang the tune at the Academy Awards ceremony the following year, there were no hit recordings made, and the song, like the film, quietly faded.

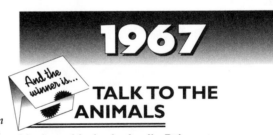

And the winner is... **TALK TO THE ANIMALS**

Music and lyrics by Leslie Bricusse
From *Doctor Dolittle*

"They would all be doing their business quite naturally, so we would then have to clear the set, sweep it up, air it, come back and start again."

No, Rex Harrison was not describing the studio executives taking meetings between shots on the set of *Doctor Dolittle*. Rather, the actor (as quoted in *Rex Harrison: The First Biography*, by Roy Moseley) was expounding on some of the less appealing experiences he had while filming the movie. "To work in close proximity with all those animals for a year wasn't the most pleasant experience of my life," Harrison explained.

The film was beset with problems, not all of them animal-related. There was the difficulty of shooting in the United Kingdom. Castle Combe in Wiltshire, reputed to be one of the most beautiful villages in England, was the original location and seemed to fit the bill for the fictitious Puddleby-on-Marsh of Hugh Lofting's series of *Doctor Dolittle* books. But the British weather was rarely equal to the scenery. Filming began at the end of June, 1966, and continued until the weather deteriorated late in the summer. The unit then moved to soundstages in Hollywood, then to Santa Lucia in the British West Indies for location work, further delayed when the rainy season interrupted the shoot.

Rex Harrison demonstrates how he "Talks to the Animals" in the Oscar-winning song from *Doctor Dolittle*.

Then there was the question of who would write the score for this screen musical, a genre that had declined over the years and was just beginning to make a comeback. Harrison wanted Alan Jay Lerner, with whom he had had a happy working relationship in Broadway's *My Fair Lady*. Lerner agreed, and signed onto the project with André Previn. But at the last minute, the pair withdrew, and producer Arthur Jacobs assigned the writing of both the score and the screenplay to Leslie Bricusse, who had collaborated with Anthony Newley for *Stop the World — I Want to Get Off*, and had co-written (with John Barry) several title songs for James Bond films. Harrison had difficulty adapting to Bricusse, who later recalled, "Our relationship at first was extremely difficult — like a headmaster (Rex) and a new pupil (me) . . . At one time while I was writing it, Rex even had writers of his own holed up secretly in London. He queried everything."

The songs included "My Friend the Doctor," "I've Never Seen Anything Like It," "Beautiful Things," "Fabulous Places," and seven others, including the one that ended up taking top honors at the Academy Awards ceremony, "Talk to the Animals." In the production number, Harrison (Dolittle) talks to his parrot, Polynesia, who we learn speaks 2,000 languages (including Dodo and Unicorn). Dolittle asks, "Could I learn to talk to animals?" He decides to give up a human medical practice to become "the greatest animal doctor in the world." He then talk-sings his way through the song, in true Henry Higgins/*My Fair Lady* form, strolling (carefully) around the barnyard, talking to pigs, cows, horses, sheep, and so on. This song, like others in the film, was recorded live, as Harrison preferred, rather than being dubbed afterwards. The animals often missed their cues, and many retakes had to be shot, inevitably leading to the unpleasant "business" that Harrison later explained to his biographer.

Unfortunately, the film was a financial flop. It earned a mere $3.5 million in North American rentals, just a fraction of its huge cost. It was overly long — 152 minutes (eight of which have been trimmed for the film's videocassette release). The members of the Academy, however, loved it and blessed the beasts and the film with the Best Song Oscar, as well as the Award for Best Special Visual Effects. The movie also received nominations for Best Picture, Best Cinematography, Best Art Direction, Best Editing, Best Original Music Score, Best Adapted Score, and Best Sound.

THE BARE NECESSITIES

Music and lyrics by Terry Gilkyson
From *The Jungle Book*

The Jungle Book was the last Walt Disney animated feature personally supervised by the maestro himself. The movie was an unqualified hit; thanks to its subsequent re-releases, the picture has become the top box office hit for films released in 1967, having earned over $60 million in North American rentals. Sadly, Disney never got to enjoy the fruits of his labors. A heavy smoker, he died of lung cancer just after turning 65 in 1966, nine months before the release of one of his most successful pictures ever.

Based on the stories of Rudyard Kipling, *The Jungle Book* chronicled the adventures of the man-cub named Mowgli, a boy abandoned at birth and raised by a wolf pack. Many famous voices of the day were used to play the various animated characters — Phil Harris as the bouncy bear, Baloo; Sebastian Cabot as Bagheera the panther; Louis Prima as the swinging ape, King Louie; George Sanders as the villainous tiger, Shere Khan; and Sterling Holloway (who later became the voice of Winnie the Pooh) as the sneaky python, Kaa. Indeed, it was the actual voices of the actors themselves, rather than

the descriptions in the script, that determined the personalities of the characters they portrayed.

The film was directed by Wolfgang "Woolie" Reitherman, one of the Disney's so-called Nine Old Men, the original group of animators who had been working with Walt since the inception of *Snow White and the Seven Dwarfs* in the mid-1930s. For the voice of young Mowgli, Reitherman used his own son, Bruce.

All but one of the songs for this animated feature were contributed by the writing team of Richard and Robert Sherman, who had been responsible for the music of *Mary Poppins* in 1964 (see page 175). But instead of one of their tunes, the Motion Picture Academy members nominated the song written by another composer, Terry Gilkyson, called "The Bare Necessities." Gilkyson had had a number four hit in 1957 with "Marianne," but hadn't done much composing for films.

"The Bare Necessities" is performed in the movie by young Mowgli (Bruce Reitherman) and his friend Baloo (Phil Harris). Baloo is a bear, hence the humor in the tune's punny title. The song sets the carefree tone of the good life in the jungle, urging Mowgli to "forget about your worries and your strife." This theme has become a constant over the years in Disney films. As recently as 1994, the hit film *The Lion King* introduced a song very similar in rhythm and meaning to "The Bare Necessities." Called "Hakuna Matata," it is also sung in the jungle (in this case African, not Indian), by elders, to a young cub. The title "Hakuna Matata" translates as "No Worries," a message not unlike the premise of Baloo's song to Mowgli.

Mowgli learns of "The Bare Necessities" from Baloo the bear in Walt Disney's *The Jungle Book.*

THE EYES OF LOVE

Music by Quincy Jones; lyrics by Bob Russell
From _Banning_

Lust, intrigue, money, gangsters — all the usual ingredients for a melodrama went into the film _Banning_. But even the lavish production values, with all the top names in art direction, costuming, makeup, and so on couldn't help this picture, whose title sounds oh-so-adventurous but turns out to be the last name of the leading character, played by Robert Wagner. Other members of the cast included Anjanette Comer, Guy Stockwell, Jill St. John, James Farentino, Susan Clark, and Gene Hackman, all part of the group of bedhoppers, hoods, and ambitious characters who peopled Banning's life.

Critics generally lambasted the picture, but reserved modest praise for Quincy Jones's musical score. _Variety,_ for example, had this to say: "Quincy Jones wrote [a] good score including a love theme. Latter, lyrics by Bob Russell and sung — twice — by Gil Bernal, is further overemphasized in background, and by the end of 102 minutes, it definitely sounds like a combination of the theme from _An Affair to Remember_ and _Face to Face_. Tune is plugged in the dialog, a bit too obviously, when Miss Comer comments on it to Wagner." The above-mentioned love theme, played ad infinitum, was "The Eyes of Love." The Academy liked it enough to include it in the year's nominations, so maybe all the plugging paid off.

This was Jones's first nomination for Best Song. He wrote his first musical score for the 1965 film _The Pawnbroker_, which was also the first movie to give full screen credit to a black composer. Soon he was writing full-time for films. He was nominated for the Oscar for the score to _In Cold Blood_ in 1967, making him a double nominee that year. Jones and lyricist Bob Russell would again be nominated, for "For Love of Ivy," the title song from the film of the same name, in 1968 (see page 194). Jones then continued solo in his film career, writing scores of scores for such pictures as _In the Heat of the Night_ (1967) and _Cactus Flower_ (1969).

Jones's biggest success in the recording world was his production of the "We Are the World" single. The 1985 hit was performed by USA for Africa, a composite group of 30 famous artists who raised millions for the starving on that continent. Jones was responsible for arranging, organizing, and producing the session that brought together such diverse talents as Harry Belafonte, Ray Charles, Bob Dylan, Michael Jackson, Cyndi Lauper, Kenny Loggins, Bette Midler, Bruce Springsteen, Dionne Warwick, and Stevie Wonder, among others. The song was Number One for four weeks and sold millions of copies.

Jones also continued his work in film and added "producer" to his résumé. In 1985, he co-produced (with Steven Spielberg, Kathleen Kennedy, and Frank Marshall) the Academy Award–nominated and critically acclaimed film _The Color Purple_. He was also a co-producer on the popular 1990s NBC television series "The Fresh Prince of Bel-Air."

Bob Russell, who wrote the lyrics for "The Eyes of Love," wrote the words to many popular tunes, including "Don't Get Around Much Anymore" (music by Duke Ellington) and "He Ain't Heavy, He's My Brother," sung by the Hollys.

THE LOOK OF LOVE

Music by Burt Bacharach; lyrics by Hal David
From _Casino Royale_

Bond, James Bond. And Bond, Sir James Bond. And Bond, Jimmy Bond. _Casino Royale_ was a veritable _Bond_anza, a spoof of the spy thriller genre, played for laughs, "suggested" by the Ian Fleming novel (any resemblance was purely coincidental). David Niven (Sir James Bond), Woody Allen (Jimmy B.), Joanna Pettet (Mata Bond) — these were just a few of the bottled-in-Bond actors camping it up. Peter Sellers headed the cast, playing Evelyn Tremble, supposedly the world's greatest authority on baccarat, recruited to simulate Bond in a confrontation with Le Chiffre, chief villain of the picture, played to the hilt by Orson Welles. The game between the two in the titular Casino Royale is just about all this picture had in common with the Ian Fleming book.

The $12 million production spent most of its budget on directors — five, count 'em, five of them — along with a big-name cast. Behind-the-camera chores fell to John Huston, Ken Hughes, Val Guest, Robert Parrish, and Joe McGrath, while those romping in front of the lens included Ursula Andress (who had appeared in the first filmed Bond movie, _Dr. No,_ in 1962), Deborah Kerr, William Holden, Charles Boyer,

Kurt Kaszner, George Raft (playing himself!), Jean-Paul Belmondo, and a last-billed Jacky Bisset (later a big star as Jacqueline Bisset) as "Miss Goodthighs."

So what was it all about? Not much. "The story line defies description," was the way *Variety* chose to phrase it. The plot never got in the way of the gags or jockeying for screen time amongst the players. Needless to say, the film lacked cohesion — and a good editor; it rambled along for two hours, 10 minutes.

Despite these flaws, *Casino Royale* featured a very successful soundtrack that, thanks to the efforts of Burt Bacharach, who wrote the score. Herb Alpert and the Tijuana Brass played the memorable "Casino Royale Theme," and Bacharach, together with his regular lyricist, Hal David, created "The Look of Love," a timeless song that received an Academy Award nomination. That tune, sung by Dusty Springfield, is heard under a scene in which a slow-motion camera tracks Sellers through a goldfish tank as he pursues the elusive Andress.

The song soon took on a life of its own as the picture passed into the realm of cult status, although most serious Bond aficionados relegated the movie to an alternative universe. Springfield's recording reached the number 22 position on the *Billboard* charts and was on the Hot 100 for 15 weeks. The following year, Sergio Mendes & Brasil '66 covered the song and bested Springfield's rendition with a surprising peak in the number four position. A third version appeared three years later, in 1971, when Isaac Hayes's recording made number 79.

THOROUGHLY MODERN MILLIE

**Music by James Van Heusen;
   lyrics by Sammy Cahn**
From *Thoroughly Modern Millie*

As far back as 1954, Hollywood producer Ross Hunter had wanted to do a 1920s movie with Julie Andrews after he had caught her performance in *The Boy Friend*. He had hoped to produce a film of that musical, with Julie in the lead, but the rights were tied up by MGM. When the script for *Thoroughly Modern Millie*, first written as a comedy without music, was presented to Hunter, he again pushed for Julie Andrews in the "flapper" lead role. "I read the script

[by Richard Morris] as a favor to Ross Hunter," said Andrews in the biography *Julie Andrews,* by Robert Windeler. "I thought it would be the last chance I'd have to do the ingenue. After all, when you're thirty-one, how many more chances can you have? So I thought I'd have a last fling at the part." George Roy Hill was signed as director and began working with Morris to create a musical out of the comedy.

Many songs of the '20s were used in the score. These included "Baby Face" (by Harry Akst and Benny David), "Do It Again" (by George Gershwin and B. G. DeSylva), "Jazz Baby" (by Blanche Merrill and M. K. Jerome), and "Poor Butterfly" (by Raymond Hubbell and John Golden). But new songs were needed, and the Oscar-winning team of Jimmy Van Heusen and Sammy Cahn was brought in to create them.

Cahn was mystified when Hunter first contacted him. "He can't want a title song called 'Thoroughly Modern Millie,' " Cahn moaned to partner Van Heusen, as told in Cahn's autobiography, *I Should Care.* " 'Sing it? I can't even *say* it.' . . . I got even because I used the title but once in the entire song. They also got even and turned it down. We went away to write another. Write a second? I never believed we could write a first." They did, though, and Cahn's memorable lyrics, with clever rhyme schemes like "What we thought was *chic, unique,* and quite *adorable* they think is *odd,* and *Sod*-om and *Gomorrable*" helped the song land an Academy Award nomination. Although it didn't win, Elmer Bernstein, who was responsible for the film's overall score, took home an Oscar for Best Original Score.

The picture was a huge hit. It ranked in the top 10 films of the year, earning $15.4 million in North American rentals at the box office. It also helped cement the resurgence of made-for-the-screen musicals, which were beginning a healthy revival in the late '60s.

The film's popularity could be attributed to many things. In addition to Julie Andrews, who was beloved by American audiences as "Mary Poppins," the movie introduced Mary Tyler Moore (a popular television star from "The Dick Van Dyke Show") to the screen, as well as Carol Channing, whose success at this point had been limited to the Broadway stage. The obvious chemistry between the three female leads, the abundance of tunes, plus the fact that the picture had fun with its spoofing of the Roaring '20s film style, using techniques like iris-ins, wipes, and title cards, all contributed to the picture's success.

1968

THE WINDMILLS OF YOUR MIND

Music by Michel Legrand;
lyrics by Alan and Marilyn Bergman
From *The Thomas Crown Affair*

The Thomas Crown Affair is often remembered for just one thing: the long, passionate kiss exchanged between the two leads. Steve McQueen played Thomas Crown, a millionaire who engineers the robbery of a Boston bank. Faye Dunaway played the female co-star, an insurance investigator out to nail Crown for the heist. Along the way, a romance between the two principals ensues, hence the prolonged pucker. The scene caught the attention of critics, many of whom seemed riveted on the moment. Renata Adler of the *New York Times* (one of several reviewers jockeying for the critic's corner vacated by Bosley Crowther, who retired in 1967, after four decades with the paper) called it a "long, soon-to-be-famous kissing scene that is so misdirected that one thinks of Edsels on a summer night."

Producer-director Norman Jewison, who became one of Hollywood's most sought-after directors in the years that followed, was uninhibited in his use of experimentation. Jewison had benefited from a visit to Montreal's "Expo '67" World's Fair the previous year, where he observed the multiple- and split-screen processes that were highly touted there. Today we take these techniques for granted, but in the late '60s, prior to which they had been used only sparingly, such innovations were considered quite daring in a conventional film.

Most outstanding was the musical score by Michel Legrand, which received a nomination for Best Original Score. Legrand wrote the music for "The Windmills of Your Mind," with lyrics by the newcomer husband-and-wife team of Alan and Marilyn Bergman. Their song captured the top prize, the first of many Oscar nominations (and wins) that the team would receive in years to come. The film was also nominated by the Academy for Best Original Score for a Non-Musical Motion Picture.

Marilyn Bergman described writing the lyrics in a special pre-Oscar radio interview with Wink Martin-dale in April, 1993: "The sequence in *The Thomas Crown Affair* for which we wrote the song with Michel Legrand was [the one with] Steve McQueen circling Boston in this glider. We did sit down and make a list of all the things that we could think of that were circular — apples and pebbles, and ripples and rings, the moon — there was a kind of technique that I guess we used." The lyrics are beautifully poetic, suggesting all things circular, objects like wheels, spirals, snowballs, and so on. And except for the repeated first verse and the imagery of the Earth being like an apple in space, nothing is repeated in this unique lyric.

The song is introduced by Noel Harrison (Rex's son) in the opening credits of the film and is sung once more during the picture. Dusty Springfield released a single of the tune in May, 1969, which peaked in the number 31 position and charted for eight weeks. Over the years, instrumental and vocal versions of "The Windmills of Your Mind" have been recorded by a wide variety of artists, including Ferrante and Teicher, John Gary, Jack Jones, Henry Mancini, Jim Nabors, Rogers Williams, and the Sandpipers.

CHITTY CHITTY BANG BANG

Music and lyrics Richard M. Sherman
and Robert B. Sherman
From *Chitty Chitty Bang Bang*

Chitty Chitty Bang Bang was the offspring of Ian Fleming, the creator of James Bond. His only children's book was brought to the screen by the same producer who had been responsible for putting the author's spy thrillers on celluloid — Albert "Cubby" Broccoli (a descendent of the Italian developer of the vegetable of the same name). The delightful children's picture had the feel of a Walt Disney-esque fantasy, a kind of *Mary Poppins* without Mary, but with the same songwriters, the Sherman Brothers, who had helped birth that Academy Award–winning film, working behind the scenes this time to birth . . . a car.

Yes, it seems that Chitty Chitty Bang Bang was the name of a fantastic automobile and the star attraction of this film. Never mind that Dick Van Dyke played Caractacus Potts ("cracked pot" — get it?) or that Sally Ann Howes, a Julie Andrews clone (she once played Eliza Doolittle on Broadway after Andrews completed her turn in *My Fair Lady*) played a character with the unlikely name of Truly Scrumptious. This, after all, was a fantasy for children. And naturally, as in *Mary Poppins*, there were two adorable English children getting into all sorts of fantastic trouble.

Richard and Robert Sherman, once described as the most successful songwriting brothers since George and Ira Gershwin, were invited by Cubby Broccoli to create the songs for the film. "I think he really kind of felt that any guys who were mad enough to write a song called 'Supercalifragilisticexpialidocious' would be nuts enough to write a song that could make sense out of the title of his movie," says Richard Sherman, referring to their title song, "Chitty Chitty Bang Bang." They thought it a great challenge, but unfortunately, they were under contract as staff writers at Walt Disney Productions. But Walt liked the idea and was also a fan of Broccoli, so he gave the brothers three months off to go to England to work on songs for *Chitty*.

"'Chitty Chitty Bang Bang' was one of the first songs that we wrote," Richard continues, "and we wanted to have fun with those words. Again, it was a matter of making the words sing and sort of feel metallic, like a machine, like the actual car. I think 'fine four-fendered friend' is a nice line," he says, referring to one of the great tongue-twisting alliterative lyrics. "Then at the end, we played with 'Oh Chitty, you Chitty, pretty Chitty' — all that kind of stuff that gives you word sounds that are fun. We were saying (without actually saying it), 'Hey, you're going to have a very good time aboard this flight of fancy.' . . . We had a chance to invent words; we said 'fantasmagorical, uncategorical, a fuel-burning oracle.'"

Dick Van Dyke, Sally Ann Howes, their kids, and the title car are up to their fenders in trouble in *Chitty Chitty Bang Bang*.

There were a total of eleven songs in the film. Asked which ones the brothers were particularly fond of, Richard replies, "'Lovely Lonely Man' was a beautiful song that Sally Anne sang, and 'Hushabye Mountain' became a rather pretty song. One of my pets was 'Truly Scrumptious,'" he adds, referring to the song named after the character. Other songs included "You Two," "Toot Sweets," and "Posh!"

"Chitty Chitty Bang Bang" was highly praised by critics and brought the Brothers Sherman their second Academy Award nomination (they won the Oscar for "Chim Chim Cheree," see page). Paul Mauriat had a recording of the song which charted for eight weeks and peaked in the number 76 position.

At the Academy Awards ceremony, the producers pulled out all the stops for the "Chitty Chitty Bang Bang" production number, performed by an improbable combination of talents — Ingrid Bergman, Sidney Poitier, Paula Kelly and the UCLA Marching Band. No doubt the event was fantasmagorical.

FOR LOVE OF IVY

**Music by Quincy Jones;
lyrics by Bob Russell**
From *For Love of Ivy*

For Love of Ivy was hailed as the final step in the transformation of actor Sidney Poitier from basically a character actor to a Hollywood superstar with, as Vincent Canby of the *New York Times* put it, "all of the mythic cool and sexual prerogatives of a Clark Gable."

In *Ivy*, Poitier, fresh from his success in *Guess Who's Coming to Dinner* — at $25 million, the number three box office hit for 1967 — played a successful Long Island businessman who has made his way in the white man's world (albeit through questionable ventures). He is persuaded to date Ivy Moore, played by Abbey Lincoln, who is working as a maid for a well-to-do white family. One of the family's teenagers, played by Beau Bridges in an early role, upon learning that Ivy wants to quit her job for secretarial school, plays matchmaker for the housekeeper, who — no surprise here — soon falls in love with Poitier.

The film was based on an original story by Poitier and was scripted by Robert Alan Aurthur, the playwright and scenarist who, a decade before, had written Poitier's first major television role. When Poitier's friend and agent, Marty Baum, shopped the treatment around as a possible vehicle for his client, no one in Hollywood would touch it because of the central story revolving around the romance of a black couple, hardly a mainstream story even for the late '60s. But Poitier and Baum persisted until Palomar Pictures, a subsidiary of the American Broadcasting Company, agreed to take on the project.

Bridges, then known only as Lloyd Bridges's son, proved he was ready to solo after this film, encouraged, no doubt, by the attention he received from critics. *Variety* noted that "Beau Bridges [continues] to register as a potential young star," and Canby commented that "Beau Bridges adds individuality to what is essentially [a] stereotyped role." Others in the cast included Nan Martin, a well-known Broadway actress, as the mother, and Carroll O'Connor, in his pre–Archie Bunker days, as the head of the household.

Poitier continued primarily as an actor until 1972, when he shifted careers to become a director. Many of his films starred Richard Pryor and/or Bill Cosby, and his directoral credits include *Uptown Saturday Night* (1974), *Stir Crazy* (1980), *Fast Forward* (1985), and *Ghost Dad* (1990). In late 1994, Poitier was named to the 12-member board of directors at the Walt Disney Company, filling the seat vacated by the late Frank Wells.

The score in *For Love of Ivy* was composed by Quincy Jones. It comprised mainly source music (music heard emanating from a radio, record player, and the like), including two songs with lyrics by the poet Maya Angelou and vocals by B.B. King — "You Put It on Me," and "The B. B. Jones" — plus a King guitar solo called "Messy But Good." The title song,

"For Love of Ivy," was sung by Shirley Horn over the end credits. The lyrics were by Bob Russell, who had collaborated with Jones on the Oscar-nominated "The Eyes of Love" the preceding year. The pair was again honored by the Motion Picture Academy with an Oscar nomination for "For Love of Ivy."

FUNNY GIRL

Music by Jule Styne; lyrics by Bob Merrill
From *Funny Girl*

In 1994, Barbra Streisand gave her first live concert in more than a decade. Those lucky enough to to have purchased a ticket from the box office, rather than from a scalper, paid "only" $350. Most people merely sat at home, content to listen to their CDs and tapes, or to watch their videos of her numerous films.

But there once was a time when you could buy a ticket to see Streisand for under $20. That would be back in the early 1960s, when the star-to-be was barely out of her teens, appearing on Broadway in the short-lived musical *I Can Get It For You Wholesale*, the play that launched her career. Composer Jule Styne caught her brief performance in that show and signed this virtual unknown to star in his upcoming musical, *Funny Girl*, based on the life of 1920s comedienne Fanny Brice. The show had a healthy run of 1,348 performances, by which time Streisand had already headed for Hollywood (Mimi Hines had taken over her role) and her future as America's most popular female vocalist.

Ray Stark, who had produced the Broadway version, also produced the film, with veteran director William Wyler at the helm. Cast opposite Streisand as Nicky Arnstein was Omar Sharif, an Egyptian national who specialized in playing very exotic parts, like the lead in *Doctor Zhivago*. For *Funny Girl*, however, he was cast against type, playing the part of Fanny Brice's Jewish husband; not only that, he also had to kiss Streisand, a Jewish woman, practically a capital offense in his native country. Initially, the film was banned in Egypt, and for a while there was even talk about revoking Sharif's citizenship.

Of the 16 songs in the original Broadway version, only seven made the cut, among them "People" (now Streisand's trademark), "You Are Woman, I Am Man," "Sadie, Sadie," and "Don't Rain on My Parade." There were a couple of new songs written especially for the

Hello, gawgeous! Barbra Streisand, Oscar-winning star of *Funny Girl.*

In addition to the Best Song nomination for "Funny Girl," there were seven other Academy Award nominations: Best Picture, Best Actress (Streisand), Best Supporting Actress (Kay Medford), Best Cinematography, Best Sound, Best Score of a Musical Picture, and Best Film Editing. Streisand won for Best Actress, tying with Katharine Hepburn for *A Lion in Winter.* It was the first time in Oscar history that there was a tie for Best Actress.

STAR!

**Music by James Van Heusen;
   lyrics by Sammy Cahn**
From *Star!*

In 1968 Julie Andrews became the latest Hollywood star to learn a hard lesson: The public is fickle. Here was Mary Poppins, Maria Von Trapp, and Broadway's former Fair Lady, playing the role of the legendary Gertrude Lawrence. The film was called simply *Star!*, proudly punctuating its presence with an exclamation mark. Furthermore, it was directed by Robert Wise, who had directed Andrews in *The Sound of Music* in 1965 and had several Oscars to show for it, including Best Picture and Best Director. Why, then, did *Star!* prove a flop?

It was not for lack of production values. The story of the British musical star was one of superlatives — the largest single wardrobe ever fitted onto an actress for one week; the most sets ever assembled for one movie, 185 in all; 20 filming sites and 14 different locations, from New York to Massachusetts to the south of France.

There were plenty of songs, too. Julie was on screen virtually all the time (of the 1,400 separate camera setups, she appeared in 1,372 of them), singing her heart out in 17 songs, by everyone from Gershwin to Cole Porter to B. G. DeSylva to Noel Coward to Jimmy Van Heusen and Sammy Cahn, who could always be counted upon to write a good tune.

But something was lacking. That something was an audience. No one, it seemed, wanted to sit through the 174-minute (plus intermission) tribute to Gertrude Lawrence, even if it meant non-stop singing in a Julie Andrews tour-de-force. Even a one-hour trim (without director Wise's input) and re-release a year later under a new title, *Those Were the Happy Times,* didn't

movie, including a title song, "Funny Girl." Surprisingly, there had been no title song for the Broadway version, so Jule Styne and lyricist Bob Merrill created one for the film. It received an Academy Award nomination.

The song "Funny Girl" is set up at the end of the picture by Nicky Arnstein saying, "So long, funny girl" after his hearing. Streisand starts the song in the courthouse and ends as she is coming out of a flashback in the film's final moments. It is rather anticlimactic, coming after the picture's 145-minute running time, especially since the real show-stopper appears at the end of the movie's first half — the "Don't Rain On My Parade" number, with Streisand's exciting dash through Manhattan, culminating in her singing from the back of a tugboat as it sails past the Statue of Liberty.

Funny Girl was the top box office hit of 1968, pulling in more than $26 million in North American rentals. A sequel, *Funny Lady,* released in 1975, earned $19.3 million in rentals, a respectable amount for a follow-up picture.

help. Nor did the seven Oscar nominations, for Best Supporting Actor (Daniel Massey, as Coward), Best Cinematography, Best Costume Design, Best Art Direction, Best Adapted Musical Score, Best Sound, and Best Song — the title song, "Star!," by Van Heusen and Cahn, sung over a clever opening montage in the film. Although title songs have often gone on to "hit" status, "Star!" failed to live up to its name and never became a popular tune.

In 1993, 20th Century-Fox scheduled some limited screenings for the film's 25th anniversary. Robert Wise, commenting in the *Hollywood Reporter* on a showing at the Directors Guild in Los Angeles, thought that the film's negative image was "maybe because it was ahead of its time, maybe because people couldn't accept Julie Andrews playing a tough, self-involved actress. But she's absolutely wonderful in the film," he continued. "I feel strongly it's the finest, most complete performance she's ever given." At the same time as the anniversary screening, Fox released a new VHS cassette as well as a letterboxed laser edition, closer to the original Todd-AO wide-screen format. "It's nice to feel vindicated," said Wise. "I've always felt it was too fine a film to be gathering dust. And it's not often, you know, a film gets a second chance, no matter what its merits, if it hasn't done well commercially the first time out."

1969

And the winner is... RAINDROPS KEEP FALLIN' ON MY HEAD

**Music by Burt Bacharach; lyrics by Hal David
From *Butch Cassidy and the Sundance Kid***

Like *Bonnie and Clyde*, Butch Cassidy and the Sundance Kid were real-life bank robbers and outlaws, so sooner or later it was inevitable there would be a film made of their lives. These two colorful characters of the Old West were immortalized in director George Roy Hill's (*Thoroughly Modern Millie; Hawaii*) film *Butch Cassidy and the Sundance Kid*. Paul Newman played Butch, while Robert Redford co-starred as Sundance, Butch's sidekick and ersatz kid brother. Katharine Ross played Butch's lady love, and the whole picture was played pretty much for laughs.

There are memorable scenes of the gang robbing a train and attempting to blow up a safe, only to blow

Paul Newman and Katharine Ross in the famous "Raindrops Keep Fallin' on My Head" sequence from *Butch Cassidy and the Sundance Kid*.

the entire baggage car to smithereens. Another now-classic scene occurs when the pair must jump into a canyon or be killed by the posse. Glancing into the water below, Redford admits his fear — "I can't swim." Replies Newman, "You're crazy! The fall will probably kill you!" It doesn't, of course, and they live to rob another day. Particularly uproarious is the scene where the pair, now transplanted to Bolivia, decide to give the local bank a try. "Eso es un robo," they inform the startled natives in their best Spanish 101 accent after failing to communicate in English. But first, time for a song.

Yes, a song. "Raindrops Keep Fallin' on My Head" turned out to be a splendid idea, winning the Best Song Academy Award and bringing millions of curious people into the theaters to see Butch and Sundance frolicking to the tune of $46 million in box office rentals, making it the top picture of the year. In the song's production number, it's Butch and Etta Place (Ross) who romp, he steering an old-fashioned bicycle, she atop the handlebars to the accompaniment of B. J. Thomas's perky singing.

It was almost Ray Stevens's singing. Composer Burt Bacharach first offered the job to Stevens, who turned the song down, as did Bob Dylan. Fortunately, Thomas was a persistent man. "We'd been working on Burt for three or four years," Thomas told Wink Martindale in a 1993 radio interview. "My personal manager was Dionne Warwick's personal manager, so we'd been trying to get him to 'cut' me for about three years. When he couldn't get Dylan, he gave me the shot. It was fantastic, doing the sessions. [At the recording sessions] they've got the scene from the movie running and a hundred musicians, and it was such an experience that it probably took me a year to relive it and remember how it went down."

Thomas's recording debuted in November, 1969, and by the first week in January it had hit Number One on the *Billboard* charts, where it remained for four weeks, charting for a total of 22 weeks and becoming a certified gold record.

It was a significant song for Bacharach and lyricist Hal David, too. Both received the Oscar for Best Song, and Burt took home another that year for *Butch Cassidy*, for Best Original Non-Musical Score. He would later describe the experience of winning two Oscars on the same evening as "one of the greatest nights in my life."

Butch Cassidy and the Sundance Kid made out like a bandit at the Academy Awards that year. Nominated for seven Oscars — Best Picture, Best Director, Best Story and Screenplay (William Goldman), Best Cinematography, Best Sound, plus the two music nominations — the 20th Century-Fox release captured the writing and cinematography awards, as well as the statuettes for song and score.

COME SATURDAY MORNING

Music by Fred Karlin; lyrics by Dory Previn
From *The Sterile Cuckoo*

A coming-of-age picture for the last year of the 1960s, *The Sterile Cuckoo* also marked the first major appearance for a rising young star — Liza Minnelli, then still being referred to as "the daughter of Vincente Minnelli and the late Judy Garland" (Judy having died while the picture was being filmed). Liza had appeared in only one previous motion picture, 1968's *Charlie Bubbles*, but she was already beginning to make a name for herself as a singer.

Liza recalled reading John Nichols's novel, on which the film is based, long before being cast in the part. "A friend had told me how much she enjoyed the story," said Liza (as quoted in the biography *Liza! Liza!*, by Alan W. Petrucelli), "so when I saw the book in an airport newsstand, I bought it. I read it straight through that night. It was a strange feeling, but I felt a deep understanding and sympathy for Pookie Adams, the lead character. It was like the same things that happened to her happened to me not very long ago. I knew that if a film was made of *The Sterile Cuckoo*, I would play it." She approached Alan Pakula, the director who co-owned the film rights, and insisted she was the only one who should play Pookie. Pakula agreed. "I couldn't separate Liza from Pookie," he commented in the same biography. At first the studio balked, but Pakula persevered. "Liza was the only person I seriously considered for the role."

The film premiered to good reviews, with Minnelli receiving the lioness's share of praise. Pauline Kael, writing in the *New Yorker,* exclaimed, "Liza's just about perfect . . . Her sad, quizzical persona — the gangling body and the features that look too big for the little face — are ideal equipment for the role. She's very funny and is probably going to be acclaimed as a great actress." Charles Champlin of the *Los Angeles Times* concurred, calling her "warm, sad-looking, serious-funny, touching and beguiling." There were predictions of an Oscar, and indeed, the part brought Minnelli her first nomination for Best Actress.

Also nominated was the film's opening song, "Come Saturday Morning." Sung over the opening credits as Pookie sits waiting at the bus stop, the tune was written by Fred Karlin and lyricist Dory Previn. Dory was still married to André Previn at the time (the couple would be divorced a year later when he left her to marry Mia Farrow, who had given birth to his twins). She had been nominated in 1960 (with André) for "Faraway Part of Town" (see page 159) from *Pepe*, under her maiden name, Dory Langdon, and again in 1962 for "Second Chance," from *Two for the Seesaw* (see page 169). "Come Saturday Morning" is a wistful, poetic tale of friendship tinged with nostalgia, establishing just the right mood for the picture. It is sung in the film by the Sandpipers, who later re-recorded the song and released it as a single.

The Sandpipers were originally known as the Grads — three young men who first met while singing in a Los Angeles boys' choir. When they grew older, the trio left to seek a career as a pop singing group, eventually landing a contract with Herb Alpert's newly formed A&M label. The Grads made one record for him, "Everything in the Garden," then changed their name to the Sandpipers. Their first big hit came with 1966's "Guantanamera." Later that year they did a cover of "Louie Louie." Their biggest success, however, came with their version of "Come Saturday Morning," which climbed to the number 17 position and charted for 20 weeks.

JEAN

Music and lyrics by Rod McKuen
From *The Prime of Miss Jean Brodie*

Maggie Smith was not that well known to American audiences, but after her tour de force performance as a Scottish schoolteacher in *The Prime of Miss Jean Brodie*, that would certainly change. Critics raved about her work in the film, which was adapted for the screen by Jay Presson Allen from her play on the London stage (starring Vanessa Redgrave) as well as in New York

(Zoe Caldwell played the role on Broadway), which was in turned based on a 1961 novel by Muriel Spark.

The film is really a character study of a scatter-brained, influential teacher in the late 1930s, Miss Jean Brodie, who lives vicariously through the lives of the girls she teaches. There had been many prior movies about outstanding members of the teaching profession — *Goodbye, Mr. Chips,* for example, was first filmed in 1939, then retooled as a musical in 1969 with Peter O'Toole. And *To Sir with Love* (1967), starring Sidney Poitier, is another example of the male-dominated plethora of films in this genre. *The Prime of Miss Jean Brodie,* however, was about a woman, a strong woman, who was allowed to express her sexuality, repressed though it may have been.

Smith received a shower of accolades for her memorable performance. "She is simply great," wrote Vincent Canby of the *New York Times*. "It's the kind of performance that not only has meaning within the context of the movie, but also can be consciously enjoyed as the work of an individual, fully developed intelligence exercising its talents for the sheer joy of it." The Academy took note too, and awarded Smith the Oscar for Best Actress.

Although the film's cumbersome title made it difficult to write a title song in the truest sense of the term, everyone was happy to settle for "Jean." Rod McKuen, a talented poet, composer, and writer created the full score for the film, as well as the "title" song, which went on to receive an Academy Award nomination. McKuen had composed for films in the 1950s before moving to New York to write music for television and begin recording his own songs. A few years later he spent some time in France, where he created the English lyrics for "Ne Me Quitte Pas" ("If You Go Away") and "Le Moribund," which was recorded by Bobby Vinton in the United States as "Seasons in the Sun"(1961). Another well-known McKuen song was Glen Yarbrough's "Baby the Rain Must Fall" (1965). In 1969 Frank Sinatra recorded an album of McKuen songs, *A Man Alone.*

"Jean" became a hit recording by William Oliver Swofford, who recorded under the name of Oliver. The single swiftly climbed the charts, peaking in the number two position, remaining on the charts for 14 weeks, and selling over a million copies. The song was also given the Golden Globe Award for the Best Original Song that year.

TRUE GRIT

Music by Elmer Bernstein; lyrics by Don Black
From *True Grit*

Actress Kim Darby came from a show business family, the "Dancing Zerbys." Her father, Jon Zerby, was a famous dancer. When his daughter, Deborah, was born, he nicknamed her Derby. "I thought Derby Zerby would be a great stage name," Jon likes to say, pointing out that he had always hoped his daughter would become a professional dancer like himself. But as the youngster grew, it became evident that her career lay not in dancing but in acting, and by her early teens she knew she needed a name change. Derby Zerby became Kim Darby. She appeared in numerous films and television shows, and in 1969 she signed to co-star opposite John Wayne in *True Grit*.

It should have been the Duke's picture, but once Darby entered Wayne's world, she nearly stole the show. Here was a 21-year-old playing a plucky 14-year-old, the daughter of a murdered man whom Federal marshal Rooster Cogburn (Wayne), assisted by a Texas ranger known only as Le Boeuf (singer Glen Campbell, in his film debut), must track down. At Oscar time, the Academy awarded John Wayne his first, long-overdue statuette for Best Actor.

The film was directed by 71-year-old Henry Hathaway, proving there's no such thing as retirement in Hollywood if you're good. Hal Wallis produced from the best-selling novel by Charles Portis. He knew the key role would be that of Mattie Ross, the young girl who stands up to Rooster. Wallis's first choice for the role was Mia Farrow, but after consulting with her then-husband, André Previn, she backed out of the deal. The film was already in preproduction, without a leading lady, and Wallis was desperate. "When I looked at the list of well-known Hollywood actresses, my heart sank," wrote Wallis in his autobiography, *Starmaker*. "None of them was right for Mattie. But one night a face jumped off the television screen at me that was. Clean-scrubbed, keen-eyed, strong-boned, full of spunk and determination, this girl *was* Mattie."

Glen Campbell was another discovery. "We were fortunate in having Glen Campbell in this picture," wrote Wallis. "After seeing him on television, I was impressed with his style and realized he had the talent and looks that would attract large audiences." Campbell, winner of four Grammy awards by then, had

never acted but had one advantage over the rest of the cast: He didn't need coaching with his accent, since he was a native of Arkansas, where a good deal of the film was set (although filmed on location in Colorado and California).

The title song, "True Grit," is sung by Campbell under the titles. It was written by Elmer Bernstein, who also scored the picture, with lyrics by Don Black, the Oscar winner for "Born Free" (see page 184). Campbell's single release of "True Grit" was a moderate success, reaching the number 35 position during a seven-week chart run.

In 1975, John Wayne again played the part of the patch-eyed marshal in a sequel to *True Grit*. *Rooster Cogburn* co-starred Katharine Hepburn, and although it did fairly good box-office ($9 million in rentals, compared to $14 for the first picture), it also, like nearly all sequels, fell short of the original.

WHAT ARE YOU DOING THE REST OF YOUR LIFE?

Music by Michel Legrand;
lyrics by Alan and Marilyn Bergman
From *The Happy Ending*

Richard Brooks wrote, produced, and directed *The Happy Ending* and therefore is due all the credit — and all the blame — for this less-than-happy picture. Brooks's credentials were impeccable — films like *Elmer Gantry* (1960), with Burt Lancaster and Jean Simmons; *The Professionals* (1966), starring Lee Marvin, Burt Lancaster, Jack Palance, and Ralph Bellamy; and *In Cold Blood* (1967), with Robert Blake and John Forsythe. With *The Happy Ending*, however, he stumbled.

The story concerns a married woman, played by Jean Simmons (Brooks's real-life wife) who seeks refuge in drugs and booze when her wedded bliss turns dull after 16 years. Silver-haired John Forsythe played her tax-lawyer husband who is practically the poster child for the Denver Chamber of Commerce. Known mainly as a television actor ("Bachelor Father" was his longest-running series at that time — 1957–62), Forsythe would eventually portray a much nicer silver-haired Denver bigwig in TV's "Dynasty" series (1981–89).

The Happy Ending had all the elements of a night-time TV soap opera too, or perhaps a mini-series (the genre had yet to be invented). Simmons played the

John Forsythe and Jean Simmons star in *The Happy Ending*.

depressed wife, subjected to clichéd lines like "One drink's too many, and a thousand's not enough" (from her bartender), or "Who wants someone else's heartache?" (from her pawnbroker, refusing her wedding band). Tina Louise, the former sexpot of TV's "Gilligan's Island," played a seductive housewife with an eye on Forsythe. Revealing her cleavage as he lights her cigarette, she whispers, "Most married men would rather switch than fight," a twist on a popular cigarette commercial of the day. "The dialog begins to sound like a three-part *Cosmopolitan* magazine article for housewives on angst, adultery and alcoholism," moaned *Variety.*

Also in the cast were pop singer Bobby Darin (billed as Robert Darin, perhaps to keep his careers separate), playing a shifty-eyed gigolo; Lloyd Bridges as a philandering tycoon; Dick Shawn as Louise's hapless husband; and Nanette Fabray in the casting mystery of the decade, actually doing a superb job as a wise-cracking, worldly-wise housekeeper.

Michel Legrand's score received critical praise. *Variety,* for example, noted, "Michel Legrand has con-tributed a slick, bluesy score with one circa-'50s-style ballad, 'What Are You Doing the Rest of Your Life?' that is bittersweet and poignant as [Henry Mancini's] 'Days of Wine and Roses' [see page 167] in context." Legrand had won the Academy Award the previous year with lyricists Alan and Marilyn Bergman (see page 193), who contributed another stirring lyric, receiving their second Oscar nomination as a team. "What Are You Doing the Rest of Your Life?" is sung by Michael Dees over scenes depicting happier times in Simmons's and Forsythe's characters' marriage — we glimpse them playing in the snow together and skiing. Later in the film, the song is played on a jukebox in a bar as Simmons drinks, smokes, and wistfully reminisces. (Interestingly the previous year's Oscar-winning song, "The Windmills of Your Mind," also appeared in this film, in the background of a scene with Darin, Simmons, and Shirley Jones in a casino bar.)

It was Simmons's performance that sustained this rather disheartening picture. In recognition of her work in *The Happy Ending,* she received an Academy Award nomination.

THE SEVENTIES

The '70s were a disaster, or at least a celebration of disasters. Tragedy figured big at the movies: ships sank, buildings burned, sharks devoured, and planes tumbled from the sky with regularity. We took a long, hard look at our lives and decided that "We May Never Love Like This Again" (unless someone made a sequel or burned down another skyscraper).

Love and sex also figured prominently up on the screen. Words and scenes that would have made our grandparents faint and our parents blush started appearing with regularity. People made love, then sang about it: Love's ways were "Strange," it was celebrated "The Morning After," and sometimes we decided that "All That Love Went to Waste." Meanwhile, a new ratings code, with its G, GP (later PG), R, and X ratings, decided for us whether we were mature enough to handle it all.

Some of the same Oscar-winning composers who had delighted us in decades past would still be with us for a few more years — people like Johnny Mercer, Sammy Cahn, Sammy Fain, Paul Francis Webster, Michel Legrand and Alan and Marilyn Bergman, the Sherman Brothers, and Henry Mancini. But new names had begun to emerge. We enjoyed Oscar-nominated and -winning songs by cinematic newcomers Marvin Hamlisch, Paul and Linda McCartney, John Williams, Joe Hirschhorn, Barbra Streisand, and Paul Williams. These were the beginnings of modern times, a new generation of standards in the making, future nostalgia for baby boomers to hold in their memories — songs of "The Way We Were."

FOR ALL WE KNOW

Music by Fred Karlin; lyrics by Robb Wilson and Arthur James
From Lovers and Other Strangers

Directed by Cy Howard and promoted as a Christian *Goodbye, Columbus* (the 1969 hit film about Jewish families and marriages, starring Richard Benjamin and Ali MacGraw), *Lovers and Other Strangers* evoked laughter out of a similar situation between families of Irish and Italian Catholic persuasions.

Lovers and Other Strangers is based on the Broadway show of the same name. The movie, which dealt with a suburban wedding and the marital and generational problems of the two families involved, was blessed with a talented cast: Bea Arthur (TV's future "Maude" and "Golden Girls" star) starred as the bridegroom's mother, Bonnie Bedelia and Michael Brandon played the young couple in love, and Richard Castellano was the boy's father. Diane Keaton (in her film debut), Anne Jackson, Harry Guardino, Cloris Leachman, Anne Meara, and Gig Young rounded out the cast.

With the new decade came a new rating system from Hollywood's self-imposed watchdogs, the Motion Picture Association of America's Production Code and Rating Administration. They doomed this pleasant comedy to a poor box office showing by branding it with an R rating, although there was no nudity and only a few mild epithets, pretty tame stuff by today's standards. An R meant that nobody under 17 could be admitted without a parent or adult guardian, shutting out a large percentage of the ticket-buying public for whom this would have been a perfect date movie. When the take was totaled, *Lovers and Other Strangers* took in a mere $6.8 million in North American rentals. By the time the picture was released on home video, the film had been downgraded to a less stringent PG rating.

Lovers and Other Strangers received three Academy Award nominations: Best Supporting Actor (Castellano), Best Adapted Screenplay (Renee Taylor, Joseph Bologna, and David Zelag Goodman), and Best Song — "For All We Know," which won the Oscar. It was written by Fred Karlin, with lyrics by Robb Wilson and Arthur

James (occasionally credited as Robb Royer and James Griffin, respectively). In addition to "For All We Know" there were two other songs — "Comin' Thru to Me" and "Keepin' Free," with vocals by Country Coalition.

"For All We Know" was performed by Larry Meredith on the movie's soundtrack, but his version was not released as a single. An up and coming duo known as the Carpenters recorded the tune and released it as a single in February, 1971. It charted for 13 weeks, reaching the number three position on the *Billboard* charts. It was a million-selling record for the brother-and-sister singing team, one of 10 such singles they would rack up during their career.

The Carpenters, Richard and Karen, were born in New Haven, Connecticut. Richard studied classical piano at Yale, while Karen excelled on drums and had a strong singing voice. By the early '70s they were producing hit after hit, including their first million-seller, "For All We Know," followed by "(They Long to Be) Close to You" (their first Number One hit), "Rainy Days and Mondays," "Yesterday Once More," "Top of the World" (also Number One), and others. The pressures of stardom weighed heavily on Karen, however, and in 1975 she collapsed from anorexia nervosa. Despite attempts to get help for this disease, she eventually succumbed to its ravages in 1983, at the age of only 32. Richard went on to produce albums after her death, including his solo album, *Time*, in 1987. In 1989, *Lovelines*, an album of previously unreleased Carpenter recordings, appeared, and 1994 saw the release of *If I Were a Carpenter*, a tribute album of Carpenters tunes performed by contemporary rock bands.

PIECES OF DREAMS

Music by Michel Legrand;
lyrics by Alan and Marilyn Bergman
From Pieces of Dreams

The story of a Catholic priest who suffers the pangs of love is a tale as old as the Church itself, and, with a little imagination, could have made a good film. Unfortunately, *Pieces of Dreams* suffered pangs of another sort at the box office, due to poor reviews and uncertain direction. It was based on William E. Barrett's novel, *The Wine and the Music*, and the author was himself a Catholic novelist from Denver who had frequently written about religious themes. Some of his previous works had also been made into films, including the highly acclaimed *Lilies of the Field*.

But somehow Roger O. Hirson's adaptation from Barrett's novel did not work. George Gent of the *New York Times* went so far as to call it "a really dreadful little movie . . . [with] unbelievably simplistic dialogue." The film centered around the relationship between Father Gregory Lind, played by Robert Forster, and his love for a wealthy, sophisticated social worker (Lauren Hutton, with a Halston wardrobe). The melodramatic film touched on all the expected topics — birth control and the pill, abortion, tippling pastors, and celibacy.

Newcomer Hutton received the critics' kindest words. "Lauren Hutton is pretty . . . and gives some evidence that she might be able to act given more favorable circumstances," wrote the *Times*, while *Variety* noted, "Miss Hutton registers strongly with a cool warmth that suggests more promise . . ."

Lauren Hutton was born Mary Hutton, in South Carolina in 1943 and began her career waiting tables in New Orleans at Al Hirt's jazz club on Bourbon Street. After a brief stint as a Playboy bunny in New York, she became a much sought-after, highly paid fashion model before playing increasingly larger roles in such lightweight films as *Little Fauss and Big Halsy* (1970), opposite Robert Redford; *The Gambler* (1974), with James Caan; *American Gigolo* (1980), with Richard Gere; and *Zorro, the Gay Blade* (1981).

Pieces of Dreams was exceptional in one way only — its musical score by Michel Legrand. There was a title song as well, written by Legrand with his previous lyric collaborators, the Bergmans, Alan and Marilyn. The trio had won the Best Song Oscar in 1968, for "The Windmills of Your Mind" (see page 193), and had been nominated for the haunting "What Are You Doing the Rest of Your Life?" in 1969 (see page 200). They were again nominated for "Pieces of Dreams" in 1970. *Variety* commented on this song and Lauren Hutton's vocal resemblance to its singer, noting: "At times [Hutton's] voice is remarkably similar to that of Peggy Lee, an impression created by Miss Lee's soundtrack vocalizing (twice) of a pop tune title theme . . . Tune's resemblance to 'Who Can I Turn To' won't hurt its exploitation. Legrand's score is okay."

Although "Pieces of Dreams" failed to become a hit song for Peggy Lee, other popular singers, such as Barbra Streisand, Jack Jones, and Sarah Vaughan, later added the now-familiar melody to their respective repertoires. The song, with its "Little boy lost" lyric,

has outgrown the film that spawned it and become a standard.

THANK YOU VERY MUCH

Music and lyrics by Leslie Bricusse
From *Scrooge*

In 1968, the Charles Dickens story of *Oliver Twist*, after having been around for several years as a popular stage musical called *Oliver!*, was finally brought to the screen. So the time seemed right for another Dickensian narrative to be produced as a screen musical as well.

Although written in 1843, the original Charles Dickens short story "A Christmas Carol" had a timelessness that has captivated audiences since it first appeared. The tale of the old tightwad Ebenezer Scrooge (the word "scrooge," meaning a miserly person, entered the English language in 1899), has had many incarnations, especially at Christmastime, when at least one version of it can be counted upon to appear on television. Memorable motion pictures of the story had been produced in 1938 (starring Reginald Owen) and in 1951 (with Alastair Sim); in 1984, another would be made, starring George C. Scott.

The musical version of this classic was called, simply, *Scrooge*. It starred Albert Finney in the title role of the cantankerous skinflint who is taken on a tour of his life — past, present, and future — in a sort of Capraesque nightmare that might be called *It's a Terrible Life*. The guides for this time-traveling banker are three ghosts, the most memorable of whom, in a creative bit of casting, is Dame Edith Evans, playing the Ghost of Christmas Past. Kenneth More played the Ghost of Christmas Present, while Paddy Stone, also the film's choreographer, played the Ghost of Christmas Yet to Come. One of the best performances, in the role of Marley's Ghost, was turned in by Alex Guiness, a veteran of two other filmed Dickens works: *Great Expectations* (1946) and *Oliver Twist* (1948).

The G-rated picture was loaded with tunes by Academy Award–winning composer Leslie Bricusse ("Talk to the Animals" — see page 188), who also served as executive producer. Songs included "A Christmas Carol," "Father Christmas," "December the 25th," "Happiness," "I Like Life," "The Beautiful Day," "I'll Begin Again," and "Thank You Very Much," which received a nod from the Academy as an Oscar nominee.

In the film, the character Tom Jenkins sings the song, accompanied by a chorus of townspeople. The tune is reminiscent of "Consider Yourself" from *Oliver!* (written by Lionel Bart), both lively songs with a music-hall feel. The lyrics to "Thank You Very Much," however, are black comedy, a celebration of the "death" of Ebenezer Scrooge (as revealed by the Ghost of Christmas Yet to Come). In the scene, people are reveling in the streets because Scrooge is dead and they don't have to pay him the money they owe. In other words, thank you very much for dying, you old &%#$!

In addition to the Best Song nomination, *Scrooge* was nominated for Best Costume Design, Best Art Direction, and Best Song Score.

In 1991, *Scrooge* was translated from film to the stage for the first time. Anthony Newley starred in the title role of *Scrooge — The Musical,* which had a limited run in Birmingham, England.

TILL LOVE TOUCHES YOUR LIFE

Music by Riz Ortolani;
lyrics by Arthur Hamilton
From *Madron*

Recognizing the financial advantages of shooting movies abroad, sometime in the 1970s producers began making westerns overseas. Frequently, their pictures were shot in Italy, where they were whimsically dubbed *spaghetti westerns.* Occasionally, they took advantage of the deserts of Israel, with the Negev and Dead Sea doubling for the American West. These "matzo westerns" brought the rugged Israeli scenery to the screen in a way that perfectly duplicated the American Southwest, at half the cost.

Such a film was *Madron.* It was actually the first western ever filmed entirely in Israel, and according to the director, Jerry Hopper, "The western terrain of the Negev photographed for the film looks more like New Mexico and Arizona than one can actually believe." The story concerned a wagon train bound for Santa Fe that is ambushed by the requisite Apaches. The chief was played by Chaim Banai, more likely from one of the so-called Lost Tribes than any Indian tribe. Or, as the *Hollywood Reporter* put it, "The Indians have a distinct Semitic appearance." Very politically incorrect by today's standards, and barely acceptable even in 1970,

After Scrooge "dies," grateful revelers sing their appreciation for this act with the song "Thank You Very Much," in *Scrooge.*

with the Indians portrayed in the usual stereotypical way as superstitious, murderous savages.

Leslie Caron played Sister Mary Joseph, a French-Canadian nun who survives the massacre, then encounters gunslinger Madron, played by Richard Boone. At first the two can't stand each other, but as they fend off the attackers together, they begin to form a bond that turns to attraction. Inevitably, Sister Mary and Madron make love — just another typical gunfighter/nun story.

Leslie Caron and Richard Boone in a scene from *Madron*.

The theme song from the film, "Till Love Touches Your Life," received quite a bit of attention when the picture opened, since it is worked into the story throughout. We first hear it near the beginning of the movie, after Caron buries the dead following the massacre. About 10 minutes into the picture, she prepares to head off on a trek across the desert on horseback, and the opening titles begin to appear while the story continues to unfold. The tune is sung by Richard Williams, a Johnny Mathis soundalike. (Mathis himself later recorded the song.) The music, with its faintly Italian sound, was written by Riz Ortolani, who composed the Oscar-nominated song "More" for *Mondo Cane* in 1963 (see page 174); the lyrics were written by Arthur Hamilton, who wrote the words to the popular song "Cry Me a River." "Till Love Touches Your Life" is sung again under the closing credits, this time by a female singer, Jan Daley.

Despite all the ballyhoo about the song, recorded releases of it didn't do very much. At the Oscar award ceremonies, neither of the two soundtrack singers performed the tune. Instead, it was sung by Lola Falana, a popular singer-dancer known for her work in nightclubs, in films, on stage, and on television.

WHISTLING AWAY THE DARK

**Music by Henry Mancini;
   lyrics by Johnny Mercer**
From *Darling Lili*

By the age of 34, Julie Andrews had already enjoyed a pretty full life. She had been the darling of Broadway in the '50s in *My Fair Lady*, she was the nanny everyone wished they'd grown up with in *Mary Poppins* (see page 175), and she'd starred in what was then the most successful film of all time when she'd played a nanny/nun in *The Sound of Music* (1965). But she'd also had her share of tragedy. Her first marriage ended, she bombed in the musical *Star!* (see page 196), and at an age when many people's careers are just beginning to blossom, she seemed on her way out.

Andrews survived all of that, no thanks to her cinematic effort in 1970 in a film called *Darling Lili*. Today the film is generally accepted as quite enjoyable, but at the time it was roundly panned by the critics — certainly not the sound of music to Julie's ears. The movie was produced and directed by Blake Edwards, who at the time was having a very open and very controversial love affair with Andrews. Her divorce was not yet final, and Hollywood still tended to frown on such situations. But Julie sailed bravely through it. "How dare 'they' judge another human being?" she said of her critics (as quoted in the biography *Julie Andrews,* by Robert Windeler). "I mostly do what I want to do and don't care what anyone thinks. I do try not to hurt anyone," she added. Eventually the couple married, with Andrews continuing to star in several Blake Edwards–produced films, including *S.O.B.* (1981), *Victor/Victoria* (1982), and *That's Life!* (1986, see page 276).

The original title of *Darling Lili* was *Darling Lili, or Where Were You on the Night You Said You Shot Down Baron von Richthofen?.* It was, in co-writer-director-producer Edwards's words, "a play with music." Set in Europe during World War I, the story (co-written by William Peter Blatty, author of *The Exorcist)* was a spoof on the life of Mata Hari, with Andrews as an English music-hall star who is really a German spy. Most of her spying is on Rock Hudson, playing a nervous flyboy who can only go aloft when he's drunk. The musical numbers get full attention, giving Julie a chance to sing such nostalgic tunes as "Keep the Home Fires Burning," "It's a Long Way to Tipperary," "Mademoiselle from Armentieres," and other tunes popular in the days of the First World War.

New songs were also a big part of the picture, and Edwards called in his old friends Henry Mancini and Johnny Mercer, who had written the Academy Award winners "Moon River" (see page 162) and "Days of Wine and Roses" (see page 167). They would pen several tunes for *Darling Lili,* including a title song, "Darling Lili," plus "The Girl in No Man's Land," "I'll Give You Three Guesses," "Smile Away Each Rainy Day," and the song that would receive an Academy Award nomination — "Whistling Away the Dark." This latter song was praised by all the critics, although it bears a strong resemblance to another of Mancini's nominated tunes, "Charade" (see page 172). It didn't win the Oscar, but it did take home the Golden Globe Award for Best Original Song from a Film.

While the movie never recouped its expensive budget — it was shot in locations all over Europe — it has become something of a cult hit today.

Richard Roundtree, as the title character in *Shaft,* is warned by shoeshine man Arnold Johnson that hoods are after him.

1971

THEME FROM *SHAFT*

Music and lyrics by Isaac Hayes
From *Shaft*

Sammy Davis Jr. didn't have to hedge his bets. As host for the production number performances of the Best Song Oscar at the 1971 Academy Awards ceremony, the odds were stacked in favor of the close ties he knew he'd feel for whomever won. "Tonight, the Academy is honoring two films about my people," joked the black entertainer who had converted to Judaism, "*Shaft* and *Fiddler on the Roof.*"

The nominee from *Shaft,* composer Isaac Hayes, then performed his "Theme from *Shaft,*" attired in a chainmail shirt. In a spectacular smoke-and-mirrors production number, Hayes rode onto the stage on a lighted organ, singing the words and music he himself had written. After the audience roared their acceptance of the bit, Davis quipped: "By the way, Mr. Hayes's shirt was by Hillcrest Hardware."

All joking aside, Hayes couldn't have been more pleased. It was the first time ever that a black songwriter had won the Best Song category. By the time the envelope was presented, Hayes had changed into a somewhat more conservative black-velvet tux with blue lapels. As he stepped up to the podium, he offered his thanks to his grandmother, "the lady who's here by me tonight, because years ago her prayers kept my feet on the path of righteousness . . . In a few days, it'll be her 80th birthday, and this is her present."

Shaft was a private eye flick with a mostly black cast, fast-paced, with lots of soul sounds from scorer Hayes. The film starred Richard Roundtree as John Shaft and was directed by the multi-talented Gordon Parks, equally famed for his writing, composing, and photography. *Shaft* was Parks's second feature, and it proved a commercial success. The script was based on the novel by Ernest Tidyman, with a script by John D. F. Black.

The story found Shaft on the trail of the kidnapped daughter of a Harlem underworld boss (played by Moses Gunn). He's assisted by a white cop, which many saw (probably justifiably) as an attempt to maintain a white market for the black-identified film. Some critics even went so far as to call *Shaft* a black movie for white audiences. Clayton Riley of the *New York Times* wrote, "Films like *Shaft* will be well received in this city because they provide whites with a comfortable image of blacks as noncompetitors." Still, it was a groundbreaker in its day, giving black people some real heroes to emulate. And in a way, *Shaft* can be seen as a prototype for all those *Beverly Hills Cop* movies.

Hayes's "Theme from *Shaft*" not only took home the Oscar, but also spent two weeks atop the *Billboard* charts as a Number One hit. The song debuted on October 16, 1971, and was on the charts for 19 impressive weeks.

THE AGE OF NOT BELIEVING

Music and lyrics by Richard M. Sherman and Robert B. Sherman
From *Bedknobs and Broomsticks*

Seven years after *Mary Poppins* descended into theaters, Walt Disney Studios dusted off a property it had acquired some years before. The project, from a story by Mary Norton, was called *Bedknobs and Broomsticks*,

and it had actually been in development around the same time as *Mary Poppins*. After it was finally filmed and released in 1971, the comparisons were inevitable. Mary Poppins, a mysterious nanny, performed magic; *Bedknobs*'s Eglantine Price, a mysterious apprentice witch, also performed magic. Both films featured children in London who related with the central female star. Both employed the time-honored Disney tradition of people and animated cartoon critters interacting. Both films had fine casts and fine songs by the Sherman Brothers, Richard and Robert.

Richard Sherman, however, is quick to point out one of the reasons for the constant comparisons. "I think if you get the same group of people from the same studio doing a musical fantasy, you are going to have that [comparison]." Actually, the songwriters had been developing tunes for *Bedknobs* back around the time when Walt Disney was still alive and very much in control of the studio. "We were working on it, and Walt liked it very much," says Richard. "But he said, 'We are going to wait awhile because it has an English background, and we don't want it to be [released] right on top of *Mary Poppins*.' Then he died . . . It was seven years before 'the committee' decided to resurrect *Bedknobs and Broomsticks*."

The Shermans, who by now were freelancing, were called back to the Disney studios to compose music for this film. According to Richard, they didn't just set out to write songs, but to find the core of the film; the rest would fall into place. "We felt it was important to have a theme," he says. He asked himself, "What's this picture about?" Once they answered that question, they not only had their theme, they had the concept for a song that would win them yet another Oscar nomination. This theme, in Richard's words, is simple: "If you believe in yourself, you can make magical things happen." The song is called "The Age of Not Believing," and Richard sees it as the central concept, "the secret to the picture."

In the film, Angela Lansbury sings the song about how children begin to doubt everything, and "worst of all you doubt yourself." It's a story of childhood's end, something everyone can relate to. Richard Sherman was disappointed, however, by the song's treatment, maintaining that it was "thrown away in the picture — it wasn't featured the way it should have been." One of the problems, as he sees it, was that the studio was somewhat adrift without Walt, who had ruled with a gentle but iron hand. It is also possible that the song wasn't given the attention it deserved because some considered Lansbury to be an unspectacular singer, although she had a convincing way of putting the point across in song (she would be used again in Disney's *Beauty and the Beast* — see page 296). In fact, she hadn't been the studio's first choice for the role, with Lynn Redgrave, Leslie Caron, Judy Carne, and Julie Andrews all in contention for the part.

Bedknobs and Broomsticks was honored with four additional nominations by the Academy: Best Art Direction–Set Decoration; Best Scoring: Adaptation and Original Song Score; Best Costume Design; and, in the film's only win, Best Special Visual Effects.

ALL HIS CHILDREN

**Music by Henry Mancini;
  lyrics by Alan and Marilyn Bergman
From *Sometimes a Great Notion***

Henry Fonda as the father and Paul Newman as the son — this rare pairing of two top actors was part of the intrigue of the film *Sometimes a Great Notion*. The story concerned a lumberjack clan in Oregon who rebuff union workers insisting that they join a statewide timber strike. Fonda, refusing to bow to intimidation, makes some remarks about "Commie pinkos who tell us when to cut," to which the union leader replies: "That's as good a statement of 19th-century philosophy as I've ever heard."

Between rounds of jacking lumber and feuding with the commie pinkos, actor Newman suddenly found himself in the director's chair. Richard Colla, the film's original director, had bowed out, citing "artistic differences," leaving Newman as the next logical choice to helm the picture. He had only directed one other film, the critically acclaimed *Rachel, Rachel*, which had starred his wife, Joanne Woodward. With *Sometimes a Great Notion* already about 20 percent over budget by the time he assumed control, Newman was at least able to maintain some consistency in style.

The music for this great-outdoors location picture was by Henry Mancini, praised by *Variety* for his "unobtrusive but effective score [that] draws on popular riffs. There is, of course, a poptune." That would be "All His Children," with words by Alan and Marilyn Bergman, and it went on to receive an Academy Award nomination. It is sung at the beginning and end of the film by country singer Charley Pride, in his soundtrack

debut. Pride released a single of the tune, arranged and conducted by Mancini. The song did little business on the charts, peaking at number 72 during a three-week chart run.

Charley Pride is sometimes called the first black country music superstar (although certainly not the first black to sing in that style). He was born in 1938 in Sledge, Mississippi, into a sharecropper family of 11 children, and grew up listening to country music on the radio. His first career choice had been baseball, but he soon traveled to Nashville, where he began cutting records, releasing a string of hits throughout the '70s and '80s.

Mancini's score was a departure from his usual style, with its country sound plus a touch of Cajun. As Mancini wrote in his autobiography, *Did They Mention the Music?*, "Paul [Newman] had found that there was a lot of country and western music on the radio and the jukeboxes [in the Oregon timber country]. So that was the kind of score I wrote — a good deal of Cajun music and country guitars." The film's producer, John Foreman, writing in the soundtrack album's liner notes, explained that in order to record the score, "Mancini assembled a group of country musicians equally at home in Nashville or Hollywood. The results displayed clearly provide another example why Henry Mancini has been able to maintain his rank among the top film composers."

BLESS THE BEASTS AND THE CHILDREN

**Music and lyrics by Barry DeVorzon
  and Perry Botkin Jr.
From *Bless the Beasts and the Children***

With its deceptively simple plot about six square-pegged kids who set out to free a herd of captive, slaughter-bound buffalo while spending a summer at a dude ranch, *Bless the Beasts and the Children* was a much-discussed film at the time of its release. Stanley Kramer produced and directed this story (based on the book by Glendon Swarthout) at a time when the country's youth were looking for ways to turn America around. The picture makes a very powerful case for ecological and environmental awareness, and also features commentary on political, social, and human values. And that's just for starters.

While violence is depicted in the film — the buffalo hunt was from stock footage Kramer purchased and matched to his own lensing, so as not to have to kill any animals — there is an emphasis on the negative side of guns. There may have been a message, but this was not a message film per se. Kramer managed to work in humor, suspense, and action along with as much characterization as time permitted with this large a cast. "Pic manages to say the important things he and the author had to say with hard-hitting courage, oft-grim or caustically tongue-in-cheek humor" was how the reviewer for *Variety* saw the movie.

Kramer produced and directed a number of prestigious films, usually with social themes, during the course of four decades. Among his well-known pictures are *On the Beach* (1959), *Inherit the Wind* (1960), *Judgment at Nuremberg* (1961), *It's a Mad, Mad, Mad, Mad World* (1963 — see page 173), *Guess Who's Coming to Dinner* (1967), and *The Runner Stumbles* (1979).

The cast consisted mostly of unknowns, with a few exceptions. Bill Mumy played Teft, one of the teens. The former child actor was best recognized for his role as Will Robinson on TV's "Lost in Space" from 1965 to 1968. In the 1990s, Mumy appeared as a regular character on the science fiction television series "Babylon 5." Another recognizable face in the film was Jesse White, who played the father of one of the boys. White was often seen on TV commercials as the Maytag repairman, "the loneliest man in town."

The title song, "Bless the Beasts and the Children," received an Academy Award nomination. It is performed on the soundtrack by the Carpenters, who also released a single version. It was not among their more successful efforts, peaking at number 67 and charting for eight weeks. The song's composers, Barry DeVorzon and Perry Botkin Jr., released their own version of the tune several years later; it made number 82.

DeVorzon had once headed a group called Barry and the Tamerlanes, whose biggest hit was back in 1963 — "I Wonder What She's Doing Tonight," which climbed to number 21. Together with Botkin, the songwriting, producing, and arranging duo had their most popular recording with 1976's "Nadia's Theme (The Young and the Restless)," which made number eight on the charts. The song was originally written as "Cotton's Dream" for *Bless the Beasts and the Children*, then used as the theme song for the daytime drama whose name appears in its title. It was also the music for the gymnastic routine performed by famed Olympian Nadia Comaneci of Romania, hence its final name change.

LIFE IS WHAT YOU MAKE IT

**Music by Marvin Hamlisch;
lyrics by Johnny Mercer**
From *Kotch*

The film *Kotch* was originally to have a title song. The movie starred Walter Matthau and was directed by his friend (and frequent co-star) Jack Lemmon, making his directoral debut. *Variety* called it "a wow," adding, "He has gotten into every single character with a remarkable objective empathy."

Walter Matthau as Kotcher is stumped by directions on how to assemble a baby's crib in *Kotch*.

When first prepping the film, Lemmon called composer Marvin Hamlisch, who was doing the score, and told him the good news. "Sammy Cahn gets a picture with a great title like *Three Coins in the Fountain*," moaned Hamlisch in his autobiography, *The Way I Was*. "Sammy Fain gets *Love Is a Many Splendored Thing*. I get *Kotch*. Believe me, there's not much you can rhyme with 'kotch,' and what you can rhyme with it is problematic." Eventually, Johnny Mercer was brought on board to create lyrics to a general tune, rather than to a true title song.

The result of this pairing was "Life Is What You Make It." Hamlisch, only 27 at the time, was naturally in awe of Mercer, who was entering his fifth decade as a writer of pop tunes and Academy Award winners. But Hamlisch found his new lyricist easy to work with. The composer presented Mercer with a tape of the melody. Five days later, he got a call from Mercer asking him to take a look at what he'd done. "And what he had done," wrote the obviously awed Hamlisch, "which no other lyricist I ever worked with before had ever done, was to come up with five — count 'em, five — different sets of lyrics; five complete versions of the song, each perfectly married to the melody." Mercer told Hamlisch to take whatever he wanted, to mix and match the lyrics any way he wished. "No vanity, take what you like," Hamlisch continued. "I cannot tell you how disarming it is to be confronted with such a total absence of ego in the music field. I was dumbfounded."

"Life Is What You Make It" was nominated for an Academy Award, and although it lost to the "Theme from *Shaft*," it won the Golden Globe Award that year for Best Original Song from a Film.

Matthau, the film's star, seemed to have been born old. At least, he was born to play old men. In *Kotch*, Matthau is supposed to be a septuagenarian whose kids want to send him off to the old folks home. But Kotch is a shrewd, independent, strong-minded sort who'll have none of it. He leaves his son's household and heads northwest, not for an ice floe but for adventure. Matthau was nominated for the Best Actor Oscar for his efforts. (The film was also nominated for Best Sound and Best Film Editing.)

Matthau and Lemmon appeared in numerous pictures together over the course of more than a quarter-century. They first worked together in *The Fortune Cookie* (1966) and have been a comedy acting team ever since. They're probably best known for the disparate characters they played in *The Odd Couple* (1968). In 1993, after a lengthy period of working on separate projects, the pair reunited for *Grumpy Old Men*, in which both set their sights on Ann-Margret.

1972

THE MORNING AFTER

Music and lyrics by Al Kasha and Joel Hirschhorn
From *The Poseidon Adventure*

In the midst of New Year's revelry, the luxury liner *S.S. Poseidon* is capsized by a 90-foot tidal wave. Obviously, the party's over, at least for the unfortunate passengers. For the audience, however, the fun was just beginning.

So was the Disaster Decade. In the 1970s, it seemed, everyone got off on watching everyone else manage to wriggle out of dangerous situations. Large all-star casts were back in vogue for these disaster films. *The Poseidon Adventure*'s passenger list was a precursor of things to come — many of these disaster-prone actors would pop up in future on-screen calamities. It's no wonder the *Poseidon* started to sink, what with all of the celebrities on board: Gene Hackman, Ernest Borgnine, Red Buttons, Shelley Winters, Stella Stevens, Carol Lynley, Jack Albertson, Roddy McDowall, Leslie Nielsen, and Pamela Sue Martin, among others.

The premise was more or less a modern-day hybrid of *The Bridge at San Luis Rey* and *Ship of Fools*, with all the technical wizardry that Tinseltown could muster adding to the excitement. Audiences gobbled it up. When the dust settled, 20th Century-Fox found that the picture had sailed away with $42 million in rentals.

The theme from *Poseidon*, "The Morning After," received the 1972 Oscar for Best Song, surprising and thrilling its young composers. Al Kasha recalled in the book *60 Years of the Oscar*, by Robert Osborne, "My father was a barber, and I lived over a store in Brooklyn. The possibility of winning an award like this seemed an impossible dream. It was an overwhelming feeling that night when my name was announced. I remembered the days over that store and said to myself, 'This can't be happening to Al Kasha!' " (Kasha and his partner Joel Hirschhorn would win Best Song

Shelley Winters gets a lift from Gene Hackman as he rescues her in *The Poseidon Adventure*.

BEN

Music by Walter Scharf; lyrics by Don Black
From *Ben*

"Ben" proved that if a song was beautiful enough, with a great melody, lyrics, and performance, it didn't matter what the song was about. "Ben" may have sounded like a love song, with its lyric about how "the two of us need look no more . . . we've both found what we've been looking for," but make no mistake. This was a love song about a boy and his beloved . . . rat.

Ben, the title rat from the movie *Ben*, was the object of a 10-year-old boy's affection. It was a sequel to the previous year's not-so-ratty hit, *Willard* (which had placed eighth in rental films of 1971, with a take of $8.2 million). *Ben* opens only minutes after Willard, the man who trained rats in the original, has been killed off by his beloved rodents. Ben was the rat "heavy" of the original film, now given his own starring vehicle in the new chiller. Wrote *Variety*: "This is not for expectant mothers."

In the film, the rat's young pal Danny Garrison (Lee Harcourt Montgomery) sits at the piano and sings the ode to his buddy. The song was recorded by Michael Jackson, formerly the cute kid in the middle of the Jackson Five. It was his first solo recording and proved a breakthrough song for him. "Ben" was released in August, 1972, and by mid-October it was ranked Number One on the *Billboard* charts. It stayed on the charts for 16 weeks.

The selection of Michael Jackson was made by the song's lyricist, Don Black, who knew that Jackson, then age 13, was especially fond of critters. "He's quite an animal lover — very sensitive, you know. He enjoys anything that crawls or flies," Black revealed to author Fred Bronson in *The Billboard Book of Number One Hits*. In later years, after Jackson became a multi-multi-millionaire, he demonstrated this affection for animals by installing his own petting zoo of exotic animals in one of his California homes and, amidst a flurry of controversy, adopting a pet baby chimpanzee, Bubbles.

"Ben" received an Academy Award nomination for Best Song and was performed at the Oscar ceremonies by Jackson himself. It was one of five nominations Don Black received during his career. He had won the Oscar for "Born Free" (see page 184) and had also been a nominee for "True Grit" (see page 200), "Wherever Love Takes Me" (see page 223), and "Come to Me." He also wrote a

Oscars again in 1974, for "We May Never Love Like This Again" — see page 220).

Following its success at the Academy Awards, "The Morning After" was released as a single, launching the career of singer Maureen McGovern and becoming a huge hit. It peaked at Number One, where it stayed for two weeks in August, 1973, becoming the first Academy Award–winning song to reach Number One *after* winning the Oscar. The song also went gold, selling over a million copies.

Although *The Poseidon Adventure* would win no other Oscars, it was nominated for seven more: Best Supporting Actress (Shelley Winters), Best Cinematography, Best Art Direction–Set Decoration, Best Sound, Best Original Dramatic Score (John Williams), Best Film Editing, and Best Costume Design. The category of Best Special Visual Effects (for which *Poseidon* would have been a shoo-in) was dropped in 1972, but the film was presented with a "Special Achievement Award" for visual effects.

number of hit songs from other films, including "To Sir with Love," "Diamonds Are Forever," "Thunderball," and "The Man with the Golden Gun." The native Londoner wrote several tunes for Jackson following the success with "Ben," and he also wrote for Smokey Robinson.

The creator of the music for "Ben," Walter Scharf, was a prominent composer who worked with many well-known motion picture lyricists, including Sammy Cahn and Ned Washington. He scored a number of motion pictures and television series, and received four Emmy Awards, a Grammy, and a Golden Globe during the course of his career. The 1972 Golden Globe was for "Ben," which received the award from the Hollywood Foreign Press Association for Best Original Song from a Film.

COME FOLLOW, FOLLOW ME

Music by Fred Karlin; lyrics by Marsha Karlin
From The Little Ark

Based on Jan de Hartog's novel about the disastrous 1953 floods in Holland, *The Little Ark* told the story of two young children, a Dutch boy and an Indonesian girl, who are refugees from the disaster. The pair, along with their assorted animals, are rescued by a compassionate sea captain, played by Israeli actor/singer Theodore Bikel, as they set out on a series of adventures before returning safely home.

The low-budget picture was filmed on location in Holland, with a mostly Dutch cast. It was produced by Robert Radnitz, who had done the successful children's film *A Dog of Flanders* (1960), also starring Bikel. Radnitz had been labeled a producer of kiddie fare, and on the surface the G-rated *The Little Ark* seemed part of that genre. But the producer insisted he made films for a family audience.

Reviews were mixed. Arthur Knight, writing in the *Saturday Review*, commented: "Radnitz has learned how to make children stay believably childlike, with the result that both children and adults can identify with his characters . . . *The Little Ark* [is] probably his best film to date. " *Variety* echoed those sentiments, proclaiming the picture "blessed with a moving story . . . A sometimes exciting, always interesting screen narrative of events . . . well told and with a satisfactory finale." But the *Los Angeles Times* was disappointed, calling The

Little Ark "a curiously plodding, uninvolving film . . . A quest without real crisis or focus . . . The kids are often as wooden as their shoes." And the critic for the *San Francisco Chronicle* opined, "Humor, suspense and excitement are missing."

Much ado was made about the four pets who figured prominently in the film's story. The menagerie consisted of a dog, cat, rabbit, and rooster. They were all trained by Frank Weatherwax, a member of the legendary Weatherwax dynasty, a Hollywood family whose main claim to fame has always been as the trainers of the original and all eight subsequent Lassies for the movies and television.

The film's theme song, "Come Follow, Follow Me," received an Academy Award nomination for Best Song. The moving song was composed by Fred Karlin, with lyrics by his wife, Marsha (a.k.a. Meg Karlin, a.k.a. Tylwyth Kymry). Karlin was born in Chicago in 1936 and enjoyed an extensive career as a composer for film and TV. In 1967 he scored the movie *Up the Down Staircase*; in 1969, *The Sterile Cuckoo* (receiving an Academy Award nomination for "Come Saturday Morning" for Best Song — see page 198). In 1970, Karlin won the Best Song Oscar for the song "For All We Know" from the movie *Lovers and Other Strangers*. He also wrote scores for *Westworld* and TV's *The Autobiography of Miss Jane Pittman*, for which he received a Best Score Emmy.

MARMALADE, MOLASSES AND HONEY

Music by Maurice Jarre;
lyrics by Marilyn and Alan Bergman
From The Life and Times of Judge Roy Bean

The old Hollywood adage about never working with children or animals because they'll steal the scene every time was put to the test in *The Life and Times of Judge Roy Bean*. The film was directed by John Huston, a bear of a man who had directed and acted in many westerns. But in this case it was a bear of a bear — one Bruno the Bear, by name — who steals the show right out from under Paul Newman and Victoria Principal. The furry, cuddly ursine gently takes cigars from mouths, guzzles beer, and is prominently featured in the movie's primary musical interlude, "Marmalade, Molasses and Honey."

Paul Newman plays the title role in *The Life and Times of Judge Roy Bean.*

The Life and Times of Judge Roy Bean was a blending of fact and fiction about the legendary Judge Bean, a real person who lived in a Texas town named after the famous English actress Lily Langtry (played by Ava Gardner). Although they never met, Langtry and Bean were pen pals, at least in this version. As the liner notes on the original Columbia Records soundtrack Perkins, Tab Hunter, Stacy Keach, Roddy McDowall, Jacqueline Bisset, Ned Beatty, and even the director himself all appeared. Huston played Grizzly Adams, a character who was later spun off into a movie (*The Life and Times of Grizzly Adams,* 1976) and a TV show, both starring Dan Haggerty as the mountain man who befriends a bear.

The Huston family was a famous Hollywood dynasty. John was the son of famed director Walter Huston and the father of actress Anjelica Huston. John had several careers — as screenwriter, actor, and director. Among his best known directorial efforts were *The Maltese Falcon* (1941), *Key Largo* (1948), *The Treasure of Sierra Madre* (1948), *Casino Royale* (1967), and *Prizzi's Honor* (1985), for which his daughter Anjelica won a Best Supporting Actress Oscar. He also co-wrote most of these pictures and occasionally did a cameo in them as well. He died in 1987 after directing his final film, a screen treatment of James Joyce's *The Dead.*

STRANGE ARE THE WAYS OF LOVE

Music by Sammy Fain;
lyrics by Paul Francis Webster
From *The Stepmother*

The Academy Award–nominated song was written by the composer of the film's score, Maurice Jarre, with lyrics by the Oscar-winning husband-and-wife team of Marilyn and Alan Bergman (for "Windmills of Your Mind" and "The Way We Were" — see pages 193 and 215, respectively). The waltz-tempoed "Marmalade" is sung by Andy Williams over scenes of Newman and Principal playing with Bruno on swings and a see-saw, as well as bathing the creature. The scene for this number, and for several other light-hearted moments in the film, is reminiscent of another of Newman's western successes, *Butch Cassidy and the Sundance Kid.* But it is the bear's scene all the way. Sadly, the bear is later killed (in the story, not in real life) protecting the couple.

With advertising catchlines like "She forced her husband's son to commit the ultimate sin! . . . *The Stepmother* . . . It's a family affair," Crown International, an independent film company noted for its quickies and cheapies, hoped to make a few bucks with their latest offering. But the 1972 picture has all but disappeared from the annals of Hollywood. This tale of lust, murder, incest, wealth, and greed among jet-setters should have had a lot going for it, but somehow it never got off the ground.

The film starred Alejandro Rey as an architect on the brink of financial ruin who discovers his wife (played by Katherine Justice) being raped by his wealthy client. They argue, and the client is accidentally killed in a fall. Rey buries the body in a secluded spot, then witnesses a man murder his girlfriend and tries to pin both killings on this young man. Later, Rey thinks his wife is having an affair with his business partner, played by Larry Linville (Major Frank Burns of TV's "M*A*S*H"). Linville accidentally falls to *his* death during an argument with Rey. Moral: If you're accident-prone, don't befriend Rey.

But there's more. Rey's son by a former marriage seduces Rey's current wife, and Rey attempts to do them both in when a police inspector, who has been dogging him throughout the picture, shows up "in the nick of time."

The film, which was written, produced, and directed by Hikmet Avedis, failed miserably at the box office and has not been seen on television in recent years; as of late 1994, it also was yet to be released on home video. Although it cost under $1 million to make, it failed to earn back its expenses.

Now the good news. Academy Award–winning songwriters Sammy Fain and Paul Francis Webster were tapped to create a mood-setting song for the film. The tune they created, "Strange Are the Ways of Love," received a nomination from the Academy for Best Song. It was one of 10 nominations Fain would receive in his career. His first was in 1937, for "That Old Feeling" (see page 15) and his last was 40 years later, in 1977, for "Someone's Waiting for You" (see page 236). He won the Oscar for "Secret Love" in 1953 (see page 123) and for "Love Is a Many-Splendored Thing" in 1955 (see page 132), both of which he co-wrote with Webster, who received 16 nominations during his extensive motion picture songwriting career.

1973
THE WAY WE WERE

Music by Marvin Hamlisch;
lyrics by Alan and Marilyn Bergman
From *The Way We Were*

"And the winner is — Marvin Hamlisch . . . !"
  "And the winner is — Marvin Hamlisch . . . !"
   "And the winner is — Marvin Hamlisch . . . !"

For Hamlisch, this was the night of Oscar, Oscar, Oscar. No sooner did the composer bound onto the stage and take his bows than he seemed to be rising once again from his seat to claim yet another statuette. The 29-year-old *wunderkind*, who had been crushed two years earlier when he didn't win the Best Song award for "Life Is What You Make It" (see page 210), now took the night and made it his own.

The tune was the title song from the box office hit *The Way We Were*, starring Barbra Streisand and Robert Redford as an unlikely pair of lovers straight out of central casting. She was the most popular female movie star, he the most popular male — what better reason to bring them together? The film was not a musical, however, but a straight acting job for Streisand, who had last sung a Best Song nominee in *Funny Girl* (see page 195).

Director Sydney Pollack hired Hamlisch to create a melody to underscore a scene in the film. Hamlisch was asked to write a tune in a minor key, but chose to write in the major. "If I'd written in a minor mode, it might have told you too much in advance that Streisand and Redford were never going to get together," he said in the book *The Top Ten*, by Gary Theroux and Bob Gilbert. Instead he created "a melody that was sad, but also had a great deal of hope in it."

At first Barbra didn't want to record it, fearing it might detract from her impact as an actress. But six months later, while the film was still being edited, she felt that it would help draw some attention away from Redford, who seemed to be running away with the picture, and she agreed to sing the theme. The song was recorded for release as a single in November, 1973, and was not an instant hit. DJs hesitated to play it because it wasn't rock. Slowly, however, the song took off, and by the following February, it had become Streisand's first chart-topper, remaining at Number One for three weeks and charting for 23. It received the *Billboard* award as the Top Pop Single of 1974, a Grammy as Song of the Year, and the Academy Award for Best Song.

The song's wistful melody, coupled with a heavy lacing of nostalgia with beautiful, poetic lyrics by the Bergmans, Alan and Marilyn, saw Hamlisch on stage for the third time Oscar night. Earlier in the evening, he'd received the Oscar for Best Song Score for *The Sting*. Next, he was announced as winner of the trophy for Best Dramatic Score for *The Way We Were*. "What can I tell you?" he cracked. "I'd like to thank the makers of Maalox for making all this possible." But the best

The way they were — Robert Redford and Barbra Streisand star in the classic romance, *The Way We Were*. The Oscar-winning theme song has become a classic too.

was yet to come. Streisand had begged off singing the nominated tune, claiming she was being honored for her acting that night (she was nominated as Best Actress), not her singing, so Peggy Lee crooned "The Way We Were." Then Burt Bacharach and Ann-Margret announced that Hamlisch had won his third Oscar of the evening. This time, the Bergmans raced to the stage first, with Marilyn telling the audience, "Marvin, it's almost obscene how many of those you have." For his part, Hamlisch, who by this point in the proceedings was a familiar face, told his assembled peers in the audience, "I think we can talk to each other as friends."

The Way We Were received a total of six Academy Award nominations. In addition to the two received by Hamlisch, it was nominated for Best Actress (Streisand), Best Cinematography, Best Art Direction–Set Decoration, and Best Costume Design.

In 1994, the readers of *People* magazine voted for their favorite song of the past 20 years. And the winner still is . . ."The Way We Were" (runner up: Whitney Houston's "I Will Always Love You"). And that same year, Hamlisch, now a mature Oscar-, Grammy- Tony-winning composer, was hired by the Pittsburgh Symphony Orchestra as its pops conductor, signing a two year contract in 1994. He also conducted the 64-piece orchestra for his old friend Barbra Streisand (they first worked together when he was 19 years old, playing

rehearsal piano for *Funny Girl* on Broadway) on her 1994 concert tour of England and the United States.

ALL THAT LOVE WENT TO WASTE

Music by George Barrie; lyrics by Sammy Cahn
From *A Touch of Class*

Melvin Frank co-wrote many of the classic Hollywood comedies of the 1940s and 1950s, including (with Norman Panama) some of the famous Bob Hope–Bing Crosby–Dorothy Lamour *Road* pictures, as well as a number of films for Danny Kaye. In 1973, he attempted to recapture some of that mirth with a romantic comedy called *A Touch of Class,* a film he produced, directed, and co-scripted (with Jack Rose).

The movie starred George Segal as a handsome, philandering American insurance company executive who has secret rendezvous with a divorcée–London fashion designer, played by Glenda Jackson. He has designs on her, and off they fly for a whirlwind week in Málaga, Spain. It is at this point that the screwball comedy sequences abound: The hotel has lost Segal's reservations, his rented car gives him endless problems, he sprains his back in bed. Nevertheless, they consummate the relationship, and by the time they return home, the affair is in full swing. Segal then sails the rough seas between his wife and his mistress, rushing at one point from a concert to Jackson's bed and back to his wife's side at the concert all in the span of time it takes to play Beethoven's Seventh.

Critics howled their approval of this refreshing comedy, *Time* magazine calling Segal "by far the most deft American actor of light comedy" and praising Jackson, whose "virtuosity and energy dazzle. Together they make an elegant pair of amorous antagonists, their smooth skills bringing great fun and fresh surprise." *Variety* proclaimed *A Touch of Class* "one howl of a picture for all age groups."

The movie had a handful of songs by George Barrie, then head of Fabergé, Inc., the company that manufactured a line of cosmetics and toiletries, including Brut cologne for men. Barrie was also president of Brut Productions, which produced *A Touch of Class* (the film was released by Avco Embassy). A self-taught musician (he played guitar, banjo, piano, clarinet, and saxophone), Barrie's first love was composing, and together with partner Sammy Cahn he wrote a title song, "A Touch of Class," and the tune that won an Oscar nomination, "All That Love Went to Waste." It is sung in the movie by Madeline Bell over a final scene with Segal and Jackson.

A Touch of Class received four Oscar nominations — Best Picture, Best Actress (Jackson, who won), Best Story and Screenplay Based on Factual Material or Material Not Previously Published or Produced, and Best Song.

LIVE AND LET DIE

Music and lyrics by Paul and Linda McCartney
From *Live and Let Die*

The James Bond franchise was alive and well in the 1970s, with some drastic changes. In the early '60s, it was decided to produce a series of films based on Ian Fleming's books about the spy who loved his martinis shaken, not stirred. The first few films, with the dashing Sean Connery cast as 007, were fairly true to Fleming's novels. But the genre began going south with the production of *Casino Royale* (see page 191) and Connery's departure. By 1973, it was time to post a new Bond.

Burt Reynolds's name had always been on the "A" list, but producer Albert "Cubby" Broccoli continued to insist that the character be played by an Englishman. During the casting of the first film, *Dr. No*, one name kept surfacing: Roger Moore. Suddenly this also-ran became the front-runner, and when the dust had settled, he found himself in James Bond-age. His approach to the character was entirely different from Connery's — light-hearted, less macho, more comedic. Audiences, however, had no trouble adapting to him, and so the world was once again safe for James Bond movies.

Live and Let Die, the eighth Bond movie and the first one starring Moore, was released in the summer of 1973 and was an instant hit. With the scripts departing more and Moore from the original Fleming stories, the writers had taken greater leeway, tailoring their story to fit Moore's style. And besides, by this time several elements were overdue for updating — the original Fleming novelization of *Live and Let Die* had been written in 1954 and was loaded with stereotypes about blacks, the story's main villains. The '70s were a sensitive time in the emergence of modern black culture, with such films such *Shaft, Lady Sings the Blues,* and *Sounder* all creating a boom in black films. Although *Live and Let Die* came under criticism as possible "blaxploitation," the nervous producers pointed out that the movie was merely following the original Fleming storyline.

The producers need not have worried. Thanks to rapid word-of-mouth during its summer release, *Live and Let Die* did excellent box office, taking in $16.9 million in North American rentals and ranking number eight for the year. Audiences eagerly embraced Moore as the new Bond. Cast opposite him was a young Jane Seymour as the latest "Bond girl," Solitaire. (She would later star in the successful CBS television series "Dr. Quinn, Medicine Woman" in the 1990s.)

The film made extensive use of the title song by Paul and Linda McCartney. "Live and Let Die" was their first venture into the realm of motion picture title songwriting. John Barry had previously been in charge of most of the Bond movie scores, but for *Live and Let Die* that task was assumed by George Martin, who had produced many of the Beatles' records. He drafted former Beatle Paul and his wife Linda to co-write the tune, performed by their group, Wings. They received their first and only Academy Award nomination for Best Song.

"Live and Let Die" also became a best-selling record; it reached number two on the *Billboard* charts, holding that position for three weeks, charting for 14, and earning a gold record for certified sales of over a million copies.

LOVE

Music by George Bruns;
lyrics by Floyd Huddleston
From *Robin Hood*

Walt Disney Productions spent four years prepping its animated version of *Robin Hood*, a film in the tradition started by the studio's late founder. Disney had done a live-acted version of the familiar Robin Hood legend back in 1952, called *The Story of Robin Hood and His Merrie Men*, starring Englishman Richard Todd. But to give the story a new twist, the artists at Disney decided to make all of the characters animals. Robin and Marian, for instance, were depicted as foxes, Little John was a bear, the evil Prince John was a tiger, his chief hench-

man (obviously cast to type) was a snake, and the narrator/balladeer, Allan-a-Dale, was a rooster.

The voices were somewhat familiar, though. Phil Harris (a Disney regular) voiced Little John; Andy Devine was Friar Tuck; Peter Ustinov played Prince John; Terry-Thomas was Sir Hiss; Pat Buttram (another frequent Disney voice-over actor) spoke the part of the Sheriff, Brian Bedford did Robin, and Monica Evans was Marian.

Roger Miller, as Allan-a-Dale, narrated and sang several songs of his own design: "Oo-de-Lally," a tune based on one of Robin's favorite sayings, "Whistle Stop," a hum-along whistling tune, and "Not in Nottingham," a ballad about the overtaxed peasants. Musical director George Bruns wrote "The Phony King of England" (with lyrics by Johnny Mercer) and "Love," with lyrics by Floyd Huddleston.

"Love" was sung by Nancy Adams, in a scene in which Robin and Maid Marian waltz through the forest paw-in-paw. The song received an Academy Award nomination, but was never successful as a single. At the awards ceremony the following spring, "Love" was performed by 10-year-old child actress Jodie Foster and young Johnny Whitaker (former child star of TV's "Family Affair" from 1969 to 1971).

Composer George Bruns had joined the Walt Disney studio in 1953 and spent more than 20 years on the studio's music payroll. The musician who had once been involved with the "Mr. Magoo" cartoon series created the theme song for the 1950s' most popular Disney TV character, Davy Crockett, and Bruns's ubiquitous "Ballad of Davy Crockett" was one of the most frequently heard tunes of the decade. In 1959, Walt assigned Bruns to adapt the score of Tchaikovsky's *Sleeping Beauty* ballet for his latest animated screen venture. In 1961, Disney produced his first totally live-action musical, *Babes in Toyland*, to showcase his favorite Mouseketeer, Annette Funicello. Bruns was again tapped to turn out 11 original songs (with lyricist Mel Leven) for the film, whose score was nominated for an Oscar. In 1963, Bruns scored the Disney film *The Sword in the Stone* (with songs by the Sherman Brothers), and again received an Oscar nomination.

Walt Disney's *Robin Hood* received critical acclaim for its innovative look at the time-honored tale. Kids ate it up, and many adults enjoyed this fanciful retelling, making it one of the most successful pictures of 1973, taking in $17.1 in rentals, ranking number seven among films released that year.

Scene from the Walt Disney animated cartoon feature *Robin Hood*.

(YOU'RE SO) NICE TO BE AROUND

Music by John Williams; lyrics by Paul Williams
From *Cinderella Liberty*

Yet another movie in the "prostitute with a heart of gold" genre, *Cinderella Liberty* was blessed with an outstanding cast, including James Caan as the sailor on leave (the title refers to his shore leave being cut short at midnight), Marsha Mason as the hooker Maggie, and Eli Wallach as Caan's former boot camp drill instructor. The picture also benefited from a talented producer/director and a reputable composer.

Mark Rydell produced and directed *Cinderella Liberty,* which was written for the screen by Darryl Ponicsan, adapted from his novel of the same title. The movie was filmed entirely on location in Seattle, with the city's beauty and starker aspects adding to the ambiance. Rydell had directed his first feature in 1966, a film called *The Fox,* starring Sandy Dennis. His other pictures include *The Cowboys* (1972), starring John Wayne; *On Golden Pond* (1981), starring Henry Fonda, Katharine Hepburn, and Jane Fonda; *The River* (1984), starring Sissy Spacek and Mel Gibson; and *For the Boys* (1991), starring Bette Midler.

Composer John Williams wrote the score for *Cinderella Liberty.* Early in his directorial career, Rydell had hired Williams to score many of his pictures. Williams, who studied music at Julliard, had been composing for films and TV since the early '60s. (Little-remembered fact: He wrote the theme to TV's "Lost in Space," credited to "Johnny" Williams.) Today he has attained superstar status, on every producer's very expensive "A" list and the composer of choice for practically every Steven Spielberg film since 1975's *Jaws,* including *Close Encounters of the Third Kind* (1977), *E.T.: The Extraterrestrial* (1982), *Jurassic Park* (1993), and *Schindler's List* (1993). It should come as no surprise that Williams's home is decorated with wall-to-wall Oscars for Best Scores.

Rydell decided to incorporate two songs into *Cinderella Liberty,* and he and John Williams brought in lyricist Paul Williams. Paul's hits included "We've Only Just Begun" and "Rainy Days and Mondays," for the Carpenters, plus "Old Fashioned Love Song" and "Let Me Be the One." He would receive numerous Oscar nominations in years to follow, winning in 1976 for "Evergreen," co-written with Barbra Streisand (see page 228). For *Cinderella Liberty,* John and Paul

James Caan and Marsha Mason stroll along Seattle's waterfront district in *Cinderella Liberty.*

Williams (no relation) wrote two songs, "Wednesday Special" and "(You're So) Nice to Be Around," the latter of which received a Best Song nomination from the Academy. (*Really* little-remembered, and quite bizarre, fact: Telly Savalas performed the song at the Academy Awards ceremony.)

The love ballad is played in the background throughout the film by the Belgian harmonica wizard Toots Thielemans. The tune is also sung by Paul Williams, a singer and actor as well as a composer, under the scene just after Caan and Mason's break-up (they reunite later on). The song was also recorded by Maureen McGovern, although it never became a hit.

Cinderella Liberty was nominated for two additional Academy Awards: Mason was a nominee for Best Actress and John Williams received a nomination for Best Original Dramatic Score.

1974

WE MAY NEVER LOVE LIKE THIS AGAIN

Music and lyrics by Al Kasha and Joel Hirschhorn
From *The Towering Inferno*

The Towering Inferno's title said it all: This was a disaster movie about fire atop a skyscraper — 'nuff said.

Little had changed since the last disaster blockbuster two years earlier, *The Poseidon Adventure*. The producer, Irwin Allen, was once again in charge behind the scenes, and the setting had shifted only slightly, with characters trapped on a sinking ship being replaced by characters trapped in a burning building. The formula, however, was still intact: a life-or-death saga of people thrown together and faced with adversity, accompanied by the best special effects money could buy.

Among those fighting for their lives this time were Steve McQueen, Paul Newman, William Holden, Faye Dunaway, Fred Astaire (in a totally serious role — no

tap-dancing his way out of this one), Richard Chamberlain, Robert Vaughn, Robert Wagner, O.J. Simpson, and dozens more.

Although the film was not intended as a comedy, a series of weakly scripted dialogue scenes threatened to inadvertently make it one (Susan Flannery, lover and secretary to Robert Wagner, amidst unseen flames after their post-coital passion: "Did you leave a cigarette burning?"). One unintentional chuckle might have come from the film's love theme, if the title were to be taken literally. Al Kasha and Joel Hirschhorn, Academy Award winners for "The Morning After" from *The Poseidon Adventure* two years before (see page 211) were again tapped to create a musical theme. This time they came up with "We May Never Love Like This Again," and it was sung, as was their effort on the previous film, by Maureen McGovern. She warbles the tune on camera during a ballroom scene at the beginning of the film. Her recording of the song was released in January, 1975, about six weeks after the film's debut, but reached only the number 83 position.

At Oscar time, Kasha and Hirschhorn were again awarded the statuette for Best Song. All of the nominated tunes that year were performed onstage at the awards ceremony by the same three singers, alone or in combination: Aretha Franklin, Jack Jones, and Frankie Laine. The three pooled their talents to sing "We May Never Love Like This Again."

Paul Newman and Steve McQueen get ready to save the day in *The Towering Inferno*.

The *Towering Inferno* received eight nominations and three wins. In addition to Best Song, the film won for Best Cinematography and Best Film Editing. Other nominations were for Best Picture, Best Supporting Actor (Astaire), Best Art Direction–Set Decoration, Best Sound, and Best Original Dramatic Score (John Williams).

BENJI'S THEME (I FEEL LOVE)

Music by Euel Box; lyrics by Betty Box
From *Benji*

Benji was an impostor. The beloved dog who starred in several movies and television series, many with some variation of his name in the title, was actually a dog named Higgins. Yet somehow, this seems appropriate for Hollywood, where nothing is as it appears. Lassie, after all, had always been played by a female impersonator — all of the actual Lassies have been males. Still, it's just a bit disillusioning to learn that Benji wasn't really Benji.

Animal trainer Frank Inn, the story goes, rescued Benji, er, Higgins from the pound just moments before the all-American breed (read: mutt) was to be sent to that big fire hydrant in the sky. By the time he became the star of *Benji*, Higgins was already a TV veteran, having appeared as a regular on "Petticoat Junction."

This warm family film was really one man's labor of love. The movie was written, produced, and directed by Joe Camp, who took his cast of humans (Peter Breck, Frances Bavier, Edgar Buchanan, Deborah Walley, and Mark Slade) to Dallas to film the simple story of how a dog rescues a brother and sister from three youthful kidnappers and ends up becoming an adopted family pet. But this film was not really about people; it was Benji's from the get-go.

Naturally, Benji needed his own special theme music. The film's scorer, Euel Box, along with his wife/lyricist Betty Box, created a tune just for the canine star. "Benji's Theme (I Feel Love)" was sung on the soundtrack by Charlie Rich, backed by a chorus of children's voices, under the opening credits (and again at the film's closing), as the unleashed Benji, that happy-go-lucky dog about town, roams freely through fields and down a busy street. This is his daily beat, and the camera follows him at his eye level, thanks to the

Benji, the irresistible mutt and star of *Benji*.

clever cinematography of Don Reddy. Much of the film is shot from about 18 inches above the ground — a sort of Benji's-eye view.

The Boxes received an Academy Award nomination for "Benji's Theme (I Feel Love)." Euel Box had worked with many top recording artists, conducting for such singers as Stevie Wonder, Boz Scaggs, Glen Campbell, Lou Rawls, Charlie Rich, and Chet Atkins. His film credits include work for *Hawmps!* (1976), *For the Love of Benji* (1977), *Double McGuffin* (1979), and *Oh, Heavenly Dog!* (1980), all of which involved Camp (and, in several cases, Benji) to some degree. Although "Benji's Theme" didn't win the Oscar for which it was nominated, it did win a Golden Globe for Best Original Song from a Film.

LITTLE PRINCE

**Music by Frederick Loewe;
lyrics by Alan Jay Lerner**
From *The Little Prince*

It was to have been *Camelot* revisited. A happy reunion between the composers of the fantasy musical that a decade earlier had captured the hearts of theatergoers (and, in 1967, filmgoers) with its perfect blending of story, characterization, and soaring score. The songwriters were Lerner and Loewe, whose portfolio also included *My Fair Lady* and *Gigi* (see page 147). They had gone their separate ways following the completion of *Camelot* after bitter disputes saw the two vowing never to work together again. Lyricist Alan Jay Lerner then went on to write with other composers, while Frederick Loewe went into virtual retirement, dividing his time between Palm Springs, New York, and the Riviera.

Then, in 1971, Lerner was tapped to write the script for a movie to be based on Antoine de Saint-Exupéry's children's classic, *The Little Prince.* It was to be a musical, produced and directed by Stanley Donen, the British director whose credits included *Charade* (1963, see page 172) and *Two for the Road* (1967). Lerner was also signed to write the lyrics. He was elated at the thought of doing a film again, rather than a play. "Writing a film does not have the sustained rigor of writing a play," he wrote in his autobiography, *The Street Where I Live.* "There are no endless days of auditioning, no agonizing weeks on the road." And he knew just who he wanted for the composer. He sent a copy of his screenplay to his old partner, Frederick Loewe, hoping they could mend their fences. "He called me, filled with his old excitement," said Lerner. "Discarding the vows and resolutions, he decided to have one last fling, and we went to work again. Eleven years slipped away in a minute, and it was 'pre-*Camelot*' again. He wrote the most beautiful score, filled with melody and bubbling with the innocence of youth. Alas, it never was heard on the screen as he had composed it." Lerner blamed director Donen for changing "every tempo, delet[ing] musical phrases at will and distort[ing] the intention of every song until the entire score was unrecognizable."

The picture was a major bomb. The story was fairly faithful to the book, about a young prince from a distant planet who meets a pilot who confronts his own innocence in the Sahara. Even the cherubic six-year-old Steven Warner, who played the title role, couldn't save it. Neither could big names Richard Kiley (famed for being the *Man of La Mancha* on Broadway), Bob Fosse, the famed actor-director-choreographer, as the Snake, or Gene Wilder, as the Fox. Most critics bashed it soundly, reserving much of their venom for the Lerner-Loewe music. "Alan Jay Lerner's adaptation is flat and his lyrics are unmemorable, as are Frederick Loewe's melodies," wrote *Variety,* while the more lenient critic for *Time* magazine wrote, "The music misses the simple, rhapsodic melancholy Saint-Exupéry achieved in his prose, but it excels at capturing the pilot's wistfulness, the Little Prince's spirit and their joy in finding each other."

Lerner and Loewe excelled at capturing the attention of the Motion Picture Academy, if not the ticket-buying audience. At Oscar time, they were honored with two nominations — one for the title song, "Little Prince," and another for Best Original Song Score and/or Adaptation. The nominated tune, "Little Prince," is a sweet lullaby sung by Richard Kiley to the little boy, but unfortunately, it had no life of its own outside the context of the film and has been forgotten since its one brief, shining moment in *The Little Prince.*

BLAZING SADDLES

Music by John Morris; lyrics by Mel Brooks
From *Blazing Saddles*

Off the wall, over the top, and out of the Old West, Mel Brooks and company rode their *Blazing Saddles* into the theaters with a style of humor that bordered on the insane. *Blazing Saddles* was Mel's tribute to and send-up of the western. Loaded with puns and inside jokes, there was no stopping this babbling Brooks film. And who would want to? With a script co-written by Brooks and a committee — Norman Steinberg, Andrew Bergman, Richard Pryor, and Alan Uger — this picture burned up the box office and became the number two movie of the year, with a take of $47.8 million in North American rentals.

Brooks's touch was everywhere. Brooks himself was everywhere — he even shows up as a Yiddish-spouting Jewish Indian chief who greets Cleavon Little's wagon train. Many of the other members of the cast were part of what was becoming Brooks's stock company, especially Gene Wilder and Madeline Kahn (who does an uproarious Marlene Dietrich impression).

The fun begins with the opening music, with Frankie Laine doing the title song, lampooning his own western style of singing. The song is so nonsensical, about a man whose blazing saddle became "a torch for justice," that there is no mistaking this for serious drama. The music for "Blazing Saddles" was written by John Morris, who scored the entire film, with lyrics by Brooks. While the pair's intent may have been comedic, the Academy deemed their work to be serious business, giving them an Oscar nomination for their efforts. Laine sang the tune live at the Oscar ceremonies the following spring.

Brooks, who also wrote three other songs for the film — "The French Mistake," "The Ballad of Rock Ridge," and "I'm Tired," the latter sung by Kahn in her best Dietrich voice — was a *shtick*ler for sight gags, as in the scene where a man KOs a horse with one punch. Or the film's ending, in which the entire cast, engaged in a classic western brawl, breaks the "fourth wall" right into the next soundstage on the Warner Bros. lot, where a Busby Berkeley white tie–and–tails musical is being filmed. After blasting this portion of the picture as the "work of men desperate for an ending," *Time* magazine's reviewer Richard Schickel succumbed. "Goldarned if it doesn't work," he enthused. "Goldarned if the whole fool enterprise is not worth the attention of any moviegoer."

Other critics eagerly bestowed their approval on the iconoclastic Brooks. Peter Schjeldahl of the *New York Times* wrote, "*Blazing Saddles* is an awesomely funny movie . . . Brooks is America's current patron saint of 'going too far,' a manic yok-artist in the checkered tradition of burlesque, the Marx Brothers and *Mad* magazine."

The Brooks/Morris title song received an Oscar nomination. It was not the first time they had worked together. Morris composed the score for all of Brooks's early films, including *The Twelve Chairs* (1970), *Young Frankenstein* (1974), *Silent Movie* (1976), and *High Anxiety* (1977). For TV, he wrote Julia Child's "French Chef" theme and the music for "The Tap Dance Kid," for which he received an Emmy Award for Best Score.

Blazing Saddles received two additional Oscar nominations: Best Supporting Actress (Kahn) and Best Film Editing.

WHEREVER LOVE TAKES ME

**Music by Elmer Bernstein; lyrics by Don Black
From *Gold***

James Bond meets the disaster genre. That was the sort of high concept envisioned for the film *Gold,* based on the novel *Goldmine,* by Wilbur Smith (who wrote the screenplay). It had many of the elements of a James Bond picture, something the producers no doubt were counting on to bring in big bucks at the box office. For starters, there was the movie's star, Roger Moore, who had slipped his bonds for a moment to take the part of the lead, Rod Slater. There was also the film's director, Peter Hunt, a former editing supervisor of the 007 romps, and the director of *On Her Majesty's Secret Service* (the 1969 Bond film starring George Lazenby in his one-time shot at playing JB; it didn't work out, and Lazenby's name is now remembered mostly as the answer to a movie trivia question). And, of course, there was plenty of bed-hopping by Moore with the film's female lead, Susannah York, the restlessly married wife of the main villain.

Like the Bond pictures, there was plenty of action and adventure in the typical good guys–vs.–bad guys scenario. This time the story concerned an evil plan to control the price of the international gold market by flooding one of South Africa's leading gold mines. Moore, tearing himself away from York's bed, naturally manages to foil the nefarious plot in the last reel.

The movie, shot on location in South Africa, took it on the chin for its blatant racism. Noted the *New York Times:* "Moore, standing up to his neck in swirling mineshaft waters, [saves the day] with the help of Simon Sabela, who plays his trusted black friend. Because *Gold* has the social conscience of a dim-witted ostrich, you expect Mr. Moore at any minute to refer to Mr. Sabela as a good darkie." Indeed, *Newsweek* echoed this sentiment, claiming, "Throughout, Hunt adopts the South African view of blacks as poor but happy darkies, making this otherwise witless entertainment something faintly disgusting."

The film had at least one redeeming quality — a score by Elmer Bernstein, the eminent Oscar-winning composer of the score for *Thoroughly Modern Millie* (1967, see page 192). Bernstein, known for his zestful, full-bodied themes, had also composed music for such well-known films as *The Magnificent Seven* (1960), *To Kill a Mockingbird* (1963), *The Great Escape* (1963), and dozens more. He was previously nominated for Best Song Oscars for "My Wishing Doll" from *Hawaii* (see page 187) and the title songs from *True Grit* (see page 200) and *Walk on the Wild Side* (see page 170).

Bernstein, along with British lyricist Don Black, received a nomination for the love theme from *Gold*, "Wherever Love Takes Me." In the movie, it is sung under a flying scene, today reminiscent of the flyover in the 1985 film, *Out of Africa.* Don Black was yet another tie to the James Bond series of movies, having written lyrics to a number of their main themes. He won an Academy Award in 1966 for the title song from *Born Free* (see page 184), with additional nominations for "True Grit" (1969, partnered again with Elmer Bernstein — see page 200), "Ben" (1972, see page 212) and "Come to Me" (1976, see page 229).

I'M EASY

Music and lyrics by Keith Carradine
From *Nashville*

Robert Altman emerged as a serious filmmaker in 1970 with *M*A*S*H*, a black comedy that established his

irreverent style. Although none of his subsequent pictures has ever matched *M*A*S*H*'s success at the box office, he has nonetheless maintained his status as one of America's top directors.

Altman is known for his large casts of celebrity-name players (many of whom he has secured by offering benefits and privileges in lieu of glamorous salaries), used mainly to attract as wide an audience as possible but also to help audiences keep track of his panoply of characters. "When you see Kim Basinger or Tim Robbins [frequent Altman actors], you remember instantly who they're supposed to be," Altman explained in a 1994 *Los Angeles Times* interview.

One of Altman's classic early pictures was Nashville. Set in a world of country music and politics, it was once described by Altman as "my distorted view of American culture." In the film, he draws a comparison between country music stars and politicians. "Our political, our elected officials . . . are also hard to shake once they get up there," he told Tom Wicker of the *New York Times* in 1975. "And their speeches are no different than the country-western songs — each new song doesn't really say anything. And that's pretty much how the thing started — the idea of making that comparison."

Nashville is chock-a-block with stars, so many that they were listed alphabetically in press releases. Among the better-known names: Ned Beatty, Karen Black, Ronee Blakley, Keith Carradine, Geraldine Chaplin, Julie Christie, Shelley Duvall, Henry Gibson, Scott Glenn, Jeff Goldblum, Elliott Gould, Barbara Harris, Lily Tomlin, and Keenan Wynn. The script was written by Altman's close friend Joan Tewkesbury, and with 24

Henry Gibson sings in a scene from *Nashville.*

characters, no one takes center stage for too long in this 159-minute picture.

Since the film was primarily about country music, a large number of songs were featured. Altman chose to have the score made up of songs written for the film by the actors and actresses. Although this did make for a bit of chaos, some good tunes emerged from the film. Karen Black performed "Memphis," Ronee Blakely sang "My Idaho Home," and Richard Baskin and R. Reicheg wrote a song called "For the Sake of the Children." But by far the best of the numbers was "I'm Easy," written and performed by Keith Carradine, a member of the Carradine acting dynasty — son of John, brother of David. "I'm Easy" won the Golden Globe Award in 1976 as Best Original Song from a Film, and also won the Oscar for Best Song. Carradine also rode it to the number 17 position on the pop charts.

Nashville received four additional Oscar nominations: Best Picture, Best Director, and two for Best Supporting Actress (Blakley and Tomlin).

HOW LUCKY CAN YOU GET?

Music and lyrics by Fred Ebb and John Kander
From *Funny Lady*

In 1975, Barbra Streisand returned to her roots. The *Funny Girl* grew up to become a *Funny Lady*. Little else was new in the continuing saga of the life of comedienne Fanny Brice, radio's "Baby Snooks." The new film found her still having husband troubles — this time it's Billy Rose (played by James Caan), who gets the Mr. Brice treatment. She still sings the blues and just about everything else at the drop of a downbeat (which of course occurs at frequent intervals). And she still looks "gawgeous."

A few things changed, however. There is plenty of nostalgic music in this sequel (one of the few sequels to a Broadway play created directly for the screen after the play itself went to the screen). Several tunes by Billy Rose crop up — songs like "Great Day" and "More Than You Know," "I Found a Million Dollar Baby," "Me and My Shadow," and "It's Only a Paper Moon." Plus there's a whole new parcel of tunes for Streisand to warble.

The original libretto for *Funny Girl* was created by Jule Styne and Bob Merrill (see page 195) — a tough act to follow for Fred Ebb and John Kander, the team that

was brought in to write new tunes for *Funny Lady*. Ebb and Kander had their own legacy to boast of, however. The composers had won Tony, Drama Critics Circle, and Grammy Awards for their score for the Broadway musical *Cabaret*, and had written hit singles for Streisand, including "My Coloring Book" and "I Don't Care Much." They were also the team responsible for the famous Emmy Award–winning TV special "Liza with a Z" and Frank Sinatra's classic "Ol' Blue Eyes Is Back." So even as they poured their hearts into the songs, comparisons of the *Girl* to the *Lady* were inevitable.

"Slavish echoes of the Bob Merrill–Jule Styne songs" was what *Newsweek* called the score. Several compared "Let's Hear It for Me" with "Don't Rain on My Parade." The *New York Times* also pointed out similarities between the newly written "How Lucky Can You Get?" and the previous film's "Who Are You Now?" *Variety*, though, insisted that "Lucky" bore a strong resemblance to "Rose's Turn," the showstopper from *Gypsy*, performed on a similarly darkened stage by Streisand in what would have been a dramatic closing number, had this been a roadshow and not a movie. Nevertheless, the Hollywood trade journal loved this number, proclaiming, "Streisand is sensational in 'How Lucky Can You Get?,' which does double duty, first as an ostensible light romantic poptune of the period recorded by Brice, then as an ironic, grim and bitter cry of emotional pain." The song stood on its own, though, and received an Academy Award nomination for Best Song.

Funny Lady received four other Oscar nominations: Best Cinematography, Best Sound, Best Original Song Score and/or Adaptation, and Best Costume Design.

NOW THAT WE'RE IN LOVE

Music by George Barrie; lyrics by Sammy Cahn
From *Whiffs*

Once again, George Barrie, president of Fabergé, makers of Brut, set out to produce a film for his Brut Productions. Twentieth Century-Fox released the picture, and hopes were high. *Whiffs* (an intriguing title, given the producer's profession) offered an excellent cast, headlined by Elliott Gould, Eddie Albert, Jennifer O'Neill (Gould's love interest in the picture, brought in mainly for window dressing), Harry Guardino, and Godfrey Cambridge. Richard Masur (from TV's "One Day at a Time"), Howard Hesseman (Dr. Johnny Fever

Elliot Gould as Frapper, a volunteer for army chemical experiments, in *Whiffs*.

of TV's "WKRP in Cincinnati"), and James Brown appeared in lesser roles.

Whiffs purported to be a comedy, but the subject matter — army chemical warfare tests on human subjects — just wasn't that laughable. Gould plays the human guinea pig who's gassed, then given a medical discharge after he's reduced to a puddle of quivering Jell-O. Once out of the Army, he turns to a life of "humorous" crime. The title has to do with the gas that sends him into uncontrollable fits and has a similar effect on an entire town when its inhabitants are given a whiff during various robberies. It's sick humor at the expense of the afflicted, with a strange message that fun crimes pay.

Critics did little laughing. The *New York Times* noted, "If Elliott Gould doesn't stop making awful movies, the notion is going to get around that he is a poorish actor . . . [*Whiffs*] is a brutally tortured comedy, potholed with intervals of the most embarrassing bad taste. The rating is PG, which in this case stands for Pathetic Garbage." *Variety* called *Whiffs* "a witless and distasteful comedy . . . The only laughs are likely to come from embarrassment." The showbiz bible also hated the film's two songs, terming them "inane."

Producer/composer George Barrie had written "All That Love Went to Waste" with lyricist Sammy Cahn

back in 1973 for *A Touch of Class* (see page 216). Now Barrie again turned to Cahn to create lyrics for two songs in *Whiffs*. Of the two, "You Can Do It Without the Army" and "Now That We're in Love," the latter tune fared better than its surroundings, rising above its sorry source to receive an Academy Award nomination.

In the movie, "Now That We're in Love" is introduced as source music. A shot of a loudspeaker on the army base is accompanied by a voice announcing, "This is KOSL-FM, Salt Lake City." The song is then performed by an unnamed singer. No hit records of the tune were released, but Steve Lawrence sang it at the Academy Awards ceremony the following spring, and again on his and wife Eydie Gorme's album *Hallelujah*.

RICHARD'S WINDOW

**Music by Charles Fox;
   lyrics by Norman Gimbel**
From *The Other Side of the Mountain*

In 1955, Jill Kinmont of Bishop, California, was considered a shoo-in for a coveted position on the United States Winter Olympics ski team. Then tragedy struck. While racing down the slopes at a trial competition in Utah, she suffered a near-fatal accident that left her a paraplegic at the age of 20. Her neck may have been broken — she was paralyzed from the chest down — but not her spirit.

E. G. Valens wrote a book about Kinmont, titled *A Long Way Up*. It seemed a natural for filming, and a screenplay was written by David Seltzer, aided by Kinmont's own personal reminiscences. *The Other Side of the Mountain* was the story of Kinmont's struggle to find new meaning in her tragic life. Naturally, romance soon enters the picture, in the form of Beau Bridges, playing a daredevil skier, motorcyclist, and skydiver. And of course she begins to find new purpose in her life. Who wouldn't with a hunk like that around? In this six-hanky film, however, he dies at the end of the picture, perishing in a plane crash.

Others in the cast included Nan Martin and William Bryant as Kinmont's parents, and Dabney Coleman as the ski coach. Several wheelchair-bound rehab patients played themselves, adding to the film's realism and pathos.

Most of the movie centers on Kinmont's rehabilitation, which would eventually see her attaining very limited mobility via a wheelchair. Kinmont herself (played by newcomer Marilyn Hassett) served as technical advisor for the film, directed with a rather heavy hand by Larry Peerce. The cinematography is outstanding, though, with picture-postcard shots of the exquisite mountain scenery.

The film has a score by Charles Fox, with one song, "Richard's Window," sung over the action by Olivia Newton-John, who also sang some transitional music in the film. Norman Gimbel wrote the lyrics to "Richard's Window," which received an Academy Award nomination. Fox and Gimbel are most remembered for writing the theme to the television series "Happy Days." Gimbel received several Oscar nominations during his career, and he and Fox would again be nominated in 1978, for "Ready to Take a Chance Again" (see page 239).

The Other Side of the Mountain did well at the box office, proving that people enjoy a good tearjerker now and then. The film took in $18 million in North American rentals, placing it among the top 10 films for 1975. Kinmont, meanwhile, proved that her spirit was indeed indomitable — she rebuilt her life and went on to teach elementary school in Beverly Hills.

THEME FROM *MAHOGANY* (DO YOU KNOW WHERE YOU'RE GOING TO?)

Music by Michael Masser; lyrics by Gerry Goffin

From *Mahogany*

Diana Ross, the former Supreme, starred in *Mahogany,* a film directed by Berry Gordy, the executive behind Motown Records. He had brought Ross to the screen in 1972, in *Lady Sings the Blues.* Now he wanted to try his hand at directing.

Mahogany is the story of a poor black girl from Chicago who becomes a top fashion model, only to renounce her career for the love of a poor but honest black politician (played by Billy Dee Williams, another Motown contract player who had appeared with her in *Lady Sings the Blues).* The title derives from the nickname given her by the photographer (played by Anthony Perkins) who helps launch her career.

Before principal photography got under way, it was decided that Ross would record the movie's "Theme from *Mahogany* (Do You Know Where You're Going To?)." According to the biography *Call Her Miss Ross,* by J. Randy Taraborrelli, "The song had been floating around Motown for years, and singer Thelma Houston had a version of it that was being readied for release as a single. When [film producer] Rob Cohen heard it, he was struck by the lovely melody and used his influence with Berry to have Thelma's version killed . . . Michael Masser, who composed the melody, played it for [Ross] on her piano one day at her Beverly Hills home. 'She looked over to a picture of her children on the wall and had tears in her eyes,' he said. 'That's how we knew we were close.' Gerry Goffin rewrote some of the lyrics, and the recording session was, said Masser, 'quick and very painless.' "

Ross sings the number over the film's opening credits. The song was released as a single and was a huge success, making a one-week stop atop the *Billboard* charts in January of 1976, and charting for 17 weeks. Soon, however, there was a controversial brouhaha surrounding this lovely song.

"Theme from *Mahogany* (Do You Know Where You're Going To?)" was not included in the preliminary nominations for Best Song, prompting the *Hollywood Reporter* to editorialize, "The failure to even nominate 'Theme from *Mahogany*' once again points out the completely antiquated and biased structure of the music branch of the Academy, whose executive committee appears to be run like a restricted private club, with the primary objective being to exclude any 'undesirables' from its membership roster." Robert Altman echoed that sentiment, angered that only one of *Nashville*'s songs ("I'm Easy" — see page 224) made the cut, accusing the Academy of "a terrible oversight and typical Academy cliquishness."

Up until this time, nominations had been decided upon by a 17-member committee representing the entire Music Branch of the Motion Picture Academy. The entire branch membership would then vote on the five nominees selected by the committee. In the face of mounting industry pressure, however, the Music Branch, in an unprecedented move, decided to reconsider. The original choices were scuttled, the committee decided to allow all 207 branch members to take part in the nominating, and when the new ballots were tallied, "Theme from *Mahogany*" had made the cut.

Composer Masser immediately sent a letter to the trades, thanking the Academy for their decision to reconsider. "I have tremendous admiration and respect for the Board of Governors who acted out of the highest principles in allowing the entire music branch to vote on eligibility this year," Masser wrote. On Oscar night, Ross performed the nominated tune via satellite from Amsterdam. Ironically, it was Altman's film's tune, "I'm Easy," that won, even though Altman still groused over the fact that no additional songs from his movie were included among the nominees.

1976

And the winner is... EVERGREEN (LOVE THEME FROM A STAR IS BORN)

Music by Barbra Streisand;
lyrics by Paul Williams
From *A Star Is Born*

As the old saying goes, nothing succeeds like success, especially in Hollywood, where a successful film is likely to be repeated — sometimes again and again. Such was the case of the movie originally called *What Price Hollywood?*, first filmed in 1932 and later remade in 1937 as *A Star Is Born*. The same story was born again in 1954, with Judy Garland cast in the role of the newborn star, a Hollywood actress whose career is on the rise even as her husband's career (and life) is on the skids (see page 131). Armed with this proven premise, screenwriters John Gregory Dunne and Joan Didion rewrote it yet again, with a rock 'n' roll feeling. This time, the two ill-fated performers would be rock stars — she on the way up, he hitting rock bottom.

Casting the right two people for the leads was one of the more difficult aspects of the film. Originally the writers sought Carly Simon and James Taylor, but they passed on the project. Other pairs considered were Liza Minnelli and Elvis Presley, Mick and Bianca Jagger, and Sonny and Cher. Once the property was obtained by Jon Peters, however, there was no question of who would star — his then-current love interest, Barbra Streisand. Eventually, Kris Kristofferson was cast as the male lead, and the chemistry between the two proved to be the proper formula for success. The picture

became the number two box office hit of the year, bringing in $37.1 million in North American rentals.

This *A Star Is Born* was a musical, like the 1954 version, with songs used to advance the story — in other words, a drama with music. No one suddenly bursts into song; instead, tunes are worked into songwriting sessions, rehearsals, recording sessions, and live concert appearances. Streisand also served as the film's executive producer and co-wrote two of the songs — "Lost Inside of You," with lyrics by Leon Russell, and "Evergreen," with Paul Williams serving as lyricist.

"Evergreen" emerged as the hit song of the film. Streisand recorded it live in a concert performance purposely staged for the production, at the Sun Devil Stadium in Tempe, Arizona. The director ordered take after take to get just the right concert footage, while 70,000 fans screamed (for mercy, probably, given the blazing sun). Finally, after soothing her audience with a performance of her signature song "People" and the Academy Award–winning "The Way We Were" (see page 215), she launched the first public performance of "Evergreen." The crowd went wild, and so did the record-buying public, pushing the tune to Number One on the *Billboard* charts by the week of March 5, 1977, where it stayed for three weeks. The song charted for nearly half a year and earned a gold record for certified sales of over a million copies. The soundtrack album with Streisand and Kristofferson fared similarly, hitting Number One with sales that eventually topped out at over four million.

At the Oscar ceremonies in the spring, a curly-haired Streisand sang the nominated tune and accepted the award for Best Song. (Other nominations, but no wins, were for Best Cinematography, Best Sound, and Roger Kellaway's original song score). "Evergreen" also cleaned up at the Grammys, winning Song of the Year and Best Original Song from a Film.

AVE SATANI

Music and lyrics by Jerry Goldsmith
From *The Omen*

From the days when our ancestors first huddled around the campfire, secure in the knowledge that the fire's light warded off unseen creatures just as surely as it dispelled the blackness of the night, the human consciousness has always had a fear of these invisible, so-called dark forces. Although we now make claims of worldly sophistication, we've only been out of our caves for the briefest of durations on the geologic timeline, and our species has retained a lingering fear of those same unknown, dark forces that once plagued our forebears. This mythos continues in our storytelling today, with the TV or movie screen's soft glow replacing the campfire's reassuring light. Sometimes these dark forces are given a name, such as Satan. And sometimes people believe they become visible, taking a form with which we are most familiar, that of a human.

Hollywood has dipped into this well of darkness on a regular basis. Modern films like *Rosemary's Baby* (1968) and *The Exorcist* (1973) raked in huge piles of money at the box office, proving that people actually enjoy being frightened by the unknown. *The Omen* was one such a chiller/horror picture, a movie that combined the literalness of the Christian Bible with the imagination of Hollywood to produce a "what if" film about the Anti-Christ, the supposed child of Satan, the personification of evil.

The film starred Gregory Peck and Lee Remick as the parents of the the Devil's spawn, a child rather appropriately called Damien (sounds like "demon," get it?), played by Harvey Stevens. At once adorable and deliciously malevolent, we learn that he was switched at birth. It soon becomes clear that this little imp is no normal five-year old — anyone who dares to cross this little devil of a child inevitably dies a most gruesome premature death, complete with the best special effects money can buy.

With sensational production values to go along with the sensationalism, *The Omen* did tremendous box office, raking in $28.5 million and ranking sixth for all films released in 1976. The opening song from the film, "Ave Satani," (which, in case you're not up on your Latin, means "Hail, Satan") was written by Jerry Goldsmith, who also wrote the film's Oscar-winning original score. "Ave Satani" was nominated for an Academy Award for Best Song, but lost to "Evergreen" (see page 228).

Sequels continued to bedevil the American filmgoer: *Damien: Omen II* (1978), the incorrectly titled *The Final Conflict* (1981), and *Omen IV: The Awakening* (a made-for-TV movie, 1991).

Goldsmith is one of Hollywood's most prolific contemporary composers, with TV credits ranging from shows like "Gunsmoke" and "The Man from U.N.C.L.E." to dozens of film scores. He has been nom-inated for over a dozen Oscars, for such scores as *The Boys from Brazil* (1977), *Star Trek: The Motion Picture* (1979), and *Hoosiers* (1986).

COME TO ME

Music by Henry Mancini; lyrics by Don Black
From *The Pink Panther Strikes Again*

The first time *The Pink Panther* struck, in 1964, audiences delighted in the Blake Edwards–created comedy about a bumbling French detective named inspector Clouseau (Peter Sellers) in this spoof on the spy thriller genre. The title was actually the name of a rare jewel and had nothing to do with the now-familiar cartoon character of the same name (although the pink feline was used in the opening credits). There was, of course, a sequel — *A Shot in the Dark*, released later that same year — again with the klutzy Clouseau cavorting clumsily. This in turn begat *Inspector Clouseau* (1968, recast, unsuccessfully, with Alan Arkin), which eventually begat *The Return of the Pink Panther* (1975), a much happier go-round. After this felicitous *Return*, with many happy returns at the box office, producer Edwards again rounded up the usual cast and crew for *The Pink Panther Strikes Again*.

The series may have been somewhat formulaic at this stage, but it certainly hadn't run out of laughs. Nearly every critic and theater-goer described the latest venture with one word: hilarious. The films were always a favorite among even the most hardened critics, and this one was no exception. *Newsweek*'s reviewer enthused, "Clouseau's near-magical obtuseness has lost none of its charm . . . The current installment is a bit funnier than its predecessor, but the success of the 'Panther' series has never depended solely on laughs. Blake Edwards's slick, seamless direction makes even the flimsiest routines seem stylish; in addition to its comic virtues, this is one of the best-looking movies of its kind in recent memory."

This cat really knew how to strut its stuff. *The Pink Panther Strikes Again* proved it was no pink pussycat at the box office, hauling in over $20 million in domestic rentals, more than triple the take of any of its three predecessors.

Once again, Henry Mancini, long associated with Blake Edwards's various films and TV series, was signed on to create the score. He also wrote a song

Chief Inspector Jacques Clouseau (Peter Sellers) tries to pacify a hostile parrot in *The Pink Panther Strikes Again.*

called "Come to Me" (with lyrics by Don Black), sung by pop singer Tom Jones over a hysterical love scene between Sellers (as Clouseau) and co-star Leslie-Anne Down (as a Russian agent/defector). Champagne bubbles over as she slips off her fur coat and into something more comfortable — the bed. Clouseau struggles to remove his tie and ends up wearing it on his head. Then he, too, sings "Come to Me," saying it was "a little song we used to sing in the resistance to keep up the courage." The scene ends with the two of them breaking through the wall and landing in the water in what then becomes an animated sequence. The tune earned Mancini (along with Black) yet another Oscar nomination for Best Song, one of 11 such nominations he would receive in his career.

The Pink Panther continued striking back. In 1978, there was *Revenge of the Pink Panther,* and 1982 saw Edwards and company on the *Trail of the Pink Panther,* (mostly a pastiche of outtakes from the previous films, as Sellers had died in 1980), followed in 1983 by *The Curse of the Pink Panther* (which starred Ted Wass as a sort of American version of Clouseau).

GONNA FLY NOW

Music by Bill Conti; lyrics by Carol Connors and Ayn Robbins
From Rocky

Rocky, the beginning of a long series of films, was the brainchild of Sylvester Stallone, who wrote this, his 33rd screenplay, after the first 32 had been turned down. "Sly" Stallone was, in many ways, a real-life Rocky: Like the underdog he would portray through five *Rocky* movies, the actor/writer (and eventually director and producer) fought on in the face of adversity, unwilling to throw in the towel. The picture became the sleeper of the decade, propelling Stallone and his property into the record books.

The story was a simple one. Club boxer Rocky Balboa is down for the count careerwise, but fate offers him the unlikely opportunity to fight for the world heavyweight championship. Given little chance, he fights the fight of his life, giving the champion fits in an epic give-and-take battle, only to have the fight declared a draw at the end. Audiences had to wait until the very end of the last reel to learn the outcome, at which point they usually rose as one to their feet and cheered Rocky's determined efforts, forgetting that only the projectionist could hear their applause.

The box office dollars flowed almost as freely as Rocky's sweat in the gym, to the tune of $56.5 million in North American rentals, making underdog *Rocky* the top dog for the 1976 box office. At Oscar time, there were nine nominations and three wins — Best Picture, Best Director (John G. Avildsen), and Best Film Editing. Other nominations were for Best Actor (Stallone), Best Actress (Talia Shire), Best Supporting Actor (two nominees — Burgess Meredith and Burt Young), Best Original Screenplay, and Best Song.

While the Best Song nominee, "Gonna Fly Now," lost to "Evergreen," it could hardly be called a loser. The music was written by the film's scorer, Bill Conti, with lyrics by Carol Connors and Ayn Robbins. The team was brought together by Conti's agent, who also represented Connors and knew of Conti's need for a lyricist. Conti played the tune for Connors and Robbins, and the ladies went home to think about possible lyrics. According to *The Billboard Book of Number One Hits*, by Fred Bronson, it was a few days later, while taking a shower, that Connors had a sudden inspiration. "I called Bill from the shower," she told Bronson, "and said I knew what the words should be. He said, 'Where

are you?' and I told him I was in the shower. 'Are you alone?' I said, 'Would I be calling you if I wasn't alone?' He said, 'Do me a favor, give me the lyrics before you electrocute yourself!' " Connors and partner Ayn Robbins then completed the song, as well as another one they were working on at Disney for *The Rescuers* (see page 236).

Conti released a recording of "Gonna Fly Now," and it did just that. It soared to the Number One position, charted for 20 weeks, and went gold. Other artists rushed to cover the tune, and many of these made the charts as well, something not seen with a motion picture–nominated song in many years. Maynard Ferguson had a version that made number 28, and two other artists — Current and Rhythm Heritage — each scraped the lower reaches of the chart at number 94.

A WORLD THAT NEVER WAS

**Music by Sammy Fain;
 lyrics by Paul Francis Webster**
From *Half a House*

Sammy Fain was 74 years old when he was tapped to write a song for a movie called *Half a House*. The tune he created with lyricist Paul Francis Webster was "A

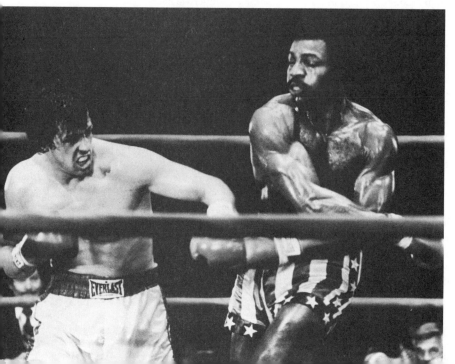

Rocky Balboa (Sylvester Stallone) takes one on the chin from Apollo Creed (Carl Weathers) in the original *Rocky*.

World That Never Was," but it may as well have been called "The song that never was," since it has been virtually forgotten by the music and motion picture industries in the years following the film's release.

Even though Fain had been a fixture in the movie world since the 1930s, he knew his latest song faced long odds. When the Oscar nominations were announced, his tune was among the five finalists, but "A World That Never Was" had little chance of winning, and Fain knew it. But he was a trooper with *chutzpah*, so, half-jokingly, he ran an ad in the Hollywood trade papers that read: "It would be nice if we had a commercial record, but we don't. It would also be nice if we were in a widely seen motion picture, but we don't have that either." Included with the ad was a telephone number for readers to "Dial-a-Song," encouraging voting members of the Academy to call up and hear Sammy's tape of the nominated tune.

The publicity gimmick paid off. The lines were jammed with curious callers. One of those phoning was a fellow nominee, lyricist Carol Connors, who, along with partner Ayn Robbins and composer Bill Conti, were nominees for "Gonna Fly Now," the theme from *Rocky* (see page 230). Connors and Robbins were in the middle of collaborating with Fain on song lyrics for the upcoming Disney movie *The Rescuers*, and Connors, curious about "A World That Never Was," decided to give her partner a ring. "The line was busy for a half hour," Connors joked in a *Los Angeles Herald-Examiner* interview, "but the song was worth waiting for."

The public, however, was not so lucky. The song was never released as a single, and the film has not been heard from much either, available neither on video nor on television in recent years. The movie starred Anthony Eisley (star of the 1960s television series "Hawaiian Eye") and Pat Delany (co-star of the obscure 1975–76 TV series "Swiss Family Robinson") as an estranged couple who decide to build their dream house with the hope that it will bring them back together. It doesn't, and it didn't do much to bring in an audience, either.

Fain already had eight Oscar nominations and two wins to his name when he was nominated for "A World That Never Was." He also won two Laurel Awards during his career, was elected to the Songwriters Hall of Fame, and served on the ASCAP board of directors. He died in 1989 at the age of 87.

1977

And the winner is...

YOU LIGHT UP MY LIFE

Music and lyrics by Joseph Brooks
From *You Light Up My Life*

The *Rocky* syndrome — the notion that perseverance will see you overcome adversity against all odds — seemed to be taking hold in the cinema. That basic storyline began cropping up again and again, as it did in 1977 — just one year after *Rocky* — in a film called *You Light Up My Life*.

The movie was the brainchild of Joseph Brooks, a former advertising writer who had won 21 Clio awards for his work in television commercials before putting his talent to work writing, producing, directing, and composing the music for *You Light Up My Life*. The plot concerns the struggles of Laurie, a former child star who writes and performs a song called — big surprise! — "You Light Up My Life." The "dramedy" — part drama, part comedy — is really a slice of life, portraying Laurie (played by Didi Conn, in her film debut) as she confronts life's little stumbling blocks, eventually emerging a winner via her song.

It was decided that Conn would not sing the title song, which was dubbed by an uncredited Kasey Cisyk. Her performance can be heard on the original cast soundtrack, along with four other songs composed for the film by Brooks. Cisyk, whose previous claim to fame had been as an obscure commercial jingle vocalist, went uncredited even on the soundtrack, listed only as "Original Cast" instead of by her name.

The single version of "You Light Up My Life," however, took on a life of its own. Debby Boone (Pat's daughter) recorded the vocal to the same music track as the one used in the film, and it was her single that became a runaway sensation. It peaked in the Number One position atop the *Billboard* charts and refused to budge from there for 10 weeks, making it the longest-running Number One single since "Don't Be Cruel" by Elvis Presley in August of 1956. "You Light Up My Life" charted for a total of 25 weeks and went platinum, ultimately selling over five million copies.

Awards organizations practically fought over the right to honor this song. "You Light Up My Life" took top honors at the Academy Awards, where it was performed by Debby Boone and a group of children "signing" the words (reportedly gibberish and not true American Sign Language, according to some newspaper accounts). The tune won a Golden Globe Award for Best Original Song from a Film in 1978. In addition, it was voted Pop/Rock Favorite Single at the American Music Awards and Favorite New Song in the music category of the People's Choice Awards. And Boone won a Grammy as Best New Artist.

Although the song's lyrics seem to address a romantic partner, Boone, who came from a conservative, deeply religious background, claimed that whenever she sang the love ballad, the words always made her think about her relationship with God.

CANDLE ON THE WATER

Music and lyrics by Al Kasha and Joel Hirschhorn
From *Pete's Dragon*

Pete's Dragon was an attempt by the Walt Disney Studios to recapture some of the magic that had blessed

Mary Poppins back in 1964 (see page 175). It was a live-acted film with humans interacting with animated characters — in this case a pudgy dragon named Elliott, with aerodynamically incorrect pink wings. Oh, and he was invisible.

The musical fantasy was based on a 13-page synopsis that Walt had prepared before his death. The story involves an orphaned boy named Pete (played by Sean Marshall) who flees from his cruel guardians, accompanied by his best friend, Elliott the dragon. All sorts of adventures befall the two as they and others sing some not-too-memorable songs in pursuit of those *Mary Poppins* box office dollars. The film wasn't exactly supercalifragilistic, but it garnered respectable notices from the critics, although it did less at the box office ($18.4 million in North American rentals) than Disney's other release that year, *The Rescuers* (which took in $30 million). Unfortunately, *Pete's Dragon* cost $11 million to produce, making it the most expensive film to that date in the history of the Disney Studios, surpassing *Mary Poppins* by $4.5 million.

The film was given life by a new generation of Disney animators, headed by Ken Anderson and Don Bluth. Bluth eventually split with Disney to form his own studio, producing and/or directing such successful animated features as *The Secret of Nimh* (1982), *An American Tail* (1986, see page 278), *All Dogs Go to Heaven* (1989), and *Thumbelina* (1994).

Helen Reddy was cast in the lead. Although a fine singer, she had little experience working in film. Her unspectacular performance didn't help things any at the box office. What Reddy did have, however, was a powerful voice. Known for roaring in her breakthrough song, "I Am Woman," she had a string of hits in the '70s, including "Ain't No Way to Treat a Lady" and "You're My World." In 1975 she became the host of the television rock show "Midnight Special," and she appeared in the film *Airport '75* before landing the female lead in *Pete's Dragon*.

Others in the cast included Jim Dale (who wrote the lyrics to "Georgy Girl" in 1966 — see page 186) as Dr. Terminus, Mickey Rooney as Lampie, Red Buttons as Hoagy, Shelley Winders as Gogan, Jim Backus as the Mayor, and Jeff Conaway as Willie.

One song, "Candle on the Water," was beautifully sung and photographed and received an Oscar nomi-

Helen Reddy, Sean Marshall, and his scaly friend in *Pete's Dragon*.

nation. Reddy performs the tune from the lighthouse where her character lives. The scene is brilliantly back-lit, one of the most striking production numbers in the film. The song itself is soft rock, obviously modern and a little incongruous, since the film is set in the 1890s. This and other songs for the movie were written by the team of Al Kasha and Joel Hirschhorn, both of whom had won Oscars for the songs "The Morning After" (see page 211) and "We May Never Love Like This Again" (see page 220).

Pete's Dragon also received a nomination in the wordy category of Best Original Song Score and Its Adaptation or Adaptation Score; Irwin Kostal, who did the arranging and conducting, was the nominee.

NOBODY DOES IT BETTER

**Music by Marvin Hamlisch;
   lyrics by Carole Bayer Sager
From *The Spy Who Loved Me***

Nobody did it better than James Bond for Albert "Cubby" Broccoli. The Bond franchise was a cash cow for producer Broccoli and United Artists, and they had been cranking out Bond films practically on an annual basis since the early '60s. For the next picture in the series, Broccoli had acquired the title only — not the story — to Ian Fleming's *The Spy Who Loved Me*.

It might have been interesting to see how a movie based on the actual book would have turned out. It was the only Bond book set almost completely in America,

written from the point of view of the heroine, with Bond as the spy who loved her. Instead, writers were hired to create a new story around the purchased title.

The screenplay went through a series of changes by a number of writers, with a final script in hand by 1976. It involved the typically formulaic Bond plot, with plenty of action and babes. *The Spy Who Loved Me* also had plenty of money behind it — $13.5 million, then the biggest budget for any Bond film. (It paid off handsomely, a take of $25.3 million in domestic rentals.) What United Artists got for their money was a script that paid homage to previous Bond movies (so much so that some cried, "Rehash!"), spectacular stunts and special effects, and great locations such as Sardinia, Egypt, the Bahamas, Scotland, Switzerland, and Canada's Baffin Island. They also got Roger Moore, in one of his better performances, and Barbara Bach as the *Me* of the title. The film introduced the character of Jaws, a super-human with really bad dental work (unless you enjoy having an all-steel mouth with a jaw like a bear trap), played by seven-footer Richard Kiel. Jaws proved such a hit, he was brought back to menace Bond in the next picture, *Moonraker*.

The producers commissioned a title song from Marvin Hamlisch. Most, but not all, of the James Bond movies had benefited from clever title songs like "Goldfinger," "You Only Live Twice," "Live and Let Die" (see page ?), "Thunderball" and so on. But although *The Spy Who Loved Me* would have a so-called title song, the title ended up cleverly buried within the tune's lyric, so technically it wasn't a title song at all. Blame it on (and thank) Carole Bayer Sager.

Nobody does it better than Jaws (Richard Kiel), chowing down on whatever's handy while holding off 007 (Roger Moore) with one enormous hand in *The Spy Who Loved Me*.

Hamlisch had completed his music and was introduced by the producers to Sager, touted as the hot new lyricist in town. Hamlisch writes of their first encounter in his autobiography, *The Way I Was:* "We met in my apartment. She was terribly attractive: dark-haired; flashing eyes. She was quick, witty, hysterically funny, and fast . . . Lyrics poured out of her. She had a good ear for language and a head filled with ideas." Soon, Sager had moved in with Hamlisch, for professional and personal reasons. "We lived and worked music," Hamlisch wrote. "We constantly turned out new songs."

Carly Simon was chosen to record the tune for the film, and her soundtrack version was released as a single at the time of the movie's debut. The record climbed to the number two position on the *Billboard* charts, where it stayed for three weeks. It remained on the charts for a lucrative 25 weeks and earned Simon a gold record.

The Spy Who Loved me received two additional Oscar nominations — for Best Art Direction–Set Decoration and for Hamlisch's original score.

THE SLIPPER AND THE ROSE WALTZ (HE DANCED WITH ME/ SHE DANCED WITH ME)

Music and lyrics by Richard M. Sherman and Robert B. Sherman
**From *The Slipper and the Rose:*
*The Story of Cinderella***

In a way, it was fitting that *The Slipper and the Rose: The Story of Cinderella* was released the same year as *Rocky*. Both were "Cinderella" stories — about people who triumph over adverse circumstances. In *Rocky* (see page 230) we see a guy who's been down on his luck but is nonetheless able to make it to the top. In *The Slipper and the Rose*, we have the traditional tale of the downtrodden young lass who also makes it to the top — by marrying a prince.

This 1977 version of the classic Cinderella story was filled with all the joy and fantasy this family movie could muster from the proven team of the Sherman Brothers, Richard and Robert, who scripted the picture along with English director Bryan Forbes. The team put their own spin on it, telling the story from the Prince's point of view. "It's not Cinderella meets the Prince," says

Richard Sherman. "It's this prince, who has all this responsibility of having to get married in a high place, and Cinderella — incidentally — is the one he falls for."

A title song was a must, but it presented some problems to these seasoned professionals. "How do you present something that everybody knows is going to happen, the love song when the Prince and Cinderella meet?" asks Sherman, rhetorically. "Everybody and his Uncle Harry has written one where they start singing at you. We said, this song is going to be the one song that they never sing at each other. They never even sing it when they first [perform] it, they just waltz to it. When the waltz concludes, Cinderella runs away from the ball. She's alone, and she starts thinking about the Prince, and she starts singing how she feels. Then, some more story evolves, and the Prince is all alone, longing for his Cinderella, and he looks for her and can't find her. He sings how it feels for him, and they both sing the song separately, as soliloquy. To have the two principals singing without each other, it becomes kind of nice." Hence the reason for the double subtitle to "The Slipper and the Rose Waltz": With each character having a song, it becomes "He Danced with Me/She Danced with Me."

The song received an Academy Award nomination, and although it didn't win the Oscar, it remains a particular favorite of the Shermans. Richard, in fact, revealed some secrets of just how clever songwriters and screenwriters can be in manipulating the audience's emotions. "*The Slipper and the Rose* was perhaps the most romantic song of ours, a song of feelings. We pretty much schemed ahead of time where we were going to tease people, and they wouldn't know they're being teased. We planned it so they were going to hear this rich, resonant waltz, and later on, she was going to be singing. [The audience would realize] 'Oh my God, that's the thing they were dancing to.' And a little bit later, 'Oh my, he's singing the same thing she was singing.' And then, later on when they finally meet, and he finds her in a field, this waltz comes sweeping in, and so we'll get tears — which we did. Basically, that's what we had the idea for, and it worked."

The film starred Richard Chamberlain as the Prince and British actress Gemma Craven as Cinderella. It never became a big hit in the United States, but according to Richard, "It's a standard over in England, played every Christmas, and it was a very big success in Europe and Japan." *The Slipper and the Rose* also earned an Oscar nomination for the Shermans and

Bernard (right) and Miss Bianca set sail on their mission to rescue a kidnapped orphan in *The Rescuers*.

Angela Morley for Best Original Song Score and Its Adaptation or Adaptation Score.

SOMEONE'S WAITING FOR YOU

**Music by Sammy Fain;
  lyrics by Carol Connors and Ayn Robbins
From *The Rescuers***

The Rescuers was one of two popular films released by the Walt Disney studios in 1977 (the other was *Pete's Dragon* — see page 233), an indication to the studio bosses that it was now all right to heave a collective sigh of relief: animation was alive and well and even thriving in a way that would have pleased Walt himself.

This was Disney's 22nd full-length animated feature, and the first one since *Robin Hood* in 1973. It was produced at a cost of $7 million — unheard of for an animated film — but returned its investment fourfold in domestic rentals, ringing up over $30 million at the box office. And with good reason — as *Variety* noted, "*The Rescuers* is the best work by Disney animators in many years, restoring the craft to its former glories."

The simple story has to do with a little girl named Penny, kidnapped by an evil witch who uses the child to search for a lost diamond. In a characteristic Disney plot development, she is rescued by two mice, repre-

sentatives of the Rescue Aid Society, an international mouse organization. Bob Newhart was the voice of mouse Bernard, while Eva Gabor, who had previously worked in the 1970 Disney animated feature *The Aristocats*, spoke the part of the other rodent lead, Bianca. Other celebrity voices included Geraldine Page as the flamboyantly evil Madame Medusa, Joe Flynn as her oafish henchman Mr. Snoops, Jim Jordan (radio's Fibber McGee) as Orville the Albatross, and the frequently used Disney voice of Pat Buttram as Luke.

As in most Disney films, the music was an important aspect of this movie. Artie Butler's evocative score was a great success, as animation directors Frank Thomas and Ollie Johnston recalled in the book *Disney Animation:* "When Artie Butler wrote the music, he felt the predicament of the mice acutely and wrote music that immediately made their task enormous, while somehow keeping them virtually helpless. When they tried to move the huge diamond from its hiding place, the score added a good one hundred pounds to the weight of the gem."

In addition to the score, five new songs made an important contribution to the movie. Disney veteran and multiple Academy Award nominee Sammy Fain composed the music, assisted by lyricists Carol Connors and Ayn Robbins (who had also written the lyrics to the Oscar-nominated "Gonna Fly Now" from *Rocky* — see page 230). One song from *The Rescuers*, "Someone's Waiting for You," received an Oscar nomination. In the number, Penny (with vocal sung by Shelby Flint) cries because she wants to be adopted and but has just been told by the evil Medusa that no one would care for a homely child like her. The young orphan sings of her hope that someday she'll be wanted.

The Rescuers was followed by a highly successful 1990 sequel, called *The Rescuers Down Under*. As the title suggests, this time the mice head to Australia to assist a young boy. Mouse voices were reprised by Newhart and Gabor, with George C. Scott and John Candy joining the cast.

LAST DANCE

Music and lyrics by Paul Jabara
From *Thank God It's Friday*

Thank God It's Friday premiered just in time for summer — Donna Summer, that is. The R&B singer made her film debut in the role of a character named Nicole Sims, an aspiring singer who cons her way to the disco stage and instant stardom. Disco was in full swing then — movie-goers had come down with *Saturday Night Fever* only the year before — and this Motown co-production relied on dozens of disco tunes to capture the attention of its young target audience. An assortment of interesting characters, some strobe lights, and the inevitable dance contest completed the package.

Although Summer was clearly the star, there were some good performances by some relative unknowns who would become bigger stars in years to come, including Jeff Goldblum (still eight years away from his 1986 breakthrough film, *The Fly*) and a tenth-billed Debra Winger. The singing group the Commodores appeared as themselves.

Billed as a 90-minute rock revue from Motown and Casablanca, the movie focuses on one night at a disco as the various types who wander in and out of the place fill us in on the sordid details of their lives. *Time* magazine probably said it best: "*Friday* is no *Saturday*." Most critics agreed that the movie came up short, pointing out that it was really just a series of vignettes strung together with songs — a snippet here, a dance there, a new tune here and there.

One of the best of the new songs, "Last Dance," was performed by Summer, whose single release of the tune peaked in the number three position, charted for 21 weeks, and sold over a million copies. It also received an Academy Award as Best Song, as well as a Golden Globe Award as Best Original Song from a Film.

At the Oscar ceremony, Donna Summer performed "Last Dance" in a lavish disco number with mirrors and strobing lights. After all the performances of the nominated songs, the Best Song Oscar was presented by Kris Kristofferson and Ruby Keeler, who was recovering from a stroke. She read off the name of the winner, songwriter Paul Jabara, who accepted the award and thanked the audience "for coming to my bar mitzvah." At the backstage press conference, Jabara explained how he was able to finally interest Summer in performing "Last Dance": "I wanted to play the song for her, but she was so busy, I finally put a cassette of the song in her bathroom and locked the door. After she heard it 10 times, she said she loved it!"

Jabara's career saw him writing songs for Barbra Streisand, Diana Ross, and Julio Iglesias. He was also an actor, and appeared onstage in *Hair* and *Jesus Christ Superstar*, and in such films as *Midnight Cowboy* (1969) and *Star 80* (1983). He also had a cameo in *Thank God It's Friday*. Sadly, the talented composer and actor died in October, 1992, at the age of only 44, from cancer.

HOPELESSLY DEVOTED TO YOU

Music and lyrics by John Farrar
From *Grease*

With the heyday of the great filmusicals long since past, *Grease* burst upon the screen fresh from its energetic Broadway production, which debuted in 1972. It started simply enough, as a five-hour amateur production in a Chicago trolley barn, a satirical look at the 1950s rock 'n' roll era. *Grease* eventually moved to off-Broadway's Eden Theatre, then to the Broadhurst, and eventually the Royale on Broadway. The surprising runaway hit ran for an incredible 3,388 performances before closing in 1980.

Even as the stage version of *Grease* was packing them in, a film was produced and rushed to theaters. John Travolta, who had taken the lesser role of Doody in one of the road shows, was cast in the lead opposite

Australian singer-actress Olivia Newton-John. The chemistry between the two young stars was magical — *Grease* was the word for big box office bucks.

A sensation on the screen as well as the boards, *Grease* proved there was still plenty of lightning in the musical genre. It pulled down $96.3 million in domestic rentals at the box office, making it the most successful live screen musical of all time, the top movie of 1978, and the number three film of the 1970s (behind *Star Wars* and *Jaws*).

Grease arrived with virtually all of its Broadway tunes intact, plus seven new ones. The songs for the Broadway version had been created by Warren Casey and Jim Jacobs, and included numbers like "Summer Nights," "Freddy, My Love," "Greased Lightnin', " "Look at Me, I'm Sandra Dee," "We Go Together," and "Beauty School Dropout." The film added such crowd-pleasers as "Grease," by Barry Gibb, "Hound Dog," by Jerry Lieber and Mike Stoller, and "You're the One That I Want" and "Hopelessly Devoted to You," both by John Farrar.

"Hopelessly Devoted to You" earned an Oscar nomination for Farrar. At the Awards ceremony the following spring, Olivia Newton-John performed the nominated song in the traditional Oscar gown. In the film, however, it is a *night*gown-clad Newton-John who sings the love ballad in her back yard, while the image of boyfriend Travolta is magically conjured up in the ripples of a pond. The song did well on the charts, peaking at number three and charting for 19 weeks.

The soundtrack also proved a hit. The album sold an astounding 24 million copies worldwide, making it the number two international best-seller to that date (right behind the soundtrack from *Saturday Night Fever*, another Travolta vehicle). Although Newton-John's recording of "Hopelessly Devoted to You" didn't reach Number One, two of the film's songs did: "You're the One That I Want," a duet by Travolta and Newton-John, and Frankie Valli's version of the title song.

A Travolta-less sequel, *Grease 2*, tried to catch greased lightning in a bottle twice, but it short-circuited before striking, earning only $6.5 in rentals. In 1993, there was a revival on Broadway, complete with most of the familiar score. However, the Oscar-nominated tune, which was not part of the original stage production, was not included.

John Travolta (left), Eve Arden (right), and cast from *Grease*, in one of the film's lavish dance numbers.

THE LAST TIME
I FELT LIKE THIS

**Music by Marvin Hamlisch;
lyrics by Alan and Marilyn Bergman**
From *Same Time, Next Year*

Same Time, Next Year found Hollywood once again dipping into the well of Broadway, this time for a film based on a two-person play starring Alan Alda and Ellen Burstyn. The story's premise revolved around a pair of married lovers (not to each other) who meet annually for an illicit tryst, renewing their passion at the same locale, while continuing their separate family lives the remaining 51 weeks of the year. The film follows the two at approximately six-year intervals, as they age (through the miracle of theatrical makeup) and catch up on each other's lives.

Nearly everyone agreed that the Broadway play was well executed, but critics couldn't seem to reach a consensus on its move to the big screen. *Time* magazine's Frank Rich, for example, thought something got lost in the translation: "Some plays transfer easily to the screen, but those built around theatrical gimmicks invariably drop dead . . . *Same Time, Next Year* . . . never stood a chance as a movie: it is a one-joke, one-set, two-character sitcom that should be allowed to retire in peace to the nation's dinner theaters." *Variety*, on the other hand, opined, "*Same Time, Next Year* is a textbook example of how to successfully transport a stage play to the big screen . . . [It is] everything you'd want from this kind of film: It's been pushed open just enough to maintain interest without altering the material . . . and it features two first class performances by Ellen Burstyn and Alan Alda."

Bernard Slade wrote the screenplay, basing it on the script for his own Broadway stage play. And the makeup, which was singled out for praise by most observers, was done by renowned Hollywood artist William Tuttle, who had the unenviable task of convincingly aging the players 26 years over the course of the film.

The other effort singled out by many reviewers was Marvin Hamlisch's score. Although he didn't receive his usual Oscar nomination for that, he and lyricists Alan and Marilyn Bergman did get the customary nod from the Academy in the form of a Best Song nomination. The tune was called "The Last Time I Felt Like This," and it is sung immediately after the opening credits, as we see tender, silent scenes of Alda and Burstyn in love.

The melody was used throughout the picture in Hamlisch's score to accent the romantic theme of the film. The song, which was performed on the soundtrack and at the Oscar ceremonies by Johnny Mathis and Jane Olivor, did not translate to a charting single.

Same Time, Next Year received three other Academy Award nominations: Burstyn was nominated for Best Actress, Bernard Slade received an Oscar nomination for Best Screenplay Based on Material from Another Medium, and director of photography Robert Surtees was nominated for Best Cinematography.

READY TO TAKE
A CHANCE AGAIN

Music by Charles Fox; lyrics by Norman Gimbel
From *Foul Play*

Blessed with a gifted cast that included two former television stars and an unknown (to American audiences) but talented British comedian-actor-musician, *Foul Play* was just the right movie to freshen the summer air in 1978. The film starred Chevy Chase, whose patented klutziness had been honed to perfection during his 1975–76 apprenticeship on TV's "Saturday Night Live." There he made a career out of tripping over his own feet, falling down in every conceivable kind of pratfall, and reporting the "news" for "Weekend Update" with his trademark opening, "Good evening. I'm Chevy Chase and you're not." But a film career beckoned, and the chase was on to find more and more suitable vehicles for this unbridled talent.

Chase had appeared in a couple of TV satire movies, *The Groove Tube* (1974) and *Tunnelvision* (1976), now both hailed as cult classics. But *Foul Play* was his breakthrough film. Since then, he's appeared in dozens more, many of them major hits, including *National Lampoon's Vacation* (1983, plus several sequels), *Fletch* (1985, plus more sequels), *The Three Amigos!* (1986), *Funny Farm* (1988), and *L.A. Story* (1991).

The movie's co-star was Goldie Hawn, a young actress who had also cut her teeth in TV comedy. She had appeared in the off-the-"joke-wall" TV comedy series "Rowan & Martin's Laugh-In" from 1968 to 1970 and had since struck it big in films, winning a Best Supporting Actress Oscar for her performance in *Cactus Flower* (1969), her first major film role.

That lovable canine, Lassie, studies a wanted poster in *The Magic of Lassie*.

the Pacific Coast near San Francisco. After the credits, Hawn hums a bar of the melody as the action begins. The song received an Oscar nomination and was a hit for Manilow, peaking in the number 11 position and charting for 16 weeks.

Charles Fox and Norman Gimbel, who had previous Oscar nominations to their credit, composed "Ready to Take a Chance Again." The pair composed for television as well as for film, and were noted for having created the "Happy Days" theme. When it came time for *Foul Play* producers Tom Miller and Eddie Milkis to select composers for their film's theme, Fox and Gimbel had the inside track: Miller and Milkis (along with Bob Boyett) had been the producers of "Happy Days" and many of its spin-offs, so they were quite familiar with the talented tunesmiths, thereby making their choice an obvious one.

WHEN YOU'RE LOVED

**Music and lyrics by Richard M. Sherman and
    Robert B. Sherman**
From *The Magic of Lassie*

Ever since Eric Knight's classic story *Lassie Come Home* came to the screen in 1943, Lassie has been a character in the literary legacy of the 20th century. She (or rather, he, since all Lassies are played by males) has been on screens big and small, working her way into hearts big and small in the process. The beloved rough-coated collie, a descendant of a class of Scottish working dogs, has been the title dog in eight sequels to the original film (which starred Roddy McDowell and Elizabeth Taylor), and at least six different TV series have been built around the beloved canine.

Audiences just couldn't seem to get enough of this wonder dog. Jack and Bonita Wrather, whose Wrather Corp. (oil, radio, TV, and hotels) owned the rights to Lassie and had been responsible for the original TV series, decided that the time was right for an eighth — and unquestionably not final — Lassie movie. To get the right feeling for this picture, they approached Richard and Robert Sherman, the writing/composing team who had won the Academy Award for their music for *Mary Poppins* (see page 175) and had written several films, including *The Slipper and the Rose* (see page 235). This time the Wrathers wanted a different direction for the Lassie franchise.

In *Foul Play*, Chase and Hawn are involved in a caper to thwart an assassination plot against the Pope during a visit to San Francisco. Dudley Moore, a British comedy actor who would soon become a household name in the United States, thanks to such pictures as *10* (1979) and *Arthur* (1980, see page 252) co-starred in this, his first important American movie. Also in the cast were Burgess Meredith, Brian Dennehy, and Billy Barty.

Barry Manilow was tapped to sing "Ready to Take a Chance Again," the opening theme from *Foul Play*. It is sung under the continuation of the opening credits as we see Hawn driving a yellow VW convertible along

"How about doing something with songs?" the Shermans ventured. "The dog's not going to sing, is he?" the Wrathers inquired of the writers. "We promised them the dog wouldn't sing," says Richard Sherman, "but he would have feelings and thoughts being expressed with song. Perhaps the camera will be on Lassie, and we'll have a song; it will be the expression of the poetry of what's going on."

One of the songs, "When You're Loved," received an Oscar nomination. It was introduced in the film by Debby Boone, who'd had great success the previous year with "You Light Up My Life" (see page 232). "She had this beautiful, pure, feeling voice . . . The record made a big stir, and her voice on the soundtrack was very thrilling," says Richard Sherman. According to the composer, the song essentially states the theme of the picture — as do all the Shermans' songs, as Richard likes to point out.

The movie's human cast was assembled in a rather unique way. The Sherman brothers came up with their dream team, a wish list that included Jimmy Stewart, Mickey Rooney, and Alice Faye. Each time they mentioned that this or that name would be perfect for a song, the Wrathers, apparently personal friends with half of Hollywood, readily complied. "Every time we opened our mouths," marvels Richard, "we got who we wanted." Others in the cast included Pernell Roberts, Stephanie Zimbalist, and, of course, Lassie (along with an assortment of Lassie doubles).

The story used in *The Magic of Lassie* follows the plot of the original: After being taken against her will to Colorado, Lassie must overcome a series of obstacles, wending her way back to her bereaved family in California, crossing mountains and deserts, fording streams, rescuing a kitten, and so forth.

As for Lassie's gender confusion, Lassie trainer Bob Weatherwax (son of Rudd, founder of the dynasty that has trained all of the Lassies), explained the situation in a 1994 interview with *Dog Fancy* magazine: "The females are just as smart, but they lose their coats noticeably during the year and look like different dogs."

In 1994, Lassie came home to her familiar place on the big screen in a new Paramount movie entitled, simply, *Lassie*. The story was updated to reflect the times but still had the age-old theme of the bond between a boy and his dog. Once again, the latest Lassie, an eighth-generation descendant of the original collie, was trained by a member of the Weatherwax clan, Bob Weatherwax.

IT GOES LIKE IT GOES

Music by David Shire; lyrics by Norman Gimbel
From *Norma Rae*

Sometime in the 1970s, when we weren't looking, Gidget grew up. The Flying Nun quit her habit, and TV's button-nosed little bundle with a bad case of the cutes was suddenly a Serious Actress. In 1977 Sally Field had won an Emmy for her remarkable performance in the four-hour TV movie *Sybil*, in which she played a mentally disturbed woman with 16 personalities.

By 1979, she was ready to fly solo. Her first major feature, *Norma Rae*, provided just the lift she needed. The story was a challenging one, about a struggling Southern textile mill worker named Norma Rae and her first encounter with big-time labor. Norma Rae is a divorced mother of two children, one of them illegitimate. Her inevitable involvement with a New York union organizer is the hub around which the film turns. But it's not truly a love story — their relationship is never consummated. It's more a film of social commentary in an entertainment guise, one that received critical acclaim, if not the undying adoration of the general public. (In a year with big films like *Kramer vs. Kramer*, *Rocky II*, and *Alien* posting blockbusting box office returns, *Norma Rae*'s take was a mere $10 million.)

Field received more than just the critical praise of which she was so worthy; she received the Academy's highest honor, the Oscar for Best Performance by an Actress (they really liked her!). The film was also nominated for Best Screenplay Based on Material from Another Medium (for writers Irving Ravetch and Harriet Frank Jr.), Best Cinematography, and Best Song.

The film's main title song, "It Goes Like It Goes," a slow country-western tune sung over opening and closing credits, was not a chart burner. Jennifer Warnes sang the number on the soundtrack, but there were no hit singles. Most people didn't recall the Academy Award–winning tune, even when Dionne Warwick sang it at the Oscar ceremonies the following spring. Actually, 1979 wasn't a particularly scintillating year for

Sally Field and Ron Leibman in a scene from *Norma Rae*.

Oscar-nominated songs; "It Goes Like It Goes" wasn't especially memorable among the song nominees — it was just the best, at least as determined by vote.

The song was written by composer David Shire, who did the film's score, and lyricist Norman Gimbel (finally winning his first Oscar after several nominations). For Shire, it was his first (and only) Best Song win, although the talented composer was nominated twice that year ("The Theme from *The Promise*" was his other entry), so the odds were certainly stacked in his favor.

Shire began his musical career collaborating with Richard Maltby Jr., writing a series of off-Broadway shows. Soon Barbra Streisand, Andy Williams, Shirley Bassey, Roberta Flack, Pearl Bailey, and Robert Goulet were recording their tunes. In 1970, Shire split with Maltby and headed to California to concentrate on the TV and film industry. Within a few years, he was a top composer, scoring such films as *Farewell, My Lovely* (1975) and *All the President's Men* (1976). He also received an Emmy nomination for his music in the 1977 TV film *Raid on Entebbe*.

THE RAINBOW CONNECTION

Music and lyrics by Paul Williams and Kenny Ascher
From *The Muppet Movie*

Kermit the Frog. You'd be hard-pressed to find a schoolchild — or an adult, for that matter — who hasn't heard of the fuzzy green amphibian. The brainchild and alter ego of Muppet master Jim Henson, Kermit and all his pals — Miss Piggy, Fozzie Bear, Gonzo, Rowlf, Dr. Teeth — and an assortment of wondrous creatures easily segued from their own TV series, which ran from 1976 to 1981, to their own movie — *The Muppet Movie*, naturally.

Jim Henson first created his beloved character of Kermit back in the 1950s, introducing him and other Muppets (the name is a coined word combining puppet and marionette) on early variety shows like "Ed Sullivan" and "Tonight." By 1969, the Muppets were making regular appearances on the award-winning children's show "Sesame Street." By the late 1970s, there were over 400 Muppet characters, and it was only a matter of time until Henson moved into the field of cinema.

The Muppet Movie was a box office bonanza for Henson and his henchmen, including Frank Oz, who was credited as creative consultant but had always been closely involved with Henson. While Henson performed Kermit, Rowlf, Dr. Teeth, and Waldorf for the *Movie*, Oz was the brains — and arm — behind Miss Piggy, Fozzie Bear, Animal, and Sam the Eagle. Other Muppeteers were Jerry Nelson, Richard Hunt, and Dave Goetz, all of whom added their own vocal characterizations to the Henson creations. Although these were the true "stars" of the picture, *The Muppet Movie* — with its perfectly suited storyline about the Muppets on the road to Hollywood — was also blessed with a plethora of cameos. Edgar Bergen, Milton Berle, Mel Brooks, James Coburn, Dom DeLuise, Elliott Gould, Bob Hope, Madeline Kahn, Carol Kane, Cloris Leachman, Steve Martin, Richard Pryor, Telly Savalas, Orson Welles, and Paul Williams all mugged for the cameras in this tribute to show biz, loaded with salutes to assorted film classics.

The film was a hit — *The Muppet Movie*'s North American rentals totaled $32 million, making it the ninth-ranked picture for the year. In 1981, the Muppets returned in *The Great Muppet Caper* (see page 253), and another sequel — *The Muppets Take Manhattan*, directed by Oz — appeared in 1984.

Paul Williams did more than pop up in a cameo. He also co-wrote (with Kenny Ascher) *The Muppet Movie*'s main theme song, an enduring tune called "The Rainbow Connection." Although *Newsweek* called the score "the least effective component of the movie," nothing could have been further from the truth, as borne out by two Oscar nominations Williams and Ascher received for their efforts: one for Best Song and one in the category of Best Original Song Score and Its Adaptation or Adaptation Score.

"The Rainbow Connection," in addition to having the perfect sing-along melody for adults as well as children, had lyrics both poetic and poignant. The song starts at the end of the opening credits, sung by Jim Henson in character as Kermit, playing left-handed banjo and singing his ballad from a swamp. The scene was a difficult one to get on film. Henson had to spend long hours in a cramped underwater chamber to perform Kermit and set just the right mood for the film to follow. It paid off, though — "The Rainbow Connec-

tion" even became a pop hit, the first song on the *Billboard* charts to be sung by a frog. Kermit's rendition peaked in the number 25 position and was on the charts for 17 weeks.

The song ends with Ascher's words that "Someday we'll find it — the rainbow connection — the lovers, the dreamers, and me." He might easily have been singing about Henson, one of those true dreamers, like Walt Disney and a handful of others, who come along once in a generation. Sadly, Henson, a gentle man who didn't like to trouble people, died in 1990 from a galloping bacterial infection (he reportedly didn't want to disturb anyone by seeking help until it was too late). His sudden death stunned millions of Muppet fans worldwide. Following Jim's death, his son Brian continued to carry on the Muppeteering tradition his father had begun. Jim Henson may be gone, but his legacy of Muppets, to paraphrase the words of "The Rainbow Connection," is keeping all of us — the lovers, the dreamers — under his spell.

SONG FROM *10* (IT'S EASY TO SAY)

Music by Henry Mancini; lyrics by Robert Wells
From *10*

10 took a chance with its title, opening itself up to the same kind of rating scale that its star, Dudley Moore, establishes as the basis of the film's plot. *Time* dubbed it "in the 6-to-7 range," but awarded the object of Moore's affection and the movie's female lead, Bo Derek, "a well-deserved 10." What was all this rating scale nonsense about?

Moore played a middle-aged, mid-life-critical man with nothing better to do than hang out on the beach ranking the attributes of various women who strolled by. He already has a lovely lover, a singing star (Julie Andrews, a.k.a. Mrs. Blake Edwards, making her customary appearance in one of hubby Blake's films), but once he spots Derek, the plot spins into motion. Does Bo know she's being stalked everywhere, from the church where she's married to her honeymoon in Mexico? Eventually she finds out, but not until several fantasy moments have been played out in this slow-motion wet dream of a picture to the beat of Ravel's "Bolero."

The comedy received surprisingly positive reviews and turned out to be the sleeper of the year, pulling down $37 million in domestic box office rentals. Much of that was due to Moore's abilities as an actor and comedian, as well as writer/co-producer/director Edwards's skills behind the typewriter and camera. "Out of such premises have come many tired and leering Hollywood farces," said *Newsweek,* "but Blake Edwards's riotous, deeply felt *10* proves just how many fresh turns are left on the well-traveled road . . . Edwards provides the side-splitting slapstick one expects from the maker of five *Pink Panther* movies, but he gives us something more: an introspective, bittersweet comedy of manners about a man whose voyeurism prevents him from seeing himself." Maybe, but viewed in a more contemporary perspective, this sort of stalking can easily be seen as sexist and dangerous.

The long-standing collaboration of Edwards and composer Henry Mancini continued with *10.* Mancini composed one of his typical scores, for which he received his typical Academy Award nomination for Best Original Score. He was not above having a bit of fun poked at him too, as some humor about the composer's music was worked into the film. Moore's character George is supposed to be a composer — a four-time Oscar winner, to be precise. Mancini's music naturally is credited to George, and at one point Derek innocently criticizes it as "elevator music."

Mancini, along with lyricist Robert Wells, also composed a song for the film. "It's Easy to Say" was performed on the soundtrack by Julie Andrews and received an Oscar nomination for Best Song. It was performed by Moore and Helen Reddy at the Academy Awards ceremonies the following April.

Dudley Moore and Julie Andrews play husband and wife Blake Edwards's *10.*

THEME FROM *ICE CASTLES* (THROUGH THE EYES OF LOVE)

Music by Marvin Hamlisch; lyrics by Carol Bayer Sager
From *Ice Castles*

"*Rocky* on ice skates" might be one way of describing *Ice Castles.* The story of a teenager from a small Iowa town overcoming every conceivable adversity, including parental opposition, lack of proper training, a late start, and even blindness, is right out of the *Rocky* mold. In the hands of the wrong director, it could have cranked out enough soap to lather up all the cornfields in Iowa, but fortunately, that didn't happen. Okay, maybe a soap bubble or two.

Newsweek attributed much of the film's credibility to its director. Donald Wrye, the magazine enthused,

"handles this chestnut with restraint, scoring points about media madness and the fear of success without getting messagy." Strong performances were also important in keeping the movie moving. Newcomer Lynn-Holly Johnson portrayed Alexis, nicknamed Lexie, the winsome farm girl who is trained under the encouragement of the local ice rink operator, played by Colleen Dewhurst. Soon Alexis is skating into the hearts of the American people, seemingly having it all, until Tragedy strikes — she's partially blinded. Her boyfriend (Robby Benson) and father (Tom Skerrit), along with her coach and family, eventually bring her out of her funk to an improbable but uplifting ending.

Despite all the fine character development, this was still a very manipulative tear-jerker. Even Marvin Hamlisch's score was designed to give a good old-fashioned tug at the heartstrings, even as it provided skatable music for Johnson. The stirringly romantic music is highlighted by the movie's love melody, "Theme from *Ice Castles* (Through the Eyes of Love)." The Oscar-nominated song, with words by Hamlisch's then–significant other, Carol Bayer Sager, augments the mood and is especially effective in the closing sequence.

In an unusual departure, Hamlisch began writing his score at the start of the film's production (rather than following the preferred method of composing — waiting for photography to wrap before beginning to compose), so that the star could skate to the love theme during the filming of some of the significant early sequences.

Melissa Manchester sang "Through the Eyes of Love" on the soundtrack and at the Academy Awards ceremony in April, 1980. Her single recording did only moderately well on the *Billboard* charts, peaking in the number 76 position and charting for four weeks.

Manchester was born in 1951 and began her professional career as a backup singer in the 1960s. She also did vocals on TV commercials, including ones for Pepsi, McDonald's, and United Airlines. In the early '70s she worked as part of Bette Midler's backing vocal group, the Harlettes. After leaving the group to strike out on her own, Manchester co-wrote a number of tunes with Carol Bayer Sager, and by the late '70s she was turning out her own successful albums. Her charting singles included "Don't Cry Out Loud," "Pretty Girls," and "Fire in the Morning." She also continued as a songwriter, co-writing "Whenever I Call You Friend" with Kenny Loggins, a major hit for him in 1978.

Lynn-Holly Johnson, on a break from location shooting of *Ice Castles*.

THEME FROM *THE PROMISE* (I'LL NEVER SAY "GOODBYE")

Music by David Shire;
lyrics by Alan and Marilyn Bergman
From *The Promise*

The Promise was a romantic Danielle Steele melodrama whose title had to do with a buried necklace and the promise of undying love and faith pledged between a young architectural student (played by Stephen Collins) and his girlfriend (Kathleen Quinlan). When Collins's domineering mother objects to the couple's wedding plans, the pair thwart her by dashing off to elope. En route, there's a horrendous automobile accident, crushing Quinlan's face and rendering Collins unconscious. While he's comatose, the conniving mother promises something too: If the girl will get out of her son's life, the mother will pay for facial reconstruction.

This sounds like a pretty square deal to Quinlan, so she goes under the skilled knife of Laurence Luckinbill, playing a top-notch San Francisco doctor. The plot works — Collins is convinced that his beloved has died in the auto wreck. But fate eventually draws the couple back together, as Collins tries to hire Quinlan for her photographic expertise, not realizing who she is. She avoids him; he pursues her across the continent and back. Cue the violins (literally) — as the picture draws to its inevitable conclusion, the lush music of composer David Shire swells in the background.

It was, in essence, a soap opera. Then, again, as *Variety* commented, "To dismiss *The Promise* as a soap opera would belittle its accomplishment. It is a soap symphony, a soap circus, a soap saga, a veritable superbowl of soap, all neatly packaged in 98 minutes instead of years or afternoons. Could be a sales plus." Actually, that last promise was broken — *The Promise* didn't live up to its title. Although the reviews were fairly kind,

most people preferred their soap in the washer, or perhaps in its true place, the TV set.

The most promising thing about the film was the fine performance by Collins. *Variety* noted that "a new, very handsome, young leading man is added to the Hollywood scene (and could they ever use him!) with Stephen Collins as the architect." Collins had a very good year in 1979 — his other big movie, *Star Trek: The Motion Picture*, premiered in December, and ended up as the year's number two hit at the box office.

David Shire's music contributed to the melodramatics quite nicely. The basis of his score was the Academy Award–nominated song "I'll Never Say 'Goodbye,' " with lyrics by the Oscar-winning husband-and-wife team of Alan and Marilyn Bergman. The tune was sung in the film by Melissa Manchester, who was having a good year of her own, recording two Oscar-nominated tunes in 1979 — "Theme from *Ice Castles* (Through the Eyes of Love)" (see page 244) and the "Theme from *The Promise* (I'll Never Say 'Goodbye')." At the Oscar ceremonies the following April, Manchester performed both tunes. And 1979 was also a banner year for Shire, who found himself with two entries in 1979's Oscar race: He was nominated for "Theme from *The Promise*" as well as for "It Goes Like It Goes" from *Norma Rae*, the song that clinched the Oscar for him (see page 241).

THE EIGHTIES

In the 1980s, the rules suddenly changed. Traditionally, the Academy had allowed only one Best Song entry per motion picture. Then, in 1980, the members decided to allow two songs from Fame. *This paved the way for future multiple nominees, a trend that continues today.*

This development was not really so surprising, since the 1980s saw the resurgence of the movie musical, which started appearing with greater frequency than in any decade since the '50s. Fame *was followed by* Flashdance, *which in turn was followed by* Yentl, Footloose, *and* White Nights. *It all added up to a remarkable rediscovery of the musical genre.*

One of the big reasons for the return of the film musical (or, at least, for the return of the featured song within a film) was MTV. Film studios quickly figured out in the early and mid-'80s that one of the easiest ways to promote a film was to feature several songs within the movie, release the songs as singles, and then load the singles' MTV videos with clips from the film, allowing the film and songs to cross-promote each other. Soundtrack sales boomed during this period.

Title songs and "Themes from" were still popular, but more and more movies were simply beginning to have a good tune as an opening or closing number — something representative of the picture, yet strong enough, perhaps, to garner a nomination (and songs were being created and worked into films for just that purpose).

One unusual thing occurred during this decade. In 1988, only three songs were nominated, the first time this had happened since the inception of the awards back in the mid-1930s. It was simply not a very prolific year in motion picture song. Perhaps this was a fluke, an oversight on the part of producers; in any event, don't look for this to happen again too soon. By the following year, the last one of the decade, the Oscar for Best Song was once again a prize sought by the traditional five nominees, each competing frantically for the coveted statuette.

1980

FAME

Music by Michael Gore; lyrics by Dean Pitchford
From *Fame*

Academy Award history was made in 1980. Not only was this a new decade, but a new era for Oscar-nominated songs was about to be entered. In an unprecedented development, two songs from the same film were nominated for Best Song. While this was the first time this had happened in the history of the awards, it would not be the last.

The film was *Fame,* and its claim was energy — the kind of youthfully energetic performances the likes of which had not been seen since the days of Mickey

Rooney and Judy Garland's "let's put on a show" time. But this time, there were fresh adolescent faces grooving to a hip disco beat. No longer lily-white and set in some milk-and-cookies suburb, these kids questing for *Fame* were urban, multiracial singers from a variety of backgrounds: There were Puerto Ricans, black kids, white kids, Jewish kids, homosexual kids, talented kids, good kids, not-so-good kids — all of them bursting with talent that just could not be contained.

"When it's cooking," wrote *Newsweek,* "it has more style and energy than any musical since *Cabaret.*" Comparisons seemed inevitable. No one had seen anything quite like *Fame* before. Was it a cross between *A Chorus Line* and Bob Fosse's *All That Jazz?* Maybe, but in the end, *Fame* owed its fame to its own uniqueness.

The story, such as it is, insisted on giving nearly every player some clichéd sort of problem, like drug abuse or an inability to deal with their sexuality. All the performers play the roles of teenagers — dancers, musicians, actors — who audition for and eventually

"I'm gonna live forever!" proclaim the stars of *Fame,* in the movie's climactic theme song production number.

graduate from Manhattan's public High School of Performing Arts (a real school). In the end, though, the exuberance of the gifted cast helped the picture rise above its own plot shortcomings.

The film's finale is a performance of the title song, "Fame," with the entire cast romping through the streets of New York, led by actress Irene Cara, wailing from atop a car. It was the kind of infectious production number that made audiences wish they could get up there and belt out the tune with her. The confident, now-familiar words proclaim that "I'm gonna live forever," an expression that connected with all the young hopefuls who felt they embodied the lyric's personal pronoun.

"Fame" was written by Michael Gore (cousin of the late Christopher Gore, who wrote the screenplay) with lyricist Dean Pitchford. The young writers received the Oscar for Best Song, competing against another song from the same movie, "Out Here on My Own" (see page 251). When "Fame" was announced as the winner at the Oscar ceremonies, Dolly Parton, whose "9 to 5" was seen as "Fame"'s primary competition for the award, pretended to block the aisle to keep Gore and Pitchford from claiming their prize. "I'm not going to let you pass," she joked, finally giving them a hug.

"Fame" also received a Golden Globe for Best Original Song from a film. Meanwhile, Irene Cara's single release of the song charted well. It peaked in the number four position and spent 26 weeks on the *Billboard* charts.

Fame received additional Oscar nominations for Best Original Screenplay, Best Sound, and Best Film Editing.

9 TO 5

Music and lyrics by Dolly Parton
From *9 to 5*

The perfect picture for the liberated woman of the '80s, *9 to 5* reflected the sentiments of a new generation of females in the work force, still struggling to free themselves from the yoke of male domination. Dabney Coleman turned in a marvelous performance as the prototypical male chauvinistic jerk of a boss, as women across America vicariously imagined hurling their typewriters from office windows with gleeful revenge.

The three females leads were perfect, too. Acting veterans Jane Fonda and Lily Tomlin shone in this comedy, directed and co-written by Colin Higgins (a man surprisingly in touch with the feminist movement). But the best performance was clearly that of Dolly Parton. A novice actress appearing in her first film, she had a plum role and proved every bit as skillful as her more experienced co-stars. What's more, she wrote and sang the movie's title song, making her a triple threat — or, more accurately, a triple joy.

The opening sequence is a gem. We see alarm clocks sounding the 7:00 A.M. wake-up call to the work force. As Parton's "9 to 5" is sung to a rock beat that sets the frenetic pace, we see people all over the city heading off to work — walking, running, commuting, bicycling. We see legs, female legs, lots of legs and feet walking and hurrying as more people are seen checking their watches and clocks. Finally, this clever opening setup (devised by Wayne Fitzgerald and David Oliver) ends with Jane Fonda arriving at her new job as the song fades.

Parton's song did anything but fade. The country singer released a single of her title tune at the time of the film's debut during the 1980 holiday season. By February of 1981, it had climbed the charts to reach Number One, where it stayed for two weeks. It remained on the charts for a full six months — 26 weeks — and went gold.

"9 to 5" was nominated for the Best Song Oscar, and Parton performed the tune at the Academy Awards ceremony. While it didn't win the statuette from the Academy (it went to "Fame" that year — see page 248), it was a Grammy winner for Best Country-and-Western Song in 1981.

The film itself proved a crowd-pleaser. Working women adored it, while men chuckled over Coleman's performance as the caricatured boss, so exaggerated that no men really identified with this personification of the lecherous, selfish supervisor. When the receipts were tallied, *9 to 5* had pulled in $59.1 million in North American rentals, making it the number two picture for the year.

In March, 1982, Jane Fonda co-produced a short-lived television series called "9 to 5." None of the original three actresses appeared in it, but Dolly Parton's sister Rachel Dennison co-starred (along with Rita Moreno and Valerie Curtin). The series was canceled after a year, but was resurrected in syndication for a short time, with "All in the Family" alumna Sally Struthers as one of the stars.

Director Jerry Schatzberg (left) rehearses with Willie Nelson, Dyan Cannon, and Amy Irving during Texas location filming of *Honeysuckle Rose*.

ON THE ROAD AGAIN

Music and lyrics by Willie Nelson
From *Honeysuckle Rose*

Willie Nelson paired with Dyan Cannon. It was an unlikely duo, the country singer and the talented actress, cast as husband and wife. One critic compared it to the Muppet romance between Kermit the Frog and Miss Piggy. Or perhaps it was closer to Leslie Howard and Ingrid Bergman, since that was the pair who starred in the original version of *Honeysuckle Rose* when it was made back in 1939. Back then it was called *Intermezzo*, the story of a married violinist (Howard) who has an affair with his protégée (Bergman, in her first English-speaking role). But Hollywood loves a remake, so just as *A Star Is Born* was updated for the '70s, screenwriter Carol Sobieski and director Jerry Schatzberg decided the time was perfect to update *Intermezzo*, featuring country-and-western star Willie Nelson in the Leslie Howard part and Dyan Cannon in the Bergman role of his illicit lover.

Honeysuckle Rose takes place in Texas and on the road. And it is while on the road that Nelson's charac-

ter gets involved with one of his pal's daughters (played by Amy Irving). Cue Nelson's "On the Road Again." The singer wrote and performed the tune, which received an Academy Award nomination. Today, Nelson is so identified with the song that most people have forgotten its origin in the movie. The tune was also a popular hit, although it peaked at only number 20 as a single. Nelson's soundtrack album, however, sold over a million copies.

Nelson was a familiar face on the country-and-western scene, with his scraggly beard and long gray hair giving him the appearance of an overaged hippie. Like the character he portrayed in *Honeysuckle Rose*, the composer-singer-actor was a native of Texas, having been born there in 1933, and his music retains a touch of the Lone Star State's honky-tonk tradition. He wrote songs for others at first, including "Crazy," a Number One country hit for Patsy Cline in 1961, and "Hello Walls," a Number One country hit for Faron Young. Nelson's breakthrough recording in 1975, "Blue Eyes Crying in the Rain," featured only his voice and an acoustic guitar. It was his first pop hit, and he soon began to find a crossover rock audience eager to hear more of his music.

Nelson's acting debut was in *The Electric Horseman* (1979), starring Robert Redford. *Honeysuckle Rose* was his second film, and some critics saw him emerging as an improbable sex symbol. *Time* described him as a "rodeo ragamuffin — with his Indian headbands, his long braided hair, a diamond stud in his left earlobe and a face as seamed and leathery as a football left out in the Texas sun," but went on to point out, "No matter, the camera loves him." Audiences however, seemed to prefer Nelson's recordings to his screen appearances. The film was only modestly successful, taking in $10.5 million in North American box office rentals.

OUT HERE ON MY OWN

Music by Michael Gore; lyrics by Lesley Gore
From *Fame*

For the first time in the history of the Oscars, two songs were nominated from the same picture. *Fame* was now famous for giving birth to two Academy Award–nominated songs — the title song, "Fame," which won the Oscar, and "Out Here on My Own."

"Out Here on My Own" was a slower, less frenetic song than the title tune. Like the film's title track, it was performed by Irene Cara and had music written by Michael Gore, who also wrote the music to the award-winning "Fame." But this time he used a different lyricist — his sister, Lesley Gore. (Their cousin, the late Christopher Gore, had written the screenplay, making this a Gore family project and a rarity among films.)

Lesley's own claim to fame had been as a pop singer back in June of 1963, when she had a Number One hit, "It's My Party." She was a mere 17 years old when the tune entered the *Billboard* Hot 100. According to *The Billboard Book of Number One Hits,* by Fred Bronson, "[The record's] ascension on the charts was swift: it debuted at 60 and moved to 26, to nine, to one." Gore continued to record songs throughout the '60s and '70s, including "Judy's Turn to Cry" and "She's a Fool," both of which peaked at number five. "You Don't Own Me" reached number two for three weeks in 1964.

The score from *Fame* had several writers. Michael Gore and Dean Pitchford, who wrote the title song, also were responsible for "Red Light" and "I Sing the Body Electric," while Michael and Lesley Gore wrote "Hot Lunch Jam," Dominick Bugatti and Frank Musker

wrote "Dogs in the Yard," and Paul McCrane wrote "Is It Okay If I Call You Mine?"

Irene Cara's single of "Out Here on My Own" gave her two songs on the charts in 1980. It peaked at number 19 and charted for 23 weeks.

Fame's fame continued on television. In 1982, NBC began airing the series "Fame," starring Debbie Allen, who'd had a bit part in the original movie. Allen became the show's chief choreographer — and later director — a stepping stone to her eventual career as a top TV director. Others from the original film who appeared in the TV series included Lee Curreri as Bruno, Gene Anthony Ray as Leroy Johnson, and Albert Hague as Mr. Shorofsky, the music teacher. Cara did not repeat her role of Coco; instead, that part went to newcomer Erica Gimpel. Janet Jackson, later a famous recording artist, actress, and composer (see "Again," page 306), had a minor role on the series from 1984–85.

The series aired on NBC for only a season and a half, from January of 1982 to August of 1983. When it was canceled due to low ratings, the series' producers decided to continue the production of new episodes, selling them into syndication to run on local stations. The series then continued in first-run syndication until the fall of 1987.

PEOPLE ALONE

Music by Lalo Schifrin; lyrics by Wilbur Jennings
From *The Competition*

All the thrills, all the chills, all the excitement of . . . a classical piano contest? Set against the intrigue and drama of two competitors in the "exciting" world of competitive classical music, *The Competition* didn't have much of its namesake — it was out there all alone with its premise.

The film had some pluses, including the excellent cast. Amy Irving, who also appeared as a musician in *Honeysuckle Rose* the same year (see page 250), was cast as the young prodigy about to turn 21, hell-bent on winning this critical contest. Richard Dreyfuss, star of *Jaws* (1975), *Close Encounters of the Third Kind* (1977), and *The Goodbye Girl* (1977), was cast opposite her as a 30-year-old, last-chance-for-the-big-time competitor. Music — and love — are in the air when these two meet, but the Big Piano Competition supersedes everything. Will they give in to each other, or will their egos and careers win this musical battle of the sexes?

Many critics abhorred this movie, which really did have some effective performances, especially from Lee Remick as Irving's piano teacher. Sam Wanamaker was also good as the lecherous conductor. Irving, who had yet to realize her full potential as an actress (she would receive such recognition in *Yentl* in 1984, see page 264), was given some good notices, especially from *Variety*, which remarked, "Irving is such a lively and attractive actress that she manages to keep whatever scenes she is in watchable and occasionally even amusing. Dreyfuss, on the other hand, seems unduly leaden."

But the sorriest commentary was reserved for the actual music itself. What should have been a joyful two-hour peek into the high-pressure world of talented musicians and their music was lambasted by *Variety*. "The classical pieces are subjected to condensation, an unconscionable violation by a film which purports to be a serious treatment of classical music. The footage devoted to actual performing reportedly was shortened after screenings for [exhibitors], on the dubious theory that the pic might do better commercially by downplaying its actual subject." The crime, as *Variety* saw it, was poor editing. The punishment? *The Competition* received an Academy Award nomination for Best Film Editing. Go figure.

Also on the Academy's list of honors was a Best Song nomination for "People Alone," the movie's theme song. Lalo Schifrin, who composed the score, and lyricist Wilbur Jennings shared the nomination. Schifrin didn't escape *Variety*'s wrath either. His music was criticized as "noisy, bombastic . . . a measure of the ham-handed tastelessness of this film . . . The entire cast boogies under the end credits to an awful disco number by Schifrin."

Schifrin took in all in stride; the talented composer was way ahead of the competition. He had been born into a musical family — his father was the conductor for the Teatro Colón in Buenos Aires for over 30 years. Lalo studied music composition in Paris while playing jazz in nightclubs during the early '50s. In 1956 he met Dizzy Gillespie, his greatest influence, and moved to New York to work with the jazz great. While there, Schifrin began arranging for Xavier Cugat's orchestra and also writing for television. Schifrin's best known TV themes were for "Mission: Impossible" and "Starsky and Hutch." Among the films whose scores he composed were *Bullitt* (1965), *Dirty Harry* (1971), and *The Eagle Has Landed* (1976).

1981

And the winner is... ARTHUR'S THEME (BEST THAT YOU CAN DO)

Music by Burt Bacharach; lyrics by Carole Bayer Sager, Christopher Cross, and Peter Allen

From *Arthur*

They called him "cuddly Dudley," that five-foot-three barrel of British dynamite who had worked his way into the hearts of Americans in his first successful Stateside picture, *10* (see page 243). In his second American film, *Arthur*, Moore starred as the title character, a rich, likable fellow with a serious drinking problem. It was, fortunately, a last gasp and gulp for the "funny drunk" role, as societal awareness and sensitivity toward alcoholism as a disease would soon make this sort of characterization a thing of the past. But while it lasted, nobody did it better than Moore in this movie.

Co-starring with him as the "faithful retainer" (quite similar to P.G. Wodehouse's Jeeves character) was Sir John Gielgud, at age 78 still proving he had what it takes. He received an Oscar — the first of his long career — for Best Supporting Actor for his role as the valet Hobson.

The film was extremely popular at the box office, earning $42 million in domestic rentals, making it one of the most successful comedies in years. There were three Academy Award nominations in addition to Gielgud's: Best Actor (Moore), Best Original Screenplay (Steve Gordon), and Best Original Song. The song, "Arthur's Theme (Best That You Can Do)," won top honors, living up to its subtitle.

"Arthur's Theme" was written by a committee of talented people in the music field. Burt Bacharach wrote the music, claiming to have composed the song in only two nights, while the lyrics were written by Peter Allen, Carole Bayer Sager (by now no longer involved with Marvin Hamlisch, musically or personally, but with Bacharach instead), and Christopher Cross, who was also tapped to record the song for release as a single. Bacharach told *Billboard Book of Number One Hits* author Fred Bronson that there was never any other choice for singer. "We wanted him, and what a logical move, too," said Bacharach, "because the year before he'd won five Grammys, and it seemed like a good career move for him as well."

"Arthur's Theme (Best That You Can Do)" did very well indeed. It reached Number One by October, 1981, and stayed there for three weeks, spending a total of 24 weeks on the charts and selling over a million copies along the way. People just couldn't get enough of the song about "the moon and New York City," as some people called it, referring to a line from the lyric — one of those "catch" lines (like "my huckleberry friend" from Henry Mancini's "Moon River") that helps cement a song in the public's mind.

A sequel, *Arthur 2: On the Rocks* lived up to *its* title as well, sounding the death knell for the funny drunk concept. Audiences may have wanted to hug the cuddly star, but not as a falling down boozer. They knew when to say when, and the sequel fizzled.

ENDLESS LOVE

Music and lyrics by Lionel Richie
From *Endless Love*

Newsweek called it "an overwrought teen make-out movie." *Endless Love,* based on the popular novel of the same name by Scott Spencer, was a lovefest for fans of Brooke Shields. The film was directed by Franco Zeffirelli, the man responsible for the highly-acclaimed screen version of a story of another pair of teenagers in love — *Romeo and Juliet* (1968). He shocked audiences then with his nude, although tastefully filmed, love scenes. By the time *Endless Love* came along in 1981, however, audiences weren't quite so prudish, but the film's young star, 16-year-old model-turned-actress Shields, was contractually excused from having to do such scenes on camera. There were nude scenes all right, but those thighs and breasts in the close-ups belonged to an anonymous body double, as called for in Shields's contract.

It really didn't matter. *Variety* noted that Shields was "the same as she's always been — gorgeous, inexpressive, fun-loving, and still a child." Despite the lackluster reviews for Shields and her young lover, played by newcomer Martin Hewitt, the film did all right at the box office, with a take of $16.5 million in North American rentals. (And if people had only known then what they

do now, it might have been even more successful: *Endless Love* marked the screen debut of future superstar Tom Cruise, in a bit part, billed third from last.)

The title song, "Endless Love," fared even better. It was a hit for writer Lionel Richie, who recorded his song with Diana Ross, at the suggestion of the film's director, Zeffirelli. These two artists were both swamped with commitments and ended up having to cut the tune at a 3:00 A.M. recording session. Ross hadn't even received a copy of the lyrics in advance, but she rose to the occasion, and by 5:00 A.M. they had laid down the final track. Their single reached Number One and stayed on top for an unbelievable nine weeks. It charted for 27 weeks and went platinum, selling over two million copies.

The song broke all kinds of records. "Endless Love"'s nine weeks at Number One made it the most successful Motown single of all time (next closest: Marvin Gaye's "I Heard It Through the Grapevine" at seven weeks, and the Jackson Five's "I'll Be There," four weeks). It was the most successful soundtrack single to that date (displacing the Bee Gees' "Night Fever" from *Saturday Night Fever*). And it was the most successful duet of all time to that date.

Nominations and awards were quickly forthcoming. The Academy of Motion Picture Arts and Sciences nominated "Endless Love" for an Oscar. At the awards ceremony, Richie and Ross sang their hit single. Lionel Richie would have to wait until 1985, however, to take home the statuette (for "Say You, Say Me" — see page 270), as "Endless Love" lost to "Arthur's Theme" (see page 252). "Endless Love" did win the American Music Awards' top honors as the Pop/Rock Favorite Single in 1982, however. "Endless Love" was also honored with the People's Choice Award in the category of Music for Favorite New Song.

In 1994, Mariah Carey and Luther Vandross recorded "Endless Love" for his new album, "Songs."

THE FIRST
TIME IT HAPPENS

Music and lyrics by Joe Raposo
From *The Great Muppet Caper*

When last seen on the big screen, the Muppets were cavorting in Hollywood. For their next adventure, Jim Henson and company moved his lovable creations to

England. Actually, they were already there, filming their syndicated television series at a studio outside London, thanks to backing from Sir Lew Grade. At the end of the fifth and final season of "The Muppet Show," the performers and workshop personnel moved from their home at ATV Studios to the site of the movie location at Elstree Studios, about a block away.

For this second Muppet movie, called *The Great Muppet Caper,* the usual gang was present and accounted for, including Kermit the Frog, Fozzie Bear, and Miss Piggy, along with some human stars. Diana Rigg, who was best known to television audiences at the time for her role as Emma Peel in "The Avengers" from 1966 to 1968, starred as Lady Holiday, a London fashion magnate. Charles Grodin co-starred as Nicky Holiday, brother of Lady Holiday but, unfortunately, a jewel thief with designs of his own — he's after her most cherished gem, the Baseball Diamond. Other humans in the cast included John Cleese, Robert Morley, Peter Ustinov, and Jack Warden.

But the movie really belonged to Jim Henson's creatures. Henson himself helmed this time, and with a reported budget of $14 million, there was no denying that his Muppets seemed every bit as alive as the human stars. *Newsweek* remarked that "Jim Henson is a real movie director, with a sense of timing Leo McCarey [director of *Going My Way,* among others] would have approved of."

Miss Piggy is the true star of this picture. She's accidentally mistaken by Kermit for Lady Holiday, and she revels in the misunderstanding. Treated with every courtesy due a major star, she even had a complete biography compiled by Frank Oz, who was performing Piggy at the time. According to the book *Jim Henson, The Works,* Oz would happily explain to visitors on the set that "Miss Piggy grew up in a small town. Her father died young and her mother wasn't very nice to her. She had to enter beauty contests to survive. She has a lot of aggressiveness, but she needs a lot in order to survive — as many women do. She has a lot of vulnerability, which she has to hide because of her need to be a superstar."

The Great Muppet Caper showcased Miss Piggy in two outstanding production numbers: a spectacular water ballet in the traditional Esther Williams style and a dramatic nightclub number featuring the beloved porcine diva singing "The First Time It Happens." The Oscar-nominated song was written by Joe Raposo, the resident composer from TV's "Sesame Street," which featured the Muppets. He was responsible for Kermit's famous theme song, "Bein' Green." The composer once explained a song he was writing to a *New York Times* reporter: "I want to describe the promise of every morning and the curiosity and hope in every child's face. I would like to think that this theme of hope and wonder is at the root of all my work."

Miss Piggy interrupts her dinner with Muppets Fozzie Bear and Kermit the Frog to dance an impromptu number in *The Great Muppet Caper.*

FOR YOUR EYES ONLY

Music by Bill Conti; lyrics by Mick Leeson
From *For Your Eyes Only*

On the ski slopes, under water, or in the air piloting a helicopter — there was no stopping 007, a.k.a. Bond, James Bond. *For Your Eyes Only* was the twelfth installment of the antics of the suave British spy, with some changes. There was considerably less emphasis on the usual gadgetry supplied by "Q." No trick cars, no technological wonders were used to help Bond save the day. He had to do that on his own — aided, of course, by a $20 million production budget and a new director.

For Your Eyes Only was the first feature film for director John Glen. Glen had worked as editor and second-unit director on several previous Bond films, including *Moonraker,* for which he directed the memorable opening free-fall sequence. Glen was also second-unit director of *On Her Majesty's Secret Service,* supervising the exciting bobsled and ski chase scenes. *For Your Eyes Only* also contains some thrilling downhill skiing scenes, as well as dazzling underwater photography.

As with most Bond films, there was the usual trek to exotic locations. Corfu, Northern Italy, the Bahamas, the Meteora mountains of central Greece, and, of course, Pinewood Studios in England, where interiors were filmed. One scene was to be filmed in the Greek mountain top village of Kalambaka, at a 600-year-old Byzantine monastery. The trouble was, although the abbot granted the production company permission to film, a couple of the monks objected strenuously to the film crew's disrupting their way of life. They made every attempt to thwart the production, hanging out their laundry in full view of the cameras and generally causing delays in any way they could. Eventually, though, the filmmakers got what they came for, and the sequence turned out to be one the movie's best.

In another Bond tradition, there was a title song, always a challenge to any songwriter. Bill Conti, who had written the music to "Gonna Fly Now" for *Rocky* (see page 230), brought a new energy to the score and main title theme, along with appropriate lyrics by Michael Leeson. It is sung by Sheena Easton (the first time a Bond theme vocalist was actually seen in the opening titles) while silhouetted female nudes swirl about her, along with images of Roger Moore as James Bond.

Lynn-Holly Johnson and Roger Moore take to the slopes to watch a biathlon competition in the James Bond thriller *For Your Eyes Only.*

"For Your Eyes Only" received an Academy Award nomination, and an elaborate production number was staged at the Oscar ceremonies the following spring, when Easton was called upon to sing the song. She performed a fantasy dance number through Bondland, complete with an onstage car, lasers, exploding pyrotechnics, and even a moving rocket ship. Easton's recording of the tune did quite well, too. It peaked in the number four position and spent 25 weeks on the *Billboard* charts.

For Your Eyes Only brought a good return for its backers. The picture came in ninth for 1981, with a take of $26.5 million in North American rentals.

ONE MORE HOUR

Music and lyrics by Randy Newman
From *Ragtime*

E. L. Doctorow's novel *Ragtime* was brought to the screen in a movie of the same name and was immediately applauded by critics. The original book was a series of montages, a kaleidoscopic look at the American psyche circa 1910. Michael Weller translated the book to the screen under the direction of Milos Forman, who replaced Robert Altman after Altman was fired by producer Dino De Laurentiis. The film also benefited from choreography by Twyla Tharp and a memorable cast, including 82-year-old James Cagney in a comeback performance that would mark his final appearance on the big screen.

Richard Corliss of *Time* lavished praise on Forman, proclaiming him "an actor's director. In *Ragtime,* he has elicited many fine performances: from [James] Olson and [Mary] Steenburgen, models of rectitude and discreet strength; from [Howard E.] Rollins Jr. [as Coalhouse Walker], who carries the film with a heroic charm that sours into fatal righteousness; from Debbie Allen [of *Fame* fame, see page 248] as Walker's doomed love; from Ted Ross and Moses Gunn as two eloquent veterans of injustice who try talking sense and restraint to Coalhouse; and from James Cagney, back on-screen after a 20-year lapse and cool as a leprechaun sphinx in the role of a wily New York City police commissioner." Jack Kroll of *Newsweek* commented on still more performances: "Elizabeth McGovern's seductive dumbness

as the first modern sex symbol, a harbinger of Brooke Shields 75 years B.C. (before Calvins) [a reference to Shields's early jeans commercials]. The film's liveliest performance comes from Kenneth McMillan as the redneck fire chief whose racial taunting of Coalhouse triggers violence and tragedy."

At Oscar time, *Ragtime* was poised to win eight statuettes. The Paramount film was nominated in the categories of Best Supporting Actor (Rollins), Best Supporting Actress (McGovern), Best Adapted Screenplay, Best Cinematography, Best Art Direction, Best Costume Design, Best Original Score (Randy Newman), and Best Song (Newman again). And the winners were — none of the above. None, that is, won an Oscar, although they were all "winners," as is always stressed at the ceremonies, merely for having been nominated.

Randy Newman's ragtime-based score was especially strong throughout the film. His wistful, waltz-time song "One More Hour," which appears during the film's closing, was sung by Jennifer Warnes and nominated for Best Song.

Newman had been scoring films since 1971, when he made his debut with Norman Lear's comedy *Cold Turkey.* He received Oscar, Golden Globe, and Grammy nominations for many films, including *The Natural* (1984, winning a Grammy for instrumental composition written for a film), *Parenthood* (1989, see page 289), and *Avalon* (1990). The nephew of Oscar-nominated composers Alfred Newman and Lionel Newman, Randy's recent scores have included *Maverick* (1994) and *The Paper* (1994), which featured his stand-out single "Make Up Your Mind."

Howard E. Rollins Jr. in a scene from *Ragtime.*

And the winner is...

UP WHERE WE BELONG

Music by Jack Nitzsche and Buffy Sainte-Marie; lyrics by Will Jennings
From *An Officer and a Gentleman*

An Officer and a Gentleman was really about three people: an officer (and a gentleman, as the saying goes), the woman in his life, and his drill instructor. The actors portraying these three characters in director Taylor Hackford's love story turned in the film's strongest performances.

Richard Gere plays the young man in training at Naval Aviation Officer Candidate School. There he meets his tough drill sergeant, played by Louis Gossett Jr. He also meets and falls in love with a local gal, played by Debra Winger, a woman who thinks a future naval officer would be just the ticket out of her dreary life.

Although these were the liberated '80s, the love aspect of the film was still a cause for some alarm in this R-rated movie, especially by an older generation that had been shocked when Rhett Butler uttered the word "damn" on-screen back in 1939 for all the world to hear. Now, on-screen for all the world to *see* were various and sundry parts of male and female anatomy. There would be no turning back.

When the fog cleared from the audience's steam-clouded glasses, it was apparent that this sleeper of a movie had all the makings of a hit. It was, in the words of Vincent Canby of the *New York Times,* "an audience picture," which he went on to define as one that "should always refer to any film that attracts a large, appreciative audience, whether the film is as good as *E.T.* or as hokey as *Rocky III.*" Both of those films were among the top five box office hits for 1982, and so was *An Officer and a Gentleman* — the movie made $55.2 million in North American rentals, placing it firmly in the number four position that year.

The film's end theme song, "Up Where We Belong," created quite a stir in music circles. As was becoming more and more frequent in love stories, the tune was sung as a duet, this time by Joe Cocker and Jennifer Warnes. It was the only original song in the film, as the tightly budgeted picture allowed only for existing songs, selected from the catalogs of director Hackford's favorite artists — Pat Benatar, Dire Straits, and Van Morrison, among others. One of scorer Jack Nitzsche's background melodies was expanded, with input by Buffy Sainte-Marie, a Native American well known as a folk singer in the 1960s. Will Jennings, who had written the lyrics for "People Alone" in 1980, was drafted to write the words to "Up Where We Belong." Finally, Cocker and Warnes (who had also sung the nominated songs "It Goes Like It Goes" from *Norma Rae,* see page 241, and "One More Hour" from *Ragtime,* see page 256) recorded the tune. It reached the top of the charts, up where it belonged, by November 6, 1982, remained there for three weeks, and charted for 23 weeks in all.

The song was among the film's six Academy Award nominations: Best Actress (Winger), Best Original Screenplay (Douglas Day Stewart), Best Original Score (Nitzsche), Best Film Editing, and the two that won the Oscar — Best Supporting Actor (Gossett) and Best Song. "Up Where We Belong" was also honored with a Golden Globe Award for Best Original Song from a Film.

Debra Winger salutes Richard Gere in *An Officer and a Gentleman.*

EYE OF THE TIGER

**Music and lyrics by Jim Peterik
and Frankie Sullivan III**
From *Rocky III*

Survivor. The term could have been applied to Rocky Balboa (played, as always, by writer-director-actor Sylvester Stallone), who had proven he was just that in two previous films about the regular-guy boxer. Survivor was also the name of the group responsible for the Number One hit song to emerge from *Rocky III*, the third contender in the motion picture ring for Stallone and his trademark character.

This time, Rocky was back and Mr. T. had him. As Clubber Lang, the menacing, chain-bedecked T was Rocky's greatest challenger so far, and the one audiences seem to remember the most, although Carl Weathers, as Apollo Creed, gave him a pretty good run for his money. For *Rocky III*, Creed went over the wall, helping to train rather than fight Rocky, after Rocky's

Rocky Balboa (Sylvester Stallone) gets in step for his latest fight, as trainer Mickey (Burgess Meredith) lends encouragement in *Rocky III*.

previous trainer, Mickey, played by Burgess Meredith, suffered a heart attack and died.

If Rocky was a survivor (he'd be back to go at least two more rounds at the box office), so was Jim Peterik. Peterik, a keyboardist, had formed the group Survivor with lead guitarist Frank Sullivan and singer David Bicker in 1978. They were recording on the Scotti Brothers label in 1981 when the trio added bassist Stephan Ellis and drummer Marc Droubay. Frank Stallone, Sylvester's brother, had recorded a single for the label a few years before, and recommended Survivor to his brother. Rather than using the Oscar-nominated "Gonna Fly Now" for a third time, Sly signed Peterik and Sullivan to create something new for this film.

The result was a song called "Eye of the Tiger." The songwriting pair got the title of their song by watching a rough cut of the film on cassette and noticing that the catch phrase "eye of the tiger" was used a half a dozen times throughout, as Creed continually tells Rocky he has to stay focused, stay determined, maintain the eye of the tiger.

The song was released as a single and went to Number One on the pop charts, where it survived at the top for six weeks, charted for 25, and sold over two million copies. The tune, which was also recorded by the group Nighthawk and reached number 71 on the rhythm and blues chart, was voted a People's Choice Award for Favorite New Song.

In the movie, the song is used at the beginning of the picture under flashbacks to Rocky's numerous career highlights. We see the champion doing various endorsements, such as a commercial for American Express, hosting a telethon, and showing off some Rocky merchandise (a bit of an inside joke — this was the real stuff spun off from the two previous films).

One problem with *Rocky III*'s plot was that Rocky wasn't an underdog any more — now that he was the champ, it became harder for Stallone to come up with new challenges for the character. And in a way, *Rocky III* suffered from the same problem — Stallone was no longer a newcomer and his films were becoming something of a Hollywood institution — the Rocky phenomenon was no longer a novelty to the Academy. The film's only nomination was for the popular new song "Eye of the Tiger." The film did, however, go the distance at the box office, where its take in North American rentals totaled $66.2 million, making it the number three film of the year. Audiences certainly hadn't seen the last of Rocky Balboa.

Burt Reynolds and Goldie Hawn play *Best Friends* who get married. Here, aboard a train, they toast their wedding night.

HOW DO YOU KEEP THE MUSIC PLAYING?

Music by Michel Legrand; lyrics by Alan and Marilyn Bergman
From *Best Friends*

Two of Hollywood's hottest properties starred in *Best Friends.* Goldie Hawn and Burt Reynolds seemed like a sure-fire combination for gold at the box office. And when Reynolds wrapped his arms around Hawn, there should have been instant sparks and the sound of money and tickets frantically exchanging hands at the box office. But there was neither. Somehow, the chemistry just wasn't right. As *Newsweek* put it, "The problem of tone is exacerbated by Reynolds's reluctance to shed his 'cute' persona — he can't help winking at the camera. Though he's trying harder than usual to create a character, he's no match for Goldie."

The script was reality-based and perhaps a little too "inside" to reach a general, non-Hollywood audience. The two screenwriters, Barry Levinson (*Diner,* 1982) and Valerie Curtin (. . . *And Justice for All,* 1979) were real-life writing partners and lovers, and *Best Friends* is the loosely autobiographical tale of their relationship, with Hawn and Reynolds playing a pair of California screenwriters who marry, just as Levinson and Curtin did, then realize the error of their ways. Things begin to fall apart for the relationship (and, unfortunately, for the film as well) when they visit their respective parents back east.

There are some clever moments, though. During the story, we learn that a filmmaker friend is ending his movie with a shot of two lovers walking into an artificial sunset. "Yeah, see, Jean-Claude wants it to be surrealistic, sort of like Coppola, so you can't tell if any of them are really happy." The surprise comes when director Norman Jewison uses this exact concept as his finale. As the song "How Do You Keep the Music Playing?" is sung over closing credits, Goldie and Burt walk out of the scene, off the set and into the streets of what is obviously Warner Bros. Studios (where this picture was filmed) and into the artificially blazing sunset.

"How Do You Keep the Music Playing?" received a nomination from the Academy for Best Song, losing to "Up Where We Belong," the year's runaway hit. The song incorporates the film's title, *Best Friends,* into the lyric, a clever gimmick used by lyricist Alan and Marilyn Bergman to give this a title-song feel. The soundtrack version (with music by scorer Michel Legrand) was produced by Johnny Mandel and sung by Patti Austin and James Ingram, continuing the trend of male-female duets for film love songs. Their single on the Qwest label peaked at number 45 on the *Billboard* pop chart (charting for 17 weeks) but fared better on the rhythm and blues charts, climbing to number six.

The song was a particular favorite of Frank Sinatra, who included it on his Quincy Jones–produced *L.A. Is My Lady* album in 1984. Other artists who have since recorded "How Do You Keep the Music Playing?" include Andy Williams, Houston Person, Susannah McCorkle, and Tony Bennett.

IF WE WERE IN LOVE

Music by John Williams;
lyrics by Alan and Marilyn Bergman
From *Yes, Giorgio*

Luciano Pavarotti, the Italian opera star with a voice as big as all Italy and a girth to match, has often been hailed as the greatest tenor of modern times, a successor to both Enrico Caruso and Mario Lanza. It seemed only fitting, then, that he should eventually have his own film in which to star. After all, Lanza had been the idol of millions of opera as well as film buffs three decades before and had made a lot of *lire* from his motion pictures, including *The Toast of New Orleans* (1950, see page 109), *The Great Caruso* (1951), and *Because You're Mine* (1952). So the time seemed right to feature Pavarotti in a major motion picture.

The film was called *Yes, Giorgio,* and it was written as a showcase for the incomparable Luciano. It cost a reported $18 million to make, betting on middle-aged viewers to recoup its investment. Unfortunately, audiences said no to *Yes, Giorgio.* Why? For starters, this so-so romantic love story suffered from a rather uninspired script by talented comedy writer Norman Steinberg (who co-wrote such classics as 1974's *Blazing Saddles,* see page 222, and *My Favorite Year,* 1982). Steinberg himself can be seen in a minor role in *Yes, Giorgio,* playing Dr. Barmen.

Then too, film acting was something new to Pavarotti, who apparently was not completely comfortable in this medium. Said *Time:* "Movies are not where he lives, and he behaves in this one like a mannerly guest, puzzled, and a bit amused by all the fuss they are going to on his behalf." However, his operatic acting was another story. No one was more at home onstage performing in classic operas, and the producers wisely gave him a large selection of tunes with which to burst forth in the movie. Audiences were treated to "La Donna e Mobile" from *Rigoletto,* "Nessum Dorma" from *Turandot,* solos of "Ave Maria" and "O Solo Mio," and half a dozen or so other classic operatic selections, along with some modern songs like "I Left My Heart in San Francisco" and a new tune by John Williams and Alan and Marilyn Bergman, called "If We Were in Love."

This latter tune, criticized by some for not being appropriate to the movie, is warbled by Pavarotti from a hot-air balloon as he sails over the California wine country. The Academy liked the tune well

Luciano Pavarotti, Kathryn Harrold, and Eddie Albert get high over Northern California's wine country in the romantic comedy *Yes, Georgio.*

enough to nominate it for Best Song, in the process helping the Bergmans to receive the most nominations in one year since Harold Arlen had received three back in 1943 (when there were 10 nominated songs, versus only five in 1982). The married lyricists received their three nominations for "If We Were in Love," "How Do You Keep the Music Playing?" (see page 259), and "It Might Be You" (see page 260). Yet despite having three of the five nominated songs — good odds, to be sure — they lost to "Up Where We Belong" (see page 257).

IT MIGHT BE YOU

Music by Dave Grusin;
lyrics by Alan and Marilyn Bergman
From *Tootsie*

She wore her high-necked dresses long and her hair short and lightly teased. She had glasses, a winning smile, a soft voice, and, if she wasn't careful, a five o'clock shadow. She was, in fact, a he.

Oscar winner Dustin Hoffman (for *Kramer vs. Kramer,* 1979, and later in 1988 for *Rain Man)* starred as the lead in *Tootsie,* playing an actor who can't get work until he masquerades as a woman to win a role on a soap opera. Hoffman played the part brilliantly, reviving the ancient theatrical tradition of cross-dressing (classic Shakespearean plays, for instance, were originally presented with young men playing the female roles). The film was a huge success, 1982's number two picture at the box office, aced out only by a creature from another planet, the unstoppable *E.T. — The Extraterrestrial.* Tootsie's take totaled an astounding $94.9 million in North American rentals for the year, making the smash Columbia movie the eleventh-ranked film of the decade and one of the most successful comedies of all time.

Critics lavished kudos on the movie. "*Tootsie* is a lulu," proclaimed the *New York Times,* "remarkably funny and entirely convincing, [the] film pulls off the rare accomplishment of being an in-drag comedy which also emerges with three-dimensional characters."

Nailing down the script for *Tootsie* didn't come easily. At least eight writers — some credited, some not — had a hand in bringing the story to life. It began with a draft by Murray Schisgal, followed by contributions from seven additional scribes, including an original script by Don McGuire, with rewrites and polishes by Robert Kaufman, Larry Gelbart (co-creator of the TV series "M*A*S*H"), Elaine May (former comedy partner of Mike Nichols), Valerie Curtin (co-writer of *Best Friends,* see page 259), Barry Levinson, and Robert Garland. After an arbitration under the auspices of the Writers Guild, screenplay credit was awarded to Gelbart and Schisgal, from a story by McGuire.

Once all that was sorted out, the production could fly. Sydney Pollack produced, directed, and played a minor role as Tootsie's agent.

The film was nominated for 10 Oscars: Best Picture, Best Actor (Hoffman), Best Supporting Actress (both Jessica Lange — the only winner — *and* Teri Garr), Best Director (Pollack), Best Original Screenplay, Best Cinematography, Best Sound, Best Film Editing, and Best Song.

The Oscar-nominated song, "It Might Be You," was composed by Dave Grusin, who scored the music for the film, with lyrics by those irrepressible Bergmans, Alan and Marilyn, up for their third Best Song Oscar of the year (see "How Do You Keep the Music Playing?," page 259, and "If We Were in Love," page 260). "It Might Be You" was performed on the soundtrack by Stephen Bishop, himself a composer (see "Separate Lives," page 273). His single climbed the *Billboard* charts to the number 25 position and remained on the charts for 20 weeks.

1983

And the winner is...

FLASHDANCE . . . WHAT A FEELING

Music by Giorgio Moroder; lyrics by Keith Forsey and Irene Cara
From *Flashdance*

Musicals with a rock beat and lots of toe-tapping, get-up-and-boogie dancing made a comeback in the 1980s. Films like *Saturday Night Fever* (1977) had paved the way for hits like *Fame* (1980, see page 248) *Footloose* (1984, see page 267), and *Dirty Dancing* (1987, see page 279). In 1983, there was *Flashdance.* Some called it "Daughter of *Saturday Night Fever,*" likening it to the disco hit of the '70s, starring John Travolta and a white suit. But *Flashdance* could strut on its own.

Its success proved it was certainly no flash in the pan, or on the screen. It proved to be the third-highest-grossing musical of the 1980s, with a box office take in domestic rentals of $36.1 million. Much of this achievement can be attributed to the film's hot soundtrack, which made viewing the movie seem like "looking at MTV for 96 minutes," claimed *Variety.* As Janet Maslin of the *New York Times* wrote, "*Flashdance* contains such dynamic dance scenes that it's a pity there's a story here to bog them down."

There was a basic plot, of course. This time, the dancer-wannabe is a welder by day and a go-go girl by night, where she works up a sweat performing improvised dances in the local bar. But what she really wants to do is study formal dance and join the local ballet company. Does she succeed? You can bet your toe shoes on it, thanks to the unbilled dancing double for the film's star, Jennifer Beals. Beals, at the time a 19-year-old Yale freshman, was chosen from a field of over 4,000 applicants. She had the right look — a lean, expressive body and, as *Time* commented, "enough sultry energy to bring heat and humidity to her role."

Beals's wardrobe caught on in a flash, too — her off-the-shoulder sweatshirt started an '80s trend. The "Flashdance" look — torn T-shirts, slashed necklines, hacked off sleeves, leg warmers, and unraveling hems — became all the rage.

Beneath, and above, it all was the music, out there on its own. The title song, "Flashdance . . . What a Feeling" (the term "Flashdance," which does not actually appear in the tune, was added to the title to tie it to the film), had music by Giorgio Moroder and lyrics by Keith Forsey and Irene Cara. Cara had become a sensation after being cast in the lead of *Fame* (1980, see page 248) and performing the Oscar-winning title song in the film, which went on to be a hit recording. She doesn't appear in *Flashdance*, but recorded this title song, which was released as a single. It climbed the charts and reached the Number One position in the last week of May, 1983. The record stayed in that position for six weeks and on the charts for 25, ultimately selling over a million copies.

The song was nominated for an Oscar and was performed at the ceremonies in a lavish production number, led by Cara and 44 young boys and girls from the

Jennifer Beals, sporting the *Flashdance* look of headband, off-the-shoulder shirt, and lots and lots of sweat.

National Dance Institute. Then presenter Jennifer Beals announced — what a surprise — that the winner was "Flashdance . . . What a Feeling." The odds were certainly loaded in favor of *Flashdance* in this category, since "Maniac," a second song from the film, had also been nominated (see page 262).

In addition, Giorgio, Keith, and Irene also received the Golden Globe Award for Best Original Song from a Film.

MANIAC

Music and lyrics by Michael Sembello and Dennis Matkosky
From *Flashdance*

Songwriting partners Michael Sembello and Dennis Matkosky rented a video cassette one evening to try to relax — if you can call *The Texas Chainsaw Massacre* relaxing. Instead, the pair found it . . . inspiring. They decided their next song would not be one of their typical love songs; it would be about a mass-murderer. Calling their new tune "Maniac," and hoping it might be worked into an upcoming *Halloween*-type thriller, they cut a rough version of it on a cassette tape, then continued their work on performer Sembello's next album.

The call was from Paramount Pictures. There was a new movie, *Flashdance*, and they needed a song. Did Michael have anything to submit? Certainly, and he immediately asked his wife, Cruz, to dub two or three songs he'd been working on onto a tape. Cruz (who, as Cruz Baca, was a former back-up singer with Sergio Mendes, for whom Sembello had written songs), was well acquainted with the music world. She happily obliged and sent the samples to the studio. The next day Paramount called back — they loved one particular song, something about a . . . maniac? Oh, and could he please change the words? This new movie was about dancing, not slashing. Sembello's wife had inadvertently found a hit song. "You know," Cruz said in *Behind the Hits,* by Bob Shannon and John Javna, "you spend so much time doing demos and finished products — and all of a sudden — it's like a fluke — you succeed with a song that you didn't even mean for someone to hear!"

Flashdance was part of a new wave of movie musicals that sprang forth in the 1980s, owing a great deal to the flashy dancing of *Saturday Night Fever*. There were a number of popular songs in the film. The title tune, "Flashdance . . . What a Feeling," received the Academy Award for Best Song and was a huge Number One hit (see page 261). Other songs in the film included "I Love Rock 'n' Roll," by Jake Hooker and Alan Merrill; "Manhunt," by Doug Cotler and Richard Gilbert; "Gloria," by Giancarlo Bigazzi, Trevor Veitch, and Umberto Tozzi; "Lady, Lady, Lady" and "Seduce Me Tonight," by Giorgio Moroder and Keith Forsey; and Sembello and Matkosky's tune, "Maniac."

"Maniac," like "Flashdance . . . What a Feeling," received an Oscar nomination and became a Number One hit, marking the first time that two songs from the same film had ever done both. Sembello also recorded his tune for the soundtrack, with words changed to reflect someone who's a maniac on the dance floor, dancing like she's never danced before. His single release of "Maniac" entered the *Billboard* Hot 100 in June of 1983, and climbed to Number One by September 10. It stayed in that position for two weeks and remained on the charts for 22 weeks.

At the Oscar ceremonies, "Maniac" was performed by Herb Alpert & the Tijuana Brass and sung by Lani Hall. The film also received Oscar nominations for Best Cinematography and Best Film Editing.

Betty Buckley plays country music singer Dixie in *Tender Mercies*.

OVER YOU

Music and lyrics by Austin Roberts and Bobby Hart
From *Tender Mercies*

Tender Mercies marked the American debut of one of Australia's major film directors, Bruce Beresford (*Breaker Morant*, 1979). It was an old-fashioned slice-of-life movie, with no sex or violence, a people story shot on location in the Texas countryside. The story concerns Mac Sledge (Robert Duvall), a down-and-out country-and-western singing star, broken up over the breakup of his marriage to fellow C&W singer Dixie (Betty Buckley). He's drowning his sorrows in alcohol when he's rescued by Rosa Lee (Tess Harper), a widow with a young son. She offers Sledge work at the filling station and motel she owns; he accepts, soon marries his angel, and remakes his life, with lots of country music by assorted composers popping up along the way.

The film was widely praised by most critics. Janet Maslin of the *New York Times* wrote, "*Tender Mercies* has a bleak handsomeness bordering on the arty, but it also has real delicacy and emotional power, both largely attributable to a fine performance by Robert Duvall. Mr. Duvall's versatility seems to know no limit; in his role here as an over-the-hill country singer, he creates yet another quietly unforgettable character." And the *Times*'s other critic, Vincent Canby, observed, "[*Tender Mercies*] is a funny, most appealing and most sharply observed film . . . likely to become the year's most unexpected hit, sometimes called 'a sleeper,' which has always seemed to me to be a phrase that contradicted itself." He was right about the word, but wrong about the film — the term *is* an oxymoron, but in this case the movie literally slept in. While brimming over with critical acclaim, the picture failed to awaken much interest in the public, earning a scant $3.1 million in domestic rentals.

At Oscar time, though, there was much deserved recognition for *Tender Mercies*. The film received five nominations: Best Picture, Best Actor (Duvall, who won), Best Director (Beresford), Best Original Screenplay (Horton Foote, another win, and his first since *To Kill a Mockingbird* in 1962), and Best Song.

The tune nominated for Best Song, "Over You," is sung by Betty Buckley in the movie. It's pure country, and she performs it dressed in an elaborately fringed outfit, as befits a country queen. Buckley, who had starred in performances on stage, film, and television, had previously won a Tony Award for her portrayal of Grizabella in *Cats* on Broadway, played the gym teacher in Brian De Palma's movie *Carrie,* and appeared as a regular on the TV series "Eight Is Enough," playing Abby.

PAPA, CAN YOU HEAR ME?

**Music by Michel Legrand;
lyrics by Alan and Marilyn Bergman
From *Yentl***

Yentl was Barbra Streisand's one-woman tour de force. It was a musical in an era when filmusicals were making a comeback, but it was a different sort of musical. There was only one singer — Streisand — and no show-stopping, heart-thumping, all-stops-out production or dance numbers. Streisand did all the singing,

and also handled the producing, directing, and half of the scripting chores.

The story, set in Poland in 1873 and filmed on location in Czechoslovakia, was based on Nobel prize laureate Isaac Bashevis Singer's tale of "Yentl, the Yeshiva Boy," a story about a young girl who wants to study the sacred Jewish writings forbidden to female members of the orthodox faith. Yentl's curiosity and thirst for knowledge is somewhat satisfied at home by an indulgent father, but when he dies, she decides she needs to know more. This was another cross-dressing story, but with a twist — Yentl, the inquisitive female, disguises herself as a male Yeshiva student. Complications, with a great deal of comedy interlaced with periodic singing by Streisand, arise when Avigdor (Mandy Patinkin), one of the Yeshiva students, finds himself inexplicably attracted to "Anshel" (Yentl's adopted male name). This causes a bit of sexual confusion and concern to Avigdor, who is must also deal with the problem of his mandated broken engagement (after the painful discovery that suicide runs in his family) to his worshipful fiancée, Hadass (Amy Irving, in one of her best screen performances). No worries — his best friend, Anshel, can marry Hadass, thus assuring his continuing closeness to his beloved ex-fiancée. After a hilarious courtship and wedding night sequence, this situation amazingly manages to work.

The film was blasted by critics but received a few nods from the Academy, although not in any of the major categories. There were nominations for Best Supporting Actress (Irving), Best Art Direction–Set Decora-

Avigdor (Mandy Patinkin) shares a tender moment with Yentl (Barbra Streisand), disguised as a young man in the romantic drama *Yentl.*

tion, two Best Song nominations, and one win, for Best Original Song Score or Adaptation Score, for Michel Legrand and Alan and Marilyn Bergman. (It was not much of a contest; there were only two other nominees in this category — *The Sting II* and *Trading Places.)*

Among the songs in the Legrand-Bergman-Bergman score were "A Piece of the Sky," "No Wonder," "Will Someone Ever Look at Me That Way?," "This Is One of Those Moments," "Where Is It Written?," "Papa, Can You Hear Me?," and "The Way He Makes Me Feel." These last two numbers were both Best Song nominees.

"Papa, Can You Hear Me?" is sung after Yentl's father dies and she is venturing out into the world disguised as a man for the first time. Having been tossed off a wagon on which she'd been hitching a ride to her new life, she finds herself at the edge of a forest, alone with only a candle and the memories of her father to comfort her and light her way. The beautiful song was released as a single but never made it to the Hot 100.

THE WAY HE MAKES ME FEEL

**Music by Michel Legrand;
    lyrics by Alan and Marilyn Bergman**
From *Yentl*

Barbra Streisand had been working on her magnum opus, *Yentl*, with a passion bordering on obsession for many years. It was her directorial debut, and the talented singer-actress also produced the film and even co-wrote the screenplay. Originally, she had planned to have an unknown actress portray the young heroine — at age 41, she felt she might be too old to convincingly play a girl/boy in her/his teens or early 20s. But United Artists insisted that the film should have a superstar in the lead, and Streisand, being closest to the project, obliged. And not only did she handle all the above chores with aplomb, but she also supervised much of the writing of the music, along with the post-production mixing and film editing.

Did critics applaud this one-woman show? Resoundingly, no. It must have been a particularly bitter pill to swallow for Streisand, since she was personally responsible for so many aspects of the picture. Vincent Canby of the *New York Times* spoke for many critics when he wrote, "*Yentl*, I guess, ought to be attended just to see just how far off the mark enormous celebrity can

lead a fine performer who, in every other way, is a woman of modest talents if unstoppable ambition. *Yentl* isn't conventionally bad. It's a big, wooden, inert ark of a movie waiting, high and dry, for someone to provide a flood so that it might float away. It never does."

The Academy, however, recognized some of the film's achievements. The score, by Michel Legrand and Alan and Marilyn Bergman, won an Oscar, and two different tunes from the movie were nominated for Best Song — "Papa, Can You Hear Me?" (page 264) and "The Way He Makes Me Feel," a love song Streisand sings to express her feelings about Avigdor, played by Mandy Pantinkin, to whom she's attracted but cannot revel her gender.

"The Way He Makes Me Feel" was released as a single, reorchestrated for the top 40 market with a modern arrangement not used in the film. The tune climbed to number 40, charting for 15 weeks. The soundtrack album fared better — the first pressing of 600,000 units was sold out before the film ever opened, selling 3.5 million copies within the first six months. And despite the lambasting from the critics, *Yentl* did just fine at the box office, pulling in $19.6 million in domestic rentals, enough to make it the 18th-ranked film of the year.

1984

And the winner is...

I JUST CALLED TO SAY I LOVE YOU

Music and lyrics by Stevie Wonder
From *The Woman in Red*

A lusty comedy that many felt would become a late summer sleeper when it was released, *The Woman in Red* failed to capture any sizable audience. Too bad. The lucky few who caught it were able to enjoy an exciting cast, including the rare sight of Gene Wilder co-starring in a movie with his bride, Gilda Radner.

Wilder (who also wrote and directed the film) played Teddy Pierce, a man determined to cheat on his wife. While the film was essentially a salute to *The Seven Year Itch*, it was actually based on a 1977 French comedy, *Pardon Mon Affaire* (no translation neces-

"I Just Called to Say I Love You" is what Gene Wilder seems to be saying in *The Woman in Red*. The Stevie Wonder song won an Oscar.

Oscar-winning Best Song, the Stevie Wonder wonder called "I Just Called to Say I Love You." Wonder's song was a breakaway hit from the film. It landed on the charts within a week of the film's release in August, 1984, and eight weeks later had become Number One, the eighth Wonder song to do that. It remained at the top for three weeks and on the charts for 26, selling a million copies in the process.

Soon the awards were piling up. "I Just Called to Say I Love You" received the Golden Globe for Best Original Song from a Film, a Grammy for Best Song of 1984, and the Oscar for Best Song. The competition at the Academy Awards ceremony was fierce that year: all five nominees had been Number One hits in 1984. After Wonder's friend Diana Ross had performed "I Just Called to Say I Love You" (and had tried unsuccessfully to coax the audience into clapping along with her rendition), Gregory Hines announced Wonder as the winner.

At the podium, the blind musician, dressed in a tieless tux with multicolored sequin-bedecked lapels, created a stir by dedicating his award to Nelson Mandela, the then-imprisoned South African civil rights leader who would later become president of his country. Immediately after Wonder's speech, his songs were banned from the state-owned South African Broadcasting Corporation. Wonder quickly responded, "If my being banned means people will be free, ban me mega-times."

sary). "Fortunately," wrote the *New York Times*, "most of the film is more appealing than its premise." When he's not plotting how to commit adultery, Wilder finds himself the object of a pursuit by a co-worker, whom he'd just as soon dodge.

This character was played by Radner, and her work was singled out for special praise by *Variety*, which noted, "A wonderful diversion through all of this is Gilda Radner, a rather plain fellow office worker who initially thinks she's the object of Wilder's wanderlust and is bitterly — and vigorously — disappointed when she finds out she isn't." In real life, however, this woman in tan, while not the character's scarlet-clad dream woman, turned out to be just fine. Radner, a gifted comedienne who had built her reputation playing various oddball characters on TV's "Saturday Night Live," married her leading man, Gene Wilder, that same year. Sadly, their lives together were cut short when Radner developed ovarian cancer in 1986; she died three years later, at the age of only 42.

Aside from its outstanding cast, *The Woman in Red* did have one other claim to fame. It produced an

AGAINST ALL ODDS (TAKE A LOOK AT ME NOW)

Music and lyrics by Phil Collins
From *Against All Odds*

Film noir was a term coined by French critics to define a type of cinema characterized by its dark tones and pessimistic mood (*noir* means *black* in French). The terminology was most often used in describing the black-and-white Hollywood films of the '40s and '50s which portrayed a gloomy underworld of corrupt criminals, abounding with night sequences and mysterious shadows. One classic film of the genre was *Out of the Past*, a 1947 movie directed, appropriately, by a Frenchman, Jacques Tourneur. It starred Robert Mitchum, Jane Greer, Kirk Douglas, and Rhonda Fleming and involved a web of murder, double-dealing, and gangsters.

In 1984, director Taylor Hackford (*An Officer and a Gentleman* — see page 259) remade *Out of the Past*, calling his film *Against All Odds*. In this full-color remake (dubbed "California noir" by *New York Times* film critic Vincent Canby), Jane Greer returns to play the mother of the character she had originally portrayed, a mean cuss whose daughter eventually flees to Mexico (where she's also dodging her possessive ex-lover, played by James Woods). The plot thickens, as they say, with characters like Jeff Bridges as the out-of-work pro football player sent by the ex-lover to track her down, plus a healthy serving of murders, corruption, real-estate scandals, gambling, car races down Sunset Boulevard, and torrid love affairs, all combining in, as *Newsweek* put it, "a cake so dense it refuses to rise." The magazine further cautioned: "The wise shopper is advised, for the price of two movie tickets, to rent a video cassette of *Out of the Past*, the taut and terrific 1947 *film noir* from which Hackford and writer Eric Hughes have greatly — and at great cost — departed." Such words cost this picture greatly at the box office; it made a mere $10.3 million in North American rentals.

But, against all odds, there *was* something of note to emerge from this movie — a Number One hit song and Oscar contender. Since it was decided that there would be a title song, the tune by composer/singer Phil Collins was called "Against All Odds (Take a Look at Me Now)," with both phrases cleverly finding their way into the lyrics. The tune is sung over the movie's closing credits, and was released as a single even as the film was preparing to be shown in theaters. The song entered the Hot 100 on February 25, and by April 21 it was atop the *Billboard* charts, replacing Kenny Loggins's "Footloose" (see page 267).

"Against All Odds (Take a Look at Me Now)" was Collins's first Number One hit. The song remained at Number One for three weeks and charted for 24, selling over a million copies. On the night of the Oscar awards the following spring, Ann Reinking performed Collins's hit tune as he looked on from the audience,[1] no doubt taking comfort in the fact that although his song did not win that evening, one of his new tunes, "One More Night," was the current Number One tune in America.

---

1. Collins wasn't invited to perform his own song. Oscar producer Gregory Peck and writer Larry Gelbart had apparently never heard of Collins, choosing instead to have the tune sung by someone in the movie industry. Reinking, having appeared in *All That Jazz* in 1979 and *Annie* in 1982, fit the bill.

FOOTLOOSE

Music and lyrics by Kenny Loggins and Dean Pitchford
From *Footloose*

Imagine a town where dancing is forbidden. A place so controlled by religious fanatics that rock 'n' roll is considered sinfully evil, a harbinger of crime, drug use, and all manner of things most foul. Sounds like something from, say, 1950s America, around the time of Elvis's first hip swivels, doesn't it? Now imagine such a town in mainstream 1980s America, a place where the local folk, inspired by their fire-and-brimstone preacher (played convincingly by John Lithgow), cling to their superstitious fear of dire consequences should a toe twitch or a heel kick up.

Such was the premise for the tenth-ranked hit of 1984, a flick called *Footloose*, derivative of *Rebel Without a Cause* and the old Judy Garland–Mickey Rooney "let's put on a show" genre. Now guess who is the most rebellious hell-raiser of all the town's teens — the preacher's very own daughter, of course, inspired, naturally, by the local "big city boy," Ren (played to the hilt by Kevin Bacon). Naturally, by the end of the picture, everybody goes "Footloose," kicking up their Sunday shoes instead of wearing them to church. And oh, the wages of sin — a box office take of $34 million in North American rentals for starters. And a slew of memorable songs, including the title track, "Footloose."

The film's opening titles, which introduced the song "Footloose," were worth the price of admission all by themselves. The credit sequence was created by Wayne Fitzgerald and David Oliver, who were also responsible for the opening sequences in *9 to 5* (see page 249). In the pulsating montage, shoes of every style, color, and shape, enclosing a similarly varied assortment of feet, tap in rhythm to the Kenny Loggins beat. It's colorful, intriguing, enticing, and in many ways a build-up to a movie that can't quite follow in these footsteps.

The title song was an Oscar nominee, although it wasn't a "shoe"-in ("I Just Called to Say I Love You" took top prize — see page 265). Still, it was yet another motion picture–based song to make Number One on the *Billboard* charts in 1984, something all five Oscar nominees achieved that year. "Footloose" was the combined effort of singer Kenny Loggins and the film's screenwriter, Dean Pitchford. As with so many memorable tunes, this one was also written under pressure of a deadline, with the work in this case being completed in four days. This is even more amazing given that both writers were suffering from physical ailments as they worked feverishly — Pitchford literally, with a strep throat and 103-degree temperature, while Loggins was nursing some broken ribs sustained when he took a header off a darkened Provo, Utah, stage.

Once recovered, and with the song safely completed and on the movie's soundtrack, Loggins was able to incorporate the new number into his concert appearances without violating Academy rules that might make the song ineligible for nomination. As Loggins explained to Fred Bronson in *The Billboard Book of Number One Hits*, "The crowds instantly got into it even though they'd never heard the song before," and he knew the song was going to be a hit. It topped the charts for three weeks in March, 1984, and charted for 23 weeks, selling over a million copies.

Footloose actually contained two songs that were Oscar nominees and Number One hits — the other one was "Let's Hear It For the Boy" (see page 269).

GHOSTBUSTERS

Music and lyrics by Ray Parker Jr.
From *Ghostbusters*

Who ya gonna call?

If you're the president of Columbia Pictures, probably your banker. *Ghostbusters* was the first mega-hit to produce a Best Song nominee. The top film of 1984, there was nothing spooky about the $132.7 million and change the picture made in North American rentals, making it the fifth-ranked film of the decade, with universal applause from critics as well as the ticket-buying public.

The movie was the brainchild of John Belushi and Dan Aykroyd, both "Saturday Night Live" alumni. But after Belushi's death from a 1982 drug overdose, Aykroyd (who co-stars in the film with another "SNL" grad, Bill Murray) worked on the screenplay with Harold Ramis, the third member of the ghostbusting team. The storyline was a fantasy about ghosts on the loose in New York City, planning a giant rendezvous in

Who ya gonna call? Probably these guys, the *Ghostbusters* (from left): Ernie Hudson, Bill Murray, Dan Aykroyd, and Harold Ramis.

Sigourney Weaver's refrigerator, or something like that. It's all harmless fun and not terribly scary, which made it a perfect family film with its PG rating.

The producers needed a catchy title song, but working the word "ghostbusters" into a lyric wouldn't be easy. There were already about 60 songs on the table, none of which pleased director Ivan Reitman when he tapped Ray Parker Jr. to do the honors. Parker, who'd begun his career as a back-up artist for Stevie Wonder, the Temptations, and Gladys Knight and the Pips before forming his own group, Raydio, was a proven songwriter, with several top 10 singles to his name. As he explained in a *USA Today* interview, "It's hard to write a song where your main objective is to use the word 'ghostbusters' . . . I wanted to make a simple, easy song people could sing along with and not have to think about." He decided upon a call-and-response pattern, with a shout-along cry of "GHOSTBUSTERS!" serving as the answer to the musical question, "Who ya gonna call?" Once Parker hit upon this approach, the rest was easy — he had his tune written and recorded for Reitman within two days.

The song was released simultaneously with the picture, in June of 1984, and by August it had reached the Number One spot. It remained on the charts for 21 weeks and sold over a million copies. A kicky production number featuring Parker and Dom DeLuise was performed at the Academy Award ceremonies the following spring.

Columbia, naturally pleased with the success of *Ghostbusters,* released a sequel, *Ghostbusters II,* in 1989, which again made good use of the Parker tune. The sequel did about half the box office of its progenitor, $60.4 million in domestic rentals, a respectable amount for any sequel. There was also a spin-off animated television series, called *The Real Ghostbusters,* which ran for a while on ABC and then moved to syndication on the USA cable network. The song "Ghostbusters" was used in this too, although sung by John Smith.

LET'S HEAR IT FOR THE BOY

Music and lyrics by Dean Pitchford and Tom Snow
From *Footloose*

Once again, Paramount Pictures had a hit on its hands with another toe-tapping musical, *Footloose.* During the '70s and '80s, Paramount clearly attempted to tie its name to the musical genre as MGM had done in the '30s and '40s. In less than seven years, Paramount had staked a claim to the modern filmusical, turning out hit after hit, ranging from *Saturday Night Fever* and (1977) *Grease* (1978) to *Flashdance, Staying Alive* (both 1983), and *Footloose,* which, as it turned out, brought this trend to a close.

Footloose certainly helped foot some bills for the studio. While not a blockbuster, it was a legitimate hit, with $34 million in domestic rentals, making it the fourth-ranked musical of the 1980s. It also had a hit soundtrack, with two singles that made it to Number One: "Footloose" (see page 267) and "Let's Hear It for the Boy."

"Let's Hear It for the Boy" was used in a scene featuring Kevin Bacon and Christopher Penn. Bacon (playing the picture's bad-boy character with his "big city ways") is determined to teach Penn (as Willard, a dull but lovable hulk of a farm boy) how to boogie. At first Willard can't quite get the hang of it, providing one of the movie's most charming and amusing numbers, as well as one to which many audience members could relate — who hasn't felt afflicted with six left feet at one time or another? Eventually, inevitably, Willard catches on, faithfully practicing all that his mentor has shown him, and we see him dancing through fields, in his room, at the gym, out in the open, and even sitting down, all to the accompaniment of "Let's Hear It for the Boy."

Deniece Williams sang the soundtrack song, although she does not appear in the film. "Let's Hear It for the Boy" climbed the charts and reached Number One by May 26, 1984, where it remained for two weeks (and on the charts for 19). In June, the song (co-written by the film's screenwriter Dean Pitchford with partner Tom Snow) received a gold record for selling a million copies. It was Williams's first solo Number One single; her previous Number One, 1978's "Too Much, Too Little, Too Late," was a duet with Johnny Mathis. This time her song scored an Oscar nomination, the second tune from *Footloose* to be so honored, making it the fourth film to feature two Best Song nominees

Footloose had a number of lively tunes on the soundtrack, including "Almost Paradise (Love Theme from Footloose)," "Holding Out for a Hero," "Dancing in the Streets," "I'm Free (Heaven Helps the Man)," "Somebody's Eyes," "The Girl Gets Around," and "Never" (with lyrics by Michael Gore, who had received the 1980 Oscar along with Dean Pitchford for "Fame" — see page 248). In all, the picture was responsible for five top 40 hits.

1985

And the winner is...

SAY YOU, SAY ME

Music and lyrics by Lionel Richie
From *White Nights*

Back in 1985, when the now-defunct Soviet Union was still intact, producer-director Taylor Hackford (*An Officer and a Gentleman,* see page 259 and *Against All Odds,* see page 266) put together a film called *White Nights.* The title refers to a time celebrated by the USSR's northernmost, winter-weary natives, when the summer "midnight sun" illuminates this land close to the Arctic Circle. It is to this land that a Russian defector unwittingly returns and finds himself placed under house arrest. His "jailer," it turns out (thanks to a huge stretch

of the imagination), is an American defector now working for the KGB. Oh, and they both just happen to be about the best dancers in the world — or else there wouldn't have been much point in putting Mikhail Baryshnikov and Gregory Hines in the same movie.

The plot was barely plausible, but the marvelous dance sequences made it is easy to overlook *White Night*'s flaws. Hines was one of the finest tap dancers around, while Baryshnikov, a real-life defector, was the embodiment of the classic Russian ballet star — lean, handsome, masculine, and a whirling blur when doing his stuff. One of the best sequences in the film involved a sort of "dance-off," in which the pair performs a breathtaking side-by-side routine. Perhaps there should have been an Oscar category for Best Choreography just so Twyla Tharp, the film's choreographer, could have been nominated. Alas, there wasn't.

There were, however, two nominations for Best Song — "Separate Lives" (see page 273) and "Say You, Say Me." Lionel Richie composed the latter tune and performed the recording on the movie's soundtrack, where it is heard over the closing credits, a line of which actually reads, "Title Song 'Say You, Say Me' written and performed by Lionel Richie" — a bit of a mystery, since the film and song titles are completely different.

Director Hackford had hired Richie to write a song called "White Nights." But after struggling with the assignment for several weeks, Richie was still stumped for a song with that title. He had something else, however, which Richie's manager suggested was better suited to the film anyway. A demo of "Say You, Say Me" was sent to Hackford, who agreed it was just what the director ordered, and this became the "title" song.

Unfortunately, due to Richie's contract with Motown, the tune could not be included on the Atlantic Records soundtrack album. Motown agreed, however, to allow Richie to release the song as a single. His recording of "Say You, Say Me" entered the *Billboard* Hot 100 on November 9, 1985, and by December 21 it was Number One, where it remained for four weeks. It stayed on the charts for 20 weeks, sold over a million copies, and, in addition to nailing down the Oscar, picked up a Golden Globe for Best Original Song from a Film for 1985.

Dancing greats Mikhail Baryshnikov (left) and Gregory Hines perform together in *White Nights.*

MISS CELIE'S BLUES (SISTER)

Music by Quincy Jones and Rod Temperton; lyrics by Quincy Jones, Rod Temperton, and Lionel Richie
From *The Color Purple*

It was supposed to be Steven Spielberg's greatest achievement The director who had brought the public such on-screen thrill rides as *Jaws* (1975), *Close Encounters of the Third Kind* (1977), *Raiders of the Lost Ark* (1981), *E.T. The Extra-Terrestrial* (1982), and *Indiana Jones and the Temple of Doom* (1984) wanted to be considered a "serious" director by his peers. He optioned Alice Walker's Pulitzer Prize–winning novel, *The Color Purple,* assigned Menno Meyjes to write the screenplay (not an enviable task — the book is written as a collection of letters), and co-produced and directed a lavish film version. Then he sat back and waited for the accolades to pour in.

They trickled. Some writers, like Vincent Canby of the *New York Times,* had fairly kind words for the film: "*The Color Purple* is a combination of *Tobacco Road, The Wizard of Oz* and *Imitation of Life.* It makes you laugh, it makes you cry and it makes you feel a little bit of a fool for having been taken in by its calculated, often phony effects." *Variety* was more succinct: "There are some great scenes and great performances in *The Color Purple,* but it is not a great film."

One of those great performances was turned in by the film's lead, Whoopi Goldberg. It was the talented actress/comedienne's motion picture debut and garnered a lot of attention, as well as a Best Actress nomination. While many thought she would win the coveted statuette for her sensitive portrayal of Celie, the Oscar instead went to Geraldine Page for *The Trip to Bountiful.* (Goldberg later won a Best Supporting Actress Oscar for her role in 1990's *Ghost*).

The Color Purple was nominated for 10 Academy Awards in addition to Goldberg's: Best Picture, Best Supporting Actress (two nominees: Margaret Avery and, in her first screen performance, Oprah Winfrey), Best Adapted Screenplay, Best Cinematography, Best Art Direction–Set Decoration, Best Original Score (Quincy Jones and 11 others), Best Costume Design, Best Make-up, and Best Song. Although Spielberg won the prestigious Directors Guild Award, his colleagues in the Motion Picture Academy didn't vote him or his picture any Oscars whatsoever. (Spielberg had to wait until 1993 to be recognized by the Academy, when his masterpiece *Schindler's List* won seven Oscars, including Best Picture and Best Director.)

The nominated song, "Miss Celie's Blues (Sister)" is a traditional bluesy tune, written as a collaboration between composers Quincy Jones and Rod Temperton, with Lionel Richie joining the two to help write the lyrics. The tune is lip-synched in the film by Margaret Avery, playing the role of Shug. The singer on the soundtrack, however, is not Avery but Tata Vega, who explains, "Although Margaret Avery was a singer, Steven Spielberg wanted her to concentrate on her acting, so he set out to find someone to sing for her." Vega says that one of the tapes Spielberg listened to was her Grammy-nominated "Oh, It Is Jesus," which she recorded with gospel performer Andrae Crouch. " 'Miss Celie's Blues' was originally a 'naughty' song," says Vega, explaining that she felt uncomfortable singing it the way it was originally written, since "I had just found the Lord. However, Spielberg felt he wanted something tender, and overnight it was rewritten to become 'Sister.' Although some people think it is about lesbians [as the character were portrayed in the book], I think Miss Celie took it to be just about love."

THE POWER OF LOVE

Music by Chris Hayes and Johnny Colla; lyrics by Huey Lewis
From *Back to the Future*

Robert Zemeckis and Bob Gale had been turned down by every major studio in town. But they believed in their script called *Back to the Future,* a sci-fi fantasy adventure about a kid who goes back in time and meets his own parents as teen-agers. "Not enough sex," the Hollywood moguls told the writers. Zemeckis and Gale persisted, however, finally getting the attention of Steven Spielberg. With Spielberg's stamp of approval, the future was bright indeed.

Back to the Future starred Michael J. Fox as Marty McFly, the teen-aged time traveler, and Christopher Lloyd as the quintessential nutty scientist who invents a time machine out of a DeLorean car. The film was imaginative and fast-paced, perfect summer escape fare. Audiences agreed, with many movie-goers going back to *Back to the Future* more than once. Their return trips

Christopher Lloyd gives Michael J. Fox some last-minute time travel instructions in *Back to the Future*.

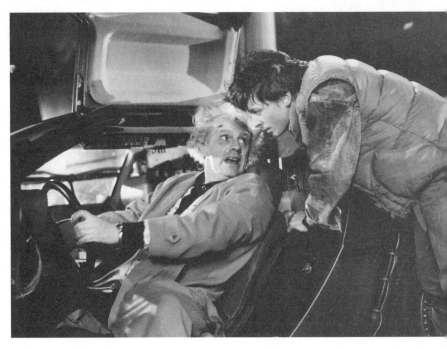

to the box office helped make the movie the year's top picture, with a North American rental total of $105.4 million, the 10th-ranked film of the decade.

Much of the film's success stemmed from its look at contemporary life versus the "olden days" of the '50s. The contrasts were fun as well as nostalgic. For example, when Marty meets his mom-to-be, she insists on calling him "Calvin Klein," thinking that the name sewn on his jeans must be Marty's name — what else would it mean? The local movie theater in town, a porno house in Marty's world of 1985, is playing a then-current Ronald Reagan starrer — *Cattle Queen of Montana* — in 1955. Times sure had changed. (It's also interesting to look back at *Back to the Future* a decade later. Clothing styles popular in 1985 may seem a bit dated now, as in the then-trendy bright orange down vest Marty wears. The people from the '50s think he's a sailor and it's his life preserver; today, it just looks a bit out of style. Such are the hazards of time-travel movies.)

Music figured prominently in the movie. Even though much of the story was set in the 1950s, there was a good deal of modern rock 'n' roll along with a nostalgic look at classic rock. In one scene, Marty, playing modern rock 'n' roll guitar with an R&B band at a high school dance, actually gives then-nascent rocker

Chuck Berry the idea for some of his songs and stage moves. (This gimmick was again used successfully in the 1994 movie *Forrest Gump*, in which Gump inadvertently influences Elvis Presley and John Lennon.)

Back to the Future received four Academy Award nominations: Best Original Screenplay, Best Sound, Best Sound Effects Editing (its only win), and Best Song. The nominated tune was "The Power of Love," by Huey Lewis and the News. The group was hot when it signed on to write the song for the film, having scored four consecutive top 10 hits in 1983 and '84: "Heart and Soul," "I Want a New Drug," "The Heart of Rock and Roll," and "If This Is It."

"The Power of Love" is used early in the film, when Marty comes out of the professor's place and heads off to school on his skateboard. Not everyone thought it would be the film's biggest hit; another Huey Lewis song in the movie, "Back in Time," was thought to be the odds-on favorite. But "The Power of Love" proved to be the smash and became the first Number One single for Huey Lewis and the News. It entered the Hot 100 at the end of June, and by August 24 it was at the top of the charts, where it stayed for two weeks and charted for 19, ultimately selling over a million copies. At the American Music Awards in 1986, "The Power of Love" was honored as Pop/Rock Favorite Single.

SEPARATE LIVES

Music and lyrics by Stephen Bishop
From *White Nights*

White Nights was not a musical, but a drama with occasional music and more than occasional dancing. In fact, without the dance sequences, there would not have been much holding this picture together at all, since there wasn't a very deep story.

Two of the world's top dancers — one American (Gregory Hines), one Russian (Mikhail Baryshnikov), are almost literally thrown together to mix it up in the film. We eventually learn that they have more in common than one would have suspected. True, one's black, one's white; one taps, one pirouettes; one's a loyal American (the former Soviet), one's a loyal Communist (the defected American). But dance conquers all in this idealized movie, shot in the days before the dissolution of the USSR, and it becomes the glue in the bond these two disparate souls manage to form.

It must have sounded great on paper, but something got lost in the translation. "Director Taylor Hackford has made a film with good looks but not style," wrote *Variety*. "The result is a vaguely uncomfortable compromise which is neither fish nor fowl, good nor bad, b.o. gold nor poison." Critiques like this can often make or break a movie, but in this case, the reviews didn't have much effect on the box office take. While no one would ever mistake *White Nights* for a blockbuster, its respectable $21.1 million in North American rentals made it the 17th-ranked picture of the year, no doubt due to the terrific dance sequences. The music didn't hurt either.

There were two nominated tunes to emerge from the film: "Say You, Say Me" (see page 270) and "Separate Lives." "Say You, Say Me" won the Oscar, and both songs became Number One hits on the *Billboard* charts. "Separate Lives," billed in the film's credits as the "Love Theme," was performed as a duet by Phil Collins and Marilyn Martin. The song appears in a scene between Gregory Hines and Isabella Rossellini (the daughter of actress Ingrid Bergman and Italian director Roberto Rossellini, making her American screen debut as Hines's wife), which concludes with her announcement that she's pregnant.

Since "Separate Lives" was performed by Phil Collins, many assumed he had also written it, as he had the title song from Taylor Hackford's previous film,

Against All Odds (see page 266). In fact, the Oscar-nominated tune was written by Stephen Bishop, who had recorded the nominated song "It Might Be You" from 1982's *Tootsie* (see page 260) and the title song for *Animal House* in 1978.

"Separate Lives" debuted on the Hot 100 on October 5, 1985, and reached Number One on November 30. It stayed on the charts for 21 weeks.

SURPRISE, SURPRISE

Music by Marvin Hamlisch;
**   lyrics by Edward Kleban**
From *A Chorus Line*

The original Broadway production of *A Chorus Line* was the longest-running show in the history of the Great White Way. When the curtain came down on its final performance on April 28, 1990, it had enjoyed a run of nearly 15 years, with a total of 6,137 performances. The show won nine Tony Awards in 1976, including Best Musical, as well as a Pulitzer Prize for drama.

While the musical was still running on Broadway, a film version was released by Columbia Pictures. There had been a trail of false starts in getting it up on the screen. Universal Pictures had paid $5.5 million for the film rights way back in 1976, and the property had passed through the hands of such talented potential directors as Mike Nichols, Sidney Lumet, and Allan Carr. At one time even John Travolta (star of *Saturday Night Fever* and *Grease* — see page 237) was being considered. Eventually *A Chorus Line* fell to the talented British director Richard Attenborough, who still had trouble overcoming the production's obvious stage-boundedness. "*Chorus* often seems static and confined, rarely venturing beyond the immediate," wrote the critic for *Variety*.

With the exception of Michael Douglas, the film's cast had no major box office names, but featured four of the original Broadway principals — Vicki Frederick, Pam Klinger, Justin Ross, and Matt West. And nearly all of the original songs used on the stage were kept for the film. The score by Marvin Hamlisch and Edward Kleban included "I Hope I Get It," "I Can Do That," "At the Ballet," "Nothing," "Dance: Ten, Looks: Three," "One," "What I Did for Love," plus two songs written especially for the screen version — "Let Me Dance for You" and "Surprise, Surprise."

1986

And the winner is...

TAKE MY BREATH AWAY

**Music by Giorgio Moroder;
lyrics by Tom Whitlock**
From *Top Gun*

Attenborough, writing in the liner notes of the film's soundtrack album, was particularly excited about these new tunes. "When I heard that Marvin Hamlisch and Ed Kleban were coming into our New York production office to play the numbers they had written just for the movie," he wrote, "I felt like a child waiting to open a special Christmas gift — full of nervous anticipation matched by an almost unbearable sense of excitement. And rarely, if ever, have I found any gift more satisfying."

One of the new songs, "Surprise, Surprise," was nominated for an Oscar. The number is sung and danced by Gregg Burge in the movie, and he also reprised it at the following spring's Academy Awards ceremony (where *A Chorus Line* was also up for the Best Sound and Best Film Editing awards). The song, a long production number in which Burge's character describes his first sexual experience, is faintly reminiscent of "Hello Twelve, Hello Thirteen, Hello Love," a tune used in the Broadway version but dropped from the film's score.

A Chorus Line may have been one singular sensation on Broadway, but there were hardly any people in the box office ticket line. The final take was just over $7 million in North American rentals. But for anyone who never got to see the live stage performance, a trip to the video store is definitely in order.

Gregg Burge performs the Oscar-nominated song "Surprise, Surprise" in the screen version of *A Chorus Line*.

Top Gun was top dog at the box office in 1986, a runaway — make that flyaway — hit. Paramount's film about Navy test pilots and the planes and women they loved seemed to have what it takes, with a box office take of $79.4 million in rentals. Part of the reason for its huge success was the picture's leading man, Tom Cruise.

Cruise had previously appeared in a string of pictures that made insufficient use of his talents, including such lightweight movies as *Endless Love* (1981, see page 253), *Risky Business* (his breakthrough film), and *Legend* (1985). *Top Gun* was his first serious film as an adult. Soon, Cruise would be top gun in Hollywood, a big-name movie star in the most traditional sense of the term. Others in the cast included Kelly McGillis as the love interest, Tom Skerritt, Val Kilmer, and an 11th-billed Tim Robbins, future star of many pictures of the '90s.

The storyline centered around the action, as F-14 Tomcats soared, swooped, and somersaulted while pulling several "g"s. Men loved the movie for this high-flying fare, while women enjoyed ogling the photogenic Cruise, who, together with McGillis, helped fill those idle moments when not storming the skies.

While not a musical, *Top Gun* was the beneficiary of a number of original soundtrack songs that were commissioned for the film. One of these, "Danger Zone," was written by lyricist Tom Whitlock and composer Giorgio Moroder, who had won an Oscar in 1983 as the composer of "Flashdance . . . What a Feeling" (see page 261). Recorded by Kenny Loggins, "Danger Zone" was the first single released from the soundtrack (it peaked at number two).

But it was another song, "Take My Breath Away," that would take the Best Song Oscar.

In the movie, "Take My Breath Away" is sung by the group Berlin over a hot-and-heavy lovemaking scene. The tune was written after "Danger Zone," both of which were originally presented to Berlin for possible recording. They selected "Take My Breath Away." The song had the usual speed-written lyric, an oft-told tale of Academy Award nominees. Whitlock, recalling the task of writing the lyric after receiving the music from Moroder, told *Billboard Book of Number One Hits* author Fred Bronson, "I hopped in my car and was driving home into Hollywood. By the time I got home, I had written the lyric. The title was a phrase that had been running through my mind, in terms of asking for that kind of awe, something so striking that you can't breathe."

"Take My Breath Away" reached Number One the week of September 13 and was on the charts for 21 weeks. In addition to winning the Oscar, the tune won the Golden Globe Award for Best Original Song from a Film for 1986. *Top Gun,* meanwhile, received three other Oscar nominations, for Best Sound, Best Film Editing, and Best Sound Effects Editing.

GLORY OF LOVE

Music by Peter Cetera and David Foster;
lyrics by Peter Cetera and Diane Nini
From *The Karate Kid II*

"A sequel that's better than the original" is what *The Hollywood Reporter* called *The Karate Kid II,* Columbia's follow-up to 1986's highly popular first *Karate Kid.* The film's star, Ralph Macchio, was really the Karate Twentysomething when he returned in the role of Daniel (now a teenager), ready to take more sage advice from his mentor, Miyagi (Noriyuki "Pat" Morita). There was also a karate girlfriend for the kid in this edition.

This time the story takes place mostly in Okinawa (actually shot in Hawaii), spicing things up a bit as Miyagi gets to settle an old score while the audience gets to ogle some lush scenery and watch a typhoon. The film properly should have been called *The Karate Master,* since it was Morita's starring vehicle more than Macchio's.

KK II was one of those rare sequels that financially bested its progenitor. While the original *Kid* took in

Noriyuki "Pat" Morita (left) and Ralph Macchio strike a contemplative pose in *The Karate Kid II.*

$43.1 million in box office rentals, its first offspring's take in North American rentals was a hefty $58.3 mil. No one (other than perhaps the astute *Hollywood Reporter* reviewer) had expected this to happen. *Variety* called *KK II* an "overlong, dumb sequel," adding that "anyone over the age of 18 is liable to start fidgeting . . . Given kids' attention spans, it's unimaginable why this simple little film was made to run nearly two hours." The *New York Times*'s Vincent Canby had even harsher words, calling the film "aimless" and "monotonous."

Bad reviews notwithstanding, *KK II* features one of the best examples of how a song can be used to underscore a film story. "Glory of Love," written by Peter Cetera, David Foster, and Cetera's wife, Diane Nini, is first heard in the film while Macchio and Yuji Oku-moto (his love interest) are standing on the rocks, preparing to race down to see the site of an ancient castle. The lyric tells of how, like a knight of long ago, he will take her to his castle far away. Then, at the end of the film, after the obligatory fight to the finish over the girl, the song reminds us that he is a man "who will fight for your honor." The tune then continues over the closing credits.

Composer Peter Cetera was with the group Chicago for 18 years, eventually soloing in 1982. His work caught the attention of the president of United Artists Records, who commissioned him to write and record a soundtrack number for *KK II*. They wanted a ballad; he sang them a few bars of what would become "Glory of Love," which they immediately loved. The next step was for Cetera to actually view the film, then tailor his lyrics to the action. His wife helped him write the words when he developed writer's block.

The song was nominated for an Oscar, and Cetera performed his tune at the awards ceremony the following spring. In addition, "Glory of Love" went to Number One on the *Billboard* charts, where it remained for two weeks, and charted for 21 weeks.

KK II's box office success virtually guaranteed that it would not mark the end of the franchise. *The Karate Kid III* appeared in 1989, and 1994 saw the release of *The Next Karate Kid*, this time starring a teenaged girl.

Sally Kellerman and Jack Lemmon share a birthday dance in Blake Edwards's comedy about aging, *That's Life!*

LIFE IN A LOOKING GLASS

Music by Henry Mancini;
 lyrics by Leslie Bricusse
From *That's Life!*

There is an adage that states that if you're going to be a writer, you should write about what you know. Writer-producer-director Blake Edwards took this message to heart during the late '70s and '80s, when many of his films reflected some aspect of his life. When he did the film *10* (see page 243), he was middle-aged, so his leading character naturally was undergoing a classic mid-life crisis. When he rounded the corner of 60, he began working on a screenplay with his therapist, Milton Wexler, about a man who turns 60. In 1986, Edwards and company unleashed their latest comedic study of life. It was called, for lack of a better title, *That's Life!* Actually, the original name was even more unique — it

was filmed on a very low budget under the working title of *Crisis,* but Columbia changed the name when they picked it up for distribution.

Jack Lemmon starred in Edwards's semi-autobiographical "celebration" of the events surrounding his 60th birthday, a movie that was "personal virtually to the point of being a home movie," as *Variety* put it. Indeed, it was filmed on location in Malibu, at Edwards's home, with many of his own (and Lemon's) family members playing key roles. For instance, Edwards's wife Julie Andrews starred opposite Lemmon (no surprise there; she starred in essentially all of Edwards's films after the pair were married); Lemmon's son Chris played the co-stars' son; Edwards's daughter Jennifer played their daughter; Andrews's daughter by another marriage, Emma Walton, played yet another of the couple's children; and Lemmon's wife, Felicia Farr, played a fortune teller.

All of these characters are brought together for a big familiy reunion. The occasion? That dreaded 60th birthday, of course, which has Lemmon freaking out. Can he face the party? His future as a grandfather? His waning libido? He can, and does, all with typical Blake Edwards good humor.

The movie was therapy for Edwards, who had undergone a series of viral illnesses yet insisted on continuing to work. "I felt if I didn't keep working I was going to die," he told *Newsweek*. His shrink, Wexler, sat in on the rehearsals with him, moderating the actors' search for their characters, prompting Edwards to quip, "It was almost like a group-therapy session."

Yet despite the fine performances and amusing situations, the film was a failure at the box office. Perhaps all this old age stuff was a turn-off to the younger crowd, who usually make or break a film. Even the film's closing theme song appealed to an older crowd. "Life in a Looking Glass" is sung under the closing credits by a slow, moody-sounding Tony Bennett. The song was written by Henry Mancini (with lyrics by Leslie Bricusse) and has that dreamy Mancini sound to it. And although it received yet another Oscar nomination for these two talented songwriters (working together in a rare collaboration), the effective cross-promotion of films and chart-topping pop tunes via MTV had made this an era when rock tunes were *de rigeur* for motion pictures, and Bennett's improbable MTV breakthrough was still many years away. The song, like the movie, failed to catch hold. As Edwards might have philosophically put it, that's life!

MEAN GREEN MOTHER FROM OUTER SPACE

Music by Alan Menken;
lyrics by Howard Ashman
From *Little Shop of Horrors*

In 1960, Roger Corman and company threw together a black-and-white motion picture quickie that would make motion picture history. Now known as "The Film Shot in Two Days," his *Little Shop of Horrors* has been an inspiration to film students and aficionados alike. This true sleeper (which pretty much kept on snoozing, financially), was a virtually unknown Jack Nicholson's fifth movie, and it is still fondly remembered as one of his best early performances. Nicholson played a dental patient who thrives on pain, a characterization that the actor, then 23 years old, captured as no one else could.

Then, in 1982, Howard Ashman and Alan Menken created an off-Broadway musical of the story about a nerdy flower shop employee named Seymour, his airheaded but loving girlfriend Audrey, and Seymour's blood-loving, human-eating plant, named Audrey II after Seymour's beloved. David Geffen, Cameron Mackintosh, and the Shubert Organization produced the show. Nearly all of the film's original characters were around to delight audiences, and their popularity saw the play through 2,209 performances. But even better than the characters was the music by Menken, with a book and lyrics by Ashman, who served as the show's director.

A translation to the screen followed four years later. Muppeteer Frank Oz, who was perhaps better qualified than anyone to tackle the complexities involved in bringing Audrey II to life on the big screen, directed a talented cast that was sort of a cross between "Saturday Night Live" and "Second City Television." Rick Moranis, who had also co-starred in *Ghostbusters* (see page 268), and whose destiny seemed to be playing the perennial nerd, was cast as Seymour, and Ellen Greene reprised her off-Broadway role as Audrey. The masochistic dental patient this time was Bill Murray, while an even juicier role went to Steve Martin as Murray's heaven-sent sadistic dentist. Other cast members included Jim Belushi, John Candy, Christopher Guest, and Levi Stubbs as the hip voice of Audrey II.

A humorous Greek chorus consisting of three ladies named after 1960s girl groups (Crystal, Chiffon, Ronette) kept things moving to a rock beat. The lively contemporary music was used in the traditional Broadway stage style, with characters stopping in at the shop to sing about the action. Catchy tunes and clever lyrics made songs like "Little Shop of Horrors," "Dentist," "Suddenly Seymour," "Suppertime," and "Mean Green Mother from Outer Space" so special.

In a year that saw the nominations dominated by sentimentality, the Academy allowed itself to admit that it had a sense of humor, proffering "Mean Green Mother from Outer Space" as one of the five entries in the Best Song derby (the film was also nominated for Best Visual Effects). The song is performed by the leading plant, Audrey II, sounding, according to composer Alan Menken, like a cross between Howlin' Wolf and Muddy Waters. As Menken tells it, "It was very much Howard Ashman's idea. Howard was the lyricist and wore many hats. He was the librettist, which means lyrics and book. He was the director. We didn't crack

Mushnik the florist (Vincent Gardenia) embraces employees Audrey (Ellen Greene) and Seymour (Rick Moranis), who holds the mysterious plant Audrey II, in a scene from *Little Shop of Horrors*.

Little Shop until we came up with creating the dark side of *Grease,* the world of Phil Spector, the apocalyptic sound of Phil Spector rock 'n' roll — a place where this particular tacky B-movie sci-fi story would take off from." Since a score written for the theater is not eligible for any Academy Award recognition unless it is augmented by new songs, Ashman and Menken were asked by producer David Geffen to create a tune "that could be sung over the final credits, that would be a single and have a life that way, [although a Hot 100 single] never happened," says Menken.

Little Shop received a Golden Globe nomination for Best Score. Menken, a future multiple Academy Award winner (see *The Little Mermaid,* page 286; *Beauty and the Beast,* page 296; and *Aladdin,* page 303), found that what should have been an honor instead caused him frustration. Says Menken: "The man who was nominated for [the Golden Globe] Best Score was named Miles Goodman, who wrote about eight or nine minutes of adaptation of my music. But because I was the composer of the theater music, I wasn't eligible for Best Score, but Miles Goodman was. That was a pretty nightmarish period for me. He's a very nice man and a very good film scorer, but I was pretty bitter about that. The Academy [of Motion Picture Arts and Sciences] remedied that by nominating 'Mean Green Mother' and not nominating Best Score, and I'm forever appreciative of their sensitivity."

SOMEWHERE OUT THERE

Music by James Horner and Barry Mann; lyrics by Cynthia Weil
From *An American Tail*

Into an animated world of WASP-ish mice named Mickey, Minnie, and Mighty came one Fievel Mousekewitz, a Jewish rodent, in a Don Bluth–directed movie called *An American Tail. Time* magazine noted the pun in the film's title and took the opportunity to make a pun of its own, running Richard Schickel's review with a headline that read, "Mousel Tov!"

The story was meant to be for children, but adults also seemed to enjoy this holiday-time tale of the little immigrant, a refugee from turn-of-the-century czarist Russia heading for the American dream, a land where, his father promises, "there are no cats, and the streets are paved with cheese." Well, not exactly, as he soon finds out. To quote Schickel: "*Oy,* does he have troubles." But, of course, there would have been no story otherwise.

Separated from his family, Fievel finds himself confronted with an unwelcome cat (voiced by Dom DeLuise, sounding a lot like Bert Lahr's cowardly Lion in *The Wizard of Oz*), a French pigeon named Henri hard at work on the still copper-colored Statue of Liberty, a con artist named Warren T. Rat, who tries to sell him the Brooklyn Bridge (at a discount, of course), society mouse Gussie Mausheimer (voiced by Madeline Kahn in a send-up of her own *Blazing Saddles* send-up of Marlene Dietrich), and so on.

The film was scored by James Horner, who composed (along with Barry Mann and lyrics by Cynthia Weil) the Oscar-nominated standout song in the film — "Somewhere Out There." In the movie, it is sung by Fievel (voiced by eight-year-old Phillip Glasser) and his friend (the voice of Betsy Cathcart) over scenes of a star-filled sky. It's cute when Glasser reaches for the high notes, but this obviously was not suitable for release as a single. So the very un-mousy Linda Ronstadt and James Ingram recorded a duet, which hit the Hot 100 on December 20 and peaked in the number two position. It remained on the charts for a total of 22 weeks — plenty of time to be noticed by award-givers.

After "Somewhere Out There" was nominated for an Academy Award, Natalie Cole filled in for Ronstadt at the Oscar ceremonies singing the tune along with Ingram. The song lost to "Take My Breath Away" (see page 274) but still managed to make a big splash at the Grammys, where it took top honors as Song of the Year. Horner, Mann, and Weil also took home Grammys in the newly created Composing category, for Best Song Written Specifically for a Motion Picture or for Television. As Fievel (or *Time* magazine) might have put it, *mousel tov!*

Fievel, meanwhile, returned in 1991, in the popular sequel *An American Tail: Fievel Goes West.*

1987

And the winner is...

(I'VE HAD) THE TIME OF MY LIFE

Music by Franke Previte, John DeNicola, and Donald Markowitz; lyrics by Franke Previte
From *Dirty Dancing*

Parents across America were wondering how a film called *Dirty Dancing* could have received a mild PG-13 rating, but it didn't take long for audiences to find out. Once the word was out that *Dirty Dancing* was truly a dance movie and that the title did not refer to sex, crowds started lining up at the box office and dance studios across the country started filling up with students eager to learn some of the "new" dances.

To be sure, some of the dancing in *DD* was suggestive, but none of it really terribly "dirty." The picture was set in 1963, when dancing with bodies pressed closely together was viewed as obscene — generally by those too old to dance that way. Patrick Swayze, whose previous credits had included *Red Dawn* and TV's "North and South," was cast in the lead as Johnny, a "Not with *my* daughter, you don't!" dance counselor at a swank upstate New York resort. Into his life comes Baby, played

Patrick Swayze and Jennifer Grey share a moment in *Dirty Dancing.*

and danced admirably by Jennifer Grey, doing most of her own dancing. Soon Baby's no baby, dancing — and loving — with Johnny, with equal enthusiasm for both.

While this may sound like a soapy plot, *Dirty Dancing* had a sound storyline with fully fleshed-out characters, each with their own needs and problems. Solid writing, directing, acting, and choreography all combined to make this the sleeper of the summer. *DD's* take at the box office was a very clean $25 million in domestic rentals.

Swayze tended to be defensive of the picture's title, as he showed in a 1987 *Newsweek* interview: "The movie isn't about bumping and grinding someone else. It's about connecting with someone. It's like the Fred Astaire movies with great dancing and a good story." A trained dancer who had worked with the Joffrey and Harkness ballet companies and studied under Russian masters, Swayze was not off-base in alluding to Astaire.

Along with the great dance numbers ("dirty," slow, fast, mambo, etc.) there were a number of oldies from the '60s plus a few new tunes. One, "(I've Had) The Time of My Life," was recorded by Bill Medley and Jennifer Warnes. It is sung under the final dance of the picture, with Grey and Swayze doing the honors. As they dance, Swayze turns to his partner and mouths the lyrics, jokingly pretending he's singing the song, since the words are so expressive of his feelings.

The song peaked at Number One and charted for 21 weeks, selling over a million copies. Medley and Warnes performed their song at the Oscar telecast, where it danced off with the Oscar for Best Song. It also won the Golden Globe Award that year for Best Original Song from a Film.

CRY FREEDOM

Music and lyrics by George Fenton and Jonas Gwangwa
From *Cry Freedom*

Set against the black struggle to overcome white oppression in South Africa, *Cry Freedom* was timely and controversial. Sir Richard Attenborough, Academy Award–winning director of *Ghandi* in 1982, produced and directed this story about the friendship forged between two men — Biko, a black activist, played by Denzel Washington, and Donald Woods, a liberal white newspaper editor, played by Kevin Kline. Through the eyes of his friend, Woods learns of the true horrors of apartheid, the legalized racism that prevailed in South Africa at the time. Human values like heroism and morality, along with excellent production values (with location shots in Zimbabwe), all combined to make this an important film, if not an overwhelmingly popular one (it made only about $2.5 million in North American rentals at the box office).

The first half of the film focuses on the bond that forms between these two unlikely friends and the tragic price the black man must pay for exposing the white government to this journalist. The screenplay by John Briley (who also co-produced) was based on two books by the real Donald Woods — *Biko* and *Asking for Trouble*. The author soon discovered he was indeed asking for trouble if he published these in his South African homeland. He narrowly escaped his house arrest, fleeing to England with his family after his brave friend was killed.

After South African activist Steve Biko is killed, over 20,000 mourners attend his funeral, as recreated in this scene from *Cry Freedom*.

Attenborough confessed that occasionally he had to tone down the actual events because they seemed more like fiction than reality. "When [the real] Donald got to the river," Attenborough told *Newsweek*, "all hell broke loose, with searchlights and dogs all over the place. Donald was convinced that he was the most wanted man since Eichmann, but it turned out that the police were looking for a couple of bank robbers. You try to put *that* in a movie."

Denzel Washington, a recent arrival on the big screen when *Cry Freedom* was made, was familiar to American audiences mainly as Doctor Phillip Chandler on the TV series "St. Elsewhere," although he had also co-starred in the 1984 movie *A Soldier's Story*. *Cry Freedom* would help him make his cinematic mark, however, as he received a nomination for Best Supporting Actor for his work. (He was later nominated for Best Actor in 1992, for his role as the lead in *Malcolm X*.)

The film's soundtrack had a chorus of native voices with a decidedly African feel to it, or, as *Vogue* called it, "The Sound of Black Music." It received a nomination for Best Original Score. The title song, "Cry Freedom," was nominated for an Academy Award for Best Song. Composed by George Fenton and Jonas Gwangwa, the tune is sung over the closing credits.

NOTHING'S GONNA STOP US NOW

Music and lyrics by Albert Hammond and Diane Warren
From *Mannequin*

In Ovid's Greek classic *Metamorphosis,* a statue of Aphrodite, lovingly sculpted by Pygmalion, the king of Cyprus, comes to life. In the 1984 movie *Splash* (1984), a man falls in love with a mermaid who is seen only in human form by others. And in a "Twilight Zone" TV episode called "The After Hours," all the mannequins come to life when a department store is closed. Put them all together and you have something a lot like the motion picture *Mannequin*.

This movie starred Andrew McCarthy (*Pretty in Pink*, 1986) as the prophetically named Jonathan Switcher, an aspiring artist who works in a mannequin warehouse. After he assembles the mannequin/woman of his dreams (as in *Metamorphosis*), he discovers his handiwork one day in the window of a department

store and lands a job there to be near his beloved creation. Predictably, the doll unwinds at night, coming to life only when he's around, dummying up whenever anyone else appears (sort of like the mermaid in *Splash*). Kim Cattrall (*Police Academy*, 1984; *Big Trouble in Little China*, 1986) played his literal sex object, but they really never do much besides kissing and cavorting through the store after hours, playing dress-up in the different departments.

Television's Meshach Taylor ("Designing Women," "Dave's World") had one of the choicer roles as a character named Hollywood, the flamboyant window dresser. Another TV regular, "The Golden Girls" co-star Estelle Getty, appeared as the store owner, while film actor James Spader (*sex, lies, and videotape*, 1989; *Stargate*, 1994) played a minor role as Getty's obnoxious preppy assistant.

Critics didn't think much of the film. Mannequin puns were frequently tossed unmercifully at the picture. "If nothing else," wrote *MacClean's*, "*Mannequin* lives up to its title: the movie is glossy, vapid and stiff." *Variety* voiced similar sentiments: "*Mannequin* is as stiff and spiritless as its title suggests." With reviews like this, the producers no doubt thought they would get stiffed at the box office. But fortunately, while returns for this film were lower than many connected with the production had hoped, they weren't really that bad, with a take in North American rentals of $18 million.

One of the happier elements connected with *Mannequin* was its theme song, "Nothing's Gonna Stop Us Now," sung by Starship over the wedding sequence, and again over the closing credits. The tune received a nomination for an Academy Award, and although it lost to "(I've Had) The Time of My Life," it became a Number One hit on the *Billboard* charts in April of 1987, remaining at the top for two weeks and charting for 15.

Starship was actually not the producers' first choice. Duos were more and more frequently being used to record movie themes, and the filmmakers considered the pairing of Patti LaBelle and Michael McDonald, as well as John Parr and Laura Branigan. Eventually, however, they hit upon the idea of Starship's Grace Slick and Mickey Thomas.

The writers, Diane Warren and Albert Hammond, wrote the song in only a day. London-born Hammond, a former member of the British group Magic Lanterns, had had a hit in 1972 with "It Never Rains in Southern California," which peaked at number five.

SHAKEDOWN

Music by Harold Faltermeyer and Keith Forsey; lyrics by Harold Faltermeyer, Keith Forsey and Bob Seger
From *Beverly Hills Cop II*

In 1982, another "Saturday Night Live" alumnus graduated to the big screen, starring in *48 Hours*. Eddie Murphy was one of that TV series' biggest success stories. He scored big in *Beverly Hills Cop* in 1984, with his comedic and acting talents propelling his vehicle into the third-biggest box office hit of the year. By 1987, he had been voted the top box office star of the year in a poll of moviegoers, putting him ahead of such important figures as Michael Douglas, Robin Williams, Kevin Costner, Arnold Schwarzenegger, and other heavy hitters. Murphy was back, and Beverly Hills had him.

Beverly Hills Cop II set out to cop as many dollars as a sequel could, and it did just fine. Audiences adored Murphy, who practically had his Axel Foley character down to a stand-up routine, which was his forte anyway. "I never had aspirations to be in the movie business," said Murphy in a Paramount Pictures press handbook. "I was always a stand-up comedian, and that's what I am more than anything."

In the film's story, Foley returns once again to assist his Beverly Hills buddies, played by Judge Reinhold and John Ashton, this time in pursuit of a female baddie, played by Brigitte Nielsen (Mrs. Sylvester Stallone at the time). Although the film was billed primarily as a comedy, it was loaded with violence. As *Time* magazine's Richard Schickel put it, "Everything anyone thinks might possibly have contributed to that initial success [of the first film] is present and noisily accounted for the second time around: the pounding rock score with the volume turned up to brain-damage level; the incomprehensible plot . . . the music-video montages of the good life in Beverly Hills alternating with sudden descents into motiveless and entirely humorless violence." Maybe so, but *Cop II* was one of the best money-making sequels of all time. It took in $80.8 million in domestic rentals, making it the number two movie at the box office for 1987 and the 15th-ranked film of the decade (its namesake was ranked ninth).

The soundtrack to the original *Beverly Hills Cop* had been a huge success, with several major pop hits emerging from the film, and the producers were out to duplicate that feat this time around. The movie's theme song, "Shakedown," is sung over the title credits as the audience sees a montage of Detroit, where Foley is seen in his real home, getting dressed and zipping off in his . . . Ferrari! (The salaries for cops in BH must be very good indeed.) The song hit the ears of the Academy just fine, and it received a nomination for the Best Song Oscar.

"Shakedown" was recorded by Bob Seger, who was pressed into service at the last minute, after Glenn Frey (who had performed the hit tune "The Heat Is On" from the original *Beverly Hills Cop* and was slated to perform the new song) came down with a bad sore throat and laryngitis. Perhaps it was just as well — Seger's recording of "Shakedown" went straight up — all the way to Number One on the *Billboard* charts.

STORYBOOK LOVE

Music and lyrics by Willy DeVille
From *The Princess Bride*

The Princess Bride was a send-up of heroic movies, poking fun at everything from swashbuckling Errol Flynn flicks to the fairy tales of our childhood memories. This was one fairy tale, however, that was just too darn good for kids — adults wanted it all for themselves. And deservedly so. "Look no further for the goodtime movie of the year," proclaimed *People* magazine. "This one's got high adventure, true love, torture, revenge, monsters, miracles and a little sex."

It also had pen-in-cheek screenwriter William Goldman (*Butch Cassidy and the Sundance Kid*, 1969 — see page 197), and director Rob Reiner (*This Is Spinal Tap*, 1984; *Stand By Me*, 1986; etc.), who also co-produced. The story starts with Peter Falk reading the medieval tale of *The Princess Bride* to his bedridden grandson. It's a yarn of a good prince (Cary Elwes) and princess (Robin Wright), an evil prince (Chris Sarandon), a giant (pro wrestler Andre the Giant), and a swordsman (Mandy Patinkin). And then there's Billy Crystal, as a Jewish wizard, who raises people from the "almost dead."

Others in the outstanding cast included Christopher Guest as Count Rugen, young Fred Savage (star of TV's "The Wonder Years") as the Grandson, Peter Cook (Dudley Moore's former comedy partner) as the Impressive Clergyman, Mel Smith (from "Not the Nine O'clock News") as the Albino, and wide-eyed Carol

Chris Sarandon (left) and Christopher Guest are up to no good in *The Princess Bride*.

Kane (best remembered from TV's "Taxi") as Valerie.

One reviewer couldn't seem to gush enough. "As you watch this enchanting fantasy," wrote Richard Corliss in *Time*, "feel free to be thrilled or to giggle, as you wish. This time, Happily Ever After lasts 98 minutes." But not everyone saw this fractured fairy tale favorably. "The shtick is stronger than the sword," *Newsweek* suggested. "A fable like this demands a visual style as rich as a Häagen-Dazs sundae — not indifferent cinematography and actors with their makeup showing. Still, if *The Princess Bride* fails to carry you away to enchantment, it's booby-trapped with sneaky wit. A good movie for browsing."

That's pretty much the way it happened at the box office. The take in North American rentals was a mere $13.3 million, hardly a blockbuster, although it proved a popular choice at the video counter and by the 1990s had begun to assume cult status with latecomers who missed it the first time around.

The movie's theme song, "Storybook Love," was written and sung by Willy DeVille over the closing credits. DeVille had originally performed with the group he founded in the 1970s, Mink DeVille. In 1986 he began working on his first solo album, assisted by Mark Knopfler of Dire Straits, who handled production and lead guitar tracks. Knopfler was also scorer for *The Princess Bride*, and was the one responsible for selecting DeVille's "Storybook Love" for the sound-

track. At Oscar time, the song was selected as one of the five nominees for Best Song, although there was no true "happily ever after" ending, since "(I've Had) The Time of My Life" won the statuette that year.

And the winner is...

1988

LET THE RIVER RUN

Music and lyrics by Carly Simon
From *Working Girl*

In *Working Girl*, Melanie Griffith starred as an ambitious brokerage firm secretary, low girl on the totem pole but determined to get ahead. Her big break comes when her boss, superbitch Sigourney Weaver — who steals Griffith's ideas and passes them off as her own — suffers a skiing accident, and Griffith has to "help out." Griffith doesn't get mad, she gets even. While the high-powered Weaver is off recuperating, Griffith steps into the boss's shoes — literally. She seduces another broker (Harrison Ford) not in the bedroom but in the boardroom, and eventually steals *him* from her boss, too.

"Give the saucy Ms. Griffith a key to the executive washroom," wrote *People* magazine in their review. "She's a winner." *Time*'s Richard Corliss had special kudos for the behind-the-scenes team responsible for pulling this one off. "Kevin Wade shows this is his smart screenplay, which is full of the atmospheric pressures that allow stars to collide. Director Mike Nichols knows this in his bones. He encourages Weaver to play (brilliantly) an airy shrew."

Much of the fun of *Working Girl* was in figuring out which time-honored movies were being sent up. There's a touch of Bette Davis's classic *All About Eve* (1950), and a vague salute to all those screwball "private secretary"–type comedies of the '30s and '40s, like *Big Business Girl* and *Wife vs. Secretary*.

The score was by Carly Simon, with many of the numbers on the soundtrack album produced together with Rob Mounsey. Although this picture is certainly not a musical, Simon's music is sensitively interwoven into the story. The film's main theme was called "Let the River Run," and its fortunes soared as much as its hymn-like words and music — the tune won the Best Song Oscar.

The song begins with a rock beat over a New York City opening title montage. We see the harbor, then on to the Staten Island Ferry as Griffith commutes to the workaday world of Manhattan and Wall Street. It's Simon's voice we hear, backed by an unidentified chorus. The song is reprised, reverently, by the St. Thomas Choir of Men and Boys later in the film. Simon joins the Men and Boys later on in a number called "Looking Through Katherine's House," and also works a few instrumentals into the film — "In Love" and "The Scar."

"Let the River Run" received a Golden Globe for Best Original Song from a Film, although it was actually tied with another song, "Two Hearts" from *Buster* (see page 285), for this prize, marking the first such tie for the award. And Simon won a Grammy in the Composing category for Best Song Written Specifically for a Motion Picture or for Television.

"Let the River Run" was selected for the Oscar from a field of only three nominees, the first time this had happened since 1935. This was due to Academy rules, which state, "If there are 25 or fewer qualified works submitted in any category, the Executive Committee may recommend to the Board of Governors that nominations be limited to three." Only 19 songs qualified in 1988, hence the lower number of nominees.

Working Girl, meanwhile, was nominated for several Oscars, including Best Picture, Best Director (Nichols), Best Actress (Griffith), and Best Supporting Actress (two nominees, Joan Cusack and Weaver).

There was a short-lived television series based on the movie. "Working Girl" starred Sandra Bullock as Tess, the role originated by Griffith. Nana Visitor (who appeared in *Star Trek: Deep Space Nine* in the 1990s) played her bitchy new boss. The show ran from April to July in 1990.

CALLING YOU

Music and lyrics by Bob Telson
From *Bagdad Cafe*

German director Percy Adlon was the driving force behind the film *Bagdad Cafe*, a movie seen by practically no one, yet commanding a lot of attention in motion picture circles. The picture made a scant $1.6 million in North American rentals, barely enough to cover the costs of the crew's catering. The picture was shot in studios in Germany and also in the sizzling California desert area surrounding Barstow.

Bagdad Cafe is a study in quirkiness. It starred mostly unknowns — German actress Marianne Sägebrecht, CCH Pounder, Christine Kaufmann — plus Hollywood's Jack Palance, playing a retired set decorator obsessed with painting Sägebrecht's portrait. Adlon is known basically as an "actor's director," and he peopled *Bagdad Cafe* with colorful characters, played mainly by character actors.

Then there was Palance. In an 1988 interview in *American Film* magazine, Adlon explained why he selected Palance: "I knew that his character, Rudi Cox, had to 'smell like Hollywood,' but I wasn't getting anywhere with casting until a friend mentioned Jack's name . . . I tracked him down in his ranch and drove up there to see him." Palance was duly impressed by this, although Adlon, best known for his documentaries, didn't think it unusual to drive all the way up to the actor's homestead. "How difficult is it to work with you?" Adlon asked the veteran actor. "Very," came the reply. The "difficulties" turned out to be things like wanting to do scenes his own way, such as wearing a headband when the director thought he should wear a hat. (The actor got his way on that one after Adlon saw him in the headband: "He looked great! What could I do?")

The movie's opening and closing song, "Calling You," was written by Bob Telson and received an Oscar nomination — quite an accomplishment for such a small film. The movie opens with Sägebrecht being dumped by the side of the road, baggage and all, left to fend for herself in the desert. Over this we see the opening titles and hear the slow ballad, sung by Jevetta Steele, accompanied by harmonica, guitar, and keyboards (played by composer Telson himself). It's a haunting melody, a bit lonely-sounding, but it sets the mood. It is also used over the closing credits.

Ironically, CCH Pounder had not been Adlon's first choice to play the curmudgeonly Brenda, owner and operator of the Bagdad Cafe diner and motel. His original choice was Whoopi Goldberg, who had impressed him with her performance in *The Color Purple* (see page 271). But he was plagued by "those managers and those agents. I hate them," he told *GQ* in 1988. In 1990, however, CBS aired a new series, "Bagdad Cafe," derived from the movie version, and guess who played Brenda? That's right, Whoopi Goldberg, starring with actress Jean Stapleton (famous for appearing for many years on "All in the Family").

Bagdad was now big time, at least for eight months — the series lasted only from March to November, 1990, and was off the air for the summer months. Goldberg and Stapleton played a sort of female "Odd Couple" in this much underrated TV series. Others in the cast included Cleavon Little and Monica Calhoun, the only one to make the transition from the film, playing 16-year-old Debbie. "Calling You" was used as the theme, still sung by Jevetta Steele.

TWO HEARTS

Music by Lamont Dozier; lyrics by Phil Collins
From *Buster*

Part romantic comedy, part crime thriller, part morality play, yet greater than the sum of its parts, *Buster* was an underrated British film that marked the big-screen debut of Phil Collins. Singer/songwriter Collins (see *Against All Odds,* page 266) had had some acting experience before his role as the real-life self-proclaimed "lucky thief" Buster Edwards. Collins's previous credits consisted of a performance onstage as a youngster in London's West End, playing the Artful Dodger in "Oliver," and an episode of TV's "Miami Vice," in the specially created role of Phil the Shill. The "Vice" episode finally caught up with director David Green back in Britain, who was planning his production of *Buster*. He decided that Collins fit the bill as the leading man who gets involved in a scheme to rob the Royal Mail train of £2.6 million (based on the actual Great Train Robbery of 1963) and then is hailed as a folk hero.

The movie was filmed on location in England, Switzerland, and Mexico. In addition to the main plot, there was a "B" story about Buster's rocky marriage, stretched to its limits while the artful, authority-dodging Buster is on the lam. He's eventually caught (the "crime doesn't pay" moral was alive and well), and the picture ends with him, now age 57 and out of jail, selling flowers by the Thames in 1980s London.

Critics were impressed with Collins's performance. "*Buster* is full of little comic gems," wrote *Variety,*

Phil Collins stars as *Buster,* the true story of a small-time crook who makes the big time by pulling off history's biggest train heist.

"mainly from Collins, who plays Buster Edwards with impish charm." And *People* commented, "Pop singer Phil Collins shows a pugnacious charm in his film acting debut . . . Green directs the robbery and the manhunt that ensued at thrill-a-minute speed."

Collins, naturally, was expected to sing, and his fans weren't disappointed. There were three Collins tunes heard on the soundtrack: "Big Noise," "Groovy Kind of Love," and "Two Hearts" (along with a song called "Loco in Acapulco" by the Four Tops). Amazingly, two of the songs — "Groovy Kind of Love" and "Two Hearts" — made it to Number One on the *Billboard* charts. "Groovy Kind of Love," written by Toni Wine and the frequent Academy Award nominee Carole Bayer Sager, was ineligible for nomination, having been used before the film, but the Academy did nominate "Two Hearts."

Hoping to concentrate more on his acting than on his songwriting, Collins approached his old friend Lamont Dozier to write music for the film. Dozier agreed, but when he flew to the location shooting in Acapulco to play his songs for Collins, the songwriter-turned-actor was so impressed that he changed his mind and asked if he could be involved with the tunes. Dozier was only too delighted.

The single climbed the charts, reaching the top position the week of January 21, 1989, and remaining at Number One for two weeks and charting on the Hot 100 for 18. The song was actually the second one from *Buster* to reach the top ("Groovy Kind of Love" had gotten there three months earlier, in October, 1988), and was the sixth Number One song of Collins's career.

Collins and Dozier were awarded a Grammy in the Composing category for Best Song Written Specifically for a Motion Picture or Television. "Two Hearts" also tied (with "Let the River Run") for the Golden Globe Award for Best Original Song from a Film.

UNDER THE SEA

**Music by Alan Menken;
   lyrics by Howard Ashman**
From *The Little Mermaid*

For the first time since 1940, a nominated song from an animated feature took top honors at the Academy Awards. Back then, it had been "When You Wish Upon a Star," from the Walt Disney movie *Pinocchio* (see page 34). Forty-nine years later, Jiminy Cricket finally had some company.

Sebastian the crab sings about the joys of life "Under the Sea" to *The Little Mermaid,* Ariel, and her companion, Flounder. The song won an Oscar.

The song was called "Under the Sea," from another Walt Disney film, *The Little Mermaid,* and both the music and the movie charmed the fins off just about everyone — young, old, and critic alike.

The story was based ever so loosely on the Hans Christian Andersen classic tale of the half-girl/half-fish who wants to venture into a world beyond the sea, to where the human boy with whom she's fallen in love lives — sort of like an animated version of 1984's *Splash* (also from the Mouse Factory).

It was a very good year for fantasy, with real popcorn movies like *Batman, Ghostbusters II,* and *Honey, I Shrunk the Kids* all jockeying for marquee space. But none could match *The Little Mermaid* for sheer fun — it was the kind of movie that most definitely would have done Walt proud.

Composer Alan Menken and lyricist Howard Ashman (the team behind *Little Shop of Horrors* — see page 277) were among the main reasons for the film's success. It is their music that really brings the picture to life and binds it all together. Menken says he and his late partner (who died in 1991) "tried to be conscious of the kind of songs that have been successful in earlier [Disney] animated features, like *Dumbo, Cinderella, Pinocchio.* I think that what we're doing is an extension of what Walt Disney started. I do think we're very much in the Disney tradition. And it's very important to me to fit into the Disney tradition."

One number in *The Little Mermaid* was a standout. Ariel, the title mer-person, is given a guardian by her solicitous father, sort of a Jiminy Cricket with pincers. He's Sebastian, the calypso-singing crab (with voice by Sam E. Wright), who gets the movie's centerpiece. The reggae-styled "Under the Sea" is "performed" in an underwater choreographed ballet, hailed by *Newsweek* as "the best of Howard Ashman and Alan Menken's musical numbers . . . a delirious Caribbean jam. It's a showstopper." *Time* chimed in, proclaiming, "The film's vocal, musical and painterly talents mesh ecstatically in the big water-ballet production number 'Under the Sea.' As Sebastian limns the aquatic virtues, a Noah's aquarium of sea creatures animates a joyous Busby Berkeley palette. If ever a cartoon earned a standing ovation in mid-film, this would be it."

How about an Oscar instead? How about two, one for Best Song and another for Best Score (for Alan Menken)? Or maybe a Golden Globe, for Best Original Song from a Film? A Grammy would be nice, in the Composing category, for the Best Song Written Specifically for a Motion Picture or for Television. When the bubbles cleared, "Under the Sea" was inundated with accolades, including all of these prestigious awards. (Another song from the film, "Kiss the Girl," also received an Academy Award nomination — see page 289).

AFTER ALL

Music by Tom Snow; lyrics by Dean Pitchford
From *Chances Are*

Reincarnation has always fascinated writers, who like to dream up storylines based on the "what if" premise — in this case, what if a man dies while his young wife is pregnant, then comes back and grows up to fall in love with his own daughter? Is it incest? What about his wife, who's been pining for him all these years, fending off suitors while practically becoming a professional widow?

There were plenty of plot twists in this derivative story, which some thought owed apologies to *Here Comes Mr. Jordan* (1941), *Heaven Can Wait* (1978), and *Made in Heaven* (1987), among others. Critics had a field day deriding this knock-off. "Here comes *Chances Are* and there goes Mr. Jordan, no doubt in a huff," wrote *Variety,* while *Newsweek* wrote it off as "a New Age romantic dilemma even Shirley MacLaine would find hard to explain."

A number of important names were attached to "Chances Are" (titled after the familiar Johnny Mathis tune, sung over the opening credits). Cybill Shepherd played a woman in her 20s at the outset, then "aged" to fortysomething so she could be the mother of 22-year-old Mary Stuart Masterson, the daughter she's raised alone. Robert Downey Jr., a former "Saturday Night Live" cast member and future star of *Chaplin* (1992) and *Natural Born Killers* (1994), played the reincarnated husband, now named Alex Finch. Ryan O'Neal played the deceased's former best friend who has stood by Shepherd's side all these years in a frustratingly platonic relationship. The film was directed by the late Emile Ardolino, who also helmed *Dirty Dancing* (see page 279) and the script was by Perry and Randy Howze, writers of the much-touted *Mystic Pizza* (1988).

The Johnny Mathis music on the soundtrack included another of his perennial favorites, "Wonderful, Wonderful." Several popular tunes were used to

Pauline Collins recreates her Tony and Olivier Award–winning role as *Shirley Valentine* for the silver screen.

THE GIRL WHO USED TO BE ME

**Music by Marvin Hamlisch;
lyrics by Alan and Marilyn Bergman**
From *Shirley Valentine*

"I'm going for the sex. Sex for breakfast; sex for lunch; sex for dinner," proclaims Shirley Valentine, the dumpy British hausfrau, as she bids farewell to her loving but neglectful husband. *Shirley Valentine* turned out to be a comic valentine, a tribute to all those women trapped in the dull sameness of their lives who have dreamed of running off for romance and escapist adventure — if only for two hours at the movies.

Shirley Valentine starred Pauline Collins, who created the role in a one-woman show in London's West End, where she first played the repressed but lusty lady. She then took her act to Broadway, where she won a Tony Award for her stage work — essentially a monologue in which she yearns to drink "a glass of wine in a country where the grape is grown." Other characters were described but not depicted, left to the audience to fill in with their imaginations.

The film version brought Shirley's fantasies to life, with a location shoot in Greece, the country of her dreams, not to mention all that sex. But this is certainly not a raunchy movie by any means; the sex is more anticipated than explicit, with an R rating due to a split-second nude scene and some racy language.

The picture is divided between Shirley's mundane Liverpool home and her travels from that dreary town to brilliantly sunny Mykonos. She has her longed-for tryst (with Tom Conti), but it's more than just a sordid little affair; she grows immensely from the experience. No longer does she feel, as she did at the beginning of the picture (in one of her continuous asides to the audience), that "Sex is like the supermarket: overrated — a lot of pushing and shoving and you still come out with very little in the end." All's well that ends well in this story by Willy Russell, based on his own play. The movie was produced and directed by Lewis Gilbert, who had teamed up with Russell in 1983 for another story about a British woman coming into her own — *Educating Rita.*

The opening song, "The Girl Who Used to Be Me," is an especially appropriate tune, sung by Patti Austin as we glimpse sketches from Shirley's ho-hum life in England. The song received an Academy Award nomi-

flesh it out, such as "Can't Get Over You" by Gregg Allman and "Forever Young" by Rod Stewart. A theme song by Tom Snow and Dean Pitchford (the team responsible for "Let's Hear It for the Boy" from *Footloose* — see page 269), called "After All," was used toward the end of the picture, sung over the wedding of Shepherd and O'Neal. The lyrics pretty much sum up the film's story as the song segues into the closing credits.

"After All" was recorded as a duet by Cher and Peter Cetera, and received an Academy Award nomination for Best Song. Geffen Records released the tune as a single, which debuted on the Hot 100 on March 11, 1989. It peaked at number six, charted for 20 weeks, and sold over a million copies. The tune has become a staple of Adult Contemporary radio stations, where it is quickly becoming a modern standard.

nation and was sung by Austin at the following spring's Oscar ceremonies by Austin. (Collins also received a nomination, for Best Actress.) Austin, the goddaughter of composer Quincy Jones, had a Number One hit in 1982 with "Baby, Come to Me," a duet that she recorded with James Ingram. In 1983 they again teamed for "How Do You Keep the Music Playing?" (see page 259).

I LOVE TO SEE YOU SMILE

Music and lyrics by Randy Newman
From *Parenthood*

The idea for *Parenthood* was born in 1985 on an airplane flight heading for Argentina. Director Ron Howard and his wife, plus screenwriters Lowell Ganz and Babaloo Mandel, plus crew members, plus all their kids, were heading to the location shooting of Howard's latest picture, *Gung Ho*. The kids were doing what any normal kids would do on a 12-hour flight: whining, crying, fighting, getting sick, making a mess of the plane. Somehow, all this chaos was an inspiration to Howard and his cohorts, who came up with just the right mix of children and antics for a movie that would pay homage to parenting.

Working on the *Parenthood* set with so many children might have been a harrowing experience in a different set of hands. But Howard, a father of four, including a set of twins, had been a child actor himself, so he knew what the kids were going through. Howard came from a showbiz family — his father and brother were actors — and as little Ronny Howard, he co-starred for years on "The Andy Griffith Show." Later, as Richie Cunningham on "Happy Days," he continued to charm audiences. He turned the many long hours on the set into a learning experience, talking to crews and learning about camera angles and lenses, and soon enough audiences were surprised to learn that little Ronny had grown up to become Ron Howard, Director.

Even before his "Happy Days" as Richie ended, Howard had left the show to pursue his directorial career. His first effort was *Grand Theft Auto* (1978). Soon he had found a niche in fantasy films. *Splash* (1984), *Cocoon* (1985), and *Willow* (1988) were clever and imaginative; in fact, he formed his own production company called Imagine. As he developed his style, he moved away from strict fantasy to produce and direct

such films as the hair-raising *Backdraft* (1991) and the stylish and beautifully photographed *Far and Away* (1992), the latter of which he also co-wrote.

Parenthood was a rollicking comedy that captured contemporary middle-class life. The story focuses on four families and four generations. Steve Martin is married to Mary Steenburgen. His sister, played by Dianne Wiest, tries to cope with her kids, Martha Plimpton and Leaf Phoenix. Other parents in the 'hood are Rick Moranis (*Ghostbusters*, see page 268, and *Little Shop of Horrors*, see page 277) and Harley Kozak. Various and sundry relatives moving through the story included Keanu Reeves, Tom Hulce, Jason Robards, and Helen Shaw.

"Howard's touch hasn't been this sure since *Splash*," said *Newsweek*. "He's woven this enormous cast into a wonderful ensemble." Still, Howard admitted it wasn't easy getting his picture on film. Some of the cast members were available only for a short time during the shoot. "I felt like an air-traffic controller instead of a director sometimes," Howard told *Newsweek*.

The mood is set right at the beginning of the movie, with Randy Newman's jaunty "I Love to See You Smile" sung over the opening credits. It's also used to wind everything up over the end titles. "I Love to See You Smile" received a nomination for Best Song, and Newman himself (a previous nominee for "One More Hour," see page 256) performed it at the Oscar ceremonies. Dianne Wiest also received a nomination, for Best Supporting Actress.

KISS THE GIRL

Music by Alan Menken;
lyrics by Howard Ashman
From *The Little Mermaid*

The Little Mermaid was the first Disney animated feature adapted from a fairy tale since *Sleeping Beauty* in 1959, and in many ways it was just a warm-up act. The film's financial success ($40.2 million in North American rentals) set the studio on a path of no return, off to far-flung places like France, Arabia, and Africa, for animated stories like *Beauty and the Beast* (see page 296), *Aladdin* (see page 303), and *The Lion King*.

The film was an amalgam forged from among a number of talents wearing many hats. John Musker and Ron Clements were writer-directors; Howard Ashman wrote the lyrics to Alan Menken's songs and also co-produced (with John Musker). Many famous actors lent their vocal talents to bringing the sea inhabitants to life. The mermaid, Ariel, was voiced by newcomer Jodi Benson (who went on to star on Broadway in the Gershwin musical *Crazy For You*). Her lord-of-the-sea father, Triton, was the voice of Kenneth Mars. Ursula, the Sea Witch, was first conceived as a Joan Collins type, but the producers eventually decided that veteran comedic actress Pat Carroll, doing a Tallulah Bankhead impression, would fit the bill. Comedian Buddy Hackett, a Disney alumnus from *The Love Bug* (1969), provided the voice of Scuttle the Seagull. René Auberjonois (familiar to TV audiences as Clayton Endicott III in TV's "Benson" and as Odo in "Star Trek: Deep Space Nine") was the voice of Louis, the sadistic slice-and-dice French chef. Samuel (Sam E.) Wright did the best-remembered voice, that of Sebastian the Crab.

From the start, writer-directors Musker and Clements knew they wanted an amphibious crab — a creature familiar with the worlds of both land and sea — to be the film's anchor. But it was lyricist Ashman who felt that Sebastian should have a decidedly Caribbean accent to give the crustacean a contemporary edge on the music.

The Disney artists then were given the task of capturing the personalities and facial expressions of these actors in their drawings, making for a not-so-coincidental resemblance between Wright's and his character's likenesses.

There was a steady stream of awards for the songs by Menken and Ashman. Menken received an Oscar for Best Original Score, while the two shared honors for Best Song ("Under the Sea," see page 286). The songwriters were also nominated for another tune, "Kiss the Girl." It too is performed by Sebastian the Crab, Ariel's mentor, as he urges the human, Prince Eric, to pucker up as they sit in a rowboat. With its mellow steel drum accompaniment, the song is a pastiche of some of Harry Belafonte's calypso numbers.

Other songs in the film included "Part of Your World," sung by Jodi Benson as Ariel, "Poor Unfortunate Souls," performed by Pat Carroll as Ursula, and "Les Poissons," sung by Auberjonois as the French chef.

THE NINETIES

As we reach the final decade of the century, it might seem that Hollywood should have reached the apex of social maturity. And to a great degree this was true, with well-crafted pictures like Philadelphia, Schindler's List, Quiz Show, and Pulp Fiction on the cutting edge of drama and technical achievement.

But producers during the '90s also catered to our basic human need for escapism, and by and large the films audiences sought out for much of the decade were of this genre. Movies about kids, dogs, dinosaurs, genies, vampires, and ghosts — as well as that old standby, romance — predominated in live-action pictures and returned top dollars at the box office. And, as in the past, music played a key role.

Films like Home Alone, Beethoven (and its cleverly titled sequel, Beethoven's 2nd), Robin Hood: Prince of Thieves, and Jurassic Park cleaned up in the live-acted department, while Disney features such as Beauty and the Beast, Aladdin, and The Lion King spearheaded an animation revival. The latter boasted full-blown musical scores from the creative geniuses Alan Menken, the late Howard Ashman, Tim Rice, and Elton John, recalling the heyday of filmusicals. And more and more, rock artists like Bruce Springsteen, Neil Young, Janet Jackson, and Whitney Houston were crossing over into the area of motion picture composing and, in many cases, performing. Hollywood, which had initially shied away from the "passing phase" of rock, now embraced the next generation with open arms — and pocketbooks.

Film soundtracks sold in abundance, with several at a time frequently jockeying for space among the nation's top 10 albums. All of the Disney albums sold well, as did CDs from 1992's The Bodyguard, 1993's Sleepless in Seattle (with its nostalgic tribute to the music of the '30s and '40s), 1993's Philadelphia, and 1994's Forrest Gump (featuring a selection of "oldies" from the '60s and '70s). Given this lucrative soundtrack market, the importance of music — a hit song plus a good score — was given almost as much emphasis as the film itself.

SOONER OR LATER (I ALWAYS GET MY MAN)

Music and lyrics by Stephen Sondheim
From *Dick Tracy*

Warren Beatty was born to play the square-jawed comic strip character Dick Tracy. At least, that's what he had always thought. As early as 1975, there had been discussions on a big-screen version of the Chester Gould comic strip, which had been done as a radio show and movie serial in the '30s and '40s and a violent, short-lived TV series in the early '50s, but never before filmed with an all-star cast.

The rights to the comic strip continued to be tossed around Hollywood for a couple of decades. Michael Eisner and Jeffrey Katzenberg became interested when they were both at Paramount, but in

Pop music superstar Madonna portrays the sultry torch singer Breathless Mahoney in *Dick Tracy*.

1983 Universal and Paramount backed out of a joint agreement to produce the picture. Clever Hollywood agents tried to package the product with top-notch producers, among them Martin Scorsese, John Landis, and Richard Benjamin. And at one time Clint Eastwood was interested in playing the title role.

Finally, Beatty, who was involved from the start and had first refusal on the role, bought the property outright in 1985 and helped work on an uncredited draft of the script. Katzenberg, by now a big-time executive at Disney, knew of Beatty's interest and finally moved forward with the project. With no animated movie being released in 1990, it was a perfect film for Disney — virtually a live-acted animated feature.

The film magically recreated all of the familiar cartoon characters, along with some new ones. Well-known cast members included Al Pacino (playing Big Boy Caprice), Dustin Hoffman (Mumbles), William Forsythe (Flattop), Charles Durning (Chief Brandon), Mandy Patinkin (88 Keys), Glenne Headly (Tess Trueheart), R. G. Armstrong (Pruneface), and Dick Van Dyke (D.A. Fletcher), with cameos by John Schuck, Charles Fleischer, Kathy Bates, James Caan, Michael J. Pollard, Estelle Parsons, Henry Jones, and Mike Mazurki.

The plum female lead went to music superstar Madonna, who was signed to play Breathless Mahoney. The pop singer had acted before, with critical approval, in 1985's *Desperately Seeking Susan*, and to somewhat less enthusiastic reaction in a few other films. And since *Dick Tracy* would be a musical, her singing talents were a plus, although she would have to drop her modern pop approach in order to get in line with the three '30s-styled songs written especially for her by legendary Broadway composer Stephen Sondheim.

Madonna described her teaming with Sondheim in Craig Zadan's book *Sondheim & Co.*, telling what it was like working with this great composer: "The first day in the studio I was so intimidated. Stephen was sitting right behind me, and I kept thinking, 'I can't do this.' When I first heard the songs, they were all in the wrong keys, and I thought, 'Oh, my God, this is impossible.' It's very hard to learn other people's material when you get used to writing and singing your own stuff." Soon, however, the Material Girl had recorded the three tunes: "More," a number with chorus girls; a duet called "What Can You Lose?," sung with an albino piano player character named 88 Keys; and the torch song, "Sooner or Later (I Always Get My Man)."

It was this last tune that proved to be the Best Song at the Oscars the following year. At the awards ceremonies, Madonna treated the audience to her show-stopping vamp number, attired in a daring, low-cut white gown as the Filmland crowd applauded their approval. Unfortunately, Sondheim had to miss the ceremonies and the chance to pick up his first Oscar — he'd broken his leg and couldn't travel to the show.

Dick Tracy did well at the box office, taking in $60.6 million in North American rentals. It was nominated for a total of seven Oscars and won three. In addition to Best Song, the well-received filmusical won for Best Art Direction–Set Decoration and Best Makeup, and received nominations for Best Supporting Actor (Pacino), Best Cinematography, Best Sound, and Best Costume Design.

BLAZE OF GLORY

Music and lyrics by Jon Bon Jovi
From *Young Guns II*

With a cast consisting of neo-Bratpackers Emilio Estevez, Kiefer Sutherland, Lou Diamond Phillips, and Christian Slater, *Young Guns II* was a sequel to the popular 1988 feature *Young Guns*, a fictitious tale of Billy the Kid and his pals. Westerns had always been a Hollywood staple, but their big-screen heyday had long since passed, or so everyone thought. The late '80s and early '90s, however, brought a new wave of revivalists who set about the task of resurrecting the genre with such films as *Dances with Wolves* (1990), *Unforgiven* (1992), *Tombstone* (1993), and *Wyatt Earp* (1994). *Young Guns* was part of this trend, an attempt to get some mileage out of the legends of Billy the Kid, who, in spite of his cult-hero status today, was a real-life mass murderer.

Reviewers were generally kinder to the film than The Kid was to his victims. *Newsweek* called *Young Guns II* the "surprise of the season" and "a stunning piece of filmmaking." *Variety* called *YG II* a "slick, glossy MTV-style Western" — not surprising, thanks to the soundtrack songs by rocker Jon Bon Jovi.

Screenwriter John Fusco knew he wanted Bon Jovi to pen some music for his film when he had first heard the singer on the radio performing "Wanted Dead or Alive." The film's star, Emilio Estevez, was also a fan of Bon Jovi's music, but more than that, he was a personal friend, so connecting the two was easy. Bon Jovi played

a selection of songs for Fusco, who was also the film's executive producer. He was especially pleased when he first heard "Blaze of Glory," but hesitated over the possible use of an anachronistic rock tune in a picture set in the 1880s. He called in the movie's other producers, and after hearing Bon Jovi play the tune again on his old guitar, they made it unanimous — the song would be used for the end credits. Bon Jovi even managed to get his face in the film, playing one of several prisoners liberated by Billy the Kid from a subterranean holding cell called the Pit.

Bon Jovi himself recorded the vocal for "Blaze of Glory," and he used some well-known musicians to record the soundtrack, including Jeff Beck, Elton John, and Little Richard. The song was nominated for an Oscar, and Bon Jovi performed it at the Academy Awards ceremony in the spring.

Although it didn't win the statuette, "Blaze of Glory" nonetheless lived up to its name. The song burned up the charts, climbing to Number One on September 8, 1990, and charting for 21 weeks. The soundtrack album also did well, peaking in the number three position. Another single release from the soundtrack, "Miracle," peaked at number 12 on the charts.

"Blaze of Glory" was selected by the Hollywood Foreign Press Association to receive a Golden Globe Award for Best Original Song from a Film. The song was also selected at the American Music Awards as the Pop/Rock Favorite Single of 1990.

I'M CHECKIN' OUT

Music and lyrics by Shel Silverstein
From *Postcards from the Edge*

Carrie Fisher was best known as the princess with the cinnamon-bun hairdo in the 1977 superhit *Star Wars*. But there was another side to Fisher, that of a talented writer. The daughter of Hollywood's 1950s lovebirds Debbie Reynolds and Eddie Fisher, Carrie wrote a semi-autobiographical novel called *Postcards from the Edge*, in which she told a bittersweet tale of a Hollywood brat and her aging actress mother, of drugs and booze, lust and sex, all with a unique sense of humor.

All this and more was alive and well in the film version of *Postcards from the Edge*. Shirley MacLaine played the mother struggling to overcome her alcoholism, but, as *Time* magazine so aptly put it, she

Meryl Streep as country singer Suzanne Vale sings "I'm Checkin' Out," the Oscar-nominated tune from *Postcards from the Edge*.

The score, which *Variety* termed "unobtrusively moving," was put together by Carly Simon (who had won the Best Song Oscar in 1988 for "Let the River Run" — see page 283). And Shel Silverstein wrote a song, performed by Streep, that was both the highlight and finale of the picture. "I'm Checkin' Out" proved that Streep was an capable singer as well as a superb actress. (She took singing lessons to be able to perform the ballads and country songs required by the role.)

"I'm Checkin' Out" is performed as a country and western number in the film-within-a-film that Streep's character Suzanne is shooting. She does the song with a great deal of energy and style, not to mention voice. This is the last scene of *Postcards from the Edge*, as well as the last scene from Suzanne's film. The "director" (Gene Hackman) yells "cut" and the assistant with the clapper rushes into the scene and says, "End mark" (typical Hollywood jargon in which the slate is used to show the editor where the scene ends). But if you look closely, ideally with the aid of a VCR's freeze-frame function, you can clearly read what is written: "Scene 229, Take 3, *Postcards from the Edge*." This was probably unintentional on the part of *Postcards* director Mike Nichols.

Streep received a nomination, the seventh of her career, for Best Actress (she had won in 1982 for *Sophie's Choice*), and Silverstein's "I'm Checkin' Out" received a nomination for Best Song. Silverstein, a former cartoonist for *Playboy* magazine, became a popular songwriter in the '60s and '70s, penning such tunes as "A Boy Named Sue" for Johnny Cash, "The Cover of the Rolling Stone" for Dr. Hook and the Medicine Show, and "The Unicorn Song" for the Irish Rovers. This was his first Oscar nomination.

"needs a drink the way a crooner needs a mike, though she claims she is no longer an alcoholic. 'Now,' she says, 'I just drink like an Irish person.'" Meryl Streep played the daughter, way too old for the role but so convincing that this minor point was soon forgotten. Mike Nichols directed, and a number of stars appeared in cameos, including Dennis Quaid, Richard Dreyfuss, Rob Reiner, Gene Hackman, and Annette Bening.

Hollywood loves pictures about itself, especially one like this, which kept its sense of humor rather than degenerating into the maudlin tale it could have become. "In this era of post-verbal cinema," said *Time*'s Richard Corliss, "*Postcards* proves that movie dialogue can still carry the sting, heft and meaning of the finest old romantic comedy."

PROMISE ME YOU'LL REMEMBER

Music by Carmine Coppola; lyrics by John Bettis
From *The Godfather, Part III*

The *Godfather* saga was an ongoing soap opera, Mafia style. Begun back in the 1970s with the original film *The Godfather*, the story of the Corleone family was surprisingly still alive and intriguing to audiences nearly two decades later. The first film starred Marlon Brando in his Academy Award–winning role as the original Godfather, Don Vito Corleone, a young Al Pacino as son Michael, and James Caan as doomed son Sonny. It became a blockbuster for Paramount Pictures, the top-ranked film of 1972 and the biggest money-making film to that date. It received 10 Oscar nominations, winning three (Best Picture, Best Actor, and Best Screenplay). Two years later, a sequel, *The Godfather, Part II*, was released, and it too proved enormously popular. Several years later, Paramount's Home Video division decided to release a re-edited cassette version, called *The Godfather Saga*, which combined elements of the first two films, edited so that the events occur in chronological order.

Enter *The Godfather, Part III*. It had been 17 years since the first picture took the nation by storm, but in 1989, Paramount's executives, after much negotiating, made producer-director-co-writer (with Mario Puzo) Francis Ford Coppola an offer he couldn't refuse. Suddenly, Coppola found himself in familiar territory as the years melted away. His star Al Pacino was back as Michael Corleone, now himself the head of the Family. Coppola's sister, Talia Shire (who had since co-starred with Sylvester Stallone in the *Rocky* movies) was back as Connie Corleone Rizzi. Diane Keaton returned as Kay Adams, Michael's ex-wife.

Coppola, a godfather type himself, was not above additional nepotism. He brought in his own 19-year-old daughter, the inexperienced Sofia Coppola, as Michael's daughter Mary. This last move was much criticized as a questionable casting choice, and Sofia's Valley Girl–accented scenes eventually had to be rerecorded. But Coppola insisted the scenes had been written with her in mind (although there were conflicting reports that the role had first been cast with Winona Ryder, who dropped out at the last minute).

Coppola's 79-year-old father, Carmine Coppola, who had worked with his son on many occasions, was brought in to do the musical score. The senior Coppola was an Oscar-winning composer, sharing the Academy Award with Nino Rota for their music from *The Godfather, Part II*. He also wrote the score for his son's *Apocalypse Now*, as well as for a number of other films. One of his songs in the soundtrack, "Promise Me You'll Remember," with lyrics by John Bettis, received a nomination for Best Song, the first *Godfather* nomination in this category. The pleasant ballad was recorded by Harry Connick Jr. on the soundtrack. Sadly, it would be Carmine's last major work. He passed away a year after the release of *The Godfather, Part III*, in May of 1991.

The Godfather, Part III didn't live up to its predecessors at the box office, taking in a mediocre $38 million in North American rentals (the film had cost a reported $55 million to make). However, it received several other Oscar nominations in addition to the nod for Best Song: Best Picture, Best Director, Best Supporting Actor (Andy Garcia), Best Cinematography, Best Art Direction–Set Decoration, and Best Editing.

SOMEWHERE IN MY MEMORY

Music John Williams; lyrics by Leslie Bricusse From *Home Alone*

Home Alone may qualify as the sleeper of the decade. Opening just before the year-end holiday time in 1990, the film was not heavily advertised. But word of mouth traveled quickly, and before you could say big box office bucks, 20th Century Fox had itself a certified hit.

The movie was written by John Hughes, writing from parental experience. Just as Ron Howard had been inspired by his own brood to come up with *Parenthood* (see page 289), Hughes got the idea for *Home Alone* from his own household. "I was going away on vacation," he told a reporter for *Time* magazine around the time of the film's release, "and making a list of everything I didn't want to forget. I thought, 'Well, I'd better not forget my kids.' Then I thought, 'What if I left my 10-year-old son at home? What would he do?'"

If his son was anything like the picture's star, he'd probably buy an armored car to help him cart all the money he would soon be making. *Home Alone* catapulted its young star, Macaulay Culkin, to unexpected stardom. Culkin played a wide-eyed 10-year-old who foils the bad guy burglars when his harried parents fly off to Paris without him (they're not child abusers, just befuddled). Director Chris Columbus auditioned at least 100 boys for the role, then settled on the future kid superstar they call Mack. "The others seemed to be playing to the moon and the stars," Columbus told *Time*. "Mack was very real and very honest. He seemed to be a real kid, one that you wouldn't be annoyed with if you had to spend two hours with."

Both Columbus and Hughes had built their reputations working with young people. Hughes directed such young-minded tales as *The Breakfast Club* (1985) and *Ferris Bueller's Day Off* (1986), while Columbus had directed *Adventures in Babysitting* (1987) and written *Gremlins* (1984) and *Young Sherlock Holmes* (1985).

There were other stars in the picture, like Joe Pesci and Daniel Stern as a pair of goofy burglars, and John Candy, playing a polka band leader who offers to let Kevin's mom hitch a ride home. But it was Culkin who drove this film. He stole every scene in which he appeared, and he appeared in virtually every one.

John Williams wrote the effective score, including a background song called "Somewhere in My Memory" (with words, barely audible, by Leslie Bricusse). The song received an Academy Award nomination and was sung by a children's choir at the Oscar ceremonies in the spring of 1991. In the movie, the tune is also sung by a chorus of children as background music when the abandoned Culkin, out walking through the neighborhood on Christmas Eve, sees people going to a party. The song was also used under the action as theme music, without lyrics, when Kevin wakes up on Christmas, and under the film's end credits. It has since become a holiday standard, played frequently in radio Christmastime medleys.

As of February, 1994, *Home Alone* was the second highest-earning film of the 1990s (right behind *Jurassic Park*), with a take in box office rentals of $140 million, making it one of the most successful movies of all time. A 1992 sequel, *Home Alone 2: Lost in New York,* reteamed Columbus, Hughes, Culkin, and most of the original cast. It was nearly as successful as the original (which made sense, since the story was virtually the same), with a bountiful box office booty of $103 million.

1991

And the winner is...

BEAUTY AND THE BEAST

**Music by Alan Menken;
    lyrics by Howard Ashman
From *Beauty and the Beast***

In 1991, the filmusical was at long last alive and well again in Burbank, home of the Walt Disney Studios. The studio had once more found a way to live up to the legacy left by the maestro himself, the man who urged others to call him simply "Walt."

It was Walt who had originated the feature-length animated film back in 1937 with *Snow White*. Live-acted musicals were all the rage back then, as they were throughout the '30s and the '40s. By the '50s, Hollywood was cranking them out at the rate of one every two or three months. Then came the long, dry spell of the '60s and '70, when musicals on screen meant something featuring either Julie Andrews or Barbra Streisand, but very little else. Traditional musicals were suddenly passe.

Then, in 1989, Alan Menken and Howard Ashman wrote the music for Disney's animated feature *The Little Mermaid* (see page 286). This smash hit led Walt Disney executive Jeffrey Katzenberg to sign up the pair for his next project, a musical version of the "tale as old as time," *Beauty and the Beast*. As *Time* put it, "Menken has almost single-handedly revived the movie musical, albeit in cartoon form."

Menken would be the first to disagree. In interview after interview, the modest composer was always quick to credit his late partner, Howard Ashman (who was also executive producer of *Beauty and the Beast*), with making an equal, if not greater, contribution to their body of work. "We had a kind of shorthand," he told a reporter for *People* magazine in late 1991, describing how they would decide when it would be appropriate for a character to suddenly sing. "Howard would have the basic idea of the number. Then he would ask what the music might sound like." Menken was devastated when he learned in 1990 that his writing partner of many years was HIV-positive. They had completed their work on *Beauty and the Beast* and most of the music for *Aladdin* when Howard passed away in March of 1991 at the age of 40.

Together, they created a host of future classics. *Beauty and the Beast* had so many knockout songs, the Motion Picture Academy couldn't decide which one to nominate. So they nominated *three*, the first time in Academy history that one movie had produced three Best Song nominees. With tunes like the title song "Beauty and the Beast," "Belle," and "Be Our Guest," Menken and Ashman, winners in 1989 for "Under the Sea" (see page 286), were virtually assured of another Oscar. And the winner was the popular "Beauty and the Beast." (An additional Oscar went to Menken for Best Original Score, and there were two other Academy Award nominations: Best Picture — a first for an animated film — and Best Sound.)

In the film, Angela Lansbury voices the part of the teapot, Mrs. Potts. Lansbury (TV's popular Jessica

Fletcher from "Murder She Wrote") sings the movie's theme in a scene where the Beast romances Belle with dinner and a dance. The song was released as a single with the combined voices of Celine Dion and Peabo Bryson, who sing the song over the movie's end titles. Their lovely harmonized rendition peaked at number nine on the charts and charted for 20 weeks. Asked if this song was written with a pop hit in mind, Menken replies, "We don't conceive songs as a hit song. With *Beauty and the Beast,* we wanted to break through and have a song that could be recorded . . . but essentially, the main priority for everyone is to create a successful filmusical."

The folks at Disney would second that. *Beauty and the Beast* became the highest-grossing animated film to that date, with a box office take of $69.4 million in North American rentals.

BELLE

Music by Alan Menken;
**   lyrics by Howard Ashman**
From Beauty and the Beast

Beauty and the Beast was Walt Disney Productions' 30th full-length animated feature since the 1937 classic, *Snow White and the Seven Dwarfs,* and it too had the promise of becoming a classic. Not surprisingly, there was a certain similarity between the two musicals. Both had female central figures — Snow White and Belle, respectively — fighting the forces of evil. Both had a cast of adorable characters to assist them: Snow White had dwarfs; Belle (whose name is French for "beautiful," or "Beauty") had a talking candlestick, clock, and teapot. And both had magic to assist them in finding their true love.

But *Beauty and the Beast* is much more sophisticated. It plays like a Broadway musical on the screen, with lavish production numbers and excellent characterization, enhanced by Alan Menken's rich score and songs by Menken and Howard Ashman.

The first big production number, "Belle," introduces our heroine to us through the eyes of her neighboring village people. This song is important in telling us about the leading lady, her hopes and dreams, and the significant people in her life. It's very Broadway, which was the way the composer and lyricist intended it. "When Howard and I were working on the songs for *Beauty and*

the Beast, in fact the first song," says Alan Menken, "I remember thinking, 'Are they just going to throw these songs back in our faces?' I was afraid they were going to hate these songs because they were so clearly Broadway. And, of course . . . the reaction was very enthusiastic."

While not released as a single, "Belle" garnered yet another Oscar nomination for the team, one of three they received for their work on *Beauty and the Beast.* *Newsweek* said of the tune, "The sensational 'Belle,' complete with Ashman's sly and quick-cutting dialogue, is reminiscent of Sondheim." At the Academy Awards ceremonies, audiences got to see the faces behind the animated characters when Paige O'Hara (Belle), Jerry Orbach (Lumiere), and Richard White (Gaston) performed the nominated song.

It is possible the audience watching that night had a strong sense of déjà vu. In animation, the voices are recorded before the artists begin their drawings, and often the real-life actors' mannerisms and facial structure become part of the characters. For *Beauty and the Beast,* animators working closely with the film's two directors (Gary Trousdale and Kirk Wise) were each assigned specific characters to develop, matching the characters' personalities and humor to the parts. Consequently, Belle turned out a lot like O'Hara, who was also a bookworm like her character. "She really is liberated," she later told *People* magazine. "Belle wants something real, and she is willing to hold out for it." This was what made the song "Belle" so special, with Ashman's lyrics achieving the formidable task of giving us this convincing thumbnail sketch of the heroine.

BE OUR GUEST

Music by Alan Menken;
**   lyrics by Howard Ashman**
From Beauty and the Beast

One of the biggest, most lavish production numbers ever to come from an animated film was the elaborate "Be Our Guest" sequence. The song scored the third Best Song nomination for *Beauty and the Beast,* but it wasn't just a nice tune. This was Hollywood animation at its pinnacle.

In the film, the characters of Mrs. Potts the Teapot, Lumiere the Candlestick, and Cogsworth the Clock, along with about a million singing and dancing dishes, knives, forks, and napkins, invite Belle (the French equivalent of the "Beauty" of the title) to a banquet. The song is reminiscent of all those Busby Berkeley musicals with high-kicking legs dancing on multi-tiered platforms. But with animation, you can have high-kicking utensils and rhythmically popping champagne bottles, a descending chandelier, and rainbow spotlights.

And then there were the singing teapot, candlestick, and clock. Mrs. Potts is the mother figure among the animated characters (she's even got a child of her own, a demitasse cup named Chip). Angela Lansbury voiced this teapot character and was one of those who sang "Be Our Guest." This was her second Disney film; her previous one had been 20 years earlier, *Bedknobs and Broomsticks* (see page 208).

Lumiere, the talking candlestick, is a character straight out of Maurice Chevalier, as Jerry Orbach, who handled the voice chores, was the first to point out. He revealed how he did the part to *People*: "You stick out your lower lip and sneer a little bit." He also claims the animators ended up giving the character "the same exaggerated nose as mine."

As for Cogsworth the Clock, David Ogden Stiers (best known as Major Winchester on TV's "M*A*S*H") described his character as "a punctilious, nagging majordomo who knows how the Beast's castle should be run but can't make it happen."

The Walt Disney Company found the lyrics to "Be Our Guest" to be readily adaptable for another use. The song, with its lyrics altered, was used in commercials for Walt Disney World, urging people to "bring a heart that's full of wonder and let Disney do the rest" at the company's Florida theme park, which is what millions of people had been doing all along.

In April, 1994, *Beauty and the Beast* landed on Broadway with a live-acted production that quickly became a hit. This seemed only fitting, since the animated version had played like a Broadway musical all along. The show retained the six original tunes from the movie and introduced one, called "Human Again," that had been cut from the film. In addition, Alan Menken, working with his *Aladdin* collaborator Tim Rice (see page 303), completed six new songs for this show, "one of which," he says, "a song called 'If I Can't Love Her,' is a song that you can just sort of feel has a tremendous future." Judging by his past track record, this would seem a certainty.

Sadly, Alan's partner Howard Ashman was not there on opening night to share in the joy of seeing their show play to a packed house. He had died in 1991 of AIDS-related causes. The final credit in the film version of *Beauty and the Beast* was a tribute to the late lyricist. It reads: "To our friend, Howard, who gave a mermaid her voice and a beast his soul, we will be forever grateful."

(EVERYTHING I DO) I DO IT FOR YOU

Music by Michael Kamen; lyrics by Bryan Adams and Robert John Lange
From *Robin Hood: Prince of Thieves*

Political correctness had entered Sherwood Forest. You remember Sherwood Forest — the place where Robin Hood and his Merry Persons hung out? Okay, so the latest Robin Hood chroniclers didn't go quite that far. But they did add a Moor to the cast to give it racial balance (Morgan Freeman, playing Azeem). And Maid Marian was suddenly a totally liberated woman, with a gutsy attitude and no small amount of fighting ability.

And then there was Robin himself. This was no Errol Flynn swashbuckling Locksley. Kevin Costner, who had spoken in Native American tongues in his previous hit, 1990's *Dances with Wolves,* played the native Englishman with probably the most pronounced American accent ever. But so what? Predecessors Douglas Fairbanks, Errol Flynn, and Sean Connery — the most memorable motion picture Robins — weren't English either (although Fairbanks, a Colorado native, was in the *silent* version, and Flynn's Australian accent and Connery's Scottish one were admittedly closer to what audiences might have expected).

No one except a few purists seemed to mind. The film was done all in good fun, seeming to bridge the gap between the 12th and 20th centuries. Filmed on location in England and France, the historic castles and lush countryside added a touch of realism that might otherwise have been missing in this latest romp through the forest. And it *was* a romp — while not quite Mel Brooks (that would come in 1993, with *Robin Hood: Men in Tights*), there was a great deal of warmth and humor in the script, along with a good love story.

Maid Marian was played by Mary Elizabeth Mastrantonio, bringing a heretofore unknown feistiness to her character. Others in the cast included Christian Slater as Will Scarlett, Alan Rickman as the Sheriff of Nottingham, Michael McShane as Friar Tuck, and Sean

Connery returning at the end of the film to be properly enthroned as King Richard. Modern special effects (such as a camera speeding along with a flaming arrow as it hit its target) contributed to the film's updating.

Audiences loved this summertime adventure. With a take of $86 million in rentals at the box office, it was the number two film of the year (right behind *Terminator 2*).

The movie had a musical theme that was easily lifted, called "(Everything I Do) I Do It for You." The ballad was sung by dusky-voiced rock star Bryan Adams over the end titles. Adams was one of the lyricists, along with Robert John, with the music written by the film's composer and conductor, Michael Kamen. Originally, Kamen saw it as Marion's song and sought a woman to record the tune. But he eventually settled on Adams.

In spite of the film's time setting, Adams insisted on using modern instruments, including electronic keyboards, which initially bothered Kamen, who had gone to great lengths not to use modern-sounding instruments in the soundtrack, but eventually he relented. The results can be seen in the music video appearing at the beginning of the laser disc version of *Robin Hood: Prince of Thieves*, which intercuts scenes of Adams and the recording artists in a sylvan setting with some actual scenes from the picture.

"(Everything I Do) I Do It for You" received an Academy Award nomination. It also became a Number One song, topping the charts for seven weeks and charting for 22.

WHEN YOU'RE ALONE

**Music by John Williams;
lyrics by Leslie Bricusse
From *Hook***

Some called it "revisionist," not surprising for a year in which all five films that spawned nominated songs turned to classic literature for their source material. In 1991, songs were from movies about beauties and beasts, outlaws and thieves, and pirates and small children who don't want to grow up. In a way, it seemed that all of the key films that year were aimed at children, or at least our collective inner child.

No one had really tampered with the Peter Pan format before. J. M. Barrie's classic had been done many times — on stage, in film, as a cartoon —but never by popcorn-and-roller-coaster director Steven Spielberg. Once he hooked up with the tale of the boy who didn't want to grow up, there were bound to be changes.

Morgan Freeman (left) and Kevin Costner take refuge in the forest in *Robin Hood: Prince of Thieves*.

Robin Williams stars as Peter Pan in *Hook,* reunited in this scene with his children, played by Amber Scott and Charlie Korsmo.

His casting for *Hook* was inspired. Robin Williams, who was pretty much a man-child anyway, was thoroughly convincing as the modern, 20th-century workaholic who's forgotten who he is; worse, once he's clued in, he still can't get the hang of flying until the picture's exciting finale.

Dustin Hoffman landed the juiciest role, that of the title pirate, Captain Hook himself. His voice alone was enough to inspire bad dreams, and Hoffman later revealed in a television interview that he patterned his interpretation after political conservative William F. Buckley. Whatever the source, Hoffman brought both terror and devilish wit to the part.

Julia Roberts also had a starring role, as Peter's pint-sized pixilated pal, Tinkerbell. Tink's obviously got the hots for Pete (not an entirely new concept — the Tinkerbell in Walt Disney's animated *Peter Pan,* which was the top movie of 1953, had a hissy fit every time Peter looked at another woman, and that included Wendy). There were tales of trouble with Roberts on the set, reportedly due to the breakup of her engagement to Kiefer Sutherland at the time, but any problems were left behind when cameras started to role, and her on-screen performance was nothing less than professional.

Wendy is now "Granny" Wendy, played by Maggie Smith. She's too old to fly, so it's Peter's kids who are off to Neverland this time. There were also cameo appearances, by musician/actor Phil Collins as Inspector Good and by Glenn Close, disguised as a male sailor victimized by Hook.

John Williams wrote his usual rousing score, exuberantly cheering on the characters when necessary, yet setting an appropriately mellow mood in the right places. He reteamed with lyricist Leslie Bricusse (they had worked together the previous year on *Home Alone,* see page 295) to write "When You're Alone." The song is sung by Peter's little girl (Amber Scott), as she remembers the way her mother sang to her back in the real world. The child's rendition of this plaintive lullaby gets the attention of everyone in Neverland, including Peter and Hook, who can hear it from the latter's pirate ship.

"When You're Alone" received an Oscar nomination, and Amber Scott recreated her song onstage at the Dorothy Chandler Pavilion during the Oscar broadcast the following spring. *Hook* was also nominated for Best Art Direction–Set Decoration, Best Costume Design, Best Makeup, and Best Visual Effects.

1992

And the winner is...

A WHOLE NEW WORLD

Music by Alan Menken; lyrics by Tim Rice
From *Aladdin*

Even as they were accepting the Academy Award for Best Song for "Under the Sea" in 1990 (see page 286), composers Alan Menken and Howard Ashman were already at work on their next Disney projects — *Beauty and the Beast* (see pages 296 and 297) and the one that would follow it.

Once again, the studio had dipped into the vast well of classic tales to select one that would serve as the basis of a feature-length animated film. Their choice this time was one in a thousand: *Aladdin*, one of the *Thousand and One Arabian Nights*.

But three days after their triumphant night at the Oscars in 1990, Ashman broke the news of his HIV-positive status to Menken. In fact, Ashman was more ill than either of them realized. He was able to complete their work on *Beauty and the Beast*, but passed away from AIDS-related complications before all the songs for *Aladdin* had been completed. Menken, though distraught, was determined not to let his partner's death affect his work, and forged ahead with a new colleague,

Tim Rice, who had written lyrics to a number of Andrew Lloyd Webber musicals, including *Jesus Christ Superstar* and *Evita*, for which he had won the Tony.

One special song from *Aladdin*, called "A Whole New World," was singled out by the Academy for the Oscar, marking the second year in a row that Menken had received the Best Song award, an unprecedented achievement for a solo composer. (Henry Mancini and Johnny Mercer, working as a team, had captured back-to-back Oscars in 1961 and '62). He also received the Oscar for Best Original Score, making him the first composer to win four Oscars in two years.

"A Whole New World," presented in the eye-opening sequence in which Aladdin takes Princess Jasmine for a spin on his magic carpet, fared as well in the pop music marketplace as it did on the big screen. It became a Number One recording by Peabo Bryson and Regina Belle, whose duet of the tune peaked at Number One on the Hot 100, charting for 23 weeks.

"A Whole New World" was a multiple Grammy winner too. At the 1994 Grammy Awards (the recording industry's calendar year for Grammy eligibility differs from the Motion Picture Academy's), it took top honors for Song of the Year (for Menken and Rice), Best Pop Performance by a Duo or Group with Vocal (the Bryson/Belle single), and Best Song Written Specifically for a Motion Picture or Television (Menken and Rice). The *Aladdin* soundtrack album also won for Best Musical Album for Children, and Menken won Best Instrumental Composition Written for a Motion Picture or Television. They left a few Grammys behind for others to win, but not very many.

Backstage, Menken told an interviewer from cable TV's "E! News Daily," "It's just telling me something really powerful, and that's 'Musicals are alive.' What we're doing are musicals, and we're getting the opportunity to actually have the 'liftable' song from a musical again, which is incredible."

All this could only help the film. *Aladdin* became Disney's highest-grossing movie to that date ($82 million in North American rentals, which has since been

The title character from *Aladdin* and his monkey pal Abu set off to discover "A Whole New World" in this top-grossing Walt Disney animated adventure. The song won the Oscar.

Armand Assante (left) and Antonio Banderas play *The Mambo Kings,* two Cuban brothers who bring their music and dreams to New York.

surpassed by 1994's *The Lion King*), and produced the industry's best-selling video cassette to that date as well. Riding the crest of this wave, "A Whole New World" soon replaced "Be Our Guest" in commercials for the Disney theme parks, which, given the song's title, seemed quite appropriate.

BEAUTIFUL MARIA OF MY SOUL

**Music by Robert Kraft; lyrics by Arne Glimcher
From *The Mambo Kings***

The Mambo Kings was the story of the rise and fall of two Cuban immigrants, brothers and musicians who

leave Havana in the 1950s for the nightclub scene of New York. The screenplay was based on Oscar Hijuelos's Pulitzer Prize–winning novel *The Mambo Kings Play Songs of Love.* The film was directed by a first-timer, Arne Glimcher, an art gallery owner and producer.

Armand Assante starred as one of the brothers, Cesar Castillo, while Antonio Banderas played the other one, Nestor. One of the movie's highlights is the brothers' appearance on the "I Love Lucy" show. Desi Arnaz Jr. played his father, Desi Sr., in a clever bit of casting and editing. The scenes were nicely intercut with some sequences of Lucille Ball in a real episode, lending an air of authenticity.

Naturally, there was plenty of music, mambo-style. *Variety* commented that the director "uses music to terrific effect" and that both Armand Assante and Antonio Banderas "are fine impersonating musicians. (Assante took voice lessons, while Banderas practiced the trumpet — and his English.)"

Director Arne Glimcher was also the lyricist for the movie's set piece, a tune called "Beautiful Maria of My Soul" (with music by Robert Kraft). The song was an integral part of the plot, as had been the case in some musicals back in the '30s and '40s (see "Faithful Forever," page 30; "Always in My Heart," page 52). The song is sung in the film by Assante and Banderas, and is the tune that supposedly makes them — the "Mambo Kings" — famous. They sing it everywhere — on "I Love Lucy," every night in their club, and, in Armand's case, by himself after his brother dies. It's also sung over the closing credits.

In addition, the tune was performed by the "Mambo All-Stars" in Spanish and in English, and was also sung by Los Lobos. The song's high-profile treatment in the film was rewarded when the Academy cried "Mambo!" and nominated the tune for Best Song.

The original soundtrack featured all sorts of renditions of this and other popular tunes of the era. Celia Cruz performed "La Dicha Mia." Tito Puente, who appears in the movie, did "Ran Kan Kan" and the ever-popular "Cuban Pete" (made famous by Desi Arnaz Sr. on "I Love Lucy," and reprised again in 1994 by Jim Carrey in *The Mask*), Arturo Sandoval did "Mambo Caliente," and Linda Ronstadt performed "Quiereme Mucho." In addition, there were 11 other tunes on the Elektra soundtrack. As several reviews of the soundtrack pointed out, listeners didn't have to be mambo experts to love the music in this film.

FRIEND LIKE ME

Music by Alan Menken;
    lyrics by Howard Ashman
From *Aladdin*

In the original *Arabian Nights* tale, Aladdin tries to polish the strange lamp he's bought at the bazaar, inadvertently summoning forth a genie. In Walt Disney's *Aladdin,* it happens a bit differently. Aladdin still rubs the lamp, but the genie who appears is no ordinary genie — it's Robin Williams, live from the Middle East!

This genie is Robin Unplugged. In what many saw as the best number in the entire animated feature, Williams (the voice and inspiration behind the likeness of the genie) does a complete animated stand-up act for Aladdin's benefit, imitating the likes of Jack Nicholson and William F. Buckley Jr. (apparently a popular celebrity to impersonate, as Dustin Hoffman also cited him as an influence for his work in *Hook* — see page 299) and doing a general line of hip patter. This was a perfect character for a song.

"Friend Like Me" was the liveliest tune in the film and a real show-stopper. Although it sounded tailor-made to fit Williams and his assorted personalties, which tend to spew forth from the talented actor/comedian's mind like exorcized demons fleeing the possessed, composer Alan Menken says that the song was not actually written with Williams in mind. "Robin's involvement in the creative process was what he improvised basically when he did dialogue sessions. He didn't add any lyrics — but he did a fantastic performance in the voices and the inflections."

"Friend Like Me" brought *Aladdin* its second Oscar nomination for Best Song. And the film had three additional nominations: Best Original Score (Menken, who won), Best Sound, and Best Sound Effects Editing.

"Friend Like Me" was one of only two surviving songs from the original score Menken wrote with partner Howard Ashman, who died before they could finalize the musical. (Tim Rice served as Menken's lyricist for the balance of the project — see "A Whole New World," page 301).

Menken also cleared up a controversy that had nearly marred the release of the *Aladdin* video cassette. Some Arab-American groups had filed protests with the Walt Disney Company, claiming the lyrics to the film's opening song, "Arabian Nights," were racist. The original film lyric had a line referring to a faraway land

"Where they cut off your ear if they don't like your face/It's barbaric, but hey, it's home." The studio bowed to pressure and had the line changed to "Where it's flat and immense and the heat is intense/It's barbaric, but hey, it's home." Unfortunately, the new generic lyric lost part of the specificity of the original's meaning — the reference to a flat, arid environ could easily apply to, say, Las Vegas rather than the Middle East

While the new lyric was inserted into the song in response to the complaints, it wasn't really *written* because of them. Menken explains: "It was not written in response to the protest. It was written before we ever recorded the song. I said, 'We'd better have another lyric in the can, because "cut off your ear if we don't like your face" could easily cause problems.' I admire my friends at Disney for saying, 'No, we want to stick with what's there; it's funny. [We] think people will understand it's a comment on a genre, not a comment on a people.' And enough people *didn't* understand, or chose not to understand, that we really had to bow to their sensitivities. We anticipated it. It was clearly a comment on the 'mysterious East.' It had nothing to do with Arab customs in particular."

I HAVE NOTHING

Music by David Foster; lyrics by Linda Thompson
From *The Bodyguard*

The Bodyguard was not a hit movie because of its stars, although it should have been. With talent on hand like top box office male star Kevin Costner and top female pop singer Whitney Houston (in her screen debut), these two could have just gazed into each other's eyes for two hours and the film would have been a blockbuster.

Fortunately, they did slightly more than that. The script wasn't much of a challenge to their acting talents: Frank Farmer (Costner) is a bodyguard with a fear of becoming too attached to his clients. He takes a job protecting superstar actress Rachel Marron (Houston) from a stalker and winds up falling for her. *Quelle surprise.*

None of this had to do with the film's huge success, financially ($56.2 million in rentals at the box office) as well as musically. For it was the music that really made this picture soar. This was not a filmusical in the classic sense; it was more akin to something like Barbra Streisand's *A Star Is Born* (see page 228), where the central figure gives live concerts. The music moments occur at these events throughout the picture. And while Houston received good notices in her acting debut, she was most at home belting out hit after hit connected with *The Bodyguard*.

Her biggest number, "I Will Always Love You," broke all records, remaining at Number One on the Hot 100 for a staggering 14 weeks, the longest run atop the charts to that date, and the full soundtrack sold over 11 million copies, ranking it among the most successful soundtracks of all time.

However, due to Academy regulations, the single "I Will Always Love You" was ineligible for an Oscar, since it had already been commercially released (by Dolly Parton) prior its use in the movie. But two other songs did make it to the finals: "Run to You" (see page 304) and "I Have Nothing." "I Have Nothing" is first heard in the film as the stalker sits watching Houston on videotape while creating hate mail. In the movie's story, the song is identified as the title tune from her last picture. It is sung again in Miami at the Fountainbleau in a performance that segues into a piano bar sequence, and then later at *The Bodyguard*'s Oscar scene. At this pseudo-Oscar ceremony, the song takes top honors, but the real Academy didn't take the hint.

David Foster co-wrote "I Have Nothing" with his wife, Linda Thompson. Although he had co-written another nominated tune, "Glory of Love" (see page 275), he was best known in the music industry as a record producer. By August of 1994, he had been nominated for a career total of 34 Grammys, and counting, and had won 12 times, including a Producer of the Year award for *The Bodyguard*'s soundtrack. Other Grammy Awards for *The Bodyguard* included Album of the Year, Best Female Pop Vocal Performance (Houston, for "I Will Always Love You"), and Record of the Year ("I Will Always Love You" again).

RUN TO YOU

Music by Jud Friedman; lyrics by Allan Rich
From *The Bodyguard*

"There was no video, no single, and the song is used for a total of two minutes in the film."

So said Jud Friedman, who, like his partner Allan Rich, was a virtual unknown in Hollywood. Yet they had their first Oscar-nominated song, "Run to You," sung by Whitney Houston in *The Bodyguard*. It was one of two nominated tunes from the picture, but the other, "I Have Nothing," was used much more prominently in the film, and they were afraid that "Run to You" would get lost in the shuffle.

"We had to do something," said Rich, in an interview with *Entertainment Weekly*. What they did was…popcorn. Well, the boxes, anyway. In their grass-roots promotion, the songwriters mailed out thousands of popcorn boxes stuffed not with the edible crunchy stuff, but with gold foil and small cassette players, which played the Whitney Houston recording of "Run to You." A similar gimmick had brought the pair to the attention of the Academy's music branch in the first place, when the nominations had taken place back in January. It was a clever idea, even though it didn't work this time (the song lost to "A Whole New World" — see page 301), but they got a lot of good publicity out of it.

Rich and Friedman knew they never really stood much of a chance. Their song was buried in the movie, never actually performed in its entirety. It is first heard as we see actress-singer Rachel Marron (Houston) listening to it on a headset while workers install security devices at her house. "Shut up!" she yells, and goes back to listening to her own voice on the headsets. The song pops up again later, but only partially, as Rachel watches a video of herself performing the tune.

David Foster produced this song along with the others on *The Bodyguard* soundtrack. He was the man responsible for the Houston's huge Number One hit "I Will Always Love You." Foster had been producing and recording throughout a 24-year career, playing keyboards and producing albums for such artists as Celine Dion, All-4-One, and Michael Jackson. He really hit his stride in the early 1990s, though — during a 20-month stretch beginning in 1992, his productions held the Number One spot on *Billboard*'s Hot 100 chart for more than 25 percent of the time.

"Run to You" and the other numbers on the soundtrack album contributed to Whitney Houston's success at the 21st annual American Music Awards in February of 1994. Houston, thanks to the boost from the album sales — among the greatest in soundtrack history — took home eight awards, including Favorite Female Artist in the soul/R&B and pop/rock categories. Her recording of "I Will Always Love You" won for favorite single, and the soundtrack to *The Bodyguard* picked up the prize for favorite album in the soul/R&B, adult contemporary, and pop/rock categories.

1993

And the winner is...

STREETS OF PHILADELPHIA

Music and lyrics by Bruce Springsteen
From *Philadelphia*

When Bruce Springsteen first recorded the soundtrack and music video song "Streets of Philadelphia" for the film *Philadelphia*, he had to do more than sing. Since the song's lyric is from the perspective of a gay man dying from AIDS, Springsteen had to assume that persona in this first-person song, which addresses the theme of the film. It was more than singing — it was essentially acting as well, quite a challenge to the man known in rock circles as the Boss, who hadn't had a hit single in years.

While many of Springsteen's biggest hits had been celebratory anthems, he'd also had success with more downbeat recordings, such as "My Hometown" (a number six hit in 1985) and the *Nebraska* album. So perhaps it wasn't surprising that "Streets of Philadelphia," a decidedly depressing song, became a big hit for Springsteen, who had never written or recorded a song specifically for a movie before.

The lyrics to the brooding song, which is sung under the opening credits, speak from the perspective of a downhearted dying man, whose "clothes don't fit me no more" and who can "feel myself fading away."

No, it didn't have a good beat and you couldn't dance to it, but it still became Springsteen's first top 10 hit single since "Tunnel of Love" in 1988.

The movie was nominated for two Best Song Oscars: the title song, "Philadelphia," by Neil Young, and Springsteen's "Streets of Philadelphia," which won the top prize. All together, the picture received five Academy Award nominations — Best Actor (Tom Hanks, who won), Best Original Screenplay (Ron Nyswaner), Best Make-up, and the two Best Song nominations.

Springsteen was signed to write and perform his hit after Glen Brunman, head of Epic Soundtrax records, contacted the artist's manager, Jon Landau, giving him the bare essentials of the movie and suggesting it might be a good project for Springsteen. Eventually, the film's director, Jonathan Demme, discussed the project with the singer-songwriter over the phone. At first Springsteen wouldn't commit, but he was reportedly so moved by Demme's description of the film (in which Hanks portrayed a gay lawyer simultaneously confronting homophobia and AIDS), that he went to work in his home studio, eventually recording a demo at his Los Angeles home.

Next came the video, with Springsteen on location, walking through the streets he was singing about. The director insisted on recording his vocal track live, with a tiny mike hidden under Springsteen's shirt. He paced through Philly's streets for two days, having to sing the tune about 30 times.

"Streets of Philadelphia" also touched the Hollywood Foreign Press Association, who awarded Springsteen a Golden Globe for Best Original Song from a Film. In accepting his award, the artist said, "Songwriting and

Tom Hanks (left), shown here with Denzel Washington, won on Oscar for his performance as a lawyer dying of AIDS in *Philadelphia*.

filmmaking got one thing in common: I think they're both acts of faith, the belief that if you tell the story well enough, there will be — and you will bring — some understanding where there was none before. So I hope that this film, and in some smaller way the song, maybe might take a little chip out of the fear and the intolerance and lack of compassion that we show for one another."

The song went on to win four Grammy Awards.

AGAIN

**Music and lyrics by Janet Jackson,
James Harris III, and Terry Lewis**
From *Poetic Justice*

When most people hear the name Janet Jackson, they immediately think of her music, her singing. But this is just one facet of the talented performer, as she demonstrated when she starred in her first major movie, *Poetic Justice*. Jackson — the youngest of the perform-

ing family that includes one of the world's most famous (and most controversial) entertainers, Michael Jackson — had been appearing in front of audiences since the age of seven, and had been acting and singing before the television camera since 1976, when the 10-year-old had joined her more celebrated Jackson 5 siblings on the family's weekly CBS musical-variety show, "The Jacksons." All eight kids (mostly young adults by then) took turns singing and dancing on the show, including Janet, who wowed the audience with her throaty impressions of Mae West and Cher.

Acting came naturally to Janet. By age 11, Norman Lear had "discovered" her and cast her in the weekly sitcom "Good Times." That ended in 1979, but by 1981 she was appearing regularly on "Diff'rent Strokes." She cut her first album in 1982, thus cementing her career in the music world as well. In 1984, after graduating from high school, she appeared on the TV series "Fame," based on the movie of the same name (see page 248). By that time, her recording career was about to take off, as she scored five top 10 pop hits during a 12-month period from 1986 to 1987.

Janet Jackson stars as Justice, a poet who discovers herself on a road trip from South Central Los Angles to Oakland in *Poetic Justice.*

In 1993, John Singleton, director of the critically acclaimed 1991 film *Boyz N the Hood,* cast her in the lead of his new film, *Poetic Justice.* It was doubly rewarding for Janet, since she both starred in the film and co-wrote the closing ballad, "Again." Her single recording of "Again" peaked in the Number One position in December of 1993 and charted for 23 weeks.

Poetic Justice's story is not for the sensitive. It opens with the murder of Justice's (Jackson's) boyfriend. In a world full of violence, Justice tries to cope with her chaotic surroundings by pouring her heart into a book of poems (hence the film's clever title). The beautiful poetry was written by renowned poet Maya Angelou, who also appears in the minor role of Aunt June. Her poems — "Alone," "In a Time," "Phenomenal Woman," "A Kind of Love, Some Say," and "A Conceit" — help carry the story forward as we follow Justice on the road to Oakland and potential happiness.

"Again" received a nomination from the Academy for Best Song. It was a particularly tough field in 1993, with two songs from *Philadelphia* as competition (see pages 305 and 307). But Janet was thrilled to be included among the nominees, calling it "a dream come true." She performed her song at the Oscar ceremonies wearing a spectacular necklace of 18-karat gold and 398 diamonds.

THE DAY I FALL IN LOVE

**Music and lyrics by Carole Bayer Sager,
James Ingram, and Cliff Magness**
From *Beethoven's 2nd*

Beethoven, that lovable, wet-nosed, four-footed hulk of a St. Bernard, returned a year later in all his scruffy elegance in a sequel to the original 1992 *Beethoven* movie. Now older (age four) and wiser (sit, jump, stay, earn big bucks at the box office), the canine returned just in time to regale audiences for the holiday season in *Beethoven's 2nd.*

And what could be more fun than 120 pounds of St. Bernard? Better make that 240 pounds of pooch, since the pup had been busy since his first celluloid appearance. It seems this dog's been going to the dogs — the neighbor's dog that is, cute, adorable Missy (we know she's a girl because she wears a pink ribbon). Soon Missy presents proud papa Beethoven with four furry little pups.

Getting all this warm fuzziness on film was a real challenge for both cast and crew. The puppy cast had to be constantly replaced with identical lookalikes, since they rapidly outgrew their roles. Then there was the problem of doggie drool — St. Bernards don't do well in hot weather, so the star dog retreated to his own private, air-conditioned trailer between takes. And whenever he returned to the set, director Rod Daniel ordered the thermostat lowered to a brisk 60 degrees. "If it gets any hotter, he becomes this canine drooling machine and poops out," Daniel explained to *Entertainment Weekly.* How did the cast fare in the deep freeze? "Some of the actors complained," Daniels said. "I told them to put on a sweater."

Beethoven (whose real name was Kris) even got to appear at the Academy Awards ceremony in the spring of 1994. The tune "The Day I Fall in Love" was nominated for a Best Song Oscar, and somebody thought it would be fun to have both Beethoven and his love interest, Missy, present at the ceremonies while Dolly Parton and James Ingram sang the number.

Things did not go well at the rehearsal down at the Dorothy Chandler Pavilion. As the two singers performed their duet, Beethoven shook his hot, slobbery jowls from side to side, giving the very tolerant Ingram a few laughs while the trainers rushed for towels. Meanwhile, Missy kept missing her mark, sniffing Parton and kissing up to Beethoven. That was Sunday. By Monday evening, the night of the Oscars, everything went according to plan, with the dogs patiently standing alongside the singers throughout the number. The ballad was performed flawlessly, by humans and dogs, although the song lost to "Streets of Philadelphia" (see page 305).

Meanwhile, the future may hold big things for Beethoven, whose namesake wrote nine symphonies and whose cinematic trailblazer, Lassie, has likewise appeared in nine films. All of which suggests that audiences may be seeing several more Beethoven movies, perhaps letting some of those puppies earn their kibble.

PHILADELPHIA

Music and lyrics by Neil Young
From *Philadelphia*

With two songs nominated from the movie *Philadelphia,* both using the word "Philadelphia" in their titles, there was some confusion among the voting members of the Motion Picture Academy. One, "Streets of Philadelphia," was written and recorded by Bruce Springsteen and sung over the film's opening titles (see page 305), while the other, called simply "Philadelphia," was written and performed by Neil Young over the closing credits. To clarify this confusion, TriStar, which released the picture, mailed out videocassettes to Academy members, with a music video of Springsteen's tune clearly distinct from the clip of the final scene in the movie in which Young's "Philadelphia" is heard. And just in case anyone was still confused, lyric sheets for both songs were enclosed.

Of course they couldn't both win, and Young's tune, although it was the picture's title song, became the also-ran. It, too, is a poignant number about the City of Brotherly Love, the famous nickname that is actually used quite a bit in the lyric. Steve Hochman of the *Los Angeles Times* called Young's song "beautiful . . . with the singer-songwriter at his most brittle, angelic and elegiac."

The film's soundtrack album did quite well, benefiting from Springsteen's and Young's specially created numbers as well as one called "Lovetown," by Peter Gabriel, along with updated versions of yesteryear's hits, like Sade's earthy version of Percy Mayfield's "Please Send Me Someone to Love" and the Spin Doctors' cover of Creedence Clearwater Revival's "Have You Ever Seen the Rain?" Young and Springsteen both performed their nominated songs at the Oscar ceremonies in the spring of 1994, helping to propel the soundtrack album from number 34 to number 12 within a week of the awards broadcast.

Young was born in Toronto in 1945 and, like so many of his generation, first became interested in rock as a child while listening to records by Bill Haley and Elvis Presley. In his teen years, he became self-taught on an Arthur Godfrey–style ukulele, later progressing to the acoustic guitar. In the early '60s, he played the coffee house circuit and formed his own folk-rock band, Neil Young and the Squires. By 1966, he had migrated south to Los Angeles, where he began concentrating on writing along with his singing. There he joined up with some old friends who had formed Buffalo Springfield. When the band broke up two years later, he tried soloing, but by mid-1969 he was persuaded to join Crosby, Stills and Nash. Soon the group was known as Crosby, Stills, Nash and Young, but not for long — by mid-1970, Young was off on his own again, purusing a solo

career that has seen him veer off into a wide variety of stylistic directions (country, rockabilly, techno, and so on) while retaining his core rock 'n' roll values.

A WINK AND A SMILE

Music and lyrics by Marc Shaiman and Ramsey McLean
From *Sleepless in Seattle*

Call it a sleeper. *Sleepless in Seattle* became the surprise hit of the summer of '93. It was romantic, lighthearted fare with a soundtrack that should have appealed to the *parents* of baby boomers, not the under-50 generation itself. Yet both movie and music captured the attention of the public like no other combination had before.

Which was exactly the way director Nora Ephron had planned it. "It's a real tribute to Nora and the way she placed the music in the film and built the movie and soundtrack simultaneously," Glen Brunman, head of Epic Soundtrax, told the *Hollywood Reporter*. Or, as Ephron herself explained to *Newsweek*, "What you hope is that people walk from the multiplex right into Tower Records."

They did, and what they found was a soundtrack full of golden oldies. Real, *real* oldies that pre-dated rock 'n' roll, like Jimmy Durante singing "As Time Goes By" and "Make Someone Happy," or "A Kiss to Build a Dream On," which had been nominated for a Best Song Oscar way back in 1951 (see page 114), or "Star Dust," "In the Wee Small Hours of the Morning," "Bye, Bye Blackbird," "I'm Back in the Saddle Again," and "When I Fall in Love." Somehow this assortment of bygone tunes appealed to contemporary record buyers, and the album became a runaway seller, passing the 1.5 million mark in sales and reaching Number One on the album chart by August of 1993.

The film had been Ephron's dream project for years. When she was still in her teens, her parents, screenwriters Henry and Phoebe Ephron, took her to see *An Affair to Remember* at the local cinema (see page 142). When Nora filmed *Sleepless in Seattle*, she found a way to work in scenes from that old movie, and also paid homage to its Empire State Building rendezvous sequence. But Ephron's love story has a twist: The two lovers never meet until the last reel.

Tom Hanks, who would win the Best Actor award for *Philadelphia* that same year, also appeared as the

Sam Baldwin (Tom Hanks) is persuaded by his young son Jonah (Ross Malinger) to participate on a radio call-in show, whose hostess has nicknamed Hanks *Sleepless in Seattle.*

lead in *Sleepless in Seattle,* playing a widower with a Machiavellian young son who'd like to see dad remarried to the right girl. That would be Meg Ryan, but the problem is, she lives on the East Coast while Hanks and son are in the title city. Ephron needed a way to keep them linked together, and composer Marc Shaiman obliged in his score.

One of the new songs Shaiman and partner Ramsey McLean created was called "A Wink and a Smile." It is subtly introduced at first, with only a few notes, as Hanks spots Ryan for the first time at the airport but doesn't know who she is. It soon becomes their theme. The song is then sung in its entirety on the soundtrack by Harry Connick Jr. as Ryan drives all around town with a map, finally finding Hanks's house. Later, a jazzy instrumental version is heard when Hanks's son flies to New York.

Actually, everyone had a musical motif in the film. Ryan's theme is "Our Love Affair," since she's such a fan of the movie. We hear it when she rides the elevator to the top of the Empire State Building. The boy has his own theme — "Bye, Bye Blackbird," which his mother, now deceased, used to sing to him when he was a baby.

Composer Marc Shaiman was an experienced scorer, with films like *City Slickers* (1991), *Sister Act* (1992), and *A Few Good Men* (1992) under his belt. So when "A Wink and a Smile" received an Academy Award nomination for Best Song, it didn't faze him. "With Bruce Springsteen being up for an award . . . being such an obvious front-runner," he said in an interview on Los Angeles TV station KTLA's "Morning Show," "it kind of takes the edge off the competitive aspect, and I can live the cliché 'It's an honor to be nominated.' When it happens to you, the cliché comes true."

TITLE SONGS

The following songs served as the title tunes for the films in which they appeared:

1930s

"Pennies from Heaven"	1936
"The Cowboy and the Lady"	1938
"Merrily We Live"	1938

1940s

"Down Argentine Way"	1940
"Blues in the Night"	1941
"Always in My Heart"	1942
"Saludos Amigos"	1943
"Love Letters"	1945
"It's a Great Feeling"	1949
"My Foolish Heart"	1949

1950s

"High Noon (Do Not Forsake Me)"	1952
"Because You're Mine"	1952
"The Moon Is Blue"	1953
"Three Coins in the Fountain"	1954
"The High and the Mighty"	1954
"Love Is a Many-Splendored Thing"	1955
"(Love Is) The Tender Trap"	1955
"Friendly Persuasion (Thee I Love)"	1956
"Julie"	1956
"Written on the Wind"	1956
"An Affair to Remember"	1957
"April Love"	1957
"Wild Is the Wind"	1957
"Gigi"	1958
"A Certain Smile"	1958
"The Best of Everything"	1959
"The Five Pennies"	1959
"The Hanging Tree"	1959

1960s

"Never on Sunday"	1960
"The Facts of Life"	1960
"Bachelor in Paradise"	1961
"Pocketful of Miracles"	1961
"Town Without Pity"	1961
"Days of Wine and Roses"	1962
"Tender Is the Night"	1962

"Walk on the Wild Side"	1962
"Charade"	1963
"It's a Mad, Mad, Mad, Mad World"	1963
"Dear Heart"	1964
"Hush . . . Hush, Sweet Charlotte"	1964
"Where Love Has Gone"	1964
"What's New Pussycat?"	1965
"Born Free"	1966
"Alfie"	1966
"Georgy Girl"	1966
"Thoroughly Modern Millie"	1967
"Chitty Chitty Bang Bang"	1968
"For Love of Ivy"	1968
"Funny Girl"	1968
"Star!"	1968
"True Grit"	1969

1970s

"Pieces of Dreams"	1970
"Bless the Beasts and the Children"	1971
"Ben"	1972
"The Way We Were"	1973
"Live and Let Die"	1973
"Blazing Saddles"	1974
"Little Prince"	1974
"You Light Up My Life"	1977

1980s

"Fame"	1980
"9 to 5"	1980
"Endless Love"	1981
"For Your Eyes Only"	1981
"Flashdance...What a Feeling"	1983
"Against All Odds (Take a Look at Me Now)"	1984
"Footloose"	1984
"Ghostbusters"	1984
"Cry Freedom"	1987

1990s

"Beauty and the Beast"	1991
"Philadelphia"	1993

FILMS FROM WHICH SONGS
HAVE BEEN NOMINATED

FILM	SONG	FILM	SONG
Affair to Remember, An	"An Affair to Remember"	*Beverly Hills Cop II*	"Shakedown"
Against All Odds	"Against All Odds (Take a Look at Me Now)"	*Big Broadcast of 1938*	"Thanks for the Memory"
Aladdin	"Friend Like Me"	*Blazing Saddles*	"Blazing Saddles"
	"A Whole New World"	*Bless the Beasts and the Children*	"Bless the Beasts and the Children"
Alamo, The	"The Green Leaves of Summer"	*Blue Skies*	"You Keep Coming Back Like a Song"
Alexander's Ragtime Band	"Now It Can Be Told"	*Blues in the Night*	"Blues in the Night"
Alfie	"Alfie"	*Bodyguard, The*	"I Have Nothing"
All American Co-Ed	"Out of the Silence"		"Run to You"
Always in My Heart	"Always in My Heart"	*Born Free*	"Born Free"
American Dream, An	"A Time for Love"	*Born to Dance*	"I've Got You under My Skin"
American Tail, An	"Somewhere Out There"	*Brazil*	"Rio De Janeiro"
Anchors Aweigh	"I Fall in Love Too Easily"	*Breakfast at Tiffany's*	"Moon River"
April Love	"April Love"	*Buck Privates*	"Boogie Woogie Bugle Boy of Company B"
Arthur	"Arthur's Theme (Best That You Can Do)"	*Buster*	"Two Hearts"
Artists and Models	"Whispers in the Dark"	*Butch Cassidy*	"Raindrops Keep Fallin' on My Head"
Babes on Broadway	"How About You?"	*Cabin in the Sky*	"Happiness Is a Thing Called Joe"
Bachelor in Paradise	"Bachelor in Paradise"		
Back to the Future	"Power of Love"	*Caddy, The*	"That's Amore"
Bagdad Cafe	"Calling You"	*Calamity Jane*	"Secret Love"
Bambi	"Love Is a Song"	*Can't Help Singing*	"More and More"
Banning	"The Eyes of Love"	*Canyon Passage*	"Ole Buttermilk Sky"
Beauty and the Beast	"Be Our Guest"	*Captain Carey*	"Mona Lisa"
	"Beauty and the Beast"	*Carefree*	"Change Partners and Dance with Me"
	"Belle"	*Casbah*	"For Every Man There's a Woman"
Because You're Mine	"Because You're Mine"		
Bedknobs and Broomsticks	"The Age of Not Believing"	*Casino Royale*	"The Look of Love"
Beethoven's 2nd	"The Day I Fall in Love"	*Cat Ballou*	"The Ballad of Cat Ballou"
Belle of the Yukon	"Sleighride in July"	*Centennial Summer*	"All Through the Day"
Bells of St. Mary's, The	"Aren't You Glad You're You?"	*Certain Smile, A*	"A Certain Smile"
Ben	"Ben"	*Chances Are*	"After All"
Benji	"Benji's Theme (I Feel Love)"	*Charade*	"Charade"
Best Friends	"How Do You Keep the Music Playing?"	*Chitty Chitty Bang Bang*	"Chitty Chitty Bang Bang"
Best of Everything, The	"The Best of Everything"	*Chorus Line, A*	"Surprise, Surprise"

APPENDIX 2

FILM	SONG	FILM	SONG
Cinderella	"Bibbidi-Bobbidi-Boo"	*Funny Girl*	"Funny Girl"
Cinderella Liberty	"You're So Nice to Be Around"	*Funny Lady*	"How Lucky Can You Get?"
Color Purple, The	"Miss Celie's Blues (Sister)"	*Gay Divorcée, The*	"The Continental"
Come to the Stable	"Through a Long and Sleepless Night"	*Georgy Girl*	"Georgy Girl"
		Ghostbusters	"Ghostbusters"
Competition, The	"People Alone"	*Gigi*	"Gigi"
Cover Girl	"Long Ago and Far Away"	*Godfather Part III, The*	"Promise Me You'll Remember"
Cowboy and the Lady, The	"The Cowboy and the Lady"	*Going My Way*	"Swinging on a Star"
Cry Freedom	"Cry Freedom"	*Going Places*	"Jeepers Creepers"
Daddy Long Legs	"Something's Gotta Give"	*Gold*	"Wherever Love Takes Me"
Darling Lili	"Whistling Away the Dark"	*Gold Diggers of 1935*	"Lullaby of Broadway"
Days of Wine and Roses	"Days of Wine and Roses"	*Golden Girl*	"Never"
Dear Heart	"Dear Heart"	*Good News*	"Pass That Peace Pipe"
Dick Tracy	"Sooner or Later (I Always Get My Man)"	*Grease*	"Hopelessly Devoted to You"
Dirty Dancing	"(I've Had) The Time of My Life"	*Great Muppet Caper, The*	"The First Time It Happens"
Doctor Dolittle	"Talk to the Animals"	*Great Race, The*	"The Sweetheart Tree"
Dolly Sisters, The	"I Can't Begin to Tell You"	*Gulliver's Travels*	"Faithful Forever"
Down Argentine Way	"Down Argentine Way"	*Half a House*	"A World That Never Was"
Dumbo	"Baby Mine"	*Hanging Tree, The*	"The Hanging Tree"
Earl Carroll Vanities	"Endlessly"	*Hans Christian Andersen*	"Thumbelina"
El Cid	"Love Theme from El Cid"	*Happy Ending, The*	"What Are You Doing the Rest of Your Life?"
Endless Love	"Endless Love"	*Harvey Girls, The*	"On the Atchison, Topeka and Santa Fe"
Facts of Life, The	"The Facts of Life"		
Fame	"Fame"	*Hawaii*	"My Wishing Doll"
	"Out Here on My Own"	*Hello, Frisco, Hello*	"You'll Never Know"
55 Days at Peking	"So Little Time"	*Here Come the Waves*	"Ac-Cent-Tchu-Ate the Positive"
Five Pennies, The	"The Five Pennies"	*Here Comes the Groom*	"In the Cool, Cool, Cool of the Evening"
Flashdance	"Flashdance...What a Feeling"		
	"Maniac"	*Hers to Hold*	"Say a Prayer for the Boys over There"
Flying Down to Rio	"Carioca"		
Flying with Music	"Pennies for Peppino"	*High and the Mighty, The*	"The High and the Mighty"
Follow the Boys	"I'll Walk Alone"	*High Noon*	"High Noon (Do Not Forsake Me)"
Footloose	"Footloose"		
For Love of Ivy	"For Love of Ivy"	*High Society*	"True Love"
For Your Eyes Only	"For Your Eyes Only"	*High Time*	"The Second Time Around"
Foul Play	"Ready to Take a Chance Again"	*Higher and Higher*	"I Couldn't Sleep a Wink Last Night"
Friendly Persuasion	"Friendly Persuasion (Thee I Love)"	*Hit Parade of 1941*	"Who Am I?"

APPENDIX 2

FILM	SONG	FILM	SONG
Hit Parade of 1943	"Change of Heart"	*Magic of Lassie, The*	"When You're Loved"
Hole in the Head, A	"High Hopes"	*Mahogany*	"Theme from *Mahogany* (Do You Know Where You're Going To?)"
Holiday Inn	"White Christmas"		
Hollywood Canteen	"Sweet Dreams Sweetheart"	*Mambo Kings, The*	"Beautiful Maria of My Soul"
Home Alone	"Somewhere in My Memory"	*Man Who Knew Too Much, The*	"Whatever Will Be, Will Be (Que Sera, Sera)"
Honeysuckle Rose	"On the Road Again"		
Hook	"When You're Alone"	*Mannequin*	"Always and Always"
Houseboat	"Almost in Your Arms"	*Mannequin*	"Nothing's Gonna Stop Us Now"
Hush . . . Hush, Sweet Charlotte	"Hush . . . Hush, Sweet Charlotte"		
		Marjorie Morningstar	"A Very Precious Love"
Ice Castles	"Theme from *Ice Castles* (Through the Eyes of Love)"	*Mary Poppins*	"Chim Chim Cheree"
		Mayor of 44th Street, The	"When There's a Breeze on Lake Louise"
It's a Great Feeling	"It's a Great Feeling"		
It's a Mad, Mad, Mad, Mad World	"It's a Mad, Mad, Mad, Mad World"	*Meet Me in St. Louis*	"The Trolley Song"
		Merrily We Live	"Merrily We Live"
Joker Is Wild, The	"All the Way"	*Minstrel Man*	"Remember Me to Carolina"
Julie	"Julie"	*Miss Sadie Thompson*	"Sadie Thompson's Song"
Jungle Book, The	"The Bare Necessities"	*Mondo Cane*	"More"
Just for You	"Zing a Little Zong"	*Moon Is Blue, The*	"The Moon Is Blue"
Karate Kid II, The	"Glory of Love"	*Mother Wore Tights*	"You Do"
Keep 'Em Flying	"Pig Foot Pete"	*Mr. Dodd Takes the Air*	"Remember Me?"
Kotch	"Life Is What You Make It"	*Muppet Movie, The*	"The Rainbow Connection"
Lady Be Good	"The Last Time I Saw Paris"	*Music in My Heart*	"It's a Blue World"
Lady Objects, The	"A Mist Is Over the Moon"	*Mutiny on the Bounty*	"Love Song from *Mutiny on the Bounty* (Follow Me)"
Las Vegas Nights	"Dolores"		
Life and Times of Judge Roy Bean, The	"Marmalade, Molasses and Honey"	*My Foolish Heart*	"My Foolish Heart"
		Nashville	"I'm Easy"
Little Ark, The	"Come Follow, Follow Me"	*Neptune's Daughter*	"Baby, It's Cold Outside"
Little Mermaid, The	"Kiss the Girl"	*Never on Sunday*	"Never on Sunday"
	"Under the Sea"	*9 to 5*	"9 to 5"
Little Prince, The	"Little Prince"	*Norma Rae*	"It Goes Like It Goes"
Little Shop of Horrors	"Mean Green Mother from Outer Space"	*Officer and a Gentleman, An*	"Up Where We Belong"
Live and Let Die	"Live and Let Die"	*Omen, The*	"Ave Satani"
Love Affair	"Wishing (Will Make It So)"	*Orchestra Wives*	"I've Got a Gal in Kalamazoo"
Love Is a Many-Splendored Thing	"Love Is a Many-Splendored Thing"	*Other Side of the Mountain, The*	"Richard's Window"
Love Letters	"Love Letters"	*Paleface, The*	"Buttons and Bows"
Love Me Or Leave Me	"I'll Never Stop Loving You"	*Papa's Delicate Condition*	"Call Me Irresponsible"
Lovers and Other Strangers	"For All We Know"		
		Parenthood	"I Love to See You Smile"
Madron	"Till Love Touches Your Life"	*Pennies from Heaven*	"Pennies from Heaven"

FILM	SONG	FILM	SONG
Pepe	"Faraway Part of Town"	*Shaft*	"Theme from *Shaft*"
Perils of Pauline, The	"I Wish I Didn't Love You So"	*Shall We Dance*	"They Can't Take That Away from Me"
Pete's Dragon	"Candle on the Water"	*She Loves Me Not*	"Love in Bloom"
Philadelphia	"Philadelphia"	*Shirley Valentine*	"The Girl Who Used to Be Me"
	"Streets of Philadelphia"		
Pieces of Dreams	"Pieces of Dreams"	*Sing, Baby, Sing*	"When Did You Leave Heaven?"
Pink Panther Strikes Again, The	"Come to Me"	*Sing Your Way Home*	"I'll Buy That Dream"
Pinocchio	"When You Wish Upon A Star"	*Singing Guns*	"Mule Train"
		Sky's the Limit, The	"My Shining Hour"
Pocketful of Miracles	"Pocketful of Miracles"	*Sleepless in Seattle*	"A Wink and a Smile"
Poetic Justice	"Again"	*Slipper and the Rose, The*	"The Slipper and the Rose Waltz (He Danced with Me/ She Danced With Me)"
Poseidon Adventure, The	"The Morning After"		
Postcards from the Edge	"I'm Checkin' Out"		
Prime of Miss Jean Brodie, The	"Jean"	*Small Town Girl*	"My Flaming Heart"
		So Dear to My Heart	"Lavender Blue (Dilly, Dilly)"
Princess Bride, The	"Storybook Love"	*Some Came Running*	"To Love and Be Loved"
Promise, The	"Theme from *The Promise* (I'll Never Say 'Goodbye')"	*Something to Shout About*	"You'd Be So Nice to Come Home To"
Ragtime	"One More Hour"	*Sometimes a Great Notion*	"All His Children"
Rescuers, The	"Someone's Waiting for You"		
Rhythm on the River	"Only Forever"	*Son of Paleface*	"Am I in Love?"
Rich, Young and Pretty	"Wonder Why"	*Song of the Open Road*	"Too Much in Love"
Ridin' on a Rainbow	"Be Honest with Me"	*Song of the South*	"Zip-A-Dee-Doo-Dah"
Roberta	"Lovely to Look At"	*Spring Parade*	"Waltzing in the Clouds"
Robin and the 7 Hoods	"My Kind of Town"	*Spy Who Loved Me, The*	"Nobody Does It Better"
Robin Hood	"Love"	*Stage Door Canteen*	"We Mustn't Say Goodbye"
Robin Hood: Prince of Thieves	"(Everything I Do) I Do It for You"	*Star!*	"Star!"
		Star Is Born, A	"Evergreen (Love Theme from *A Star Is Born*)"
Rocky	"Gonna Fly Now"		
Rocky III	"Eye of the Tiger"		"The Man That Got Away"
Romance on the High Seas	"It's Magic"	*Star-Spangled Rhythm*	"That Old Black Magic"
		State Fair	"It Might As Well Be Spring"
Royal Wedding	"Too Late Now"	*Stepmother, The*	"Strange Are the Ways of Love"
Saludos Amigos	"Saludos Amigos"		
Same Time, Next Year	"The Last Time I Felt Like This"	*Sterile Cuckoo, The*	"Come Saturday Morning"
		Story of GI Joe, The	"Linda"
San Antonio	"Some Sunday Morning"	*Strike Up the Band*	"Our Love Affair"
Sandpiper, The	"The Shadow of Your Smile"	*Strip, The*	"A Kiss to Build a Dream On"
Scrooge	"Thank You Very Much"	*Sun Valley Serenade*	"Chattanooga Choo Choo"
Second Chorus	"Love of My Life"	*Susan Slept Here*	"Hold My Hand"
Second Fiddle	"I Poured My Heart into a Song"	*Suzy*	"Did I Remember?"

FILM	SONG	FILM	SONG
Sweet and Lowdown	"I'm Making Believe"	*Under Western Stars*	"Dust"
Swing Time	"The Way You Look Tonight"	*Up in Arms*	"Now I Know"
Tammy and the Bachelor	"Tammy"	*Vogues of 1938*	"That Old Feeling"
10	"Song From *10* (It's Easy to Say)"	*Wabash Avenue*	"Wilhelmina"
		Waikiki Wedding	"Sweet Leilani"
Tender Is the Night	"Tender Is the Night"	*Walk on the Wild Side*	"Walk on the Wild Side"
Tender Mercies	"Over You"	*Way We Were, The*	"The Way We Were"
Tender Trap, The	"(Love Is) The Tender Trap"	*Wet Blanket Policy*	"The Woody Woodpecker Song"
Thank God It's Friday	"Last Dance"		
Thank Your Lucky Stars	"They're Either Too Young or Too Old"	*What's New Pussycat?*	"What's New Pussycat?"
		Where Love Has Gone	"Where Love Has Gone"
That Certain Age	"My Own"	*Whiffs*	"Now That We're in Love"
That Lady in Ermine	"This Is the Moment"	*White Christmas*	"Count Your Blessings Instead of Sheep"
That's Life!	"Life in a Looking Glass"	*White Nights*	"Say You, Say Me"
Thomas Crown Affair, The	"The Windmills of Your Mind"		"Separate Lives"
Thoroughly Modern Millie	"Thoroughly Modern Millie"	*Why Girls Leave Home*	"The Cat and the Canary"
		Wild Is the Wind	"Wild Is the Wind"
Three Coins in the Fountain	"Three Coins in the Fountain"	*Wizard of Oz, The*	"Over the Rainbow"
Time, the Place and the Girl, The	"A Gal in Calico"	*Woman in Red, The*	"I Just Called to Say I Love You"
Toast of New Orleans, The	"Be My Love"	*Wonder Man*	"So in Love"
		Working Girl	"Let the River Run"
Tonight and Every Night	"Anywhere"	*Written on the Wind*	"Written on the Wind"
Tootsie	"It Might Be You"	*Yentl*	"Papa, Can You Hear Me?"
Top Gun	"Take My Breath Away"		"The Way He Makes Me Feel"
Top Hat	"Cheek to Cheek"	*Yes, Giorgio*	"If We Were in Love"
Touch of Class, A	"All That Love Went to Waste"	*You Light Up My Life*	"You Light Up My Life"
		You Were Never Lovelier	"Dearly Beloved"
Towering Inferno, The	"We May Never Love Like This Again"	*You'll Find Out*	"I'd Know You Anywhere"
Town Without Pity	"Town Without Pity"	*You'll Never Get Rich*	"Since I Kissed My Baby Goodbye"
Trail of the Lonesome Pine	"A Melody from the Sky"	*Young Guns II*	"Blaze of Glory"
True Grit	"True Grit"	*Young Land, The*	"Strange Are The Ways of Love"
Two for the Seesaw	"Song from *Two for the Seesaw* (Second Chance)"	*Youth on Parade*	"I Heard That Song Before"
Umbrellas of Cherbourg, The	"I Will Wait for You"		
Unchained	"Unchained Melody"		

THE MOST OSCAR NOMINATIONS, BY LYRICIST

SAMMY CAHN (26)

"All That Love Went to Waste"	1973
"All the Way"	1945
"Anywhere"	1945
"Be My Love"	1950
"Because You're Mine"	1952
"Best of Everything, The"	1959
"Call Me Irresponsible"	1963
"High Hopes"	1959
"I Fall in Love Too Easily"	1945
"I'll Never Stop Loving You"	1955
"I'll Walk Alone"	1944
"I've Heard That Song Before"	1942
"It's a Great Feeling"	1949
"It's Magic"	1948
"(Love Is) The Tender Trap"	1955
"My Kind of Town"	1964
"Now That We're in Love"	1975
"Pocketful of Miracles"	1961
"Second Time Around, The"	1960
"Star!"	1968
"Thoroughly Modern Millie"	1967
"Three Coins in the Fountain"	1954
"To Love and Be Loved"	1958
"Where Love Has Gone"	1964
"Wonder Why"	1951
"Written on the Wind"	1956

JOHNNY MERCER (18)

"Ac-Cent-Tchu-Ate the Positive"	1945
"Blues in the Night"	1941
"Charade"	1963
"Days of Wine and Roses"	1962
"Dearly Beloved"	1942
"Facts of Life, The"	1960
"I'd Know You Anywhere"	1940
"In the Cool, Cool, Cool of the Evening"	1951
"Jeepers Creepers"	1938
"Life Is What You Make It"	1971
"Love of My Life"	1940
"Moon River"	1961
"My Shining Hour"	1943

"On the Atchison, Topeka and Santa Fe"	1946
"Something's Gotta Give"	1955
"Sweetheart Tree, The"	1965
"That Old Black Magic"	1943
"Whistling Away the Dark"	1970

PAUL FRANCIS WEBSTER (16)

"April Love"	1957
"Certain Smile, A"	1958
"Friendly Persuasion"	1956
"Green Leaves of Summer, The"	1960
"Love Is a Many-Splendored Thing"	1955
"Love Song from Mutiny on the Bounty"	1962
"Love Theme from El Cid"	1961
"Remember Me to Carolina"	1944
"Secret Love"	1953
"Shadow of Your Smile, The"	1965
"So Little Time"	1963
"Strange Are the Ways of Love"	1965
"Tender Is the Night"	1962
"Time For Love, A"	1966
"Very Precious Love, A"	1958
"World That Never Was, A"	1976

MARILYN AND ALAN BERGMAN (14)

"All His Children"	1971
"Girl Who Used to Be Me, The"	1989
"How Do You Keep the Music Playing?"	1982
"If We Were in Love"	1982
"It Might Be You"	1982
"Last Time I Felt Like This, The"	1978
"Marmalade, Molasses and Honey"	1972
"Papa, Can You Hear Me?"	1983
"Pieces of Dreams"	1970
"Theme from The Promise"	1979
"Way He Makes Me Feel, The"	1983
"Way We Were, The"	1973
"What Are You Doing the Rest of Your Life?"	1969
"Windmills of Your Mind, The"	1968

NED WASHINGTON (11)

"Baby Mine"	1941
"High and the Mighty, The"	1954
"High Noon (Do Not Forsake Me)"	1952

"My Foolish Heart"	1949
"Rio De Janeiro"	1944
"Sadie Thompson's Song"	1953
"Saludos Amigos"	1943
"Strange Are the Ways of Love"	1959
"Town Without Pity"	1961
"When You Wish upon a Star"	1940
"Wild Is the Wind"	1957

LEO ROBIN (10)

"Faithful Forever"	1939
"For Every Man There's a Woman"	1948
"Gal in Calico, A"	1947
"Love in Bloom"	1934
"My Flaming Heart"	1953
"So in Love"	1945
"Thanks for the Memory"	1938
"This Is the Moment"	1948
"Whispers in the Dark"	1937
"Zing a Little Zong"	1952

MACK GORDON (9)

"Chattanooga Choo Choo"	1941
"Down Argentine Way"	1940
"I Can't Begin to Tell You"	1946
"I'm Making Believe"	1944
"I've Got a Gal in Kalamazoo"	1942
"Through a Long and Sleepless Night"	1949
"Wilhelmina"	1950
"You Do"	1947
"You'll Never Know"	1943

MACK DAVID (8)

"Bachelor in Paradise"	1961
"Ballad of Cat Ballou, The"	1965
"Bibbidi-Bobbidi-Boo"	1950
"Hanging Tree, The"	1959
"Hush, Hush, Sweet Charlotte"	1964
"It's a Mad, Mad, Mad, Mad World"	1963
"My Wishing Doll"	1966
"Walk on the Wild Side"	1962

HOWARD ASHMAN (7)

"Be Our Guest"	1991
"Beauty and the Beast"	1991
"Belle"	1991
"Friend Like Me"	1992
"Kiss the Girl"	1989
"Mean Green Mother from Outer Space"	1986
"Under the Sea"	1989

IRVING BERLIN (7)

"Change Partners and Dance with Me"	1938
"Cheek to Cheek"	1935
"Count Your Blessings Instead of Sheep"	1954
"I Poured My Heart into a Song"	1939
"Now It Can Be Told"	1938
"White Christmas"	1942
"You Keep Coming Back Like a Song"	1946

RAY EVANS (7) AND JAY LIVINGSTON (6)[1]

"Almost in Your Arms"	1958
"Buttons and Bows"	1948
"Cat and the Canary, The"	1945
"Dear Heart"	1964
"Mona Lisa"	1950
"Tammy"	1957
"Whatever Will Be, Will Be (Que Sera, Sera)"	1956

HAROLD ADAMSON (5)

"Affair to Remember, An"	1957
"Change of Heart"	1943
"Did I Remember?"	1936
"I Couldn't Sleep a Wink Last Night"	1944
"My Own"	1938

DON BLACK (5)

"Ben"	1972
"Born Free"	1966
"Come to Me"	1976
"True Grit"	1969
"Wherever Love Takes Me"	1974

LESLIE BRICUSSE (5)

"Life in a Looking Glass"	1986
"Somewhere in My Memory"	1990
"Talk to the Animals"	1967
"Thank You Very Much"	1970
"When You're Alone"	1991

JOHNNY BURKE (5)

"Aren't You Glad You're You?"	1945
"Only Forever"	1940
"Pennies From Heaven"	1936

---

1. The pair were always billed as a team, rather than separately. However, for "The Cat and the Canary," they were billed as follows: Music by Jay Livingston; lyrics by Jay Evans.

"Sleighride in July"   1945
"Swinging on a Star"   1944

OSCAR HAMMERSTEIN II (5)
"All Through the Day"   1946
"It Might As Well Be Spring"   1945
"Kiss to Build a Dream On, A"   1951
"Last Time I Saw Paris, The"   1941
"Mist Is Over the Moon, A"   1938

FRANK LOESSER (5)
"Baby, It's Cold Outside"   1949
"Dolores"   1941
"I Wish I Didn't Love You So"   1947
"They're Either Too Young or Too Old"   1943
"Thumbelina"   1952

RICHARD M. SHERMAN
AND ROBERT B. SHERMAN (5)
"Age of Not Believing, The"   1971
"Chim Chim Cheree"   1964
"Chitty Chitty Bang Bang"   1968
"Slipper and the Rose Waltz"   1977
"When You're Loved"   1978

THE MOST OSCAR NOMINATIONS, BY COMPOSER

James Van Heusen (14)

"All the Way"	1957
"Aren't You Glad You're You?"	1945
"Call Me Irresponsible"	1963
"High Hopes"	1959
"(Love Is) The Tender Trap"	1955
"My Kind of Town"	1964
"Pocketful of Miracles"	1961
"Second Time Around, The"	1960
"Sleighride in July"	1945
"Star!"	1968
"Swinging on a Star"	1944
"Thoroughly Modern Millie"	1967
"To Love and Be Loved"	1958
"Where Love Has Gone"	1964

Henry Mancini (11)

"All His Children"	1971
"Bachelor in Paradise"	1961
"Charade"	1963
"Come to Me"	1976
"Days of Wine and Roses"	1962
"Dear Heart"	1964
"Life in a Looking Glass"	1986
"Moon River"	1961
"Song from *10*"	1979
"Sweetheart Tree, The"	1965
"Whistling Away the Dark"	1970

Harry Warren (11)

"Affair to Remember, An"	1957
"Chattanooga Choo Choo"	1941
"Down Argentine Way"	1940
"I've Got a Gal in Kalamazoo"	1942
"Jeepers Creepers"	1938
"Lullaby of Broadway"	1935
"On the Atchison, Topeka and Santa Fe"	1946
"Remember Me?"	1937
"That's Amore"	1953
"You'll Never Know"	1943
"Zing a Little Zong"	1952

Sammy Fain (10)

"April Love"	1957
"Certain Smile, A"	1958
"Love Is a Many-Splendored Thing"	1955
"Secret Love"	1953
"Someone's Waiting for You"	1977
"Strange Are the Ways of Love"	1972
"Tender Is the Night"	1962
"That Old Feeling"	1937
"Very Precious Love, A"	1958
"World That Never Was, A"	1976

Jule Styne (10)

"Anywhere"	1945
"Change of Heart"	1943
"Funny Girl"	1968
"I Fall in Love Too Easily"	1945
"I'll Walk Alone"	1944
"I've Heard That Song Before"	1942
"It's a Great Feeling"	1949
"It's Magic"	1948
"Three Coins in the Fountain"	1954
"Who Am I?"	1940

Harold Arlen (9)

"Ac-Cent-Tchu-Ate the Positive"	1945
"Blues in the Night"	1941
"For Every Man There's a Woman"	1948
"Happiness Is a Thing Called Joe"	1943
"Man That Got Away, The"	1954
"My Shining Hour"	1943
"Now I Know"	1944
"Over the Rainbow"	1939
"That Old Black Magic"	1943

Alan Menken (8)

"Be Our Guest"	1991
"Beauty and the Beast"	1991
"Belle"	1991
"Friend Like Me"	1992
"Kiss the Girl"	1989
"Mean Green Mother from Outer Space"	1986
"Under the Sea"	1989
"Whole New World, A"	1992

DIMITRI TIOMKIN (8)

"Friendly Persuasion"	1956
"Green Leaves of Summer, The"	1960
"High and the Mighty, The"	1954
"High Noon (Do Not Forsake Me)"	1952
"So Little Time"	1963
"Strange Are the Ways of Love"	1959
"Town Without Pity"	1961
"Wild Is the Wind"	1957

IRVING BERLIN (7)

"Change Partners and Dance with Me"	1938
"Cheek to Cheek"	1935
"Count Your Blessings Instead of Sheep"	1954
"I Poured My Heart into a Song"	1939
"Now It Can Be Told"	1938
"White Christmas"	1942
"You Keep Coming Back Like a Song"	1946

MARVIN HAMLISCH (7)

"Girl Who Used to Be Me, The"	1989
"Last Time I Felt Like This, The"	1978
"Life Is What You Make It"	1971
"Nobody Does It Better"	1977
"Surprise, Surprise"	1985
"Theme from *Ice Castles*"	1979
"Way We Were, The"	1973

JEROME KERN (7)

"All Through the Day"	1946
"Dearly Beloved"	1942
"Last Time I Saw Paris, The"	1941
"Long Ago and Far Away"	1944
"Lovely to Look At"	1935
"More and More"	1945
"Way You Look Tonight, The"	1936

MICHEL LEGRAND (7)

"How Do You Keep the Music Playing?"	1982
"I Will Wait for You"	1965
"Papa, Can You Hear Me?"	1983
"Pieces of Dreams"	1970
"Way He Makes Me Feel, The"	1983
"What Are You Doing the Rest of Your Life?"	1969
"Windmills of Your Mind, The"	1968

BURT BACHARACH (5)

"Alfie"	1966
"Arthur's Theme (Best That You Can Do)"	1981
"Look of Love, The"	1967
"Raindrops Keep Fallin' on My Head"	1969
"What's New Pussycat?"	1965

NICHOLAS BRODSZKY (5)

"Be My Love"	1950
"Because You're Mine"	1952
"I'll Never Stop Loving You"	1955
"My Flaming Heart"	1951
"Wonder Why"	1951

RAY EVANS AND JAY LIVINGSTON (5)

"Almost in Your Arms"	1958
"Buttons and Bows"	1948
"Mona Lisa"	1950
"Tammy"	1957
"Whatever Will Be, Will Be (Que Sera, Sera)"	1956

RICHARD M. SHERMAN AND ROBERT B. SHERMAN (5)

"Age of Not Believing, The"	1971
"Chim Chim Cheree"	1964
"Chitty Chitty Bang Bang"	1968
"Slipper and the Rose Waltz, The"	1977
"When You're Loved"	1978

TOP-CHARTING OSCAR NOMINEES

The following Oscar-nominated songs were as big off the screen as on —
they went all the way to Number One on the pop charts.

1934

"The Carioca" — Enric Madriguera and His Orchestra (Vocal: Patricia Gilmore)
"The Continental" — Leo Reisman
"Love in Bloom" — Bing Crosby

1935

"Cheek to Cheek" — Fred Astaire
"Lovely to Look At" — Eddy Duchin
"Lullaby of Broadway" — Dorsey Brothers Orchestra

1936

"Did I Remember?" — Shep Fields
"Melody from the Sky" — Jan Garber
"Pennies from Heaven" — Bing Crosby
"The Way You Look Tonight" — Fred Astaire
"When Did You Leave Heaven?" — Guy Lombardo

1937

"Remember Me?" — Bing Crosby
"Sweet Leilani" — Bing Crosby
"That Old Feeling" — Shep Fields
"They Can't Take That Away from Me" — Fred Astaire
"Whispers in the Dark" — Bob Crosby

1938

"Change Partners" — Fred Astaire; Jimmy Dorsey
"Jeepers Creepers" — Al Donohue
"Thanks for the Memory" — Shep Fields

1939

"Over the Rainbow" — Glenn Miller
"Wishing" — Glenn Miller

1940

"Only Forever" — Bing Crosby
"When You Wish upon a Star" — Glenn Miller

1941

"Blues in the Night" — Woody Herman
"Chattanooga Choo Choo" — Glenn Miller
"Dolores" — Tommy Dorsey

1942

"I've Got a Gal in Kalamazoo" — Glenn Miller
"I've Heard That Song Before" — Harry James
"White Christmas" — Bing Crosby

1943

"That Old Black Magic" — Glenn Miller
"You'll Never Know" — Dick Haymes

1944

"I'll Walk Alone" — Dinah Shore
"I'm Making Believe" — Ella Fitzgerald & Ink Spots
"Swinging on a Star" — Bing Crosby

1945

"Ac-Cent-Tchu-Ate the Positive" — Johnny Mercer

1946

"I Can't Begin to Tell You" — Bing Crosby
"Ole Buttermilk Sky" — Kay Kyser
"On the Atchison, Topeka and Santa Fe" — Johnny Mercer

1948

"Buttons and Bows" — Dinah Shore
"The Woody Woodpecker Song" — Kay Kyser

1950

"Be My Love" — Mario Lanza
"Mona Lisa" — Nat "King" Cole
"Mule Train" — Frankie Laine

1953

"Secret Love" — Doris Day

1954

"Three Coins in the Fountain" — The Four Aces

1955

"Love Is a Many-Splendored Thing" — The Four Aces
"Unchained Melody" — Les Baxter

1957

"April Love" — Pat Boone
"Tammy" — Debbie Reynolds

1969

"Raindrops Keep Fallin' on My Head" — B. J. Thomas

1971

"Theme from *Shaft*" — Isaac Hayes

1972

"Ben" — Michael Jackson
"The Morning After" — Maureen McGovern

1973
"The Way We Were" — Barbra Streisand

1975
"Theme From *Mahogany* (Do You Know Where You're Going To?)" — Diana Ross

1976
"Evergreen" — Barbra Streisand
"Gonna Fly Now" — Bill Conti

1977
"You Light Up My Life" — Debby Boone

1980
"9 to 5" — Dolly Parton

1981
"Arthur's Theme (Best That You Can Do)" — Christopher Cross
"Endless Love" — Diana Ross and Lionel Richie

1982
"Eye of the Tiger" — Survivor
"Up Where We Belong" — Joe Cocker & Jennifer Warnes

1983
"Flashdance . . . What a Feeling" — Irene Cara
"Maniac" — Michael Sembello

1984
"Against All Odds" — Phil Collins
"Footloose" — Kenny Loggins
"Ghostbusters" — Ray Parker Jr.
"I Just Called to Say I Love You" — Stevie Wonder
"Let's Hear It for the Boy" — Deneice Williams

1985
"Power of Love" — Huey Lewis & The News
"Separate Lives" — Phil Collins & Marilyn Martin

1986
"Glory of Love" — Peter Cetera
"Take My Breath Away" — Berlin

1987
"(I've Had) The Time of My Life" — Bill Medley and Jennifer Warnes
"Nothing's Gonna Stop Us Now" — Starship
"Shakedown" — Bob Seger

1988
"Two Hearts" — Phil Collins

1990
"Blaze of Glory" — Jon Bon Jovi

1991
"(Everything I Do) I Do It for You" — Bryan Adams

1992
"A Whole New World" — Peabo Bryson and Regina Belle

1993
"Again" — Janet Jackson

"LOVE" SONGS

There have been scores of Oscar-nominated songs with the word *Love*, or one of its variations, in the title. Here's a list of these lovely songs:

"All That Love Went to Waste"
"Am I in Love?"
"April Love"
"Be My Love"
"Benji's Theme (I Feel Love)"
"The Day I Fall in Love"
"Endless Love"
"Evergreen (Love Theme from *A Star Is Born*)"
"The Eyes of Love"
"For Love of Ivy"
"Friendly Persuasion (Thee I Love)"
"Glory of Love"
"I Fall in Love Too Easily"
"I Just Called to Say I Love You"
"I Love to See You Smile"
"I Wish I Didn't Love You So"
"I'll Never Stop Loving You"
"If We Were in Love"
"The Look of Love"
"Love"
"Love in Bloom"
"Love Is a Many-Splendored Thing"
"Love Is a Song"
"(Love Is) The Tender Trap"

"Love Letters"
"Love of My Life"
"Love Song from *Mutiny on the Bounty* (Follow Me)"
"Love Theme from *El Cid* (The Falcon and the Dove)"
"Lovely to Look At"
"Now That We're in Love"
"Our Love Affair"
"Power of Love"
"Secret Love"
"So in Love"
"Storybook Love"
"Strange Are the Ways of Love (1959)"
"Strange Are the Ways of Love (1972)"
"Theme from *Ice Castles* (Through the Eyes of Love)"
"Till Love Touches Your Life"
"A Time for Love"
"To Love and Be Loved"
"Too Much in Love"
"True Love"
"A Very Precious Love"
"We May Never Love Like This Again"
"When You're Loved"
"Where Love Has Gone"
"Wherever Love Takes Me"

MISCELLANEOUS OSCAR FACTOIDS

Compiled by Marcia Rovins

NOMINATED SONGS WITH THE SAME TITLE:

"Strange Are the Ways of Love"　　From *The Young Land* (1959)

"Strange Are the Ways of Love"　　From *The Stepmother* (1972)

NOMINATED SONGS FROM FILMS WITH THE SAME TITLE:

"Always and Always"　　From *Mannequin* (1938)

"Nothing's Gonna Stop Us Now"　　From *Mannequin* (1987)

"The Man That Got Away"　　From *A Star Is Born* (1954)

"Evergreen"　　From *A Star Is Born* (1976)

FILMS WITH MULTIPLE NOMINEES:

Aladdin	"Friend Like Me"
	"A Whole New World"
Beauty and the Beast	"Be Our Guest"
	"Beauty and the Beast"
	"Belle"
The Bodyguard	"I Have Nothing"
	"Run to Him"
Fame	"Fame"
	"Out Here on My Own"
Flashdance	"Flashdance...What a Feeling"
	"Maniac"
Footloose	"Footloose"
	"Let's Hear It for the Boy"
The Little Mermaid	"Kiss the Girl"
	"Under the Sea"
Philadelphia	"Philadelphia"
	"Streets of Philadelphia"
White Nights	"Say You, Say Me"
	"Separate Lives"
Yentl	"Papa, Can You Hear Me?"
	"The Way He Makes Me Feel"

BIBLIOGRAPHY

Adler, Bill. *Fred Astaire: A Wonderful Life*. New York: Carroll & Graf Publishers, Inc., 1987.

Arce, Hector. *The Secret Life of Tyrone Power*. New York: William Morrow and Company, Inc., 1979.

Bach, Bob, and Ginger Mercer. *Our Huckleberry Friend*. New Jersey: Lyle Stuart, Inc., 1982.

Barnes, Ken. *The Crosby Years*. New York: St. Martin's Press, 1980.

Belafonte, Dennis, with Alvin H. Marill. *The Films of Tyrone Power*. Secaucus, N.J.: The Citadel Press, 1979.

Benny, Mary Livingstone, and Hilliard Marks with Marcia Borie. *Jack Benny*. Garden City, N.Y.: Doubleday & Company, Inc., 1978.

Benson, Raymond. *The James Bond Bedside Companion*. New York: Dodd, Mead & Company, 1984.

Bookbinder, Robert. *The Films of the Seventies*. Secaucus, N.J.: Citadel Press, 1982.

Bordman, Gerald. *Jerome Kern: His Life and Music*. Oxford: Oxford University Press, 1980.

Brode, Douglas. *The Films of the Fifties*. New York: The Citadel Press, 1976.

Brode, Douglas. *The Films of the Sixties*. Secaucus, N.J.: Citadel Press, 1980.

Bronson, Fred. *The Billboard Book of Number One Hits*, 3rd Edition. New York: Billboard Books, Watson-Guptill Publications, 1992.

Brooks, Tim, and Earle Marsh. *The Complete Directory to Prime Time Network TV Shows*, Fifth Edition. New York: Ballantine Books, 1992.

Cahn, Sammy. *I Should Care: The Sammy Cahn Story*. New York: Arbor House, 1974.

Callinicos, Constantine, with Ray Robinson. *The Mario Lanza Story*. New York: Coward-McCann, Inc., 1960.

Cassiday, Bruce. *Dinah!* New York: Franklin Watts, 1979.

Cole, Maria, with Louie Robinson. *Nat King Cole, An Intimate Biography*. New York: William Morrow & Company, Inc., 1971.

Considine, Shaun. *Barbra Streisand: The Woman, the Myth, the Music*. New York: Delacorte Press, 1985.

Costello, Chris, with Raymond Strait. *Lou's on First*. New York: St. Martin's Press, 1981.

Croce, Arlene. *The Fred Astaire and Ginger Rogers Book*. New York: Outerbridge & Lazard, Inc. Distributed by E. P. Dutton & Co., 1972.

Culhane, John. *Special Effects in the Movies*. New York: Ballantine Books, 1981.

Deschner, Donald. *The Films of Cary Grant*. Secaucus, N.J.: The Citadel Press, 1973.

Eames, John Douglas. *The MGM Story*. New York: Crown Publishers, Inc., 1977.

Eells, George. *The Life That Late He Led*. New York: G. P. Putnam's Sons, 1967.

Ewen, David. *All the Years of American Popular Music*. Englewood Cliffs, N.J.: Prentice-Hall, Inc., 1977.

Ewen, David. *American Popular Songs*. New York: Random House, 1966.

Ewen, David. *Popular American Composers*. New York: The H. W. Wilson Company, 1962.

Ewen, David. *The World of Jerome Kern*. New York: Henry Holt and Company, 1960.

Fehr, Richard, and Frederick G. Vogel. *Lullabies of Hollywood*. Jefferson, North Carolina: McFarland & Company, Inc., 1993.

Finch, Christopher, and Justine Strasberg. *Jim Henson, The Works*. New York: Random House, Inc., 1993.

Fitzgerald, Michael E. *Universal Pictures*. New Rochelle, N.Y.: Arlington House, 1977.

Freedland, Michael. *Irving Berlin*. New York: Stein and Day Publishers, 1974.

Furia, Philip. *The Poets of Tin Pan Alley*. New York: Oxford University Press, 1990.

Godfrey, Lionel. *Cary Grant, The Light Touch*. New York: St. Martin's Press, 1981.

Green, Stanley. *Broadway Musicals, Show by Show*, Third Edition. Milwaukee: Hal Leonard Publishing Corp., 1990.

Green, Stanley. *Hollywood Musicals, Year by Year*. Milwaukee: Hal Leonard Publishing Corp., 1990.

Grossman, Gary H. *Saturday Morning TV*. New York: A Dell Trade Paperback, 1981.

Hamlisch, Marvin, with Gerald Gardner. *The Way I Was*. New York: Charles Scribner's Sons, 1992.

Hardy, Phil, and Dave Laing. *The Faber Companion to 20th-Century Popular Music*. London: Faber and Faber, 1990.

Harmetz, Aljean. *The Making of the Wizard of Oz*. New York: Limelight Editions, 1984.

Harris, Warren G. *Natalie & R. J., Hollywood's Star-Crossed Lovers*. New York: A Dolphin Book, Doubleday, 1988.

Hemming, Roy, and David Hajdu. *Discovering Great Singers of Classic Pop*. New York: Newmarket Press, 1991.

Hemming, Roy. *The Melody Lingers On*. New York: Newmarket Press, 1986.

Higham, Charles. *Warner Brothers*. New York: Charles Scribner's Sons, 1975.

Hope, Bob, and Bob Thomas. *The Road to Hollywood*. Garden City, N.Y.: Doubleday & Company, Inc., 1977.

Hotchner, A. E. *Doris Day: Her Own Story*. New York: William Morrow and Company, Inc., 1976.

Jacobs, Dick. *Who Wrote That Song?* White Hall, Virginia: Betterway Publications, Inc., 1988.

Jaques Cattell Press. *ASCAP Biographical Dictionary*. New York: R. R. Bowker Company, 1980.

Jewell, Richard B. with Vernon Harbin. *The RKO Story*. London: Arlington House, 1982.

Katz, Ephraim. *The Film Encyclopedia*. New York: A Perigee Book, 1979.

Kimbrell, James. *Barbra: An Actress Who Sings*. Boston: Branden Publishing Company, 1989.

King, Norman. *Madonna, The Book*. New York: William Morrow and Company, Inc., 1991.

Kinkle, Roger D. *The Complete Encyclopedia of Popular Music and Jazz, 1900-1950*, Various Volumes. New Rochelle, N.Y.: Arlington House, 1974.

Lax, Roger, and Frederick Smith. *The Great Song Thesaurus*. New York: Oxford University Press, 1984.

Lees, Gene. *The Singers and the Song*. New York: Oxford University Press, 1987.

Lenburg, Jeff. *The Encyclopedia of Animated Cartoon Series*. Westport, CT: Arlington House Publishers, 1981.

Lerner, Alan Jay. *The Street Where I Live*. New York: W. W. Norton & Company, 1978.

Lyon, Richard Sean. *The 1989 Investor's Guide to Films*. West Los Angeles: LyonHeart Publishers, 1989.

Maltin, Leonard. *The Disney Films*. New York: Crown Publishers, Inc., 1973.

Maltin, Leonard. *The Disney Films*, New Updated Edition. New York: Crown Publishers, Inc., 1984.

Maltin, Leonard. *The Great Movie Comedians*. New York: Crown Publishers, Inc., 1978.

Maltin, Leonard. *Leonard Maltin's Movie and Video Guide*, 1994 Edition. New York: Plume, 1993.

Mancini, Henry with Gene Lees. *Did They Mention the Music?* Chicago: Contemporary Books, 1989.

Minnelli, Vincente, with Hector Arce. *I Remember It Well*. Garden City, N.Y.: Doubleday & Company, Inc., 1974.

Morella, Joe; Edward Z. Epstein & Eleanor Clark. *The Amazing Careers of Bob Hope*. New Rochelle, N.Y.: Arlington House, 1973.

Morella, Joe; Edward Z. Epstein & John Griggs. *The Films of World War II*. Secaucus, N.J.: The Citadel Press, 1973.

Morella, Joe, and Edward Z. Epstein. *Jane Wyman*. New York: Delacorte Press, 1985.

Morella, Joe, and Edward Z. Epstein. *Loretta Young: An Extraordinary Life*. New York: Delacorte Press, 1986.

Morella, Joe, and Edward Z. Epstein. *Rita: The Life of Rita Hayworth*. New York: Delacorte Press, 1983.

Moseley, Roy, with Philip and Martin Masheter. *Rex Harrison*. New York: St. Martin's Press, 1987.

Nash, Jay Robert, and Stanley Ralph Ross *The Motion Picture Guide*, Various Volumes. Chicago: Cinebooks, Inc., 1986.

Nite, Norm N. *Rock On: The Solid Gold Years*, Updated Edition. New York: Harper & Row, Publishers, 1982.

BIBLIOGRAPHY

Nite, Norm N. *Rock On: The Years of Change 1964-1978*. New York: Harper & Row, Publishers, 1984.

Osborne, Robert. *60 Years of the Oscar*. New York: Abbeville Press, Publishers, 1989.

Owens, Harry. *Sweet Leilani: The Story Behind the Song*. Pacific Palisades, Calif.: Hula House, 1970.

Palmer, Christopher. *The Composer in Hollywood*. London: Marion Boyars, 1990.

Parish, James Robert. *The Fox Girls*. New Rochelle, N.Y.: Arlington House, 1971.

Parish, James Robert. *The Hollywood Death Book*. Las Vegas: Pioneer Books, Inc., 1992.

Petrucelli, Alan W. *Liza! Liza!* New York: Karz-Cohl, 1983.

Powell, Jane. *The Girl Next Door...and How She Grew*. New York: William Morrow and Company, Inc., 1988.

Previn, Andre. *No Minor Chords*. New York: Doubleday, 1991.

Ragan, David. *Who's Who in Hollywood*. New Rochelle, N.Y.: Arlington House, 1976.

Reynolds, Debbie, with David Patrick Columbia. *Debbie: My Life*. New York: William Morrow & Co., Inc., 1988.

Ringgold, Gene, and Clifford McCarty. *The Films of Frank Sinatra*. New York: The Citadel Press, 1971.

Rolling Stone Rock Almanac. New York: Macmillian Publishing Company, 1983.

Rooney, Mickey. *Life Is Too Short*. New York: Villard Books, 1991.

Sackett, Susan. *The Hollywood Reporter Book of Box Office Hits*. New York: Billboard Books, An Imprint of Watson-Guptill Publications, 1990.

Sackett, Susan. *Prime-Time Hits*. New York: Billboard Books, An Imprint of Watson-Guptill Publications, 1993.

Sadie, Stanley. *The New Grove Dictionary of Music and Musicians*, Various Volumes. London: Macmillian Pub. Ltd., 1980.

Shannon, Bob, and John Javna. *Behind the Hits*. New York: Warner Books, 1986.

Shipman, David. *Judy Garland: The Secret Life of an American Legend*. New York: Hyperion, 1992.

Siegman, Gita; Editor. *World of Winners*, Second Edition. Detroit: Gale Research Inc, 1992.

Simon, George T. *Glenn Miller and His Orchestra*. New York: Thomas Y. Crowel! Company, 1974.

Spoto, Donald. *Stanley Kramer, Film Maker*. New York: G. P. Putnam's Sons, 1978.

Stambler, Irwin. *Encyclopedia of Pop, Rock and Soul*, Revised Edition. New York: St. Martin's Press, 1989.

Taraborelli, J. Randy. *Call Her Miss Ross*. Secaucus, N.J.: Birch Lane, 1989.

Taylor, Theodore. *Jule: The Story of Composer Jule Styne*. New York: Random House, 1979.

Theroux, Gary, and Bob Gilbert. *The Top Ten*. New York: Simon and Schuster, 1982.

Thomas, Bob. *Astaire: The Man, the Dancer*. New York: St. Martin's Press, 1984.

Thomas, Frank, and Ollie Johnson. *Disney Animation*. New York: Abbeville Press, 1981.

Thomas, Tony. *The Films of the Forties*. Secaucus, N.J.: The Citadel Press, 1975.

Tietyen, David. *The Musical World of Walt Disney*. Milwaukee: Hal Leonard Publishing Corporation, 1990.

Ulanov, Barry. *The Incredible Crosby*. New York: Whittlesey House, McGraw-Hill Book Company, Inc., 1948.

Walker, Leo. *The Big Band Almanac*, Revised Edition. New York: A Da Capo Paperback, 1989.

Wallis, Hal, and Charles Higham. *Starmaker, The Autobiography of Hal Wallis*. New York: Macmillan Publishing Co., Inc., 1980.

Warner, Alan. *Warner/Chappell Music Inc. Song Catalog*. New York: Billboard Publications, 1991.

Whitburn, Joel. *Pop Memories 1890-1954*. Menomonee Falls, Wis.: Record Research Inc., 1986.

Whitburn, Joel. *Top Pop Singles 1955-1990*. Menomonee Falls, Wis.: Record Research Inc., 1991.

BIBLIOGRAPHY

White, Adam. *The Billboard Book of Gold & Platinum Records.* New York: Billboard Books, An Imprint of Watson-Guptill Publications, 1990.

Widener, Don. *Lemmon.* New York: Macmillan Publishing Co., Inc., 1975.

Wilder, Alec. *American Popular Song.* New York: Oxford University Press, 1972.

Wiley, Mason, and Damien Bona. *Inside Oscar.* New York: Ballantine Books, 1993.

Wilk, Max. *They're Playing Our Song.* New York: Atheneum, 1973.

Willis, John. *Screen World 1971.* New York: Crown Publishers, Inc., 1971.

Windeler, Robert. *Julie Andrews.* New York: G. P. Putnum's Sons, 1970.

Worth, Fred L. *Rock Facts.* New York: Facts On File Publications, 1980.

Zadan, Craig. *Sondheim & Co.,* Third Edition. New York: Harper & Row, 1990.

INDEX

INDEX